THE PAPERS
OF
JOHN MARSHALL

Sponsored by
The College of William and Mary
and
The Institute of Early American History and Culture
under the auspices of
The National Historical Publications Commission

John Marshall

by Henry Inman (1831)

THE PAPERS
OF
JOHN MARSHALL

Volume 1

Correspondence and Papers, November 10, 1775—June 23, 1788
Account Book, September 1783—June 1788

HERBERT A. JOHNSON, *Editor*

CHARLES T. CULLEN, *Associate Editor*
NANCY G. HARRIS, *Assistant Editor*

The University of North Carolina Press, Chapel Hill
in association with the
Institute of Early American History and Culture,
Williamsburg, Virginia

*The Institute of Early American History and Culture
is sponsored jointly by The College of William and Mary in Virginia
and The Colonial Williamsburg Foundation*

*The ornament on the title page is based upon John Marshall's personal seal, as it appears on
a gold watch fob that also bears the seal of his wife, Mary Willis Marshall. It was drawn
by Richard J. Stinely of Williamsburg, Virginia, from the original, now owned by the Association for the Preservation of Virginia Antiquities, Richmond, Virginia, and is published with
the owner's permission.*

Library of Congress Cataloging in Publication Data

Marshall, John, 1755–1835.
  The papers of John Marshall.

  CONTENTS: v. 1. Correspondence and papers, November 10, 1775–June 23, 1788. Account
book, September 1783–June 1788.
  1. Marshall, John, 1755–1835. I. Johnson, Herbert Alan, ed. II. Institute of Early American
History and Culture, Williamsburg, Va.
E302.M365   347'.73'2634   74–9575
ISBN 0–8078–1233–1

Dedicated to

DAVIS YOUNG PASCHALL
President of The College of William and Mary
1960–1971

CONTENTS

CORRESPONDENCE AND PAPERS
November 10, 1775—June 23, 1788

1775

1777

1778

ACCOUNT BOOK
September 1783—June 1788

INTRODUCTION

This volume initiates a series of approximately ten volumes that will constitute the first appearance in print of the papers of Chief Justice John Marshall. As such, it symbolizes the achievement of a scholarly goal that has been intermittently pursued from the earliest years of the twentieth century. In 1906 Waldo G. Leland and William E. Dodd announced to the profession their intention to collect and publish the papers of the chief justice, adding to their call for assistance the statement that "inasmuch as there is no single large collection, so far as is known, of Marshall papers, in existence, it is necessary that an extensive search shall be made, particularly among the papers of Marshall's contemporaries. . . ."[1] Although that collection never reached the stage of publication, it did provide materials for the more extensive transcription of documents assembled by Albert J. Beveridge in the preparation of his four-volume biography.[2]

After the appearance of Beveridge's work, Marshall's career continued to be the subject of serious historical study, but it took the 1955 bicentennial celebration of the chief justice's birth to revive serious discussion about publishing his papers. The College of William and Mary, because of its historical connection with its prominent alumnus, held a scholarly conference on John Marshall in May 1955, and from that meeting emerged an outstanding collection of essays that stimulated study of Marshall and, coincidentally, an interest in the publication of his papers.[3] Simultaneously the librarian of the College of William and Mary, James A. Servies, prepared *A Bibliography of John Marshall*, which was published under the auspices of the United States Commission for the Celebration of the Two Hundredth Anniversary of the Birth of John Marshall.[4]

---

1. *American Historical Review*, XI (1906), 747.

2. *The Life of John Marshall* (Boston, 1916–1919).

3. W. Melville Jones, ed., *Chief Justice John Marshall: A Reappraisal* (Ithaca, N.Y., 1956).

4. (Washington, D.C., 1956). The bibliography covered printed works by JM and printed works about him. Mr. Servies subsequently assembled a mimeographed check list of manuscript materials concerning JM, which has been particularly helpful in the collection of documents for the files of *The Papers of John Marshall*.

Quite independently from the College of William and Mary's activities, Irwin S. Rhodes of Cincinnati, Ohio, began to collect Marshall manuscripts with an eye toward scholarly publication in a definitive edition. Working alone, with some financial assistance from the American Bar Association and local bar associations, Rhodes gathered a large file of documents. Upon the basis of this remarkably devoted effort, he published a descriptive calendar of Marshall's papers.[5] Until the appearance of all the volumes in *The Papers of John Marshall*, Rhodes's calendar will continue to be the most complete directory to the manuscript and printed materials that relate to Marshall's life.

The next practical step was taken in May 1960, when the Council of the Institute of Early American History and Culture adopted a resolution unanimously "endorsing the publication of the Marshall Papers in the Williamsburg area," thereby opening the way to a collaboration between the College of William and Mary and the Institute in a joint effort to establish an editorial project and obtain the necessary financial support for the venture. A committee consisting of Louis B. Wright, Walter Muir Whitehill, and Lester J. Cappon was appointed by the Council to investigate the problems that would be involved in establishing a publication project. At the suggestion of the college's president, Alvin D. Chandler, the Institute and its committee assumed full responsibility for planning and advancing the project on behalf of the joint interests of the Institute and the college. In November 1960 this planning committee was designated the administrative board of *The Papers of John Marshall* and was authorized, by action of the Institute Council and the college's Board of Visitors, to supervise the project on behalf of the two institutions.

By the spring of 1961 the administrative board received from the National Historical Publications Commission a detailed statement of the known surviving Marshall material in various depositories, and from this information projected an edition of approximately ten volumes. At the same time the board appointed James Morton Smith, editor of publications at the Institute, to serve as editor of *The Papers of John Marshall*. The publication under the auspices of the Institute and the college was endorsed by the National Historical Publications Commission on March 6, 1962. Actual editorial work on *The Papers of John Marshall* did not commence until September 1966, when the project was funded by a challenge grant

5. *The Papers of John Marshall, A Descriptive Calendar* (Norman, Okla., 1970).

from the National Historical Publications Commission, matched by an appropriation to the College of William and Mary by the General Assembly of the Commonwealth of Virginia. Stephen G. Kurtz, who had succeeded Mr. Smith as editor of publications, was named the new editor and to him fell the direction of the project for the next five years.

In the six and one-half years since the inception of work, the staff has continually been engaged in the search for Marshall manuscripts. As Dodd and Leland anticipated in 1906, the absence of any single large collection has made necessary an extensive exploration for widely scattered sources of material. Using a frequently updated list of Marshall's correspondents, the editors have searched through those repositories that are likely to contain Marshall documents or information that might lead to other manuscript collections. They have corresponded with over a hundred descendants of the chief justice and with an even larger number of private autograph collectors and dealers in an effort to include all extant manuscripts in these volumes.

JOHN MARSHALL AND HIS PAPERS

As historian, lawyer, and judge, John Marshall should have been strongly motivated toward careful record-keeping. Yet the state of his surviving papers, coupled with what we know of his carelessness in preserving documents, suggests that no large collection of personal or professional papers existed at the time of his death. Such papers could not have been voluminous at any given time, for Marshall broke with the tradition of the day and did not retain drafts or letterbook copies of his letters. One suspects that he would have disdained the maintenance of a correspondence log or registry; certainly none has survived. His Account Book reveals a declining interest in accurate bookkeeping throughout the years from 1783 to 1795, and the scraps of accounts that have survived from Marshall's later years are more suitable for carrying in the brim of a hat than for permanent records. Some of the letters that may have come from his personal files have been used for unrelated arithmetic computations and other scribblings.

The disarray of the chief justice's records cannot be explained by frequent family moves from place to place, for the Marshalls were firmly rooted in Richmond, Virginia. From the time that John Marshall built his house there in 1790 until a few months before his death, he continued in the same residence and worked in the old law office on the premises. Although the office was torn down some years after his death, the house remains standing to this day, untouched by the 1865 fire that destroyed a major portion of the old city. Now open to the public under the administration of the Association for the Preservation of Virginia Antiquities, it was owned or occupied until 1907 by Marshall's direct descendants.

James Keith Marshall, the chief justice's eldest surviving son, meticulously gathered every conceivable financial and business record concerning his father. A large collection of papers in the possession of a descendant of James Keith Marshall evidences the extent to which he as executor attempted to trace his father's investments and verify his legal debts. For our purposes it is helpful, although discouraging, to note that the bulk of the papers that came into the hands of James Keith Marshall are dated from the last two or three years of Marshall's life.

For many years Marshall scholars have suspected the virtual nonexistence of any other significant body of papers in the family's possession. It has also been accepted that Marshall did not keep regular records of his financial dealings and his correspondence. None of the files from his law office appears to have survived; there is no mention of any substantial number of Marshall legal documents in his letters, nor do they appear in institutional collections or auction catalogs.

Fortunately the public records pertaining to John Marshall's career are reasonably complete, and the meticulous record-keeping of many of his private correspondents has preserved a substantial amount of information and documentation. The Virginia State Library houses the archives of the Commonwealth of Virginia, including the executive papers and executive letterbooks of the governors, the legislative papers of the House of Delegates, and a large collection of court records, including the papers of the Richmond City Hustings Court during Marshall's term as recorder. The National Archives in Washington, D.C., has provided the editors with a great amount of information concerning John Marshall and a substantial percentage of the documents that will be printed in this edition of his papers. Most prominent are the collection of Revolutionary War records, the diplomatic archives concerning the XYZ mission to France and Marshall's term as secretary of state, and the records of the Supreme Court of the United States. A cursory statement of the major classes of material obtained from these two public depositories cannot fully discharge the debt that Marshall scholars owe to the archivists who have preserved the public record of the chief justice's career. The publication of these materials alone would justify the issuance of this edition of Marshall's papers.

Every particle of the archival material concerning Marshall has not survived, however, for there are gaps in the record created by the destruction of public buildings and archives. Portions of the domestic letterbooks of the secretary of state for 1800 and 1801 are missing, having been destroyed by the fire in the United States Capitol set by British troops in 1814. The court records of the higher courts of Virginia, with the single exception of the minute-book of the Court of Appeals, were burned in 1865 during the evacuation of Richmond and its occupation by federal troops. Luckily these documentary losses can be partially remedied from materials in other depositories. The diplomatic archives of foreign missions to Washington, D.C., have been searched for Marshall letters that otherwise might have been more easily located in the domestic letterbooks and notes to legations letterbooks. Cases in the Virginia district courts, established in 1788, frequently contain transcripts of proceedings in the General Court or the High Court of Chancery, whose original records have been totally destroyed. Similarly the intact records of the United States Circuit Court for Virginia, maintained in the Virginia State Library, contain transcripts of certain proceedings in the higher courts of the Commonwealth of Virginia. Another source for Virginia court records is the Treasury 79 series in the Public Record Office in London. This is a collection covering the claims of British merchants against their pre-Revolutionary American debtors, and as such it includes transcripts of certain court records and memoranda of legal precedents in Virginia concerning the recovery of these obligations.

Many of John Marshall's correspondents retained their private papers, including letterbooks containing the text of letters addressed to Marshall. The papers of John Adams, Timothy Pickering, James Monroe, and John Breckinridge are among those that have been most valuable for the reconstruction of Marshall's correspondence. For the most part, however, the extant Marshall letters addressed to correspondents are widely scattered, and their systematic collection from a variety of depositories has contributed to the comprehensive body of materials to be presented in this and subsequent volumes. Of course, the editors' reliance upon these surviving documents of Marshall's correspondence results in the presentation of far more letters written by him than are printed from manuscripts addressed to him. In every instance where a Marshall letter has been located in the papers of a given individual, an effort has been made to locate letterbooks, drafts, or letterpress copies of outgoing letters to Marshall, as well as any additional correspondence from Marshall. The scarcity of Marshall's autograph, coupled with the sentimental appeal his name has in the legal profession, has resulted in an active trade in those Marshall manuscripts not in archives or institutional collections. Several of these privately owned manuscripts have been identified through dealers' catalogs, and a number of them have been generously made available for publication in this edition. However, it is clear that a small amount of manuscript material that should properly be noted in this edition has not come to the editors' attention despite strenuous efforts to publicize the scholarly need for the text of these manuscripts. Whatever manuscripts may appear after the publication of the appropriate chronological volumes will be published or noted in an addendum volume covering the entire series.

While the editors of *The Papers of John Marshall* have encountered unusual problems in locating and obtaining copies of the chief justice's extant papers, it has become readily apparent in the course of work that the available materials concerning Marshall are far more extensive than originally anticipated. A number of hitherto unknown manuscripts will be available for scholarly use for the first time upon their publication in this series; many others will be identified by date and recipient, providing a helpful guide to those documents that may become available for scholarly use at some future date. It is the editors' hope that as each volume of *The Papers of John Marshall* is published it will stimulate new interest in Marshall and his manuscripts. Ideally this series should begin a new era of studies concerning Marshall and serve as a point of departure for future generations, who will profit from the editors' achievements and transcend their shortcomings.

SELECTION AND ORGANIZATION OF THE PAPERS

More than three-quarters of the papers presented in this volume have never been printed previously, although scholars have from time to time used many of the manuscript originals to good purpose. The editors have adopted a policy of publishing, or calendaring with a short synopsis, every known document signed by or prepared by John Marshall. Where Marshall's role has been merely that of a scrivener, a specific reference to the document has been eliminated, but its existence has been noted in an appropriate place in the annotations. The editors have also included, either in their entirety or by synopsis, all papers that were addressed to Marshall (or that came to his attention in the course of his work) and that required some action on his part. However, for manuscripts that are but one of many formal documents, a characteristic example has been printed, and the similar remaining documents have been synopsized.

From these general rules of selection the editors have made three departures that appeared justified by the nature of the materials and the needs of those who will use this edition. (1) Only the first quarter of Marshall's law notes has been printed in this volume, although the entire document is in his handwriting. The editors believe that such an extract amply demonstrates the process of commonplacing, as well as the general nature of Marshall's source material. The original manuscript is available on microfilm from the Earl Gregg Swem Library at the College of William and Mary for those who may wish to study the complete text of the law notes. (2) John Marshall's arguments in the higher courts of Virginia from 1786 to 1788 are taken from the manuscript notes made by St. George Tucker, which are now in the Swem Library at the College of William and Mary. Because the arguments are reported in such detail and the citations are so accurate, it is most probable that Tucker's summaries were based upon Marshall's handwritten points for argument in these cases. However, certain of Tucker's notes on cases, published in the fourth volume of Call's *Reports*,[6] have not been included, except for the landmark argument in *Hite v. Fairfax*. Instead these previously printed notes are discussed in calendared synopses, which assist the reader in finding Marshall's printed arguments. (3) Finally, the editors have included the text of John Marshall's speeches before the Virginia ratifying convention of 1788, as published in David Robertson's stenographic report of the debates.[7] The parallels between Marshall's speech on the judiciary and a prior speech on the same topic by George Mason leave little doubt that Marshall's oral presentations at the convention were carefully planned and delivered from notes. In the absence of these manuscript notes, Robertson's stenographic transcript is the best evidence of their content.

6. Daniel Call, *Reports of Cases Argued and Decided in the Court of Appeals of Virginia*, IV (Richmond, 1833).

7. *Debates and other Proceedings of the Convention of Virginia, Convened at Richmond, on Monday the 2d of June, 1788* . . . (Petersburg, Va., 1788).

The recent practice of editors of the papers of major statesmen has been to separate legal papers from the chronological series of letters and documents. While there are valid reasons for this practice in terms of editorial clarity, the editors of John Marshall's papers have decided that an arbitrary isolation of legal materials not only would detract from the general usefulness of the chronological volumes but also would deprive the reader of any reference to what must be considered the most important segment of Marshall's papers, those dealing with the law. Consequently this volume includes a group of Marshall's arguments in the appellate courts of Virginia, selected on the basis set forth above, as well as calendared synopses of all extant legal documents known to have been prepared or signed by Marshall. Other materials related to Marshall's law cases, including extensive editorial annotations concerning his legal practice, have been withheld here but will be selectively published in a separate volume arranged in a topical format to highlight the nature of Marshall's law practice.

Every extant Marshall paper from the time of his birth to June 30, 1788, is printed or calendared in this volume. The material presented actually covers Marshall's life from his entry into military service in the Culpeper Minutemen Battalion to the end of the Virginia ratifying convention. It is admittedly a fragmentary collection, assembled chronologically for the use of the reader—and not a continuous record—but even this residuum of business and legal records, correspondence, and other official and private papers provides ample justification for its preparation and publication.

The early documents show Marshall as a militia officer and company grade officer in the Continental Line, where he performed extra duties as a deputy judge advocate. Marshall participated in many major events of the War for Independence, including the deadly winter encampment at Valley Forge, and although historians have tended to overemphasize the influence of military service on his career, it undoubtedly broadened his horizons as well as his circle of friends. Upon his discharge, Marshall began his long involvement with the legal profession. His law notes demonstrate his method of commonplacing as he studied at the College of William and Mary in 1780, the same year that he gained admission to the bar. Papers from the following years reveal Marshall's growing stature as a legal practitioner; the publication of his legal arguments, as recorded by St. George Tucker and preserved in Tucker's notes, adds still more evidence about his proficiency in legal study and practice. A frequently elected member of the House of Delegates, he also served on the Council of State from 1782 to 1784 and as recorder of the city of Richmond from 1785 to 1788. Of special interest too is Marshall's Account Book for 1783 to 1788, which provides new insights into his social activities, relationships with his family, management of his home, and the growth of his library. The volume concludes with Marshall's speeches to the Virginia ratifying convention in June 1788, where he helped secure ratification of the Constitution he was later to expound with such force and wisdom.

The thirteen years of public service covered by the documents in Volume I were clearly a time of growth and maturation for both the future chief justice and the political and judicial life of Virginia. Approaching the age of thirty-three Marshall could look back upon a career of notable achievement and forward to an active and prosperous future in the years ahead.

EDITORIAL STAFF

At a recent gathering of historical editors, one of the most distinguished scholars present suggested that a good editor should possess the "head of a scholar, and the soul of a clerk." In other circumstances the remark might have been resented, but among those who have experienced the challenges and drudgery of day-to-day editorial work, it can only be taken as a compliment. All editorial projects rely upon the precise, painstaking, and often tedious work of each individual on the staff.

The Papers of John Marshall has been blessed in having a fine group of people assisting in the editorial work, either on a part-time or full-time basis during the past seven years. Although only three names appear on the title page of the volume as editors, there is a much larger group whose contributions deserve mention for making possible the publication of this, as well as successive volumes in this series.

In the introduction the contributions of Lester J. Cappon, James Morton Smith, and Stephen G. Kurtz have been acknowledged, but it is nevertheless proper that their leadership, planning, and foresight be referred to at this point. Although Mr. Kurtz as the first editor of *The Papers of John Marshall* was the only one to serve as a member of the staff while editorial work was in progress, Mr. Cappon has always maintained a lively interest in the operational aspects of the project. As a member of the editorial advisory committee and more recently as chairman of the Council of the Institute, Mr. Smith has continued to aid in the work of the project and to extend encouragement and advice.

While the text of the first volume was being edited, the staff was augmented in 1970–1971 and again in 1972–1973 by the addition of a specialist in diplomatic history, Professor William C. Stinchcombe of Syracuse University. The bulk of the editorial work done under Mr. Stinchcombe's direction will appear in subsequent volumes dealing with John Marshall's diplomatic career. However, the editors have drawn upon his scholarly judgment at frequent intervals during the course of the editing of the first volume, and he has assisted in their search for manuscripts covering Marshall's entire career. Lest his title as diplomatic editor conceal the contribution he has made to this volume, the editors here gratefully acknowledge his assistance.

In the 1968–1969 academic year the staff was supplemented on a part-time basis by Stella Duff Neiman, who served ably as editorial assistant. Mrs. Neiman was particularly helpful in searching for printed materials pertaining to John Marshall. Her comprehensive knowledge of Virginia history was invaluable to the work of the project.

The Papers of John Marshall has benefited from the opportunity to train three young scholars in editorial procedures under the National Historical Publications Commission's fellowship program. Funded by a grant from the Ford Foundation, this fellowship provides on-the-job training to men and women who have expressed an interest in editorial careers and who are competitively selected for a one-year term with an editorial project conducted under the auspices of the commission. In 1967–1968 Joan M. Corbett served as a fellow with *The Papers of John Marshall*, and while learning editorial methods, she contributed immeasurably to the accuracy of documentary research in the National Archives and the Library of Congress. Since that time she has continued to provide the editors with occasional references to Marshall documents, discovered in the course of her work as assistant editor of *The Papers of George Washington*. The second NHPC fellow, Charles T. Cullen, was appointed in September 1970; upon the conclusion of his fellowship term, he remained with *The Papers of John Marshall* as associate editor. During the 1972–1973 academic year a third NHPC fellow, Professor W. Allan Wilbur of Purdue University, joined the staff.

Mr. Wilbur has been involved in the preparation of the text of this volume for the printer and has also worked closely with Mr. Stinchcombe on the diplomatic papers, thus making a substantial contribution to the progress of the project's work while learning the skills of an editor.

Two research assistants, Carolyn D. Hensley and Susan H. Elias, have assisted the editors in annotating this first volume, and Mrs. Hensley has contributed her secretarial skills by retyping a substantial portion of the text and annotations before submission to the printer.

The Institute of Early American History and Culture's apprenticeship program in the editing of historical books and magazines has provided the editors with the opportunity to participate in the training of two graduate students for future work as editors. Fredrika J. Teute served as an apprentice with *The Papers of John Marshall* in 1970–1971 and is now associate editor of *The Papers of James Madison*. Susan L. Patterson served as an apprentice on the staff in 1971–1972 and is presently assistant editor of the *New England Historical and Genealogical Register*.

A number of graduate students from the department of history at the College of William and Mary have also assisted the editors at various stages in the editorial work of *The Papers of John Marshall*. Gerald Cowden, John Dann, Daniel Kemp, and Joan Rezner Gundersen are entitled to notice for their contributions to this and subsequent volumes.

Particular acknowledgment is due to the dedication and precision that has characterized the work of the typists who have prepared the text for publication. Doris L. Buchanan served with *The Papers of John Marshall* from 1968 to 1971 and, as the senior typist, was responsible for the preparation of typescripts covering a substantial part of the material that will be published in *The Papers of John Marshall*. Ably assisted by E. Rachel Fausack and Kathleen M. McCall, she performed this task with patience and determination, and the editors wish to thank these typists, in addition to Mrs. Hensley, for the outstanding contribution they have made to the work of the project.

EDITORS' ACKNOWLEDGMENTS

We are indebted to a number of depositories and individuals for preserving and making available for our use the manuscripts of John Marshall printed or calendared in this volume. Although the name of each institution and individual is contained in a source line preceding the printed document or calendar entry, we nevertheless wish to acknowledge our gratitude to the following benefactors who materially assisted our work in this regard.

The materials upon which this volume is based were provided by the Office of the Clerk of the Circuit Court, Augusta County, Staunton, Virginia; the University of Chicago Library, Chicago, Illinois; the Connecticut Historical Society, Hartford, Connecticut; the Office of the Clerk of the Circuit Court, Fauquier County, Warrenton, Virginia; The Filson Club, Louisville, Kentucky; the Office of the Clerk of the Circuit Court, Fredericksburg, Virginia; the Office of the Clerk of the Circuit Court, Henrico County, Richmond, Virginia; the Collection of Mrs. Nancy G. Harris, Williamsburg, Virginia; the Collection of Mrs. Kenneth R. Higgins, Richmond, Virginia; the Indiana Historical Society, Indianapolis, Indiana; the Land Office, Kentucky Secretary of State's Office, Frankfort, Kentucky; The Library of Congress, Washington, D.C.; the Collection of Mr. Thomas B. Marshall, West Chester, Pennsylvania; The James Monroe Memorial Library, Fredericksburg, Virginia; The National Archives, Washington, D.C.; the Manuscript Division, New York Public Library, the Astor, Lenox, and Tilden Foundations, New York, New York; The New York Society Library, New York, New York; The Historical Society of Pennsylvania, Philadelphia, Pennsylvania; the Office of the Clerk of the Circuit Court, Prince Edward County, Farmville, Virginia; Princeton University Library, Princeton, New Jersey; the Office of the Clerk of the Circuit Court, Prince William County, Manassas, Virginia; the Office of the Clerk of the Richmond City Law and Equity Court, Richmond, Virginia; the Manuscript Department, Division of Special Collections, Stanford University Libraries, Stanford, California; The Virginia Historical Society, Richmond, Virginia; the Virginia State Library, Richmond, Virginia; the Alderman Library, University of Virginia, Charlottesville, Virginia; the Swem Library, College of William and Mary, Williamsburg, Virginia; and the State Historical Society of Wisconsin, Madison, Wisconsin.

The editors have received the cooperation of a large group of people who have given freely of their time and advice to help in the collection of Marshall documents and subsequent editorial work. To identify them is to run the risk of unintentionally omitting some individuals who deserve mention, for the list of benefactors is large and extends through six and one-half years of editorial work. Mrs. Kenneth R. Higgins of Richmond deserves special mention for her unfailing interest in the work of the Marshall Papers and her knowledge of the Marshall family, which she has made available on innumerable occasions. Dr. and Mrs. H. Norton Mason have also guided the editors' relations with Marshall's descendants and, from their knowledge of Marshall and his life, have freely provided advice and guidance. The Honorable Elliott Marshall of Front Royal, Virginia, has been generous in providing advice concerning the descendants of James Markham Marshall, and Fauquier County history. Mrs. James R. Green of Markham, Virginia, has been helpful in facilitating our research in Fauquier County, as has her sister, Mrs. John D. McCarty of Delaplane. Countless other members of the Marshall family have provided us with suggestions concerning the location of the chief justice's extant manuscripts, and although we do not acknowledge them by name, we are nevertheless indebted to them for their valued assistance.

The editors have received scholarly advice and assistance from James R. Bentley, curator of manuscripts at The Filson Club; Colonel James R. Case of Bethel, Connecticut; Harold B. Gill, Colonial Williamsburg Foundation; Professor Robert M. Ireland of the University of Kentucky; Mary-Jo Kline, associate editor of *The Papers of John Jay*; and Professor Patricia S. Watlington of Quinnipiac College. Also to be acknowledged at this point is the extensive help received from the editorial advisory committee of *The Papers of John Marshall*. Each member of this committee has rendered special service to assist in the preparation of this and subsequent volumes, and each should be considered a contributor to the scholarly excellence of this volume, although the editors alone must bear the responsibility for the errors that the diligence of this distinguished editorial advisory committee has not been able to prevent.

At a critical stage in the editorial work, the editors were benefited by an editorial critique and valuable suggestions from Julian P. Boyd, editor of *The Papers of Thomas Jefferson*, which were of inestimable help in bringing this volume into its present format. Acceptance of some of Professor Boyd's suggestions does not implicate him in any of the editors' shortcomings in this volume. The volume has also benefited from readings at various stages of its development by Norman S. Fiering, editor of publications at the Institute of Early American History and Culture, and Thad W.

Tate, the present director of the Institute. The editors are also indebted to Joy Dickinson Barnes, associate editor of publications at the Institute, who has been responsible for copy editing the text and expediting this first volume through the various stages of preparation for publication.

We have already acknowledged in our dedication our indebtedness to Dr. Davis Y. Paschall, former president of the College of William and Mary, for his strong and enthusiastic support of our work. From his initial efforts to obtain funds to match the challenge grant made by the National Historical Publications Commission in 1965, Dr. Paschall has overextended himself to insure a sound financial basis for our scholarly work. His own personal interest in *The Papers of John Marshall* has pervaded the entire college community, and we are deeply grateful to the past and present administrative officers and faculties of the college for the many evidences of their interest and support.

The National Historical Publications Commission, and its dedicated staff headed by Dr. Oliver W. Holmes and Mr. Fred Shelley, have contributed in countless ways to this edition of Marshall's papers. Through its original challenge grant the commission showed its recognition of the importance of Marshall's papers and the need for their publication. That initial expression of encouragement resulted in the first steps toward the establishment of *The Papers of John Marshall*, but the commission has not thereafter lagged in exertions upon behalf of this project, which continues to rely upon the commission for a sizable portion of its annual operating budget. The editors have been awarded the privilege of training three Ford Foundations fellows, and the Washington office staff members of the commission have undertaken the burden of searching the abundant files of the National Archives for Marshall documents. A predominant part of the documents printed in this first volume were photocopied through their efforts, and they are entitled to share the credit for assembling these manuscript sources for publication.

During the past two years *The Papers of John Marshall* has been fortunate in obtaining a grant from the American Council of Learned Societies to cover a short-term need for funds to continue the editorial staff at its present strength. In addition the American Philosophical Society provided funds to defray the expenses of research trips to London to gather materials on Marshall's law practice and diplomatic career and to Paris to search the governmental archives concerning the XYZ mission.

Finally, the editors wish to express their thanks to the National Endowment for the Humanities, which provided a matching-funds grant to cover the period October 1972 to September 1974. The generosity of the Association for the Preservation of Virginia Antiquities, C. Waller Barrett, Robert T. Barton, Jr., the John Stewart Bryan Memorial Foundation, the Society of the Cincinnati in the Commonwealth of Virginia, the Friends of the College of William and Mary, the Henry C. Hofheimer Family Foundation, Jay W. Johns, the Charlotte Palmer Phillips Foundation, and the Langbourne Williams Foundation has permitted *The Papers of John Marshall* to take full advantage of this grant. While the funds so obtained will be applied toward the editing of the diplomatic papers of John Marshall and a special volume on the portraits of John Marshall, it is appropriate that this first volume should acknowledge this additional source of financial support.

EDITORIAL APPARATUS

RENDITION OF TEXT

In accordance with modern editorial standards, the editors have attempted to render the text as faithfully as possible. However, the dateline on each letter and document has been modernized and standardized to indicate the place and date of composition. The editors have also made a standard practice of bringing the signatures to letters flush with the right margin, wherever those signatures may appear upon the original. Should a letter contain the designation "private," or bear a dispatch number, or both, this material has been placed at the left margin above the salutation and in line with the place and dateline of the letter. Likewise acknowledgments or jurats to a document have been arbitrarily brought to the left margin and included, as well as the signatures of witnesses or notaries. All postscripts also have been placed at the left margin, regardless of where they might appear on the face of a letter.

Each document and calendared synopsis has been given a heading, composed by the editors to provide a brief key to the nature of the document. These headings are reflected in the table of contents and are designed solely for the convenience of the reader in locating particular classes of documents. Letters are identified by the name of the individual who wrote to John Marshall or the person to whom Marshall wrote. In the case of multiple authors or addressees, the editors have endeavored to identify the group to which these individuals belonged and to use such a group identification in heading the letter. Documents other than letters are, as a rule, identified by the category of document that is being printed or synopsized, such as "Petition," "Speech," or "Legislative Bill." For legal documents the heading has been expanded to include not only the category of the document but also the title of the case.

Within the text of documents copy has been followed as far as modern printing methods would permit. In most cases superscript letters have been lowered to the line, and omitted letters in a word have been inserted only when necessary to preserve the meaning of the word as written in the original. The ampersand (&) has been retained, but the editors have expanded "&c" and "&ca" to "etc." to conform to modern usage and typography. The tailed "p" (ꝑ) has been rendered as either "pro" or "per," depending upon the context in which it appears in the original. Finally, the editors have followed the tradition that all sentences begin with capital letters and terminate with periods, question marks, or exclamation points, and these corrections have been silently inserted in the text as necessary to preserve the original intention of the writer. All dashes at the end of sentences and paragraphs have been silently omitted from documents other than those that reproduce a previous imprint. Because of the uncertainties involved in correcting any given writer's use of the comma, the text has been followed in this and in all other matters of punctuation. Should considerations of clarity dictate some explanatory insertion, the editors have added punctuation in square brackets, thereby permitting the reader to reach his own decision concerning the propriety of the editorial decision.

Signatures to documents are uniformly rendered in large and small capitals, regardless of their appearance on the original. However, where the editors have not examined the original signature or have no reason to believe that the signature as reflected on the edited document was copied from an original signature, the signature has been rendered as it appears in the text being copied. This situation usually occurs in the case of printed documents where the original manuscript copy and all contemporary copies and later transcripts from the original manuscript have been lost.

Where insertion has become necessary, the editors have been sparing and cautious in their exercise of imagination. If the meaning of a word was clear, although some letters may have been missing because of mutilation or illegibility, up to four missing letters have been silently supplied without the use of brackets. However, if the meaning was not clear, or there might have been more than one meaning, the editors have inserted their preferred choice in square brackets ([ ]) and, if necessary, have supplied the explanation in a footnote. Where more than one word was missing, or the text was supplied through editorial conjecture, this has been indicated by brackets and the inserted matter rendered in italics rather than roman. Where material in a manuscript text appears to have been inserted through a slip of the pen, the editors have followed the text and explained the error by means of a footnote annotation. However, in the case of printed materials where typesetting errors are not uncommon and where they reflect a printer's error rather than that of the writer, the editors have silently corrected the typographical error.

Matter deleted by the writer has, as a general rule, been deleted from the text as printed in this edition. However, in those circumstances where the editors believe that the significance of the material deleted is sufficient to justify an exception to this general policy, the canceled word or passage has been placed *before* the matter that replaced it, and enclosed in angle brackets (⟨ ⟩). A deletion within a deletion has been indicated by double angle brackets (⟨⟨ ⟩⟩), and the preceding rule concerning its placement in the text has been applied.

Throughout, the editors have avoided attributing their own conjectures in interpreting an ambiguous text. Inserted editorial materials appear in bracketed italics whenever the insertions have been too tentative to entitle them to the more definite roman. If necessary, additional information has been supplied in a footnote. The editors have tried to limit the use of brackets, thereby permitting easier reading of the text, but when this jeopardized the integrity of the original text, brackets have been inserted.

Material that Marshall originally wrote as a marginal notation has been brought into the text of a document, printed in a small type size, indented from the left margin, and set following the part of the text to which it pertains. The major portion of this former marginalia occurs in Marshall's law notes.

The presentation of seals in a printed edition is a matter of some difficulty. For purposes of clearer rendition, the editors have divided seals into two categories. One group covers the official and corporate seals, which are rendered [SEAL], provided the document indicates that such a seal was at one time attached to the original. The other seal, be it a wafer seal or simply a signature followed by "L.S.," has been considered a hand seal and rendered "L.S." The number of variations in practice concerning the hand seal of an individual results in the following renditions in our printed text:

J. Marshall L.S.	is shown as	J. Marshall L.S.
J. Marshall (LS)	is shown as	J. Marshall (LS)
J. Marshall (Seal)	is shown as	J. Marshall [LS]
J. Marshall (SEAL)	is shown as	J. Marshall [LS]
J. Marshall (L.S)	is shown as	J. Marshall (L.S)

In presenting documents containing seals, the editors have attempted to conform the appearance of the seal on the printed page to its place on the original manuscript.

ANNOTATION OF DOCUMENTS

While the editors have preferred a policy of sparse annotation, they have attempted to provide the reader with as much guidance as possible concerning the interpretation of Marshall's papers, including essential explanations and a reasonably complete identification of individuals upon their first appearance in the text of the papers. (The volume index will facilitate cross-reference to the first mention of a given name or individual.) Biographical references to well-known individuals listed in the *Dictionary of American Biography* or *Dictionary of National Biography* are intentionally brief, and the editors similarly have not expansively discussed individuals of slight importance to Marshall's career or those whose identity is not material to an understanding of the text of the document. When an identification has not been possible, the editors upon occasion have advanced a supposition based upon knowledge of Marshall's activities and associations, but in most cases they have chosen the safer policy of permitting the reader to speculate upon the identity of an unknown person.

In identifying individuals and business firms the editors have frequently relied on several basic reference works and have used information from them without citation in each instance. In addition to the *DAB* and the *DNB*, these include Lyon G. Tyler's *Encyclopedia of Virginia Biography* and Earl Gregg Swem's *Virginia Historical Index*. Information derived from the periodicals indexed in the latter also has not been named as to source. To identify military figures the editors have similarly depended on Frederick B. Heitman's *Historical Register of the Officers of the Continental Army* and two publications of the Daughters of the American Revolution, the *DAR Patriot Index* and the *Lineage Book*.[1] Definitions of little-used or archaic terms taken from the *Oxford English Dictionary* have not been given a citation, nor have definitions of legal terms obtained

1. Lyon G. Tyler, *Encyclopedia of Virginia Biography* (New York, 1915); E[arl] G. Swem, *Virginia Historical Index* (Richmond, 1934); Frederick B. Heitman, *Historical Register of the Officers of the Continental Army during the War of the Revolution, April, 1775, to December, 1783* (Washington, D.C., 1893); the *DAR Patriot Index* (Washington, D.C., 1966); *Lineage Book, National Society of the Daughters of the American Revolution* (Harrisburg, Pa., 1895; Washington, D.C., 1896–1939).

from *Black's Law Dictionary*. For all other sources, the editors have provided a full bibliographic citation in the appropriate footnote, immediately after the information to which it pertains, or, for works that have been assigned short titles, in the short title list below. Whenever possible, book-length biographies have been cited at the first mention of a given individual in one of Marshall's papers.

The source of each document is identified in full in the line immediately below its heading. In cases where this description is not adequate, the first footnote provides further material and also identifies the writer or recipient if he has not been previously identified. The additional descriptive information is included to give the reader those additional materials available to the editors that may be helpful to one who uses the printed version rather than the original manuscript or imprint. In the case of a particularly delicate problem of documentary analysis, there is, of course, no adequate substitute for viewing the original document, but the editors believe that their annotation policy will reduce the need to consult original documents to a minimum.

In preparing calendared synopses of documents not printed in this edition, the editors have tried to summarize concisely the contents of the manuscript or printed source. As a general rule the synopsis includes a notation concerning John Marshall's connection with the document, and an attempt has been made to identify individuals mentioned in the synopsis. Additional details, if available, have been provided by way of footnote annotations, but in the interest of economy of space, these have been kept to a minimum. Synopses dealing with Marshall's law practice include, if possible, sufficient information for the reader to identify the case involved, the nature of the litigation, and the court in which the case was pending when the calendared document was prepared.

When a document or group of documents has required more extended discussion than could be conveniently included in a footnote annotation, an editorial note has been added immediately preceding the document to which it pertains. Although these notes are intended to be definitive discussions, they obviously are limited in scope to a consideration of the basic document and the situation that gave rise to the documentary material. The editorial notes also contain editorial commentary about interpretive difficulties that have arisen concerning the paper or papers being edited.

ABBREVIATIONS AND SHORT TITLES

The editors have tried to avoid ambiguous abbreviations and have made short titles in citations sufficiently complete to permit ease in bibliographic reference. The following lists contain, first, explanations of abbreviations that may not be readily understood and that have a special meaning in this series and, second, full citations for short titles that are used frequently throughout this volume. Generally accepted abbreviations, such as months of the year, have not been listed, nor have short titles that occur in a limited section of the volume. The latter can easily be expanded by going to the first reference to a work in each document or editorial note; there a full citation is provided.

ABBREVIATIONS

AD	Autograph Document
ADS	Autograph Document Signed
AD[S]	Autograph Document Signed, but with the signature cropped or obliterated
[A]DS	Autograph Document Signed, the text probably in the hand of the signer
AL	Autograph Letter
ALS	Autograph Letter Signed
AL[S]	Autograph Letter Signed, but with signature cropped or obliterated
[A]LS	Autograph Letter Signed, the text probably in the hand of the signer
DS	Document Signed
LS	Letter Signed

SHORT TITLES

Adams, ed., *Autobiographical Sketch*	John Stokes Adams, ed., *An Autobiographical Sketch by John Marshall . . .* (Ann Arbor, Mich., 1937)
AHR	*American Historical Review*
AJLH	*American Journal of Legal History*
Ammon, *Monroe*	Harry Ammon, *James Monroe: The Quest for National Identity* (New York, 1971)

Bacon, *Abridgment* — Matthew Bacon, *A New Abridgment of the Law* . . . , 3d ed. (London, 1766–1769)

Barton, *Va. Colonial Decisions* — Robert T. Barton, ed., *Virginia Colonial Decisions: The Reports of Sir John Randolph and Edward Barradall of the Decisions of the General Court of Virginia, 1728–1741* (Boston, 1909)

Beveridge, *Marshall* — Albert J. Beveridge, *The Life of John Marshall* (Boston, 1916–1919)

Blackstone, *Commentaries* — Sir William Blackstone, *Commentaries on the Laws of England* . . . (Oxford, 1765–1769)

CVSP — William P. Palmer *et al.*, eds., *Calendar of Virginia State Papers and other manuscripts* . . . (Richmond, 1875–1893)

Chitty, *On Pleading* — J[oseph] Chitty, *A Treatise on the Parties to Actions, Forms of Actions, and on Pleading*, 3d Am. ed. (Philadelphia, 1819)

Cullen, "St. George Tucker" — Charles T. Cullen, "St. George Tucker and Law in Virginia, 1772–1804" (Ph.D. diss., University of Virginia, 1971)

Fitzpatrick, *Writings of Washington* — John C. Fitzpatrick, ed., *The Writings of George Washington from the Original Manuscript Sources, 1745–1799* (Washington, D.C., 1931–1944)

Freeman, *Washington* — Douglas Southall Freeman, *George Washington, A Biography*, 6 vols. (New York, 1948–1957); 7th vol. by J. A. Carroll and M. W. Ashworth (New York, 1957)

Hamilton Papers — Harold C. Syrett *et al.*, eds., *The Papers of Alexander Hamilton* (New York, 1961–)

Jefferson Papers — Julian P. Boyd *et al.*, eds., *The Papers of Thomas Jefferson* (Princeton, N.J., 1950–)

JCC	Worthington C. Ford *et al.*, eds., *Journals of the Continental Congress, 1774–1789* (Washington, D.C., 1904–1937)
JVCS	Wilmer L. Hall *et al.*, eds., *Journals of the Council of the State of Virginia . . .* (Richmond, 1931–)
JVHD	*Journal of the House of Delegates of the Commonwealth of Virginia. . . .* This short title will be followed by the year and month in which the General Assembly session commenced.
Madison Papers	William T. Hutchinson *et al.*, eds., *The Papers of James Madison* (Chicago, 1962–)
Marshall, *Washington*	John Marshall, *The Life of George Washington . . .* , 2d ed. rev. (Philadelphia, 1839)
Mason, *Dearest Polly*	Frances Norton Mason, *My Dearest Polly: Letters of Chief Justice John Marshall to His Wife, with Their Background, Political and Domestic, 1779–1831* (Richmond, 1961)
Mason Papers	Robert A. Rutland, ed., *The Papers of George Mason, 1725–1792* (Chapel Hill, N.C., 1970)
PMHB	*Pennsylvania Magazine of History and Biography*
Rhodes, *Marshall Papers Calendar*	Irwin S. Rhodes, *The Papers of John Marshall, A Descriptive Calendar* (Norman, Okla., 1969)
Sellers, "Virginia Continental Line"	John R. Sellers, "The Virginia Continental Line, 1775–1780" (Ph.D. diss., Tulane University, 1968)
Tucker, *Blackstone's Commentaries*	St. George Tucker, [ed.], *Blackstone's Commentaries: With Notes of Reference, to the Constitution and Laws, of the Federal Government of the United States; and*

	of the Commonwealth of Virginia (Philadelphia, 1803)
Tyler's Quarterly	*Tyler's Quarterly Historical and Genealogical Magazine* (1919–1952)
VMHB	*Virginia Magazine of History and Biography*
WMQ	*William and Mary Quarterly*

In addition to the foregoing abbreviations and short titles, the editors have followed the policy of using legal form citations when discussing or citing the reports of cases in courts and statutes passed by legislative bodies in England or the United States. These generally conform to *A Uniform System of Citation*, 11th ed. (Cambridge, Mass., 1967), adopted for use by several law reviews. All other legal citations follow the Institute of Early American History and Culture's *Style Sheet for Authors*, with the following exception:

Hening	William Waller Hening, ed., *The Statutes at Large; Being a Collection of All the Laws of Virginia . . .* (Richmond, 1809–1823)

MARSHALL CHRONOLOGY

1755–1788

September 24, 1755	Born in the vicinity of Germantown, Fauquier County, Virginia.
ca. May 1775	Commissioned a lieutenant in the Fauquier County militia.
ca. September 1775– *ca.* April 1776	Commissioned first lieutenant in the Culpeper Minutemen Battalion; served in Great Bridge-Norfolk campaign.
ca. August 1776	Commissioned first lieutenant in Virginia Continental Line; assigned to Eleventh Virginia Regiment; ordered to active service *ca.* January 1777.
August 30, 1777– September 11, 1777	Assigned to light infantry, participated in skirmish at Iron Hill, Delaware, and battle at Chadd's Ford on Brandywine Creek.
October 3, 4, 1777	Participated in battle of Germantown; wounded in hand.
November 20, 1777	Appointed deputy judge advocate.
December 19, 1777– June 18, 1778	Stationed with troops at Valley Forge winter encampment.
June 28, 1778	Witnessed the battle of Monmouth while defending artillery emplacement.
July 15, 16, 1779	Detached for duty with troops supporting Brig. Gen. Anthony Wayne's assault on Stony Point.
August 19, 1779	Accompanied relief party sent to assistance of Maj. Henry Lee after battle at Paulus Hook.
ca. December 9, 1779	Released from active service when Virginia Continental Line ordered south to defend the Carolinas; subsequently discharged as a supernumerary officer on February 12, 1781.

ca. May 1– July 29, 1780	Attended lectures on law and natural philosophy at the College of William and Mary.
August 28, 1780	Admitted to the practice of law in Fauquier County Court.
ca. May 25– July 2, 1782	Served as member of the Virginia House of Delegates representing Fauquier County.
ca. November 9–29, 1782	Served as member of the House of Delegates representing Fauquier County.
November 30, 1782– April 1, 1784	Served as member of the Council of State (Privy Council).
January 3, 1783	Married Mary Willis Ambler.
May 12–July 1, 1784	Served as member of the House of Delegates representing Fauquier County.
October 30, 1784– January 1, 1785	Served as member of the House of Delegates representing Fauquier County.
April 29, 1785	Admitted to practice before the Virginia Court of Appeals.
July 7, 1785– March 10, 1788	Served as recorder of the city of Richmond.
October 15, 1787– January 8, 1788	Served as member of the House of Delegates representing Henrico County.
June 2–27, 1788	Served as delegate to the Virginia convention called to consider the Constitution proposed by the Philadelphia Convention, representing the Henrico County district.

CORRESPONDENCE AND PAPERS

November 10, 1775—June 23, 1788

Williamsburg Public Store Day Book Entry

DS, Virginia State Library

Williamsburg, Va., November 10, 1775

Culpeper Battalion
for Capt. Pickett[1]...........................Dr.

Per Necessary List

To 9 Yards flannel......................@ 2/6	1	2	6
To 8 Yards frize[2].......................@ 4/8	1	17	4
To 2 doz Small butts. 1/, 1 doz large.......@ 1/		2	
To 42 Yards Oznabr. for body Shirts[3] ......@ 1/6	3	3	
To 2 P ribd. hoes.......................@ 5/		10	
To 13 P Shoes @ 7/, 3 P Virga @ 8/[4]...........	5	15	
To 2 felt hatts 8/..............................		8	
	12	17	10

JOHN MARSHALL
for Wm. Pickett

1. The Culpeper Minutemen Battalion was raised in Sept. 1775 by an ordinance of the Provincial Congress that authorized additional training and equipment for certain militia units. JM's participation in a muster and a description of the unit's uniform are in John F. Dillon, ed., *John Marshall: Life, Character and Judicial Services* (Chicago, 1903), III, 286–288. See also Peter Force, ed., *American Archives*, 4th Ser. (Washington, D.C., 1837–1853), III, 400–404, 687–688, 693; Philip Slaughter, *A History of St. Mark's Parish, Culpeper County, Virginia* (Baltimore, 1877), 107.

JM's company marched from Williamsburg, Va., on or after Nov. 14, was present at the battle of Great Bridge on Dec. 9, and occupied Norfolk from Dec. 14 to about Mar. 1. The company marched to Williamsburg before being dismissed and returned home sometime in Apr. 1776. Journal of the Public Store, 22, Records of the Williamsburg Public Store, Virginia State Library; pension files of David Jameson, S 5607, William Payne, S 8938½, and Samuel Templeman, S 6204, Record Group 15, National Archives.

William Pickett (1735–1798) was a resident of Fauquier County who had received land grants from the Fairfax proprietor on July 18, 1766, Dec. 29, 1772, and Mar. 31, 1779. See Northern Neck Loose Surveys, Fauquier County A-Z, Va. State Lib.

2. Frieze is a coarse woolen cloth with a nap, usually on one side.

3. Osnaburg is a coarse linen cloth that was commonly used for clothing in the American colonies. From the amount issued by the Williamsburg Public Store, it would appear to have been the principal fabric for uniforming the American troops. Hunting shirts were made at public expense and cost 1s. 8d. each. See entry for Nov. 23, 1775, Day Book, Records of the Williamsburg Public Store, Va. State Lib.

4. The distinction seems to be between shoes of Virginia manufacture and those imported from outside the province. Even at this early date there was difficulty in providing adequate footwear to the troops, and the lack of shoes is cited as a hardship during the Great Bridge-Norfolk campaign.

Muster Roll

ADS, RG 93, National Archives[5]

[Falls of the Schuylkill, Pa.], August 7, 1777
A Muster Roll of Capt. Wm. Blackwell's Compy. of the 11th. Virga.
Regt. of Foot in the Service of the United States, commanded by
Colo. Danl. Morgan.[6] From the first of July to the 7th of Augt.
1777.

Commissioned Officers

Wm. Blackwell Capt.

John Marshall 1st. Lieut.

James Wright[7] 2d.   Do.   Sick at Morris Town

Thomas Ransdell[8] 3d. Do.   On Furlough

5. The muster roll is in JM's hand to the "proof of the effectives"; the oath is in an unknown hand.

6. The company under the command of Capt. Blackwell (1738–1782) was raised in Aug. and Sept. 1776, marched to Philadelphia for inoculation in Jan. 1777, and joined the American forces at Princeton in Apr. 1777. The company joined the main army in early May 1777; during this time JM served as regimental adjutant. During the summer Blackwell's company participated in a long march from Morristown, N.J., to the western shores of the Hudson River near Nyack, N.Y., and then south by way of Hackettstown, N.J., to the Delaware River. This muster roll was executed a week after the army crossed the Delaware and marched south to repel the British landing expected to take place at the head of Chesapeake Bay or on the shores of Delaware Bay. Lyon G. Tyler, "The Old Virginia Line in the Middle States during the American Revolution," *Tyler's Quarterly*, XII (1930), 19, 22, 118, 130–131, XIII (1931), 284–287; Sellers, "Virginia Continental Line," 65, 238, 242–243; pension files of Clement Hasty, W 8919, John Krytsar, S 38902, William Stark, S 7592, and William Suddoth, S 40538, RG 15, National Archives. The regimental orderly book for Apr.–May 1777 is entirely in JM's hand. Christian Febiger Orderly Book, 1777, Febiger Papers, Historical Society of Pennsylvania; for functions of adjutants, see John W. Wright, "Some Notes on the Continental Army," *WMQ*, 2d Ser., XI (1931), 99–100. On the army's route of march see Philip Slaughter, Manuscript Diary, Swem Library, College of William and Mary.

Col. Daniel Morgan (1736–1802) was appointed commander of the regiment on Nov. 12, 1776, after previous service in the siege of Boston and the attack on Quebec. At this time, and during most of the war, he was on detached duty with his light infantry brigade.

7. Wright (d. 1823) was appointed second lieutenant in the regiment on July 31, 1776; after the war he returned to Fauquier County.

8. Ransdell (1755–*ca.* 1802) was subsequently promoted to second lieutenant on Feb. 11, 1777.

No.	Serjts.	Time Enlisted for	Remarks
1	John Morgan[9]	3 Years	In Colo. M. R. B.
2	Saml. Phillips[1]	Do.	Sick at Trenton
3	John Anderson	Do.	Sick at M. B.[2]
4	Joseph Garner	Do.	Sick in Phila.[3]

No.	Corpls.	Time enlisted for	Remarks
1	Edwd. Fielding[4]	3 Years	
2	Wm. Suddoth[5]	Do.	In Colo. M. R. B.
3	Thos. Lawler	Do.	
4	Thos. Ryecroft	Do.	Sick at M. Town[6]

No.	Drs. & Fifes	Time Enlisted for	Remarks
1	John Bates	3 years	

No.	Privates	Time enlisted for	Remarks
1	John Lawless[7]	3 years	
2	John Williams	Do.	Sick in Virga.
3	Spencer Edwards[8]	Do.	
4	John Lee	Do.	At M. Town[9]
5	Benjn. Kenton	Do.	Died July 26th.
6	John Grant	Do.	In Colo. M. R. B.
7	Danl. Grant[1]	Do.	[Do.]
8	John Mitchel	Do.	Waiter on G. Woodd.[2]

9. Sgt. Morgan died in service, according to a certificate of Lt. James Wright dated Apr. 28, 1783. See Fauquier County Court, Box 1783, Bundle-May, Office of the Clerk of the Fauquier County Circuit Court, Warrenton, Va.

1. Phillips (d. 1780) enlisted on Sept. 6, 1776.

2. Anderson enlisted on Aug. 10, 1776; at this muster he was hospitalized at Middlebrook, N.J.

3. Garner (*ca.* 1754–1840) enlisted from Fauquier County. It is possible that his hospitalization at Philadelphia was the result of his smallpox immunization the previous January; however, he rejoined the regiment in Sept. 1777 and was wounded in the battle at Brandywine Creek. Pension file, W 7496, RG 15, Natl. Arch.

4. Fielding enlisted on Aug. 20, 1776.

5. Suddoth, or Sudduth (b. *ca.* 1752), indicated in 1820 that he had been enlisted into Blackwell's company by JM and that his enlistment took place in Fauquier County. Pension file, S 40538, RG 15, Natl. Arch.

6. Ryecroft, Rycraft, or Ryecraft, enlisted on Aug. 1, 1776. He was hospitalized at Morristown, N.J.

7. Lawless (*ca.* 1751–*ca.* 1840), a farmer from Fauquier County, enlisted on Aug. 10, 1776. Pension file, W 9109, RG 15, Natl. Arch.

8. Edwards enlisted on Sept. 14, 1776.

9. Lee enlisted on Sept. 14, 1776, and died in service. At this time he was on detached duty at Morristown, N.J.

1. Grant (1759–1831) had served with JM in William Pickett's company of the Culpeper Minutemen Battalion; he enlisted in Blackwell's company in Aug. 1776.

2. Mitchel, or Mitchell, was assigned as a waiter at the table of Brig. Gen. William Woodford (1734–1780), the brigade commander.

9	John Laws[3]	Do.	
10	John Hasty[4]	Do.	At M. Town
11	Clem Hasty[5]	Do.	[Do.]
12	Mach Robinson[6]	Do.	In Colo. M. R. B.
13	James Ash	Do.	
14	Baylis Stone[7]	Do.	
15	Richd. Hervey[8]	3 Years	
16	Edwd. Ransdell	Do.	
17	Richd. Broddus	Do.	at Trenton[9]
18	Wm. Shumate[1]	Do.	
19	John Straughn	Do.	In Colo. M. R. B.
20	Charles Garner[2]	Do.	On Furlough
21	John Phillips[3]	Do.	
22	Wm. Dennis	Do.	In Colo. M. R. B.
23	Danl. Healey[4]	for the War	
24	Wm. Healey	[Do.]	
25	David Harris	Three Years	
26	Saml. Elliot[5]	Do.	At M. Town
27	Charles Morgan	Do.	In Colo. M. R. B.
28	Charles Duncan	3 years	⟨Sick⟩[6]
29	Wm. Kearns[7]	Do.	

3. Laws, or Lawes (1757–1840), a farmer, enlisted in Fauquier County on Aug. 1, 1776. Pension file, S 41754, RG 15, Natl. Arch.

4. Hasty (*ca.* 1753–1826) enlisted from Fauquier County in Aug. 1776. Pension file, W 8919, RG 15, Natl. Arch.

5. Hasty (b. *ca.* 1756) enlisted from Fauquier County in Aug. 1776, and in 1818 JM recalled being present at his enlistment. Pension file, S 38003, RG 15, Natl. Arch.

6. McKinney Robinson (*ca.* 1750–1829) was born in Augusta County, Va.

7. Ash and Stone died in service on Dec. 1 and Dec. 2, 1777.

8. Possibly Richard Harvey (1759–1817).

9. Probably Richard Broadus (*ca.* 1759–*ca.* 1814) from Virginia. The Broddus in JM's company enlisted on Jan. 1, 1777; he was on detached duty at Trenton, N.J.

1. Probably William Shumate (1745–1810).

2. Garner (b. *ca.* 1756) enlisted from Fauquier County, and his pension file indicates that he was discharged because of a swollen leg on June 11, 1777. His affidavit, filed in 1818, claimed that his injury was permanent, and in 1783 he applied to the Fauquier County Court for tax exemption because of lameness. Pension file, S 37950, RG 15, Natl. Arch.; petition, May 22, 1783, Fauquier County Court, Box 1783, Bundle-May, Office of the Fauquier County Circuit Court.

3. Phillips (1739–1794) died in Isle of Wight County, Va.

4. Healey, or Heally, or Haley (d. 1782), enlisted on May 4, 1777.

5. Elliot (*ca.* 1754–1821) enlisted from Fauquier County on Aug. 20, 1776. Pension file, W 19225, RG 15, Natl. Arch.

6. Duncan (*ca.* 1761–1838), a farmer, enlisted on Jan. 12, 1777. A line through the entry "sick" may indicate that Duncan returned to duty after the muster roll was prepared but before the muster was held.

7. Kearns (*ca.* 1757–1842) claimed enlistment in 1775 or 1776 in his pension application and stated that he resided in Fauquier County after his discharge. Pension file, W 7965, RG 15, Natl. Arch.

| 30 | Simon Barré[8] | Do. | |
| 31 | John Chrytser[9] | Do. | On Furlough |

August 4th 1777 Mustered then Capt. Blackwells Company as specified in the above Roll

Jos. Clark D.M. Master[1]

Proof of the Effectives

	Capt.	Lieuts.	Ensign	Serjts.	Corpls.	Dr. & Fifes	Privates
Present	1	1	—	—	2	1	15
Absent		2	—	4	2	—	15
Total	1	3	—	4	4	1	30

The within Muster Roll is Just to the best of Our Knowledge, without Fraud to the united States or Any Individual.

WILLIAM BLACKWELL Capt.

JNO. MARSHALL 1st. Lieut.

Sworn before me this 7th Day of Augt. 1777
WM WOODFORD Bridgr: Genl:

Payroll

DS, RG 93, National Archives

[Skippack, Pa.], October 1, 1777
A Pay Roll of Capt. Wm. Blackwell's Company in The 11th Virginia Regt. Commanded by Colol. Daniel Morgan—from the first of Septr. to the firs[t] of Octobr 1777.[2]

---

8. Barré was also known as Barry and Berry.

9. Chrytser, or Krytsar (b. *ca.* 1752), enlisted from Fauquier County on Jan. 8, 1777. After the company joined the main army at Middlebrook, N.J., in May 1777, Chrytser was assigned to a scouting party. In the course of this duty he was wounded in the groin by an enemy musket ball and remained disabled until Jan. 1778. Pension file, S 38902, RG 15, Natl. Arch.

1. Joseph Clark (1751–1813) was an adjutant from New Jersey.

2. This payroll documents JM's return to duty with his company. In the skirmishes leading up to the battle at Brandywine Creek he had served with the light infantry under Brig. Gen. William Maxwell (*ca.* 1733–1796). The light infantry unit saw combat at the "battle" of Iron Hill and harrassed the British advance toward Chadd's Ford, Pa. Adams, ed., *Autobiographical Sketch*, 6; Marshall, *Washington*, 2d ed., I, 154–155, 158. See also Evan W. H. Fyers, "General Sir William Howe's Operations in Penn-

Names	Rank	pay pr. Month		Time Drawn for M. W	Who[l]e pay Dols
William Blackwell	Capt.	40	Dos	1	40
John Marshall 1st.	Leit.	27		1	27
James Wright 2nd	Leiut.	27		1	27
Thos. Ransdell 3rd.	Leiut.	27		1	27
Samuel Phillips	Sergent	8	Dols	1	8
John Anderson	Do.	8		1	8
Joseph Gardner[3]	Do.	8		1	8
Edwerd Fielding	Corporal	7 1/3		1	7 1/3
Thos Lawler	Do.	7 1/3		1	7 1/3
Thomas Rycroft	Do.	7 1/3		1	7 1/3
John Bates	Drummr	7 1/3		1	7 1/3
John Lawless	Private	6 2/3		Do.	6 2/3
Spencer Edwerds	Do.	6 2/3		Do.	6 2/3
John Lee	Do.	6 2/3		Do.	6 2/3
John Mitchell	Do.	6 2/3		Do.	6 2/3
John Laws	Do.	6 2/3		Do.	6 2/3
John Hastey	Do.	6 2/3		Do.	6 2/3
Clem Hastey	Do.	6 2/3		Do.	6 2/3
James Ash	Do.	6 2/3		Do.	6 2/3
Richard Harvey	Do.	6 2/3		Do.	6 2/3
Edwerd Ransdell	Do.	6 2/3		Do.	6 2/3
William Shumate	Do.	6 2/3		Do.	6 2/3
Charles Garner	Do.	6 2/3		Do.	6 2/3
John Phillips	Do.	6 2/3		Do.	6 2/3
William Haley	Do.	6 2/3		Do.	6 2/3
David Harris	Do.	6 2/3		Do.	6 2/3
Samuel Elliot	Do.	6 2/3		Do.	6 2/3
Charles Duncan	Do.	6 2/3		Do.	6 2/3
William Keirnes	Do.	6 2/3		Do.	6 2/3
John Critser	Do.	6 2/3		Do.	6 2/3
Daniel Hailey	Do.	6 2/3		Do.	6 2/3
Simon Barrey	Do.	6 2/3		Do.	6 2/3
Richard Broaddos	Do.	6 2/3		Do.	6 2/3
Baliss Stone	Do.	6 2/3		Do.	6 2/3
		327 2/3		Dollars	327 2/3

JOHN MARSHALL Lieut.

sylvania, 1777," *Society of Army Historical Research Bulletin*, VIII (1929), 235, IX (1930), 33–34.
    3. The name should read "Joseph Garner."

Muster Roll

DS, RG 93, National Archives

[Towamensing, Pa.], October 13, 1777
A Muster Roll of Captn. Blackwells Company in 11th Virga. Regt. of foot Commanded by Colol. Daniel Morgan. To 13th of Octobr 1777.[4]

Commissiond: Officers
Wm. Blackwell, Capt.   Sick
John Marshall. 1st Leit.
James Wright. 2 Leit
Thos. Ransdell 3 Leit

No	Sergts.	Remarks	Term Enlistment
1	John Morgan	In Colol. M. R. B.	3 years
2	Saml. Phillips		Do.
3	John Anderson	Sick Middlebrook	Do.
4	Jos. Garner	On Command	Do.
No	Corpos & Drums	Remarks	Term of Enlist.
1	Edwd Fielding		3 years
2	Wm. Suddoth	In Colol. M. R. B.	Do.
3	Thos. Lawler	Sick	Do.
4	Thos. Rycraft		Do.
1	John Bates, Drum		Do.
	[Privates]		
1	John Lawles		3 years
2	Spenr. Edwards		Do.
3	John Lee		Do.
4	John Grant	In Colol. M. R. B.	Do.
5	Jno. Mitchell	Wa[i]ter on Genl. Woodford	Do.
6	Jno. Laws		Do.

4. This muster roll was prepared after the battle of Germantown, probably in accordance with the general order of Oct. 13. See Fitzpatrick, *Writings of Washington*, IX, 362. JM's regiment was assigned to the division commanded by Maj. Gen. Adam Stephen (*ca.* 1716–1791), and during his company's engagement in the siege of the house of Benjamin Chew, JM was wounded in the hand. Marshall, *Washington*, 2d ed., I, 168–169; pension file of William Kearns, W 7965, RG 15, National Archives; Freeman, *Washington*, IV, 510–519. See also Alfred B. Lambdin, "Battle of Germantown," *PMHB*, I (1877), 377–379, 383–384.

7	Jno. Hastey	Sick	Do.
8	James Ash	Sick	Do.
9	Richd. Harvey		Do.
10	Edwd. Ransdell		Do.
11	Wm. Shumate		Do.
12	Chars. Garner	on Furlough	Do.
13	Jno. Phillips		Do.
14	Wm. Dennis	In Colol. M. R. B.	Do.
15	Wm. Hailey		for the War
16	Clem Hastey		for 3 years
17	Daniel Grant	In Colol. M. R. B.	for 3 years
18	David Harris		Do.
19	Saml. Elliot		Do.
20	John Straughn	In Colol. M. R. B	Do.
21	Charles Duncan		Do.
22	Wm. Keirnes		Do.
23	Charles Morgan	In Colol. M. R. B	Do.
24	John Cretser	on Furlough	Do.
25	Mack Robinson	In Colol. M. R. B	Do.
26	Daniel Hailey		for the War
27	Simon Barry		for 3 years
28	Richard Broaddus		Do.
29	Bailey Stone	Sick	Do.

JOHN MARSHALL, Let
JAMES WRIGHT Leit

Octob 13, Mustered, then Capt. Blackwells Company as specified above

JOS. CLARK D.M. Master

Proof of the Affective

	Capt.	Leiut.	Ensigns	Sergt.	Corpls.	Drum fife	Privates
Present		3		1	2	1	16
Absent	1			3	2		13
Total	1	3		4	4	1	29

We do Swere that the Within Muster Roll is a true State of the Company Without fraud to the United States or to Any Individual According to the Best of our knowledge.

JOHN MARSHALL
JAMES WRIGHT

Sworn Before me this 13th. Day of   1777
T. MARSHALL Colo. Com[manding][5]

Muster Roll

DS, RG 93, National Archives

[*November 4, 1777* (*White Marsh, Pa.*). JM signs the muster roll in the absence of Capt. Blackwell, who is sick; the company remains at about half its full strength, with several men sick and a number detached for duty with Col. Morgan's rifle brigade.]

Assignment

AD, RG 93, National Archives[6]

Sir   [Valley Forge, Pa.], *ca.* December 23, 1777
   You will please to pay Lieut. Marshall my wages from the first of October to the 23d. of Decr. 1777.

CHARLES TYLER[7]

To the Pay Master of the 11th V. Regt.[8]

Muster Roll

DS, RG 93, National Archives

[*January 11, 1778* (*Valley Forge, Pa.*). JM signs the muster roll as first lieutenant; the company remains at half strength.]

5. Brig. Gen. William Woodford had been wounded at the battle of Germantown. JM's father, Thomas Marshall (1730–1802), then colonel of the Third Virginia Regiment, was apparently senior colonel present for duty and thus succeeded to the command of the brigade.

6. The document, with the exception of the signature, is in JM's hand.

7. Tyler (1740–*ca.* 1800) was commissioned an ensign in Capt. Charles Gallahue's (d. 1777) company of the Eleventh Virginia Regiment on Nov. 25, 1776, and resigned on Dec. 23, 1777.

8. Although not negotiable in form and unwitnessed, it would appear that this document was a sufficient assignment of two months' salary.

Payroll for Extra Pay

[A]DS, RG 93, National Archives

[Valley Forge, Pa., *ca.* January 11, 1778]
A Pay Roll[9] of the late Capt. William Blackwells Comp. in the
11th. Virga. Regt. commanded by Capt Charles Porterfield,[1] for
the extra pay agreable to Genl. Orders—Jany. 11th 1778.

No.	Names	Rank	For one Month	Pay per Month in Dollars	Whole pay in lawful Money		Casualties
	John Marshall	Lt.	—	27	8	2	
	James Wright	Lt.	—	27	8	2	On Furlough since the 29th. of Decr. 1777[2]
	Thomas Ransdell	Lt.	—	27	8	2	
1	Saml. Phillips	Serjt.	—	8	2	8	
2	John Anderson	Serjt.	—	8	2	8	
1	Edwd. Fielding	Corpl.	—	7 1/3	2	4	
2	Thos. Ryecroft	Do.	—	7 1/3	2	4	
	John Bates	Drumr.	—	7 1/3	2	4	
1	John Lawless	Private	—	6 2/3	2	0	
2	Spencer Edwards	Do.	—	6 2/3	2	0	
3	John Lee	Do.	—	6 2/3	2	0	
4	John Mitchel	Do.	—	6 2/3	2	0	Waiter on Genl. Woodford

9. The extraordinary pay of one month's wages was voted by Congress on Dec. 30, 1777, and this payroll was required by a subsequent resolution of Jan. 1, 1778. *JCC,* IX, 1067–1068, X, 8; Fitzpatrick, *Writings of Washington,* X, 266, 284. On Feb. 17, 1778, Congress authorized payment to all men under Washington's direct command, either present for duty or on authorized furlough. *JCC,* X, 178. We have assumed that the payroll was prepared on or about Jan. 11. It does not contain the names of 13 men in the company, presumably because they did not fall within the categories established by the resolution of Congress.

1. Porterfield (d. 1780), a veteran of the Quebec expedition, was appointed captain in the Eleventh Virginia Regiment on Feb. 3, 1777.

2. Under the terms of the resolution of Dec. 30, 1777, it was unclear whether men on furlough as of that date would be eligible. The Feb. 17 clarifying resolution established the entitlement of Lt. Wright and Pvt. Elliot.

5	John Laws	Do.	—	6 2/3	2	0	
6	Clemn Hastey	Do.	—	6 2/3	2	0	
7	Richard Hervey	Do.	—	6 2/3	2		
8	Edward Ransdell	Do.	—	6 2/3	2		
9	Wm. Shumate	Do.	—	6 2/3	2		
10	John Phillips	Do.	—	6 2/3	2		
11	William Healey	Do.	—	6 2/3	2		
12	David Harris	Do.	—	6 2/3	2		
13	Samuel Elliot	Do.	—	6 2/3	2		On Furlough since the 29th. of Decr. 1777
14	Charles Duncan	Do.	—	6 2/3	2		
15	Wm. Kearns	Do.	—	6 2/3	2		
16	John Chrytser	Do.	—	6 2/3	2		
17	Daniel Healey	Do.	—	6 2/3	2		
18	Simon Barri	Do.	—	6 2/3	2		
19	Richard Broddus	Do.	—	6 2/3	2		

£ 73 14   Equal to 245 2/3 Dollars

JOHN MARSHALL Lt. commanding[3]

Payroll

DS, RG 93, National Archives

[*January 31, 1778 (Valley Forge Pa.*). JM draws $27 monthly pay as a first lieutenant; he also signs the payroll as "Lt comdg" the company.]

Honoraria

DS, Emmet Collection, New York Public Library

Valley Forge, Pa., February 22, 1778

It is offered to the consideration of the Officers of the Virginia Line to contribute something as a reward to Mrs Hay & her Daughter for their great attention & Tenderness to our Brother Officers, Prisoners in the City of Philadelphia, it is well known to several

3. Capt. Blackwell resigned his commission on Jan. 10, 1778. Muster roll of Feb. 6, 1778, RG 93, National Archives.

Officers of Rank, that they have come out at different times purely to serve the distressed at the risque of their Lives, & have actually assisted some officers in makeing their escape, besides nursing the sick & takeing particular care of the affects of the Deceased. Mrs Hay is a poor Widow, & any Little matter that Gentlemen chuse to contribute, can't fail of being acceptable & will be considered as a greatfull acknowledgement on their part for the Voluntary & Benevolent part she has acted.

Majr Day[4] is obligeing enough to receive what the Gentlemen of Genl. Woodfords Brigade chuse to contribute.

JOHN MARSHALL[5]

N B. The Gentlemen of the Brigade have with the greatest Chearfulness contributed the Sums affixed to their names, and flatter themselves if all the Officers of the Brigade had been present the Amount would have been more worthy the Acceptance of the Persons for whom it is intended.

BENJN: DAY M B[6]

Assignment

AD, RG 93, National Archives[7]

Sir   [Valley Forge, Pa.], February 27, 1778
    Please to pay Lt. Marshall my wages for the[8]

                                               his
                              Robert   X   Colwell
                                             mark

The Pay Master of Colo. Grayson's Regt.

4. Benjamin Day was appointed adjutant of the Second Virginia Regiment in June 1777.
    5. The document was signed by JM and 42 other officers of the Virginia Continental Line. JM subscribed 15s. of a £50 10s. total.
    6. "M B" stands for brigade major.
    7. The document, with the exception of the signature, is in JM's hand. An endorsement reads "Robert Caldwell's / Order / Ent'd." A list of orders and proved accounts not entered in the receipt book shows an obligation of £2 10s. in favor of "Jno. Marshall," based upon an order signed by Robert Caldwell against Capt. Hebart Smallwood's company in the Additional Regiment commanded by Col. William Grayson (1736–1790). Loose Manuscripts, RG 93, National Archives. The sum of £2 10s. was the monthly pay of a private in the Continental Line.
    8. Mutilated at the end of the paper, this was probably a date such as "February 1778."

Payroll

Copy, RG 93, National Archives[9]

[*February 28, 1778 (Valley Forge, Pa.)*. JM receives $27 for month's pay as a first lieutenant and signs the payroll as lieutenant commanding.]

Muster Roll

DS, RG 93, National Archives

Valley Forge, Pa., March 15, 1778
MUSTER ROLL Captain Wm. Blackwells Compy: of the 11th. Virga. Regt. Command. by Major Thos. Snead[1] taken for February 1778.

COMMISSION'D

July 31st	1776	John Marshall	1st Lieut:	acting as Judge advocate[2]
July 31	1776	James Wright	2d. do.	on furlow
July 31	1776	Thos. Ransdell	3d. do.	

9. In a clerk's hand, JM's signature is in an unusually round hand, using the old style "s."

1. Maj. Thomas Snead resigned from the service on Mar. 8, 1778, the day following the muster of troops in this company.

2. JM had been appointed a deputy judge advocate by general orders on Nov. 20, 1777. Fitzpatrick, *Writings of Washington*, X, 88. The 1776 articles of war provided that the judge advocate general, or some person deputed by him, should prosecute al courts-martial in the name of the United States. Deputy judge advocates were appointed for each of the three territorial departments, and additional deputy judge advocates were appointed by field commanders as the need for their services arose. *JCC*, V, 801, VII, 391, X, 178, XII, 1131. See also William F. Fratcher, "History of the Judge Advocate General's Corps, United States Army," *Military Law Review*, IV (1959), 89–92, 116–117. JM's first experience with a court-martial in the Continental army was on Apr. 16, 1777, when he served as a member of the regimental court-martial that tried Sgt. Athanasius Farber and Pvt. John Burk. Christian Febiger Orderly Book, Febiger Papers, Historical Society of Pennsylvania.

Presumably JM was at the court-martial when the muster of the unit was held on Mar. 7, 1778. The proof of the effectives leads us to believe that the court was convened at the Valley Forge encampment; otherwise JM would have been shown as absent on detached duty. He returned to duty and was available to sign and swear to the contents of the muster roll on Mar. 15.

No.	Serjeants	War	3 Yrs	Remarks
1	Sam. Phillips			
2	John Anderson			On Guard
3	Joseph Garner			On Furlow

No.	Corporals	War	3 Yrs.	Remarks
1	Edwin Fielding			
2	Thos. Ryecroft			on Command

No.	Drums & Fifes	War	3 Yrs	Remarks
1	Jno. Bates			

No.	Privates	War	3 Yrs	Remarks
1	John Lawless			
2	Spencer Edwards			Command
3	John Lee			Do.
4	John Mitchell			Waitg on Gl. Woodford
5	John Laws			
6	John Hasty			Sick prest:
7	Clem Hasty			
8	Richd Harvey			on Command
9	Edwd Ransdell			
10	Wm Shumate			on Guard
11	Chas. Gardner			on Furlow
12	John Phillips			
13	Willm. Heally			
14	David Harris			
15	Saml. Elliott			on Command
16	Charles Duncan			
17	Wm Cairnes			
18	Jno. Crytser			Sick present
19	Danl. Hayley[3]			
20	Richd Broddus			Sick present
21	Simon Barry			

VALLEY FORGE March 7th: 1778 then Mustered Captn Wm Blackwells Compy as Specified above

JOS CLARK DMM

3. Daniel Heally.

PROOF OF THE EFFECTIVES

	Lieutents.	Serjts:	drums & fifes	Corps.	Privts:
Present	2	1	1	1	14
Absent	1	2		1	7
Total	3	3	1	2	21

I DO SWEAR that the within Muster Roll is a true State of Captn: Wm. Blackwells Compy. without fraud to the United States or any Individual to the best of my knowledge.

JOHN MARSHALL Lt.

SWORN to before me this 15th day of March 1778
WM WOODFORD Brigdr. Genl.

Acknowledgment

ADS, RG 93, National Archives[4]

[Valley Forge, Pa.], March 24, 1778

Danniel Willett, Dr
   To Six Dollars For Clothing £1.16.0

DAVD. WILLIAMS[5]

Proved this 24th. day of March 1778 before me

JOHN MARSHALL D.J.A.G.[6]

Payroll

ADS, RG 93, National Archives

[*ca. March 31, 1778 (Valley Forge, Pa.*). JM signs the payroll as commanding officer; he draws $27 monthly pay as a first lieutenant.]

4. In Williams's hand with the attestation beginning "proved" in JM's hand.

5. Three officers of this name are listed as being from Virginia. Very likely the individual mentioned here is David Williams (1750–1831), who became ensign in the Eleventh Virginia Regiment on July 1, 1777.

6. "Deputy Judge Advocate General." This and the following group of acknowledgments taken by JM as deputy judge advocate are the only documentary evidence of his activities in that office. They indicate that deputy judge advocates possessed notarial powers not dissimilar to those assigned to summary courts officers today.

Payroll

ADS, RG 93, National Archives

[*May 1, 1778* (*Valley Forge, Pa.*). JM draws $27 pay as a first lieutenant and signs the payroll as commanding officer of company.]

Acknowledgment

ADS, RG 93, National Archives[7]

[Valley Forge, Pa.], May 8, 1778

Jeremiah Goldsburry

Dr to Richard Conner[8]

	£	S	D
To Cash Lent	0 .	15 .	0
Do.	0 .	12 .	6
	£1 .	7 .	6

Sworn before me this 8th. day of May 1778

JOHN MARSHALL DJAG

Acknowledgment

ADS, RG 93, National Archives

[*May 8, 1778* (*Valley Forge, Pa.*). An account between Duncan Cowen and William Pope, dated Apr. 6, 1778, and proved before JM as deputy judge advocate general on May 8.]

7. A scrap of paper with writing in a hand other than JM's but with the acknowledgment in JM's hand. On the verso is an endorsement "Goldsbery Paid by Conner 75."
8. Richard Conner (1753–1824) was a member of the company commanded by Capt. William Johnston (1751–1815) in the Eleventh Virginia Regiment.

Acknowledgment

ADS, RG 93, National Archives[9]

[Valley Forge, Pa.], May 10, 1778

Serjt. Nollen of Capt. Ricees Compy.[1] Dr. to John Rooke Seven Dollore

Proved this 10th. day of May 1778 before me.

JOHN MARSHALL DJAG

Acknowledgment

ADS, RG 93, National Archives

[*May 10, 1778 (Valley Forge, Pa.).* JM takes acknowledgment of Jeremiah Goldsburry's two-dollar debt to John Rooke.]

Payroll

DS, RG 93, National Archives

[*May 31, 1778, Valley Forge, Pa.* JM signs the payroll as commanding officer and receives monthly pay of $27 as a first lieutenant.]

Acknowledgment

ADS, RG 93, National Archives[2]

[Valley Forge, Pa.], June 8, 1778

Andrew Dunn, Dr.

To yr wages from the 1st Decr. 1777 untill the 1st April 1778

---

9. The last sentence and the signature are in JM's hand. It is possible that Sgt. Nollen may be James Noland (1760–1835), although Noland's age in 1778 would have been young for a sergeant.

1. George Rice (1748–1800) had been promoted to captain in the Eleventh Virginia Regiment on Mar. 9, 1777.

2. An irregular sheet of paper in a hand other than Williamson's; last sentence and signature are in JM's hand.

which you agreed to give me to Exchange Companys,[3] 26⅔ Dollars.

JOHN WILLIAMSON[4]

Proved this 8th: day of June 1778 before me.
JOHN MARSHALL DJAG

Acknowledgment

ADS, RG 93, National Archives

[*June 16, 1778* (*Valley Forge, Pa.*). JM takes acknowledgment of an account between Thomas Thomas, possibly Ens. Thomas Thomas (1752–1836), and Isaac Brown for 15s. 6d.]

Acknowledgment

ADS, RG 93, National Archives

[*August 10, 1778, White Plains, N.Y.* JM as deputy judge advocate takes acknowledgment of an account between George Taggert and Capt. George Rich (Rice) for two dollars. The account is for "cash lent." A Pvt. George Tiggart (Teggart, Tygart, Tagart) was in Capt. George Rice's company of the Eleventh Virginia Regiment.]

Acknowledgment

ADS, RG 93, National Archives

[*August 10, 1778, White Plains, N.Y.* JM takes acknowledgment of an account between Anthony Meaday and Timothy Sheehan for $12. Meaday, or Mayday, was a corporal and drum major assigned to Capt. Charles Porterfield's company of the Eleventh Virginia Regiment; Sheehan was a private in Capt. William Johnston's company in the same regiment.]

3. It may have been customary for a private to pay his company commander for the privilege of changing to another unit. The salary assigned amounts to four months' pay as a private soldier in the Continental Line.

4. Probably John Williamson (1726–1794), who was appointed first lieutenant in the Fourth Pennsylvania Battalion on Jan. 6, 1776.

Acknowledgment

ADS, RG 93, National Archives

[*August 10, 1778, White Plains, N.Y.* JM takes acknowledgment of an account between Sgt. Aquilla Narvell and Roger McMahon showing a balance of £3 7s. 6d. due to Narvell. Narvell was a sergeant in Capt. Charles Gallahue's company in the Eleventh Virginia Regiment; McMahon (1759–1823) was a private in Capt. George Rice's company in the same regiment.]

Acknowledgment

DS, RG 93, National Archives

[*August 12, 1778, White Plains, N.Y.* JM takes acknowledgment of a debt of William Berry, a soldier in Capt. Charles Porterfield's company of the Eleventh and Fifteenth Virginia Regiment (combined), to Daniel Collett (1752–1835), a private in the same company, for £2 12s. 6d.]

Acknowledgment

DS, RG 93, National Archives

[*August 13, 1778, White Plains, N.Y.* JM takes acknowledgment of an account between Lt. Jesse Davis (1755–1818) of the Eleventh Virginia Regiment and James Thompson (*ca.* 1738–*ca.* 1809) of Capt. George Rice's company in the same regiment.]

Acknowledgment

DS, RG 93, National Archives

[*August 16, 1778, White Plains, N.Y.* JM takes acknowledgment of an account between George Tagart (Tiggart, Tygart, Taggart) and Robert Sharman, probably Robert Shearman (*ca.* 1745–1816), warrant officer and pipe major in the Eleventh and Fifteenth Virginia Regiment (combined).]

Acknowledgment

ADS, RG 93, National Archives

[*August 18, 1778, White Plains, N.Y.* JM takes the oath of Capt. John Blackwell[5] that Blackwell has examined the account book of Capt. John Chilton, deceased,[6] and has found that Duncan Meade[7] owed Chilton £5 11s. for clothing.]

Acknowledgment

ADS, RG 93, National Archives

[*August 20, 1778, White Plains, N.Y.* JM takes acknowledgment of an account between Capt. John Blackwell and Lt. Jesse Davis of the Eleventh Virginia Regiment.]

Payroll

DS, RG 93, National Archives[8]

[White Plains, N.Y.], August 30, 1778
A Pay Roll of Lieut. Colo. Croppers[9] Companey in 11th and 15th Virginia Regmt. in the Service of the United of America Commanded by Colo. Daniel Morgan—Taken for the Month of August 1778.

5. Blackwell (1755–1831) became captain in the Third Virginia Regiment on Sept. 15, 1777.

6. Chilton (1739–1777) was killed at the battle of Brandywine; presumably Blackwell, a close friend of the deceased, had been appointed to administer his estate. See *Tyler's Quarterly*, XII, 91–93.

7. Duncan Meade was a fifer assigned to Capt. Charles Porterfield's company in the Eleventh Virginia Regiment.

8. The marginal notations and footings are in JM's hand. Under the "new military establishment" implemented on May 27, 1778, battalions were formed to consist of nine companies of the line and one light infantry company. Sellers, "Virginia Continental Line," 299. This payroll reflects a substantial influx of men into JM's company. A muster roll for July 23, 1778, indicates that the company was reinforced by men selected from the companies of Capt. William Grymes (1730–1777) and Capt. James Harris (1740–1796) in the Fifteenth Virginia Regiment. Muster roll, RG 15, National Archives. During Dec. 1778 these men were withdrawn from JM's command, reducing the size of the company from 58 to 21. Payrolls, Dec. 2, *ca.* Dec. 30, 1778, RG 15, Natl. Arch.

9. John Cropper (1755–1821) was appointed lieutenant colonel in the Eleventh Virginia Regiment on Apr. 18, 1778, according to the regimental muster rolls in RG 93, Natl. Arch. Frederick B. Heitman, *Historical Register of Officers of the Continental Army* (Washington, D.C., 1893), 140, gives Oct. 26, 1777, as the date of his assignment to the regiment.

[No.]	Names	Rank	Commencement of pay	Pay Per Month	Subsistence	Whole amt of pay and subsistence £ S. D.			Remarks
1	John Marshall	Liut.[1]	Augt. 1	26 2/3	10	11	—	—	
	John Townes[2]	Ensign	Do.	20	10	9	—	—	
1	Samuel Phillips	Sergts.	do.	10	—	3	—	—	
2	Thomas Lawler	do.	do.	10	—	3	—	—	
3	William Cox	do.	do.	10	—	3	—	—	
4	Nathaniel Quarles	do.	do.	10	—	3	—	—	
5	George Flack[3]	do.	do.	10	—	3	—	—	
1	Edward Fielding	Corpl.	do.	7 1/3	—	2	4	—	
2	Thomas Rycroft	do.	do.	7 1/3	—	2	4	—	
3	James Duffay[4]	do.	do.	7 1/3	—	2	4	—	
4	Robert Watterson[5]	do.	do.	7 1/3	—	2	4	—	
5	Simon Butt[6]	do.	do.	7 1/3	—	2	4	—	

1. A field and staff muster roll of Aug. 4 listed JM as a captain lieutenant of a company in the combined Eleventh and Fifteenth Virginia Regiment. RG 93, Natl Arch. His listing here as a lieutenant is noteworthy. Since Col. Morgan continued to command the regiment, Lt. Col. Cropper's company could not contain a captain lieutenant. However, Col. Morgan was serving as brigade commander, and Lt. Col. Cropper was in actual command of the Eleventh and Fifteenth Virginia Regiment (combined). Thus there is a certain amount of confusion concerning JM's position and rank.

2. Townes (1758–ca. 1830) was appointed ensign in the Eleventh Virginia Regiment on Nov. 25, 1776; he was promoted to first lieutenant effective July 1, 1777, but like JM, who was promoted to captain effective on that date, his promotion had not yet been announced.

3. Flack enlisted on Feb. 14, 1778, and was discharged Feb. 15, 1779.

4. Duffay, or Duffy, enlisted on Dec. 5, 1776.

5. Watterson enlisted on Dec. 26, 1776.

6. Butt enlisted on Dec. 24, 1776.

[No.]	Names	Rank	Commencement of pay	Pay Per Month	Subsistence	Whole amt of pay and subsistence £	S.	D.	Remarks
1	Spencer Edwards	Private	Augt. 1	6 2/3	—	2	—	—	
2	Keder Dobbs[7]	do.	do.	6 2/3	—	2	—	—	
3	William Hardy[8]	do.	do.	6 2/3	—	2	—	—	
4	Timothy Wood[9]	do.	do.	6 2/3	—	2	—	—	
5	James Bailey	do.	do.	6 2/3	—	2	—	—	
6	Jessey Jones[1]	do.	do.	6 2/3	—	2	—	—	
7	George Long[2]	do.	do.	6 2/3	—	2	—	—	
8	John Hufman[3]	do.	do.	6 2/3	—	2	—	—	
9	William Roland[4]	do.	do.	6 2/3	—	2	—	—	
10	Abden Duff[5]	do.	do.	6 2/3	—	2	—	—	
11	William Haily	do.	do.	6 2/3	—	2	—	—	
12	Alexdr. Ronalds[6]	do.	do.	6 2/3	—	2	—	—	
13	Simon Berrey	do.	do.	6 2/3	—	2	—	—	

7. Dobbs enlisted on Sept. 14, 1776.

8. Hardy (ca. 1720–ca. 1790) enlisted as a private in Capt. William Grymes's company of the Fifteenth Virginia Regiment on Feb. 14, 1778.

9. Wood enlisted on Dec. 13, 1776.

1. Jones enlisted on Jan. 9, 1776.

2. Long enlisted on Nov. 17, 1776.

3. Hufman, probably John Hoffman (1728–1802), enlisted on Feb. 14, 1776.

4. Roland, or Rowland, enlisted on Nov. 19, 1776.

5. Duff enlisted on Feb. 14, 1778; he had been hospitalized at Valley Forge and was still sick, either there or at West Point, when this payroll was executed.

6. Ronalds, or Reynolds, enlisted on May 1, 1777.

[No.]	Names	Rank	Commencement of pay	Pay Per Month	Subsistence	Whole amt of pay and subsistence £. S. D.			Remarks
14	William Shoemate	do.	do.	6 2/3	—	2	—	—	
15	Clem Hastey	do.	do.	6 2/3	—	2	—	—	
16	William Dolbey[7]	do.	do.	6 2/3	—	2	—	—	
17	Henry Mathias[8]	do.	do.	6 2/3	—	2	—	—	
18	Joshua Stafford[9]	do.	do.	6 2/3	—	2	—	—	
19	Mathew McDougle[1]	do.	do.	6 2/3	—	2	—	—	
20	Joseph Davis	do.	do.	6 2/3	—	2	—	—	
21	Holida Rival[2]	do.	do.	6 2/3	—	2	—	—	
22	Howell Underhill[3]	do.	do.	6 2/3	—	2	—	—	
23	Alexandr. Campbell[4] [do.]		do.	6 2/3	—	2	—	—	
24	Willson Leversage[5]	do.	do.	6 2/3	—	2	—	—	
25	Charles Duncan	do.	do.	6 2/3	—	2	—	—	
26	William Creamore[6]	do.	do.	6 2/3	—	2	—	—	
27	John Hastey	do.	do.	6 2/3	—	2	—	—	

7. Dolbey enlisted on Dec. 7, 1776, and received an invalid's pension in 1802. Pension file, S 25033, RG 15, Natl. Arch.

8. Mathias enlisted on Dec. 29, 1776.

9. Stafford enlisted on Feb. 14, 1778, and was discharged on Feb. 15, 1779.

1. McDougle enlisted on Nov. 30, 1776.

2. Holida Rival, or Holliday Revell (b. *ca.* 1753), enlisted on Sept. 2, 1777. He was a lifelong resident of Southampton County, Va. Pension file, S 39034, RG 15, Natl. Arch.

3. Underhill enlisted for one year on Feb. 14, 1778.

4. Campbell (1744–*ca.* 1786) enlisted on Nov. 16, 1777.

5. Leversage enlisted on Dec. 26, 1776.

6. Creamore, or Cremour (also known as Cramour and Kreamour), enlisted on Nov. 27, 1776.

[No.]	Names	Rank	Commencement of pay	Pay Per Month	Subsistence	Whole amt of pay and subsistence £	S.	D.	Remarks
28	John Laws	do.	do.	6 2/3	—	2	—	—	
29	William Kernes	do.	do.	6 2/3	—	2	—	—	
30	John Kernes	do.	do.	6 2/3	—	2	—	—	
31	George Rose	do.	do.	6 2/3	—	2	—	—	
32	David Harris	do.	do.	6 2/3	—	2	—	—	
33	Henry Simons[7]	do.	do.	6 2/3	—	2	—	—	
34	Richard Harvey	do.	do.	6 2/3	—	2	—	—	
35	Adam McCormack[8]	do.	do.	6 2/3	—	2	—	—	
36	Daniel Hailey	do.	do.	6 2/3	—	2	—	—	
37	Nathaniel Millington	do.	do.	6 2/3	—	2	—	—	
38	John Lawless	do.	do.	6 2/3	—	2	—	—	
39	John Ore	do.	do.	6 2/3	—	2	—	—	
40	John Mitchell	do.	do.	6 2/3	—	2	—	—	
41	Samul Elliot	do.	do.	6 2/3	—	2	—	—	
42	William Flora[9]	do.	do.	6 2/3	—	2	—	—	
1	Joseph Gaines	Sergt.	—	10	—	3	—	—	Hospl. June Since Joined & Discharged
1	John Baites	Drummer	do.	7 1/3	—	2	4	—	

£ 135   4   Equal to 450 2/3 Dollrs.

JOHN MARSHALL Lt.

7. Simons, or Symons, enlisted on Jan. 21, 1776.
8. McCormack enlisted on May 14, 1777.
9. Flora, or Florea, enlisted on Nov. 22, 1776.

Payroll

DS, RG 93, National Archives

[*ca. May 31, 1779* (*Smith's Clove, N.Y.*). JM signs the payroll showing his receipt of $40 monthly pay and $20 monthly subsistence.]

Muster Roll

DS, RG 93, National Archives

Smith's Clove, N.Y., June 13, 1779
Muster Roll of Capt. John Marshalls Company in the 7th. Virga. Regiment[1] of Foot in Genl. Woodfords Brigade Commanded by Colo. Daniel Morgan for the Month of May 1779.

Commissiond. Officers
John Marshall Captain   July the 5th. 1777[2]
John Barnes[3] Lt. & Quarter Masr.   March the 18th. 1778
Robert Porterfield[4] Lt. & Acting Aid to Genl. Woodford

1. JM was listed as a captain in a rank roll prepared on Sept. 8, 1778, by a board of Virginia Continental Line officers under the presidency of Col. James Wood (1750–1813). He is listed as the 54th-ranking captain with a July 1, 1777, date of rank, but 26 of the officers preceding him are marked absent from duty. In the course of the realignment of Virginia Continental Line regiments on Sept. 14, 1778, absent and imprisoned officers were eliminated from the rank rolls, and the old Eleventh Virginia Regiment was designated the Seventh Virginia Regiment. JM was then appointed the fifth-ranking captain in the new Seventh Virginia Regiment. This "White Plains" arrangement of Sept. 14, 1778, became effective on Feb. 7, 1779. "Rank roll of Virginia Line Officers," Sept. 8, 1778, "Arrangement of the several regiments in the First Virginia Brigade," Sept. 14, 1778, Orderly Book No. 28, RG 93, National Archives; Sellers, "Virginia Continental Line," 321–323. From Dec. 1778 to early May 1779, JM was on furlough in Virginia.
   2. JM's date of rank is incorrect; it should read "July 1, 1777."
   3. Barnes (1740–1817), ensign in the old Eleventh Virginia Regiment, was promoted to first lieutenant on May 13, 1779. The date of rank on this muster roll does not correspond to his date of rank as second lieutenant, Mar. 7, 1777.
   4. Porterfield (1752–1843) had been appointed second lieutenant in the Eleventh Virginia Regiment on Dec. 24, 1776, and promoted to first lieutenant on June 1, 1777. He remained with his regiment when it was redesignated the Seventh Virginia Regiment.

No.	Serjeants	Time of Enlistmt.	term of Years	Remarks
1	Samuel Phillips	Aut. 10th, 76	3 yrs.	
2	John Anderson	Do.	Do.	
3	Archable Botts⁵		Do.	
4	Tobias Bourk		war	

No.	Corperals	time of Enlistmt.	term of Years	Remarks
1	Edward Fielding	Aut. 20th, 76	3 yrs.	
2	Thomas Ryecraft	Do. 1, 76	Do.	
3	Willm. Copeland⁶		Do.	
4	John Godbolt		war	

No	Drum & Fife	time of Enlistmt.	term of Years	Remarks
1	John Bates	Aut. 20th, 76	3 year.	

No	Privates	time of Enlistmt.	term of Years	Remarks
1	Spencer Edwards	Sepr. 14th, 76	3 yrs.	
2	John Ore		war	
3	Sylvester Hurley		Do.	
4	Clem Hasty	Aut. 22d, 76	3 years	
5	Peter Barrett		war	
6	William Kearns	Aut. 10, 76	3 years	
7	Thomas Roberts		war	
8	John Laws	Aut. 1st, 76	3 yr.	
9	George Winters	Decr. 76	Do.	
10	Benjm. Cook⁷		Do.	
11	Willm. Rexter		war	
12	Thomas Sherry		Do.	
13	Felty Frits⁸		3 yrs.	
14	Thomas Bryan		war	
15	John Hasty	Aut. 10, 76	3 yrs.	
16	David Harris		war	
17	Richd. Harvey	Novr. 7, 76	3 yrs.	
18	Charles Dunkin	Jany. 7, 77	3 yrs.	
19	Richd. Broadhouse	Do. 1, 77	Do.	on Command
20	John Crytser	76	Do.	waiter to Colo. Morgan

5. Botts enlisted on Feb. 1, 1777.
6. Copeland (ca. 1754–1822) enlisted on Nov. 21, 1776.
7. Benjamin Cook enlisted on Nov. 20, 1779.
8. Frits enlisted on July 1, 1777, and had served with the light infantry.

21	Michal Murphy		war	on Tatterage[9]
22	Willm. Hynes[1]		Do.	on Command
23	James Bayley	Der. 26 76	3 yrs.	Sick in Camp
24	John Phillips	Sepr. 6, 76	Do.	Taylor
25	Abraham Wigley		war	on Command
26	Willm. Healy		Do.	Do.
27	John Halfpenny		Do.	on Guard
28	Simon Berry	Aut. 28th 76	3 yrs.	Do.
29	James Thompson[2]		war	Do.
30	Edwd. Marlow		Do.	Do.
31	William Dennies	76	3 yrs.	Do.
32	Thomas Jeffs[3]		war	Do.
33	Daniel Burcher		Do.	on Command
34	Thomas Stuthard		Do.	on Guard
35	Willm. Whiteall		war	on Guard
36	Saml. Elliott	Aut. 20, 76	3 yrs.	waggoner
37	John Mitchell	76	Do.	waiter to Genl. Woodford
38	James Lynch[4]		war	Do. to Lt Porterfield
39	Michl. McNelly		Do.	sick at summerset[5]
40	David Phillips		Do.	Do. at Morris Town
41	James Noland[6]		3 yrs.	Do. at summerset
42	Zacha. Butt		Do.	Waggoner to the Comm.[7]
43	James Fitzgerald		Do.	Deserted Feby. 79
44	John Armond[8]		Do.	waggoner

9. "Tatterage" probably refers to gathering rags for bandages or wadding.

1. Probably William Hinds (1736–1816).

2. Thompson enlisted in the company of Capt. Peter Bryan Bruin (1754–1827) in the Eleventh Virginia Regiment. When he enlisted in Dec. 1776, he was a resident of Frederick County, Va.

3. Possibly Thomas Jeffers (1756–1815).

4. Possibly James Lynch (1732–ca. 1805).

5. McNelly, or MacNelly (b. 1749), enlisted at Winchester, Va., in Nov. 1776, and served in Capt. Peter Bryan Bruin's company of the Eleventh Virginia Regiment. When Bruin became an aide to Brig. Gen. Woodford, Capt. William Johnston took command of the company. In Nov. 1777 MacNelly was transferred to JM's company because he was a tailor and his services were required by JM's company. Pension file of Michael MacNelly, S 38943, RG 15, Natl. Arch. MacNelly was hospitalized at Somerset, N.J.

6. Noland (1760–1835), born in Liverpool, England, had served in Morgan's Rifle Regiment from June 1, 1777, to Nov. 30, 1778. He was discharged on July 24, 1779. Payroll, ca. July 31, 1779, RG 93, Natl. Arch.

7. Zachariah Butt enlisted on Nov. 20, 1776. At this time he was doing detached duty as a wagon driver for the commissary.

8. Armond enlisted on Dec. 6, 1776.

45	Willm. Shoemake		war	on Furlough at Vir- ga till Apl. 15th 79
46	Danl. Healy		Do.	Do.
47	John Lee		Do.	Do.

Camp Smiths Cloves June the 10th. 79 Musterd. then Capt. John Marshalls Compy. as Specified Above.

JOS: CLARK DMM

Proof of the Effectives

	Capt.	Lieut.	Serjts.	Corpl.	Drumr.	Privates
Present	1	1	4	4	1	18
Absent	—	1	—	—	—	28
Total	1	2	4	4	1	46

I do swear that the within Muster Roll is a true state of the Compy. without fraud to the United States or to any Individual, according to the best of our Knowledge.

JOHN MARSHALL Capt

Sworn before me this 13th day of June 1779
WM WOODFORD Brigdr. Genl.

Payroll

ADS, RG 93, National Archives

[ca. June 30, 1779 (Smith's Clove, N.Y.). JM writes the payroll, on which he is listed as receiving $40 pay and $20 subsistence for the month.]

Muster Roll

DS, RG 93, National Archives

[July 5, 1779, Smith's Clove, N.Y. JM signs the muster roll as captain.]

Muster Roll

DS, RG 93, National Archives

[*August 4, 1779, Ramapo, N.J.* JM signs the muster roll as captain.]

Legislative Petition

DS, Legislative Petitions, Miscellaneous, Virginia State Library

[Smith's Clove], N.Y., August 26, 1779
To the Honble. the Speaker and House of Delegates[9]

The memorial of the Military Officers, Citizens of the State of Virginia, on behalf of themselves and the Troops under their command; beg leave respectfully to Represent.

That your memorialists took an Early and Active Part in the Present Glorious and Necessary war with Great Britain; by entering into the Service of their Country, Since which, they have Continued in it with Patience and Unremited Assiduity, they hope, with the Approbation of their Countrymen, and some Degree of Reputation to themselves,—that they have During the Contest, with Chearfulness foregone the Opportunity which has been Presented to Every Other Citizen, with a Common Degree of Industry, of Bettering their Fortunes, of which a Great Number in Private life have Availed themselves. Your memorialists are sensible that the Measure of laying Heavy Taxes is wise, and salutary, and the Only Possible Means of raising the Credit of Our Depreciated Currency; at the same time they must think, the army bear an Unequal and Disproportioned part of the Burthen; which they Concieve the Justice of this Honble. House must Acknowledge, when they Consider, that the memorialists are Possessed of Estates most of them Unprofitable, which are rendered so, by their being Absent; that many of them have Families; that their Pay is Altogether inadequate to their Expences; that a great part of the Public Expenditure has been in high Bounties given to men for entering into the Service; and as they Concieve all the Citizens of a free

9. The petition was introduced in the House of Delegates on Nov. 4, 1779, and referred to the Committee on Propositions and Grievances, which rejected it on Nov. 22. *JVHD*, Oct. 1779, 39, 67.

State, Equally Bound to Afford their Country Personal Service, whenever the Public Exigencies require it, they think it Altogether Unreasonable, that the Army who are rendering Personal Service, Shoud Contribute Equally with those who really Owe the Service, & fail to give it. Your memorialists beg leave to Suggest to this Honble. House, that they Labour under a great and real Inconvenience, by their managers, or Overseers, being Called Out Under the Militia Laws, that their Crops are frequently Neglected, by which they Suffer irreparable Injury.

Your memorialists therefore take the Liberty of Recommending the Consideration of those Grievances, to the Honble. House, Trusting, they will think it Just and reasonable, that such Parts of their Estates as are Unprofitable, or rendered so by their Absence, may be Exempt from Taxation, by any mode of Discrimination this Honble. House may Judge Proper; and that the managers or Overseers, of your memorialists, during the time they Continue in the Service, may be Excused from giving their Attendance at musters, or from being Called into Service under the Militia Laws.

JOHN MARSHALL[1]

Payroll

DS, RG 93, National Archives

[ca. *August 31, 1779* (*Smith's Clove, N.Y.?*). JM signs the payroll as a captain; he is listed as receiving $40 pay and $97 subsistence for the month.]

To Thomas Posey

ALS, Indiana Historical Society

Dear Major[2]   Smith's Clove, N.Y., September 1, 1779
Yours, inclosing Genl. Wayne's second letter to Congress[3] relative to the reduction of Stony Point, I received just as I was setting

1. JM and 115 other officers signed the document.
2. Addressed to "Major Thomas Posey, Light Infantry." Posey (1750–1818) commanded the second battalion of the light infantry regiment commanded by Col. Christian Febiger (1746–1798) and was the sixth or seventh man to enter the British fort at Stony Point, N.Y. Henry P. Johnston, *The Storming of Stony Point* (New York, 1900), 69,

out from Ramapough.[4] I read the Genl.'s letter with attention &
will give my sincere sentiments upon it. You recollect that in your
letter to Genl. Washington[5] you only complaind because you was
not mentioned. You did not claim particular attention. Your sole
wish was not to be totally neglected. You are now mentioned. The
cause of your complaint is removed, & you cannot, in my opinion,
without acting inconsistantly demand anything farther. Though I
say you can demand nothing farther yet I must confess that I think
Genl. Wayne ought to have done more. When the Man who pos-
sesses a great, a generous Soul has inadvertently injured another
he will not stop at barely giving him such satisfaction as will prevent his discovering resentment. He will repair the injury in the
most ample manner immaginable. Was Genl. Wayne regardless of
you he ought I think to have said more for his own sake. He committed an error in omitting you. This he did not attempt to correct
till your complaints obliged him to it, & even then he has said
nothing which he could possibly avoid. Your being mentioned ap-

82. The other battalion commander, Lt. Col. François Louis de Fleury (ca. 1740–1794),
who preceded Posey into the fort, was awarded a gold medal by Congress. Lt. George
Knox of the Pennsylvania Line, who had command of the "forlorn hopes" assigned to
clear the abattis from the path of the American charge, also preceded Posey and was
given a brevet promotion to captain. Resolution of July 26, 1779, *JCC*, XIV, 890–891;
Freeman, *Washington*, V, 119, n. 76. JM served with the support troops during the
Stony Point assault and did not visit the fort until the morning after its capture. Pension file of Churchill Gibbs, S 46002, RG 15, National Archives; Marshall, *Washington*,
2d ed., I, 310–311.

3. This refers to the second letter from Brig. Gen. Anthony Wayne (1745–1796) to
George Washington (1732–1799), who, as commander-in-chief of the army, transmitted Wayne's report to John Jay (1745–1829), president of the Continental Congress.
Wayne's first letter, written at 2:00 A.M. on July 16, was a short note informing Washington of the success of the American attack; his second letter was a detailed statement
that particularly identified those officers who had distinguished themselves. Posey was
not mentioned in this second letter, although Wayne did commend all the field officers
for their diligence and courage. Papers of George Washington, Ser. 4, July 16, 17,
1779, Library of Congress (microfilm ed., reel 60); Papers of Continental Congress,
Item 152, VII, 503–511, Natl. Arch. (microfilm ed., reel 169).

4. Near present-day Suffern, N.J. The main road from Ramapo to Haverstraw Bay
ran east-northeast through a pass between the mountains, a few miles inland from the
west bank of the Hudson River. A settlement called Smith's, presumably near Smith's
Clove or an alternative name for the same place, was located in the pass at an intersec-
tion between the road from Ramapo and another road that led north to the vicinity of
West Point, N.Y. "Surveys done for His Excellency General Washington," 1778–1779,
No. C, West Bank of the Hudson River, Newburgh Bay to Haverstraw Bay (Negative
48, 744), Erskine-DeWitt Papers, New-York Historical Society.

5. Posey, complaining to Washington that he had not been mentioned as a partici-
pant in the attack, set forth particular details as evidence of his early arrival within the
walls of the fort and the capture of a battery by troops under his command. He specifically claimed he wanted more recognition than "being mentioned." Posey to Washington, Aug. 10, 1779, Wayne Papers, Historical Society of Pennsylvania.

pears to proceed from constraint as much as choice. The Man who has seen with what a liberal hand the Genl. has, in his first letter, dealt out praises to Men who could not have deserved much more than yourself will confess that he has been rather sparing in his encomiums on Major Posey.

I have shewn the letter to several of your Friends. They perfectly agree with me in thinking that you can ask nothing farther but that Genl. Wayne might & ought to have done more. What news have you Major? What does our movement to this place indicate? Is an attack on West Point apprehended?[6] I assure I am somewhat fearful we may yet have bloody noses. Never was I a witness to such a scene of lewdness as about Ramapough particularly at the very venerable Mrs. Sydmon's. I should certainly have thought had I staid there much longer that all the virtue of the fair sex was centered in our Camp Ladies & should very possibly have begun to think of choosing one of them as a Partner for life.

You have heard that Congress have at length done something cleaver for us by way [of] subsistence.[7] One hundred Dollars per Month for each ration will do pretty well. It will serve to purchase *milk & sopaun*[8] for some time. Farewell I am dear Major with much esteem, Yours

JOHN MARSHALL

Muster Roll

ADS, RG 93, National Archives

[*September 7, 1779 (Smith's Clove, N.Y.?*). JM writes the muster roll as captain; one of his men is detached for service with the light infantry.]

6. After Stony Point fell to Wayne's troops, the British moved a large force up the river, but Washington had already decided to evacuate Stony Point after destroying the fortifications. The increased British strength in Haverstraw Bay troubled Washington and his general officers, and their fears were increased by the arrival of fresh British troops at New York City on Aug. 27. Johnston, *Storming of Stony Point*, 91; Freeman, *Washington*, V, 123, 134; Fitzpatrick, *Writings of Washington*, XV, 26–28, 488–489, XVI, 18–19, 189. We have been unable to find an order directing the movement of JM's regiment to Smith's Clove.

7. Congress, after six months of consideration, resolved that because of the monetary inflation, subsistence allowances made for officers of the Continental Line should be increased. A major was to receive subsistence of $300 per month under the new schedule, and a captain was to receive $200 per month. Resolution of Aug. 11, 1779, *JCC*, XIV, 946–948. The congressional action was reported to the troops by general orders of Aug. 29, 1779. Fitzpatrick, *Writings of Washington*, XVI, 202–204.

8. "Sopaun," or sopum, probably refers to a bread or doughy substance used to sop up milk or water to form an edible but unappetizing meal.

Payroll

DS, RG 93, National Archives

[*ca. September 30, 1779 (Ramapo, N.J.?)*. JM signs payroll listing him as a captain drawing $40 monthly pay and $200 subsistence.]

Payroll

DS, RG 93, National Archives

[*ca. October 30, 1779 (Haverstraw, N.J.)*. JM receives $40 pay and $200 subsistence.]

Muster Roll

DS, RG 93, National Archives[9]

Morristown, N.J., December 9, 1779
MUSTER ROLL of Capt. John Marshalls Company of Foot in the 7th. Virga. Regt. commanded by Colo. Danl. Morgan for Novr. 1779.

			Commissioned
July	1st.	77	John Marshall Capt.
June	1st.	77	Robt. Porterfield Lt. & Aid to Genl Woodford
May	13th.	79	John Barnes Lt. & Q.M.
			Benjn. Ashby Lt.[1]
July	4th.	79	Saml. Phillips Ensign Light Infantry
July	4th.	79	Peyton Powell Ensign[2]

9. In a clerk's hand, except the names of commissioned officers, which are entered in JM's hand. This is the last documentary record of JM's service in the Continental Line.

1. Ashby was appointed ensign in the Eleventh Virginia Regiment on Nov. 30, 1776.

2. Powell (*ca.* 1763–post 1828), a brother of Col. Leven Powell (1737–1810), joined the Eleventh Virginia Regiment as cadet in Mar. 1777. His pension claim indicates that he was promoted to ensign four or five months later. Pension file, S 46407, RG 15, National Archives.

No.	Serjeants	Date of enlistment	war 3 yr.	Remarks
1	Archibal Botts	Decr. 25th. 76	x	

No.	Corpls.	Enlistment	war 3 Yr.	Remarks
	Wm. Copland	Novr. 20th.	x	Dischargd.
	John Godbolt		x	

No.	Drums & Fifes	Enlist.	war 3 yr.	Remarks
	[Privates]			
1	James Thompson		x	
2	David Harris		x	
3	Wm. Whitehall		x	
4	Wm. Rexter		x	
5	Thomas Roberts		x	
6	John Ore		x	
7	George Winters			x	
8	Thomas Stuthard			x	
9	Chas. Dunken			x	
10	John Halfpain		x	
11	Wm. Hailey		x	
12	Henry Tinchman			x	
13	Thomas Bryan		x	
14	Edward Marlow		x	
15	James Bailey	Decr. 26th. 76		x	
16	Michl. McNelly		x	Abst. wt. leave
17	Thos. Sherry		x	On Guard
18	Abraham Whigley		x	Sick present
19	David Philips		x	Infantry
20	Sylvester Hurley		x	Do.
21	Peter Barrett		x	Do.
22	Wm. Hynes		x	Do.
23	Danl. Burcher		x	Do.
24	Michl. Murphy		x	Infantry
25	Richd. Broadhouse	Jary. 1st.		x	Waggoner
26	Thomas Jeffs		x	On furlough
27	Wm. Shoemate		x	On furlough
28	John Lee		x	Supposed to be w[ith] Gl. S[cott][3]

3. Charles Scott (ca. 1739–1813) was the brigadier commanding Scott's Brigade of the Virginia Continental Line.

29	Danl. Hailey		x		
30	Benja. Cook	Novr. 20th.		x	Disch'd
31	Zecha. Butt				Novr. 17th. Do.
32	John Armond	Decr. 6th. 79		x	Do.
33	James Lynch		x		Waiter on Lt Porterfield

Camp Morristown Decr. 9th. 79—Then Mustred Capt. Marshalls Co. as Spacified Above

W. CROGHAN Major[4]

Proof of the Effectives

Rank	Capt.	Lieuts.	En-signs	Sejts.	Copls.	D. & Fifes	Pri-vates	Non Effec-tives	3 Years	War
Present	I	2	I	I	I	—	16			
Absent	—	I	I	—	I	—	15			
Total	I	3	2	I	2	—	31	—	11	23

I do Swear that the within Muster Roll Containes a true State of my Company without fraud to the United States or to any Individual According to the best of my Knowledge.

JOHN MARSHALL Capt.

SWORN to before me this 9. Day of Decr. 1779
JAMES WOOD,[5] Colo Com

Law Notes

EDITORIAL NOTE

In the spring of 1780, while awaiting further military orders, John Marshall visited his father, who was stationed at Yorktown with the Virginia State Artillery. At some time prior to May 1, he decided to attend the lectures to be delivered at the College of William and Mary by the newly appointed professor of law and police, George Wythe (1726–1806). During the period of his attendance, from May

4. Croghan (1752–1822) was promoted to major on May 16, 1778.
5. Wood, of Winchester, Va., was colonel of the old Twelfth Virginia Regiment, redesignated the Eighth Virginia Regiment on Sept. 14, 1778. He acted as brigade commander in the absence of Brig. Gen. Woodford and all colonels superior to him in rank.

1 to July 29, 1780, he was elected to membership in Phi Beta Kappa, but other than the minutes reflecting his attendance at meetings of that society, his "Law Notes" are the only documentary record of his presence at the college.[1]

Marshall scholars have differed on the approximate date of the manuscript volume of law notes and have also ventured conflicting opinions concerning the method of preparing the notebook.[2] But until the recent work by Professor William F. Swindler, little close attention had been given to the substance of the document, either for dating purposes or for assessing its significance. By careful comparison Swindler has been able to show Marshall's reliance upon the 1766–1769 edition of Matthew Bacon's *A New Abridgment of the Law* and upon *The Acts of Assembly Now in Force in the Colony of Virginia*, printed in Williamsburg in 1769. Only a part of Professor Swindler's study has been completed, and a short extract from the law notes has appeared in print.[3]

Based on the work of Professor Swindler and the evidence in the extract from Marshall's law notes published here, there can be no doubt that the notebook was prepared after the Declaration of Independence was promulgated, since Marshall avoided all mention of the king of England, and after the enactment of the 1776 Virginia statute abolishing entail. At the same time, certain inaccuracies in his transcription indicate that it was written at a very early stage in his acquaintance with the law, most likely before his contact with practice had sharpened his attention to procedural details. A comparison of the law notes with the legal arguments printed later in this volume will demonstrate the relative lack of professionalism evidenced by the law notes.

It also seems clear that the law notes were actually prepared by commonplacing Bacon's *Abridgment*, the 1769 compilation of Virginia statutes, and occasionally Sir William Blackstone's *Commentaries on the Laws of England*. It is inconceivable that such precision could be obtained in notes from George Wythe's oral lectures, even if one were willing to believe that Wythe would have limited himself to reading Bacon's text as a substitute for an original lecture. The fidelity of Marshall's transcription is reflected in our annotations, which are designed to provide the reader with a reasonably accurate index to the degree of correspondence that exists between Marshall's handwritten version and the printed passage in the cited text. We have used the terms "verbatim" or "verbatim extract" to describe a Marshall transcript that is identical in wording to the original. There may of

---

1. Adams, ed., *Autobiographical Sketch*, 6; pension file of Humphrey Marshall, S 31234, RG 15, National Archives. For a general discussion of JM's attendance at the College of William and Mary see Beveridge, *Marshall*, I, 154–160. The manuscript minutes of Phi Beta Kappa are at the Swem Library, College of William and Mary; they were printed in *WMQ*, 1st Ser., IV (1896), 213–241.

2. Beveridge, *Marshall*, I, 174, claimed that the law notes were taken according to topics Prof. George Wythe announced he would discuss and that they were not the result of commonplacing. Mrs. Mason surmised that the outlines may have been entered in the book before the war, based upon JM's readings in Blackstone. Mason, *Dearest Polly*, 7, 20. Rhodes, *Marshall Papers Calendar*, I, 23, asserted that the notes were made in the rear of the book after JM began his accounts in the front in 1783.

3. William F. Swindler, "John Marshall's Preparation for the Bar—Some Observations on His Law Notes," *AJLH*, XI (1967), 207–213. Prof. Swindler has very generously permitted the editors to use his Xeroxed copies from Bacon's *Abridgment*, marked to indicate JM's parallel text, and has provided guidance and advice in this phase of the editorial work.

course be some variation in capitalization, spelling, or abbreviation, and these we have considered not sufficiently important to eliminate the transcript from the category of a verbatim copy. Next in a decreasing order of fidelity to the original text is what we have called a "paraphrase"—a free rendering of the text, which nevertheless substantially retains the word order and content of the original. Finally, we have used the term "summary" to cover a brief and comprehensive presentation of the original that involves Marshall's attempt either to précis a substantial portion of the text in fewer words or to change significantly the manner in which the original material was presented. The portion of the law notes printed here shows that only a small amount of the material can be considered a product of Marshall's mind. Also, the reliance on three major printed sources, and the alphabetic development of the subjects, clearly make it unlikely that these notes were taken in a lecture hall or that they followed a lecture outline.

The pedestrian character of Marshall's work in compiling the law notes tends to obscure some useful information that can be gained from a close study of his transcription. At a number of points Marshall translated Latin legal phrases into English, presumably with some ease, during the course of copying from the printed text. We know that prior to his attendance at William and Mary he had been given instruction in Latin. The Reverend James Thomson (*ca.* 1745-1812), a Scottish clergyman of the Church of England and a family friend, tutored him in early life, and in 1769 Marshall attended the Campbelltown Academy and received instruction from the Reverend Archibald Campbell (*ca.* 1710-*ca.* 1774).[4]

The young law student's infrequent citation of Blackstone's *Commentaries* also offers insight into his background and legal training. A passage in his autobiography, referring to his giving up the study of Blackstone to begin military training in 1775, coupled with the 1772 purchase of the American edition of Blackstone by his father, would lead us to believe that young Marshall should have been more familiar with the work than is evidenced by his law notes. In addition, his citations are to the London edition, rather than the American edition, which indicates that his father's set of Blackstone was not in his possession when the law notes were prepared. However, at least two volumes of the 1772 Philadelphia imprint later came into Marshall's possession, for they bear both his signature and that of his father.[5]

Comparison of the citations that Marshall extracted from Bacon's *Abridgment* shows which English authorities were considered important for his purposes. The case citations are strongly weighted toward King's Bench and High Court of Chancery reports. While this may be simply a reflection of the group of reports known by the law student to be available in Williamsburg, it may also show a general Virginia preference for the law emanating from those two English tri-

4. JM was a classmate of James Monroe's (1758-1831), the future president, at Campbelltown Academy. Ammon, *Monroe,* 3. See also Adams, ed., *Autobiographical Sketch,* 4; Beveridge, *Marshall,* I, 57; William Meade, *Old Churches, Ministers and Families of Virginia* (Philadelphia, 1857), II, 159-161.

5. A copy of the 1772 American edition of Blackstone, published in Philadelphia, was in the hands of Thomas Marshall well before the war, leading Mrs. Mason to assert that JM's mind was "steeped" in Blackstone before his military service. Mason, *Dearest Polly,* 7. If so, he must have forgotten most of his Blackstone during the war, since relatively few Blackstone passages appear in the law notes. The fourth volume of the American edition and an appendix volume, owned by Thomas Marshall and later by JM, were presented to the College of William and Mary in 1923 by the Hon. James K. M. Norton of Alexandria, Va.

bunals. Marshall's citations to English treatises are more wide-ranging, but seem concentrated upon Sir Matthew Hale's *Historia Placitorum Coronae* . . . [History of Pleas of the Crown] (London, 1736); William Hawkins, *A Treatise of the Pleas of the Crown*, 4th ed. (London, 1762); and Sir Edward Coke, *The first part of the Institutes of the laws of England: or A commentary upon Littleton*, 12th ed. (London, 1738), commonly called Coke on Littleton. Marshall's law notes give no indication that the cited reports or treatises were consulted, but his care in retaining these portions of the marginal citations by Bacon and Blackstone indicates that these were important sources of law for a Virginia practitioner and that copies of these books were reasonably available if closer study might be required at a future time.

In Marshall's gleaning of certain citations from Bacon and Blackstone, we may perhaps find some of the influence of his law teacher, George Wythe. Although Marshall's relationship to his mentor was not as close as that enjoyed by men who had served as Wythe's law clerks, the newly appointed professor undoubtedly provided some instruction to his pupils concerning the citations that would prove most useful to them. Quite possibly the selection of citations to particular works was guided by their knowledge of what volumes were in Wythe's library and thus available for study. Throughout his law notes Marshall ignored certain topics covered by Bacon, usually because they did not apply to American conditions, and this decision probably was the result of advice from Wythe or some other experienced Virginia practitioner.

The manuscript copy of the law notes terminates with a series of blank pages headed "Mayhem," "Maintenance," "Mandamus," and "Master & Servant," which indicates that Marshall intended to continue his commonplacing beyond the topic "Libel," but was prevented from doing so. Remaining pages in the same volume were used to begin his Account Book in September 1783. The manuscript volume remained in family hands and was used by Albert J. Beveridge in preparing his biography of Marshall; on June 13, 1962, it was presented to the College of William and Mary by Dr. H. Norton Mason of Richmond and Gloucester Point, Virginia. The extract printed here covers approximately one-fourth of the text of the law notes, from the beginning of the manuscript to the end of the topic "Condition." We believe that it provides an accurate representation of the remaining portion of the law notes and that it will give the reader a good understanding of their nature and content.

Preparation of the law notes did not engross all of the time Marshall devoted to his studies. George Wythe's curriculum for law study included two lectures per week, supplemented by moot courts and model legislatures held to instruct his students in judicial and legislative procedure. At one moot court Marshall headed a team of four students that tried a case against a similar team led by William Short (1759–1849), one of the founders of Phi Beta Kappa. In addition to these law lectures, Marshall attended lectures in natural philosophy delivered by the president of the college, the Reverend James Madison (1749–1812). While no description of Madison's 1780 course survives, lecture notes from the natural philosophy courses he taught from 1800 to 1810 suggest that he devoted a substantial amount of time to topics that today would constitute a course in Newtonian physics.[6]

6. Walker Maury to Thomas Jefferson, *ca.* Apr. 20, 1784, *Jefferson Papers*, VII, 112; John Brown to William Preston, July 6, 1780, *WMQ*, 2d Ser., II (1922), 41; William

Marshall's attendance at the College of William and Mary began with the commencement of the spring term on May 1 and extended for nearly three months until July 29, the last day of that term.[7] A clothing account prepared for Marshall by the clerk in the state store at Richmond shows that he was in the capital city on July 31.[8] He received his license to practice law sometime between July 31 and August 14, for on August 15, Governor Thomas Jefferson left Richmond for a two-week period and did not return until about the time Marshall took his oath of admission before the Fauquier County Court on August 28, 1780. According to the best evidence concerning admission practices in 1780, the governor's license to practice was granted after the candidate had been examined in the law and approved by two lawyers appointed by the governor.[9] Unfortunately no copy of Marshall's license or any record of his examination has survived.

GUIDE TO CITATIONS

Ab. E.   See Eq. Ca. Abr.
Ab. Eq.

B   Matthew Bacon, *A New Abridgment of the Law* . . . , 3d ed. (London,
Ba   1766–1769)

Bl.   Sir William Blackstone, *Commentaries on the Laws of England* . . .
        (Oxford, 1765–1769)

B.   Sir Robert Brooke, *La Graunde Abridgement, Collecte & Escrie per le*
Br.   *iudge Tres Reverend Syr Robert Brooke, Chiualier* . . . (London, 1576)
Brk.
Bro.
Broke

Short to Greenbury Ridgely, Nov. 10, 1817, in *Maryland Historical Magazine*, LXIV (1969), 367; Adams, ed., *Autobiographical Sketch*, 6; William and Mary College Papers, Bound Volumes, Notes on Professors' Lectures A-M, Swem Library, College of William and Mary.

7. The law classes were organized on May 1, and we have assumed JM was present at that time; vacation time was to begin on Aug. 1, in accordance with a faculty resolution of June 25, 1780. Minute Book, William and Mary Faculty, Swem Library, College of William and Mary. Beveridge, *Marshall*, I, 154, 160, after noting the abrupt cessation of JM's law notes, asserted incorrectly that JM left the college when the Ambler family moved to Richmond in June 1780. Since we do not accept his evaluation of the law notes as having been taken from lectures, we are not persuaded by his argument that JM attended his classes for only six weeks.

8. Accounts of Military Stores, under date July 31, 1780, Box 37, War Office Papers, Virginia State Library.

9. Dudley Digges to Charles Magill, Aug. 16, 1780, and Thomas Jefferson to Dudley Digges, Joseph Prentis, and Meriwether Smith, Aug. 28, 1780, in *Jefferson Papers*, III, 553, 564. JM's appearance to take his oath as an attorney is recorded in the minutes of the Fauquier County Court for Aug. 28, 1780. Minute Book, Office of the Clerk of the Fauquier County Circuit Court, Warrenton, Va. For licensing in 1778 and 1782 see *JVCS*, II, 133, III, 165. On admission to practice in Virginia see also Alan M. Smith, "Virginia Lawyers, 1680–1776" (Ph.D. diss., The Johns Hopkins University, 1967), and George M. Curtis III, "The Virginia Courts during the Revolution" (Ph.D. diss., University of Wisconsin, 1970). For an expanded discussion on JM's Virginia bar admission see Charles T. Cullen, "New Light on John Marshall's Legal Education and Admission to the Bar," *AJLH*, XVI (1972), 345–351.

Brown. Brownl.	Richard Brownlow and John Goldesborough, *Reports of Diverse Choice Cases in Law* [1569–1624] (London, 1675)
Bulst. Bulstr.	Edward Bulstrode, *The Reports of Edward Bulstrode . . . in King's Bench* [1609–1638] (London, 1688)
Bur. Rep.	Sir James Burrow, *Reports of Cases Argued and Adjudged in the Court of King's Bench* [1756–1772] (London, 1766–1777)
C.L. Co. L.	Sir Edward Coke, *The first part of the Institutes of the laws of England: or A commentary upon Littleton*, 12th ed. (London, 1738)
Carth.	Thomas Carthew, *Reports of Cases Adjudged in the Count of King's Bench* [1687–1700] (London, 1743)
Ch. Ca.	*Cases in Chancery* [1660–1688] (London, 1735)
Ch. Re. Chan. Rep.	*Reports of Cases Taken and Adjudged in the Court of Chancery in the Reign of King Charles I, Charles II and James II, . . . being Special Cases* [1625–1688], 3d ed. (London, 1736)
Co. Coke	Sir Edward Coke, *The Reports of Sir Edward Coke, Kt.* [1572–1616] (London, 1738)
Co. Ent.	———, *A Booke of Entries* (London, 1671)
Comyns	Sir John Comyns, *Reports, King's Bench, Common Pleas and Exchequer, Special Cases in Chancery and before the Delegates* [1695–1741] (London, 1744)
Cr. Ch.	Sir George Croke, *Reports of Sir George Croke, Kt. . . . . of the Court of King's Bench, and . . . the Court of Common Bench . . . during the Reign of Charles the First* [1625–1641] (London, 1657)
Cr. El.	———, *Reports of Sir George Croke, Kt. . . . . of the Court of King's Bench, and . . . the Court of Common Bench . . . during the Reign of Queen Elizabeth* [1582–1603] (London, 1661)
Cr. Ja. Cro. Ja.	———, *Reports of Sir George Croke, Kt. . . . . of the Court of King's Bench, and . . . the Court of Common Bench . . . during the Reign of James the First* [1603–1625] (London, 1658, 1659)
Doct. & Stu. Doct.	Christopher Saint German, *Doctor and Student*, 16th ed. (London, 1761)
Dyer	Sir James Dyer, *Les Reports des Divers Select Matter & Resolutions des Reverend Judges & Sages del Ley* [1513–1582], 6th ed. (London, 1688)
Eq. Ca. Abr. Ab. E. Ab. Eq. Eq. Abr.	*General Abridgment of Cases in Equity . . .* (London, 1756)

F.N.B. Sir Anthony Fitzherbert, *New Natura Brevium*, 8th ed. (London,
Fitz. B. 1755)

G.H.C. Sir Geoffrey Gilbert, *History and Practice of the High Court of Chan-
Gil. His. Ch. cery* (London, 1758)

Godb. John Godbolt, *Reports of Certain Cases Arising in the Courts of Record
at Westminster* [1575–1638] (London, 1652)

Godol. John Godolphin, *The Orphan's Legacy; or a Testamentary Abridgment* (London, 1701)

Hale P.C. Sir Matthew Hale, *Pleas of the Crown* (London, 1759)

H.P.C. William Hawkins, *A Treatise of the Pleas of the Crown*, 4th ed. (Lon-
Haw. don, 1762)
Haw. P.C.
Hawk. P.C.

Hob. Sir Henry Hobart, *The Reports of that Reverend and Learned Judge,
The Right Honorable Sr. Henry Hobart, Knight and Baronet, Lord
Chiefe Justice of His Majesties Court of Common Pleas* [1603–1625]
(London, 1724)

Hutt. Sir Richard Hutton, *Reports Containing Many Choice Cases, Judgments, and Resolutions on Points of Law in the Court of Common Pleas*
[1612–1638] (London, 1656)

Inst. Sir Edward Coke, *The Second Part of the Institutes . . .* (London,
1681)
————, *The Third Part of the Institutes . . .* (London, 1680)
————, *The Fourth Part of the Institutes . . .* (London, 1681)

Keb. Joseph Keble, *Reports, King's Bench, at Westminster* [1661–1679]
(London, 1685)

Ld. R. Robert, First Baron Raymond, *Reports of Cases Argued and Adjudged
in the Courts of King's Bench and Common Pleas* [1694–1732] (London,
1765)

Leon. William Leonard, *Reports and Cases of Law; Argued and Adjudged in
the Courts of Law at Westminster* [1540–1615], 2d ed. (London, 1686–
1687)

Lit. Sir Thomas Littleton, *Littleton's Tenures in English Lately Perused
and Amended* (London, 1661)

March John March, *Some New Cases in the Time of Henry VIII, Edward VI
and Queen Mary, collected out of Brooke's Abridgment* [1540–1558]
(London, 1651)

Mo. Sir Francis Moore, *Cases Collect et Report per Sir Fra. Moore . . .*
Moor. [1512–1621], 2d ed. (London, 1688)

Mod.   *Modern Reports; Or Select Cases Adjudged in the Courts of King's Bench, Chancery, Common Pleas and Exchequer* [1668–1726], 4th ed. (London, 1757–1769)

Owen   Thomas Owen, *Reports in the King's Bench and Common Pleas* [1556–1615] (London, 1656)

Pop.   Sir John Popham, *Reports and Cases* [King's Bench, Common Pleas, and Chancery, 1592–1597], 2d ed. corr. (London, 1682)

Preced. in Ch. *Precedents in Chancery; Cases, Court of Chancery, 1689–1722*, 2d ed. (London, 1750)

Ray.   Sir Thomas Raymond, *Reports, King's Bench, Common Pleas, and*
Raym.   *Exchequer* [1660–1683], 2d ed. (London, 1743)

Rep. in Eq.   Sir Geoffrey Gilbert, *Reports of Cases in Equity, Courts of Chancery and Exchequer* [1705–1726], 2d ed. (London, 1742)

Rol. Ab.   Sir Henry Rolle, *Un Abridgment des Plusiers Cases et Resolutions del*
Rolls Abr.   *Commun Ley* . . . (London, 1668)

Rol. Rep.   ———, *Les Reports de Henry Rolle . . . de Divers Cases en le Court del' Banke le Roy* [1614–1625] (London, 1675–1676)

Sal.   William Salkeld, *Reports of Cases Adjudg'd in the Court of King's Bench . . . Chancery, Common Pleas and Exchequer* . . . [1689–1712] (London, 1717–1742)

San.   Sir Edmund Saunders, *Les Reports du Tres Erudite Edmund Saunders, des Divers Pleadings et Cases en le Court le Bank le Roy en le Temp del Reign de le Roy Charles II* [1660–1685], 2d ed. (London, 1722)

Show.   Sir Bartholomew Shower, *The Reports of Sir Bartholomew Shower, Knt. of Cases Adjudged in the Court of King's Bench* [1678–1694] (London, 1708, 1720)

Sid.   Sir Thomas Siderfin, *Les Reports des Divers Special Cases Argue & Adjudge en le Court del Bank le Roy et Auxy en le Co. Ba., & l'Exchequer* [1657–1670], 2d ed. (London, 1714)

Skin.   Robert Skinner, *Reports of Cases Adjudged in the King's Bench* [1681–1697] (London, 1728)

Stile   William Style, *Narrationes Modernae, or Modern Reports Begun in the*
Style   *Now Upper Bench Court at Westminster* [1646–1656] (London, 1658)

Str.   Sir John Strange, *Reports of Adjudged Cases in the Courts of Chancery, King's Bench, Common Pleas, and Exchequer* [1716–1749] (London, 1755)

Vaugh.   Sir John Vaughan, *The Reports and Arguments of . . . Sir J. V. . . . in the Common Pleas* [1665–1674], 2d ed. (London, 1706)

Ven.   Sir Peyton Ventris, *The Reports of Sir P. V. . . . in Two Parts* [King's

Vent.   Bench, 1668–1684], 2d ed. (London, 1726)

Ver.   Thomas Vernon, *Cases Argued and Adjudged in the High Court of*
Vern.   *Chancery* [1681–1720] (London, 1726–1728)

Yel.   Sir Henry Yelverton, *The Reports of Sir Henry Yelverton . . . of Divers
Special Cases in the Court of King's Bench . . .* [1602–1613], 3d ed.
(London, 1735–1742)

Extract from AD, Marshall Papers, Swem Library, College of William and Mary
[Williamsburg, Va., *ca.* June 1780]

ABATEMENT[1]

Abatemt. is a plea put in by the Deft. in which he shews cause to the Ct. why he should not be impleaded or if impleaded not in the manner & form he then is.

    1. B. 2.; [Gil.] His. of the crown 186.[2]

A plea in Abatemt. to the jurisdiction of the Ct. [must][3] be put in by the Deft. in person & before any imparlance. He must make but half defence.[4]

    1. B. 2.; Gil. H. crown 187.; Show. 386.; C.L. 127.

There are several pleas to the person of the Pf.[5] Outlawry does not entirely abate the writ but only suspends it.[6]

    1. B. 2.; G.H.C. 196.

This disability is not pleadable when the action is brought in Auter droit.[7]

    1. On the page where this title appears JM had written the names of "Polly Ambler" and "Peyton Short," and the additional notation "Richmond." JM met his future wife, Mary Willis Ambler (1766–1831), in the spring of 1780. Peyton Short (1761–1825), a brother of William Short, attended the College of William and Mary from 1780 to 1781 and with JM was a member of Phi Beta Kappa. The reference to Richmond may perhaps pertain to Mary Willis Ambler's residence there during the summer of 1780. See William F. Swindler, "John Marshall's Preparation for the Bar—Some Observations on His Law Notes," *AJLH* (1967), XI, 209, n. 6.

    2. JM's first sentence on abatement is a paraphrase of the first paragraph in Matthew Bacon, *A New Abridgment of the Law . . .* , 3d ed. (London, 1766–1769), I, 2. From this work JM obtained the major portion of his notes and citations. For expanded bibliographic information on JM's citations see the guide printed above. The second work cited would appear to be an unpublished treatise by Sir Geoffrey Gilbert. See Percy H. Winfield, *The Chief Sources of English Legal History* (Cambridge, Mass., 1925), 242–243.

    3. Bacon at this point reads "must"; JM's writing of this word is illegible.

    4. A summary from Bacon, *Abridgment*, I, 2. JM omitted Bacon's observation that a full defense would submit the defendant to the jurisdiction of the court.

    5. This sentence is JM's insertion.

    6. Bacon stated that outlawry is a "temporary Impediment," which can be removed by the plaintiff obtaining a charter of pardon, whereupon the defendant must answer to the same writ. *Abridgment*, I, 2.

    7. "In the right of another." This is a summary of Bacon's material, *ibid.*

Excommunication, Premunire & popish recusancy are pleas in abatement.

C.L. 128.[8]

An Alien Enemy can bring no action. 4. Mod. 285. An Alien in Lague[9] may bring personal actions.

Secus Ld. R. 282.[10]

Officers of a court are privileged in actions brought in their own right.[11]

1. B. 5.

If a writ vary materially from that in the register or be defective in point of substance the party may [take] advantage of it; so if the declaration varies from the writ.[12]

1. B. 6; 12 Mod. 273; Fitz. B. 219, 231.

Tis a genl. rule that where any party dies & the plea [is in] the same condition as if such party [were living] death makes no abatement of the writ.[13]

1. B. 7; G.H.C. 242; 12 Mod. 251.

Two Exrs. bring debt—one dies—the writ does not abate. Secus if one was dead when the writ was brought.
Action agt. several Defts. one dies—the writ does not abate.[14]

1 B. 8.

Actions originally maintainable by & against Exrs. etc. not to abate after interlocutory judgmt.

8. Excommunication was a penalty imposed by ecclesiastical courts for contempt, perjury, and certain other misdoings; praemunire was a procedure for punishment of individuals who sought to invoke papal jurisdiction in medieval England, and included a group of related offenses later subjected to the same penalty. Popish recusancy involved punishment for nonattendance at services of the established Anglican church. JM ignored the extended discussion of these topics in Bacon, *ibid.*, 3–4. Ecclesiastical courts did not exist in colonial Virginia, and even in colonies with English-patterned ecclesiastical courts, excommunication was not used. It is most likely that praemunire and prosecutions for popish recusancy were also unknown in Virginia. The citation to Coke on Littleton refers to materials on outlawry and not excommunication, praemunire, and recusancy.

9. "League," that is, an alien friend as discussed in Bacon, *ibid.*, 83.

10. A summary from Bacon, *ibid.*, 4; the exception cited to Lord Raymond's reports is also from Bacon. "Secus" means "on the contrary" or "otherwise."

11. This summarizes 10 paragraphs in Bacon, *ibid.*, 5, covering the nature of the privilege and the manner in which privilege applied in various English courts. While JM's statement does not so indicate, the privilege was available to defendant-officers as well as plaintiff-officers.

12. The statement is composed of two verbatim extracts from Bacon, *ibid.*, 6.

13. A paraphrase from Bacon, *ibid.*, 7. JM omitted a paragraph concerning abatement of writs by the demise of the king.

14. JM's extracts from several paragraphs in Bacon, *ibid.*, 8. "Secus" means "on the contrary" or "otherwise."

Death of either party between verdict & judgemt. not to be pleaded in abatement.

    22. G. 2; Ch. 5, 180, 181.[15]

Process agt. one returnd, no inhabitant shall abate.

    Do. 184.[16]

Coverture is a good plea in Abatement & may be either before the writ sued or pending the writ. By the first the writ is abated de facto, by the second tis only abateable. Coverture pending the writ must be pleaded since the last continuance. If a feme sole takes out a writ & after marries the deft. may plead in Abatemt. or in chief.[17]

    1. B. 9; Doct. pl. 3, Sid. 140; Leon. 168, 169

If a writ is false when sued out it shall abate.[18]

    Fitz. B. 476.

If a writ is de facto a nullity & destroyed so that judgmt. thereupon would be erroneous there the writ is de facto abated. As if an action be brought agt. a feme covert as sole, or where the Plaintiff by his own shewing had no cause of action at the time the writ was brought.[19]

    1. B. 10; Doct. pl. 3; Cr. El. 121, 185, 193, 330; Cart. 172, the Ct. gave [*leave to*] a[*mend*].

Where the writ is only abateable it must be abated by pleading in time; for matters in & before the writ cannot be taken advantage of in error.[20]

    sal. 2. pl. 5; Ld. R. 853.

Tis a good plea that a stranger in tenant in common with the Plaintiff.[21]

    Cr. El. 554; 1. B. 10.

15. A summary from 22 Geo. 2, c. 5, sec. 5 (1748) in *The Acts of Assembly Now in Force in the Colony of Virginia* (Williamsburg, Va., 1769), 180–181, printed in 5 Hening 510.

16. A summary from 22 Geo. 2, c. 6, sec. 5 (1748), *Va. Acts in Force* (1769), 184, printed in 5 Hening 512.

17. A paraphrase from Bacon, *Abridgment*, I, 9, but JM confused the material he abstracted in his last sentence. Bacon stated that if a defendant was legally attached in the action and the female plaintiff thereafter married, the defendant might plead in chief but presumably could not plead in abatement. However, if a couple sued out a writ as husband and wife, and thereafter married, the defendant might plead in abatement, for the writ was false when sued out.

18. A summary from Bacon, *ibid.*, 11.

19. Extracted verbatim from two paragraphs in Bacon, *ibid.*, 10.

20. Verbatim from Bacon, *ibid.*

21. Extracted verbatim from a longer passage from Bacon, *ibid.*, indicating that such a plea must be made in abatement, for it will not be accepted later in arrest of judgment. JM meant "stranger is tenant."

Whenever it appears on record that the Plaintiff has sued out two writs against the same Defendants for the same thing the second writ shall abate.[22]

    1. B. 13; 12. Mod. 418; 5 Coke. 61.

Whatever destroys the Plfs. action & disables him forever from recovering may be pleaded in bar but the Deft. may sometimes plead it in Abatemt. As in Replevin the Deft. may pl[e]ad property in himself or in a stranger either in bar or in Abatemt.[23]

    1. B. 14; Vent. 249; 2. Ld. R. 984.

If a Deft. pleads matter in bar & concludes in abatemt. or matter in abatemt. & concludes in bar this shall be deemed a plea in bar.[24]

    1. B. 14; 2. Mod. 64; Ld. R. 593; 6. Mod. 203; Con.[25] 2. Ld. R. 1018.

Where the matter of Abatemt. appears on the face of the record the plea shall begin & end with a petit judicium de brevi but where the matter is dehors the Deft. shall only end his plea with a petit judicium.[26]

    1. B. 15.; Moor. 30; 5 Mod. 136.

Pleas in abatemt. are not to be recd. but on oath.[27]

Suits shall not abate for want of form if there be matter sufficient in the Declara[tion.]

ACCOUNT

Account, at common law, lay only agt. a Guardian in socage, Bailiff or Receiver, or by one in favor of trade & commerce. The statutes on that subject have given this action to the Execrs. of Merchants, the Exrs. of Exrs. & to Administrators.[28]

    1. B. 17; C.L. 90.

Action of account is by the laws of Virga. given agt. the Exrs. or Admrs. of every Guardian Bailiff or Receiver & also to one joint

    22. Extracted verbatim from Bacon, who began his paragraph with the maxim, "The Law abhors a Multiplicity of Actions. . . ." *Ibid.*, 13. The remaining paragraphs were ignored by JM.

    23. Summarized from Bacon, *ibid.*, 14.

    24. A summary of two paragraphs in Bacon, *ibid.*

    25. Bacon's citation reads "See contr. 2 Ld. Raym. 1018." *Ibid.*

    26. Verbatim from Bacon, *ibid.*, 15. A "petit judicium de brevi" is a shortened judgment from the writ; a "petit judicium" is a shortened judgment. "Dehors," not of record.

    27. This material was extracted from Bacon, *ibid.*, 1 n., 11, 12, and the absence of citations concerning it seems to indicate that JM added it as an afterthought.

    28. A paraphrase from Bacon, *ibid.*, 17. JM did not include Bacon's observations that the law demanded privity between the parties before account would lie, a defect that he cured somewhat later in his abstracting. The statutes mentioned in the second sentence are English statutes cited in Bacon.

tenant or tenant in common his Exrs. or Admrs. against the other as Bailiff for receiving more than comes to his proportion, or agt. his Exrs. or Admrs.[29]

22. G. 2, Ch. 3, p. 166.

An infant appointed Factor etc. not accountable in law or equity but by his sureties.[30]

1. B. 17; 4. Leon 32.; Sec. 1. Vern. 208.

If I make J.S. my Bailiff etc. who appoints a Depy. I cannot have account against his Deputy.[31]

Do.

An apprentice by the name of an apprentice is not chargeable in account.[32]

11. Co. 89.

To maintain an action of account there must be a privity either in law or by the provision of the parties.[33]

1. B. 18; Co. L. 172.

Equity will make all persons account for the profits of lands they have received to such as have the equitable title.[34]

1. B. 18; The case of coventry vers. Hall.

A Bailiff cannot be charged as receiver—whether the same person may be charged as Bailiff & Receiver. Quere.[35]

1. B. 19.

No action of account lies for a thing certain.[36]

1. B. 19.

29. A summary from 22 Geo. 2, c. 3, sec. 37 (1748), *Va. Acts in Force* (1769), 166, printed in 5 Hening 468.
30. A summary from Bacon, *Abridgment*, I, 17, but JM ignored the statement that an infant might be an executor, or liable in trover, which preceded this passage in Bacon.
31. A paraphrase from Bacon, *ibid.* JM deleted the remainder of the sentence, which indicates that account would still lie against the original bailiff or receiver.
32. Verbatim from Bacon, *ibid.* Bacon's marginalia, ignored by JM, make the point that, while an apprentice is not chargeable as to ordinary receipts of his master's trade, he is chargeable as any other might be, as a bailiff or receiver.
33. A verbatim extract from Bacon, who then provided examples of those individuals who are not chargeable in account. *Ibid.*, 18. This was JM's first mention of privity.
34. This was JM's summary from Bacon's extensive discussion of the 17th-century development of account as an appropriate action to recover mesne profits from land wrongfully withheld. *Ibid.*, 18. Bacon stated that after Coventry v. Hall "Equity began to make all Persons account for the mesne profits they had received, to such Persons as had the equitable Title." JM's synopsis was therefore somewhat inaccurate.
35. A summary from Bacon, *ibid.*, 19, which described the differing functions of a bailiff and a receiver and asserted that if the action is to be brought against the same person in both capacities the receivership should be pleaded specially. The query was also Bacon's.
36. A paraphrase from Bacon, *ibid.*, eliminating the examples.

If a man by obligation acknowleges that he has recd. money ad proficiendum & computandum[37] the obligee may either sue the bond or bring account.[38]

    1. B. 19; Cr. El. 644.

Where account would lie Assumpsit may be brought on an express promise. Wherever one acts as Bailiff he promises to render an account.[39]

    1. B. 19, 20; Sal. 9. pl. 1.

A release or submission to an award are good pleas in bar of account. It is no good plea that the Deft. has paid the money.[40]

    1. B. 20; Cr. Ch. 116; Br. 48.

In an action of account the first judgment is quod computet[41] after which the Ct. assigns Auditors armed with authority to convene the parties before them from day to day at any day & place that they shall appoint till the account be settled: the time by which the account is to be settled is prefixed by the Ct. but may be enlarged.[42] Either of the parties on injustice may apply to the Court. If the Deft. denies any article or demurs to any demand it is to be tried in court.[43]

    1. B. 21; Mod. 42; Co. Ent. 46.

Whatever may be pleaded to the action shall never be allowed of as a good discharge before the Auditors.[44]

    1. B. 21; Cr. Ch. 116.

ACCORD AND SATISFACTION

Accord can not be pleaded in bar unless satisfaction be actually made.[45]

    1. B. 22; Ray. 450.

37. A receipt of money for safekeeping, and perhaps investment, with an account to be rendered. In other words, the transaction would be more in the nature of a bailment of cash than a loan.

38. A paraphrase from Bacon, *Abridgment*, I, 19.

39. JM's summary was inaccurate in that Bacon indicated that where there is an express promise a party may proceed in assumpsit or in account, at his election, and that failure to proceed in account may not be pleaded in abatement of an assumpsit action. The last sentence is a verbatim extract from Bacon, *ibid.*

40. A summary by JM from Bacon's discussion of matters that would bar an action of account. *Ibid.*, 20.

41. "That he account."

42. Bacon's statement was that if the account be exceptionally long or confusing, the time of settlement may be extended by application to the court. *Abridgment*, I, 21.

43. A paraphrase from Bacon, *ibid.*

44. Standing alone, JM's verbatim extract is rather ambiguous, but the material following in Bacon indicates that absent a defendant's plea of a former settlement in bar to the action, he may not introduce the settlement before the auditors. *Ibid.*

45. A summary from Bacon, *ibid.*, 22.

An accord must appear to be advantageous to the party otherwise it can be no satisfaction.[46]

    1. B. 22; 9 Ed. 4, 19; Rol. Ab. 128.

An accord with satisfaction is no good plea to an action real.[47]

    1. B. 22; 4 Co. 1.

When a duty in certain accrues by a deed tempore confectionis scripti[48] it ought to be avoided by matter of as high a nature.[49]

    1. B. 22; 6 Co. 43; Cr. Ja. 254.

If an accord be pleaded by way of accord a precise execution thereof in every part must be pleaded,[50] if by way of satisfaction, the Deft. need plead no more but that he paid the Plf. 10/ in full satisfaction of the action which he received. Accord cannot be plead without satisfaction.[51]

    1. B. 25; 9. Co. 80; Rolls Abr. 129.

ACTIONS IN GENERAL

It is clear that for every injury a man shall have an action & for every right he has a remedy—where a person has several remedies he may chuse which he pleases, but in this he must follow the rules of that society of which he is a member, for though a man has a right & is barred by the Statute of limitations yet he can have no remedy.[52]

    1. B. 28; Co. L. 145; Stile 4.

Also in cases where there may be damnum absque injuria[53] the party can have no action.

    Roll. Abr. 107; 1 Mod. 69.

46. A verbatim extract from Bacon, *ibid.*, but JM omitted subsequent passages that stress the contractual nature of accord and satisfaction.

47. A verbatim extract from Bacon, *ibid.* JM's extract is somewhat misleading. According to the Bacon passage, real actions brought by writ of right could not be barred by an accord and satisfaction, but accord and satisfaction might be pleaded in bar to ejectment actions.

48. Written in the manner of the time.

49. JM omitted Bacon's explanation that if the duty arises from a covenant, bill, or writing obligatory, the accord and satisfaction must be executed with equal formality. *Ibid.*

50. Here JM omitted Bacon's admonition that failure in pleading any part of the performance of the accord will render the plea insufficient and that it is therefore better to plead the satisfaction. *Ibid.*, 25.

51. The first sentence is a paraphrase from Bacon; the second sentence may be drawn from Bacon's statement, "*Note*; It [i.e. an accord and satisfaction] cannot be pleaded without Performance." *Ibid.*

52. A summary from three paragraphs in Bacon, *ibid.*, 28.

53. "Damage without injury" (in the legal sense). This paragraph is a verbatim extract from Bacon, *ibid.*, but JM omitted an example.

None are excluded from bringing an action except on account of their crimes or their country.[54]

    Co. L. 128.

A man that hath a special property in goods shall have an action agt. a stranger who takes them away because he is answerable in damages to the absolute owner.[55]

    Mod. 30.

A man who has cause of action agt. two may bring it agt. which he pleases.[56]

    Dyer. 98.

In real actions in those writs which contain the time place & demand particularly several lands by several titles cannot be demanded in the same writ. Secus where there is only a genl. complaint as in the writ of trespass quare clausum fregit.[57]

    8. Co. 87; F.N.B. 209; Dyer 145.

In personal actions several wrongs & trespasses may be joined. Fraud & warranty may be joind.[58]

    1. Ba. 30; 8 Co. 87; Ray. 233.

But actions founded on a tort & a contract cannot be joined as Assumpsit & trover.[59]

    Ld. Ray 58.

Where one hath a right to recover in the same kind of action though he derives his right from difft. titles, yet being conjoined in him he may recover in one action.[60]

    1. Ba. 31; Yel. 63; Cro. Ja. 68.

But one cannot in the same action join a demand in his own right & one which he hath in right of another.[61]

    Cro. El. 486.

---

54. A summary of the material, *ibid.*, 29, but Bacon cited felons, traitors, outlaws, excommunicants, and alien enemies as individuals who because of criminal record or nationality could not bring actions.

55. A paraphrase from Bacon, *ibid.*

56. A paraphrase from Bacon, *ibid.*, but JM omitted the examples that follow, which limit the general statement to tortious wrongs.

57. "Trespass to land," one of the common law actions for damages resulting from an unlawful entry upon land. The paragraph summarizes Bacon, *ibid.*

58. A summary from Bacon, *ibid.*, 30.

59. Assumpsit, the ancestor of the modern action for breach of contract, arose from the fraudulent refusal to perform one's promises. At this time assumpsit was still considered a tort, rather than a contract, action. The statement is a verbatim extract from Bacon, *ibid.*

60. A paraphrase from Bacon, *ibid.*, 31.

61. A verbatim extract from Bacon, *ibid.*, but JM omitted examples that follow.

Several persons may join in an action where their interest is joint.[62]
  Roll. Ab. 31.

ACTIONS LOCAL & TRANSITORY

All actions real or mixd must be laid in the county where the lands
lie.[63]
  1. Ba. 34.

All personal actions may be brought in any Cty. & laid in any
place & the Deft. cannot traverse it.[64]
  1. Ba. 35; Co. L. 282; 7. Co. 3.

The Deft. cannot by his plea oblige the Plf. to lay his action in a
dift. Cty. unless the matter pleaded be local. The motion must be
on affadavit.[65]
  2 Sal. 669 pl. 6.

ACTIONS QUI TAM[66]

Wherever a statute prohibits a thing as being an immediate offence agt. the publick good, under a certain penalty the whole or
part of which is given to him who will sue for it, any person may
bring such action or information & lay his demand with a qui tam.
Also where a Statute prohibits or commands a thing the doing or
omission of which is both an immediate damage to the party &
also highly concerns the good of the publick, the party may & some
say ought to bring his action with a qui tam.[67]
  Co. En. 375; 4. Co. 13; 2. Haw. [P.]C. 265.

An action on a publick stat. need not recite the stat. But if the
prosecutor recites the Stat. & materially varies from a substantial
part this is fatal.
  Cro. El. 236; 2 Haw. P.C. 246.

If an information contain several offences & be well laid as to some
but defective as to others the informer may have judgt. for such as
are well laid.
  Cr. Ja. 104.

62. A paraphrase from Bacon, *ibid*.
63. A verbatim extract from Bacon, *ibid.*, 34. JM ignored Bacon's extensive discussion of venue in real property actions.
64. A verbatim extract from Bacon, *ibid.*, 35, omitting types of action that are
personal.
65. The first sentence is a verbatim extract from Bacon, *ibid*. The second sentence
is extracted from the remainder of the paragraphs that specify the method of moving
for a change of venue.
66. Bacon's marginal definition was that a qui tam action is one where the penalty,
or a part thereof, will be given to anyone who will institute the action. *Ibid.*, 37.
67. A paraphrase from Bacon omitting mentions of the king. *Ibid.*

An action or information need not conclude contra pacem[68] or in contemptum[69] as an Indictment must.[70]

Cr. Ja. 529.

Every informer on any penal statute shall exhibit his suit in person & pursue it by himself or attorney.

18. El. Ch. 5.[71]

The Deft. cannot plead specially & the genl. issue either to the whole or to part of the charge.[72]

Rol. rep. 49, 134.

If there be more than one deft. they ought not to plead jointly.

2 H.P.C. 276.[73]

Where a Stat. gives a certain penalty to the party grieved he is entitled to his costs.[74]

2. Hawk. P.C. 274.

Any informer (not grieved) who willingly delays his suit etc. shall pay costs charges & damages to be assigned by Ct. & no informer shall compound without leave of Ct. under penalty of standing in the pillory, of being disabled to sue in any popular or penal statute & of forfeiting ten pounds.

18. El. ch. 5.[75]

ACTIONS ON THE CASE

If A delivers goods to B to deliver to C & B does not deliver them but converts them to his own use either A or C may have an action agt. B. They cant join.[76]

Bulster 68.

If a servant is cozened of his Masters money the Master may have an action agt. the cozener.[77]

Cr. Ja. 223.

68. "Against the peace."

69. Bacon, *Abridgment*, I, 38, says "in contemptum Domini Regis," or "in contempt of the Lord King," but JM avoided mention of the king.

70. This and the preceding two passages are verbatim extracts from four paragraphs in Bacon, *ibid.*, 38.

71. Substantially as in Bacon, *ibid.*, 40. JM's citation was to the English statute 18 Eliz. I, c. 5.

72. A summary from Bacon's statement in *Abridgment*, I, 40.

73. A verbatim extract from Bacon, *ibid.*, 41.

74. A verbatim extract from Bacon, *ibid.*, 42.

75. A summary from two paragraphs in Bacon referring to the Elizabethan statute. *Ibid.*, 42, 43.

76. The first statement paraphrases Bacon, *ibid.*, 45. The second sentence is a JM summary.

77. A paraphrase from Bacon, *ibid.*, 46.

No action lies by a Master agt. his sert. for the bare breach of his comd. but if a Servt. does any thing falsely & fraudulently to the damage of his Master an action lies.[78]

Sid. 298.

No master is chargeable with the acts of his Servant but when he acts in execution of the authority given by his Master & then the act of the Sert. is the act of the Master.[79]

Sal. 282 pl. 11.

If I deliver goods to A who delivers them to B to keep to the use of A[80] who wastes them I may have an action[81] against B.[82]

Though an injury happens to a Man in his property by the neglect of another yet if by law he was not obliged to be more careful no action lies.

If a man uses or abuses the thing he finds he shall answer for it.[83]

Cr. El. 219.

If by the wrongful act of A, B. becomes chargeable to C B may have his action against A before he is sued by C.[84]

Cr. Ja. 474; Cr. El. 53.

If a man forges a bond in my name 'tis possible I may be injured by it, but 'till it be put in suit agt. me I have no action agt. the forger.[85]

Hob. 267; vide 6 Mod. 46.

Where a man has the possession of any personal chattel & sells it, the bare affirming it to be his amounts to a warranty & gives an action.[86]

Sal. 210. pl. 2; Ld. Ray. 284; Cr. Ja. 474.

If on a treaty for the purchase of a house the Deft. affirms the rent of the house to be £30 whereas it was but £20 & thereby the Plf. is

78. A paraphrase from Bacon, *ibid.*
79. A verbatim extract from Bacon, *ibid.*, 47.
80. Bacon here also said "and B." JM inserted "who," which does not appear in Bacon. *Ibid.*, 48n.
81. Bacon here also said "upon the Case." *Ibid.*
82. Bacon here also said "though I did not deliver them to him." *Ibid.*
83. A paraphrase from Bacon, *ibid.*, 48. Bacon listed situations in which a finder of goods will not be held liable for negligence, but he stated that if the finder realizes gain or advantage from the thing found and then abuses it, he shall be liable for damages. The citation is to this latter point.
84. A summary from material in Bacon, *ibid.*, 49; however, Bacon's example was limited to the illegal sale of sheep from *A* to *B*, and JM's generalization does not seem to be a valid one.
85. A paraphrase from Bacon, *ibid.*, 50.
86. A summary from Bacon's discussion, *ibid.*

induced to give so much more than the house is worth an action lies.[87]

Sal. 211. pl. 3.

If I sell unsound goods & knowing them to be unsound affirm them to be sound, or not knowing them to be unsound warrant them to be sound an action lies.[88]

Cr. Ja. 469.

If a man rides an unruly horse in places much frequented[89] & the horse breaks from him & runs over B & hurts him, B shall have an action. For an injury accruing to a Man in his real estate of freehold or inheritance the action lies.[90]

Vent. 295; Ld. Ray. 38.

If a Man lend or hire anothers horse & for want of safe keeping the horse dies an action lies.[91]

Cr. El. 777.

If A obtains a judgt. in debt agt. B as Exr. to his Father, & thereupon A takes out a Fi. Fa.[92] but before the sheriff can execute it B[93] removes & disposes of all the Testators goods so that the sheriff is forced to return nulla bona[94] an action on the case lies agt. B for the sheriff could not return a devastavit & if this action does not lie the party is without remedy.

Godb. 285, 2. Rol. Rep. 312, vide con.[95] Mod. 286.

In genl. where by the covin[96] of a third person a man loses his debt an action on the case lies agt. him.[97]

87. A paraphrase from Bacon, *ibid.*, 51.
88. A summary from Bacon's marginal note, *ibid.*, 52.
89. Bacon specified that the purpose of the riding was to break and tame the horse. *Ibid.*, 53.
90. The passage is a summary from three paragraphs in Bacon, *ibid.*
91. A paraphrase from Bacon, *ibid.*, 55.
92. "Fieri facias," a writ of execution against a judgment debtor's goods and chattels.
93. Bacon here inserted "*secrete & fraudulenter*," that is, secretly and fraudulently. *Abridgment*, I, 55.
94. "No goods." Bacon appended "&c," referring to the return "nulla Bona testatoris nec propria," or that the goods of the estate are not available for execution. The plaintiff's next step would be to apply for an execution against the person and goods of the executor or administrator, called a devastavit. The passage is a paraphrase from Bacon, *ibid.*
95. "See to the contrary."
96. "Covin" is a secret conspiracy or agreement to defraud.
97. A summary from a lengthy paragraph in Bacon; JM did not note that the debt Bacon discussed was a judgment debt. *Abridgment*, I, 56.

Also for injuries done to a man with respect to his wife his child or his servant an action lies.[98]

Carth. 3, 4.

If a minister of justice have a warrant to attach the goods of another & can do it & does it not an action lies against him.[99]

3. Bul. 212; Cr. El. 873.

If a smith refuses to shoe my horse or if he pricks him; if a farrier kills my horse with bad medecine or by neglect in curing him; or if a client receives an injury by the neglect or fraud of his attorney an action lies.[1]

San. 312; 2 Bulster 373; Cr. Ja. 395.

If by a common nusance I suffer a particular damage an action lies, so too for continuing a nusance.[2]

Cr. Ja. 446; Ld. Ray 370.

It seems agreed that for a false & malicious prosecution for any crime whether capital or not by which a man may be endangered of his life, suffer in his liberty reputation or property an action on the case in nature of a writ of conspiracy lies whether an indictment was exhibited or not.[3]

Cr. El. 70; 134, Sal. 15.

If a stranger brings an action in the name of J. without consulting[4] J. an action lies.

Ray. 503; Cr. El. 629.

If an action on the case is brought for a civil action special grievance must be shewn.[5]

Style 379; Sand. 228.

It seems the better opinion that a person guilty of felony & pardoned or burnt in the hand[6] may be proceeded agt. at the suit of the party injurd.[7]

Stile 346; Yel. 99.

98. JM's summary from Bacon, *ibid.*, does not distinguish between the seduction of the wife and the enticement away of a child or servant.

99. Nearly verbatim from Bacon, *ibid.*, 58, which also included the words "upon the case" after "action."

1. A paraphrase from three paragraphs in Bacon, *ibid.*, 60.

2. A summary from two paragraphs in Bacon; JM omitted Bacon's definition of a common nuisance. *Ibid.*, 61.

3. A paraphrase from Bacon, *ibid.*

4. Bacon's statement was "without the consent of"; the rest of the passage is verbatim from Bacon, *ibid.*, 62.

5. JM's summary of Bacon's discussion and marginal note, *ibid.*; however, this material occurs prior to the Bacon passage summarized at n. 4 above.

6. One was burned in the hand if he successfully pleaded benefit of clergy after being convicted of a felony.

7. Two verbatim extracts from Bacon, *Abridgment*, I, 64.

Action lies for a virgin of good fame married by a man who had a wife.[8]

> Skin. 119.

AFFADAVIT[9]

AGREEMENTS

A person non compos, an infant & a feme covert[10] are generally incapable of entering into agreements.

> see Eq. ca. ab. 25. pl. 6.

The ancestor seised in fee may by his agrt. bind his Heir.[11]

> 2. Ver. 215.

Tis a genl. rule that wherever the matter of the bill is merely in damages the remedy is at law, but if there be matter of fraud mixt with the damages the remedy is in chancery. So where the agreemt. is to do something in specie.[12]

> Ab. Eq. 16; chan. rep 158; Ch. ca. 42.

A court of equity has decreed a performance of covenants & directed a trial in a quantum damnificat.[13]

> Ver. 189 pl. 190; 2 Ch. ca. 146.

Agreemts. out of which an equity can be raised for a decree in specie ought to be obtaind with all imaginable fairness & without any mixture tending to surprise or circumvention and that they be not unreasonable in themselves.[14]

> Ab. Eq. 17; 2. Ch. ca. 17; Ver. 227 pl. 225.[15]

8. A summary from a paragraph in Bacon, *ibid*.

9. Bacon's discussion of affidavits covered about three pages. JM left blank the remainder of the page after the heading, presumably intending to return to the subject later. On the page appear two signatures with elaborate scrolls surrounding the "J" of his name.

10. JM substituted "feme covert" for Bacon's English translation "a wife during marriage." The sentence is a summary from three short paragraphs in Bacon, *Abridgment*, I, 67, 68.

11. Bacon's examples that follow indicate that this verbatim extract by JM referred to specific performance of a contract to sell land being decreed against the owner's heirs. *Ibid.*, 68.

12. A summary from three paragraphs in Bacon, *ibid.*, 69. Bacon and JM used the term "in specie" to refer to the rendering of a particular item or service, rather than the more general use of the term to refer to coined money.

13. By quantum damnificat a court of equity directed that the issue of damages be tried as in a court of law. JM roughly paraphrased the paragraph in Bacon, *Abridgment*, I, 69; his version omitted the alternative method of determining damages by referral to a master in chancery. Possibly the parallel administration of law and equity in the Virginia county courts, and the General Court, before Independence, resulted in an exclusive reliance upon a jury inquest into damages.

14. A verbatim extract from Bacon, *ibid.*, 70.

15. The last two citations do not pertain to this paragraph, but to another paragraph in Bacon, *ibid.*, that JM did not copy.

A ct. of eqty. will much sooner[16] dismiss a bill which prays a specific execution of an unreasonable agrt. than set aside an agrt. though not strictly fair on a bill for that purpose and when such agreements are set aside it must be on refunding what was[17] paid, making reasonable allowances for improvemts. etc.

2. Ch. Ca. 136; Ver. 271; Rep. in Eq 155; 2 Ver. 127.

In law & equity[18] voluntary conveyances are good agt. the parties & cannot be revoked, nor will the Ct. interpose in behalf of one volunteer agt. another. But if they affect creditors purchasers or younger children the Ct. will set them aside.

Ver. 100, 464.

If there be a defective conveyance without an equitable consideration[19] equity will not oblige the party to make it good though there be a covenant for farther assurances.

2. Ven. 365; 2 Ver. 40.

If the agreemt. be to quit the possession of lands the ct. will not decree a conveyance.[20]

Ver. 121.

If one is bound to transfer £300 Stock before such a time which he does not do, & the stock is much risen he shall transfer the stock in specie & account for dividends since the time.[21]

2 Ver. 394, Preced. in ch. 533.

No estate for life or any higher estate shall be made to take effect, nor shall an use thereof be created unless it be by deed indented sealed & recorded in the Genl. Ct. or the ct. of that coty. where the land lies. The deed of residents to be recorded in 8 months of non residents in 2 Years.[22] The Deed to be acknowleged[23] by the

16. JM substituted "sooner" for "will much easier be prevailed on to," in this paraphrase from Bacon, *ibid.*

17. Here JM omitted *"bona fide."* Except for this the paragraph is a verbatim extract from Bacon, *ibid.*

18. The sentence in Bacon begins "Also in Equity"; otherwise verbatim from Bacon, *ibid.*, 71.

19. Here JM omitted Bacon's words, "a Court of." Otherwise this is a verbatim extract. *Ibid.*

20. A verbatim extract, JM omitting the next clause that if the agreement were for a conveyance, it would be so decreed, even if the party did not know the nature of his estate in the land. *Ibid.*

21. Bacon concluded the sentence with "that it ought to have been transferred"; otherwise a close paraphrase of Bacon's statement. *Ibid.*

22. JM omitted the statutory provision that these times be computed from the time of execution of the document transferring title.

23. JM omitted the statutory requirement that the acknowledgment be made in court.

grantor or proved by three witnesses before it can be admitted to record. Deeds of inheritance, for term of years, or for marriage settlement; all deeds of trust & Mortgages whatsoever not recorded etc. to be void as to subsequent purchasers & creditors but binding between the parties & their heirs.

19. G. 2 Ch. 1 p. 142, 143.[24]

The foregoing act is very similar to the stat. of frauds & perjuries on which the following determinations have been made by the Judges in England.[25]

Note the stat. of Frauds etc. does not require recording.

If the Deft. in his answer confesses the substance of a bill setting forth a parol agrt. & demanding a specific execution the Ct. will decree it.[26]

Ab. E. 19 pl. 3; Ver. 151, 159.

A parol agreemt. which is intended to be reduced to writing but is prevented by fraud may be decreed in specie.[27]

Ab. eq. 20.

A letter from a father promising a portion & a marriage had in consequence thereof has been deemed sufficient.[28]

2. Ver. 322; 2 Vent. 361; Prec. in Ch. 361.

It seems to be admitted that if an agreement be made concerning lands etc. though not in writing & the whole or part of the money is recd. by the party equity will decree a specific execution. The doubt is what evidence shall be admitted as proof of the receipt. If the Deft. confesses it in his answer 'tis sufft.[29] if he denies[30] it the Plaintiff must prove it by written evidence.

Ver. 151; 2. Ch. Ca. 135; Str. 426; Gil. His. Ch. 239, Contra, 2. Ch. ca. 36, Gil. His. Ch. 231.

---

24. A summary from 19 Geo. 2, c. 1, secs. 1, 4 (1745), *Va. Acts in Force* (1769), 142, 143, not in Hening.

25. JM's comment.

26. A summary of Bacon's statement, but JM omitted the fact that Bacon was discussing a bill demanding specific performance of a contract for the sale of real property. *Abridgment*, I, 73.

27. Bacon reads "in Equity"; JM's "in specie" is probably a copying error. Otherwise this is a verbatim extract from Bacon, *ibid.*

28. A paraphrase from Bacon's marginal note, *ibid.*

29. In JM's manuscript text the line ends at this point, and for a correct paraphrase JM should have inserted a semicolon here. *Ibid.*, 74.

30. Bacon stated that if the defendant confessed receipt but asserted that the money was loaned and not given in execution of the agreement, then the plaintiff must prove the receipt for purposes of the agreement. The sentences here printed are a paraphrase from an extended discussion in Bacon, *ibid.*

If a man on the promise of a lease lays out money on improvements he shall oblige the lessee[31] to execute a lease. Secus if he has been at no expense.[32]

Ver. 159; 2. Vent. 361.[33]

If a man purchases lands in anothers name & pays the money it shall be a trust for him.[34]

Ver. 366.

AMENDMENT AND JEOFAIL[35]

ANNUITY AND RENT CHARGE

Whenever the remedy by way of charge for the rent is not commensurate to the rent, the rent is called seck[36] & the charge is only appurtenant.[37]

Co. L. 147; 7 Co. 151.

If I bind my land & goods for the payment of a rent,[38] or if I grant that if such a rent be arrear B may distrain for it in the manor of C. This is a good rent charge.[39]

Co. L. 147; Broke rent. 14.

If an original grant be made of a rent charge to commence after the death of J.S. it is good, secus of a rent in being.[40]

Broke grant 86; 2 Vent. 204; B. grant 86.

If a man grants by his deed an annual rent out of certain lands with distress & does not provide that the grant shall not charge his person, the grantee may distrain for the rent or have a writ of annuity.[41]

Lit. Sec. 219, 220; 6 Co. 58.

31. A mistake in transcribing "lessor" from Bacon, *ibid.*, 75.

32. That is, the bare promise would fall within the statute of frauds and be unenforceable without its being incorporated in a written instrument. The paragraph is a summary from Bacon's paragraph, *ibid.*

33. The citation to Ventris's King's Bench reports pertains to the next paragraph in JM's notes.

34. A paraphrase from Bacon, *Abridgment*, I, 75.

35. The law notes page is headed with this title and contains the name Thomas Marshall and John May (b. 1737), and the word "ambassadors" in handwriting other than that of JM. The notes also skip materials on aliens, ambassadors, and ancient demesne.

36. "Rent seck" is a barren rent, without provision for distress as a method of collection.

37. A short verbatim extract from Bacon's paragraph, *Abridgment*, I, 115.

38. Bacon here added "with Power to distrain." *Ibid.*, 116.

39. A paraphrase from Bacon, *ibid.*

40. A verbatim extract from Bacon, *ibid.*, 117; the material after "secus" is summarized from a marginal note. JM ignored Bacon's queries and speculations concerning the application of the rule against perpetuities to this situation.

41. A summary from two paragraphs in Bacon, *ibid.*

If a rent be granted out of lands in which the grantor has no interest, or in which the grantee cannot by the deed distrain, with a proviso that it shall not charge his person the proviso is void.[42]
Co. L. 146; 6. Co. 41; 6. Co. 58.

A grant that a man may distrain in certain lands if a certain sum be unpaid does not charge the person.[43]
Co. L. 146.

A rent is granted out of an inheritance & term for years.[44] The grantee may distrain in both but must avow for a rent issuing out of the inheritance.[45]
Co. L. 147; Cr. Ja. 390.

If such power is given in the deed the grantee may when rent is arrear enter & hold the lands till he is satisfied by the perception of the profits.[46]
Ray. 135; San. 112.

An action of debt does not lie for the arrearages of an annuity if the grantee be seised of it for life or in fee,[47] secus if for years.[48]
Co. L. 162; 4 Co. 49; Cr. El. 268.

If the grantee distrains & avows or brings a writ of annuity and declares he has determined his election & shall ever after be confined to the remedy he has adopted.[49]
Lit. S. 219; Co. L. 145.

If the grantee of a rent charge before he has made his election purchases a part of the land he is without any remedy.[50]
C.L. 148; see 2. Ver 143–4.

ARBITRAMENT & AWARD[51]

A right of freehold cannot be transferd, an Annuity determind,

---

42. A summary from two paragraphs in Bacon, *ibid.*, 118.
43. A summary from Bacon's discussion, *ibid.*
44. That is, two parcels, one held in fee and one held for a term of years. *Ibid.*
45. JM's paragraph is a summary from Bacon's discussion, *ibid.*
46. A summary from Bacon, *ibid.*, 118, 119.
47. JM omitted Bacon's mention of grantee's title in fee tail. *Ibid.*, 119. Virginia abolished entails of land and slaves in Oct. 1776. 9 Hening 226–227.
48. The material after "secus" is a summary of Bacon's marginal note. The remainder is verbatim from Bacon, *Abridgment*, I, 119.
49. A summary from Bacon, *ibid.*, 120.
50. JM omitted Bacon's statement that the rent was extinguished by the purchase. The passage is a paraphrase. *Ibid.*, 121.
51. JM moved directly to this title in Bacon, omitting the titles "Appeal" and "Ap-

partition made by award.[52] But if the parties are bound in mutual obligations to stand to the award & a transfer etc. is awarded the party refusing forfeits his obligation.[53]

9. Co. 78.

Debt certain & fixed cannot be discharged by naked award, nor causes criminal or matrimonial decided.[54]

6. Co. 44; Cr. Ja. 99; 2 Vent. 109.

Chattels & actions personal may be determined by arbitrament & transfered by award without deed. The submission is to be taken largely & according to the intent of the parties, where tis made by word the remedy to enforce a performance of the award is by reciprocal actions on the case. An action of debt will lie if money be awarded.[55]

9 Co. 78.

Ex nuda submissione non oritur actio,[56] but notice must be given. If the submission be by deed tis still revocable but the party forfeits his obligation. Marriage of a feme sole is a revocation.[57]

8 Co. 81; 8. Co. 82; 2 Keb. 845.

In debt on a bond to perform an award if non submisit[58] must be pleaded no breach need be alledged.[59]

Sid. 290.

An award must be made according to the submission. It ought to be certain, equal, & mutually satisfactory. It must be lawful & possible. It must be final.[60]

If the award is good as to one party & void as to the other party tis void in the whole.[61]

---

prover." The appeal section deals with appeals of felony. Approver is the body of English law dealing with the receipt of testimony against coconspirators by one who has confessed his treason or felony; the traitor or felon so admitted to testify was known as an approver.

52. JM's synopsis is misleading; Bacon contended that a right of freehold cannot be transferred by an award; neither could an annuity be determined or a partition be made by such a procedure. *Abridgment*, I, 132.

53. The paragraph is a summary from three paragraphs in Bacon, *ibid.*

54. A summary from three paragraphs in Bacon, *ibid.*, 133.

55. A summary from two paragraphs in Bacon, *ibid.*

56. Out of a "bare parole" submission, no cause of action arises.

57. A summary from five paragraphs and marginal notes in Bacon, *Abridgment*, I, 133, 134.

58. "He did not submit."

59. A summary from Bacon, *Abridgment*, I, 134.

60. A summary from Bacon, *ibid.*, 139–147, followed by Bacon's subtitles.

61. A paraphrase from Bacon, *ibid.*, 148.

If money be awarded & not paid the party may either have his first action or action of debt.[62]

8 Co. 98.[63]

In pleading a man should set forth the award & therein how he hath performed it.[64]

Moor. 3. pl 9.

Where any thing is awarded in satisfaction the award is a bar, but where releases are awarded 'tis no bar till performance.[65]

Carth. 378; Ld. Ray. 247.

Not necessary to lay time & place of the award.[66]

2. Brownl. 137.

ASSAULT & BATTERY

Any injury whatever actually done to the person of a man, in an angry revengeful, rude or insolent manner is a battery.[67]

6 Mod. 149; Ld. Ray. 62; Salk. 407 pl. 2.

The least touching of anothers person wilfully or in anger is a battery.[68]

3. Bl. 120.

A Parent may moderately chastise his child, a Master his servt. or his scholar. An officer having a warrant agt. one who will not be arrested may beat or wound him in the attempt to take him. A man may beat wound or maim one who makes an assault on his person or on that of his wife parent child or master, or who attempts to kill a stranger.[69]

I may justify an ass[aul]t in defense of my land or goods. In an action on the case the Deft. must plead the matter of justification specially.[70]

Hawk. P.C. 130; 3. Bl. 120;[71] 6 Mod. 172.

Every ass[aul]t will not justify every beating.[72]

2 Inst. 316; 2 Haw. P.C. 159.

62. A verbatim extract from Bacon, *ibid.*, 149.
63. This citation refers to the material at n. 61 above.
64. A paraphrase from Bacon, *Abridgment*, I, 150, 153.
65. A summary from Bacon, *ibid.*, 151.
66. A summary from Bacon, *ibid.*, 152.
67. A summary from Bacon, *ibid.*, 154.
68. A verbatim extract from Blackstone, *Commentaries*, III, 120.
69. A paraphrase from a long paragraph in Bacon, *Abridgment*, I, 155. It should be noted that Bacon said a parent may chastise a child "in a reasonable manner." Blackstone said "gives moderate correction." *Commentaries*, III, 120.
70. The first sentence is from the material paraphrased at n. 65 above. The second sentence is a summary from a short paragraph in Bacon, *Abridgment*, I, 155.
71. The Blackstone citation does not appear in Bacon, *ibid.*, but is JM's insertion.
72. A verbatim extract from Bacon, *ibid.*

ASSIGNMENT

In assignments of a lease for life or years a man parts with his whole property & the assignee stands in the place of the Assignor.[73]

2. Bl. 326–7.

Assignment of lease etc. to be recorded etc.

19. G. 2. ch. 1. 143.[74]

To avoid maintenance[75] a possibility, right of entry thing in action, cause of suit or title for a condition broken cannot be granted or assignd over.[76] Assignee of bond or note for money or tobacco may sue in his own name allowing all discounts the Deft. can prove either agt. the Plf. himself or the first obligee before notice of assignment.[77]

A personal trust not assignable.[78]

Co. L. 214; 27. G. 2. 249.[79]

ASSUMPSIT[80]

In assumpsit damages are recovered in proportion to the loss sustaind by the violation of the contract. Indebitatus will lie in no case but where debt woud lie.[81]

4 Co. 92.

Obligor in a bond witht. any new considn. promises to pay the Money Ass[umpsi]t will not lie but debt.[82]

Hutt. 34; Cr. El. 240 cont.

Neither debt nor a genl. Ind. ass.[83] will lie agt. the acceptor of a bill of exchange but action on the case.

Hard. 485; Sal. 23. pl. 3.

73. A summary from Blackstone, *Commentaries*, II, 326–327.

74. A summary from 19 Geo. 2, c. 1, sec. 4 (1745), *Va. Acts in Force* (1769), 143, not in Hening.

75. "Maintenance" is the unauthorized and officious interference in a suit by one who has no interest in the subject matter.

76. This sentence is a paraphrase of the material in Bacon, *Abridgment*, I, 157.

77. JM inserted the mention of tobacco, but the remainder of the sentence is a summary statement of the modern rule from Bacon's text and marginal note, *ibid*.

78. Summarized from Bacon, *ibid*., 158. To JM and Bacon a personal trust was an obligation to perform services that rests in a particularly selected individual, not an equitable trust in personal property.

79. The citations apply to the matter at n. 77 above; the second citation is to the Virginia statute on assignment of bonds, 22 Geo. 2, c. 27, secs. 6, 7 (1748), *Va. Acts in Force* (1769), 249, printed in 6 Hening 87.

80. JM ignored Bacon's discussion of "Assise," which covered the assize of novel disseisin and the assize of mort d'ancestor.

81. A paraphrase from Bacon, *Abridgment*, I, 163.

82. Bacon said the obligee "must still pursue his Remedy by Action of Debt." *Ibid*., 164.

83. "General indebitatus assumpsit."

But debt or a genl. Ind. may be brought agt. the drawer.[84]
> Ld. Ray. 175.

An Ind. lies for money won at play,[85] paid by mistake.[86]
> 2 Vent. 175.[87]

An indet. lies for money recd. to the Pl. use on an implied contract.
Lies agt. sheriff for money levied on a Fi. Fa.[88]
All promises are to be taken most strong agt. the promisor & are
not to be rejected if they can be reduced to certy.[89]
> Salk. 27. pl. 14.[90]

Wherever a person promises without a benefit arising to the promisor or loss to the promissee tis a void promise as being without sufft.
consideration.[91]
> 2 Buls. 269.

If the father of A & B lying sick declares his intention of devising a
rent to his younger son during life & the elder in consideration his
father will not charge the lands promises to pay the rent in consequence of which the land is not charged, this is a good consideration.[92]

A consideration altogether executed & past, unless moved by a
precedent request will not maintain ass[umpsi]t.[93]
> Leon. 192; Cr. El. 163.[94]

Where the consideration is agt. law promise void.[95]
> Cr. Ja. 103.

The Plf. must set forth every thing essential to the Gist of the action
with such certainty that it may appear there was cause of action.
But the law requires no greater certainty than the nature of the
thing requires.

84. Except for the abbreviation at n. 83 above, a verbatim extract from Bacon,
Abridgment, I, 165.

85. Bacon indicated that there was a division of opinion on the question of gaming
debts, but JM's summary merely recorded Bacon's tentative conclusion that indebitatus assumpsit probably lies in such cases. *Ibid.*

86. Bacon stated that in the case of receipt of money by mistake, assumpsit, that is,
special assumpsit, would lie. JM's inclusion of this matter in the sentence discussing
indebitatus assumpsit unduly confused the two forms of action. *Ibid.*, 165, 167.

87. The citation pertains to matter at n. 85 above.

88. A summary from Bacon, *Abridgment*, I, 166.

89. A paraphrase from Bacon, *ibid.*, 168.

90. The citation applies to material at n. 88 above.

91. A paraphrase from Bacon, *Abridgment*, I, 170.

92. A paraphrase from Bacon, *ibid.*, 171.

93. A paraphrase from Bacon, *ibid.*, 173.

94. The citations apply to material at n. 92 above.

95. A summary from Bacon, *Abridgment*, I, 174.

The Deft. must shew there was no contract, or that the contract was void & without consideration or that he has performed it.

An entire promise cannot be apportioned.[96]

March 200.

The Deft. cannot plead that he has revoked the promise.[97]

Cr. Ja. 483.

ATTACHMENT

Attachmt. is a process that issues at the discretion of the Judges Of a Ct. of record agt. a person for some contempt for which he is to be committed & may be awarded by them upon a bare suggestion or on their own knowlege.[98]

All courts of record have a discretionary power over their own officers & will punish them for disobeying their commands for executing them oppressively or otherwise misdemeaning themselves in their office.[99]

Dyer. 218; 2 Haw. P.C. 142, 145.

Attachmts. have been granted for speaking contemptuous words concerning the rules of Ct., for disobedience of those rules & for the abuses of the process.[1]

Sal. 84. pl. 4; Mod. 21; 2 Haw. P.C. 154.

AUDITA QUERELA[2]

An Audita querela is a writ to be releived against an unjust judgement or execution by setting them aside for some injustice of the party that obtaind them which could not be pleaded in bar to the action.

If A being within age becomes bail for B & judgement is given against him he may avoid it by Audita querela.[3]

AUTHORITY[4]

A naked authority must be strictly executed. Several persons named in a will to sell lands, one dies, the survivors cannot sell.[5]

Co. L. 181, 113.

96. A summary from Bacon, *ibid.*, 177, 179.
97. A verbatim extract from Bacon, *ibid.*, 180.
98. A verbatim extract from Bacon, *ibid.*
99. The first clause is a verbatim extract from Bacon, while the second summarizes the following material in Bacon, *ibid.*, 181.
1. A series of three summaries from three paragraphs in Bacon, *ibid.*, 182.
2. JM ignored Bacon's section on "Attorney."
3. A paraphrase from Bacon, *Abridgment*, I, 193.
4. "Authority" in this sense is similar to the modern legal term "power."
5. A summary from Bacon, *Abridgment*, I, 200. A "naked authority" is one uncoupled

Deed not delivered till after the day of date, attorney makes livery on the delivery of the deed good.[6]

    Cr. Ja. 153.

Letter of Attorney to make livery absolutely, he delivers on condition good. Secus if to make livery on condi[ti]on & he delivers absolutely.[7]

    Co. L. 258.

Feofment made to A & B, livery by attorney to one in name of both good. Authority cannot be transfered. 9. Co. 77.[8]

    Co. L. 49.

Must be executed during the life of the person that gives it.[9]

    Co. L. 52.

BAIL IN CIVIL CAUSES

When the Shf. arrests anyone he is obliged to take bail otherwise an action on the case lies agt. him.[10]

    Vent. 55; 3. Bl. 290.[11]

Deft. failing to appear, or give special bail when ruled thereto, the bail returned shall be subject to the same judgement & have the same liberty of defense as Deft. would have had.

No bail to be taken after judgement.

    22. G. 2.ch. 4, 171; 27. G. 2.Ch. 1, 296.[12]

In suit on a penal stat. the Deft. not held to Bail.[13]

    22. G. 2.ch. 4.172.[14]

----

with an interest. The distinction that Bacon made is between executors empowered to sell a testator's land and executors devised land to be sold by them on behalf of the estate.

6. A summary from Bacon, *ibid.*, 201.

7. A summary from two paragraphs in Bacon, *ibid.*

8. Summarized from two paragraphs in different sections of Bacon, *ibid.*, 201, 203. The citation immediately follows the text of JM's summary, but does not appear in Bacon.

9. A verbatim extract from Bacon, *ibid.*, 204.

10. A verbatim extract from Bacon, *ibid.*, 206.

11. The first citation is from Bacon, *ibid.* The second citation to Blackstone, *Commentaries*, III, 290, does not appear in Bacon.

12. A summary from 22 Geo. 2, c. 4, sec. 16 (1748), *Va. Acts in Force* (1769), 171, printed in 5 Hening 495, and 27 Geo. 2, c. 1, sec. 16 (1753), *Va. Acts in Force* (1769), 296, printed in 6 Hening 331–332.

13. A paraphrase from Bacon, *Abridgment*, I, 210.

14. A summary from 22 Geo. 2, c. 4, sec. 17 (1748), *Va. Acts in Force* (1769), 172, printed in 4 Hening 496. JM failed to note that this was the general rule, which could be altered by specific statutory provisions covering certain crimes.

Heir, Exr., or Admr. not held to special bail.[15]
> 2. Brown. 293.

Bail subject to judgement of Genl. Ct. in appeals.[16]
The Bail liable to judget. etc. agt. Deft. unless he render his body in execution.[17] If the Bail plead a render of the principal he must plead prout patet per recordum.[18]
> 22. G. 2. ch. 4. 178.[19]

BAIL IN CRIMINAL CAUSES

Two Justices Quorum unus[20] having examined the prisoner & put in writing so much as is material, as also the information of those who bring him may bail any person who is replevisable.
> 1 & 2. Ph. & Ma. Ch. 13.[21]

No justice of peace can bail 1. on an accusation of treason, 2. of Murder, in case of Manslaughter if the prisoner be clearly the slayer or if an indictmt. be found agt. him, 4th. such as being committed for felony have broken prison, 5. Outlaws, 6. such as have abjured the realm 7. Approvers & such as are by them accused, 8. Persons taken with the mainour,[22] 9. those charged with Arson 10. Excommunicated persons. Others are of a dubious nature as 11. Theives openly defamed & known, 12 persons charged with other felonies or manifest & enormous offenses not being of good fame, 13. Accessories to felony who labor under the same want of reputation. Others must be bailed on offering sufft. surety, as 14. persons of good fame charged with a bare suspicion of Manslaughter or other inferior homicide, 15. Such persons being charged with petty larceny or other felony not before specified, or 16 with being Accessory to any felony.[23]
The Ct. of Kings Bench may admit any person whatever to bail,

15. A paraphrase from Bacon, *Abridgment*, I, 210.
16. Not in Bacon.
17. This material roughly summarizes the discussion in Bacon, *Abridgment*, I, 216–218.
18. This sentence is a paraphrase from Bacon, *ibid.*, 218. "Prout patet per recordum," as it appears by the record.
19. A summary from 22 Geo. 2, c. 4, secs. 26–27 (1748), *Va. Acts in Force* (1769), 177–178, printed in 9 Hening 504–506. JM's discussion omitted portions of the Virginia statute that pertained to witnesses.
20. Bacon's phrase was "two justices at the least, and one to be of the *Quorum*."
21. A summary from Bacon's printing of the English statute. *Abridgment*, I, 222.
22. "Mainour" is stolen goods found in the hands of the thief.
23. A paraphrase from Blackstone, *Commentaries*, IV, 295–296.

yet will it pay due regard to the rules prescribed by St. west. 1. ch. 13.[24]

    stat. West. 1; 3. Ed. 1. ch. 15; 1 & 2 Ph. & Ma. ch. 13; 4. Bl. 295–6.

No person shall be bailed for felony by less than two.[25]
Justice taking insufft. sureties, the party not appearing fineable.[26]
    2. Hawk. P.C. 88.[27]

Justices before they bail a man under commitment must at their peril inform themselves of the cause of the commitment. Bailing a man not bailable punishable by sevl. stat. West. 1. ch. 15, 27. E. 1. ch. 3. 1 & 2. P.M. 13.[28]

    2 Haw. P.C. 90.

To delay or deny or obstruct bail where it ought to be granted punishable by indictment as well as action.[29]
    Do.

Where a person in Ct. is bailed for a crime punishable with loss of life or member, a recogn. may be taken from each bail in a certn. sum of money, body for body or both ways but bail is only liable to be fined.[30]

    [2] Haw. 97.

For crimes of an inferior nature the recog. only in certn. sum.[31]
    2. Do. 115.

Recog. not forfeited if the Principal stands mute.[32]
    Do.

BAILMENT[33]

Bailmt. is a delivery of goods on a contract express or implied that the trust shall be faithfully executed on the part of the Bailee.
    2. Bl. 452.[34]

24. A summary of the material in two paragraphs from Bacon, *Abridgment*, I, 223.
25. A verbatim extract from Bacon, *ibid.*, 226.
26. That is, the justice may be fined; the summary is from Bacon, *ibid.*, 227.
27. The citation applies to the material at n. 25 above.
28. A summary from Bacon, *Abridgment*, I, 227, 228.
29. A paraphrase from Bacon, *ibid.*, 228.
30. A paraphrase from Bacon, *ibid.*, 230.
31. A summary from Bacon, *ibid.*
32. Bacon stated that the recognizance shall not be forfeited by the defendant's failure to plead, in spite of the fact that the standard form required that the bail returned the defendant to answer the indictment. *Ibid.*, 231.
33. JM ignored Bacon's section on "Bailiff."
34. A paraphrase from Blackstone, *Commentaries*, II, 452.

If A leave a chest locked with B without acquainting B with the particulars & take away the key the goods are still in possession of A.[35]

Co. L. 89; 4 Co. 83.

The naked possession of chattels personal cannot be aliened.
If the goods of A are bailed by B to C—C must redeliver them to B, but if C dies his Exr. is chargeable only to A.[36]

Broke. att. on Assise 20.

Where goods are pledged for money lent the pawnee may use them without injuring them & if they are stolen he shall not answer for them unless the money for which they were pledged had been tendered.[37]

Doc. & Stu. 130; 2 Sal. 522. pl. 1; Co. L. 89; Cr. Ja. 243; Do.

If the money be tendered or the goods decay the duty remains.[38]
The Pawnbroker hath a special property though the goods be not delivered to him at the time of the money lent, provided they be delivered for the livery[39] is not countermandable.[40]

2. Leon. 30; Yel. 164.

If goods be pawned without mentioning time of redemption the pledger has time during life though the pledgee dies.[41]

2 Co. 79.

If a carrier, ferryman or hostler be robbed he shall answer the value of the goods.[42]

4. Co. 84; Cr. Ja. 162.

If A takes a gelding to pasture & he be stolen no action lies agt. A without a special assumpsit to restore him.[43]

Moor. 543.

35. A summary from Bacon, *Abridgment*, I, 236.
36. A summary from Bacon, *ibid.*, 237.
37. A summary from Bacon, *ibid.*
38. A summary from Bacon, *ibid.*, 238.
39. The unusual use of the word "livery" seems to be JM's misreading of Bacon's text, which referred to "delivery" of the goods. While the word "livery" could be used to describe such a transfer of personalty, it was generally restricted to formal transfers of title to real property.
40. A summary from Bacon, *Abridgment*, I, 238, 239.
41. A paraphrase from Bacon, *ibid.* JM's paraphrase obscured Bacon's point that the death of the pawnbroker does not terminate the right to redeem but that the death of the pledgor who deposited the property does terminate that right.
42. A verbatim extract from Bacon, *ibid.*, 242.
43. A paraphrase from Bacon, *ibid.*, 243.

My Lord Holt has laid down the following rules with regard to Bailment.

There are six sorts of bailment which lay a care & obligation on the party to whom tis made.

1. A bare bailt. to another to keep for the use of the bailor, bailee not answerable witht. gross neglect.

2. A delivery of goods to another which are in themselves useful to keep; bailee if guilty of the least neglect or abuse of the loan answerable.

3. A delivery of goods for hire, hirer to take all imaginable care & to restore them at the time.

4. A delivery by way of pledge if the goods are not the worse for using pawnee may use them at his peril as also if the keeping them be a charge, if notwithstanding all his diligence the goods be lost he shall have his debt.

5. Goods to be carried for a reward; if you deliver them to a public or common carrier he must be chargeable at all events, but if to one who has a particular private employment he is not chargeable at all events: though he receive a hire.

6. Where goods are delivered to do some act about them as carrying witht. a rewd.[44] The person to whom they are delivered only chargeable if they are lost by his own particular neglect.[45]

Sal. 26 pl. 12; 2. Ld. Ray. 209.

BARGAIN & SALE[46]

Bargain & sale is a kind of a real contract whereby the bargainor bargains & sells, that is contracts to convey, for some pecuniary consideration, the land to the bargainee, & thereby becomes seised to his use.[47]

2. Bl. 338.

No person can bargain & sell who cannot be seised to an use.[48] Though words of bargain & sale be used if no consideration of money be inserted it can only operate as a covt. to stand siesed.[49]

Bro. Feof. to uses. 33; 7. Co. 40; Cr. El. 394.

44. "Without a reward."
45. The rules of bailment are paraphrased from Bacon's statement of the principles enunciated by Chief Justice Sir John Holt (1642–1710), *ibid.*, 243–245.
46. JM ignored Bacon's section on "Bankrupt."
47. A paraphrase from Blackstone, *Commentaries*, II, 338.
48. Paraphrased from Bacon, *Abridgment*, I, 274. Bacon's principal point was that the king could not bargain and sell, for he could not be compelled to execute a use by the chancery court, which was the instrument of his conscience.
49. A summary from Bacon, *ibid.*, 275, 276.

Any freehold or inheritance & possession remainder on reversion on an estate for life or years may be bargaind and & sold.[50]

    2. Co. 54.

A man seised of a freehold may bargain & sell it for years but a man possessed of a term cannot bargain & sell it so as to be executed by the statute.[51]

    8. Co. 93; 2. Co. 35.

BARON & FEME [52]

The age of consent in an inft. male is fourteen & in a female twelve. Both must be bound or neither.[53]

    Co. L. 33; 6. Co. 22.

A wife seperated by articles, in consideration of money recd. by the Husbd. & covenants by him, cannot be seised & forced to live with him.[54]

    Bur. rep. 542.

If a man marries a woman seised in fee he gains a freehold.[55] Baron & feme may by deed (the wife being privately examd.) transfer a freehold of which he is seised in her right.[56]

    Co. L. 351.[57]

Marriage is a gift in law to the husbd. of the wifes chattels real, but if he does not dispose of them in his life they survive to her & he cannot devise them away.[58] If the husbd. survives the wife they are absolutely his.[59]

    Br. 24; Co. L. 46; 2. Bl. 434; Co. L. 300.

If a husbd. possessed of a term for seventy years makes a lease for twenty years to begin after his death this is good because a present interest passes. Secus if a rent be granted to issue out of the lands because the term comes entire to the wife by a title paramount the grant.[60]

    Pop. 5. 97; Co. L. 46, 351; Cr. Ch. 344.

---

    50. A summary from Bacon, *ibid.*, 275. JM omitted mention of an estate in fee tail.

    51. That is, the statute of uses. This passage is a verbatim extract from two sentences in Bacon, *ibid.*

    52. JM ignored Bacon's section on "Barratry."

    53. A paraphrase from Bacon, *ibid.*, 283.

    54. Nearly verbatim from Bacon, *ibid.*, 285.

    55. A verbatim extract from Bacon, *ibid.*, 286.

    56. This may be a summary from Bacon's discussion, *ibid.*, 301–303.

    57. The citation applies to material at n. 55 above.

    58. A paraphrase from Bacon, *Abridgment*, I, 286.

    59. A summary from Blackstone, *Commentaries*, II, 434, 435.

    60. A summary from Bacon, *Abridgment*, I, 286–287.

Choses in action do not survive to the husbd. on the death of the wife nor has he any right to them but as Admir. [61]

2 Bl. 433–4; 3. Mod. 186.

Husbd. & wife divorced from bed & board, the wife having alimony brings suit [62] & is allowed costs, husbd. cannot release them. [63]

Salk. 115 pl. 4.

A legacy was given to a feme covert who lived seperate from her husbd., the Exr. paid it to the feme & took her receipt for it, decreed to pay it over again to the husbd. with interest. [64]

Ver. 261.

Lease at will not determined by marriage. [65]

1 Co. 10.

A will or submission to an award made by feme sole are revoked by her subsequent marriage. [66]

4 Co. 60.

Contracts or debts in presenti [67] from husbd. to wife, also such as are contingent & may happen during coverture are extinguished by marriage. [68]

Salk. 325; Ld. Ray. 315. [69]

A man enters into a bond to his intended wife conditioned to leave her £1000 & mortgages his estate [70] not leaving personal assets to discharge the bond. Decreed in equity though void in law. [71]

2. Ver. 480; ch. Ca. 21; 2 Vent. 343.

Equity will set aside the intended wife's contracts enterd into before marriage when they appear to have been made with an intent to deceive & cheat the husbd. & are in derogation of the rights of marriage. [72]

2. Ch. re. 81, 79; 2. Ver. 17.

61. A rough summary from Bacon, *ibid.*, 289, and Blackstone, *Commentaries*, II, 434–435.
62. JM deleted Bacon's limitation that the suit, presumably against a third party, be for defamation or other injury. *Abridgment*, I, 290.
63. A summary from Bacon, *ibid.*
64. A paraphrase from Bacon, *ibid.*
65. A summary from Bacon, *ibid.*, 291.
66. A summary from Bacon, *ibid.*
67. "At the present time," as distinguished from those to take effect in the future.
68. A summary from Bacon, *Abridgment*, I, 291.
69. The citation should be "Ld. Raym. 515." *Ibid.*
70. JM here omitted the words "and died." *Ibid.*, 292.
71. A close paraphrase from Bacon's discussion, *ibid.* By the last sentence JM intended to convey Bacon's meaning that the bond would be decreed enforceable in equity, even though it was void at law.
72. A paraphrase from Bacon, *ibid.*

Widow before her marriage with a second husbd. may, without his knowledge, make provision for her children by the first.[73]
Ver. 408.

The husbd. is liable for the wifes debts contracted before marriage whether he had any portion with her or not.[74]
Moor. 468.

Husbd. not liable for her debts before coverture unless recovered in her life time.[75]
3 Mod. 186.

Feme covert not punishable for theft if committed in compy. with or by coercion of her husbd. Secus if the theft be only by the command of her husband.[76]
Haw. P.C. 65.

If the wife incur the forfeiture of a penal statute the husbd. may be made a party to an action or information for the same.[77]
Haw. P.C. 3.

Sevl. goods were devised to A's wife for life & after her death to B. Though A & his wife were parted & there had been great suits for alimony, & she, during the seperation had wasted the goods yet husbd. charged for this conversion of the wife's.[78]
Ver. 143.

A husbd. may by law be compelled to find his wife with necessaries suitable to his degree circumstances or estate of which & of the wifes necessity the jury are to determine. The wife has no absolute power, by any contract of hers though for necessaries, to bind the husbd. without his assent precedent or subsequent of which likewise the jury are to judge. If she cohabits with her husbd. & bought necessaries for herself children or family the husbd. is liable for them: so if he runs from her, or turns her away, or forces her by cruelty to go away from him. But if he allows her a seperate maintenance or prohibits particular persons from trusting her he shall not be liable during the time he pays that maintenance or for goods taken from the particular persons prohibited.[79] If the wife pawns

73. A summary from Bacon, *ibid.*
74. A verbatim extract from Bacon, *ibid.*
75. A summary of the discussion and marginal notes in Bacon, *ibid.*, 293.
76. A summary from Bacon, *ibid.*, 294.
77. A verbatim extract from Bacon, *ibid.*
78. A paraphrase from Bacon, *ibid.*, 295.
79. A series of verbatim extracts from Bacon summarizing an extended discussion, *ibid.*

her cloaths & borrows money to redeem husbd. not liable.[80]

> Mod. 128; 2 Vent. 155; Salk. 116, 118, pl. 10; 2d. Ld. Ray. 1006; Str. 647; 2 Show. 283.

If Baron or stranger disseise another to the use of a feme covert her agreement signifies nothing. But if a Feme covert actually enters & commits a disseisin, binding.[81]

> Br. Disseisin 67.

Husbd. & wife make a lease by indenture of the wifes lands reserving rent, he dies, she marries again, the second husbd. receives the rent & dies she cannot avoid the lease.[82]

> Dyer 159.

A feme covert is capable of purchasing, but the husbd. may disagree & it shall avoid the purchase, though the husbd. should agree to the purchase yet after his death she may waive it & if she does no act which proves her assent to it her heirs may waive it after her.[83]

> Co. L. 3.

In those cases where the debt or cause of action will survive to the wife husbd. & wife are regularly to join in the action.[84]

> Moor. 432; Str. 229.

The fruit of the labor of the wife belongs to the husbd. for which he only shall bring the action unless there is an express promise to the wife.[85]

> Salk. 114.

For a personal tort done to the wife they must join & if the wife dies the action dies with her.[86]

> Vent. 328.

All actions for which the wife stood attached at the time of the coverture, also for all her torts or trepasses during coverture, the action must be brought agt. both baron & feme.[87]

> Co. L. 133.

80. A summary from Bacon's marginal note, *ibid.*, 300.
81. A summary from Bacon, *ibid.*, 302.
82. A summary from Bacon, *ibid.*, 303.
83. A series of verbatim extracts and a close paraphrase summarizing the material in a paragraph from Bacon, *ibid.*
84. A verbatim extract from Bacon, *ibid.*, 304.
85. A paraphrase from Bacon's marginal note, *ibid.*, 305.
86. Bacon's statement was "For a Battery or other Personal Tort. . . ." *Ibid.*, 306. Otherwise JM's copy is verbatim.
87. A summary from Bacon, *ibid.*, 307.

If goods come to feme covert by trover the action may be brought agt. both but the conversion must be laid solely in the husbd.[88]

Co. L. 351; Yel. 166.

A husbd. who has abjured the realm or who is banished is civiliter mortuus,[89] his wife must be considered as a feme sole.[90]

Bro. B & F 66; Co. L. 133.

A woman whose husbd. had left her about twelve years had carried on a trade & given receipts in her own name, being sued for debt contracted in the course of her trade gave coverture in evidence & her husband was proved to have been lately alive in ireland. Jury found for Deft.[91]

BASTARDY

All persons born in lawful wedlock are deemed legitimate unless there is an apparent impossibility that they should be generated by the husband.[92]

Sal. 122 pl. 5.

If a person be castrate, be under the age of fourteen or out of the realm the issue are bastards.[93]

Br. bas. 36, Co. L. 344.[94]

The usual time for the legitimation of children born after the death of the husbd. is nine solar months & ten days.[95]

Godol. 281.

A lewd woman immediately after her husbds. death married her adulterer & within six months had a child—adjudged to be her first husbands.[96]

Co. L. 8.

Widow marries immediately child born within nine months & eleven days adjudged the secd. husbds.[97]

Co. L. 8.

88. A close paraphrase from Bacon, *ibid.*
89. "Civilly dead."
90. A paraphrase from Bacon, *Abridgment*, I, 308.
91. JM omitted the fact that the jury was directed to bring in a verdict for the defendant. The paragraph is a close paraphrase from Bacon, *Abridgment*, I, 308.
92. A paraphrase from Bacon, *ibid.*, 310.
93. A summary from Bacon, *ibid.*
94. The citation in Bacon reads, "Co. Lit. 244."
95. A summary from Bacon, *Abridgment*, I, 312, but JM omitted Bacon's explanation that the time in this circumstance might be as long as 11 months.
96. A paraphrase from Bacon, *ibid.* The word "immediately" is JM's insertion.
97. A summary from Bacon, *ibid.* JM omitted Bacon's explanation that the period

If there be bastard eigne[98] & a mulier & on the death of the father the bastard enters & enjoys the land during life the mulier cannot enter on his issue.[99]
 Co. L. 245.

No man can bastardize another after his death.
To exclude the mulier from his inheritance the possession of the bastard must be uninterupted & a descent cast to his issue.[1]
 7 Co. 44; Sal. 120.

BILLS OF SALE [2]

Blood & natural affection a void consideration agt. creditors.[3]
 3. Co. 81.

If goods continue in the possession of the vendor after a bill of sale of them, though there is a clause in the bill that the vendor shall account annually with the vendee for them, yet it is fraud.[4]
 Mo. 638.

A genl. conveyance of them all without any exception, also a secret manner of transacting the said bill also unusual clauses contained in it, as that it be made honestly, truly, & bona fide are marks of fraud & collusion.[5]
 3. Co. 81.

Possession of a lease for years after an absolute conveyance or gift fraudulent, secus if the conveyance or sale be conditional as that on payt. of so much money it shall go to the vendee.[6]
 2 Bulstr. 226.

Fraud need not be pleaded but may be given in evidence.[7]
 5 Co. 60.

---

of gestation was one day more than that accepted by law and that the legally accepted time is the only way to distinguish paternity in this case.
 98. Bacon defined a "bastard eigne" as a son born to a couple before their marriage. A "mulier" is a legitimate child. See *ibid.*, 315.
 99. A summary from Bacon, *ibid.*
 1. Two verbatim extracts from Bacon, *ibid.*, 315, 316.
 2. JM ignored Bacon's section on bigamy.
 3. Bacon's passage from which this is summarized referred to a bulk sale of goods. *Abridgment*, I, 323.
 4. A verbatim extract from Bacon, *ibid.*
 5. A summary from Bacon, *ibid.*
 6. A summary from Bacon, *ibid.*
 7. This summarizes Bacon's statement that fraud could be given in evidence to defeat a fraudulent conveyance, even if the party offering to prove fraud did not plead it. *Ibid.*, 324.

BILL OF EXCEPTIONS

At common law a writ of error lay not for an error in law not appearing in the record & therefore 13th. of Ed. 1. ch. 30. gives a bill of exceptions in such case.[8]

2 inst. 426.

The Stat. extends to all pleas dilatory or peremptory to prayers to be received, oyer of records & deeds etc. also to any material evidence offered & overruled.[9]

2. Inst. 427; Dyer 231, pl. 3; Ray. 46.

The party must pray the justices to put their seals to his bill before judgement & after judgement they may (if they have before refused) be commanded to it.[10]

2. Inst. 427.

The Ct. will not suffer the party to move any thing in arrest of judgement on the point on which the bill of exceptions has been before allowed.[11]

Vent. 366.

BURGLARY[12]

Burglary is a breaking & entering the mansion house of another or a church or the walls or gates of a walled town with an intent to commit some felony.[13]

Hale P.C. 80.

One who comes down a chimney, opens a window, or breaks the glass thereof, unlocks the door or draws the latch of a door, or if persons coming to a house with an intent to rob it, are let in under pretence of business & then rob the house, or take lodgings in the house & then fall on the Landlord & rob him, or having brought a Constable with hue & cry bind the constable & rob—these cases have been adjudged burglary.[14]

Any the least entry either with the whole or with a part of the body or with a pistol or weapon is sufficient.[15]

8. A paraphrase of Bacon's discussion and marginal note, *ibid.*, 325.

9. A paraphrase of Bacon's paragraph, *ibid.*, but JM omitted challenges to jurors as being included within the provisions of the English statute.

10. A paraphrase from Bacon, *ibid.*, 326.

11. A paraphrase from Bacon, *ibid.*, 327.

12. JM ignored Bacon's discussion of borough English and bridges.

13. Two verbatim extracts from Bacon, *Abridgment*, I, 332. JM omitted Bacon's qualification that burglary must be committed at night.

14. A paraphrase from two paragraphs in Bacon, *ibid.*, 333.

15. A summary from Bacon, *ibid.*, 334.

There may also be an entry in law as where sevl. come to commit a felony[16] & some stand in parts adjacent while[17] others enter & rob.[18]

It must be in the night, not day light to distinguish the face.[19]

A house which a man dwells in but for part of the year or which he has hird & brought part of his goods in but has not yet lodged in, or which his wife has hird though withot. his privity & lives in will satisfy the wds. mansion house.[20] Also outbuildings which are part of the mansion house, or a lodging in one of the Inns of Ct. or in a house actually divided for the rent with a door to the street in which case the indictmt. shd. term it the mansion house of the proprietor.[21] There must be an intention to commit a felony.[22]

Hale P.C. 81; Hawk. P.C. 102; 4. Bl. 227.[23]

CARRIERS[24]

All persons carrying goods for hire come under the denomination of common carriers.[25]

Co. L. 89.

The master of a stage coach who only carries passengers for hire not liable for goods of those passengers.[26]

Sal. 282 pl. 11; Comyns 25 pl. 16.

If a carrier be robd he shall answer the value of the goods.[27]

4 Co. 84.

If A delivers a box to a carrier to carry & he asks what is in it & A tells him a book & tobacco, though there is a hundred pounds besides if the carrier is robd he shall answer for the money.[28]

Vent. 238.

But if A being a common carrier receives by his book keeper from the servt. of B two bags of money seald up containing as was told

---

16. Bacon said "burglary." *Ibid.*

17. JM copied "while" twice, first at the end of a line in his notebook and again at the beginning of the next line. We have deleted the second word as a slip of the pen.

18. A paraphrase from Bacon, *Abridgment*, I, 334.

19. A summary from Bacon, *ibid.*

20. Nearly verbatim from Bacon, *ibid.*, 335.

21. A summary of three paragraphs from Bacon, *ibid.*

22. A summary from Bacon, *ibid.*, 336.

23. The Blackstone citation, not in Bacon, referred to the paragraph on felonious intent. *Commentaries*, IV, 227.

24. JM ignored Bacon's discussion of the bylaws of corporations.

25. Two verbatim extracts from Bacon, *Abridgment*, I, 343.

26. A paraphrase from Bacon, *ibid.*

27. A verbatim extract from Bacon, *ibid.*, 345.

28. A paraphrase from Bacon, *ibid.* JM did not mention Bacon's limitations on this rule, that a carrier may limit his liability by means of a special acceptance.

him £200 & the book keeper gives a receipt to this effect Recd. of etc. two bags of money seald up said to contain £200 which I promise to deliver such a day at Exeter to——he to pay 10/pr. Ct.[29] for carriage & risk. Though the bags contained £450 & the Carrier is robd he shall be answerable only for the £200 for this is a particular undertaking;[30] & the fraud of the Plaintiff.[31]

Carth. 485.

A carrier may maintain trover & conversion agt. a stranger by reason of his special property.[32]

Co. L. 89; 4 Co. 83.

If a Carrier opens a pack & takes out part of the goods, or if he having brought the goods to the place appointed takes them away again secretly animofurandi[33] he is guilty of felony.[34]

Hawk. P.C. 90; Hale P.C. 60.

CERTIORARI

Certiorari is an original writ issuing out of Chancery or the Kings bench[35] to the judges[36] of an inferior ct. comd. them to return recds. of a cause depending before them.[37]

F.N.B. 543.

Certiorari is not to be allowed after issue or demurrer joind. Cause once removed by certiorari & sent back by procedendo etc. never after to be removd.[38]

22. G. 2. Ch. 4.

Certiorari not to be granted where the matter in dispute was not originally cognizable in Genl. Court.[39]

27. G. 2. Ch. 1.

29. That is, 10 shillings per £100.
30. The passage to this point is a close paraphrase from Bacon, *Abridgment*, I, 345.
31. This summarizes Bacon's statement that the plaintiff's fraud against the carrier should deprive him of the reward covering the amount so misrepresented. *Ibid.*, 346.
32. A summary from Bacon, *ibid*.
33. That is, with intent to steal.
34. Two verbatim extracts from two paragraphs in Bacon, *Abridgment*, I, 346.
35. After this point JM deleted the words "in the King's Name," as found in Bacon, *ibid.*, 349.
36. JM omitted Bacon's reference to officers of the court to whom certiorari might be directed in England.
37. A paraphrase from Bacon, *Abridgment*, I, 349.
38. A summary from 22 Geo. 2, c. 4, sec. 28 (1748), *Va. Acts in Force* (1769), 178, printed in 5 Hening 506.
39. A summary from 27 Geo. 2, c. 1, sec. 29, cl. 3 (1752), *Va. Acts in Force* (1769), 302, printed in 6 Hening 342.

COMMITTMENTS [40]

All persons who are apprehended for offences not bailable as also those who neglect to offer bail for offences which are bailable must be committed.

Also wherever a justice has power to bind a person over or to compel him to do such a thing he may commit quousque [41] etc. if in his presence he shall refuse to be bound or to do such a thing. [42]

2. Haw. P.C. 116.

Previous to commt. the justice must take the examination of the Prisoner & the information of those that bring him & certify the same in writing. [43]

2 & 3. P. & M. Ch. 10.

Every commitmt. must be in writing, under the hand & seal of him that made it, shewing his authority & directed to the keeper of the prison. It ought to set forth the crime with convenient certainty.

Every Mittimus ought to have a lawful conclusion.

And if grounded on an act of Parliament ought to be conformable to the method prescribed by that Statute. [44]

2. Haw. P.C. 119, 120.

CONDITION [45]

The word condition or sub conditione does most properly create a condition. Other words create a condition as proviso; but it must depend on another sentence, also it must be the words of the grantor & compulsory to enforce the grantee to do some act. [46]

C.L. 203.

As the intent of the testator chiefly governs in wills these words faciendum, faciendo ea intentione, ad effectum [47] etc. create a condition. [48]

Co. L. 204.

---

40. JM ignored Bacon's sections on champerty, charitable uses and mortmain, and churchwardens.

41. That is, until he post bond, or do what is commanded.

42. A close paraphrase from Bacon, *Abridgment*, I, 377.

43. A summary of the English statute printed in Bacon, *ibid.*, 380.

44. A series of verbatim extracts and paraphrases from Bacon, *ibid.*, 380–381.

45. JM ignored Bacon's section on "common," or common lands.

46. A summary from Bacon, *Abridgment*, I, 396.

47. "Ad faciendum," to do; "faciendo ea intentione," to do or pay with that intent; "ad effectum," to the effect or end.

48. Two verbatim extracts from Bacon, *Abridgment*, I, 398.

Conditions cannot be annexed to estates of inheritance, or freehold estates without deed.[49] Secus of Rents, annuities, warranties etc. Executory interests. Also of chattels.[50]

A person cannot resign or a condition be released on condition. A man cannot release a personal thing on a condition subsequent. Secus on a condn. precedent.[51]

Owen 12; 9. Co. 85.

Conditions can only be reserved to parties & privies—their Heirs.[52] Feme covert & infant bound by express conditions.[53]

Moor 92; 8. Co. 44.

Conditions which defeat an estate are to be taken strictly[54] therefore if a man leases lands for years on condition that the lessee nor his assigns shall not alien but to one of his brothers & the lessee aliens to[55] one of his Brothers the assignee is not within the condition but he may alien to whom he pleases.

5. Co 68; Cr. Ja. 398; Vaugh. 31; Co. L. 163.

If a man makes a lease for years by indenture provided always & it is covenanted & agreed between the parties that the lessee shall not alien this is both a condition & a covenant.[56]

Co. L. 203.

When the estate is so expressly confined & limited by the words of its creation that it cannot endure for any longer time than till the contingency happens upon which the estate is to fail this is denominated a limitation.[57] These words are proper for its creation while, so long as, until, etc.[58] In such cases the estate determines so soon as the contingency happens & the next subsequent estate which depends on such determination becomes immediately vested without any act to be done by him who is next in expectancy.[59] But

49. Verbatim from Bacon, *ibid.*, 399.
50. A summary from Bacon, *ibid.*
51. A summary from Bacon, *ibid.*, 400.
52. A summary from Bacon, *ibid.*
53. That is, the feme covert is bound because the condition charges the land; the infant is bound because there is an express condition. *Ibid.*, 401.
54. A paraphrase from Bacon's marginal note, *ibid.*, 402.
55. Bacon here inserted "any but one of his brothers, and after the Lessee aliens to"; JM's deletion was probably an error in transcription. *Ibid.*, 401, 402. Otherwise a close paraphrase from Bacon.
56. A paraphrase from Bacon, *ibid.*, 402.
57. A verbatim extract from Blackstone, *Commentaries*, II, 155.
58. Summarized from Blackstone, *ibid.*
59. Two verbatim extracts from Blackstone, *ibid.*

though strict words of condition be used in its creation yet if on breach of the condition the estate be limited over to a third person the law construes it into a limitation.[60]

2. Bl. 154; 1 Vent. 202; 10. Co. 42.[61]

In equity with respect to conditions precedent & subsequent the prevailing distinction seems to be to releive agt. the breach or non performance of a condition where a composition can be made.[62]

Ver. 79, 167; 2 Vent. 352.[63]

As where one devised Lands to J.S. his kinsman paying £1000 a piece to his two daughters who were his heirs at law and J.S. made default & the daughters recovd. in ejectmt. Yet J.S. was releived on paymt. of principal, interest & costs.[64]

2. Ver. 366.

If a condition be impossible at the time of its creation or afterwards become impossible by the act of God, or the act of the feoffer himself, or if it be contrary to law, or repugnant to the nature of the estate tis void.[65]

2. Bl. 156; 2. Vent. 109; 10 Co. 38.[66]

If the condition of a bond be impossible at the time of making it the condition is void & the obligation stands single. But if the condition is possible at the time of making it & becomes impossible by the act of God of the law or of the Obligee etc. the obligation is saved.[67]

Co. L. 206.

The condition of a bond was to settle certain lands in such a manor by such a day; the obligor died before the day, the bond saved at law, but a specific execution decreed in chancery.[68]

Eq. Abr. 18.

60. A paraphrase from Blackstone, *ibid.*

61. The citation to Ventris's reports is from Blackstone. The citation to Coke's reports is also from Blackstone, and refers to the list of words that create a condition. *Ibid.*, I, 155, n. "p.," 156, n. "q."

62. Two verbatim extracts from Bacon, *Abridgment*, I, 406.

63. The citation to Ventris is not clear due to JM's handwriting at this point, but it would appear that the citation is as shown, which appears in Bacon, *ibid.*, 407.

64. A verbatim extract from Bacon, *ibid.*

65. A paraphrase from Blackstone, *Commentaries*, II, 156.

66. The citations to Ventris's and Coke's reports are from Bacon, *Abridgment*, I, 410, and pertain to Bacon's discussion of cases on this point.

67. The first sentence is a verbatim extract from Bacon, the second a paraphrase. *Ibid.*, 412, 413.

68. A paraphrase from Bacon's marginal note, *ibid.*, 413.

If there be lessee for years on condn. not to alien witht. the assent of the Lessor, makes his Exr. & devises it to him & the Exr. enters generally the testator not being indebted to any body, this is a forfeiture of the condition.[69]

Cr. El. 815.

If there be a nomine penae[70] given to the lessor for the non payment of the rent he must demand the rent before he can be entitled to the penalty. Or if the clause had been that if the rent were behind that the estate of the lessee should cease & be void. In these cases a demand must be made at the day prefixed for the payment & alledged expressly to have been made in the pleadings.[71]

7. Co. 56; Vaug. 32.

But where the power of reentry is given to the lessor for default of payment without any farther demd. the lessee has undertaken to pay it whether demanded or not.[72]

Dyer. 686.

If words of limitation be used the Lessee must at his peril pay the rent.[73]

If a man leases land on condn. that he shall not alien the land or any part thereof & after aliens part with the assent of the lessor, the whole condition is dispensed with.[74]

Vaugh. 31.[75]

It is laid down as a rule that he who enters for a conditn. broken shall be in of the same estate he was before & therefore shall avoid all mesne incumbrances.[76]

Co. L. 202.

But a man entitled to be tenant by the Curtesy makes a feoffment in fee on condition, enters for condition broken & then his wife dies he shall not be tenant by the Curtesy.[77]

Co. L. 30.

If a man makes a feoffmt. in fee with condition to be void if the feoffer pays a certain sum of money to the feoffee & he dies before

69. A paraphrase from Bacon, *ibid.*, 415.
70. That is, in name of a penalty, or a coercive condition.
71. A series of verbatim extracts from Bacon, *Abridgment*, I, 417.
72. A paraphrase from Bacon, *ibid.*
73. A summary from Bacon, *ibid.*, 417–418.
74. A summary from Bacon, *ibid.*, 418.
75. The citation is to the material at n. 73 above.
76. Two verbatim extracts from Bacon, *Abridgment*, I, 420.
77. A paraphrase from Bacon, *ibid.*, 421.

paymt. the heir cannot pay it. But when a day of paymt. is limited & the feoffer dies before the day his heir may tender the money.[78]

　　Lit. sec. 337; Co. L. 308.

If A enfeoffs B on condition that B shall pay money on a day & before the day B enfeoffs C either of them may tender the money.[79]

　　Co. L. 207; 5 Co. 96.

If a man bargains & sells lands with a proviso that if the vendor before such a day pay so much money to the vendee his heirs or assigns then the sale to be void a tender to the Exr. is not good. Secus if a feoffee be to pay money to the feoffer.[80] Designatio unius est exclusio alterius.[81]

　　Co. L. 210; 5 Co. 97.

If the condition of an obligation be to pay a less sum & no day of paymt. be limited, the obligor ought to pay it presently that is in convenient time.[82]

　　Cr. El. 798.

The intent of the condition must be honestly performed.[83]

If the condition be in the copulative & it is not possible to be performed it shall be taken in the disjunctive.[84]

　　Cr. El. 363.

If the condition of an obligation be that the obligor shall pay £10 to the obligee which is for the rent of certn. lands & the obligee enters on the land & so suspends the rent yet this shall not excuse the paymt. for it is but a recital that it is for rent & therefore not material.[85]

　　Hob. 103.

If the condition of an obligation be to pay a small sum at a certain day & the obligee refuses it at the day, though this saves the penalty yet the principal must be paid. Secus if the condition be for the performance of an act collateral to the obligation.[86]

　　Co. L. 207; Cr. El. 755.

78. Two verbatim extracts from Bacon, *ibid.*, 422.
79. A paraphrase from Bacon, *ibid.*, 423.
80. A paraphrase from Bacon, *ibid.*, 424.
81. That is, the specification of one is the exclusion of others. This is the maxim adopted by JM, which does not appear in Bacon, to explain the rule that in the case of a feoffment in fee where the rent is to be paid to the feoffor or his heirs or assigns, the rental, even after assignment, must be paid to the feoffor or his executor. *Ibid.*
82. A paraphrase from Bacon, *ibid.*, 426.
83. This phrase does not appear in Bacon or in Blackstone.
84. Verbatim from Bacon, *Abridgment*, I, 431.
85. A paraphrase from Bacon, *ibid.*, 436.
86. A summary from two paragraphs in Bacon, *ibid.*, 436, 437.

Regularly if the condition be to be performed by a stranger & he refuses the obligation is forfeited.[87]

If the condition be to make a gift in tail to a stranger who refuses obligation saved because it was intended that the obligee should have the reversion.[88]

Cr. El. 755; Cr. Ja. 14.

To Nathanael Greene

[*December 22, 1780*. Listed in Calendar of Papers of Gen. Nathanael Greene,[1] Box 4, "National Institute," District of Columbia College, Library of Congress. Not found.]

To Nathanael Greene

[*April 23, 1781*. Listed in Calendar of Papers of Gen. Nathanael Greene, Box 4, "National Institute," District of Columbia College, Library of Congress. Not found.]

Oaths of Office

DS, Virginia State Library[2]

Richmond, May 25, 1782

I [*John Marshall*] do declare myself a citizen of the Commonwealth of Virginia; I relinquish and renounce the Character of Subject or

87. A verbatim extract from Bacon, *ibid.*, 437.

88. A summary from Bacon, *ibid.*

1. Greene (1742–1786) was commanding general of the Southern Department at the time this letter was written.

2. In a box marked "House of Delegates Attendance Book, 1781–1782," there is a manuscript volume labeled "Resolutions of House of Delegates, 22 May 1776 and 28 May 1781–24 July 1784." This book was apparently used to enter the official roll of the House of Delegates for several sessions during the 1780s. The clerk copied the oaths of office into the book and then passed it to each member to sign. See also similar documents under May 4, 1784, and Oct. 15, 1787.

JM had been elected to the House of Delegates from Fauquier County on Apr. 22, 1782, and took the official oath of office in the presence of Sampson Mathews (1737–1807), a member of the Council of State, on May 25, prior to attending his first session. Election Certificate, Apr. 22, 1782, and Qualification Certificate, May 25, 1782, Election Records, Virginia State Library. The law requiring the administration of oaths of office by a member of the Council of State is in 10 Hening 22–23.

citizen of any Prince or other State whatsoever, and abjure all allegiance which may be claimed by such Prince or other State. And I do swear to be faithful and true to the said Commonwealth of Virginia, so long as I continue a citizen thereof. So help me God.

I [*John Marshall*] do solemnly promise and swear, that I will faithfully, impartially, and justly perform the duty of my office of [*delegate*] according to the best of my skill and judgement. So help me God.

JOHN MARSHALL

Pay Voucher

AD, Virginia State Library[3]

Richmond, *ca*. July 1, 1782

The Commonwealth of Virginia to John Marshall Dr.
May Session 1782

To 38 days attendance as a Delegate at 10/ per day	£ 19	
To travelling to & from the Assembly 260 miles[4] at two pounds of Tobaccos per mile 520 lb at 20/ per Ct.	5	4
	£ 24	4

Advertisement

Printed, *Virginia Gazette, or, the American Advertiser* (Richmond), November 2, 1782, 2

[Richmond], November 1, 1782

THE SURVEYOR FOR THE COUNTY OF Fayette[5] has desired me to

3. In Auditor's Item 292, Pay Vouchers, Officers of Government, 1781–1782. On the bottom of the voucher is written in another hand, "1782, July 1: Entered, J. Beckley C. h. d." and on the reverse, "John Marshall, £24-4, July 3, 1782, wages to mem-[bers]."
    In addition to writing this voucher, JM also entered a copy in the attendance book of the House of Delegates. See House of Delegates Attendance Book, 1781–1782, Virginia State Library.
    4. To and from Fauquier County.
    5. Thomas Marshall, JM's father.

give public notice to all those who have lands to locate or survey in that County, that his office[6] is now opened.

JOHN MARSHALL.

Pay Voucher

DS, Virginia State Library[7]

[*November 25, 1782, Richmond*. JM draws £2 14s. travel reimbursement for 135 miles from Fauquier County to Richmond and £18 for 36 days' attendance at the General Assembly.]

Legislative Bill

AD, House of Delegates Papers, Virginia State Library[8]

Richmond, November 30, 1782

WHEREAS by the Laws of this Commonwealth no Entry for vacant & unappropriated Lands can be made with any person except the Principal Surveyor of the County in which such vacant and unappropriated Land lies,[9] And in many of the Counties on

6. Thomas Marshall's office was located on the south fork of Elkhorn Creek, about one mile west of Lexington, Ky. See map by John Jillson, 1784, The Filson Club.

7. In Auditor's Item 292, Pay Vouchers, Officers of Government, 1781–1782. The clerk also copied the voucher into the attendance book of the House of Delegates. See House of Delegates Attendance Book, 1781–1782, Virginia State Library.

8. This draft of the bill concerning surveyors is endorsed "November 29th, 1782, Read the first Time/November 30, Read 2d Time and committed to Mr. Tazewell, Mr. Marshall & Mr. Campbell." Henry Tazewell (1753–1799) had been a member of the House of Burgesses in 1771 and a delegate to the state constitutional convention in 1775–1776. From 1776 through 1778 he represented Brunswick County in the House of Delegates, but from 1779 to 1785 he represented Williamsburg. He was made a judge of the General Court in 1785 and was elevated to the Court of Appeals in 1793, only to leave that post the following year to accept election to the U.S. Senate, which office he held until his death. Arthur Campbell (1743–1811) had attended the state constitutional convention and the House of Delegates in 1776 as a representative of Fincastle County. After moving to Washington County, he represented that county in the House of Delegates at five sessions between 1778 and 1788 and was active in the movement to separate Kentucky from Virginia.

The draft appears to be a fair copy of the bill and includes the preamble and first two paragraphs; the third enacting paragraph is in JM's hand; the phrase "At the end of the Bill add" and the material that follows are in the same hand as the preamble and first enacting paragraph.

9. This system for surveying entries dated from 1705, but the controlling statute

the Eastern Waters great inconveniences have arisen from having no Surveyor nor any person residing within the County willing to undertake the said Office.

Be it therefore enacted that where the Court of any County on the Eastern Waters shall recommend any person not resident in their County to the Governor & Council who shall be found qualified by the president and Masters of William and Mary College[1] to execute the Office of Surveyor the Governor may & he is hereby authorized to Commission such person in the same manner as if he was actually resident within the County from which such recommendation came, and when thus commissioned as Surveyor such person may and shall act and do in all respects as the Surveyor of such County.

And where any person shall hold a Warrant from the Land Office, or be desirous to make an Entry in any County on the said Eastern Waters for vacant and unappropriated Land and there shall be no surveyor qualified to act in such County then it shall and may be lawfull for such person to make such Entry with the Clerk of the County Court, and the same surveyed by any legal Surveyor of the next or neighbouring County shall be good & sufficient to enable such person to obtain a Pattent or Grant therefore.

And[2] be it further enacted that it shall & may be lawful for the principal surveyor of any County within the Commonwealth to appoint one deputy for whose conduct the principal shall be answerable, who shall in the absence or indisposition of such principal keep the office & transact the business of the same in the same manner as such principal surveyor might have done.

At the end of the Bill add

And whereas the Death of the right Honble Thomas Lord Fairfax, may occasion great inconvenience to those who may incline to make Entries for vacant Lands in the Northern Neck.

Be it therefore further enacted that all Entries made with the Surveyors of the Counties within the northern Neck and returned

---

was the comprehensive act of 1779 (10 Hening 50–65) that continued the 1763 requirement that a surveyor reside in the county (7 Hening 645). The act of 10 Geo. 2, c. 11, sec. 4 (1736), in 4 Hening 511–512, invalidated any survey made by one other than the principal surveyor of the county.

1. The college received one-sixth of the surveyors' fees in accordance with the 1779 statute. 10 Hening 53.

2. The matter beginning with this word to the end of the paragraph is in JM's handwriting.

to the office formerly kept by the said Thos Lord Fairfax shall be held deemed & taken as good and valid *in Law* as those heretofore made under the direction of the said Thos Lord Fairfax untill some mode shall be taken up and adopted by the Genl Assembly concerning the Territory of the northern Neck.[3]

Land Bounty Certificate

ADS, Land Office Military Certificates, Virginia State Library

Richmond, November 30, 1782

I certify that Captain John Marshall is entitled to a Captain's allowance of land for three years service[4] as an officer in the army.

WILLIAM DAVIES.[5]

Military Land Warrant

Record Book, Land Office, Kentucky Secretary of State's Office[6]

[Richmond], November 30, 1782

Land-Office Military Warrant, No. 30

To the principal SURVEYOR of the Land, set apart for the Officers and Soldiers of the Commonwealth of Virginia.

THIS shall be your WARRANT to survey and lay off in one or more surveys, for John Marshall his Heirs or Assigns; the Quantity of four thousand acres Acres of Land, due unto the said John Marshall in consideration of his Services for three Years as Captain in

3. After JM left the House of Delegates to become a member of the Council of State, the bill was reported out with amendments on Dec. 17; it was read a final time and passed on Dec. 18 and sent to the Senate. On Dec. 19 Senate approval was received, and the bill signed on Dec. 28. The text in 11 Hening 159–160 is identical except for minor variations in capitalization, punctuation, and paragraphing. *JVHD*, Oct. 1782, 44, 45, 68, 71, 73, 90.

4. Virginia military land grants find their statutory authority in the acts of 1776 and 1780. 9 Hening 179; 10 Hening 373, 375. The best description of the allocation of acreage is continued in "Digest of Laws, on the Subject of Land Bounties," 11 Hening 559–565. Under the terms of the two Virginia statutes, JM was entitled to 4,000 acres.

5. Davies (1749–*ca.* 1825), a former colonel in the Virginia Continental Line, was commissioner of the War Office.

6. The entry is on a printed page with blanks for the number, name, quantity, length of service, and rank, which are filled in a clerk's hand. "Commissioner of War" is written over "Governor and Council" on this form.

the army agreeably to a Certificate from the Commissioner of War, which is received into the Land-Office.[7]

GIVEN under my Hand, and Seal of the said Office, this 30th. Day of November in the Year One Thousand Seven Hundred and 82.

JOHN HARVIE Re L Off[8]

Pay Voucher

DS, Virginia State Library[9]

[*December 2, 1782, Richmond.* JM draws two pounds for four days' attendance at the House of Delegates, his final voucher before becoming a member of the Council of State.]

Marriage Bond

DS, Vault, Office of the Clerk of the Henrico County Circuit Court, Richmond

[Henrico County, Va.], January 1, 1783
KNOW[1] ALL MEN by these presents that we John Marshall & Henry Young[2] of the County of Henrico are held & firmly bound unto his Excellency Benjamin Harrison[3] Esq. Governor

7. For statutory authority supporting this grant see 11 Hening 83–84. For method of obtaining a military land grant see Patricia Watlington, *The Partisan Spirit: Kentucky Politics, 1779–1792* (New York, 1972), 13–14.

8. Harvie (1742–1807) was register of the Land Office from 1780 to 1791.

9. In Auditor's Item 292, Pay Vouchers, Officers of Government, 1781–1782. See House of Delegates Attendance Book, 1781–1782, Virginia State Library, where the clerk also copied the voucher.

JM had been elected to the Council of State on Nov. 20 but did not take the oath until Nov. 30. He probably intended to take his seat on Nov. 25, when he drew the voucher printed above, but delayed his departure perhaps to vote on two important bills, one dealing with finances and another with the militia. See *JVHD*, Oct. 1782, 27, 37–38, 45; Qualification Certificate, Nov. 30, 1782, Executive Papers, Va. State Lib.

1. According to the 1631–1632 code of laws in Virginia, marriages could be performed by authority of a license granted by the governor or his authorized agents. 1 Hening 156. In 1660 a law was passed requiring a marriage bond. Because some areas had few ministers and the governor could not be expected to know everyone applying for licenses, the new law required persons wanting to marry to appear before the county clerk and give bond with sufficient security that there was no lawful cause to prevent the marriage. The clerk then prepared the license, which was presented to the minister who performed the ceremony. 2 Hening 28, 55.

2. Young (1741–1817).

3. Harrison (*ca.* 1728–1791) was governor of Virginia from Nov. 30, 1781, to Nov. 30, 1784.

or Chief Magistrate of this CommonWealth in the sum of fifty pounds, to be paid to the said Governor & his Successors for the use of the CommonWealth; to which paiment well & truly to be made We bind ourselves & each of us our Heirs, Executors & Administrators jointly & severally firmly by these presents Sealed with our Seals & dated this first day of January 1783.

THE CONDITION of the above Obligation is such, that Whereas a License is desired for a marriage intended between John Marshall Esq. & Miss Mary Willis Ambler[4] of the parish and County of Henrico; If therefore there is no lawful cause to obstruct the said intended marriage, then the above Obligation to be void, otherwise to remain in full force & Virtue.

Sealed & Delivered   JOHN MARSHALL (LS)
In the presence of   HENRY YOUNG (LS)
ADAM CRAIG[5]

Richmond, January 1, 178[3]

John Marshall Esqr. has my approbation for obtaining a license to intermarry with my Daughter Mary Willis. Given under my Hand & Seal the day & Year above written.

Test   J. AMBLER [LS][6]
JOHN SYNE
HENRY YOUNG

From George Hay

ALS, Gratz Collection, Historical Society of Pennsylvania[7]

Dear Sir,   [Richmond], February 6, 1783

In consequence of your and Mr. Lee's[8] directions, such farther

4. Polly Ambler married JM on Jan. 3, 1783, at The Cottage, a Hanover County plantation. Mason, *Dearest Polly*, 19–20.

5. Craig (*ca.* 1760–1808) had been clerk in the office of the secretary of the colony in Williamsburg before and during the Revolution. He moved to Richmond and became clerk of Henrico County Court, then the Richmond Hustings Court, and finally the General Court.

6. Jaquelin Ambler (1742–1798) was treasurer of Virginia from 1782 to 1798. Mr. Ambler's name is also spelled "Jacquelin" by several authors, but we have adopted JM's spelling, which follows the general use by Ambler, his family, and descendants.

7. Addressed to JM in Richmond, apparently in the care of Mrs. Ramsay. Enclosed in the letter is a list of names, written in two hands, with no explanation of why they are there. The names on the list are John Thweat, John Beard, Chs. Duncan, Wm. Stainbeck, Richd Williams, Richeson Booker, Richard Williams (second depo.), Alexander Taylor, Daniel Sturdevant, Edward Markes, and Anthony Laparke.

8. Probably Charles Lee (1757–1815), the future U.S. attorney general.

evidence as can be procured to counteract M. C. Hays[9] report in Mrs. Ramsay's cause,[1] will be taken tomorrow. The necessity of adducing testimony to prove the inaccuracy, I might say, the atrocious injustice of that report, does not appear to me; but I acquiesce with readiness, satisfied that the strict and regular practice of the Chancery requires it. But my object in now troubling you is to inform you of a fact, perhaps material in Mrs. Ramsay's cause. At the time of the sale of the lot in question, there were several houses on it, two of which have been suffered to stand. For these Mr. Bolling[2] and his representatives have received annually a rent of about £25. or £30. The depositions of the tenants Anthony Leparke and Lancelot Stone were taken to prove these circumstances. M. C. Hay in his report has not noticed these depositions. Perhaps it may be proper to inquire into the reason why he has not. I am, with great respt., yr. ob. Svt.

GEO HAY[3]

To William Pierce

Photostat, Von Hemert Collection, Princeton University Library[4]

Richmond, February 12, 1783

Never more dear Pierce shall pique at your not answering my letters deprive me of the pleasure of writing to the soldier I esteem. I will not again think myself neglected or beleive that our friendship had on your part lost its former warmth. You shall have my thoughts as freely as they rise in my own bosom.

What, says my friend, is Virginia about? Upon my word I can

9. This Mr. Hay, unidentified, was most likely acting as master in chancery in this case.

1. Mrs. Ramsay was defendant in this case, Bolling v. Ramsay.

2. Bolling was plaintiff against Mrs. Ramsay.

3. Hay (1765–1830) was later U.S. attorney and then judge of the U.S. District Court in Virginia.

4. Photostat of a four-page ALS. "No. 70" is written in an unknown hand at the top of the first page. William Leigh Pierce, Jr. (1740–1789), was at the College of William and Mary with JM in 1780 and was also a member of Phi Beta Kappa. [Earl G. Swem], *A Provisional List of Alumni, Grammar School Students, Members of the Faculty, and Members of the Board of Visitors of the College of William and Mary in Virginia, from 1693 to 1888* (Richmond, 1941), 32; Phi Beta Kappa Minute Book, June 3, 1780, Swem Library, College of William and Mary.

Pierce had served with Washington's army in 1778 and 1779; he returned to active duty in 1780 or 1781 and served with distinction in the southern campaign.

scarcely tell you. The grand object of the people is still, as it has ever been, to oppose successfully our British enemies & to establish on the firm base of certainty the independence of America. But in the attainment of this object an attention to a variety of little interests & passions produces such a distracted contrariety of measures that tis sometimes difficult to determine whether some other end is not nearer the hearts of those who guide our Counsels. We have not perhaps so much virtue as we ought to have but we are possessed of much more than our neighbors will give us credit for. But you wish to know what measures we have taken to bring men into the field & Money into the Treasury. You are acquainted with our recruiting bill.[5] It has producd a considerable sum & the money has been religiou[s]ly applied to the purpose for which it was raised. We have not however been so successful as I could have wished. We have not yet recruited in the course of the winter 300 men. Those officers who have been most successful are continued in the business & the money is taken out of the hands of those who have raised no men. The financier tis said has discontinued the post at Winchester in consequence of which our continental recruits have no provisions or are a burthen on the state. We have paid into the continental Treasury 37000 Dollars. The Continent will receive from us in the Spring £50000. Other States have paid more money than Virginia & other States exult in having done so. It is not remembered that the property of our citizens to an immense amount, has been wrested from them for Continental purposes, that could accounts ever be fairly settled (a thing I know to be impossible) the Continent could now have no demands on Virginia. We are exerting ourselves to put our arms in repair & to place ourselves in a defensible situation. So much for politics.

How my dear Pierce in that relaxation from business which is the consequence of the evacuation of Charles Town is your time employed?[6] But I need not ask. You are in a Country where your *gallantry* may be as serviceable in peace as in war. I know your skill in maneuvering under the banners of Venus & I doubt not but several hearts can testify your success. But have you among the rice birds & polloos[7] of Carolina a particular object? Have you totally forgot the Virginia *genius* to whom you was so long an humble Servant? Write me everything which interests you. I expect it be-

5. 11 Hening 14–20.
6. Charleston was evacuated by the British on Dec. 14, 1782.
7. Bobolinks and parakeets.

cause you know 'twill interest me: Am I not uncommonly dull? I[']ll give you a reason for it. I have been setting up all night at an Assembly. We have them in Richmond regularly once a fortnight. The last was a brilliant one; 'twas on the Generals birth night.[8] Never did I see such a collection of handsome Ladies. I do not beleive that Versailles or saint James's ever displayed so much beauty. I wish you had been present. The Virginia[ns] would have retained their high place in your opinion.

Adieu my dear Sir. Mrs. Marshall presents her compliments to you. I am your

JOHN MARSHALL

We have vague accounts of peace but they will [reach] you as soon as this letter. [   ][9]

J. M.

Council of State Opinion

Printed, Wilmer L. Hall, ed., *Journals of the Council of the State of Virginia . . .*, III (Richmond, 1952), 221-222

Richmond, February 20, 1783

The Governor having laid before the Board a Memorial from the Honble Bartholomew Dandridge[1] representing that Mr. John Price Posey[2] one of the Magistrates for the County of New Kent had been guilty of diverse gross misdemeanors, disgraceful to the Character which should be preserved by a Justice of the peace, and praying that the Executive would give their opinion and advice

8. George Washington's birthday on the "old style" calendar would fall on Feb. 11.

9. Part of the postscript, written on the left margin of the first page, is rendered inaccessible by binding.

1. The Board was the Council of State, to which JM had been elected by the House of Delegates on Nov. 20, 1782, while he was representing Fauquier County at the fall session of the General Assembly. He took his seat on Nov. 30, 1782, and served until Apr. 1, 1784. See *JVHD*, Oct. 1782, 27; Qualification Certificate, Nov. 30, 1782, Executive Papers, Virginia State Library; *JVCS*, III, 184; and JM to Benjamin Harrison, Apr. 1, 1784.

Dandridge (1737–1785) was a judge of the General Court and a resident of New Kent County.

2. Posey was convicted of arson and hanged in 1788. A good account of the entire Posey affair is given in *Madison Papers*, VI, 347, n. 5. See also Thad W. Tate, "The Social Contract in America, 1774–1787: Revolutionary Theory as a Conservative Instrument," *WMQ*, 3d Ser., XXII (1965), 384, for the constitutional significance of the Council's action.

whether the said John Price Posey is worthy to be continued in the office of Magistrate and whether for the malpractices aforesaid he ought not to be displaced & removed from the said office——The Board, on consideration thereof, are of opinion that the Law authorizing the Executive to enquire into the Conduct of a Magistrate and determine whether he has or has not committed a certain fact[3] is repugnant to the Act of Government contrary to the fundamental principles of our constitution and directly opposite to the general tenor of our Laws; And therefore it is advised that the Complaint made against the said John Price Posey be not considered unless the facts are found in a Court of Justice.

S: HARDY[4]

BEVERLEY RANDOLPH[5]

J: MARSHALL

To Arthur Lee

Copy, Lee-Ludwell Papers, Virginia Historical Society[6]

Dear Sir   Richmond, February 26, 1783

I inclose you a Bill for fifty pounds. I drew one hundred pounds for you & have retaind the other forty five pounds for the fees due on your western lands.[7] I am Sir etc. etc.

Signed JOHN MARSHALL

3. 9 Hening 478.

4. Samuel Hardy (ca. 1758–1785) attended the College of William and Mary with JM and later served as a delegate to the Continental Congress from 1783 until his death.

5. Randolph (1754–1797) became governor on Nov. 12, 1788.

6. Arthur Lee (1740–1792) was a delegate from Prince William County and one of Virginia's delegates to the Continental Congress. From "Extracts of Letters from Col. J. Marshall to A. Lee" in Lee's hand, item no. Mss1L51f. Lee added the following to this letter: "N B. forty five pounds is mistaken for fifty the remainder of the hundred; it is surprising how Mr. Marshall coud have made such a mistake."

7. In late 1782 Lee had asked JM's father to locate two tracts of land in the western country amounting to approximately 10,000 acres. Thomas Marshall notified Lee on Oct. 22, 1783, that he had not been able to finish locating the land. He asked Lee for money to pay the deputy and register's fees, which money should be delivered to JM in Richmond. See "Extracts of Letters from Col. T. Marshall to Mr. A. Lee," Aug. 20, 1782, and Oct. 22, 1783, Lee-Ludwell Papers, Mss1L51f, Virginia Historical Society. Seie also JM to Lee, Jan. 2, 1784.

To William Heth

ALS, Heth-Selden Manuscripts, University of Virginia Library[8]

My dear Sir   Richmond, March 1, 1783

With all that heart felt pleasure which a letter from Colo. Heth ever has & ever will give his humble servant did I yesterday receive your letter by Mr. Briggs.[9] I will plainly speak to your ifs. If any Officers have upper Rapahanock Tobacco it must I think have been drawn before your certificates were entrusted to me, if this is not the case the quantity was certainly so very small that it would not have taken up your smallest warrant. At present there is no tobacco in the Treasury. Some is soon expected. Mr. Banks[1] is not in town, should he not come in time I will consult Mr. Ross[2] provided I fall in with him, if I do not I will do the best I can. Lower York or James River may probably suit you as well [as] any. I made the application to the Treasurer[3] which you requested. His answer was what I expected. He would wish to oblige Colo. Heth but this was out of his power.

Pryor,[4] the other day wished to purchase a fine horse from Colo. T. M. Randolph,[5] his price was £100 in cash payable in six months or £130 in Military certificates. I tell you this that you may attend to it in the disposal of yours.

Now for the confidential communication. There are I beleive three naval Offices in this State. In time of peace they will certainly be profitable, but they are filled up by three young Gentlemen who promise to live there many years to come. Should a vacancy happen soon the appointment is with the Executive. You know that no Man on earth might command my services sooner

8. Addressed to Heth (1750–1807) at Wales (presumably his estate), "Hond. by Mr. Briggs." Heth noted on envelope "Answd. the 4th," but his letter has not been located.

9. Not found.

1. Probably John Banks (ca. 1757–1784) of Hunter, Banks, & Co., a mercantile firm in Richmond.

2. David Ross (ca. 1736–1817) had been commercial agent for Virginia from 1780 to 1782.

3. Jaquelin Ambler.

4. Probably Maj. John Pryor (ca. 1735–1785), former Virginia commissary of military stores.

5. Thomas Mann Randolph (1741–1793), father of the future Gov. Thomas M. Randolph (1768–1828), had represented Goochland County in the House of Burgesses from 1769 to 1775 and was appointed lieutenant of that county by the Committee of Safety on Sept. 30, 1775.

than Colo. Heth, but this is so distant a prospect that tis not worth a moments thought to a Gentleman who would choose immediate employment. I shall not therefore mention this matter to Monroe [or] Lawson[6] unless you wish me to do so. Ten thousand loves etc. etc. etc. does Polly join me in sending to your Eliza.[7] I just received a letter from my sisters.[8] Colo. Heth & his sweet girl are complimented etc. Adieu, My dear Sir, I am your

JOHN MARSHALL

My compliments to Mr. Briggs & his lady.

Report to the Council of State

Journal, Council of State, Virginia State Library[9]

Richmond, March 25, 1783

Agreeable to the desire of your Excellency[1] in Council we have examined the Books and proceedings of the Solicitor in drawing off the Accounts of this State against the United States, a Duty vested in him by an Act of the late General Assembly.[2] By this Act the Accompts aforesaid are directed to be drawn off in two distinct formes; the one of which to comprehend all advances of the State in money for Continental purposes, and the other all advances in Specifics, with this State of said Accompts and upon this principle the law instructs him to commence the thirty first of January 1781, and to support every article with Vouchers and positive proof, for performance also of which Duty he is authorized by the Legislature to appoint two Clerks each to manage a Distinct branch.

The Solicitor hath appointed One Clerk only who hath been and

6. James Monroe and Robert Lawson (1748–1805), JM's fellow members of the Council of State.

7. Heth's wife, Eliza Briggs Heth.

8. Not found.

9. This report, in a clerk's hand, is preceded by "Mr. Monroe and Mr. Marshall who were appointed to examine into the progress made by the Solicitor in the settlement of the accompts of this State against the continent, report as follows to wit." This entry in the journal is on pp. 130–132. See also *JVCS*, III, 234–235. The original report has not been found. Both JM and James Monroe were members of the Council of State.

1. Benjamin Harrison.

2. *JVCS*, III, 230, 234–235. The solicitor general of Virginia was Leighton Wood (1740–1805). The "act" of the General Assembly was actually a resolution adopted on Dec. 28, 1782. See *JVHD*, Oct. 1782, 14, 16, 88, 90.

is still employed in drawing of the pecuniary Accompt which he hath brought down to the 15th Day of August 1781. The Specific Accompt he hath as yet not meddled with because, as suggested by him, the Commissioners have not yet brought in their returns, and many other Officers through whose hands Specifics have passed have not been called to a settlement. Upon enquiry & examination into the Settlements in this branch of the public revenue upon the Documents we have been able to collect we have reason to suspect great abuses have taken place and very dishonourable misapplications of the public money; We therefore take the Liberty to suggest to your Excellency & the Council the propriety of making some pointed exertion to call those who have been thus employed and entrusted with the public property in every line to an immediate Settlement.

Marshall's Kentucky Lands

EDITORIAL NOTE

Under the authority of the Commonwealth of Virginia, land claims in Kentucky were predicated upon three types of documents: settlement and preemption warrants for those already living on the land in May 1779, military warrants issued to veterans of the French and Indian War and Revolutionary War for military services rendered to the colony or state, and treasury warrants issued on the basis of payment into the state treasury of a fixed sum of money for the purchase of acreage.[3] John Marshall's interests in Kentucky lands were based upon his location of two thousand acres of land under his four-thousand-acre allotment for military service and a substantial number of entries founded upon his acquisition of treasury warrants, either directly from the Land Office or by assignment from original purchasers.[4] We have printed the documents pertaining to Marshall's

3. The statute erecting the Virginia Land Office and specifying the procedures to be followed to obtain land grants upon treasury warrants is in 10 Hening 50–65. It also sets a priority for the claims of Kentucky settlers and military bounty warrant holders. For a discussion of the statute and its historical background see Patricia Watlington, *The Partisan Spirit: Kentucky Politics, 1779–1792* (New York, 1972), 12–13.

4. Some confusion arises from the appearance of two John Marshalls in the Kentucky land grant indexes, and Irwin S. Rhodes speculated that the names of "John Marshall" and "John Marshall, Jr." may have been a trading device used by Col. Thomas Marshall, or that the "Jr." may have been added to distinguish JM from his uncle. Rhodes, *Marshall Papers Calendar*, I, 16. A closer examination, coupled with the assignment printed below, leads us to believe that prior to 1783 "John Marshall," when used in Kentucky, does not apply to JM or his relatives, but rather to an older John Marshall in another Marshall family. Prior to 1783, JM was known as "John Marshall, Jr." in Kentucky. However, in Virginia, JM was never referred to as "Jr.," and warrants issued to "John Marshall" cannot be arbitrarily assigned to the elder Kentucky "John Marshall."

military land warrants elsewhere in this volume; a group of documents pertaining to one of his many entries under a treasury warrant is printed after this editorial note.

The Virginia Land Office at Richmond began to issue treasury warrants on October 15, 1779, enabling direct purchasers to establish claims to land in the district of Kentucky. Although the statute erecting the Land Office and stipulating the method for obtaining land had been passed five months previously, the legislature had wisely delayed the issuance of treasury warrants to insure that settlement claims and preemption certificates issued to settlers in Kentucky might be processed and given priority over later entries on treasury warrants. The statute also provided that no entry, other than on preemption warrants, might be made with the county surveyors before May 1, 1780. In addition, due allowance was made for the land reserved to the use of soldiers of the Continental Line and Virginia Line under existing legislation. An excessive number of acres was covered by the treasury warrants issued, and in a short time the treasury warrants depreciated in value, for most of the good available land had been entered within the first year.[5]

John Marshall was particularly well situated to take advantage of the opportunities presented by Kentucky land speculation. His residence at Richmond facilitated access to the Virginia Land Office, as well as serving as a central point for the purchase of treasury warrants from Virginia residents who wished to assign them for entry by Marshall or a subsequent assignee. At the same time, his father's appointment as surveyor of Fayette County in 1780 provided him with accurate information concerning land that had not been previously entered, or if so entered, had not been surveyed and therefore possibly abandoned.[6] Professor Patricia Watlington has commented upon the existence of such partnerships between men residing in Virginia and others in Kentucky,[7] and it is readily apparent from a study of land entries that Marshall and his father were closely allied in their dealings in Kentucky land.

While the financial benefits secured to Marshall through his dealings in Kentucky lands remain obscure, the pattern of operations is obvious from the documentary records of these transactions. John Marshall either obtained land warrants at the Land Office in his own name or acquired them by assignment from a purchaser or an intermediate assignee. The warrant was then sent to Colonel Thomas Marshall in Kentucky, who would enter the acreage in his son's name and arrange for a survey. Unlike other speculators in Kentucky lands, John Marshall and his father seem to have acted promptly to survey the lands they entered. Of course, the difficulty of making entries that would remain uncontested increased with the passage of time, and after 1783 a decreasing number of surveyed acres was obtained from each entry. We have uncovered a total of 292,813¾ acres in treasury warrants issued from the Land Office that were used in connection with Marshall's entries. Of these, 229,823¾ acres were entered with the surveyor, the entire amount being in what then constituted Fayette County but what in later years included Bourbon County. Based on these entries, tracts of 201,815

5. Watlington, *Partisan Spirit*, 18–19.
6. An example of an entry being located by Col. Thomas Marshall on behalf of JM, in an area between two disputed tracts, can be seen in the case of Ward v. Fox's Heirs, 1 Kentucky (Hughes) 406, 432–434.
7. Watlington, *Partisan Spirit*, 20–21.

acres were surveyed for John Marshall and registered in the survey books of the Land Office. Marshall obtained grants to 41,503½ acres in his own name; 108,525½ acres were assigned to Colonel Thomas Marshall, and grants were issued to him;[8] 1,700 acres were assigned and granted to Thomas Marshall, Jr., while 500 acres were assigned and granted to Benjamin Ashby. The total number of acres granted to Marshall or his assignees was 152,229 acres.

Unquestionably there was a prior agreement between John Marshall and his father concerning Marshall's Kentucky land purchases. Although Colonel Marshall served as surveyor of Fayette County, this did not automatically exclude him from entering land there. However, it did make it necessary for him to enter his lands with the county court, and this could have resulted in expensive delays. Conceivably John Marshall merely acted as his father's agent, and his grant of 41,503½ acres may have represented compensation for these efforts. On the other hand, there may have been a pooling of resources in partnership, with the resulting land grants being divided in proportion to the parties' original investment in the enterprise. John Marshall's Account Book does not reflect any substantial transfers of funds between him and his father, other than amounts that might easily be Colonel Marshall's remittance of one-sixth of his surveyor's fees to the College of William and Mary. There is also no item in the Account Book that reflects disbursement of funds for the purchase of treasury warrants. Possibly a separate ledger, no longer available, was maintained for these transactions.

In the absence of such a formal record of land investments, it is conceivable that we have not located all of Marshall's entries and land grants in Kentucky. However, we have examined the treasury warrant books and all of the appropriate entry books; we have also scanned the survey books maintained in the Land Office Papers in the Virginia State Library. As a result of this research we believe that we have identified all of the Kentucky land transactions with which Marshall had any connection up to 1792, when the Virginia Land Office ceased to have authority over Kentucky land.[9] We have also identified a few scattered land grants in the panhandle area of western Virginia, made after Kentucky independence, which are based upon John Marshall's treasury warrants. For the most part, however, the evidence indicates that Marshall's principal interest was in Kentucky and that subsequent acquisitions elsewhere were merely attempts to recoup the unused portion of his investment in treasury warrants. We have also examined the deed books of Fayette County, which date from 1803, and have found no record of grants by John Marshall, which suggests the possibility that he sold his acreage prior to that time.[1] Whatever premise one may have concerning the motivation

8. JM's assignments to his father amounted to a substantial portion of the 127,841 acres granted to Col. Marshall. *Ibid.*, 43.

9. A few JM grants were made under the Kentucky state government after it was divided from Virginia in 1792. See Rhodes, *Marshall Papers Calendar*, I, 352–353. These will be treated in a later volume of this edition. For the period of JM's greatest activity in Kentucky lands, from 1782 to 1784, the most complete survey and grant books are those that were maintained by the Virginia Land Office at Richmond. After Nov. 1781 a deputy register was authorized to register land titles in Kentucky, but registry with him was not made mandatory until after Nov. 1, 1783. All of the deputy register's records were transmitted to Richmond for recording purposes. See 10 Hening 445, 11 Hening 292.

1. The Fayette County deed books, in the Office of the Fayette County Clerk, Lex-

for John Marshall's investment in Kentucky realty, it is abundantly clear that his intentions after 1784 did not include settling in the area.[2]

Theoretically the steps necessary to obtain a land grant in Kentucky were reasonably well defined by statute. A payment of the necessary sum of money, computed at £40 per hundred acres, was made into the Virginia state treasury, and the treasurer's receipt was presented to the register of the Land Office, who thereupon issued the treasury land warrant, authorizing the surveyor of any county to accept an entry and conduct the survey. The owner of the warrant then determined what land he wished to obtain and, after carefully noting its location through reference to natural landmarks and man-made boundary marks, entered this description with the surveyor of the county in which the land was located.[3] The original entry books for Kentucky are presently in the Jefferson County Archives at Louisville, and so some of John Marshall's earliest entries are contained in those volumes. When Fayette County was established in 1781 a separate surveyor's office was authorized, and the bulk of John Marshall's entries are in the entry books of that office, now maintained at the Land Office in the Kentucky Secretary of State's Office in Frankfort.[4]

Once the entry was filed and the surveyor's schedule permitted, the owner of the land was to be notified to appear at the surveyor's office with his chainmen and line marker, ready to survey the land contained in the entry. The large number of land claims entered, coupled with the general unavailability of claimants, caused difficulties in arranging for the prompt survey of lands. As a result, a substantial amount of land remained unsurveyed several years after the original entry had been made; in Marshall's case the average delay was slightly more than twenty-three months, with the shortest period being one month and the longest seventy-four months between entry and survey.[5]

Upon the completion of the survey, the owner was provided with a plat and a verbal description of the land surveyed. This document, with the treasury warrant, was then presented to the Land Office for examination by the register. If all was found in order and no caveat had been filed in the Land Office contesting the claimant's entitlement to the land, a grant was issued to the claimant or his as-

---

ington, Ky., are fairly complete after 1803; however, the records prior to that date reportedly were destroyed by fire.

2. Toulmin refers to lands of JM's brother, Thomas Marshall, Jr. (1761–1817), which were rented for three lives at a fixed annual rental, on terms similar to those applicable to the manor lands in the Northern Neck of Virginia. Whether JM or his father held lands and rented them in this fashion is unclear, but the practice may have been common in the better farming areas of Kentucky. Harry Toulmin, *The Western Country in 1793: Reports on Kentucky and Virginia*, ed. Marion Tinling and Godfrey Davis (San Marino, Calif., 1948), 61, 76–77.

3. See 10 Hening 50–65; Tucker, *Blackstone's Commentaries*, II, app. D, 66–67, synopsizes the statutory requirements. See also Watlington, *Partisan Spirit*, 14.

4. On the division of Kentucky into three counties and provisions for separation of entry books, see 10 Hening 315, 317.

5. While priority of entry determined entitlement to lands accurately located, a proper survey might defeat an earlier incorrect survey on a senior entry. Ammons v. Spears (1787), 1 Kentucky (Hughes) 10. For a good discussion of legislative attempts to encourage prompt surveys, see Watlington, *Partisan Spirit*, 14–15. See also 11 Hening 441 (1784) and 12 Hening 99 (1785). For complications that might arise from conflicting surveys, see Ward v. Fox's Heirs (1801), 1 Kentucky (Hughes) 406 *et seq.*

signee under the hand of the governor and the privy seal of the Commonwealth of Virginia. Remarkably, no caveats were entered against the issuance of land grants surveyed for Marshall, perhaps because of his father's diligence in locating and surveying land for him. On the other hand, the entries by Marshall seem to have been subject to frequent modification, either by location elsewhere or by withdrawal of acreage from one or another border of the entry, and this would seem to show a clear intention upon his part to avoid the expensive and time-consuming litigation that might ensue from conflicting land claims.[6]

Warrant

Printed DS, Surveys, Land Office, Kentucky Secretary of State's Office

[Richmond], April 7, 1780

Land-Office WARRANT, No. 4583

To the principal Surveyor of any County within the Commonwealth of Virginia.

THIS shall be your WARRANT to Survey and lay off in one or more Surveys, for John Marshall his Heirs or [SEAL]   Assigns, the Quantity of four hundred Acres of Land, due unto the said Marshall in Consideration of the Sum of one hundred & Sixty pounds current Money paid into the publick Treasury; the Payment whereof to the Treasurer hath been duly certified by the Auditors of publick Accounts, and their Certificate received into the Land Office. GIVEN under my Hand, and the Seal of the said Office, on this Seventh Day of April in the Year One Thousand Seven Hundred and Eighty.

S: CARR D.R.L.O.[7]

[Lexington?], September 4, 1783

As Heir at law to the within John Marshall deceased I hereby assign all my right and title to the within warrant to John Marshall junr. his heirs or assigns in case the division of the said Estate

6. Kentucky's early judicial history was characterized by litigation over disputed land titles, the complexity of which can be seen by examining James Hughes's reports in 1 Kentucky Reports. Prof. Watlington observes that "almost every inch of Kentucky land was disputed." *Partisan Spirit*, 16. St. George Tucker used most of the appendix devoted to land grants to rail against the fraud, litigation, and speculative activity that was involved in Kentucky land grants. Tucker, *Blackstone's Commentaries*, II, app. D, 68–72.

7. "Deputy Register of the Land Office."

stands as it is now made. Given under my hand this fourth day of September one thousand seven hundred and Eighty three.
Test GRANT ALLIN   DIXON MARSHAL

Entry

Record Book, Fayette Entries, Fayette County Clerk's Office, Lexington, Ky.

[Lexington], April 10, 1785

John Marshall Junr Enters 1000 acres of land on two Treasury Warrants No. 4580 and 4583 Beginning at the North East Corner of Samuel Blankenbakers 517¾ Acre Entry thence South with his Line to his South East Corner thence East so far that a North West Line Shall Include the quantity.

Survey

ADS, Surveys, Land Office, Kentucky Secretary of State's Office

[Lexington?], August 17, 1787

August the 17th 1787

Surveyd for John Marshall 1000 Acres of Land by virtue of an entry made April the 10th 1785 Situate lying and being on the Waters of Sandy and in the County of Bourbon[8] and bounded as follows (to

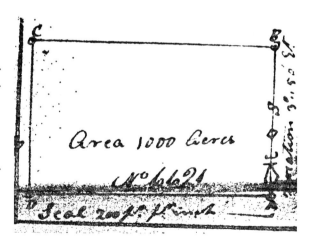

---

8. Bourbon County was formed from Fayette County in an act passed in Oct. 1785, to become effective May 1, 1786. 12 Hening 89–91.

wit) (on two Treasury warrant No. 4580–4583), BEGINNING at the N. East corner of Samuel Blankenbeckers Survey of 517½ Acres at the Letter (A) two White oakes thence south with his line 320 poles to two Black ashes thence East 500 poles to a Sugar tree and Poplar thence North 320 poles to a Poplar & Ash thence West 500 poles to the Begining.

ISRAEL TULLY   ⎰   GEO. LEWIS D.S.B.C.[9]
RICHARD BARTLETT   ⎱   CC[1]
JOHN CURTIS   ⎰ L Marker[2]

Ex[amine]d JAMES GARRAND, Reg.[3]

Grant

Record Book, Land Office, Kentucky Secretary of State's Office

Richmond, February 8, 1791

BEVERLEY RANDOLPH Esquire Governor of the Commonwealth of Virginia To all to whom these presents shall come Greeting: Know ye that by virtue and in consideration of two Land Office Treasury Warrants Numbers 4,580 & 4,583, Issued the seventh day of April 1780, There is Granted by the said Commonwealth unto John Marshall, a certain tract or parcel of Land containing One thousand acres by Survey bearing date the 17th day of August 1787, lying and being in the County of *Bourbon*, on the waters of *Sandy*, and bounded as followeth To wit: Beginning at the North East corner of Samuel Blankenbeckers Survey of five hundred seventeen and a half acres, to two white oaks, thence South with his line three hundred and twenty poles to two black oaks, thence East five hundred poles to a Sugar tree & Poplar, thence North three hundred and twenty poles to a Poplar & ash, thence West five hundred poles to the Beginning: with its Appurtenances, To have and to hold the said tract or parcel of land with its Appurtenances, to the said John Marshall and his Heirs forever. In Witness whereof the said Beverley Randolph Esquire Governor of the Commonwealth of Virginia hath hereunto set his hand and caused

9. "Deputy Surveyor, Bourbon County."
1. "Chain Carrier."
2. "Line Marker."
3. "Register."

the lesser Seal of the said Commonwealth to be affixed at Richmond on the eighth day of February, in the year of our Lord one thousand seven hundred & Ninety one, and of the Commonwealth the fifteenth.

BEVERLEY RANDOLPH.

Land Bounty Certificate

ADS, Bounty Warrants, Virginia State Library

[Richmond], October 20, 1783

John Grant enlisted in the 11th. Virginia Regt. as a soldier for three years sometime in August 1776. He served out his time, & was then dischargd.[4]

JOHN MARSHALL
then Capt. 11th. V. R.

Land Bounty Certificate

ADS, Bounty Warrants, Virginia State Library

[Richmond], November 6, 1783

I do certify that John Anderson Serjeant served in the 7th. Virga. Regt. three years, the term for which he was inlisted & was then dischargd.[5]

JOHN MARSHALL
then Capt. 7th. V. R.

Land Bounty Certificate

Copy, Bounty Warrants, Virginia State Library

[Richmond, ca. November 10, 1783]

I do certify that Richard Marshall[6] enlisted into the 11th

4. For information on land bounty certificates, see note at JM's certificate, Nov. 30, 1782.
5. For information on land bounty certificates, see note at JM's certificate, Nov. 30, 1782.
6. Marshall (1730–1798) was not related to JM and did not serve in JM's company

Virg[*inia Regimen*]t in the Novr. 1776 & servd as a Sergt in the Same Regt till the first Janury. 1779 When He listed in cavalry.

JOHN MARSHALL Capt.

Land Bounty Certificate

Copy, Bounty Warrants, Virginia State Library

[Richmond], November 11, 1783

Daniel Haley enlisted with me for the war in 1776 & served in the 7th Regt. till the last of 1780, when I left the Regimt.

JOHN MARSHALL
then Capt. 7th V. Regt.[7]

To Leven Powell

Printed, *The John P. Branch Historical Papers* . . . , II (June 1902), 130–131

Dear Sir,[8]—   Richmond, December 9, 1783

No step whatever has been taken in your suit against Burwell.[9] If the matter is not arbitrated, will without question be tried next Court. I should be glad to see your depositions. If you have not a certain opportunity sooner, I shall be at Fauquier March Court,

during the war. The May 1779 act concerning military land warrants required that a noncommissioned officer receive a certificate from the colonel or commanding officer of his regiment and present it and such other proofs of service as might be necessary to a court of record in the Commonwealth of Virginia. 10 Hening 51. Upon the court's certification of the proceedings, the War Office was to issue a certificate similar to that printed under date Nov. 30, 1782. This War Office certificate was in turn exchanged for a military land warrant. JM's certificate for Richard Marshall probably formed part of the record transmitted to the War Office by the court that determined the sergeant's entitlement to a land bounty.

7. The copy was written by John Pendleton, Jr. (*ca.* 1749–*ca.* 1807), on another certificate. Pendleton had been appointed a temporary state auditor by the Council of State on July 1, 1783. He was elected to the position by the General Assembly on Nov. 20, 1783. He also served a term on the Richmond City Common Council in 1783–1784. *JVCS*, III, 276; *JVHD*, Oct. 1783, 22, 25, 26; *Madison Papers*, I, 190.

Haley actually enlisted on May 4, 1777, and JM left the regiment at the end of 1779. See Muster Roll, Aug. 7, 1777. For information on land bounty certificates, see note at JM's certificate, Nov. 30, 1782.

8. Powell (1737–1810), of Loudoun County, was later a Federalist congressman in the Sixth Congress.

9. See Account Book, Receipts, Apr. 8, 1786.

when I shall with pleasure take charge of them. Judgment is given against you at the motion of the Commonwealth. The Solicitor[1] swore that you in conversation with him admitted the receipt of the money, the Court, however, have only given judgment for the value of the money when it was supposed to have passed into your hands, which I confess was more justice than I expected.—The Solicitor has written to you on the subject, and the costs of an execution may be saved.

Your Delegates, I presume, give you the news of the Assembly. Never could there have been less to give. This long session has not produced a single bill of Public importance, except that for the re-admission of Commutables.[2] You will get the bill before you receive this. It ought to be perfect as it has twice passed the House. It fell the first time (after an immensity of labor and debate), a sacrifice to the difference of opinion subsisting in the House of Delegates and in the Senate with respect to a money bill. A bill for the regulation of elections and enforcing the attendance of members is now on the Carpet, and will probably pass.[3] It contains a good deal of necessary matter with some things that appear to me to be impracticable. It is surprising that Gentlemen of character cannot dismiss their private animosities, but will bring them in the Assembly.

Adieu my dear friend, I am Yours Truly,

J. MARSHALL.

To James Monroe

ALS, Draper Collection, State Historical Society of Wisconsin[4]

Dear Sir   [Richmond], December 12, 1783

The letters to Genl. Clarke & Mr. Banks enclosed in yours of the 5th. inst. I yesterday delivered.[5] Should a letter to Majr. Critten-

1. Leighton Wood.

2. Allowed in "An act to amend the several acts of assembly for ascertaining certain taxes and duties, and for establishing a permanent revenue." 11 Hening 299–306.

3. This bill was finally rejected on Dec. 19. *JVHD*, Oct. 1783, 73. A related bill was debated at the following session. See JM to Charles Simms, June 16, 1784.

4. This letter was printed, somewhat incorrectly, in *AHR*, X (1904–1905), 815–817, where Jefferson was named the recipient. The mistake was repeated in John Edward Oster, *The Political and Economic Doctrines of John Marshall* (New York, 1914), 86–88, but Beveridge recognized that Monroe was the correct recipient in Beveridge, *Marshall*, I, 208n. There can be little doubt this letter was to Monroe. See JM to Monroe, Jan. 3, 1784.

5. George Rogers Clark (1752–1818) and probably John Banks. The subject of

den[6] arrive by the next post I can give it a certain & immediate conveyance. I gave you in my last some account of the proceedings of the Assembly. The Commutable bill has at length passed & with it a suspension of the collection of taxes till the first of January next.[7] I told you the principle speakers for & against the measure. Colo. R. H. Lee has not attended this Session. This is not all. His services in the Assembly are lost for ever. 'Tis conjectured that Colo. Harry Lee of the Legionary corps, will take his place. You know the character of that Gentleman better than I do & can best determine whether the public will be injured by the change. The idea of rendering Members of Congress eligible to the Genl. Assembly has not been taken up.[8] Indeed the attention of the house since the passage of the Commutable bill has been so fixed on the citizen bill that they have scarcely thought on any other subject. Since the rejection of the bill introduced by Taylor, Colo. Nicholas[9] (a politician not famed for hitting a medium) introduced one admitting into this Country every species of Men except natives who had borne arms against the state. When the house went into Committee on this bill Mr. Jones[1] introduced by way of amendment, one totally new & totally opposite to that which was the subject of deliberation. He spoke with his usual sound sense & solid reason. Mr. Henry[2] opposed him. The Speaker replied with some degree of acrimony &

Monroe's letter to Clark may be seen in Monroe to Clark, Oct. 19, 1783, in James Alton James, ed., *George Rogers Clark Papers, 1781–1784* (Illinois Historical Library, *Collections*, XIX [Springfield, Ill., 1926]), 248–250. Neither Monroe's letter to Banks nor his Dec. 5 letter to JM has been found.

6. John Crittenden (1756–1806).

7. See 11 Hening 299–306.

8. Richard Henry Lee (1732–1794) of Westmoreland County and Henry "Light Horse Harry" Lee (1756–1818). Harry Lee was elected a delegate to the Oct. 1785 session. See Earl G. Swem and John W. Williams, *A Register of the General Assembly of Virginia, 1776–1918* . . . (Richmond, 1918), 21.

Members of Congress had been ineligible for election to the House of Delegates by a law adopted at the May 1777 General Assembly but repealed in 1779. There were several attempts to restore that restriction, partially sponsored by the anti-Lee faction in the House of Delegates, and they finally succeeded at the May 1783 General Assembly. Sentiment against the bill, however, was strong enough to repeal the measure at the May 1784 session. JM was among those who opposed the restriction. 9 Hening 299; 10 Hening 75; 11 Hening 249, 365.

9. John Taylor of Caroline (1753–1824) introduced a bill defining citizenship on Nov. 10, and it was defeated on Dec. 2. See *JVHD*, Oct. 1783, 13, 42. George Nicholas (1754–1799) of Albemarle County introduced his bill on Dec. 6. See *ibid.*, 50.

1. Probably Joseph Jones (1727–1805), Monroe's uncle, delegate from King George County and future judge of the General Court from 1789 to 1805, who had helped draft the bill in committee. This debate occurred on Dec. 9. See *ibid.*, 56.

2. Patrick Henry (1736–1799), then a delegate from Henry County, had also served on the committee that drafted the bill.

Henry retorted with a good deal of tartness but with much temper; 'tis his peculiar excellence when he altercates to appear to be drawn unwillingly into the contest & to throw in the eyes of others the whole blame on his adversary. His influence is immense. The house rose for the day without coming to any determination & the bill is yet in suspense. The principle point on which they split is the exclusion of the Statute Staple[3] men. I really am uncertain what will be the determination on this subject.

The Officers will soon begin to survey their lands on the Cumberland. Has Crittenden your Military warrant? The report from Congress with respect to the 'cession has not yet reached us; of course the Assembly can have determined nothing about it.[4] My Father set out for the western Country about the 5th. of Novr. I have not heard a syllable from Crittenden since his departure. Adieu, I am, with the greatest esteem, Your

J MARSHALL

Banks has applied to me for a considerable sum on your account but I presume your letter to him was on that subject. I hurry every applicant as well as possible. Your

J. M.

Land Bounty Certificate

ADS, Bounty Warrants, Virginia State Library

[Richmond], December 18, 1783

Lt. Benjamin Ashby engaged in the Continental Service in the

3. A statute staple would have confined foreigners to specific ports where exports could be made. "Statute Staple men" were presumably foreign merchants. No such clause was in the bill that finally passed on the last day of the session, Dec. 22. See *JVHD*, Oct. 1783, 82, and 11 Hening 322.

4. JM was referring to the involved negotiations between Congress and Virginia over Virginia's attempt to cede the territory northwest of the Ohio River to the Confederation. The report from Congress had arrived by the date of this letter. Gov. Benjamin Harrison sent the report to the House with a letter dated Dec. 11, and the House proceeded to agree to the terms of the deed on Dec. 15. JM attended the Council of State meeting on Dec. 11 and must have known the report had arrived. This suggests JM wrote this letter before Dec. 12 and perhaps added the date when it was mailed, if in fact he did not simply write the incorrect date initially. See *JVHD*, Oct. 1783, 53, 62, 71, 82; Gov. Harrison to Speaker of House of Delegates, Dec. 11, 1783, Executive Letterbook, Virginia State Library; *JVCS*, III, 315; JM to Monroe, Jan. 3, 1784.

7th. Virga. Regt. in the year 1777 as an Ensign. He was afterwards promoted & continued in service more than three years.[5]

JOHN MARSHALL
then Capt. 7th. V. R.

Land Bounty Certificate

ADS, Bounty Warrants, Virginia State Library

[Richmond, *ca.* 1783]
I certify that Richard Harvy enlisted in my company in the 11th. Virginia Regt. some time in the year 1776 & that he served faithfully the time for which he was enlisted which was three years.[6]

JOHN MARSHALL
then Capt. 11th. V. R.

Land Bounty Certificate

DS, Bounty Warrants, Virginia State Library

[*ca. 1783, Richmond.* JM certifies that John Hasty had enlisted in his company in 1776 for three years.[7] JM's certification is written on a similar statement by William Woodford.]

To Arthur Lee

Copy, Lee-Ludwell Papers, Virginia Historical Society[8]

Richmond, January 2, 1784
I cannot tell you with certainty what the expence of patenting

5. Actually Ashby had been appointed an ensign on Nov. 30, 1776. See Muster Roll, Dec. 9, 1779. For information on land bounty certificates, see note to JM's certificate, Nov. 30, 1782.

6. For information on land bounty certificates, see note at JM's certificate, Nov. 30, 1782.

7. See note at JM's land bounty certificate, Nov. 30, 1782.

8. From "Extracts of Letters from Col. J. Marshall to A. Lee" in Lee's hand, item no. Mss1L51f. This letter was probably in reply to a letter from Lee, written after receiving Col. Thomas Marshall's request for money to finish locating the warrants. See JM to Arthur Lee, Feb. 26, 1783, n. 7.

your western lands may be. If there is but one tract, the Surveyors fees will (including the payment to the College & deputy)[9] will[10] amount to £10.9.4½. But a much more considerable charge remains, the Registers fees with the tax on patents—both wch. it will be absolutely necessary to settle immediately with Col. Harvie)[1] will amount to upwards of £22. The expence of Chain, chainmen, markers etc. with their provisions I can only guess at. The calculation is, that the collected charges are about, or very near five pounds per Acre.[2]

To James Monroe

ALS, Monroe Papers, Library of Congress[3]

Dear Sir   Richmond, January 3, 1784
    At length then the military career of the greatest Man on earth is closed.[4] May happiness attend him whereever he goes. May he long enjoy those blessings he has secured to his Country. When I speak or think of that superior Man my full heart overflows with gratitude. May he ever experience from his Countrymen those attentions which such sentiments of themselves produce.
    Let me assure you that I will punctually comply with every requisition you may make on pecuniary subjects or any other within my reach. Your letter to Majr. Crittenden shall be put today into the hands of Genl. Clarke who will be in the western country

9. Surveyors and their deputies were examined and certified by the president and professors of the College of William and Mary, after which one-sixth of all fees collected by them went to the college in an annual payment. Deputies were paid the same fees as principals but were entitled to keep only half the money, out of which one-sixth went to the college. See 10 Hening 53 and 11 Hening 352–353.
    10. The second "will" is a slip of the pen.
    1. John Harvie, register of the Land Office.
    2. Lee continued to have difficulty learning the disposition of his warrants and finally wrote Charles Lee in 1789, complaining that he had "not been able to obtain a line from [Thomas Marshall] on the subject, nor any thing satisfactory from [John Marshall]. I have written frequently on the subject to both." Lee wanted Charles Lee to obtain some information for him on the warrants, but he cautioned: "I wish to possess this information without any communication with Mr. J. Marshall & have my reasons for requesting that you will not let him know any thing on the subject. I cannot but think, that they [JM and his father] intend to force me to acquiesce in the loss or seek redress at Law. It is too great a loss to submit too quietly, & I think the acknowlegements they have made will be sufficient to support a demand at Law." Arthur Lee to Charles Lee, May 8, 1789, Lee-Ludwell Papers, Virginia Historical Society.
    3. Addressed to Monroe at Annapolis.
    4. George Washington resigned his commission on Dec. 23, 1783. See Freeman, *Washington*, V, 473–477, and *Jefferson Papers*, VI, 6, 402–414, for accounts of the ceremony attending the resignation.

in February next, or in march at furthest. I will request his particular attention to your military warrant.[5] I am sure his friendship for you will induce him to pay it chearfully. The Speaker[6] has for some time left Richmond & may not perhaps be here till the next session. Should I see him I will mention to him your certificate. I lament as sincerely as you can do the exclusion of our Delegates in Congress from a seat in our Legislature.[7] There is no one quality perhaps which we more need than wisdom. Severely very severely indeed have we experienced the want of it. And surely no one measure can have a greater tendency to continue & even increase the misfortune than those exclusions, those unnecessary exclusions of men whose virtue & abilities have secured the esteem & good opinion of their Country. Fears of the power of Congress I have ever considerd as chimerical. I never could bring myself to think that Gentlemen who urged really felt them but conceived they were usd as a political engine to effect particular purposes. And I have ever observed that our Countrymen in the general may be persuaded from an apprehension of a distant evil, to adopt measures which ⟨may⟩ must produce a certain one. This arises from refining too much, & this they will do in all cases except those where money is to be [drawn] from their purses.

While the sending the resolution of Congress with respect to our cession of Western territory shews your attention to the information & interests of your Country, I cannot but lament that my letter should have produced to you unnecessary trouble & to us expense. For the thursday after I had written to you the Resolutions of Congress made their appearance under a cover from our friend Colo. Mercer[8] dated in Septr. last. Adeiu I am with the most affectionate esteem, Your

J MARSHALL

5. Monroe's military warrant was no. 2368, for 5,333 acres, dated Feb. 2, 1784. See Willard Rouse Jillson, *Old Kentucky Entries and Deeds* (Louisville, Ky., 1926), 350.

6. John Tyler (1747–1813), father of the future president of the same name, was an attorney and Revolutionary War leader. He had been elected Speaker of the House of Delegates in 1781 and again in 1783. He later was judge of the Virginia admiralty court until 1788, when he was made a judge of the newly reorganized General Court. He resigned that position in 1808 to become governor and left that post in 1811 to become a federal district judge for Virginia until his death.

7. Act passed at the May 1783 session of the General Assembly, but repealed at the May 1784 session. See JM to Monroe, Dec. 12, 1783; 11 Hening 249–250, 365.

8. John Francis Mercer (1759–1821) was a delegate from Virginia to the Continental Congress from 1782 to 1785. The congressional resolution accepting Virginia's cession of the northwest territory is in *JCC*, XXV, 559. For a discussion of the western cession, see *Jefferson Papers*, VI, 571–580. JM's letter to Monroe is Dec. 12, 1783.

To James Monroe

ALS, James Monroe Memorial Library

Dear Sir   Richmond, February 7, 1784

The post is just setting out & I have only time to tell you that the enclosed bill[9] is the best method of transmitting you the money due to you as a Delegate to Congress which was within my reach. The sum drawn for you was one hundred Dollars, four Dollars were expended on your Land warrant which is now in the hands of the Surveyor.

Farewell. With earnest wishes for your happiness, I am your

JOHN MARSHALL

Land Bounty Certificate

ADS, Bounty Warrants, Virginia State Library

[Richmond], February 13, 1784

The within mentioned William Tomlin enlisted out of the infantry into the cavalry some time in 1777, he belonged to this state.[1]

JOHN MARSHALL
then Capt. 7th. V. R.

To James Monroe

ALS, New York Society Library[2]

Dear Sir   Richmond, February 19, 1784

By a Gentleman of whom I have just been informed & who is now in waiting I have an opportunity of sending to Mr. Maury[3]

9. The enclosed bill of exchange has not been found.

1. JM wrote this certificate on the verso of Tomlin's discharge from the Fourth Regiment of Light Dragoons, dated Dec. 5, 1780. For information on land bounty certificates, see note at JM's certificate, Nov. 30, 1782.

2. Addressed to Monroe at Annapolis, "Hond. by Mr. Maury."

3. Probably James Maury (1746–1840), of Fredericksburg, who was delivering some of Madison's letters to Jefferson at Annapolis on the same trip. See *Madison Papers*, VII, 406, 421.

who will deliver to you duplicates of bills I transmitted sometime past by post[4] but which may possibly be detained by the hard weather. Will you permit me to request that you will receive Mr. Maury as a gentleman of a most amiable character & introduce him as such to your *Compeers* in Congress. But Mr. Jefferson[5] is better acquainted with him than I am.

Will you deliver the bills to those for whom they are drawn. I am your

J. MARSHALL

To James Monroe

ALS, Monroe Papers, New York Public Library[6]

Dear Sir   Richmond, February 24, 1784

I wish it was possible to releive your wants by your Boy, but it is impossible. The exertions of the Treasurer & of your other friends here have been ineffectual. There is not one shilling in the Treasury & the keeper of it coud not borrow one on the faith of government. The extreme inclemency of the season has rendered it impossible for the Sheriffs to make collections and I have my fears that you will not receive an adequate supply till some time in April. I transmitted to you by post three weeks past a bill for a small sum drawn since the £100. I hope you have received it.

I am pressed warmly by Ege[7] for money & your old LandLady Mrs. Shera begins now to be a little clamarous. I shall be obligd I apprehend to negotiate your warrants at last at a discount. I have kept them up thus long in hopes of drawing Money for them from the Treasury & shall keep them up till about April next by which time I may receive som[e] instructions from you on the subject.

This excessive cold weather has operated like magic on our youth. They feel the necessity of artificial heat, & quite wearied with lying alone, are all treading the broad road to Matrimony. Little Stewart, (coud you beleive it?) will be married on thursday to Kitty Hair & Mr. Dunn will bear of your old acquaintance Miss

4. Probably a reference to bill enclosed in JM's letter of Feb. 7, 1784, printed above.

5. Thomas Jefferson (1743–1826), then a delegate to the Continental Congress.

6. Addressed to Monroe at Annapolis.

7. Probably Samuel Ege (1742–1801), an inspector of flour in Richmond.

Shera.[8] Tabby Eppes[9] has grown quite fat & buxom, her charms are renovated & to see her & to love her are now synonimous terms. She has within these six weeks seen in her train at least a score of Military & civil characters. Carrington, Young, Selden, Wright (a merchant) & Foster Webb[1] have alternately bowed before her & been discarded. Carrington tis said has drawn off his forces in order to refresh them & has marched up to Cumberland where he will in all human probability be reinforced with the dignified character of Legislator. Webb has returnd to the charge & the many think from their similitude of manners & appetites that they were certainly designd for each other.

The other Tabby is in high spirits [*with the*] success of her antique sister & firmly beleives her time will come next, she looks quite spruce & speaks of matrimony as of a good which she yet means to experience. Lomax is in his County.[2] Smith is said to be electioneering.[3] Nelson has not yet come to the board.[4] Randolph is here & well.[5] Short[6] has a certain complaint which you will probably be a judge of before you return from Annapolis. Farewell, I am your

J MARSHALL

8. John Stewart and Catherine Hare (b. *ca.* 1766) were issued a marriage license on Feb. 24, 1784, in Henrico County. See Henrico County Marriage Bonds, Virginia State Library. They were married on Feb. 26. See *Virginia Gazette, and Weekly Advertiser* (Richmond), Feb. 28, 1784. Dunn and Shera cannot be identified.

9. Probably Tabitha Eppes, daughter of Richard and Martha (Bolling) Eppes. She was not yet married in 1789. See Thomas Jefferson to William Short, Dec. 14, 1789, *Jefferson Papers*, XVI, 27.

1. Edward Carrington (1749–1810), Matthew Wright (b. *ca.* 1757), and Foster Webb, Jr. (1756–1812). Young and Selden cannot be identified positively.

Carrington had served in the Revolution as a lieutenant colonel and he was elected to represent Cumberland County in the House of Delegates in 1784 and 1785. He was a delegate to the Continental Congress in 1785–1786, and in 1789 President Washington appointed him U.S. marshal of Virginia. He married JM's sister-in-law, Eliza Ambler Brent, in 1790. He later served as foreman of the jury in the trial of Aaron Burr in 1807. See Garland E. Hopkins, *Colonel Carrington of Cumberland* (Winchester, Va., 1942).

Wright was a Richmond merchant. See "Return of the Inhabitants," 1784, Richmond City Common Hall Records, 358, Va. State Lib.

Webb worked in the state treasury office at this time.

2. Thomas Lomax (1746–1811), of Caroline County, had served on the Council of State with JM during 1783.

3. Meriwether Smith (1730–1794), of Essex County, was serving as a member of the Council of State with JM. Smith attended no sessions after Dec. 22, 1783, and finally resigned more than a year later on Apr. 16, 1785, having won election to the Oct. 1785 session of the General Assembly.

4. William Nelson, Jr. (1754–1813), had been elected to the Council of State on Nov. 27, 1783; he did not take his seat until Mar. 6, 1784. See *JVHD*, Oct. 1783, 36, and *JVCS*, III, 331.

5. Beverley Randolph was president of the Council of State at this time. See *JVCS*, III, 305.

6. William Short was also a member of the Council of State.

Land Bounty Certificate

ADS, Bounty Warrants, Virginia State Library

[Richmond], March 8, 1784

I do certify that William Suddoth has servd three Years in the Virginia Continental line & was then discharged.[7]

JOHN MARSHALL
then Capt. 7th. V. Regt.

To Benjamin Harrison

ALS, Executive Communications, Virginia State Library

Sir   Richmond, April 1, 1784

The situation of my private affairs having rendered it impossible for me to continue longer a member of the Executive I have to request that your Excellency will receive my resignation & permit me to retire from the Council Board.[8]

I have only to add my wishes that the same happiness which has hitherto accompanied your Excellency's Administration may attend its close. I have the honor to be, with the most respectful esteem, your Excellency's most obedt.

JOHN MARSHALL

To Arthur Lee

Transcript, Lee Family Papers, Virginia Historical Society[9]

Dear Sir,   Richmond, April 17, 1784

A temporary absence from this place has prevented my answer-

7. JM placed additional information in Suddoth's file several months later. See Addendum to Land Bounty Certificate, Nov. 3, 1784. For information on land bounty warrants, see note at JM's certificate, Nov. 30, 1782.

8. JM later informed James Monroe that his resignation was caused by an opinion of the judges concerning "a Counsellors standing at the bar." While the opinion does not survive, it is most likely that the courts held that a member of the Council of State could not practice law, causing JM to resign his seat on the Council. See JM to Monroe, Apr. 17, 1784.

9. Addressed to Lee at Annapolis. This letter is copied in vol. 2, pp. 249–253, of a book of transcripts of Lee family letters, item no. Mss1L51a.

ing earlier your two last letters.[1] Of the tobacco you left in my hands I have sold eight Hoxheads—six lying in the warehouses of Byrd & Shockoe[2] & two at Petersburg. Their weights amounted to 8697 lbs. & I sold them at 35/ per Ct. the amount of sales £152.3.10 for which sum I now transmit you a bill.

If you recollect you had four notes issued from the Rocky ridge inspection two of which were heavy & the other two considerably under crop. Our papers have informed you of the capital misfortune sustained by the publick & by individuals in the burning of those houses & I doubt not you have apprehended the total loss of your Tobacco there as no resort for payment of notes more than twelve months old is to be had to the publick. Two of the Hoxheads I have certainly found the other two I am persuaded I have found likewise though of this I am not sure as they are in a very indifferent state—some of the staves with the marks on them being loose.

I could have sold the heavy tobacco very readily for a good price but if I part with it t'will be impossible to sell the light notes for anything you could think of receiving. I will endeavor for the coming week to sell the whole together, but if as I apprehend the case will be, that should be out of my power I will sell them seperately. Perhaps it may be even necessary to reprize them. Tis my hope & opinion that Tobacco is rising in its price but as your tobacco pays a monthly tax in consequence of its age, loses in its weight, & is entirely at your own risk, I thought it not safe to hazard the passing away of the present market.

These disadvantages obliged me too to be content with 35/ for your tobacco at a time when the current price for your commodoty (where the notes are new) was 36 shillings. I was the more determined on selling from an incident some time past—on the Saturday evening tobacco was as 36/ I held up yours for a better market—on the Monday it had fallen to 32/6. This was occasioned by a combination among the Merchants & such combinations may again take place.

As I interest myself much in the happiness of the western country a country to which my nearest connexions will certainly move[3] & which in all probability will be ultimately my place of residence too I feel real pleasure at the hint you drop that your attention like-

1. Not found.

2. JM had been in Fauquier County. See JM to Monroe, Apr. 17, 1784. Byrd and Shockoe were the two public tobacco warehouses in Henrico County.

3. JM's father had already moved. See JM to Monroe, Dec. 12, 1783.

wise may be turned to the New world. Surely Sir no people on earth possess a fairer prospect of political happiness than do the inhabitants of Kentucky. The constitution of the thirteen United States having been formed by persons whose political ideas grew entirely under a Monarchy it is not matter of surprize if they have in some instances introduced principles unnecessary & perhaps improper, in a Republic by guarding against the influence of the crown where no crown exists.

The constitution of a new state may be formed with more experience & less prejudice. Happy will they be if on their separation from Virginia they can draw from this & the neighboring States a few of the wise & virtuous. I receive the most flattering accounts of that Country from Mr. Daniel.[4] Their commerce & their society have improved beyond the hopes of the most sanguine. The uncertainty of, tog[e]ther with the disagreeable circumstances attending publick office have induced me to resign my seat in the Executive & I am now standing at the General Court bar. I shall probably remain in Richmond at any rate during the session of the next Assembly & while I stay here I shall with a great deal of pleasure execute any commands you may lay on me. I am dear Sir, with every sentiment of esteem, Your obedt Servt

J. MARSHALL

I transmit you likewise a bill for £100. The few additional shillings are discount on the notice.

To James Monroe

AL, Monroe Papers, New York Public Library[5]

Dear Sir   Richmond, April 17, 1784

Yours of the 12th. of March I did not till yesterday receive.[6]

I had made a small excursion into Fauquier to enquire into the probability of my being chosen by the people should I offer as a Candidate at the next election.[7]

I am no longer a member of the Executive, the opinion of the Judges with respect to a Counsellors standing at the bar determined

4. Probably Walker Daniel (d. 1784), attorney general for the Kentucky District Court, who was killed by the Indians later that summer. See *CVSP*, III, 605.

5. The conclusion and signature are missing from this two-page letter.

6. Not found.

7. At an election in Fauquier County on Apr. 26, JM was elected to the House of Delegates. Election Certificate, Apr. 26, 1784, Election Records, Virginia State Library.

me to retire from the Council board. Every person is now busied about the ensuing election. Your friend Wilson Nicholas is the first Representative of Albemarle. Grayson is chosen with Bullitt for Prince William.[8] Carrington will certainly come for Cumberland & either Wallace or Brent for Stafford.[9] Mann Page is I am told a candidate for the chair. Dick Lee I expect will come from Loudoun.[1] In almost every County except this changes have taken place. Here Wilkinson supports himself against every attack Mayo[2] & the town can make on him. I had forgot to tell you that Hawes with Taylor are chosen for Caroline.[3] I have been maneuvering amazingly to turn your warrants into cash.[4] If I succeed I shall think myself a first rate speculator. I can tell you that you will not lose more[5]

The ten shillings added to the £100 is the discount on the negotiation of the bill which I have insisted on your being allowd for.[6]

8. Wilson Cary Nicholas (1761–1820) was a member of the House of Delegates from 1784 to 1788, a delegate to the Virginia ratifying convention of 1788, U.S. senator from 1799 to 1804, a member of the House of Representatives for 1807 to 1809, and governor of Virginia from 1814 to 1817.

William Grayson was a member of the Continental Congress from 1784 to 1787, a delegate to the Virginia ratifying convention of 1788, and U.S. senator from 1789 to his death in 1790.

Alexander Scott Bullitt (1761–1816), son of Cuthbert Bullitt, later moved to Kentucky, where he helped frame the state's first constitution, served as the first Speaker of the Kentucky House of Representatives from 1792 to 1804, and then became the first lieutenant governor of that state.

9. Edward Carrington; Gustavus Brown Wallace (1751–1802), who had served as a captain and lieutenant colonel in the Third Virginia Regiment during the Revolution, and who had been taken prisoner in Charleston in 1780; and William Brent, Jr. (ca. 1750–1785), who had served as colonel of the First Virginia Regiment in 1777 and the Second Virginia Regiment from 1778 to 1781. Brent married JM's sister-in-law, Eliza Ambler, who later married Edward Carrington after Brent's death. See Marriage Bond, Mar. 26, 1785.

1. Mann Page, Jr. (1749–ca. 1810), of Spotsylvania County, had been a member of the county Committee of Safety in 1775 and the Virginia conventions of 1775–1776. He then served in the Continental Congress in 1776–1777 and was elected to most of the House of Delegates sessions from 1776 to 1787 and that of 1795–1796. See Madison Papers, IV, 137–138. If Page had been a candidate for Speaker of the House of Delegates, he evidently withdrew before the election. See JM to Monroe, May 15, 1784.

Richard Bland Lee (1761–1827) represented Loudoun County from 1784 to 1788 and was elected to three sessions of Congress from 1789 to 1795, after which he returned to the House of Delegates in 1796 and 1799.

2. Nathaniel Wilkinson represented Henrico County at every session of the House of Delegates from 1776 to 1794 and again in 1807. John Mayo, Jr., was elected from Henrico County to the 1785 session and several sessions in the 1790s.

3. Samuel Hawes, Jr., represented Caroline County from 1784 until 1787. After this session, John Taylor did not serve again until 1796.

4. See Account Book entry under Receipts, July [3], 1784.

5. The remainder of the letter is missing.

6. This appears as a marginal note on the first page, left margin.

Oaths of Office

DS, Virginia State Library[7]

[*May 4, 1784, Richmond.* As a delegate to the General Assembly, JM signs the oaths of office in the roll book of the House of Delegates.[8]]

To John Ambler

ALS, Collection of Mrs. Nancy G. Harris, Williamsburg, Va.

Dear Sir[9]   Richmond, May 7, 1784

Mr. Ambler[1] shewd me this morning your letter to him in which you request me to give you my opinion on your Fathers will with respect to Masons claim on a part of the slaves. I have been reading the will & really think it to intricate to determine on the question without mature consideration. When the court rises[2] I will pay more particular attention to it than it is now in my power to pay & will write you fully on the subject. At present I can only say that I am rather inclined to think his claim not a good one though it is a point on which I am by no means yet a while decided. It shall be the first object of my attention when the court rises. My best wishes wait on Mrs. Ambler.[3] I am dear Sir, your

J MARSHALL

7. See May 25, 1782.

8. JM had been elected a representative of Fauquier County on Apr. 26, 1784. Election Certificate, Election Records, Virginia State Library.

9. John Ambler (1762–1836) was the only surviving son of Edward Ambler (1733–1768), Jaquelin Ambler's brother. He was therefore the cousin of JM's wife. In 1782 he inherited Jamestown Island as well as several other estates in Virginia. After his first wife died in 1787, he married JM's sister, Lucy (1768–1795), in 1792. He represented James City County in the House of Delegates in 1793 and 1794. Ambler moved to Richmond in 1806 and served on the jury during the trial of Aaron Burr. He was made a major in the Nineteenth Regiment of Virginia Militia and commanded the troops sent to Norfolk after the attack on the *Chesapeake*. During the War of 1812 he attained the rank of colonel. Louise Pecquet DuBellet, *Some Prominent Virginia Families* (Lynchburg, Va., 1907), I, 35–42.

The letter is addressed to Ambler at The Cottage, Ambler's residence in Hanover County where JM and Polly had married on Jan. 3, 1783.

1. Probably Jaquelin Ambler.

2. The General Court, the Court of Appeals, and the High Court of Chancery met in that order each April and May in Richmond. The General Court and Court of Appeals had already risen, the latter adjourning on Monday, May 3. JM therefore is referring to the High Court of Chancery, which had convened on May 5. 10 Hening 455; Court of Appeals Order Book, I, 39, Virginia State Library.

3. Frances Armistead Ambler (d. 1787).

To James Monroe

Photostat, Monroe Papers, Library of Congress[4]

Dear Sir   Richmond, May 15, 1784

Receive my thanks for the enclosure containd in your last. Colo Grayson is not yet here. Mr. Nicholas is &, I presume will write to you by this post.[5] We made a house on wednesday. Nothing has yet been done but the common business of going through the different papers prepared for us & appointing the Committees.[6] Mr. Henry arrived yesterday & appears as usual to be chargd high with postponement of the collection of the taxes. If you wish to see a part of the first speech he will make on this subject versified turn to Churchill's prophecy of famine & read his description of the highlands of Scotland.[7] I wish you woud write me your sentiments pretty fully on this subject. I beleive the subject of citizenship will again be taken up. On this point I have ever been a moderate man & I beleive the moderate party will be much the strongest in the house.

We had no contest about the chair tho one was expected.[8] Give my compliments to Colo Mercer & let him know that there now lies in the Treasury for him £100 of which I will give immediate information to his Brother in Frederecksburg.[9] Major Crittenden[1] is again elected for Fayette County & has returnd from the western Country but I have not yet seen him. I shall be very inquisitive about your lands there. The bell rings. I am dear Sir, Your

                                                     J MARSHALL

If Doctor Lee is not in Annapolis will you take up my letters to him?[2]

4. Addressed to Monroe at Annapolis. The location of the original is unknown.

5. Probably William Grayson and Wilson Cary Nicholas.

6. Scheduled to convene on May 3, the House did not form a quorum until May 12. JM was appointed to the Committee on Propositions and Grievances and the Committee for Courts of Justice. *JVHD*, May 1784, 5.

7. Patrick Henry's concern over taxes was aroused by the widespread economic suffering left by the war, especially in the northern counties. For an interesting account of his speech against the tax law, see George Morgan, *The True Patrick Henry* (Philadelphia, 1907), 314–315.

JM's reference to the "subject versified" is from Charles Churchill, *The Prophecy of Famine* (London, 1763), where he writes "The Scots are poor, cries surly English pride; / True is the charge, nor by themselves denied."

8. John Tyler of Charles City County was chosen Speaker of the House of Delegates on May 12.

9. Probably John Francis Mercer and James Mercer (1736–1793), who was then a General Court judge residing in Fredericksburg.

1. John Crittenden.

2. Arthur Lee, who was a medical doctor by training. Letters not found.

To Charles Simms

ALS, Simms Papers, Library of Congress

Dear Sir[3]   Richmond, June 16, 1784

I received your two favors the one on the subject of the petition & the other enclosing a bond.[4] Mr. Henderson[5] promisd to write you immediately to let you know that by a standing order of the house no petition concerning private property could be received till it had been publishd in the County & in the Gazette. If this is done by the next session I flatter myself we may be able to carry it through the house. I see no prospect of amending the mode of distributing justice in this Commonwealth. The circuit Court system meets with too much opposition from selfish individuals to be adopted. Those Magistrates who are tenacious of authority will not assent to any thing which may diminish their ideal dignity & put into the hands of others a power which they will not exercise themselves. Such of the County Court lawyers too as are suspicious that they do not possess abilities or knowledge sufficient to enable them to stand before judges of law are opposd from motives of interest to any plan which may put the distribution of justice into the hands of judges. Every attempt to alter & amend the County Court establishment has been alike ineffectual.[6] Indeed there are many members who really appear to be determind against every Measure which may expedite & facilitate the business of recovering debts & compelling a strict compliance with contracts. These are sufficient to throw impediments in the way of any improvements on our judiciary system tho they are not so powerful as to shut up our courts altogether.

A bill is now under the consideration of the house which has employd its ablest members & will I beleive end in being printed for the consideration of the people. Tis to restrict vessels from foreign nations to certain ports. Norfolk & Alexandria are the two which are now in contemplation. Tis calculated to agrandize very much those two commercial Towns & shoud it be adopted will I trust produce many happy effects.[7]

3. Simms (1755–1819), a former Continental Line officer, lived in Fairfax County.
4. Not found.
5. Alexander Henderson (1738–1815) was a delegate of Fairfax County.
6. On June 2 JM had been added to a committee to prepare a new county court bill, but the group was discharged from further proceedings on the same day. *JVHD*, May 1784, 29, 32, 34.
7. In the bill that passed, foreign vessels were restricted to Norfolk, Alexandria,

We seem at length to have determined to hold but one session in the year. A bill for that purpose has gone through a committee of the whole house, it has not yet passd into a law but the greatest obstacles are I hope surmounted.[8]

As soon as the Assembly rises I shall go up to Fauquier.[9] My present plan is to pass my summers there & my winters here. I am uncertain whether or not 'twill hold in practise.

Present my compliments to your Lady. I am dear Sir with the greatest esteem, Your

J. MARSHALL

Pay Voucher Copy

AD, Virginia State Library[1]

Richmond, June 30, 1784

John Marshall

Travelling to & from the Assembly 270 miles[2] }		
at 2 lb Tobo. per mile 540—@ 20/ per Ct. }	£ 5	8
Ferriages 5/ To 58 days attendance @ 10/	29	5
	34	13

Birth of Thomas Marshall

Entry, Marshall Family Bible, Collection of Mrs. Kenneth R. Higgins, Richmond

[*July 24, 1784 (Richmond)*. A notation in JM's hand indicates his son Thomas[3] was born on this day.]

Bermuda Hundred, Tappahannock, and Yorktown. 11 Hening 402. JM voted against the final bill. *JVHD*, May 1784, 61.

8. "An act altering the time of the annual meeting of the general assembly. . . ." 11 Hening 387.

9. After the General Assembly session ended on June 30, JM stayed in Richmond until early August before leaving for Fauquier County. One reason for delaying his departure was no doubt the expected birth of his first child, who was born on July 24, 1784. See Account Book entries for late July and early August 1784.

1. In House of Delegates Attendance Book, 1783–1785. The actual pay voucher is missing, but JM penned this copy in the attendance book. See entry in Account Book, Receipts, July 1, 1784, where JM was 9 shillings short.

2. To and from Fauquier County.

3. Thomas Marshall attended Princeton University and graduated in 1803. He

Bayless v. Morton

Petition for Supersedeas

AD, University of Virginia Library

[*October 24, 1784, Richmond*. A petition to the General Court to stay execution of a judgment of the county court of Frederick County, in an action upon a bond signed by petitioner William Bayless and William Craig. Bayless states that the plaintiff in the court below, William Morton, waited until Craig absconded before suing Bayless, that no declaration was filed in the action, and that he is informed there is error in the proceedings below. JM certifies his opinion, as an attorney practicing in the General Court, that there is error in the judgment. The petition is endorsed with an order that a supersedeas[4] should issue upon the petitioner's posting bond and security for costs.]

Notice of Richmond Lawyers

Printed, *Virginia Gazette and Weekly Advertiser* (Richmond), November 6, 1784, 3

Richmond, October 25, 1784

WE BEG LEAVE TO INFORM those, who may wish to employ us in the business of the Court of Appeals, High Court of Chancery, or the General Court, that we have pledged ourselves to each other, not to undertake any cause after the 1st day of January next, without the fee and the tax of the writ in hand. We except, however, the cases, in which we choose to engage *gratis*. Those clients, whose punctuality we have no reason to doubt, will consider us, as com-

---

studied law and began practicing in Richmond, where he remained until failing health forced his retirement to Oak Hill. He attended the Virginia Constitutional Convention in 1829. In 1835 he was called to Philadelphia, where JM was dying. In Baltimore en route he took shelter from a storm under some scaffolding of the courthouse. A brick fell, striking his head, and he never regained consciousness. He died on June 29, one week before his father succumbed.

4. A "supersedeas" is a writ from an appellate court prohibiting the issuance of an execution upon a judgment rendered in a lower court until an appeal can be heard.

pelled to involve them in the same resolution, from the pain of making invidious distinctions.

EDMUND RANDOLPH,	JOHN TAYLOR,
THOMPSON MASON,	J. MARSHALL,
JERMAN BAKER,[5]	A. STUART,[7]
HENRY TAZEWELL,	CHARLES LEE.
WILLIAM DU VAL,[6]	

Addendum to Land Bounty Certificate

ADS, Bounty Warrants, Virginia State Library

[Richmond], November 3, 1784

The soldier I settled for was not a Corporal as well as I can recollect, nor can he be the same alluded to in the within certificate,[8] though his company shoud have been mentioned in the discharge to prove him a different person.

JOHN MARSHALL

5. Randolph (1753–1813) became attorney general of Virginia in 1776 and was a member of the Continental Congress from 1779 to 1782. He served as governor from 1786 to 1788, when he was elected to the House of Delegates, where he worked for the completion of the revisal of the laws of Virginia. Appointed attorney general in Washington's first cabinet, he became secretary of state in 1794 but resigned in 1795 amid charges that he had promoted pro-French projects during the Whiskey Rebellion.

Thomson Mason (1733–1785) practiced law and served in the House of Burgesses before the Revolution. He was elected one of the first judges of the General Court but apparently refused to serve and was elected to the 1779 General Assembly from Elizabeth City County. He later served as a delegate from Stafford County in 1783. Here the printer made a common error in misspelling Mason's first name.

Jerman Baker (d. 1799) was a prominent lawyer from Chesterfield County who, soon after serving in the House of Delegates in 1779, moved his practice to the General Court and Court of Appeals in Richmond.

6. William DuVal (1748–1842) had represented Louisa County in the House of Delegates in 1782.

7. Archibald Stuart (1757–1832) studied law with Thomas Jefferson after the Revolution and represented Botetourt or Augusta County in the House of Delegates during the 1780s. He served as attorney general in the early 1790s. In 1797 he was chosen to finish the term of the senator from his western district of the state, and he remained in the Virginia Senate, serving as Speaker in 1799, until his election to the General Court in 1800. He was a General Court judge until 1831.

8. JM added this note to the file of William Suddoth several months after he had written a certificate for Suddoth. See Land Bounty Certificate, Mar. 8, 1784.

Pay Voucher

AD, Virginia State Library[9]

Richmond, *ca.* November 27, 1784
The Commonwealth of Virginia to John Marshall Dr.
October session 1784

To travelling 135 miles[1]	£ 2	14	
To ferriages 2/6		2	6
To 40 days attendance	20		
	22	16	6

Legislative Bill

AD, House of Delegates Papers, Virginia State Library

Richmond, *ca.* December 1, 1784
Whereas[2] *it has been represented to this General Assembly that the*[3] act
entitled "an act to amend the Act entitled an act for adjusting &
settling the titles of claimers to unpatented lands under the present
& former government previous to the establishment of the Com-
monwealths land office," *has been so misconstrued that some County
Courts have given certificates of a right to a settlement & preemption to per-*

9. In Auditor's Item 292, Pay Vouchers. At the bottom of the voucher is written in
another hand, "1784 Novr. 27th, Entered J. Beckley, C. h. d." JM also entered the
voucher in House of Delegates Attendance Book, 1783–1785, Virginia State Library.
He did not enter the receipt in his Account Book.
    1. From Fauquier County.
    2. Again representing Fauquier County at the fall session of the General Assembly,
JM was appointed chairman of a committee to prepare this bill on Nov. 29. Edward
Carrington and John Breckinridge (1760–1806) were the other members of the committee. Breckinridge was representing Montgomery County at this session, but he had
been a delegate from Botetourt County from 1781 to 1783. He was elected to the U.S.
House of Representatives in 1792 but moved to Kentucky before taking his seat. In
Kentucky he became attorney general in 1795 and moved into the state House of Representatives in 1798, where he became Speaker in 1799. Elected a U.S. senator in 1801,
he remained in that office until 1805, when he accepted an invitation to become U.S.
attorney general. See Lowell H. Harrison, *John Breckinridge, Jeffersonian Republican*
(Louisville, Ky., 1969).
    JM introduced the bill, entirely in his hand, on Dec. 2. After discussion on Dec. 8,
it was tabled but on the next day it was reconsidered and accepted with amendments.
The bill passed the House on Dec. 10 and the Senate on Dec. 30. *JVHD*, Oct. 1784, 45,
51, 62, 63, 64, 96; 11 Hening 507–508.
    3. An amendment in a clerk's hand included with the AD indicates the italicized
portion was omitted and "by" inserted.

sons not having been in the service of this Country & have likewise granted similar certificates to persons not having made an actual settlement as is required by the law contrary to the true intent & meaning of the said act and to the great injury of many good Citizens of this Commonwealth; [4]

And whereas also it has been doubted whether any person claiming lands by virtue of a treasury warrant & caveating a person claiming the same lands under such certificate of settlement & preemption, or being caveated by him, be allowed to examine into & contest the legality of such certificate in the trial of the cause, even though he had no previous notice that such certificate was to be applied for. BE IT ENACTED that in all cases where any caveat has been or shall be enterd by or against any person claiming lands by virtue of a certificate granted by a County Court of a settlement & preemption right or of a preemption right only, such certificate shall not of itself be considered as conclusive proof of the title of the person holding the same, but the opposite party by or against whom such Caveat may have been entered shall be allowed to adduce any testimony proving that such Certificate was granted contrary to law or in any manner invalidating the said Certificate. And the Court where such Caveat may be tried, after hearing all the proofs of the parties against & in support of such certificates shall determine as the very right of the cause may appear to them.

PROVIDED always that any Magistrate or Officer belonging to the court granting such Certificate as aforesaid and who was present at the time of granting the same may be admitted as a witness for either party to prove on what testimony such Certificate was granted.

To James Monroe

Photostat, Monroe Papers, Library of Congress [5]

Dear Sir   Richmond, December 2, 1784

Yours of the 14th. of Novr. I have just received. I congratulate

---

4. A second amendment, also in a clerk's hand, indicates the italicized portion was replaced by "County Courts were empowered to grant Certificates of settlement and preemption rights in certain Cases."

5. Addressed to Monroe at Trenton, where the Continental Congress had convened. ALS not found.

you sincerely on your safe return to the Atlantic part of our world.[6]

I wish with you that our Assembly had never passed those resolutions respecting the British debts which have been so much the subject of reprehension throughout the States.[7] I wish it because it affords a pretext to the British to retain possession of the forts on the lakes but much more because I ever considered it as a measure tending to weaken the federal bands which in my conception are too weak already. We are about, though reluctantly to correct the error. Some resolutions have passed a Committee of the whole house & been received by the house on which a bill is to be brought in removing all impediments in the way of the treaty & directing the payment of debts by instalments. The resolutions were introduced by your Unkle.[8] As the bill at present stands there are to be seven annual payments, the first to commence in April 1786.

We have as yet done nothing finally. Not a bill of public importance, in which an individual was not particularly interested has passd. The exclusive privilege given to Rumsey & his assigns to build & navigate his new invented boats, is of as much perhaps

6. Letter not found. Monroe had spent the summer touring parts of the Northwest, going as far as Montreal. Ammon, *Monroe*, 45–48.

7. The House of Delegates had considered resolutions pertaining to the payment of British debts at their May 1784 session. On June 7 a committee was appointed to propose resolutions regarding the failure of the British to return slaves taken from the state. A report was given on June 14, and the House debated the resolutions on June 22 and 23. They agreed to instruct their delegates in Congress to ask that a remonstrance be sent to the British, complaining about the infraction of article 7 of the Treaty of Paris and requesting reparations for slaves not returned. Virginia would refuse to comply with article 4, providing for debt recovery, if reparations were not paid. As soon as reparations were paid, the General Assembly would repeal all laws inhibiting the recovery of British debts and provide for a systematic repayment. Finally, the House agreed that all laws concerning escheats and forfeitures from British subjects ought to be repealed, and a committee was appointed to prepare appropriate legislation. Amendments to the resolutions were suggested, perhaps by James Madison, which would have asked Congress's approval of a plan to withhold debts to British creditors up to the amount of reparations sought by Virginia claimants and which would have authorized the governor to begin collecting claims of Virginia property owners to be forwarded to Congress. Both amendments were defeated by substantial margins. See *JVHD*, May 1784, 41, 54, 72–75, 81; Emory Evans, "Private Indebtedness and the Revolution in Virginia, 1776 to 1796," *WMQ*, 3d Ser., XXVIII (1971), 349–374.

8. Monroe's uncle was Joseph Jones. JM had voted for a similar bill at the spring session but it was handily defeated. *JVHD*, May 1784, 41. The resolutions, listed in the journal as being introduced by Edward Carrington of Cumberland County, are printed *ibid.*, Oct. 1784, 48. A bill "to prevent the future operation of the laws concerning escheats and forfeitures from British subjects" was introduced on Dec. 3, debated on Dec. 21, and approved by the House of Delegates as "an act, respecting future confiscations." *Ibid.*, 78, 79. See also 11 Hening 446.

more consequence than any other bill we have passed.[9] We have rejected some which in my conception woud have been advantageous to this country. Among these I rank the bill for encouraging intermarriages with the Indians. Our prejudices however oppose themselves to our interests & operate too powerfully for them. The two subjects which now most engross the attention of the Legislature are the General Assessment & circuit court bills. I am apprehensive they will both be thrown out. When supported by all the Oratory & influence of Mr. Henry the former coud scarcely gain admission into the house & now, when he is about moving in sphere of less real importance & power his favorite measure must miscarry. I am sorry the members of Council were appointed before your letter recommending Colo. Mercer had reachd me.[1] Had I known that that Gentleman wished an appointment in the Executive I should certainly not have been unmindful of the debt I contracted with him on a former similar occasion. Mr. Jones supplies the vacancy made by the resignation of Mr. Short & Mr. Roane & Mr. Selden take the places of our old friend Smith & of Colo. Christian.[2] I exerted myself though ineffectually for Carrington.[3] He was excessively mortified at his disappointment & the more as he was within one vote of Selden & as that vote was lost by the carelessness of Colo. Jack Nicholas who walked out just as we were

9. James Rumsey (d. 1792) had invented a steam engine that he wanted to protect with a monopoly. The 1784 General Assembly granted him a 10-year monopoly to develop the machine in a steamboat. *JVHD*, Oct. 1784, 23, 30; 11 Hening 502; James Madison to Thomas Jefferson, Jan. 9, 1785, *Jefferson Papers*, VII, 592–593. See also *JVHD*, May 1784, 84, for a detailed description of the planned boat.

1. John Francis Mercer was at this time a member of the Continental Congress from Virginia. He later moved to Maryland and attended the Constitutional Convention in 1787. He was a member of the House of Representatives from 1792 to 1794 and governor of Maryland from 1801 to 1803.

2. Joseph Jones, William Short, Spencer Roane (1762–1822), Miles Selden, Jr. (d. 1811), Meriwether Smith, and William Christian (*ca.* 1743–1786).

Roane served on the Council of State until 1786. He was elected a judge of the General Court in 1789 and was moved up to the Court of Appeals in 1794, where he remained until his death.

Selden had served three terms in the Virginia Senate before he was elected to the Council of State. After leaving the Council in 1788, he represented Henrico County in the House of Delegates at various sessions until 1800 and ended his career back in the Senate from 1806 to 1810.

Christian had studied law with Patrick Henry and then represented Fincastle County in the House of Burgesses from 1773 to 1775. He was a member of the Committee of Safety in 1775 and served as a lieutenant colonel in the First Virginia Regiment of the Continental Line in 1776. Elected to the Council of State in 1783, he moved to Kentucky in 1785.

3. Probably Edward Carrington.

about to ballot the last time & did not return till it was too late to admit his ticket.[4] I endeavored too to promote the interests of your friend Wilson Nicholas who is just about to form a matrimonial connexion with Miss Smith of Baltimore,[5] but he was *distanced*.

I shewd my Father that part of your letter, which respects the western Country. He says he will render you every service of the kind you mention which is within his power with a great deal of pleasure. He says tho that Mr. Humphry Marshall a Cousin & Brother of mine[6] is better acquainted with the lands & would be better enabled to [*work*] for your advantage than he woud. If however you wish rather to depend on my Father I presume he may avail himself of the knowledge of his son in law.

I do not know what to say to your scheme of selling out. If you can execute it you will have made a very capital sum, if you can retain your lands you will be poor during life unless you remove to the western country but you will have securd for posterity an immense fortune. I shoud prefer the selling business & if you adopt it I think you have fixd on a very proper price.

Adieu. May you be very happy is the wish of your

J. MARSHALL

To Patrick Henry

ALS, Stanford University Libraries[7]

Sir   Richmond, January 3, 1785

The enclosed petition signed by the most respectable inhabitants of Prince William was committed to my charge with a request that I would deliver it to your Excellency.[8] I should not, Sir, take the

4. John Nicholas, Jr., of Buckingham County.

5. Wilson Cary Nicholas married Margaret Smith, daughter of John Smith, in 1784.

6. Humphrey Marshall (*ca.* 1756–1841) married JM's sister, Anna Maria (Mary) (*ca.* 1757–1827), in Sept. 1784, after moving to Kentucky from Isle of Wight County. Later he attended the Kentucky Constitutional Convention that met at Danville in 1787, where he opposed the separation of Kentucky from Virginia. He served in the Kentucky legislature after statehood and was a U.S. senator from 1795 to 1801. He wrote the first history of Kentucky, published in 1812.

7. Marked "To the Governor" in an unidentified hand.

8. Petitions to the governor were usually requests for mercy on a convicted felon. The governor might either commute a sentence to hard labor for years or pardon the felon and release him from custody. Coming at this time, just after the meetings of the General Court and Court of Appeals, it is most probable the petition was on behalf of one of the criminals mentioned in *JVCS*, III, 410–422. The petition JM enclosed has not been found.

liberty to add any thing to what is said by the petitioners had they not mistated one fact to the injury of the unfortunate young Man for whom they pray your merciful interposition. He did not, Sir, ask for the gun, 'twas called for by another, & rather forced upon the prisoner at a time when his mind seems to have been in a state of listless torpor—rather fitted to be moved by the impulse of others than to act from any formed design of his own. I have the honor to be Sir, with the highest respect, Your Excellency's Obedt. Sert.

JOHN MARSHALL

Pay Voucher

AD, Virginia State Library[9]

Richmond, *ca.* January 6, 1785

The Commonwealth of Virginia to John Marshall Dr.

To forty one days additional attendance }			
On the Genl. Assembly }	£ 20	10	
to travelling 135 miles[1]	2	14	
To ferriages 2/6		2	6
	£23	6	6

To George Muter

Printed, "Reminiscences of Kentucky and Her Early Patriots," *Tyler's Quarterly Historical and Genealogical Magazine*, I (1919–1920), 28

Dear Sir:[2]   Richmond, January 7, 1785

Let me thank you for the full account you have given me of the situation of affairs in the western country. I begin to think that the time for a separation is fast approaching, and has perhaps actually arrived. All I am solicitous about is, that the business be done with wisdom and temperance. If honor and public faith should be distinguished features in the character of the new State, she will soon

9. In Auditor's Item 292, Pay Vouchers. At the bottom of the voucher is written in another hand, "1785 January 6th, Entered, J. Beckley C. h. d." JM also copied the voucher in House of Delegates Attendance Book, 1783–1785, Virginia State Library. He did not enter the receipt in his Account Book.
    1. Return to Fauquier County.
    2. Muter (b. *ca.* 1730) was an attorney formerly in practice in Richmond.

attract very many of the wise and virtuous from her sister States, and Kentucky may be the seat of happiness as well as wealth. It is impossible that we can, at this distance, legislate wisely for you, and it is proper that you should legislate for yourselves. I presume you heard that Mr. Innes was chosen attorney general for your district court.[3] We had you nominated as judge in his place, and I am persuaded you would have been appointed in preference to any other person who was in nomination, had not Cyrus Griffin been put on the list. Your friends withdrew you. There is some doubt whether that gentleman will serve or not. If he should decline it, you may depend on my applying for you to the executive, and using my best endeavors to procure the appointment for you.[4] The salary is £300 per annum.

We have passed two bills this session of the utmost consequence, both to you and us. They are, to open the communication between the James and Potomac rivers with the western waters.[5] Should this succeed, and should Mr. Rumsey's scheme for making boats to work against the stream answer the expectation of our sanguine gentlemen, the communication between us will be easy, and we

3. Harry Innes (1752–1826), chief justice for the western district of Kentucky, was elected attorney general for that region on Nov. 17, 1784. *JVHD*, Oct. 1784, 26, 27. He had been appointed a judge of the Kentucky District Court on Oct. 30, 1782. *JVCS*, III, 164–165.

4. Upon Innes's resignation, the General Assembly elected Griffin (1748–1810), president of the federal court of appeals in cases of capture, to serve as chief justice for the western district on Jan. 5, 1785. *JVHD*, Oct. 1784, 107. Griffin declined the appointment, and George Muter was named to the position on June 2, 1785. *JVCS*, III, 449.

5. "An act for clearing and improving the navigation of James River," 11 Hening 450–462, and "An act for opening and extending the navigation of Potowmack river," 11 Hening 510–525. George Washington was the strongest supporter of these projects, especially the Potomac River Company. After a trip up the Potomac in Sept. 1784, he became convinced a system of canals could open navigation between the Ohio River and the Potomac. He recommended such a proposal to Gov. Benjamin Harrison upon his return in October and began lobbying for cooperation from Maryland. He appeared before the General Assembly in Nov. 1784 to encourage passage of an act creating a private company to develop the canals. At the same time plans were being made to develop navigation between the James River at Richmond and the Great Kanawha River in West Virginia, which emptied into the Ohio. JM was especially interested in the James River plan, although he supported both. The object in all of this, of course, was a substitute system of commerce that would replace the Mississippi River and help develop Virginia ports. It was no accident that James Rumsey's steamboat monopoly was granted by the General Assembly at the same session. The best recent summary of these commercial companies is in Kent Druyvesteyn, "With Great Vision: The James River and Kanawha Canal: A Pictorial Essay," *Virginia Cavalcade*, XXII (Oct. 1972), 22-47, but see also Wayland Fuller Dunaway, *History of the James River and Kanawha Company* (New York, 1922), 9–28, and James Thomas Flexner, *George Washington and the New Nation (1783–1793)* (Boston, 1969), 73–82.

shall have but little occasion to contest the navigation of the Mississippi.[6] My father sets out early in the spring.[7] Will you present my compliments to my acquaintances in your country, and believe me to be, dear colonel, with esteem and affection, yours,

J. MARSHALL.

Deed

Record Book, Office of the Clerk of the Law and Equity Court, Richmond[8]

Richmond, March 15, 1785

THIS INDENTURE made the fifteenth day of March in the Year of our Lord one thousand seven hundred & eighty five BETWEEN Jaquelin Ambler of the City of Richmond of the one part and John Marshall of the said City of the other part WITNESSETH that the said Jaquelin Ambler for and in consideration of the sum of ten pounds current money[9] to him in hand paid by the said John Marshall the receipt whereof the said Jaquelin Ambler DOTH hereby acknowledge; he the said Jaquelin Ambler HATH granted, bargained and sold, aliened and confirmed and by these presents DOTH grant, bargain and sell, alien and confirm unto the said John Marshall his Heirs and Assigns forever one half acre Lot in the said City of Richmond on Shockoe Hill known in the plan of the said City by the number 480 (four hundred and eighty)[1] and also all Lands, woods, trees, commons, common of pasture, profits, commodities, advantages, heheditaments,[2] ways, waters and Appurtenances whatsoever to the said Lot above mentioned belonging or——any wise appertaining, and also the reversion and remainder and Remainders rents and Services of the said premises and of every part thereof and all the estate, right, title, interest, claims and demands whatsoever of him the said Jaquelin Ambler of in and to the said Lot and premises and every part thereof. To HAVE AND TO HOLD

6. See JM to James Monroe, Dec. 2, 1784, n. 5.

7. Col. Thomas Marshall had returned from Kentucky for his family in 1783 and departed with them in 1785. Beveridge, *Marshall*, I, 170n; John A. M'Clung, *Sketches of Western Adventure* (Philadelphia, 1832), 195–196.

8. This warranty deed is entered on p. 29 and is marked "Ambler to Marshall" in margin.

9. This token sum would indicate the property was a gift.

1. Part of the city block now occupied by the Federal Building, 400 N. 8th Street, Richmond.

2. Should be "hereditaments."

the said Lot and all and singular the premises above mentioned and every part and parcel thereof with the Appurtenances unto the said John Marshall his Heirs and Assigns forever. And the said Jaquelin Ambler for him and his Heirs the said Lot and Premises and every part thereof against him and his Heirs and against all and every other person and Persons whatsoever to the said John Marshall his Heirs and Assigns shall and will warrant and forever defend by these presents. IN WITNESS whereof the parties to these presents have hereunto set their hands & Seals the day and year above written.

J. AMBLER (LS)

City of Richmond.

At a Hustings Court held the 21st. day of March 1785. This Indenture was acknowledged by Jaquelin Ambler Esqr. one of the parties thereto & Ordered to be Recorded. Teste

ADAM CRAIG C.C.

Deed

Deed Book, Office of the Clerk of the Fauquier County Circuit Court, Warrenton, Va.

[Markham], March 16, 1785

THIS INDENTURE made the sixteenth day of March in the Year of our Lord one thousand seven hundred and eighty five BETWEEN Thomas Marshall of the Parish of Leeds in the County of Fauquier of the one part and John Marshall of the same Parish and County of the other part WITNESSETH that for and in Consideration of the sum of five shillings to him in hand paid by the said John Marshall at or before the signing and delivery of these presents the receipt whereof he doth hereby acknowledge and for and in consideration of the love and natural affection which he bears to his Son the said John Marshall hath given granted enfeoffed and confirmed and by these presents doth give grant enfeoff and confirm unto the said John Marshall all that tract or parcel of land[3] which he the said

3. This tract is the Oak Hill plantation, which JM's father had purchased for £912 10s. in Jan. 1773. JM had gone to Fauquier County to see off his father, mother, and

Thomas Marshall purchased from Thomas Turner Esq.[4] then of the County of King George now Westmoreland lying in the County of Fauquier at the north Cobler mountain and bounded as followeth BEGINNING at three red oaks corner trees to the lands surveyed for Capt. James Ball & for John Blowers and extending thence north three degrees east five hundred and forty poles crossing a branch of Goose Creek to a box oak and three white Oaks standing on an hill thence North eighty six degrees West three hundred and forty poles to a great white oak on the west side of a drain, thence south fifty one degrees west two hundred and sixty poles to two white oaks and a red oak on a point nigh the foot of the north Cobler then binding on the mountain South three degrees west three hundred and sixty poles thence south eighty six degrees East and binding on the land formerly of John Blowers now of Burr Harrison[5] five hundred and thirty six poles to the BEGINNING containing one thousand eight hundred and twenty four Acres except one thousand Acres sold by the said Thomas Marshall and conveyed to Thomas Massey of the County of Frederick by deed indented and recorded in the County Court of Fauquier TO HAVE AND TO HOLD the said above granted premises to the said John Marshall & his heirs forever to the only proper use and behoof of him the said John Marshall and his heirs forever. IN WITNESS whereof the said Thomas Marshall hath hereunto set his hand and affixed his Seal the day and year first above written.

Test   T MARSHALL (LS)
MARTIN PICKETT
JOSEPH BLACKWELL JUR.
THOMAS MADDUX
THOMAS CHILTON[6]

---

several brothers and sisters as they departed for Kentucky. See Account Book, Disbursements, Mar. 1785; Beveridge, *Marshall*, I, 55.

4. Turner (d. 1787) had served on the Committee of Safety of King George County from 1774 to 1776 and, after the change in the county boundary by the Oct. 1777 General Assembly, lived the rest of his life in Westmoreland County. 9 Hening 432.

5. Harrison (1738–1822), of Fauquier County, had served as a corporal in the Third Virginia Regiment.

6. Pickett's daughter Lucy later married JM's brother Charles; Blackwell (1750–1826) had served as a major with the Subsistence Department of the Virginia Line and obtained a large grant of Kentucky land for his service; Maddux (1755?–1811?) was a longtime Fauquier County resident, whose house was used for monthly court sessions for a while after 1789 while a new courthouse was under construction; Chilton was from another entrenched Fauquier County family and was probably a cousin of Joseph Blackwell, Jr.

At a Court Continued and held for Fauquier County the 26th day of April 1785. This Indenture was proved to be the act and deed of the said Thomas Marshall by the oaths of Martin Pickett Thomas Maddux and Thomas Chilton Witnesses thereto and ordered to be recorded.

Teste H BROOKE CC[7]

To Cuthbert Bullitt

Printed extract, Paul C. Richards Catalog No. 47, Item 156

[*March 16, 1785.* "In the suit brought by Col. Thomas Marshall & Martin Pickett against Katharine Rector, Exec. of John Rector[8] dec'd in the County Court of Fauquir in which I confessed Judgement as Attorney to Mrs. Rector, you have permission to file a declaration. . . ."[9]]

To an Unknown Person

ALS, John S. and Elizabeth Milligan Gulick Autograph Collection, Princeton University Library

Dear Sir[1]   [Warrenton], March 17, 1785

I receivd yours by Mr. Brooke.[2] I cannot inform you what papers I have respecting the suit you engaged me in unless I was in Richmond as I do not recollect them all. I had drawn the ejectment

7. Humphrey Brooke (1730–1802) was the veteran clerk of the court of Fauquier County.

8. Bullitt (*ca.* 1740–1791), a prominent Fauquier County attorney, had been a member of the Prince William County Committee of Safety, the provincial convention of 1776, and the House of Delegates in 1777. He later served in the Virginia ratifying convention and as a judge of the General Court.

Martin Pickett (*ca.* 1735–1804) later represented Fauquier County in the Virginia ratifying convention. He and JM's father had been cosigners of a bond to Burgess Ball (1749–1800), as sureties for John Rector (*ca.* 1713–1773). When the bond was placed in suit, the cosigners paid, but Rector refused to perform his promise to indemnify them against loss. Subsequent to his death this action was brought against his widow and executrix, Katharine (1714–*ca.* 1785). The amount in litigation was £600, covered by the bond dated Mar. 6, 1771. See declaration and bond, Fauquier County Court, Box 1783, Bundle-Sept., Office of the Clerk of the Fauquier County Circuit Court, Warrenton, Va.

9. JM's confession of judgment has not been found.

1. Address leaf missing.

2. Probably Humphrey Brooke.

some time past & meant to have brought it up with me but when I searched I found I had left it behind me. I will send it to the sheriff as soon as possible from Richmond. I am dear Sir, your obedt. Sert.

J MARSHALL

To Charles Simms

ALS, Simms Papers, Library of Congress

Dear Sir   Falmouth, March 20, 1785

I send you your interest warrant. I keep the Certificate because you do not want it & there would be some risk in sending it. Your bond amounted to a considerable sum higher than your former interest warrant woud discharge. I have engagd to pay it off this April & by doing so prevented the institution of a suit against you. The bond was put into a Lawyers hand. Colo. Grayson[3] promisd to leave either with you or my Unkle Keith[4] a considerable sum of money for me, will you write me whether he has done so or no? I am dear Sir, your

J MARSHALL

Marriage Bond

Copy, University of Chicago Library

[Richmond], March 26, 1785

Know all men by these presents that we William Brent[5] & John Marshell are held and firmly bound unto his Excellency Benjamin Harrison Esqr. Govenor of the Commonwealth of Virginia in the sum of fifty pounds; to be paid to the said Govener and his successors for the use of the said Commonwealth to which payment well & truly to be made we bind ourselves and each of us, our and each and every of hours Executors & administrators jointly & sev-

3. William Grayson. See Account Book, Receipts, June 1, 1785.
4. "Major" James Keith (1734–1824), of Alexandria, was the oldest brother of JM's mother.
5. Brent had served in the Second Virginia Regiment from Dec. 20, 1776, to Apr. 1782 and had been promoted to colonel in Jan. 1779. He was the son of William Brent (1733–1782) of Stafford County.

erally firmly by these presents, Sealed with our seals and dated this 26th. day of March 1785.

The Condition of the above obligation is such that whereas a License is desired for a marriage intended between Mr. William Brent & Miss Elizabeth Jaquelin[6] if therefore there be no Lawful cause to obstruct the said marriage then this obligation to be void otherwise to remain in full force and virtue.

Sealed and delivered   W Brent (LS)
in the presence of   J Marshall (LS)

Virginia Constitutional Society
Subscription Paper

Printed, *Virginia Gazette, or, the American Advertiser* (Richmond), April 23, 1785, 2

Williamsburg, April 13, 1785

A MEETING of the members who form the Constitutional Society[7] is intended to be held at Mr. Anderson's tavern,[8] in the City of Richmond, on Tuesday the 24th day of the next month.

JOHN BLAIR,[9] President.

It having been resolved at a late meeting of the Society, that the President make such notification of the above institution as he may think proper, he judges that he cannot do it better than by publish

6. Miss Ambler (1765–1847) was the sister of JM's wife. The couple were married on Mar. 31. Brent lived only three months after the wedding. See Eliza Ambler Brent to Mildred Smith, July 18, 1785, Ambler-Carrington Letters, Collection of Mrs. John L. Lewis, Williamsburg, Va., and entry in Account Book, Disbursements, June 23, 1785.

7. The Constitutional Society was organized in June 1784 when the declaration printed herein was signed by the members. Copies of the society's declaration and brief minutes of some of its meetings were found in the Library of Congress in 1937. Existence of the society had been first discovered in 1927 by J. G. de Roulhac Hamilton of the University of North Carolina. The society met at least three times after signing its declaration, on June 11, 15, and 29, 1784, but the minutes indicate JM was not present. Little is known about this society, but see Bess Furman, "Signed, Sealed—and Forgotten! The Story of a Premier Promoter of the Constitution," *Daughters of the American Revolution Magazine*, LXXI (1937), 1004–1009; J. G. de Roulhac Hamilton, "A Society for Preservation of Liberty, 1784," *AHR*, XXXII (1927), 550–552, 792–793. E. C. Branchi, trans., "Memoirs of Philip Mazzei," *WMQ*, 2d Ser., X (1930), 12, suggests one of the reasons the society was formed was to discuss matters scheduled to come before the Virginia General Assembly.

8. This tavern was a popular meeting place for such celebrations as Independence Day. It was burned in the fire of 1787. *Jefferson Papers*, X, 110; W. Asbury Christian, *Richmond: Her Past and Present* (Richmond, 1912), 30.

9. John Blair (1732–1800) was at this time a judge of the High Court of Chancery and later an associate justice of the Supreme Court of the United States.

ing the subscription paper, which is the basis of the same, together with such extracts from the subsequent proceedings as it may concern those desirous of becoming members and the public at large to be acquainted with, both which are hereto subjoined, viz.

We, the underwritten, having associated for the purpose of preserving and handing down to posterity those pure and sacred principles of liberty which have been derived to us from the happy event of the late glorious revolution, and being convinced that the surest mode to secure republican systems of government from lapsing into tyranny is, by giving free and frequent information to the mass of people, both of the nature of them, and of the measures which may be adopted by their several component parts, have determined, and do hereby most solemnly pledge ourselves to each other by every holy tie and obligation which freemen ought to hold inestimably dear, that every one in his respective station will keep a watchful eye over the great fundamental rights of the people.

That we will without reserve communicate our thoughts to each other and to the people on every subject which may either tend to amend our government, or to preserve it from the innovations of ambition and the designs of faction.

To accomplish this desirable object, we do agree to commit to paper our sentiments, in plain and intelligible language, on every subject which concerns the general weal, and transmit the same to the President of the said society, who is empowered to congregate the members thereof, either at Richmond or Williamsburg, whenever he may suppose that he has a sufficient quantity of materials collected for publication. It is further agreed, that it shall be a rule of the said society, that no publications shall be made till after mature deliberation in the convocation it shall have been so determined, by at least two-thirds of the present members.—John Blair, James Madison,[1] Robert Andrews,[2] James M'Clurg,[3] John Page,[4] James Innis,[5] Mann Page, James Madison, Jun.,[6] Patrick

1. The Rev. James Madison was president of the College of William and Mary.

2. Robert Andrews (d. 1805) was a professor of mathematics at the College of William and Mary and the son-in-law of John Blair.

3. James McClurg (1748–1823), formerly professor of medicine at the College of William and Mary and a member of the Council of State, also practiced medicine in Richmond.

4. John Page (1743–1808) was a Revolutionary leader and future U.S. representative from Virginia and governor.

5. James Innes (1754–1798) was a graduate of the College of William and Mary and a future attorney general of Virginia.

6. James Madison, Jr. (1751–1836), was the future president of the United States.

Henry, Thomas Lomax, Edmund Randolph, William Short, William Fleming,[7] John Breckenridge, Archibald Stuart, Joseph Jones, William Nelson, Jun., B. Randolph, J. Marshall, Richard H. Lee, William Lee,[8] Ludwell Lee,[9] William Grayson, Francis Corbin,[1] Philip Mazzei,[2] Wilson C. Nicholas, John Nicholas, John Taylor, J. Brown,[3] Richard B. Lee, Spencer Roane, Alexander White,[4] James Monroe, Arthur Lee.

At a meeting held on the 15th of June, 1784, *Resolved*, That the following declaration be added to the paper originally signed by the members: viz. The society being persuaded, that the liberty of a people is most secure, when the extent of their rights and the measures of government concerning them are known, do declare, that the purpose of this institution is to communicate by fit publications, such facts and sentiments as tend to unfold and explain the one or the other.

As the intention of this society is to be useful to the community, and not merely to shew a desire of being so, *Resolved*, That it is expected that each member should send to the President, every six months, an essay or problem on some political thesis of importance, which it is hoped will be confined to the subject thereof; and that any one failing in this duty, be informed by the Secretary, that two essays or problems will be expected from him during the next six months; and that any member, on a second delinquincy herein, shall not thereafter be considered as a member of this society.

Resolved, That candidates to become members of this society shall be nominated by a member at a meeting preceding his election or rejection.

7. William Fleming (1736–1824) was a judge of the General Court.
8. William Lee (1739–1795), former alderman and sheriff of the city of London, served as an American diplomat during the Revolution.
9. Ludwell Lee (1760–1836), son of Richard Henry Lee, was an attorney.
1. Francis Corbin (1759–1821), then a member of the House of Delegates from Middlesex County, had been educated at Cambridge and the Inner Temple.
2. Philip Mazzei (1730–1816), formerly Virginia's financial agent in Europe, was instrumental in establishing the Constitutional Society.
3. John Brown (1750–1810) was clerk of the General Court.
4. Alexander White (1739–1804), formerly at the Inner Temple and Gray's Inn, was a member of the House of Delegates from 1783 to 1789, and thereafter a member of the federal House of Representatives.

Eggleston v. Chiles

Declaration

Record Book Copy, District Court Records, Office of the Clerk of the Circuit Court, Fredericksburg, Va.

[*April 1785, Richmond.* A declaration in debt on bond to secure payment of £70, filed in the General Court by JM as attorney for the plaintiff and signed by JM.[5]]

McGeehee v. Carter

Declaration

Record Book Copy, District Court Records, Office of the Clerk of the Circuit Court, Fredericksburg, Va.

[*April 1785, Richmond.* A declaration in debt on bond to secure payment of £140, filed in the General Court by JM as attorney for the plaintiff and signed by JM.[6]]

Coleman v. Wyatt

Declaration

Record Book Copy, District Court Records, Office of the Clerk of the Circuit Court, Fredericksburg, Va.

[*October 1785, Richmond.* A declaration in indebitatus assumpsit on a promissory note, filed in the General Court by JM as attorney for the plaintiff and signed by JM.[7]]

5. The case was subsequently transferred to the newly established District Court in Fredericksburg, and, after trial, judgment was entered for the plaintiff on Oct. 1, 1789. District Court Records, 1789–1792, 30, Office of the Clerk of the Circuit Court, Fredericksburg, Va. See Account Book, Receipts, Mar. 25, 1785.

6. The case was subsequently transferred to the newly established District Court at Fredericksburg, where the defendant withdrew his plea and judgment was entered for the plaintiff on Oct. 2, 1789. District Court Records, 1789–1792, 33, Office of the Clerk of the Circuit Court, Fredericksburg, Va. See Account Book, Receipts, Dec. 11, 1784.

The ADS has not been seen by the editors, although the Charles Hamilton Sale Catalog No. 61, Sept. 14, 1972, 45, printed a description of the document indicating the case originated in Stafford County, probably on Nov. 8, 1783.

7. The defendant pleaded non assumpsit, and the case was subsequently transferred

Leitch v. Thomas

Declaration

Record Book Copy, District Court Records, Office of the Clerk of the Circuit Court, Fredericksburg, Va.

[*October 1785, Richmond.* A declaration in debt on bond to secure payment of £50, filed in the General Court by JM as attorney for the plaintiff and signed by JM.[8]]

Pollard v. Gaines

Declaration

Record Book Copy, District Court Records, Office of the Clerk of the Circuit Court, Fredericksburg, Va.

[*October 1785, Richmond.* A declaration in debt on bond to secure payment of 1,286 pounds of crop tobacco, filed in the General Court by JM as attorney for the plaintiff and signed by JM.[9]]

Souther v. Thompson

Declaration

Record Book Copy, District Court Records, Office of the Clerk of the Circuit Court, Fredericksburg, Va.

[*October 1785, Richmond.* A declaration in debt on bond to secure payment of £42 2s., filed in the General Court by JM as attorney for the plaintiff and signed by JM.[1]]

---

to the newly established District Court at Fredericksburg. After jury trial and verdict, judgment was entered for the defendant and costs awarded against the plaintiff. District Court Records, 1789–1792, 474, Office of the Clerk of the Circuit Court, Fredericksburg, Va.

8. The case was subsequently transferred to the newly established District Court in Fredericksburg, and, after trial, judgment was entered for the plaintiff on Oct. 5, 1789. District Court Records, 1789–1792, 47–48, Office of the Clerk of the Circuit Court, Fredericksburg, Va. See Account Book, Receipts, Oct. 4, 1785.

9. The case was subsequently transferred to the newly established District Court at Fredericksburg, where the defendant withdrew his plea and judgment was entered for the plaintiff on Oct. 5, 1789. District Court Records, 1789–1792, 54–55, Office of the Clerk of the Circuit Court, Fredericksburg, Va. See Account Book, Receipts, Mar. 14, 1786.

1. The case was subsequently transferred to the newly established District Court at

Seekright ex dem Dade v. Saunders

Declaration

Copy, Land Causes, 1789–1793, Office of the Clerk of the Prince William County Circuit Court, Manassas, Va.

[*ca. October 1785, Richmond*. A declaration in ejectment for 500 acres of land in Fairfax County, filed in the General Court by JM as attorney for plaintiffs Townshend Dade, William G. Stuart, John Fitzhugh, George Fitzhugh, William Fitzhugh, Thomas Fitzhugh, Nicholas Fitzhugh, and Sarah Fitzhugh, against defendant Lewis Saunders, and signed by JM as attorney for the plaintiffs.[2]]

Receipt

ADS, Dabney Family Papers, Virginia Historical Society

[Richmond], December 21, 1785

Recd. from Mr. Samuel Dabny forty eight shillings for a suit instituted by him in the Genl. Court against John Hawkins.

J. MARSHALL

N.B. Paid Capt. Marshall for Saml. Dabney after giveing this receipt. 6/.[3]

CHA. DABNEY

Fredericksburg, and, after trial, judgment was entered for the plaintiff on Oct. 5, 1789. District Court Records, 1789–1792, 52–53, Office of the Clerk of the Circuit Court, Fredericksburg, Va. See Account Book, Receipts, Apr. 14, 1786.

2. Charles Lee entered a not guilty plea, and the General Court ordered a survey at the following Apr. 1786 term. The cause was continued until 1789, when it was transferred to the District Court at Dumfries. Afterwards the declaration was amended, objections were overruled, and exceptions were made. The trial was held on Oct. 14 and 15, 1791. Judgment was finally entered for the plaintiffs on May 12, 1792. It is not known who took the case after it was transferred in 1789. Land Causes, 1789–1793, 361–421, Office of the Clerk of the Prince William County Circuit Court, Manassas, Va.

3. This is item no. Mss1D1124631 in the Virginia Historical Society collections. See Account Book, Receipts, Dec. 20, 1785, "From Dabney v. Hawkins covt.," and Receipts, Nov. 9, 1788.

Seekright ex dem Lloyd v. Osborne

Answer

DS, University of Virginia Library

[*January 10, 1786, Richmond.* A declaration in ejectment brought in the General Court of Virginia for a 400-acre plantation in Hardy County,[4] claimed by Ephraim Lloyd and in the possession of Zara Osborne. JM answers "not guilty" on behalf of the defendant.[5] Endorsements on the declaration indicate that the matter continued in litigation until Apr. 1791, when additional costs were assessed in the District Court at Winchester.[6]]

Seekright ex dem Lloyd v. Smith

Answer

DS, University of Virginia Library

[*January 10, 1786, Richmond.* A declaration in ejectment filed against John Smith, similar in all other respects to the one against Zara Osborne, described immediately above.]

Seekright ex dem Lloyd v. Lambert

Answer

DS, University of Virginia Library

[*January 11, 1786, Richmond.* A declaration in ejectment filed against Barnet Lambert, similar in all other respects to the two described immediately above.]

4. Hardy County is now in West Virginia.
5. Edmund Randolph was attorney for the plaintiff.
6. The case came before the General Court at its Apr. 1786 term and was continued until after the reorganization of that court in 1788, when pending cases were transferred to district courts. Hardy County cases were assigned to the District Court that met at Winchester. See 12 Hening 730–763, and Cullen, "St. George Tucker," 100–103, 113–117, 272. Also see Account Book, Receipts, Oct. 3, 1786.

Acknowledgment

ADS, Morris Papers, University of Virginia Library[7]

[*January 24, 1786, Richmond.* Two bills sworn to by Zena Tate, before JM as a magistrate of the city of Richmond,[8] which contain lists of materials required for construction of a building for Capt. Overton,[9] with certificates of Dabney Minor[1] concerning the number of running board feet involved.]

Douglass's Executor v. Bruin

Declaration

ADS, University of Virginia Library

[*March 30, 1786, Winchester, Va.* A declaration in debt on a writing obligatory in the penal amount of £594 19s. 6d., payable upon demand, with the pleading drawn by JM as attorney for the plaintiff, Hugh Douglass, executor of the estate of William Douglass, deceased, against Bryan Bruin.[2] Action was in the General Court, with venue in Frederick County. An endorsement indicates that the subsequent jury verdict was for the plaintiff in the amount of £156 19s. 9d., with interest.[3] The verdict was returned in Apr. 1790.]

7. Attestation on verso in JM's hand.

8. Tate had been keeper of public buildings in Richmond and was appointed city sergeant and constable in Sept. 1785. As recorder of the city of Richmond, JM was a magistrate empowered to take oaths. See discussion at Sept. 28, 1786, below.

9. It is impossible to distinguish whether this is John or Thomas Overton.

1. Minor (b. *ca.* 1750) was a building contractor.

2. The estate involved is probably that of Col. William Douglass (d. 1783), of Loudoun County. William Douglass, the son of Hugh Douglass, was born in Scotland. A Bryan Bruin resided in Frederick County in 1758 and was among those who cast their ballots for George Washington as a member of the House of Burgesses. See Account Book, Receipts, Sept. 29, 1785.

3. In actions upon penal bonds it was customary to demand the full amount of the bond in the declaration, although the amount of money lent was usually considerably less. In Virginia it was the practice that the jury would award the full amount of the bond in its verdict but provide that the defendant would be discharged from the judgment debt upon his payment of the actual amount due, with interest and costs of the action.

Receipt

ADS, Land Papers, Clark-Hite Papers, The Filson Club[4]

[*April 8, 1786 (Richmond)*. A receipt annexed to a note from Jonathan Clark[5] to a Mr. Chew, authorizing Chew to retain JM as counsel in the General Court and deliver the bond to him in the case of *Clark v. Free*; JM acknowledges delivery to him of the bond, as well as his institution of the action and collection of his fee.]

Gilbert v. Taylor

Notes on Argument in the General Court

Extract from Casebook, Tucker-Coleman Papers, Swem Library, College of William and Mary

Richmond, April 1786

This was an appeal as I[6] understood from the Court of Henrico County. The plaintiff in the beginning of his Declaration demanded the penalty of his Bond; but assigned Breach that the Defendant had not paid the sum mentioned in the Condition—Judgement by Default. (Quaere.)—for principal & Interest.

Marshall, for the appellant said that this Error was not cured by any of the Statutes of Jeoffails.[7]

Randolph, for the Same—The Error is two fold; Judgt. is rendered for more than the plt has assigned breach in; & in settling sterling money in Dollars, instead of current money.[8]

4. Notation on verso "50 / sent." See Account Book, Receipts, Apr. 13, 1786.

5. Clark (1750–1811) lived in Spotsylvania County until 1802, when he moved to Kentucky.

6. St. George Tucker (1752–1827) began practice before the General Court in Apr. 1786 and took extensive notes upon cases argued and decided in that and subsequent terms. See Cullen, "St. George Tucker," 69, 77–80.

7. In Nov. 1753 the English statutes concerning amendment and jeofailes were declared in force in Virginia; this colonial statute was later continued in force by an Oct. 1788 act of the General Assembly. 6 Hening 339; 12 Hening 749. The statutes of jeofaile, enumerated and discussed in Blackstone, *Commentaries*, III, 406, were designed to permit amendment of pleadings prior to judgment, thereby eliminating unnecessary appeals by writ of error.

8. Edmund Randolph's argument relied upon the impropriety of a default judgment being entered for an amount in excess of the amount of the bond. He also argued that it was error to give judgment in pounds sterling rather than current money. In the absence of any contrary provision in the bond, current money of the place of execution customarily should have been the amount awarded in judgment.

Nelson, Contra: insisted there was no distinction between Judgements by nil dicit & by Default: he contended that the Error is aided by the Statutes of Jeoffails—NB. They extend only to Judgements by Confession, nil dicit, or non sum informatus; or after verdict.[9]

I could not distinctly hear what was said on the Bench—Lyons & Carrington appeared to think that this Case was aided by the Statutes of Jeofails—Mercer and Fleming contra.[1] Tazewell said something of a Case in Lord Raymond, & of one in 2d. Burrow, & seemed to incline to support the Judgement below.[2] But a day or two after he said that he was satisfied the Error was not cured, as it would have been after a verdict.

Judgement reversed.

Smith v. Lowry

Declaration

Copy, District Court Order Book, Office of the Clerk of the Augusta County Circuit Court, Staunton, Va.

[*April 1786, Richmond.* A declaration in debt on a bond, filed in the General Court by JM as attorney for the plaintiff and signed by JM.[3]]

9. William Nelson represented the appellee. A judgment by nil dicit, or "says nothing," is one rendered where the defendant fails to plead or fails to plead again after his original plea is stricken. A judgment non sum informatus, "I am not informed," is one entered after appearance by the defendant's attorney, who has stated that he has not been informed of any answer to be made on behalf of the defendant. Nelson's argument on behalf of the plaintiff below was designed to protect the validity of the judgment, which otherwise would have been declared null and void because of the variance between the amount due and that actually awarded in judgment.

1. Peter Lyons (*ca.* 1725–1809) had been a judge of the General Court since 1779. Paul Carrington (1733–1818), a lawyer and judge under the royal government, had been a judge of the General Court since 1778. James Mercer had been appointed a judge of the General Court in 1780.

2. Henry Tazewell, the junior judge on the bench, having been appointed in 1785, probably referred to Morris v. Gelder, 1 Lord Raymond 317, 91 Eng. Rep. 1107 (K.B., 1699), in support of the liberal application of the statutes of jeofaile to uphold the judgment. Similarly the case of Nedriffe v. Hogan, 2 Burrow 1024, 97 Eng. Rep. 687 (K.B., 1760), referred to the practice of pleading the penal amount of a bond as a set-off, as a "clearly unjust" procedure. However, the case of Wray v. Lister, 2 Strange 1110, 93 Eng. Rep. 1064 (K.B., 1733), clearly held that in an action of debt upon a bond, where judgment was given for more than the amount due, the judgment was void and not amendable under the statutes of jeofaile.

In this case the General Court followed the strict English precedent concerning the statutes of jeofaile; however, the general practice in Virginia was to permit liberal amendment of pleadings. See Tucker, *Blackstone's Commentaries*, III, 407, n. 4.

3. The defendant defaulted in pleading after the case had been transferred to the

Hite v. Fairfax

EDITORIAL NOTE

John Marshall's appellate argument in the case of *Hite v. Fairfax* marked the commencement of his long professional concern with the legal defense of the proprietary interests in the Northern Neck of Virginia. As a native of the region, Marshall's personal knowledge of the land and its history was further supplemented by his father's connection with the case as a surveyor while *Hite v. Fairfax* was pending before the General Court of Virginia at the end of the colonial period. This familiarity with the prior litigation aided Marshall in his argument on behalf of those residents of Virginia who claimed title to their lands on the basis of grants made to them by Thomas, Sixth Lord Fairfax of Cameron (1693–1781), who in 1719 had succeeded to his mother's interests in the Northern Neck proprietary.

Hite v. Fairfax arose from the terms of an agreement entered into between the crown and Lord Fairfax in the course of determining a boundary dispute. An April 11, 1745, order of the Privy Council awarded Lord Fairfax the title to a large tract of disputed land on the southern boundary of the Northern Neck, including the acreage involved in the *Hite v. Fairfax* case. In conjunction with that award, and presumably as a condition for the determination favorable to him, Lord Fairfax promised that he would take title "subject to the Grants made of any parts thereof by his Majesty or any of his Royal Predecessors and . . . the said Lord Fairfax . . . [would] comply with his proposal" that "all the Grantees of Lands under the Crown within his boundaries . . . [should] quietly enjoy their Lands according to their respective Grants. . . ."[4]

An Alsatian from Strasbourg, Joist Hite (*ca.* 1685–1761) migrated to Virginia by way of Kingston, New York, and Philadelphia County, Pennsylvania. In 1731 he purchased the interests of John and Isaac Vanmeter in forty thousand acres, which were to be settled with thirty families within two years before a formal patent would issue from the Virginia royal government. Hite also succeeded in obtaining an additional order of council from the Virginia government, covering a hundred thousand acres to be settled in two years by a hundred families as a condition precedent to the issuance of a patent. Almost immediately caveats were filed by the agent of Lord Fairfax, preventing the issuance of any patents for these lands.[5] Consequently Hite and a number of his partners and fellow

---

newly established District Court at Staunton. On inquest, damages of £159 were awarded to the plaintiff. District Court Order Book, 1789–1793, 37–38, Office of the Clerk of the Augusta County Circuit Court, Staunton, Va. See Account Book, Receipts, May 19, 1785.

4. The Privy Council order is in Transcript of Hite v. Fairfax, 22–23, 250–298, Additional Manuscripts, 15317, British Museum, and portions are printed in Josiah L. Dickinson, *The Fairfax Proprietary* (Front Royal, Va., 1959), app., xix. On the litigation generally, see *ibid.*, 9–11; Stuart E. Brown, Jr., *Virginia Baron: The Story of Thomas 6th Lord Fairfax* (Berryville, Va., 1965), 74–78, 80–100; Fairfax Harrison, *The Proprietors of the Northern Neck* (Richmond, 1926), 128. See also John A. Treon, "*Martin v. Hunter's Lessee*: A Case History" (Ph.D. diss., University of Virginia, 1970), 18–20.

5. Transcript of Hite v. Fairfax, 12–13, Add. MSS, 15317, Brit. Museum; William J. Hinke and Charles E. Kemper, eds., "Moravian Diaries of Travel through Virginia," *VMHB*, XI (1903–1904), 119.

settlers had not obtained patents by the time the April 11, 1745, order of the Privy Council was issued.

Upon learning of Lord Fairfax's success in obtaining title to the disputed tract, Hite and his associates applied to the proprietor, requesting that he issue them proprietary grants confirming the titles they claimed to possess by virtue of the Virginia orders of council. This Lord Fairfax refused to do, basing his denial upon two grounds. First, he contended that his promise to the Privy Council pertained to "grants," or more properly "patents," issued by the Virginia governor and Council for lands in the hitherto disputed area and not to unpatented surveys filed in the Virginia colonial secretary's office. Second, Lord Fairfax objected to the irregularity of the plats as surveyed and filed in the secretary's office, noting that the patenting of lands in such a manner destroyed the value of the surrounding land by rendering it inaccessible and uninhabitable.[6]

Hite and his associates, after several attempts to persuade Lord Fairfax of the rectitude of their position, began the lengthy litigation of *Hite v. Fairfax* by filing their bill in chancery with the General Court of Virginia on October 17, 1749. Dated seven days earlier, the bill asserted that in common parlance orders of council entered concerning land matters were known as "grants" and that this terminology had been used in the orders of council themselves to refer to the Virginia royal government's promises to issue patents when settlements were made. As far as the irregularity of their surveys was concerned, the bill asserted that Hite and his associates offered to acquire such additional land as would satisfy Lord Fairfax's objections and to pay the usual fees and charges for the additional acreage. It concluded with a demand for an examination of Lord Fairfax under corporal oath concerning the facts of the dispute and a request that Lord Fairfax be ordered to issue a grant to Hite and his partners for the 140,000 acres in dispute and that he be made to account for rents, services, profits, and emoluments from the lands during the course of the wrongful detention from Hite.[7]

Difficulties in serving process, as well as the normal delays in colonial chancery procedure, resulted in slow progress in bringing the case of *Hite v. Fairfax* to a hearing by the General Court. Lord Fairfax's answer was executed on March 22, 1751, but it was not until April 11, 1760, that sworn answers were obtained from codefendants George Wright and William Ewing. From then until September 23, 1769, the parties were occupied in obtaining formal depositions from witnesses.[8]

On October 13, 1769, *Hite v. Fairfax* came on for a hearing before the General Court, which, after considering the various documents, the depositions and pleadings, and after hearing arguments by counsel, entered its decree in favor of Joist Hite's representatives, Hite having died in 1761. The court decreed that Hite had been entitled to all of the lands granted by the Virginia orders of council and actually surveyed before December 25, 1735, the date Lord Fairfax's caveat was filed, and for which gubernatorial patents had not been obtained prior to April 11, 1745, the date of the Privy Council order. In all cases where Lord Fairfax had not conveyed these lands subsequent to the commencement of the suit, he was ordered to do so. If he had conveyed the petitioners' lands to others, those parties

6. A good discussion of the events leading to Hite v. Fairfax is in Brown, *Virginia Baron*, 110–114.

7. Transcript of Hite v. Fairfax, 10–46, 47–91, Add. MSS, 15317, Brit. Museum; Dickinson, *Fairfax Proprietary*, app., ii–vii, vii–xxi; Brown, *Virginia Baron*, 114–117.

8. Transcript of Hite v. Fairfax, 68, 90–102, 114, Add. MSS, 15317, Brit. Museum.

were directed to transfer title to Hite's representatives or his grantees, or to show cause within six months why such conveyances should not be made. The General Court further ordered that seven commissioners, including John Marshall's father, be appointed to examine the surveys of the petitioners and to state who occupied the lands, what were the boundaries, and whether the titles were derived from Joist Hite or Lord Fairfax.[9]

When the commissioners' report was filed, the General Court, on October 13, 1771, proceeded to a final decree in the case, awarding to Hite's representatives and associates all of the forty thousand acres included in the tracts originally promised to John and Isaac Vanmeter by the Virginia Council. It also decreed that fifty-four thousand acres of the hundred-thousand-acre tract promised by the Council to Joist Hite had been settled and thus belonged to Hite's representatives or his assigns. From this decree both parties took their appeals to the Privy Council, but the outbreak of the American Revolution stayed further proceedings.

On August 29, 1780, the Hite representatives, citing the statutory transfer of authority from the Privy Council to the Court of Appeals of the Commonwealth of Virginia, moved in the Court of Appeals for additional time to obtain a transcript of the record of the case in the colonial General Court.[1] From that time until April 1786 *Hite v. Fairfax* remained on the dockets of the Court of Appeals and was continued from term to term, Lord Fairfax's executors having been substituted as parties defendant on October 29, 1782. It came up for argument on April 29, 1786, a Saturday, and presentations by counsel continued from Monday, May 1, until Friday, May 5. The decision of the court, affirming the General Court decree as to Lord Fairfax, was announced on Saturday, May 6. Although final in regard to the Fairfax interests, the decree permitted all other parties to submit their petitions for equitable relief from the decree at any term of the High Court of Chancery held within the following three months.[2]

Hite v. Fairfax was significant far beyond the narrow controversy between the proprietor and the settlers under Hite. As Professor John Treon has indicated, the case resulted in judicial recognition of the property interests of Lord Fairfax's heirs precisely at a time when the Virginia legislature was proceeding toward a sequestration of the proprietary lands and a renunciation of the Fairfax title as one vested in alien enemies.[3] In this way *Hite v. Fairfax* served as a spur to further claims predicated upon Lord Fairfax's grants and was the beginning, rather than the end, of litigation over titles in the Northern Neck. Because of his family con-

9. For the decree, see *ibid.*, 115–116; the commissioners' report is transcribed, *ibid.*, 116–217. An original copy signed by the commissioners and probably served upon one of Hite's heirs is in f. 103, Clark-Hite Papers, The Filson Club. See also Brown, *Virginia Baron*, 163, 166–167.

1. Court of Appeals Order Book, 1779–1789, 8–9, Virginia State Library; 10 Hening 89, 91 (1779).

2. Court of Appeals Order Book, 1779–1789, 14–15, 17–18, 23–24, 30, 35, 43, 70–80, Va. State Lib. Although no notes on the rehearing of this case are available, the decree of the Court of Appeals entered on Nov. 14, 1787, indicates that the matter in issue was Lord Fairfax's liability for rents and profits. This was reaffirmed with leave to the other parties to file objections to the account of rents and profits filed in the High Court of Chancery after May 6, 1786. See *ibid.*, 108, 110, 117–118. The May 6, 1786, decree of the Court of Appeals is printed in 4 Call 81–83.

3. Treon, "*Martin v. Hunter's Lessee*," 44.

nections, and later because of his personal investments in Northern Neck lands, John Marshall was to be closely involved in these various controversies for the rest of his life.

The minutes of the Court of Appeals do not specify the date of Marshall's argument, but since it is the last in the printed report of the case, we have assigned a May 5 date as most probable. Because of the loss of file papers in the Court of Appeals and of all the records of the High Court of Chancery, we are unable to provide any further documentation concerning Marshall's participation in this litigation.

Hite v. Fairfax

Argument in the Court of Appeals

Printed, Daniel Call, *Reports of Cases Argued and Decided in the Court of Appeals of Virginia*, IV (Richmond, 1833), 69–81

[Richmond, May 5, 1786]

Marshall, for such of the tenants as were citizens of Virginia.[4] From a bare perusal of the papers in the cause, I should never have apprehended that it would be necessary to defend the title of lord *Fairfax* to the Northern Neck. The long and quiet possession of himself and his predecessors; the acquiescence of the country; the several grants of the crown, together with the various acts of assembly recognizing, and, in the most explicit terms, admitting his right, seemed to have fixed it on a foundation, not only not to be shaken, but even not to be attempted to be shaken. I had conceived, that it was not more certain, that there was such a tract of country as the Northern Neck, than that lord *Fairfax* was the proprietor of it. And if his title be really unimpeachable, to what purpose are his predecessors criminated, and the patents, they obtained, attacked? What object is to be effected by it? Not, surely, the destruction of the grant; for gentlemen cannot suppose, that a grant made, by the crown, to the ancestor for services rendered, or even for affection, can be invalidated, in the hands of the heir, because those services and affection are forgotten; or because the thing granted has, from causes which must have been forseen, become more

4. The original bill named Lord Fairfax and 78 other individuals. Some of these settlers had obtained their grants directly from Lord Fairfax, while others had applied to him on the basis of claims that had been obtained from Joist Hite and then confirmed by Fairfax.

valuable, than when it was given. And, if it could not be invalidated in the hands of the heir, much less can it be in the hands of a purchaser. Lord *Fairfax* either was, or was not, entitled to the territory: If he was, then it matters not whether the gentlemen themselves, or any others, would, or would not, have made the grant, or may now think proper to denounce it as a wise, or impolitic, measure; for still the title must prevail: If he was not entitled, then why was the present bill filed; or what can the court decree upon it? For if he had no title, he could convey none, and the court would never have directed him to make the attempt. In short, if the title was not in him, it must have been in the crown; and, from that quarter, relief must have been sought. The very filing of the bill, therefore, was an admission of the title, and the appellants, by prosecuting it, still continue to admit it.

But, if it is not seriously to be denied, that lord *Fairfax* was rightful proprietor of the Northern Neck, with as little reason can it be contended, that the bounds of that territory were really more contracted, originally, than they are now admitted to be. It is impossible to accede to that reasoning, which says, that the expression in the grant, which confines it to the heads of the rivers, and the courses of the said rivers, as they are commonly called and known by the inhabitants and descriptions of those parts, (as the inhabitants did not then know where the heads actually were,) can restrain the grant to places known, by the inhabitants, not to be the heads of those rivers. Besides, the reference made to the knowledge of the inhabitants seems to be of the courses, rather than the heads of the rivers. The words "*&c.,*" bounded the grant absolutely by the heads of those rivers, wherever they might be, and where the rivers were known by their reputed courses. But it is sacrificing a great deal for certainty, to say, that where an extensive grant is made, the boundaries of which are not perfectly known, although they may easily be discovered, the grant shall be limited by an object known certainly not to be the boundary designed, and which bears no analogy to it. The middle part of a line can never be its termination. Whether lord *Fairfax's* grant extended, originally, beyond the forks of the rivers or not, will no more admit of an argument, than it ever could have admitted of a doubt. But whether it should be bounded by the north, or south fork of the Rappahanock, was a question involved in more uncertainty, and, about which, men might have had different opinions. It is, however, no longer a question; for it has been decided, and decided by that tribunal, which had the power of determining it.[5] That decision did not create, or extend lord *Fairfax's* right, but determined what the right originally was. The bounds of many patents are doubtful; the extent of many titles uncertain; but when a decision is once made on them, it removes the doubt, and ascertains what the original boundaries were. If this be a principle universally acknowledged, what can destroy its application to the case before the court? It is said that the dispute, between the crown and lord *Fairfax*, was accommodated on terms, not decided on principles: But an appeal to the decision itself will refute the argument, as may be seen in the answer of lord *Fairfax*, the report of the commissioners, and the sentence of the king and council.

The gentlemen, however, argue, as if the north was really the main branch of the Rappahanock, although the king and council decided otherwise, and adduce in support of their assertion, the report of the king's commissioners. But that report, the survey and map accompanying it; together with the report, the survey and map of the commissioners on the part of lord *Fairfax*, and perhaps other evidence, were all laid before the king and council; who, after solemn debate and mature deliberation, determined in favour of lord *Fairfax*. And can this court say, they determined against the weight of the testimony? Nay, more, if the point were now open for reconsideration, it cannot be said that a contrary judgment would be given. For if, on the one hand, the king's commissioners report that the northern branch of the Rappahanock is the largest, the longest, and drains more land; those of lord *Fairfax*, on the other, report, that the southern branch passes through a longer tract of country, (in support of which they urge the relative position of the blue ridge of mountains, and the course of the river), and contains, in its channel, more water, and is, of consequence, the main branch of the river. Such was the evidence; and, as those, to whom, all these facts were submitted, and who could have had no private motives for it, decided in favour of lord *Fairfax*, this court will not now impair the force of the decision, or say it was erroneous.

The judgment of the king and council, then, was no concession of the rights of individuals on the part of the crown; nor any exten-

5. On Apr. 11, 1745, the Privy Council issued an order in council establishing the boundaries of Lord Fairfax's lands in Virginia and fixing the tenure of those settled on lands under grants from the Virginia governor and Council. See entry under date July 25, 1745, *Journal of the Commissioners for Trade and Plantations from January 1741/2 to December 1749* (London, 1931), 176; Transcript of Hite v. Fairfax, 250–258, Additional Manuscripts, 15317, British Museum.

sion of the boundaries of the Northern Neck; but a fair and impartial determination of the boundaries of that territory, as described in the first grant of it.

Through this medium then, let the cause be viewed:

If, as seems to be certain, the grant to lord *Fairfax* and his predecessors, did comprehend the lands in question, have the appellants, independent of the promises made by lord *Fairfax* to the lord commissioners,[6] or to *Hite*, any equitable claim to the lands they contend for? They dilate upon their hardships as first settlers; their merits in promoting the population of the country; and their claims as purchasers without notice. Let each of these be examined.

Those who explore and settle new countries, are generally bold, hardy and adventurous men, whose minds as well as bodies, are fitted to encounter danger and fatigue; their object is the acquisition of property, and they generally succeed. None will say, that the complainants have failed; and, if their hardships and dangers have any weight in the cause, the defendants shared in them, and have equal claim to countenance; for they, too, with humbler views and less extensive prospects, "have explored, bled for, and settled a, 'til then, uncultivated desert."

With as little pretensions do the appellants claim the merit of having strengthened the frontier, and contributed to the general population of the country. There is no evidence of the fact. For who have they drawn from the other colonies and fixed in Virginia? Who was allured here by their persuasions; or, when here, protected by their efforts? The mere grant of principalities to individuals, without correspondent exertions on their part, do not render a country populous. The true reason for the rapid increase of our western frontier, seems to have been the ease with which lands were procured. The fame of their fertility and cheapness reached the northern colonies, and invited emigration. All the testimony in the cause supports this assertion; and there is no evidence that a single inhabitant was obtained, who would not have come if the orders of council in favour of *Hite* and his associates, had never been made. The claim to extraordinary favour on this score, therefore, is without foundation. But, were it otherwise, what right does that give them against lord *Fairfax*? For they do not pretend, that, at his request, they possessed themselves of his lands; or

6. The reference is to the 1745 proposal and consent by Lord Fairfax, by which he agreed to ratify grants made to Hite and his associates by the Virginia royal government.

that, in consequence of any contract with him, they parcelled out his territory. Their only pretension is a purchase from those who had no right to sell.

Neither are the appellants purchasers without notice. For there is no proof of the fact: And whether *Joist Hite* and his associates had or had not actual notice of the bounds of lord *Fairfax's* grant, when he received permits from the governour and council, to take up lands within the proprietary, is not material; for he ought to have enquired, and there were such circumstances attending his lordship's claim to the extent contended for by him, as will be deemed sufficient notice to a purchaser. To penetrate into the human mind, and determine with absolute certainty how far particular facts have actually come to the knowledge of a man, is sometimes beyond the reach of the court, but that which a prudent man might and ought to have known, the court will presume him to have known; and that which should have excited enquiry, and prompted him to have searched into the title, will be always deemed notice to a purchaser. By this rule let the question be tried.

Lord *Fairfax's* claim for the now acknowledged extent of his boundary, could not have been unknown to any body. For the report of the commissioners to the general court, in 1705,[7] was a public transaction, which could not have escaped general observation: and the report itself must have convinced every man, that it was extremely doubtful which branch of the Rappahanock bounded the north. To this, add the *caveats* by *Robert Carter*, which were matters of record, and had actually reached the ear of *Vanmeter*,[8] and probably *Hite*, before the date of either order of council;[9] to

7. The 1705 survey of the north and south branches of the Rappahannock, undertaken by Lord Fairfax's father in conjunction with the Virginia colonial government, was an attempt to determine whether the north branch or the south branch (the Rapidan) was the longer, and hence the main stream. Because the results were inconclusive, this survey had no significance for the determination of this case, but it did serve as evidence of public knowledge that title to the region was in dispute. See the answer of Lord Fairfax, Transcript of Hite v. Fairfax, 47, Add. MSS, 15317, Brit. Museum.

8. Robert Carter (1663–1732), also known as "King Carter," was agent for the Fairfax interests from 1702 to 1713 and from 1722 to 1732, and in this capacity in 1731 he filed a caveat against the issuance of patents to land in the Northern Neck by the Virginia governor. John and Isaac Vanmeter had obtained orders of council promising them patents to some of the land in dispute in this case, and subsequently assigned their interests to Joist Hite. William J. Hinke and Charles E. Kemper, eds., "Moravian Diaries of Travel through Virginia," *VMHB*, XI (1903–1904), 119.

9. This refers to the Virginia orders of council authorizing the issuance of patents to the Vanmeters and Hite upon their settlement of the lands in dispute within two years of the date of the orders. See Charles E. Kemper, ed., "Early Westward Movement in Virginia," *ibid.*, XIII (1905–1906), 133, 134, 354–356.

say nothing of the obligation to take notice of all matters of record, and the pendency of controversies in courts respecting titles. All these circumstances refute the idea of ignorance, and affect the appellants with knowledge of lord *Fairfax's* title.

But lord *Fairfax's* title to the Northern Neck, was a legal title; and he was in possession according to his title and boundaries: Therefore, no mistake, with respect to the boundaries, could give a purchaser a legal, or an equitable title: and, consequently, independent of the promise of lord *Fairfax* to the royal commissioners for plantation affairs, and that to *Hite* himself, the appellants have not even a shadow of equity.

Consider those promises then:

That to the royal commissioners, was to confirm the grantees under the crown, in the possession of the lands granted. Under which, the appellants say, their claims, growing out of the orders of council, are included: This, the appellees deny, and insist that no construction of the promise can reach the case: and therefore it becomes necessary to enquire what a *grant* is, and what the nature of the orders of council.

The word *grant*, as to subjects, according to *Co. Litt.* 172, *a.* "is in the common law a conveyance of a thing that lies in grant, and not in livery, which cannot pass without deed; as advowsons, services, rents, commons, reversions, and such like." And *Blackstone* defines those from the crown as matters of public record, as "no freehold may be given to the king, or derived from him, but by matter of record." 2 *Black. Com.* 346. Both these definitions require a seal; and prove that the term cannot be satisfied without one: whereas the orders of council were never under seal; but were mere permits to the applicants, to take up vacant lands, in which no body had a better right. The applicant, therefore, was to find the land, and government promised nothing but to grant it when found. The pretensions of the complainants, therefore, do not meet the definitions; which suppose a conveyance of the legal estate by instrument, under seal, so as to enable the grantee to prosecute or defend his rights upon the legal title, the last act having been done to complete it: whereas the appellants rest their claims upon agreement to make a *grant*, if certain conditions were performed: which, by no fair interpretation, can be denominated a *grant*, according to a just exposition of the term.[1]

1. JM's argument emphasized that, because a formal grant had not been made by the Virginia royal government, Lord Fairfax was under no obligation to convey lands

I admit, however, that if the crown and lord *Fairfax* intended by the convention in 1745, to include surveys, that the intention ought to prevail. But how does such intention appear? That reasoning which is founded on the idea that the decision of the king and council was a new grant to lord *Fairfax*, of a more extended territory, and therefore incapable of affecting the rights of individuals, cannot persuade for a moment: For it is a conclusion drawn from premises evidently untrue. The decision of the king and council is clearly no enlargement of the Northern Neck, but a determination how far the Northern Neck actually extended, as described in the original grant. The reservation, therefore, in the judgment of that tribunal, a reservation produced by the voluntary offer of lord *Fairfax*, cannot be considered as a royal grant; because the king had before granted the lands in question to his lordship's predecessors. Nor does the omission of the word *patent* or *seal* in the decision, afford any argument in favour of the complainants; because that is the judgment of a court, and not a grant from the crown; and it would have been, too, glaringly improper to have framed a judgment in the words of a grant. Of as little weight, is the argument drawn from the distinction between grants on which quit-rents are reserved, and those which contained no such reservation: for if it were true, (although the fact does not appear,) that there were some grants on which no quit-rents were reserved, it is impossible that the orders of council could have been alluded to; because they were not grants at all. Again, the words are, "and where, upon such grants, quit-rents have been reserved." Plainly referring the word *such* to those grants, from the terms of which some advantages, profits and emoluments arose to the crown. So that the grants on which quit-rents were, or were not reserved, were such as afforded some profits to the grantor. But there is no reservation of any kind, in the orders of council; and therefore that part of the agreement between lord *Fairfax* and the crown, rather disproves than proves an intention to comprehend orders of council. Not stronger is the observation of the opposite counsel,[2] drawn from the caution, as it

to the appellants according to their surveys. His promise in 1745 had only been to confirm *grants* previously made by the Virginia governor.

2. Edmund Randolph, as attorney general of Virginia, argued on behalf of Hite and his associates, as did John Taylor. Randolph's argument on this point is printed in 4 Call (Va.) 59. It should be noted that Randolph had previously acted on behalf of the Fairfax estate in the attempt to obtain legislative clarification of title to the Northern Neck lands. See Bryan Fairfax to Lord Fairfax, Mar. 20, 1782, Jan. 6, Oct. 21, Nov. 10, 1783, Feb. 21, 1785, Fairfax Family Correspondence, II, Add. MSS, 30301, Brit. Museum.

is said, used by the crown for securing grantees under the crown, extending not only to security against disturbance from lord *Fairfax*, but to his consent to all such acts as might be necessary to secure their quiet possession and enjoyment of the lands they had taken up. The true construction of all this seems to be, that lord *Fairfax* would not only permit the *patentees* quietly to enjoy, but that he would pass titles to them from himself, if it should be requested. For the titles under the crown being clearly defeated by the decision, that no right to the lands existed in the crown when the patents issued, it might, perhaps, be deemed necessary that lord *Fairfax* should engage not only that he would not disturb actual patentees, but would, if required, give them sufficient titles from himself: a precaution not unusual, as most deeds contain a covenant for quiet enjoyment, and further assurance. It is plain that the two provisos in this case, were intended for the same subject; because the words are *such* grant, and *said* lands: and, if orders of council were included, the patent from lord *Fairfax* would have been inapplicable.

But other circumstances shew, that orders of council were not intended: 1. The contest, between the king and lord *Fairfax*, was of immense value; and the government, here, seems to have interested itself a good deal in the decision: which was not made in haste, but drawn up advisedly. It is therefore extremely improbable, that cases like those of the complainants, would have been left unexpressed, had there been a design to include them. For, in all legal transactions, the same cases are more frequently repeated, than any one, intended to be comprehended, totally omitted. 2. The promise of lord *Fairfax* probably owes its existence to the recommendation, with which the address of the king's commissioners to the governour of Virginia, is closed; and that recommends patentees only. 3. The contrast, between the words used, by the crown, in the grant to lord *Culpeper*;[3] and those in the decision in favour of lord *Fairfax*. In the one, the crown articles for the confirmation of *contracts*: In the other, for the confirmation of *grants* only: because, in the one case, the interest was enlarged, and therefore any conditions might be inserted; but the other being only a legal decision, no condition could be inserted, which lord *Fairfax* did not, expressly, assent to. It is extremely probable, from these circumstances, that had the intention, in the one, as well as in the other case, been to save contracts, it would have been so declared in

3. John, First Lord Culpeper (d. 1660).

terms, as well in the one case, as in the other. 4. The act of assembly in 1748, shews that the legislature designed to enact into a law the promise of lord *Fairfax* to the lords commissioners of plantation affairs;[4] and manifests their idea of the extent of that promise. But the act must, necessarily, have met with the assent of the governour and council, or it could not have been a law; and, if in their conception, it had narrowed rights originating with themselves, they never would have consented to the passage of it. That act, then, expresses the idea which the governour and council had of their own orders of council, and shews that the government, here, did not mean to perplex the compromise.

The insinuation in the bill respecting the means by which that act was obtained, is both refuted by the answer of lord *Fairfax* and the deposition of *G. W. Fairfax*;[5] and is, upon the face of it, improbable. It is strange too, that the complainants should have supposed their case to have been unknown and unconsidered by their own representatives, and by that power which gave it being, while it was particularly attended to, and preserved by the king and council.

If it be reasonable, to suppose, that the king did not consider the promise of lord *Fairfax* as comprehending cases similar to that of the complainants, it is almost certain, that lord *Fairfax* himself, annexed no such idea, to the words he used on that occasion, as his answer denies it, and sets forth his own conception of it, without being disproved by any evidence in the cause.

Thus, then, as it appears, that the words, in the provision for the *grantees* under the crown, can, by no construction, be so extended, as to embrace the case of the complainants; that the king in council and the lords commissioners could not have supposed it to have been comprehended; and that lord *Fairfax* himself did not design it should, the court will not extend it beyond the plain meaning of the words, and the intention of the parties.

On the promise of lord *Fairfax*, then, to the complainants themselves, unconnected with their former supposed title; on his naked promise uninfluenced by any preexisting circumstances, must they

4. The text of the statute is in 6 Hening 198–199.

5. George William Fairfax (*ca.* 1725–1787), Lord Fairfax's first cousin and a defendant in this case, detailed in his deposition the proprietary land office procedures and asserted that Lord Fairfax's refusal to issue grants upon the basis of the Hite surveys was based upon their irregularity and tendency to engross the existing waterways and springs. Transcript of Hite v. Fairfax, 103–105, 106, Add. MSS, 15317, Brit. Museum.

rely for success. As this is the most important point in the cause, some time will be necessary to investigate it.

The bill states the promise according to the plaintiffs' own view of it; but that statement is denied by lord *Fairfax's* answer, which shews, very clearly, that surveys, made after the *caveat*, were not comprehended. The question then is, whether, among the surveys made before the *caveat*, any discrimination was intended? If the answer of lord *Fairfax* is to have the same weight as those of other people, the question is decided. The promise stated, in it, is universal and unqualified, as to patents; but, with respect to unpatented lands, it extends, only, to such surveys as were made in an honest and equitable manner. *Hite* must have so understood it, at the time of the promise, or he would have required further explanation: and lord *Fairfax*, not only, uniformly, declared it, but practised upon that idea, giving patents to fair locators, after having the irregularity of the surveys corrected; and with this they were satisfied.

There is no testimony to invalidate the answer of lord *Fairfax*: on the contrary, it is confirmed by those of *Peter Scholl*[6] and others, to whom he gave patents, after their lands had been re-surveyed in a regular manner. The deposition of *Peter Wolfe*[7] does not contradict it. He seems only to state detached parts of the conversation; but says nothing of any expression from lord *Fairfax*, relative to the irregularity of the surveys; nor does he say, that there was no such expression. Then, as there is other evidence of lord *Fairfax's* general declarations, and of his particular declarations to the complainants themselves, the silence of *Peter Wolfe*, on this subject, proves nothing. Suppose he did not mention it to the settlers in general, they are satisfied: the complainants knew, from lord *Fairfax* himself, that the lands must be surveyed regularly:[8] and this conversation seems to have been designed for the contentment of the people at large; who, in event, appear to have been pleased with the conduct of his lordship. What, indeed, were his motives, what the object he

6. In 1744 Peter Scholl, also known as Peter Schull, lived in present-day Rockingham County and served as captain of the militia. He was a grantee of 420 acres from Benjamin Burdin located on Smith's Creek in Augusta County. Answer of Lord Fairfax, *ibid.*, 67; Josiah L. Dickinson, *The Fairfax Proprietary* (Front Royal, Va., 1959), app., xxxi.

7. The deposition of Wolfe (*ca.* 1700–1779) is printed in Dickinson, *Fairfax Proprietary*, app., xxxi.

8. JM's personal knowledge of the Fairfax survey requirements dated to Nov. 1770, when he had served as a chain carrier in Fauquier County. Northern Neck Loose Surveys, Fauquier County A–Z, Virginia State Library.

designed to effect, in all these conversations? We cannot doubt, but it was to increase the number of inhabitants in that country, and to multiply his quit-rents. These seem to have been the points to which all his exertions tended; and his whole conduct appears to have been calculated to effect them. These were clearly promoted by giving patents to the settlers for lands in such shapes as not to destroy the value of the adjoining lands: but these were, as certainly, obstructed, by permitting the lands to be parcelled out, in such a manner, as to render it probable that the greater part of them would remain, for a long time, totally unoccupied: and this makes it reasonable to suppose, that the promises and assurances of lord *Fairfax* were as they appear, in evidence, to have been, that patents should issue for all lands regularly and equitably surveyed, but for no others. The time and the situation of the parties, when these promises were made, are leading circumstances, to their probable extent. Lord *Fairfax* struck at the very root of their titles; he claimed their lands; and asserted that the crown, from whom they derived their titles, had no right to grant them. This was, at once, to defeat their patents, as well as to destroy their inchoate rights; and therefore the whole settlement, as well those whose lands were patented, as those who had not then obtained patents, spoke of removing and settling themselves on some less contested spot. Their fears were not, that the shape of such surveys, as grants had not been issued on, would be so changed, as to give their neighbours some water, and some meadow, but that they would lose their lands entirely. To quiet these fears, lord *Fairfax's* promises were made; and therefore he repeatedly assures them, that they will only change their landlord: that he means not to exact, from them, higher returns than the king; that he means to be easier than the king; because he will, sometimes, be content with the produce of the lands, instead of money for his quit-rents. The statements, made of the promises, look as if they were designed for the settlers in general, rather than for *Hite*; and, if there could be any doubt, that doubt would be removed, by observing the deposition of *John Dyer*,[9] where, after lord *Fairfax* had made his promise as usual, he is asked how Mr. *Hite* would come off? Clearly, indicating, that, in the opinion of those who heard him, *Hite* was included in those declarations, which he made to the people. And will any man say, that those promises have not been religiously complied

9. For the deposition of Dyer (b. 1704), see Dickinson, *Fairfax Proprietary*, app., xxxi, and Transcript of Hite v. Fairfax, 107, 108, Add. MSS, 15317, Brit. Museum.

with? Who, among those settlers, is dissatisfied with lord *Fairfax*? They enjoy their lands as quietly, and on as easy terms, as they would have enjoyed them, if his lordship had failed in his suit. That they have obtained patents from his lordship has contributed to the bringing of the present suit, and is one subject of complaint in their bill. 'Tis strange that these promises of lord *Fairfax* should be urged as arguments against him, when his compliance with those promises would be set aside! or that they would appropriate, entirely to themselves, that which was evidently designed for others, and not for themselves.

On this view of the case, then, the promises of lord *Fairfax* give the complainants no claim upon him, but in consequence of those surveys, which were made according to the rules of proportion, which were wisely established throughout the country.

In short, neither the words of the compromise, nor those of the promise, and much less the intention, warrant the pretentions of the complainants.

                                                        Cur. adv. vult.[1]

Letters Patent

Extract from Record Book, Land Office, Kentucky Secretary of State's Office

Richmond, June 15, 1786

PATRICK HENRY Esquire governor of the Commonwealth of Virginia To all to whom these presents shall come: greeting. Know ye that by virtue of a military Warrent Number 30 and Issued the 30th day of November 1782[2] There is granted by the said Commonwealth unto John Marshall Esquire a Certain Tract or Parcel of land Containing one thousand Acres by Survey bearing date the 4th. day of January 1785[3] lying and being the District Set apart for the officers and Soldiers of the Virginia Continantal line and on the waters of Clay lick Creek and bounded as followeth to wit Beginning at two white oaks near Thomas Edmunds[4] one thousand

---

1. *Curia advisari vult,* "the court takes the case under advisement." The phrase is used to indicate that the court took cognizance of the arguments and suspended rendering its judgment until it might hold further deliberations upon the matter.

2. The warrant is printed above at Nov. 30, 1782.

3. The text of the survey follows the text of the grant.

4. Edmunds, or Edmonds (d. 1794), served as a captain in the Third Virginia Regiment.

Acres Survey running north Seventy five degrees west four hundred poles to a white oak and hickory thence north fifteen Degrees East four hundred poles to three dogwoods Corner to William Taylors[5] one thousand Acres Survey thence with his line South Seventy five degrees East four hundred poles Crossing the west fork of the Creek to two white oaks and dogwood South east Corner to Taylor and in Edmunds line thence South fifteen degrees West with Edmunds line and passing his corner four hundred poles to the Beginning with its appurtenances to have and to hold the said Tract or parcel of land With its appurtenances to the Said John Marshall and his heirs forever. IN WITNESS where of the Said Patrick Henry Esqr. Governor of the Commonwealth of Virginia hath here unto Set his hand and caused the lesser Seal of the said Commonwealth to be affixed at Richmond on the fifteenth day of June in the year of our Lord one thousand Seven hundred and Eighty six and of the Commonwealth the Tenth.

P. HENRY

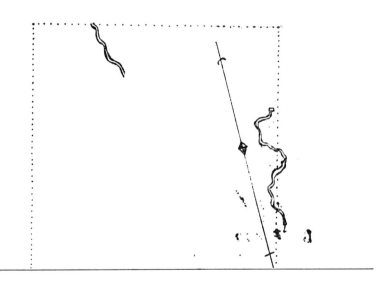

Surveyed for John Marshall 1000 Acres of Land part of a Military Warrant No. 30. On the Waters of Clay lick Creek, beginning at

5. Taylor (ca. 1745–1830) served as a captain in the Second Virginia Regiment.

two White Oaks near Thomas Edmonds's 1000 Acre Survey Running N.75°W. 400 poles to a White Oak, and Hickory, thence N.15°E. 400 poles to three Dogwoods, corner to William Taylors 1000 Acre Survey thence with his line S75°E. 400 poles, crossing the West fork of the Creek to two White Oaks, and a Dogwood S.E. corner to Taylor and in Edmonds's line thence S.15°W. with Edmonds's line and passing his corner 400 poles to the beginning.

WILLIAM PATTEN M   RO BRECKINRIDGE Asst.[6]
JOHN ROGERS   } C.M.[8]   4th. January 1785
JOSEPH CLEGHORN   }   RICHARD C ANDERSON. S.[7]
No. 30 Dated the 30th day of November 1782.

Letters Patent

Extract from Record Book, Land Office, Kentucky Secretary of State's Office

Richmond, June 15, 1786

PATRICK HENRY Esquire Governor of the Commonwealth of Virginia To all to whom these presents shall come Greeting; know ye that by Virtue and in consideration of part of a military warrant Number 30 & and Issued the 30th. day of november 1782 There is Granted by the said Commonwealth unto John Marshall Esqr a Certain Tract or parcel of Land Containing one thousand Acres by Survey bearing date the 20th. day of may 1785 lying and being in the District Set apart for the Officers and Soldiers of the Virginia Continantal line and on the Waters of Lost Creek a branch of the Ohio and bounded as followeth to wit BEGINNING at a black oak dogwood and Sassafras in a line of Thomas Pemberton[9] Survey number 323 running South thirty two degrees west three hundred and ten poles Crossing a branch at twenty one, at thirty eight and one at three hundred poles to two Elms and ash in the line of Richard Eastins[1] Survey number Eleven hundred and ninety three thence with his line and the line of Edmund Taylors Survey Num-

6. Breckinridge (d. 1833?) acted as assistant surveyor to Anderson.
7. Anderson (1750–1826) was appointed principal surveyor on behalf of the Continental Line on Jan. 15, 1784.
8. Presumably "C.M." represents "Chain Men" and "M" represents "Marker."
9. Capt. Pemberton served in the Continental Dragoons to Jan. 1783.
1. Probably Lt. Richard Easton, who resigned his commission June 7, 1778.

ber thirteen hundred and Sixty three and the line of Andrew Waggoners[2] Survey number Eleven hundred and three South fifty eight
degrees East five hundred and Sixteen poles to a gum black oak and
dogwood South west corner to George Lewis[3] Survey number Eighteen and in Waggoners line thence with Lewiss line north thirty
two degrees East three hundred and ten poles Crossing a branch at
one hundred and Sixteen poles to a honey locust ash and Elm
Lewises' north west Corner and in the line of Richard Taylors[4] Survey number fourteen hundred and forty three thence with his &
Pembertons [to] north fifty eight degrees west five hundred & Sixteen poles Crossing a branch at Eighty eight poles and one at two
hundred [and] ninety Seven poles to the BEGINNING with its appurtenances To Have and to hold the Said Tract or parcel of land
with its appurtenances to the Said John Marshall and his heirs forever in Witness whereof the Said Patrick Henry Esqr. Governor of
the Commonwealth of Virginia hath here unto set his hand and
caused the lesser Seal of the Said Commonwealth to be Affixed at
Richmond on the fifteenth day of June in the year of our Lord one
thousand Seven hundred and Eighty Six and of the Commonwealth the Tenth.

P. HENRY

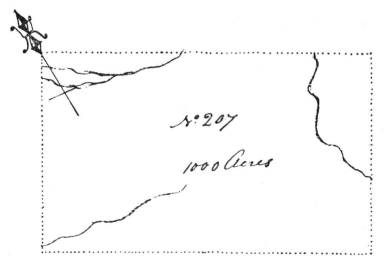

No. 30 Dated the 30th day of November 1782.
   Surveyed for John Marshall 1000 acres of Land part of a Military

2. Waggoner (1743–1813) served as major in the Eighth Virginia Regiment.
3. Capt. Lewis (1757–1821) served in the Continental Dragoons.
4. Taylor (1744–1829) served as major in the Ninth Virginia Regiment.

Warrant No. 30 on the Waters of Lost Creek a Branch of the Ohio Beginning at a Black oak dogwood and sassafras in the Line of Thomas Pembertons Survey No. 323 Running S32W 310 poles crossing a Branch at 20 one at 38 and one at 300 poles to Two Elms and an Ash in the line of Richard Eastens survey No. 1193 Thence with his line and the line of Edmund Taylors survey No 1363 and the line of Andrew Waggoners survey No. 1103—S58°E 516 poles to a gum Black Oak and dogwood S.W Corner to George Lewis's Survey No. 18 and in Waggoners line. Thence with Lewis's line N32°E 310 poles crossing a Branch at 116 poles to a honey Locust ash & Elm. Lewis's N.W Corner and in the line of Richard Taylors Survey No. 1443 Thence with his and Pembertons line N58W 516 poles Crossing a Branch at 88 and One at 297 poles to the Beginning.

ISAAC HITCHCOCK. M   P ROBERTSON[5]
AMOS GOODWIN   }   May 20th. 1785
WILLIAM DRENNEN } C.C.[6]   RICHARD C ANDERSON. S.

Birth and Death of Rebecca Marshall

Entry, Marshall Family Bible, Collection of Mrs. Kenneth R. Higgins, Richmond

[*June 15–20, 1786 (Richmond)*. A notation in JM's hand indicates his daughter Rebecca was born on June 15 and died five days later.[7]]

To William Branch Giles

ALS, Marshall Papers, Swem Library, College of William and Mary[8]

Dear Sir   Richmond, September 22, 1786
   I receivd your letter enclosing one to Major Magill while I was

5. Robertson was probably Anderson's assistant.
6. Here "C.C." represents "chain carriers."
7. This death, followed some months later by the abortion or miscarriage of another pregnancy, reportedly caused Mrs. Marshall to have a mental breakdown; "Mrs. Marshal, once Miss Ambler, is Insane, the loss of two Children is thought to have Occationed it." Martha Jefferson Carr to Thomas Jefferson, Feb. 26, 1787, *Jefferson Papers*, XV, 635. See also Account Book, Disbursements, June 15, Sept. 22, 1786.
8. Addressed to Giles (1762–1830), as an attorney-at-law, the envelope is marked "Hond. by Mr. Bell," that is, the letter was delivered by a Mr. Bell.

in Winchester[9] & immediately delivered the enclosure to that gentleman. I think on looking at the law the gaming act ought to be pleaded & cannot be given in evidence on the plea of payment.[1]

A Mr. Bell[2] a client of yours has been with me shewing me some errors you have filed to arrest a judgement hanging over him for a breach of covenant. He requested my opinion & I gave it to him that errors were sufficient. Doubtless the original institution of the suit was wrong & there can be no question but the error woud have been deemd fatal on demurrer. The only question is whether it is cur[e]d by verdict, I think now it is not—though I have not examined the statutes of jeofail[3] particularly with an eye to this case. If I should alter my opinion I will write to you. My Brother James[4] has just come in from Kentucky. He will be here in the course of October next. I need not tell you how glad he woud be to see you. I heard you was in town when I first came home & searched for you but coud not find you. I am dear Sir, your obedt Servt.

J MARSHALL

Hustings Court Session

EDITORIAL NOTE

At the triennial municipal election held on July 5, 1785, John Marshall was elected a member of the Richmond governing body, the Common Hall. He attended the organizational meeting on July 7 and at that time was chosen to serve as recorder.[5] Although the Richmond City incorporation statute did not specif-

9. Charles Magill (1760–1827). Letter not found. See Account Book, Disbursements, Aug. 1786, reflecting JM's expenditure of £15 for "expenses going to and returning from Winchester."

1. Gaming debts were unenforceable at law in colonial Virginia, and continued to be so. See 5 Hening 102 and 10 Hening 205. JM discussed whether the gaming act ought to be specially pleaded and, if it were not, whether the defendant could give evidence of the gaming act's applicability after pleading payment of the debt. The plea and the evidence, in the latter case, would be inconsistent, and the weight of authority seems to have been in favor of pleading special matters. See Blackstone, *Commentaries*, III, 305, 306; Chitty, *On Pleading*, I, 346–347.

2. JM received £1 6s. for advice to Bell. See Account Book, Receipts, Sept. 22, 1786.

3. The English statutes of amendment and jeofaile, applicable in Virginia since 1753, permitted amendment of pleadings at any stage of trial up to the entry of final judgment. Since Bell already had judgment entered against him, this form of amendment would not have been available; however, his failure to avail himself of this relief could preclude success in his appeal by writ of error. JM had argued a matter concerning the statutes of jeofaile in Apr. 1786. See Gilbert v. Taylor, Apr. 1786, above.

4. James Markham Marshall (1764–1848).

5. At the organizational meeting the successful candidates elected from their number a mayor, a recorder, and four aldermen. Those not selected to serve in those offices

ically require that the recorder be a lawyer, this had been traditional in Virginia municipal government since 1723, when the recorder of the city of Williamsburg was required to be a man "learned in the law."[6] During John Marshall's term of office as recorder, he was called upon by the Common Hall to prosecute actions in the courts on behalf of the city of Richmond, and reference to Marshall in the resolution as "Mr. Recorder" suggests that this was considered part of his official duties.[7] For these reasons it would appear that Marshall's selection to serve as recorder was a recognition of his professional competence as well as an acknowledgment of the substantial number of votes cast in favor of his candidacy for the Common Hall.

As recorder, John Marshall was expected to participate in the activities of the two local government bodies of the city of Richmond, the Common Hall and the Richmond City Hustings Court. The duties of the Common Hall were mainly legislative in character and need not concern us here, although it is readily apparent from the minutes of that body that Marshall's participation in its deliberations was active and regular. In judicial and certain administrative matters the mayor, recorder, and aldermen acted separately, forming a panel known as the Richmond City Hustings Court. This court exercised authority over criminal and civil matters arising within the magisterial limits of the city of Richmond.

The criminal jurisdiction of the Hustings Court of the city of Richmond can be divided into four categories for purposes of discussion. Individually each member of the court was a magistrate with powers equal to those of a county justice of the peace; this permitted him to examine an accused person and to imprison him until a "called court" was assembled to examine the evidence against the prisoner.[8] The "called court," denominated a Hustings Court in the minutes, then either discharged the accused or referred the matter to the county court of Henrico County, for a misdemeanor, or to the next sitting of the General Court, for a felony.[9] Sitting as a "Court of Oyer and Terminer" the Hustings Court tried

---

continued in the Common Hall and constituted the Common Council, which met with the mayor, recorder, and aldermen to conduct administrative and legislative business. Minutes of the Richmond City Common Hall, I, 104–107, Virginia State Library; 11 Hening 45–51 (1782).

6. 4 Hening 139 (1723).

7. Resolution of Feb. 13, 1786, Common Hall Minutes, I, 121, Va. State Lib.

8. Authority to hold an accused person for examination was derived from the 1748 statute, 5 Hening 541, and was recognized subsequent to Independence by the 1780 statute concerning crimes injurious to the Independence of America, 10 Hening 268, 270. Clause 6 of the Richmond incorporation act conferred powers of justice of the peace upon the mayor, recorder, or alderman. 11 Hening 49.

9. The "called court" procedure for examination of criminals other than slaves derived from the 1748 act, which was included by reference in the Richmond incorporation act. 5 Hening 541; 11 Hening 48. This limited criminal jurisdiction was typical of the borough courts established in colonial Virginia, which were the lineal ancestors of the subsequently created city hustings courts. See 3 Hening 409–411 (1705) and 4 Hening 139 (1723, Williamsburg incorporation act). The petty criminal jurisdiction of the borough courts gave rise to the term "hustings courts." 3 Hening 410.

The Richmond Hustings Court, unlike the Williamsburg Hustings Court, did not absorb the jurisdiction of its adjacent county court over misdemeanors. See the Williamsburg court's authority as defined in 4 Hening 139 (1723) and 5 Hening 205 (1742); Richmond City Hustings Court powers are spelled out in 11 Hening 48 (1782). See also Minutes of the Richmond City Hustings Court, I, 70, Office of the Clerk of the

Negro slaves for all degrees of malfeasance, including felonies, and passed judgment upon them up to and including death sentences.[1] Finally, the court exercised statutory jurisdiction over all persons committing offenses against the laws of the corporation in cases where the fines imposed did not exceed forty shillings.[2] Although the number of criminal matters was not particularly large, each one required special attention and an extraordinary session of the Richmond City Hustings Court. The extract from the Hustings Court minutes printed below provides an example of the activities of the Richmond City Hustings Court in the administration of criminal justice and is only one of several court proceedings that bear Marshall's signature as presiding officer in the absence of the mayor.[3]

The civil jurisdiction of the Richmond City Hustings Court extended to all inhabitants of the city, to those arrested and brought within its cognizance, and also to the attached goods of those who fled the city of Richmond to avoid process of the Hustings Court. In all other actions where the defendant or his attorney proved that no arrest had been made and that the defendant resided outside the court's jurisdiction, the cause was summarily dismissed. For the most part the civil causes before the Hustings Court were those that might be denominated "collection matters" and some insignificant tort cases. The calendar was always lengthy and a substantial number of matters were dismissed for failure to prosecute, nonresidence of the defendant, or a *pendente lite* settlement between the parties.[4]

Routinely the Hustings Court took proofs of wills and granted certificates for letters testamentary to be issued. Similarly the court was empowered to admit administrators to manage the affairs of intestate decedents, at the same time taking bond for their faithful performance and appointing appraisers to inventory the assets. Upon the completion of an estate appraisal, the inventory was recorded in the Hustings Court. In addition the court was charged with the power of granting naturalization to such alien residents of the city of Richmond as might be entitled to the privileges of citizenship. The Hustings Court took acknowledgments to real property deeds and mortgages and accepted them for recording in the files

---

Law and Equity Court, Richmond, for a misdemeanor bound over for trial at Henrico County Court in 1783.

1. The procedures for the trial of slaves suspected of capital offenses were derived from the 1748 statute. 6 Hening 104. The issuance of an oyer and terminer commission, required by the 1748 law, was altered by a 1765 statute that permitted a blanket oyer and terminer commission to issue to county court justices upon their appointment to the county court and empowered them to impose the death penalty upon convicted slaves. 8 Hening 137–138. Up to and including the period of JM's service as recorder, the Richmond City Hustings Court had not condemned a slave to death, and it is unclear from the statutory language whether they possessed this authority. However, they could, and did, impose heavy corporal punishment in several cases. For examples of the court's work under its oyer and terminer commission, see Hustings Court Minutes, I, 4, 5, 7, 178, Office of the Clerk of the Law and Equity Court.

2. See clause 5 of the Richmond incorporation act, 11 Hening 48.

3. The calendar prepared by Irwin S. Rhodes identifies each session of the court at which JM presided and signed the minutes. Rhodes, *Marshall Papers Calendar*, I, 35.

4. Under the Richmond incorporation act, the Hustings Court was granted substantial civil jurisdiction within the city magisterial limits. See 11 Hening 48. Although a thorough discussion of its jurisdiction and practice is beyond the proper scope of this note, the limitations discussed are readily ascertainable by a cursory examination of the minute books of the court.

of the court. Certain evidences of indebtedness, powers of attorney, and partnership agreements were also accepted for recording in the court.[5]

Supplementary to its judicial duties, the Hustings Court acted as the executive body of the Common Hall. It appointed and supervised the work of city officials. Applications to operate ordinaries and taverns were brought before the Hustings Court for approval, as were requests for permission to maintain billiard tables. The court at regular intervals reviewed the rates for services rendered by taverns and ordinaries and made such adjustments in the legal fees as seemed most proper to the members of the court.[6]

As recorder Marshall was most conscientious in his attendance at sessions of the Hustings Court, and he did more than his share of the work in the "called court" and oyer and terminer courts summoned to hear criminal matters. Although his presence was not required to give validity to the recording of deeds and other matters, he was not infrequently the principal officer of the Hustings Court present at such sessions. In the absence of any documentary evidence concerning Marshall's decision to resign from his position as recorder, we can only speculate that his political activities in support of the proposed federal Constitution, coupled with the demands of his growing law practice, made his duties in the Common Hall and Hustings Court most onerous. His last appearance on the bench of the Richmond City Hustings Court was on January 29, 1788, and on March 10, 1788, he submitted his resignation to the Common Hall and was succeeded by William Hay.[7]

5. The court might order production of a will for probate and admit proof in common form. For these procedures and proof of wills in general, see Matter of Carson (1783), Hustings Court Minutes, I, 10, 14, 44, Office of the Clerk of the Law and Equity Court. Recording of an estate appraisal is in Matter of Leitch (1783), *ibid.*, 60. For naturalizations see Honoré Giroud (1784) and John McCaul (1785), *ibid.*, 194, 250. Acknowledgments occurred on nearly every court day; see *ibid.*, *passim.*

6. On July 18, 1785, the first day that JM sat on the Hustings Court bench, four constables and one clerk of the city market were appointed. By direction of the Common Hall, the Hustings Court in Dec. 1786 investigated charges that the city sergeant, Mathew Moody (*ca.* 1741–1803), was delinquent in serving executions; apparently it was found that he was overburdened with work, for he was subsequently reappointed and a deputy sergeant appointed to assist him. *Ibid.*, 299, 669, 673; 11 Hening 48.

Tavern and ordinary licenses were granted for one year, renewable upon application to the Hustings Court. See licenses to William Winston (July 17, 1786), William Holderby (Sept. 18, 1786), James Burnet (Dec. 18, 1786), Francis Pearce, and Thomas Scott (both Mar. 29, 1787), Hustings Court Minutes, I, 508, 566, 670, II, 40, Office of the Clerk of the Law and Equity Court. Tavern rates were established for 1786–1787 on May 16, 1786. See *ibid.*, I, 461. See also 11 Hening 47.

7. Hustings Court Minutes, II, 264–265, Office of the Clerk of the Law and Equity Court; Common Hall Minutes, I, 160, Va. State Lib. Hay (*ca.* 1749–1813) was a Richmond merchant. "Return of the Inhabitants," 1784, Richmond City Common Hall Records, 359, Va. State Lib.

Commonwealth v. Garrett and Johnson

Arraignment

Extract from Minute Book, Richmond City Hustings Court, Office of the Clerk of the Law and Equity Court, Richmond

Richmond, September 28, 1786

At a Court of Hustings called for the City of Richmond, and held at the Courthouse in the said City, on Thursday the twenty-eighth of September 1786, for the Examination of Patrick Garret and William Johnson, charged with Burglary and felony, in breaking and entering the dwelling house of John Tisdall, of the County of Hanover, and stealing from thence, Cash, and other articles to the amount of twenty pounds. [8]

Present

John Marshall, Recorder; Robert Mitchell, Robert Boyd, Foster Webb Jun. & Alexander McRobert, Aldermen. [9]

The said Patrick Garret and William Johnson were set to the bar in custody of the Jailer of this City, to whose custody upon the Charge aforesaid they were Committed, and upon examination denied the Charge, with which they are accused. Whereupon sundry Witnesses were sworn and examined,[1] as well on behalf of the Commonwealth as the prisoners, and they heard in their defence. On consideration whereof, It is the Opinion of the Court, that for the

8. The court was assembled at the call of Foster Webb, Jr., an alderman of the city of Richmond since July 1785, who had held the first hearing in this case and committed the defendants to jail to await arraignment. Mittimus, Sept. 22, 1786, Summons, Sept. 22, 1786, Richmond City Hustings Court Papers, Virginia State Library. Burglary was a nonclergyable felony if the goods taken exceeded 20s. in value. Hugh F. Rankin, *Criminal Trial Proceedings in the General Court of Colonial Virginia* (Williamsburg, Va., 1965), 149; 4 Hening 272 (1730).

9. Mitchell (*ca.* 1746–1811), Boyd (1750–1812), and McRobert (1755–1800) had been elected aldermen in July 1785. Boyd was probably the son of Spencer Boyd (d. 1779), a wealthy merchant from King and Queen County; Robert Boyd had been prominent in Richmond political affairs since 1781. McRobert later served as grand treasurer of the Grand Lodge, Ancient Free and Accepted Masons of Virginia, while JM was grand master in 1792 and 1793.

1. The appearance bond of witnesses, executed before Alderman Webb, required the presence of John Tisdall, William Tisdall, and Hood Wade at the called court to be held on Sept. 28. Possibly Wade was the individual sentenced to death for horse stealing in 1782 and later pardoned because of his youth and military service. Appearance bond, Sept. 22, 1786, Richmond City Hustings Court Papers, Va. State Lib.; *CVSP*, III, 395, 401; *JVCS*, III, 201.

Offence aforesaid the said Patrick Garret and William Johnson ought to be tried at the next General Court to be held at the Courthouse in this City on the first day of October next, And thereupon they are remanded to Jail.[2]

John Tisdall, Frances Tisdall, William Tisdall and Hood Wade, of the County of Hanover, come into Court and severally acknowledge themselves indebted to his Excellency Patrick Henry, esqr. Governor or Chief Magistrate of this Commonwealth, in the sum of One hundred, to be levied of their respective goods and Chattels, lands and Tenements, and to the said Governor & his successors for the use of the Commonwealth rendered; Yet upon this condition that if the said John Tisdall, Frances Tisdall, William Tisdall & Hood Wade shall make their personal appearance, before the next General Court to be held at the Courthouse in the said City on the first day of October next, then and there to give evidence on behalf of the Commonwealth against Patrick Garret & William Johnson, touching a certain Burglary and felony whereof they are accused, and shall not depart thence without the leave of the said Court, then this Recognizance to be Void, or else to remain in full force.[3]

"The minutes of the preceeding Examination were signed."

J. MARSHALL, Recorder.

Ashton v. West

Notes on Argument in the General Court

Extract from Casebook, Tucker-Coleman Papers, Swem Library, College of William and Mary

Richmond, October 13, 1786

Ejectment. The Case was—John West devised "to his Grandson Hugh West 300. acres of Land, to him & to the heirs of his body

---

2. The case was considered at the General Court session in Oct. 1786, and Patrick Garret was ordered recommitted. The matter does not appear in newspaper accounts of General Court trials for Apr. or Oct. 1787. Presumably the prosecution was discontinued. See the *Virginia Gazette, or, the American Advertiser* (Richmond), Oct. 11, 1786.

3. This was an appearance bond for the witnesses expected to appear before the General Court.

lawfully begotten, and in default of such lawful heirs, to his Grandson John West, & the heirs of his Body lawfully begotten—Item; to
his Grandson John West 313. Acres to him & the heirs of his Body
lawfully begotten, and in default of *such* heirs lawfully begotten, my
Will is that the aforesaid 300. Acres bequeathed to my Grandson
Hugh West & the 313. Acres to John West, be given, granted and
bequeathed unto my loving son John West, his heirs or assigns forever." [4] John West the *son* of the Testator was his youngest son by a
second venter. [5] John West the *Grandson* entered, and died siezed
under age, & without issue: on his death John West the *son* entered
into the premises, Hugh West (who was Brother of John West the
Grandson, & son of the testators *eldest* son by a former Wife) being
then an infant; and by Deeds of Lease and release in March 1735.
conveyed the 313. Acres, the premises in question, to John Minor.
In 1740. Hugh West brought an Ejectment against Minor, & recovered the possession; & died siezed in 1754. leaving issue John
West, his eldest son; who also dying hath left issue a son called
Thomas West, now living. The Defendant is widow of Hugh West,
and hath been in possession ever since the death of her husband.
John Minor in 1750. by Deeds of Lease & release reconveyed the
premises to John West the son: who, by his will devised "all his
Lands which he can or may lawfully or justly claim or demand["]
particularly the 313. Acres above mentioned to the Lessors of the

4. This summary of the will is obviously incomplete, but no other evidence concerning the terms of the devise has been located. A cross-remainder arose under a conveyance or devise to two or more persons as tenants in common in fee tail. In other words,
each held an undivided partial interest in the realty as a tenant in fee tail during his
lifetime, and upon his death with issue surviving him, his interest passed to that descendant or those descendants. However, if the tenant in common did not leave issue that
survived him, his part interest in the realty was added either to the portions of his other
cotenants or to the portions held by the descendants of his deceased cotenants. For a
discussion of the historical development of the rules concerning cross-remainders see
Thomas Jarman, *A Treatise on Wills*, ed. Joseph F. Randolph and William Talcott,
5th Am. ed. (Jersey City, N.J., 1880–1881), III, 344.

The arguments of counsel leave little doubt that a tenancy in common, and hence a
cross-remainder problem, must have been present in Ashton v. West, although the
summary of the will omits this vital fact. In this light, however, the identification of an
unequal number of acres as the portions of the two grandsons is perplexing, for even
in the event of a voluntary partition of the realty after the testator's death but before
the litigation, the shares should have been equal. In addition, it should be noted that
unlike the usual situation with cross-remainders, the will dealt with the two parcels of
realty in separate phrases, and the devolution of the property does not appear to have
been expressed in parallel terms.

The argument is discussed in Cullen, "St. George Tucker," 91–94. JM's Account
Book indicates he received a fee in this case on Apr. 1, 1786.

5. That is, a second wife.

plaintiff [6]—John West the son hath left a son named Roger West, who is now living.

Taylor,[7] for the plt; contended here are no cross remainders between Hugh West, & John West the grandson: Consequently that the remainder to John West the son took effect immediately on the death of John West the Grandson. He cited the Case of Holmes & West, Tho. Raym. 452. & the Cases there cited arguendo.[8] That Case was, "Isaac Meynell by his will devised *all* his Lands in Derbyshire unto his two Daurs. Elizabeth & Anne, and their heirs equally to be divided between them; & in Case they happen to die without issue, remainder over: Anne died without issue—adjudged that this was a cross remainder." He also cited Comber v Hill, 2. Strange 969.[9] where a Devise to the Testators "Grandson Richard Holden, & to Elizabeth Holden his Grand-daughter equally to be divided, and to the heirs of their *respective* bodies, and for default of *such* issue, to his Grand-daughter Anne Holden in fee;" was adjudged "not to create any cross remainder between Richard & Elizabeth; but that Anne should have the moiety of Elizabeth presently, on her death without issue." In this Case the reporter lays much stress on the word *respective* in the devise, to which the word *such*, it was insisted had reference: otherwise the word respective must be rejected. He also cited 2. Bacon's Abr: 75. Clatche's Case. & 4. Bacon's abr: 333.[1]—but as I[2] was employed in taking down the Case I could not follow his Argument.

Lee,[3] for the deft. In the former argument three points were made. 1st: possession above twenty years. 2d. That here were cross Remainders. 3d. That John West the son not being in pos-

6. This would appear to be an attempt on the part of the son, John West, to disentail the 313 acres originally devised to the grandson, John West, who died without issue. However, under neither of the opposing interpretations of the will would such a procedure to eliminate the entail be necessary. Either the exact terms of the will, as relied upon by Ashton, would govern, in which case son John West would take title in fee simple absolute upon the death of grandson John West without surviving issue; or, under the defendant's view that cross-remainders were intended by the will, son John West could not take steps concerning the 313 acres until the death of grandson Hugh West without issue or the death of the last descendant of grandson Hugh West.

7. John Taylor.

8. Holmes v. Meynel, T. Raymond 452–456, 83 Eng. Rep. 236–238 (K.B., 1682).

9. 93 Eng. Rep. 973–975 (K.B., 1734).

1. Clanch's Case, 3 Dyer 330–331a, 73 Eng. Rep. 747–748 (Ch., 1573), held that cross-remainders could not be implied in law when the expressed intention of the testator was contrary to the implication. The other citations are to Bacon, *Abridgment*.

2. St. George Tucker.

3. Charles Lee.

session at the time of his death could pass no Interest in the Lands by his Will.

1st: point—A possession within twenty years must be proved in order to support an Ejectment: there must be an actual Entry—12. Mod: 573. Bullers nisi prius 102. nor will the Confession of Lease Entry & ouster bring it out of the Statute of Limitations—Runnington's Ejectm: 17.[4]

2d. point. John West the son, under whom plt claims was not in possession at the time of the devise. The Statute agt. maintenance & champerty would have operated against a Conveyance by Deed, under such Circumstances[5]—and he contended that a Devise was not a more effectual Conveyance. For a devise of Lands is not good, if the Testator hath nothing in them at the time of making the devise. 1. Salk: 237. Bunter v Coke.[6] The Lands must be *sua*[7] at the time of the devise.

3d. point—Here are cross remainders. The Testator's Intention is to be regarded. He had found no Case aptly to fit it. It should be remember that the Defendant is the Testator's heir at Law,[8] and

4. Hayward v. Kinsey, 12 Modern Rep. 568–579, 88 Eng. Rep. 1526–1531 (K.B., 1702), held that the confession of an entry and ouster in an ejectment action would not suspend the running of the statute of limitations. The other citations are to Charles Runnington, *A Treatise on the Action of Ejectment* (London, 1781), and Sir Francis Buller, *An Introduction to the Law relative to Trials at Nisi Prius*, 5th ed. (London, 1768).

5. The English statute, 32 Hen. 8, c. 9, sec. 2 (1540), required that a party be in actual possession of realty for at least one year before a conveyance, or the conveyance would be void. See William S. Holdsworth, *A History of English Law* (London, 1945), IV, 521. The old common law rule that lands in possession of a stranger could not be conveyed even by the owner applied in Virginia until 1849. Clay v. White, 1 Munford (15 Va.) 162–175 (Sup. Ct. App., 1810); Carrington v. Godden, 13 Grattan (54 Va.) 587–614 (Sup. Ct. App., 1855).

6. Bunter v. Coke, 1 Salkeld 237–238, 91 Eng. Rep. 210–211 (K.B., 1707), held that lands acquired after the execution of a will did not pass under the devises in that will; "a man cannot give that which he has not." The thrust of this argument seems to have been that the son, John West, had an estate in expectancy, which because of the survival of Thomas West, grandson of the original grantee, Hugh West, had not come into the son's, John West's, possession at the time of his death and devise of the realty. While the rules against champerty and maintenance were formal objections to the validity of title based on the devise, the broader ground of argument revolved about the postponement of the son's, John West's, estate.

7. That is, "his."

8. The defendant in this case would be Thomas West, heir-at-law to his father, John West, who was heir-at-law to his father, Hugh West, the grandson of the testator; joined in the action was Thomas West's grandmother, the widow of Hugh West, presumably as holder of dower rights in the realty. Unfortunately it is not clear to which testator the argument refers. The grandsons of testator John West, who executed the will creating these estates, could not have been his heirs-at-law. Rather, his son by the second marriage, John West, upon whose will the plaintiff based his case, was the heir-

therefore to be favoured in the construction of the will: By the last clause it is clear that *both* tracts of Land were to go over to John West the Son, at the same time. Consequently not till the death of *both* the Grandson's without issue, for they had severally Estates of Inheritance. He cited the Cases in the margin.

Cowper 777, 797; 4. Leon: 14; Sir Tho. Jones 172; Dyer 330.[9]

Marshall, on the same side: The Testators words shew a clear intention in him in him[1] to postpone his Son's Estate to that both his grandsons. As the Testator in the last clause speaks of both tracts of Land, the words *such heirs*, must relate to the heirs of the Body of *both*. There is but *one* Contingency & *both* tracts must vest when that contingency happens. Cross remainders are favoured at this day, where they occur between two alone, nor are they altogether discountenanced where they occur between more than two. vi. Cowper's rep: 780, 800.

2: Blacks. Com: 381; Cowper 780, 800.[2]

Randolph,[3] for the plt. Had John West the son a right to devise this Land, under the will of his Father? To determine this Question he would resort to the Doctrine of cross remainders. They must

---

at-law of the elder John West. Since cross-remainders are implied to defeat intestacy, and hence a delivery of the property to the heir-at-law, this argument and its purpose are quite obscure.

9. Pery v. White, 2 Cowper 777–781, 98 Eng. Rep. 1356–1359 (K.B., 1778), and Phipard v. Mansfield, 2 Cowper 797–803, 98 Eng. Rep. 1367–1370 (K.B., 1778), involved the presumptions of law relating to the implications of cross-remainders. The rule was that cross-remainders between two parties would be presumed but that the presumption was against cross-remainders between three or more parties. An anonymous case in 4 Leonard 14, 74 Eng. Rep. 695 (K.B., 1590), also upheld the two-person limitation and may have been cited because it was decided before 1619. While the two-person limitation is said to have been short-lived and of little judicial weight, it seems to have survived in opinions as late as 1843. See Jarman, *Wills*, III, 345. The citation to Thomas Jones's reports is to Holmes v. Meynel, T. Raymond 452–456, 83 Eng. Rep. 236–238 (K.B., 1682); the citation to Sir James Dyer's reports is to Clanch's case, discussed at n. 1 above.

1. The second "in him" is a slip of the pen.

2. The citation to Blackstone, *Commentaries*, II, 381–382, and JM's return to the argument of Pery v. White and Phipard v. Mansfield (see n. 9 above) indicate that he was arguing that cross-remainders were clearly intended by testator and, even if testator's meanings were unclear, that there is a presumption of law in a case when only two persons take cross-remainders.

Old English law required precision in the devise of cross-remainders in realty, but at the time this case was argued in Virginia, the law of England seems to have been gradually changing to permit the courts to take into consideration the testator's intent and his presumed intent to provide for the individuals named to take cross-remainders. See Comber v. Hill, 2 Strange 969, 93 Eng. Rep. 973–975 (K.B., 1734), and Gorges v. Webb, 1 Taunton 239, 127 Eng. Rep. 823 (C.P., 1808), which overruled Comber v. Hill.

3. Edmund Randolph.

arise from express words, or a necessary implication. 1. Atk: 579.[4] The words *such heirs* refer to their respective heirs. The word *Item*, disconnects the clauses, so far as to shew that the Testator had taken up a new subject. Testator appears throughout the will to favor his son John. Here then there is no necessary implication. Lord Hardwicke's[5] reasoning in 1. Atk. 579. well applies to this Case: no Case can be cited where cross remainders have been determined to exist, merely from the word *in default* of *such issue*. 1. Atk: 580. Cowper 797. is not against the Authority of Ld. Hardwicke, for there the decision turns upon other points.

Nor is the plaintiff's remedy barred by the Act of Limitations.[6] The Land was recovered in 1740. John West brought an Ejectment in 1742. Hugh West died in 1754. before his possession had acquired strength by Lenth of time. In 1754. John West brought a new Ejectment which was not decided until 1758. This Ejectment was brought in 1782.—12. Mod. 573. a strong Case, & may be sound Law, yet does not apply here. Possession to bar the Act of Limitations must have been uninterrupted. Is not a claim by Ejectment such an interruption? Continual claim is a bar to Act of Limitations. An Assize amounts to continual claim. Co. Litt: 263.[7] Why not an Ejectment? If it be so, this ejectment was brought within twenty years after the decision in 1758. if the Time when the act of Limitations did not operate, during the war be deducted from that period, to the Commencement of this suit in 1782.

Marshall—Contra. We need not shew a continual possession within twenty years, but the plaintiff, on his part must shew a possession, in order to maintain an Ejectment.

October 27. The court delivered their opinions. Tazewell, Judge.

4. Davenport v. Oldis, 1 Atkyns 579–581, 26 Eng. Rep. 363–365 (Ch., 1738), held that cross-remainders were never favored by law and could only arise by implication when absolutely necessary to avoid an intestacy.

5. Philip Yorke, first earl of Hardwicke (1690–1764), served as lord chancellor from 1737 to 1756.

6. At this time actions to recover land by ejectment, based upon an ancestor's possession, had to be brought within 40 years; if based on one's own possession, the actions had to be commenced within 30 years; the references to a 20-year limitation are not in line with the Virginia statutes. 5 Hening 408, 416 (1748). However, a 1784 statute provided that the period from Apr. 10, 1771, to Apr. 10, 1784, should be counted as one day in computing limitations on actions at law. 11 Hening 294.

7. Sir Edward Coke, *The first part of the Institutes of the laws of England; or, A commentary upon Littleton*, 16th ed. (London, 1809), 262–263b, indicates that a continual claim is an entry by construction of law for the advantage of the disseisee and not for his disadvantage. *Ibid.*, 263b. Randolph's argument, asking that this rule be applied to ejectment actions contrary to the precedent of Hayward v. Kinsey (see n. 4, p. 177, above), seems rather technical and was rebutted by JM's final argument to the court.

The plaintiffs claim is founded on their being no cross remainders established by the will of John West the elder. To this claim the Defendants make three objections—1st. Want of possession in John West the son, at the time of devise to the plaintiffs. 2d. The Act of Limitations. 3d. Cross remainders. As to the 1st. point he was clearly of Opinion that a vested interest might be devised. The 2d. point he had not considered. 3d. The Intention of the Testator in this Case clearly was to create cross remainders between his grandsons—otherwise Hugh would loose the Land devised to him at the death of his Brother; which could never be the Testators meaning.

Fleming, Lyons, & Carrington, accordant.

Judgement for the Defendant. vi: Gilbert v Witty, 2. Cro: 655, Cumber v Hill 2. Str: 969, Holmes v Meynell, T. Ray. 452, Marriot v Townley, 1. Vezey 102, Perry v White, Cowper 777, & Phippard v Mannsfield, Ib: 797.[8]

Sandford v. Conn

Notes on Argument in the General Court

Extract from Casebook, Tucker-Coleman Papers, Swem Library, College of William and Mary

Richmond, October 25, 1786

This was a sups.[9] to the Court of Fairfax County. The Case was thus. In novr. 1773. A will of Michael Regan,[1] dated 1759. was admitted to record. In may 1784. another will, dated March 1, 1773. was exhibited for probate, by one of the Devisees under it. The heir at law, though affected by it, does not appear to have been summoned.[2] The Objections made to this will were, That one

8. Gilbert v. Witty, Cro. Jac. 655–656, is printed in 79 Eng. Rep. 566–567 (K.B., 1623); Marryat v. Townley, 1 Vesey Sr. 102–105, is printed in 27 Eng. Rep. 918–920 (Ch., 1748).

9. "Supersedeas." A writ issuing from an appellate court that directs the suspension of proceedings in the trial court by staying the issuance or execution of a writ of execution until the matter can be heard upon appeal.

1. Possibly the Michael Regan, Jr., who was a trooper in the Fairfax County militia in 1756.

2. Virginia procedure, following the English model, permitted proof in "common form." Such an ex parte proceeding dispensed with the appearance of subscribing witnesses to a will or a citation to the heir-at-law of the testator; however, it was available

Margaret Johnson one of the subscribing Witnesses had a Legacy of £5. which she had released in consideration of thirty shillings.[3] And, That the other subscribing witness was interested, having taken a Lease of some Lands held under the former will; which he still holds. This witness wrote the will—He had drawn another by the Testor.'s direction, but having omitted some legacies to his Grandchildren his wife prevailed on him to destroy it—In this will they were inserted as dictated by the wife. The testator said nothing when the will was read to him, but signed it, & then acknowledged it in presence of the Witnesses: he lived six months after, without revoking it.

Lee,[4] for the plt. Here are two Objections to this will—1st. The competence of the witnesses—2d. The Wife's Interposition. He cited 2. Ld. Ray. 1008.

2. Ld. Raym. 1008, 1 Salk: 286. s.c.[5]

Marshall, contra: Sandford was a disinterested Witness at the time of his subscription. He became interested by his own subsequent act. Sandford knew of the secretion of this will; and knowing that, accepted a Lease under the heir at Law, from whom the Land was devised away—Were such a practise admitted, numerous Combinations would take effect to defeat Wills & Deeds. He cited

only if there was no contest concerning the validity of the will. John Godolphin, *The Orphan's Legacy; or a Testamentary Abridgment* (London, 1701), 62, 65; William Nelson, *Lex Testamentaria* (London, 1724), 463; Henry Swinburne, *A Briefe Treatise of Testaments and Last Willes* . . . (London, 1640 [orig. publ. 1591]), II, 69–70; Berryman v. Booth, Apr. 1734, Barton, *Va. Colonial Decisions*, II, B42–B43. However, in this situation, where a prior will was on file with the court and questions of its revocation and the validity of the subsequent will were raised by the existence of an earlier will, "solemn form" proof would have been required, necessitating citation of the heir-at-law.

3. A 1752 English statute provided that a subscribing witness named as a legatee in a will might renounce his legacy and testify concerning the execution of the will. Before this statutory change the legatee was not permitted to testify, and thus the will might be invalidated if a sufficient number of subscribing witnesses were not available. 25 Geo. 2, c. 6; Thomas Wentworth, *The Office and Duties of Executors* . . . (London, 1728), 5, 6; Henry Swinburne, *A Treatise of Testaments and Last Wills* . . . (London, 1677), 295–296. In Apr. 1735 the Virginia General Court, passing upon other matters, ventured the dictum that a legatee must release his legacy before testifying concerning the execution of the will. Harwood v. Grace, Barton, *Va. Colonial Decisions*, II, B45. Virginia law, in this regard, seems to have anticipated the English statutory development; however, since the colonial decisions were not available to JM and other counsel arguing this case, the question of a legatee's testifying as a subscribing witness was open to renewed argument.

4. Charles Lee.

5. Tilly's Case, 2 Lord Raymond 1008, 92 Eng. Rep. 171 (K.B., 1703), also reported in 1 Salkeld 286, 91 Eng. Rep. 254, concerned a witness whose deposition was taken in a chancery proceeding to perpetuate his testimony. In a subsequent ejectment action, brought after the witness had become an interested party, the court held that his deposition might not be read, nor might he testify.

—Holt's rep: 754, 1: Strange 1: 406, Buller's nisi prius 290.—to shew that a subscribing witness is compellable to give Testimony.[6]

NB. As to the competency of the subscribing Witness Margaret Johnson, see the Case of Ansty v Dowsen—1. Blacks: rep: 8, 2. Strange 1253. S.C., Wyndham v Chetwynd 1. Blacks: rep: 98, 1. Burrow, 416 to 431. S.C. Where this point is fully illustrated.[7]

Randolph[8] for the plt. Rests the point on the court's compelling Sandford to prove the will against his own Interest. He does not object to his Competency. The only Question with him is, whether the court had power to oblige him to swear, in this Case.

Tazewell, Judge. The Court have clearly that power.

Lyons, Judge—said he should never hesitate to grant an Attachment against a subscribing witness who refused to testify. He had no notion of turning the party over to a court of Equity.

Carrington, accordant. Fleming & Mercer, absent.

The witnesses were called into court but before they were sworne.

Lee, cited, Swinburne 479.[9] Where a Will is made in extremis,

6. An anonymous case in Holt 754, 97 Eng. Rep. 1314–1315 (K.B., 1695), involved a fraudulent scheme in connection with wagers at a horse race; a witness who had bet upon the same race as the parties to the litigation was permitted to testify, although the court observed that his interest would impair his credibility. The number 1 following the page citation indicates that this is the first case appearing on p. 754 of Holt's reports.

Clark v. Elwick, 1 Strange 1, 93 Eng. Rep. 346 (K.B., 1715), held that a witness to an arbitration award must testify, even if he objected to the terms of the award as unfairly given, for "every witness does by his signing undertake to prove when required." In Hawkins v. Perkins, 1 Strange 406, 93 Eng. Rep. 600 (K.B., 1718), it was held that if one of a party's bailsmen in an action was also a subscribing witness to a bond, he could be compelled to testify concerning the handwriting. The last citation is to Sir Francis Buller, *An Introduction to the Law relative to Trials at Nisi Prius*, 5th ed. (London, 1768).

7. The material following "NB." is probably St. George Tucker's collection of authorities on this point of law and not JM's argument. Holdfast ex dem Anstey v. Dowsing, 2 Strange 1253–1255, 93 Eng. Rep. 1164–1165 (K.B., 1747), also reported in 1 Blackstone Rep. 8–18, 96 Eng. Rep. 5–9, had held that a legatee who was a subscribing witness was precluded from testifying concerning the execution of the will by the English statute of frauds of 1676. Wyndham v. Chetwynd, 1 Blackstone Rep. 96–103, 96 Eng. Rep. 53–57 (K.B., 1752), also reported in 1 Burrow 414–431, 97 Eng. Rep. 377–387, criticized Anstey v. Dowsing and, after an extended historical discussion, held that it was absurd to make credibility a ground for disqualifying a witness. Interest, the court stated, was certainly a basis for objection to the witness's competency, but was not a positive disability or one imposed by the statute of frauds. Interest was only a presumptive disability in the eyes of the law.

8. Edmund Randolph.

9. Henry Swinburne, *A Treatise of Testaments and Last Wills* . . . , 5th ed. (London, 1728), 503, indicated that a subsequently executed will did not revoke the prior will when it was executed under the influence of fear or threat of violence, when it was obtained through fraud or deceit, when it did not mention and specifically revoke the

at the instigation of another person, it shall be set aside in favor of a Testament made before that time.

The witnesses were then sworn, & the latter will established.

Kuhn v. Hoomes

Declaration

Record Book Copy, District Court Records, Office of the Clerk of the Circuit Court, Fredericksburg, Va.

Richmond, October 1786

October General Court 1786

Caroline County to wit.

Jacob Kuhn complains of John Hoomes[1] in Custody etc. for this to wit that he the defendant on the   day of   in the year 1786 with force and Arms to wit sticks, staves, and fists at the parish of   in the County aforesaid made an assault upon him the Plaintiff and him the plaintiff he the defendant did then and there beat, wound and evilly treat and other wrongs and injuries to him the plaintiff he the defendant then and there did against the peace and dignity of the Commonwealth of Virginia and to the damage of the plaintiff two thousand pounds wherefore he brings Suit etc.[2]

J: MARSHALL p q.

---

prior will and was made at the interrogation or suggestion of another person and the testator was very sick or in peril of death. However, a later will in favor of a child of the testator or the testator's heirs-at-law might be upheld in spite of these circumstances.

1. The defendant may be identifiable with Col. John Hoomes (*ca.* 1745–1805), former justice of the peace of Caroline County, whose will mentions John Taylor of Caroline. See *VMHB*, XXXVIII (1930), 74–79.

2. Hoomes, represented by John Taylor, pleaded not guilty on Aug. 30, 1787. After the reorganization of the courts, the case was transferred to the District Court in Fredericksburg. The case went to trial in Sept. 1789, but the jury was withdrawn and the case continued until May 6, 1791, when judgment was entered for Hoomes. On Kuhn's behalf JM asked the High Court of Chancery for an injunction against the judgment but it was refused on Oct. 28, 1791. This decree was appealed to the Court of Appeals, which affirmed it on Oct. 20, 1792. See Account Book, Receipts, Apr. 23, 1787. JM also received fees in this case in Oct. 1791 and Sept. 1792. District Court Records, 1789–1792, 498–499, Office of the Clerk of the Circuit Court, Fredericksburg, Va.; Wythe 136; Court of Appeals Order Book, II, 187, 188, Virginia State Library; 4 Call 274–279.

Robertson's Will

Notes on Argument in the General Court

Extract from Casebook, Tucker-Coleman Papers, Swem Library, College of William and Mary

Richmond, October 1786

Martha Robertson being extremely ill, Doctor Bennet[3] who attended her, at the instance of some person present, asked her to whom she intended to leave her estate, her Brother, Uncles, Aunts or Cousins? At the same time he informed her of the danger of her situation. She answered—"To my mother." He repeated—"Do you desire to give all to your Mother." She answered "Yes." The substance of this conversation was committed to paper by some other person, it being now late at night, & in the morning it was read to her by Bennet, but was never signed, although the witnesses say that she assented to it when read to her. She was in her perfect senses at the time, and continued so during that whole day: the next day she died.

Carrington, junior; in favor of the will cited, 2. Blacks: Com: 376, Swinburne 6: 54: 55. 59.—5. Ba. ab: 505.[4]

Baker,[5] contra: Is this a Will in writing made by Miss Robertson according to her instructions? If it be not, is it a nuncupative will?[6]

As to a written will he cited 2. Blacks. Com: 501. and took a dis-

3. A Martha Field Archer married the Rev. George Robertson (d. 1724) of Bristol Parish; she was his second wife and survived him. The Dr. Bennet mentioned could not have been Dr. Jesse Bennett (1769–1842), a surgeon from the Shenandoah Valley of Virginia noted for performing a Caesarian section in 1794.

4. Paul Carrington, Jr., was an attorney from Prince Edward County who served as commonwealth attorney for that county in 1794. He does not appear to have been related to Paul Carrington, a judge of the General Court at the time this case was argued, although he was called "Jr." to distinguish him from the jurist. Henry Swinburne, *A Treatise on Testaments and Last Wills* . . . , 5th ed. (London, 1728), 6, states that, before the 1676 English statute of frauds, any notes in writing taken at the direction of or by the testator and put into the form of a will would be adequate to devise title to real property, even if the testator died before he signed the document or it was shown to him. The passages at pp. 54 and 55 refer to soldiers' and sailors' testaments, and the subject on p. 59 is testaments *ad pias causas* ("in favor of charities").

5. Jerman Baker.

6. A nuncupative will is an oral declaration of testamentary intentions, later proven in court by the witnesses to the declaration; this form of testament could not devise title to real property. See Thomas E. Atkinson, *Handbook of the Law of Wills* . . . , 2d ed. (St. Paul, Minn., 1953), 363–367.

tinction between a question proposed to a sick person, & instructions first moving from the sick person herself.

Marshall—advocated the will, & relied wholly on the Authorities adduced by Carrington.

Randolph,[7] Contra—what was read to Miss Robertson was really not a will, but the Evidence which the Witnesses were about to give.

The Court established the will as a Will in writing.[8]

McElheny v. Hughes

Declaration

Copy, District Court Order Book, Office of the Clerk of the Augusta County Circuit Court, Staunton, Va.

[*October 1786, Richmond.* A declaration in indebitatus assumpsit on a promissory note, filed in the General Court by JM as attorney for the plaintiff and signed by JM.[9]]

7. Edmund Randolph.

8. A similar factual situation confronted the Prerogative Court of colonial New York in regard to the 1743 will of Lewis Pintard, which was also accepted as a will in writing even though Pintard had died before he was able to sign the completed document. Folio 1243, New York County Wills (New Ser.), Historical Documents Collection, Queens College, Flushing, N.Y. The English rule after the 1676 statute of frauds was that if a person declared his will and called in a scribe to commit it to writing, but died before he could sign it, the will would not be a will in writing but rather might constitute a nuncupative testament. On the other hand, if a testator wrote his will in a regular and complete manner, but did not sign it, it nevertheless would be valid as a "holographic" will in writing. Swinburne, *Treatise of Testaments*, 498, 500. In other words, under the English rule Martha Robertson's will would have been valid as a will in writing only if she had written it entirely in her own hand. The more liberal Virginia rule, accepted here by the court and later evidenced by the Kentucky decision, Sarah Miles's Will, 34 Kentucky (4 Dana) 1–5 (1836), permitted the document to be a will in writing even if not prepared in testator's hand. See discussion of the varying American rules in Atkinson, *Wills*, 299–302.

9. The defendant pleaded non assumpsit, and the case was transferred to the newly established District Court at Staunton. After jury trial and verdict, judgment was entered for the plaintiff on Sept. 1, 1790. District Court Order Book, 1789–1793, 83, Office of the Clerk of the Augusta County Circuit Court, Staunton, Va. See Account Book, Receipts, May 29, 1786.

Edmundson v. Hunt

Declaration

Record Book Copy, Records at Large, District Court, Office of the Clerk of the Prince Edward County Circuit Court, Farmville, Va.

[*ca. October 1786, Richmond.* A declaration in debt on bond to secure payment of £120, filed in the General Court by JM as attorney for the plaintiff and signed by JM.[1]]

Rice v. Jones

Argument

Printed, Daniel Call, *Reports of Cases Argued and Decided in the Court of Appeals of Virginia* (Richmond, 1833), IV, 89–91

[*November 3, 1786, Richmond.* JM argues for Edward Rice in the Court of Appeals.[2] The judgment, for Rice, was returned on Nov. 9, 1786.[3]]

Dudley v. Crump

Notes on Argument in the High Court of Chancery

Extract from Casebook, Tucker-Coleman Papers, Swem Library, College of William and Mary

Richmond, November 16, 178[6]
In Chancery, Nov: 16, 1785.[4] abt. Devise of Slaves. Devise to one *for Life*—& if Devisee should die in the Life time of A. then to A.

1. The case was transferred to the newly established District Court at Prince Edward County, where it came on for trial in Apr. 1790. The jury returned a verdict for plaintiff, and judgment was entered thereon. Records at Large, District Court, 1789–1792, 94–95, Office of the Clerk of the Prince Edward County Circuit Court, Farmville, Va.

2. See Account Book, Receipts, Oct. 4, 1788; Court of Appeals Order Book, 1779–1789, 93, Virginia State Library.

3. Court of Appeals Order Book, 1779–1789, 99, Va. State Lib.

4. St. George Tucker did not begin taking notes on cases until 1786, and this case is on p. 23 of his notebook. Although he occasionally copied notes from other attorneys,

A died living the devisee—Heir at Law claims the Reversion, on the Death of Devisee.[5] There was allso a residuary clause in the will—date of will 1750.

Qu: The Devise being expressly for Life, can the death of A. in the Lifetime of the Devisee give her a greater Estate in the Slave than is expressed in the will.

2: If it does not, will the residuary Clause embrace the reversion in this Slave, after the death of the first Devisee,* or will the Slave go to th[e h]eir at Law of the Testatrix.

Marshall—1. point. Can a Reversion exist after a Devise for Life—Remr. may be limitted after Disposition of a personal thing for Life. 1: P. Wms. Mattox v Staines.

1: P: Wms. 1; 2: P. Wms. 421; 1. Vern: 234; 1 Ld. Ray. 325; 2. Atk: 314.[6]

these do not seem to have been copied. Apparently Tucker made a mistake and wrote 1785 instead of 1786.

5. In other words, the individual entitled to the slaves after the death of the holder of the life estate predeceased the life tenant. It is not clear whether the heir-at-law is the heir of the life tenant or the heir of the testator; however, since there was a residuary clause in the will, normally the executor or residuary legatee of the testator would claim the slaves if they reverted to the testator's estate.

6. JM's argument undoubtedly was quite elaborate, since this was a difficult point in English law further complicated by the ambiguities of Virginia law concerning the status of slaves as either real or personal property. The weight of English authority was that chattels personal might be granted for life but that any future estates were void. However, by 1766 English law had progressed to the point that Blackstone could state that remainders after life estates in personalty, created by deed or by will, were valid. See John C. Gray, *The Rule against Perpetuities*, ed. Roland Gray, 4th ed. (Boston, 1942), 70–71; Blackstone, *Commentaries*, II, 298. Remainders after life estates in realty had been long recognized in English law.

The cases cited by JM applied to both real and personal property, which would indicate that he had prepared his argument to anticipate a determination that slaves were either real property or personal property. Maddox v. Staines, 2 Peere Williams 421–423, 24 Eng. Rep. 796–797 (Ch., 1727), held that a devise of personalty to a wife for her life, and upon her death with children, the interest and profits to be divided equally among the children until the sons reached 21 years of age and the daughters 18 years of age, at which ages each should receive his share of the estate, was a valid executory devise. This decision was subsequently affirmed by the House of Lords, 3 Brown 108–112, 1 Eng. Rep. 1209–1212 (1728). Hyde v. Parrat, 1 Peere Williams 1–6, 24 Eng. Rep. 269–272 (Ch., 1695), held a devise of household goods to the testator's wife for life, with the remainder to their son, was good as a devise over. Nicholls v. Osborne, 2 Peere Williams 420–421, 24 Eng. Rep. 795–796 (Ch., 1727), held that in the case of a devise of personalty to the testator's niece, to be paid upon her attaining 21 years of age, in which the niece died before reaching that age, the interest on the legacy would be payable to her estate. The court termed the estate of the niece a devise on a condition subsequent. Massenburgh v. Ash, 1 Vernon 234–237, 23 Eng. Rep. 437–438 (Ch., 1684), involved a trust estate in real property and hence does not seem pertinent to JM's argument, as Dudley v. Crump raised only the issue of legal estates. However, Massenburgh involved a series of successive equitable interests in children, vesting upon their reaching the age of 21 but passing to the next eldest child if the child entitled to the benefit of the use died before reaching 21. Ayres v. Falkland, 1 Lord Raymond 325–326, 91 Eng. Rep. 1112–1113 (K.B., 1697), held that a devise of a term of

Wythe[7]—Do you suppose, Sir, that this Doctrine of a Remr. in a Slave after Gift for Life will be contested?[8]

2. point. Is reversion disposed of by residuary clause.[9]

3. point. Whether Complt's right is destroyed by a Deed which his wife privately made the day before marriage.

1: Eq: Ca: ab. 59; 2: Ch: rep: 79–81; 2: Vern: 17; 2. Ba: abr: 600.[1]

*vi: Cole v Claiborne, 1 Wash: 265. That the Slave passes thereby.[2]

Browning's Representatives v. Hite's Representatives

Bill in Chancery

Copy, Clark-Hite Papers, The Filson Club

[*ca. November 1786, Richmond.* A petition by Joshua Browning, John Ritson Browning, William Keating, and Roseman Keating for an order

---

99 years to *A* for life, then to six others successively for their lives, with all seven life tenants dying before the end of the term, resulted in a reversion of the residue of the term to the testator's executors. Here the court observed that a devise of realty to *A* for life, and the remainder to *B*, was a good devise; this was probably JM's reason for citing this case. Beauclerk v. Dormer, 2 Atkyns 308–315, 26 Eng. Rep. 588–592 (Ch., 1742), involved a will that designated an individual the testator's sole heir and executrix and provided that, if she should die without issue, the property should go to *B*. The executrix obtained a fine and recovery and died without issue. The court held the limitation over invalid, since the personal estate had vested in the sole heir and executrix. JM may have distinguished this case as having involved an entailed estate, contrary to the situation in Dudley v. Crump.

7. George Wythe, who was then a judge of the High Court of Chancery.

8. Wythe's willingness to concede the point of law presumably ended JM's argument here. Later case law supports the contention that a remainder after a life estate in slaves was valid. In Medley v. Jones, 5 Munford (19 Va.) 98–101 (Sup. Ct. App., 1816), the court upheld a chancery order protecting reversionary interests against the attempt by a life tenant to remove the slaves from the state.

9. Unless the residuary clause of the will, disposing of all property not specifically devised and bequeathed, were limited in its scope, it ordinarily would transfer title to the testator's estate and bar a claim by his heir-at-law. The problem was one of construction of the will, hence no legal arguments were needed.

1. Lance v. Norman, 2 Chancery Reports 79–80, 21 Eng. Rep. 621–622 (Ch., 1673), also discussed in 1 Equity Cases Abridged 59, 21 Eng. Rep. 872 (Ch., 1673), held that when a woman on the day before her marriage, without the consent or knowledge of her future husband, executed a recognizance in favor of her brother, the recognizance was void. Carleton v. Dorset, 2 Vernon 17, 23 Eng. Rep. 622 (Ch., 1686), held that a conveyance to trustees made before marriage but without the future husband's privity, in which the property was for the separate use of the wife, was void and that the husband was entitled to possession of the property. The relationship of these legal precedents to the facts in Dudley v. Crump is unclear. JM's final citation on the same point was to Bacon, *Abridgment.*

2. St. George Tucker's later notation of a 1794 opinion of the Virginia Court of Appeals, which upheld JM's contention that a reversion passed by way of the residuary clause in a testator's will.

awarding title to 1,200 acres of land on Potomac Run in Berkeley County, sold to John Browning, deceased, by Joist Hite. Citing the decree in *Hite v. Fairfax*, it requests that the complainants' equitable claims be determined by the High Court of Chancery and is signed by JM as attorney for the complainants.]

Cunninghame v. Hite's Representatives

Bill in Chancery

Copy, Clark-Hite Papers, The Filson Club

[*ca. November 1786, Richmond.* A petition by Adam Cunninghame for an order awarding title to a portion of a 7,000-acre tract of land called the South River Tract, in Shenandoah County. The land had been sold to the complainant or his predecessor in title by Robert McKay, a partner of Joist Hite. Citing the decree in *Hite v. Fairfax*, it requests that the complainant's equitable claims be determined by the High Court of Chancery[3] and is signed by JM as attorney for the complainant.]

Denton v. Hite's Representatives

Bill in Chancery

Copy, Clark-Hite Papers, The Filson Club

[*ca. November 1786, Richmond.* A petition by John Denton and John Crockinhour for an order awarding title to land on North River in Shenandoah County, sold by Joist Hite to their predecessors in interest on Mar. 26, 1735. Citing the decree in *Hite v. Fairfax*, it requests that the complainants' equitable claims be determined by the High Court of Chancery and is signed by JM as attorney for the complainants.]

3. On Aug. 5, 1790, the High Court of Chancery held that the bill should be dismissed since the complainant failed to prove his title to be included within those covered by the decree of May 8, 1786. See chancery decree, folder 143, Clark-Hite Papers, The Filson Club.

Hyatt v. Hite's Representatives

Bill in Chancery

Copy, Clark-Hite Papers, The Filson Club

[*ca. November 1786, Richmond.* A petition by Simeon Hyatt, George Cloke, John Daniel, John Bees, Jr., and Adam Livingston for an order awarding title to land in Berkeley County, granted to the complainants or their predecessors in interest by Joist Hite. Citing the decree in *Hite v. Fairfax,* it requests that the complainants' equitable claims be determined by the High Court of Chancery[4] and is signed by JM as attorney for the complainants.]

Keller v. Hite's Representatives

Bill in Chancery

Copy, Clark-Hite Papers, The Filson Club

[*ca. November 1786, Richmond.* A petition by George Keller and Henry Somewalt for an order awarding title to 500 acres of land in Powell's Fort, Shenandoah County, sold by Robert McKay and Joist Hite to Abraham Delbach. Citing the decree in *Hite v. Fairfax,* it requests that the complainants' equitable claims be determined by the High Court of Chancery[5] and is signed by JM as attorney for the complainants.]

Leith v. Hite's Representatives

Bill in Chancery

Copy, Clark-Hite Papers, The Filson Club

[*ca. November 1786, Richmond.* A petition by James Leith for 200 acres of land on the South Branch of the Shenandoah River, sold by Joist Hite

4. An endorsement to the bill indicates dismissal for failure to specify the land claimed or the persons under whom the petitioners claimed. See folder 153, Clark-Hite Papers, The Filson Club.

5. On Aug. 5, 1790, the High Court of Chancery decreed that the complainants had failed to adduce sufficient evidence to prove the contract and that the bill was dismissed with costs. See chancery decree, folder 154, Clark-Hite Papers, The Filson Club.

and his associates to the complainant's grandfather, James Leith, in 1736. Citing the decree in *Hite v. Fairfax*, it requests that the complainant's equitable claims be determined by the High Court of Chancery[6] and is signed by JM as attorney for the complainant.]

Lindsay v. Hite's Representatives

Bill in Chancery

Copy, Clark-Hite Papers, The Filson Club

[*ca. November 1786, Richmond.* A petition by John Lindsay, Jr., Thomas Lindsay, Albion Throckmorton (*ca.* 1740–1796), Isaac Laine, Warner Washington, Jr., and Edmund Clair for 860 acres of land on Long Marsh in Berkeley County, sold by Joist Hite to Nathaniel Doherty. Citing the decree in *Hite v. Fairfax*, it requests that the complainants' equitable claims be determined by the High Court of Chancery and is signed by JM as attorney for the complainants.]

Matthews v. Hite's Representatives

Bill in Chancery

Copy, Clark-Hite Papers, The Filson Club

[*ca. November 1786, Richmond.* A petition by Solomon Matthews for an order awarding title to land in the Great Cove survey in Shenandoah County sold by Joist Hite to William Clark and David Carlock. Citing the decree in *Hite v. Fairfax*, it requests that the complainant's equitable claims

6. By answer sworn to on Sept. 29 and Oct. 16, 1789, the defendants denied information sufficient to answer the bill, but defendant James McCoy admitted that years earlier he had seen a bond securing the grant of some land to James Leith in the area described by the bill, although he did not recall the amount of land involved in the transaction. After taking depositions, the High Court of Chancery on Aug. 5, 1790, decreed that complainant was entitled to quiet possession of 200 acres of land, provided he pay the remaining portion of the purchase price within 21 days after being served with a copy of the court's decree. On Mar. 1, 1792, this decree was affirmed on appeal by the Court of Appeals. See folder 157, Clark-Hite Papers, The Filson Club.

be determined by the High Court of Chancery[7] and is signed by JM as attorney for the complainant.]

Taylor v. Hite's Representatives

Bill in Chancery

Copy, Clark-Hite Papers, The Filson Club

[*ca. November 1786, Richmond*. A petition by William Taylor, John Milton, and William Booth (d. 1790) for an order granting title to 147 acres of land on Buck Mouth sold to one Pennington by Joist Hite and also granted to Isaac Pennington by Lt. Gov. William Gooch (1681–1751) in 1734. Citing the decree in *Hite v. Fairfax*, it requests that the complainants' equitable claims be determined by the High Court of Chancery and is signed by JM as attorney for the complainants.]

Washington v. Hite's Representatives

Bill in Chancery

Copy, Clark-Hite Papers, The Filson Club

[*ca. November 1786, Richmond*. A petition by John Augustine Washington (1736–1787) for an order awarding title to land on Bullshin in Berkeley County sold by Joist Hite to Patrick Matthews. Citing the decree in *Hite v. Fairfax*, it requests that the complainant's equitable claims be determined by the High Court of Chancery and is signed by JM as attorney for the complainant.]

7. An Aug. 5, 1790, decree of the High Court of Chancery awarded title to the complainant on his payment of the purchase price or balance remaining. On appeal to the Court of Appeals, it was held that, since it had been proved that the purchase price had been paid, the decree of the High Court of Chancery ordering payment was reversed. A revised decree was issued by the High Court of Chancery on Mar. 19, 1792. See transcript of decree, folder 159, Clark-Hite Papers, The Filson Club.

To Edmund Randolph

DS, Executive Papers, Virginia State Library[8]

Sir   Richmond, December 24, 1786

In Pur[s]uance of the request of your Excellcy. & Honble. Board, we have made Such enquiry into the Intellect & Soundness of mind of *James Goss* as fully Sattisfie us on this Subject; & tho the unhappy object is ignorant & Stupid to a great degree, yet we are perfectly convinced he does not come under the Terms of Idiotism or insanity, but is a Competent Judge of Right from Wrong.[9] We are, Sir, Your Excellcy.'s Most Obt. Servts.

W. FOUSHEE
J. MARSHALL
ROBT. BOYD[1]

Legislative Bill

AD, House of Delegates Papers, Virginia State Library

Richmond, *ca.* December 25, 1786

Whereas[2] the delays inseparable from the present constitution of the General Court, do in many cases unavoidably amount to a de-

8. Written from the Richmond public jail, marked received on Dec. 25, "formerly postpd. to 26th decr. Done."

9. Goss had been convicted by the General Court for horse stealing and was sentenced to death. He and a few others escaped from the public jail in Richmond on May 31, 1786, but Goss was apprehended in a few days. On June 5 the governor pardoned him on the condition that he "perform bodily labor" for three years. In October he escaped again but was soon caught. *JVCS*, III, 554, 565, 587. After his return to jail, Goss's pardon was revoked and he was sentenced to die. Apparently an appeal was made to the governor and Council to reconsider Goss's conviction on the grounds that he was insane. At this point, on Dec. 21, JM, Foushee, and Boyd were asked to examine him. The report was presented to the Council on Dec. 26, and they advised unanimously that "no further pardon or reprieve be granted." *Ibid.*, IV, 10, 12, 13.

1. Foushee (1749–1824) and Boyd were members of the Richmond City Common Hall with JM, and Foushee was a physician. The governor obviously used as a model the procedure outlined for commitment of insane persons adopted in 1769, which required examination by three members of the local government. 8 Hening 379.

2. Although JM was not a delegate in the House of Delegates this session, this bill s unquestionably in his hand. It was ordered drawn on Dec. 20, presented on Dec. 25, debated and accepted with no changes by the Committee of the Whole House on Jan. 3, and adopted by a 64–44 vote on Jan. 4, 1787. The Senate failed to report any action on the bill before the session ended, and so it did not become a law. *JVHD*, Oct. 1786, 111, 121, 124, 137, 138–139.

nial of justice so that one great object for which government is instituted cannot be completely afforded to the good people of this Commonwealth; and whereas also it is reasonable that the burthen of administering justice shoud be borne equally by those who are selected from their fellow citizens for that purpose.

Be it therefor enacted that henceforth there shall be four sessions of Oyer & terminer holden by the Judges of the court of admiralty in the city of Richmond in every year; to wit one on the tenth day of March one on the first day of June one on the ⟨tenth⟩ first day of September and one on the tenth day of December, but if any of the said several days of session shall happen on a sunday then that session shall commence on the munday thereafter. Before any Judge of the said Court shall enter on the duties of his office he shall take & subscribe the oath of fidelity to the Commonwealth & shall also take the oath prescribd by law to be taken by the Judges of the General Court adapting the same to the particular occasion. The said oaths shall be administerd to the ⟨senior⟩ presiding Judge by some one other Judge & then by him to the other Judges of the court. Any two of the said Judges shall constitute a court and may continue to sit untill the business depending before them be completed and for this purpose shall have power to adjourn from day to day. And if two of the said Judges shall not attend on the first day of any term one Judge shall have power to adjourn the court till next day & so on from day to day for six days, and if another Judge shall not then attend the said court shall be adjournd till the court in course and thereupon all causes matters and things depending before the court shall stand continued till their next court.

The said court shall be a court of record & shall have jurisdiction & cognizance of all treasons, murders, felonies, misdemeanors, ⟨and other pleas of the commonwealth⟩ and also all motions against public debtors and other pleas of the Commonwealth, now cognizable in the General Court at their sessions holden in the months of June and December, except those made triable by the constitution before the General Court; And against such as shall be found guilty by the verdict of the petit jury the said court shall proceed to judgement according to law & award execution thereupon as hath been heretofore done by the Genl. Court & shall also in like manner discharge those not so found guilty.

The said court shall have power to appoint a Clerk one or more assistant Clerks, a crier and Tipstaf who shall hold their offices during good behavior. The Clerk shall receive for his services the same fees & other compensation now received by the Clerk of the Genl. court for the same services, and shall have power to do all things appertaining to the duty of Clerk which the Clerk of the General Court at their additional sessions is now by law authorized to do, and all subpoenas & other process issuing from the said court shall be signd by the Clerk & bear teste in the name of the oldest judge. The Crier & Tipstaf shall be allowed and paid for their services as the crier and tipstaf of the Genl. Court now are.

⟨And be it further enacted that it shall and may be lawful for the sheriff of the county of Henrico for the time being upon a writ to him directed by the Clerk of the ⟨⟨County of Henrico⟩⟩ court of oyer and terminer which writ⟩

And be it further enacted that a Grand Jury constituted as the law now requires shall be summond in the same manner ⟨and⟩ for the same purposes and with the same powers that a Grand Jury is now summond to attend the General Court and shall proceed in the same manner that Grand Juries in the General Court may now by law proceed.

The Clerk of the General Court shall be considerd as Clerk of the court of oyer and terminer and shall perform all the duties thereof until the said court shall meet and appoint a Clerk.

All proceedings of any county or other inferior court which were heretofore returnable to the General Court and which are concerning any matter or thing hereby made cognizable in the ⟨Gener⟩ court of oyer & terminer shall hereafter be made returnable to the court of oyer & terminer, And where an examining court shall direct any person to be removed to the public jail for further trial he shall be tried before the court of oyer & terminer, and the sheriff ⟨and⟩ shall proceed in the same manner, have the same power, be subject to the same penalties and have the same compensation for his services as is now directed by law in similar cases triable in the General court, and all Witnesses and venire Men shall be recognizd & summond to attend the court of oyer and terminer in the same manner, shall be subject to the same penalties and shall have the same allowance for their travelling & attendance as is by law directed in case of Witnesses and venire men recognizd or summond to attend the Genl. Court.

And be it further enacted that in all cases not herein otherwise particularly directed the court of oyer and terminer shall have the same power & be governd by the same laws & regulations that the General Court at their additional sessions in June and December hath heretofore been governd by.

The Judges of the General Court shall henceforth ceace to ⟨perform⟩ exercise those powers and perform those duties which are by this act directed to be exercised and performd by the Judges of the court of admiralty, except that the General Court may at their next session proceed as usual to the trial of such prisoners as have been or may be orderd by an examining court for further trial before the first day of March next where the witnesses ⟨shall⟩ may happen to be recognized to appear before the General Court instead of the court of oyer & terminer & therefor a Grand Jury shall be summond in the usual manner to attend the next Genl. Court, and the General court shall likewise have power at their next term to ⟨grant⟩ render judgement on motions made in behalf of the Commonwealth as usual, but all business which now is or which may be depending in the General Court & which is hereby made cognizable in the court of Oyer & terminer and which shall not be tried by the General Court during their next sessions shall be transferd to the court of oyer & terminer & taken up and tried by the said court in the same manner as the same woud have been tried in the General Court had this law never passed; and in such cases the General court shall cause the recognizance of all witnesses ⟨appearing before them⟩ to be taken for their appearance at the following court of oyer & terminer. ⟨And the notices of the sollicitor General shall hereafter be given to the notify those⟩

The General court at their sessions ⟨to⟩ which now commence in the months of April & October shall henceforth continue to sit ⟨ten⟩ twenty days, sundays exclusive in addition to their present terms, unless the business depending before them shall be finishd in less time; and the Clerk shall observe the same rules respecting the regulation of the court docket for those terms thus lengthened as he is now by law directed to observe and the said terms shall henceforth commence on the 20th. of March & the 10th. of September in every year, if not on Sunday & then on the munday thereafter.

The two additional sessions of the General court hitherto holden in June and December shall ceace and the court shall hold one session with power to receive the probat of deeds and wills & to try & determine ⟨for the trial of⟩ all questions of law brought before them from any inferior Court by appeal writ of error supersedeas or by any other legal ways or means whatever or which shall arise in the General court on any special verdict or case agreed: The said term shall commence on the second Munday of June—in each year and shall continue eighteen days sundays exclusive unless the business depending before them shall be sooner finishd.

In each year ⟨directly⟩ on the day after the expiration of the said last mentioned term unless the same shall be on a sunday & then on the munday thereafter one Judge of the General Court shall sit for the execution of all writs of ⟨all⟩ enquiry which may be depending before the Court and for this purpose the Clerk shall after every term holden in the month of april take from his general docket those suits on which writs of enquiry have been or shall be awarded & make out a separate docket of the same for the Judge and for each Attorney practising in the court who shall require the same and shall issue subpoenas in like manner as subpoenas are now issued in such cases in the General court. Any defendant who will appear before the said Judge by himself or Attorney & plead to issue and go to trial immediately may be permitted to do so. The said Judge may adjourn from day to day & may continue to sit for six days unless the business depending before him shall be sooner ended. Executions may be awarded on all writs of enquiry thus executed & on all judgements thus obtaind, in like manner as hath been heretofore practisd in the General Court in similar cases.

That session of the ⟨High⟩ Court of appeals which hath hitherto commencd on the 29th. day of April in each year shall henceforth commence on the tenth day of May unless the same shall happen on a sunday & then on the Munday following and the May session of the High court of Chancery shall commence the day after the rising of the ⟨High⟩ court of appeals if the same be not on a sunday & then on the Munday following.

And whereas the services required to be performd by the Judges of the General Court by this act are ⟨very much⟩ considerably encreasd be it further enacted that the sum of five hundred pounds per annum in addition to their present salaries shall be divided among the Judges of the General Court in proportion to their attendance, and warrants shall issue for the same in like manner as warrants are issued for their present salaries. So much of all & every act and acts of Assembly as comes within the purview of this act & is contrary to anything herein containd shall be and the same is hereby repeald.

Arbitrators' Award

DS, Executive Communications, Virginia State Library

Richmond, December 28, 1786

WE the underwritten, nominated and appointed, to hear and determine a Controversy subsisting between the Commonwealth of Virginia and Mr Simon Nathan, respecting certain Bills of Exchange, drawn upon the said Commonwealth, assigned to Mr Nathan, and accepted by the Executive,[3] having inspected the proofs to us submitted, and considered the Arguments of the late Attorney General[4] on the part of the Commonwealth and also the arguments of the said Mr Nathan, each of which were delivered in writing, DO FIND

FIRST that there is no convincing Testimony, that the Bills in question were drawn for depreciated money;

SECONDLY that there are considerable proofs that the Bills in question were purchased by Mr Nathan as Bills drawn for specie Value.

WE are of Opinion that Evidence of fraud on the part of Mr Nathan could alone discharge the Commonwealth from the full Payment of those Bills.

No such Evidence of fraud has been adduced in the proofs before us.

THEREFORE WE award and determine that the Acceptance of all the Bills by the Executive is binding upon the Commonwealth of Virginia both in Law and equity and that they ought to be paid accordingly, with the legal Interest arising thereupon.

GIVEN under our Hands and Seals at Richmond this 28th of December 1786.

JOHN MARSHALL [LS]
CYRUS GRIFFIN [LS][5]

3. Simon Nathan (1746–1822), merchant of Philadelphia, claimed that he had accepted 13 bills of exchange from Gen. George Rogers Clark for military supplies and was due the face value of the bills in specie. See *Madison Papers*, III, 21, for background of the case. On Jan. 10 and 11, 1787, the General Assembly acquiesced in this award by resolutions authorizing the executive to issue warrants in settlement of the claim. *JVHD*, Oct. 1786, 152, 155; *JVCS*, IV, 30.

4. Edmund Randolph, the former attorney general, was then governor of Virginia.

5. Griffin was at this time judge of the Confederation's Court of Appeals in Cases of Capture and also a delegate to the House of Delegates from Lancaster County.

To [   ] Hall

ADS, Innes Papers, Library of Congress[6]

[Richmond, *ca.* 1786]

Mr. Perkins will please request Mr Hall to pay Mr. Jones the ballance due me from Genl. Clark[7] & also inform Mr. Jones how he may get the money due me on the execution vs Pope[8] which I beleive is about £10. He will be so good also as to write an order in my name on Capt. Easton to tran[s]fer my credit which I beleive is about £2. to him. I will also thank Mr P. to settle with Mr. Hall for what he owes me at Picquett.[9] I won 9 dollars but he has a small acct. against me in the store.

J M.

To James Wilkinson

Printed, "Letter of John Marshall to James Wilkinson, 1787," *American Historical Review*, XII (1906–1907), 346–348[1]

Dear Sir,   Richmond, January 5, 1787

It is with a great deal of mortification I tell you that I have failed in obtaining the passport I applied for. On my mentioning the subject to the Governor he said he was acquainted with you and would with great pleasure do any thing which was proper to serve you. He took time to consider the subject and after several applications, told me to-day that to grant the passport as an official act was entirely improper because it could only extend to the limits of Virginia to which you had a right to go without his permit and that he could not write a private letter of recommendation to the Governor without having some acquaintance with him. On these reasons sir, my

6. Noted on the document "Memo of Chief Justice John Marshall in 1786. [signed] Geo. D. Dodd, 1886." In the Kentucky Historical Society is a copy in Mr. Dodd's hand to which he added "Endorsed on back, J. Marshall to Dr. Hall . . . found in Mr. Thos. Perkins papers . . . at Danville, Ky." That copy is dated Jan. 1895.

7. Probably Gen. George Rogers Clark.

8. See Account Book, Receipts, Apr. 3, 1786.

9. Picquet, or piquet, is a two-handed card game in which a pack of 32 cards is used.

1. The letter and information about it were furnished to the *American Historical Review* by Reuben T. Durrett of Louisville, Ky.

application in your favor was rejected. I am much chagrined at my disappointment.[2]

I am much indebted to you for the clear and succinct account you have given me of the two expeditions against the Indians. I fear with you that so long as you remain connected with Virginia it will be absolutely impossible to act on any great occasion with reputation or success. Just information from such a distance will never be obtained by government without a solicitude about intelligence which seldom exists in a proper degree on the eve of a separation. You are considered as being certainly about to part with us and therefore less attention will be given to any regulations respecting your country than if the disunion was not expected.

All is gloom in the eastern states. Massachusetts is rent into two equal factions and an appeal I fear has by this time been made to the God of battles. Three of the leaders of the opponents to Government have been taken and imprisoned in Boston. The whole force of the party is collected for their releif. The last intelligence gives us reason to fear that before this time the attempt to relieve them has been made with the whole power of one party and opposed by the whole power of the other. But of this I suppose you receive better information than I can give you. We have contradictory accounts of the motives and views of the insurgents.[3] We are sometimes informed that they are a British faction supported secretly from Canada whose immediate object is to overthrow the present and restore the former government, at other times we are told that it is a mere contest for power between Bowdoin and Hancock[4] and that the Hancock faction are aiming at the destruction of all public securities and the subversion of all public faith. Whatever may be the cause of these dissentions or however they may terminate, in their present operation they deeply affect the happiness and reputation of the United States. They will, however, I presume tend to people the western world if you can govern yourselves so wisely as

2. Apparently Wilkinson (1757–1825) wanted a passport for safe passage down the Mississippi River to New Orleans, the river having been closed by the Spanish pending the adjustment of several disputes with the United States. The governor of Virginia was Edmund Randolph; the other governor referred to was no doubt Rodriguez Esteban Miró (1744–1795), Spanish governor of Louisiana from 1785 to 1791. Arthur Preston Whitaker, "James Wilkinson's First Descent to New Orleans in 1787," *Hispanic American Historical Review*, VIII (1928), 82–97; James Ripley Jacobs, *Tarnished Warrior: Major-General James Wilkinson* (New York, 1938), 76–77.

3. JM refers to reports of the insurgency led by Daniel Shays in western Massachusetts.

4. James Bowdoin (1726–1790), the governor of Massachusetts, and John Hancock (1736–1793), his predecessor.

to present a safe retreat to the weaker party. These violent, I fear bloody, dissentions in a state I had thought inferior in wisdom and virtue to no one in the union, added to the strong tendency which the politics of many eminent characters among ourselves have to promote private and public dishonesty cast a deep shade over that bright prospect which the revolution in America and the establishment of our free governments had opened to the votaries of liberty throughout the globe. I fear, and there is no opinion more degrading to the dignity of man, that these have truth on their side who say that man is incapable of governing himself. I fear we may live to see another revolution. I am dear sir, with high esteem and respect, Your obed't serv't.

JOHN MARSHALL

To Thomas Marshall

Printed extracts, William Littell, *Political Transactions in and concerning Kentucky* (Frankfort, Ky., 1806). Reprinted, with an Introduction by Temple Bodley, Filson Club Publications, No. 31 (Louisville, Ky., 1926), 76, 79[5]

[Richmond, *ca.* January 11, 1787]

The act is not precisely such as I wished it to be,[6] nor is it conformable to the resolutions of the committee before whom I appeared, but it may perhaps be formed on more prudent and cautious principles; on principles which will finally conduce more to

5. The style and tone of this letter make JM's authorship questionable, especially when the letter is compared with others written on the same subject on Feb. 11 and Mar. 5, 1787. JM rarely wrote formally and one would least expect him to write this way to his father. The editors suspect the letter probably is to Thomas Marshall but think it may have been written by someone other than JM. Because the ALS has not been found, and handwriting examination is thus impossible, and because we have no evidence JM refuted the attribution after this extract was first published, we have elected to include it in this edition.

6. Referring to "An act making further provision for the erection of the district of Kentucky into an independent State," passed by the House of Delegates on Dec. 18 and concurred in by the Senate on Dec. 21, 1786. See 12 Hening 240–242; *JVHD*, Oct. 1786, 106, 114, 153, 156.

Upon the failure of a quorum in the Kentucky convention assembled under the 1786 law, the members present at Danville prepared a memorial to the Virginia legislature and sent it to JM, who was appointed their agent to deal with the statehood question. See John M. Brown, *The Political Beginnings of Kentucky* (Louisville, Ky., 1889), 73–74, and William Littell, *Political Transactions in and concerning Kentucky* (Frankfort, Ky., 1806), also reprinted in Filson Club Publications, No. 31 (Louisville, Ky., 1926), 16–18. The Kentucky convention of 1786 continued to meet while this application was pending in Richmond under JM's guidance.

the peace and harmony of the district, than had my wishes (which were to enable the present convention to decide the question finally) prevailed. Those, sir, who introduced and passed the law, reasoned thus: the power delegated to the convention by the people, to decide upon a separation, was limited in point of time to a decision to be made in such time that Congress might consider and determine on the admission of your state into the union, by the first day of June, 1787, that an existence for twelve months was given for other purposes pointed out in the law, that as you are very much divided among yourselves, and there does not appear to be in the minority a disposition to submit it with temper to the decision of the majority, and the measures of the convention, in consequence of a defect in the original law, would be liable to some objection, the most safe, unexceptionable & accommodating plan is, to pass a law, in which the defects of the former act may be corrected, and which shall enable the present convention either to sit till their term has expired,[7] or to call immediately a new convention, to the decisions of which the disappointed can make no objection. . . . The negociation which has been opened with Spain, for ceding the navigation of the Mississippi—a negociation so dishonourable and injurious to America, so destructive of the natural rights of the western world, is warmly opposed by this country, and for this purpose the most pointed instructions are given to our delegates in congress.[8] I persuade myself that this negociation will terminate in securing, instead of ceding that great point.

To Cadwalader Jones

ALS, Etting Collection, Historical Society of Pennsylvania[9]

Sir   Richmond, January 17, 1787
    An order of yours on Mr. William Constable[1] Mercht. of Philadelphia for 2000 wt. of tobo. in favor of Mr. Gratz & which is re-

---

7. Delegates to the 1786 Kentucky convention were to serve for one year after taking office, presumably until Sept. 1, 1787. See 12 Hening 37, 38.

8. By resolution dated Nov. 29, 1786, concurred in by the Senate on Dec. 7, the House of Delegates instructed the governor and Council to instruct Virginia's delegates in Congress to "oppose any attempt that may be made in Congress to barter or surrender . . . the right of the United States to the free and common use of the river Mississippi." See *JVHD*, Oct. 1786, 67, 93.

9. Addressed to Maj. Jones (1755–1796), "near Petersburg."

1. Constable later moved to New York City and retained JM as his attorney.

turnd unpaid has been in my hands upwards of twelve months & Mr. Gratz is now anxious about payment.[2] I wrote to you on the subject but had not the pleasure of receiving your answer.

Will you be so obliging as to send me a line concerning it. The Tobo.[3] I hope you will enclose in it. I am Sir respectfully, your obedt. Servt,

J MARSHALL

Brame v. Haley

Declaration

Record Book Copy, Records at Large, District Court, Office of the Clerk of the Prince Edward County Circuit Court, Farmville, Va.

[*ca. January 1787, Richmond.* A declaration in debt on a bond to secure payment of £20, filed in the General Court by JM as attorney for the plaintiff and signed by JM.[4]]

To John Alexander

ALS, Marshall Papers, Library of Congress[5]

Dear Sir   Richmond, February 10, 1787

Mr. Randolph[6] is not now in Richmond, when he returns I will speak to him about the amendment to your bill.[7] The Judges seem rather to incline to continue the injunction untill the final hearing of the suits & to decide on the whole together.

I remember to have had some conversation with you while you

2. Probably Bernard or Michael (1740–1811) Gratz, Philadelphia merchants who traded in Virginia.

3. A warehouse receipt for tobacco is presumably what is meant.

4. The case was transferred to the newly established District Court at the Prince Edward County courthouse and came on for trial about Sept. 1789. The jury returned a verdict for the plaintiff, and judgment was entered thereon. Records at Large, District Court, 1789–1792, 42–43, Office of the Clerk of the Prince Edward County Circuit Court, Farmville, Va.

5. Addressed to Alexander in Loudoun. Added on address leaf in an unknown hand "annexed to the examination of John Orr taken 7 of November 1791."

6. Gov. Edmund Randolph.

7. See Account Book, Receipts, Feb. 2 and Mar. 28, 1787.

were here about your suit with Belfield but I do not recollect what it was. He has spoken to me since & has offerd me very high fees indeed to take his cause. I have refused him till I see or hear from you because no consideration woud tempt me to engage for him if I had promised to appear for you. I do not recollect or beleive that I did but I wish to be certain on the subject. I am Sir with respect & esteem, Your obedt. Servt.

J. MARSHALL

To George Muter

ALS, Marshall Papers, Library of Congress[8]

My dear Sir   Richmond, February 11, 1787

How do you approve of the measures of the last assembly so far as they affect your district? But before you can answer this I expect to hear your sentiments & those of your country. A separation I expect either has or will be decided on. I had the other day some conversation with Colo. Carrington[9] one of our Delegates in Congress on the subject and he seems to entertain some doubt whether Congress will consent to your admission into the union. Do not imagine that any difficulties will be generated by virginia or her Delegates—I beleive I can assure you that you will experience from them every good office. What prospect have you of obtaining the navigation of the Mississipi & what are your sentiments of the treaty about the cession of it for a term of years? People in general here are decidedly against it & yet some who are deeply interested in the prosperity of the western country appear to wish for it as being beneficial to you. I cannot conjecture how this opinion is to be supported but I assure it is the opinion of some very rational men who are I beleive sincere friends to the prosperity of the western country. I suppose you have before this [colle]cted all the comfortable things [of] this world except one to share them with you. How do you feel on that subject? Are you not beginning to think tis time to take up the consideration of that subject? Farewell I am my dear Sir with the warmest wishes for your happiness, your

J MARSHALL

8. Addressed to Muter in Danville, Ky., to be delivered by Mr. Fields.
9. Edward Carrington.

Acknowledgment

ADS, Executive Papers, Virginia State Library

[*March 2, 1787, Richmond*. JM, as a magistrate of Richmond, affirms that James Harris,[1] "a Quaker," appeared before him and swore that two felons had escaped from their jobs. Their death sentences had been commuted to hard labor by the governor.]

To Arthur Lee

Copy, Lee Family Papers, Virginia Historical Society[2]

Dear Sir   Richmond, March 5, 1787

Your favor of the 10th of Jany. is now before me. I have not sent the letter you enclosed me in search of Mr. Imlay[3] because I am told by my brother who is much better acquainted with him than I am that he either now is or will very soon be in New York.

I have in my possession the notes you enquire for. I very much fear that the conduct of some unthinking men in the western country will embroil us with Spain unless there be some more vigorous interposition of government than we seem disposed to make. A memorial signed by some of the most respectable persons of Kentucky has lately been presented to the Governor on this subject in which the conduct of General Clarke[4] I am told is a good deal

1. Harris was manager of construction of the canal being built by the James River Company around the falls of the river at Richmond. One of the escaped felons may have been Edward Watkins, who was captured and returned to work on the canal in October. *JVCS*, IV, 89, 152.

2. Addressed to Lee in New York, where he was a member of the Treasury board (1785–1789). ALS advertised for sale in 1940 in Goodspeed's *The Flying Quill* (Jan.), 3, as a Mar. 3, 1787, letter. The printed extract in Goodspeed's catalog also contains some variations in the text. John Edward Oster, *The Political and Economic Doctrines of John Marshall* (New York, 1914), 40, printed a copy of the letter under Mar. 5, 1787, and contained fewer variations, but he copied his version from Richard Henry Lee, *Life of Arthur Lee* . . . (Boston, 1829), II, 321–322. This copy is item no. Mss1L51a, vol. 2, p. 235, in the Virginia Historical Society.

3. Imlay is most likely Gilbert Imlay (*ca.* 1754–*ca.* 1828), who had purchased a tract of Kentucky land in 1783 and began speculating after he moved there in 1784. He left Kentucky in 1785 or 1786 and went to Europe at about the time of this letter. Reputedly he was in financial difficulty. In England he published *A Topographical Description of the Western Territory of North America* . . . (London, 1792) and became involved in French politics.

4. On Feb. 24, 1787, the Council of State received several letters with enclosures addressed to the governor by Thomas Marshall, among others, and sent from Danville, Ky., on Dec. 22, 1786. One of the things complained of was that Gen. George Rogers Clark had been recruiting soldiers, nominating officers, and seizing supplies for the

criminated. Whether the cession for a time of the navigation of the Mississipi would conduce to the interests of the western country or not must depend on facts of which I have but little information & therefore have never formed a decided opinion on the subject; but the people of this as well as of the Kentucky country who seem to form no adequate ideas of the magnitude of danger while at a distance have pronounced upon it without hesitation.

Mr. Henry whose opinions have their usual influence has been heard to say that he would rather part with the confederation than relinquish the navigation of the Mississipi—but as we have been fortiter in modo, I dare say we shall be suaviter in re.[5]

I congratulate you on the prospect of reestablishing order & good government in Massachusetts. I think their government will now stand more firmly than before the insurrection provided some examples are made in order to impress on the minds of the people a conviction that punishment will surely follow an attempt to subvert the laws & government of the Commonwealth.

Our attention is now entirely turned towards the next elections— the debtors as usual are endeavoring to come into the Assembly & as usual I fear they will succeed. I am dear Sir with the highest esteem, your obedt Servt.

J. MARSHALL

Acknowledgment

DS, Executive Papers, Virginia State Library

[*March 26, 1787, Richmond.* As a magistrate of the City of Richmond, JM takes the oath of George Nicholson (1758–1802), pursuant to the statute concerning naval officers and collection of the duties (11 Hening 182 [1782]), that the sloop *Nancy* was built in Virginia and is owned by Pennock, Nicholson, and Skipwith, inhabitants of Virginia.]

---

support of Ft. Vincennes and that he had seized some Spanish property without authority. On Feb. 28 the Council of State voted to notify Clark that it disapproved his actions. Steps were ordered taken to disclaim any Spanish property seized, and all those guilty of taking such property were ordered punished. *JVCS*, IV, 46–47.

5. JM twisted the idiomatic "fortiter in re, suaviter in modo" ("strongly in deed, gently in manner") to "strongly in manner, gently in deed."

To Battaile Muse

ALS, Collection of Thomas B. Marshall, West Chester, Pa.

Dear Sir   *ca*. April 1, 1787
I have receivd the three fees you mention. The defendants have employd a lawyer to keep off judgement so that it will be a considerable time before judgements can be obtained. So soon as it is possible I will obtain them for you. I am your obedt.

J MARSHALL

Dandridge's Executor v. Allen

Notes on Argument in the General Court

Extract from Casebook, Tucker-Coleman Papers, Swem Library, College of William and Mary

Richmond, April 7, 1787
Appeal from N. Kent. In an Action of Detinue for two negroes. Writ laid value of each of the Slaves, but no Value laid in Decl[arati]on.[7] Non detinet & Issue.[8] Spl verdict finds that Thomas Lyon by his will devised Hannah the mother of the Slaves in Ques-

6. Addressed to Muse (1751–1803) in Berkeley County, "hond. by Mr. Milton." Written on the address leaf, presumably in Muse's hand, "John Marshall/£7.10.0/ Enter this amt. in Ledger." In the same hand on the letter appears "Decr. 1787/Lee, Mason, Mason: The three this Money was paid for." See Account Book, Receipts, Apr. 1, 1787.

7. Detinue was a common law form of action for the recovery of a chattel, or its value as determined by a jury, if specific recovery was not possible. Chitty, *On Pleading*, I, 91–94. Although a description of the chattel was required, its value was not important to the cause of action; on the other hand, appeals to the General Court were limited to cases exceeding £10, exclusive of costs. 5 Hening 481 (1748); 9 Hening 412 (1777). While slaves were considered real property for certain purposes, the usual form of action for their recovery was detinue. See Marston v. Parrish (Apr. 1730), Edmonds v. Hughs (Apr. 1730), and Brooking v. Dudley (Apr. 1737), Barton, *Va. Colonial Decisions*, I, R35–R39, II, B256–B261; 3 Hening 334 (1705).
Replevin or trover might also have been used. Edmund M. Morgan, *Introduction to the Study of Law*, 2d ed. (Chicago, 1948), 89–92, 111–112. However, there is no record of their being so employed in Virginia. Replevin awarded possession to the plaintiff pending determination of the action; trover permitted either recovery of the chattel or its value. Either of these characteristics may have been considered undesirable in an action for the recovery of slaves.

8. The plea of "non detinet," that the defendant did not detain the chattel, raised the general issue and denied all of the allegations in the declaration.

tion to his son after the death of his wife, to whom he devised his whole Estate during Life, & many other facts which I[9] can not trace. Verdict finds the price as in the writ.

vi. 2. Blacks: rep: 854.[1]

But the most important Question arising from any of the facts found appeared to be,

Whether a Husband entituled in right of his wife to the Reversion of a Slave, has a right to dispose thereof. The plt adduced his Title to the Slaves under such a grant.

This point was not contested by Defts Council.

There were also some exceptions taken to the Decl[arati]on & the special Verdict, as below.

Baker, for the appellant, began to attack the Decl[arati]on, for the omission of the price. This he did not press. The Cases of Gordon & Bates & Posey & Curtis[2] appeared to conclude him. He took an Exception to the Verdict, which finds that the Slaves named Harry & Betty are the Children of Hannah named in Thomas Lyons will and *are in possession of Deft. but does not find that they are the same Slaves in Decl*[arati]*on mentioned.*[3] Here is a vacuum, which cannot be supplied.

Marshal, on the same side took a further Exception to the Verdict, which finds *a Deed in the words following*, but does not find *one word* in the Deed, so as to ascertain the Identity of the Deed found. The Deed however was annexed *to the record* of the Special Verdict.[4]

April 27, 1787

Where the finding of the Jury is such as to shew that they might have found something more without which the Court cannot give Judgement a venire de novo,[5] must be awarded. Per Tazewell.

9. St. George Tucker.

1. Pawley v. Holly, 2 Blackstone Rep. 853–854, 96 Eng. Rep. 504 (C.P., 1772), held that it was unnecessary that the articles sued for in detinue be separately valued in the declaration, provided that the jury verdict properly assessed their value.

2. Jerman Baker did not cite English cases but earlier Virginia decisions that are no longer available.

3. Since the slaves in question were the children of Hannah, they were considered subject to the same rules as other children in regard to legitimacy, namely that illegitimate children are offspring of the mother but not the father. However, the action of detinue is for the recovery of specific property, which, according to Chitty, "must be distinguishable from other property, and their identity ascertainable by some certain means." *On Pleading*, I, 92. This lack of specificity in the jury's special verdict would defeat the plaintiff's action and result in a reversal upon appeal.

4. JM's contention was that the deed should have been exemplified within the text of the special verdict and not merely attached as a supplement to the verdict.

5. A *venire de novo*, or more properly, a *venire facias de novo*, was a writ issued when the

Fleming, accordant. Lyons & Carrington of the same opinion.

Cause sent back for further proceedings & venire de novo awarded.

Chrisman v. Trents

Notes on Argument in the General Court

Extract from Casebook, Tucker-Coleman Papers, Swem Library, College of William and Mary

Richmond, April 9, 1787

Appeal from Montgomery County. This was an Action brought by the Appellees, who were plantiffs in a former suit against one [6] in which the now defendant promised to become bail for the then Defendants appearance, which the now Defendant (after the Sheriff had set the then Defendant at large) refused to do. The Decl[arati]on also states that Deft protected   from Any future arrest, whereby plaintiffs lost their Debt. Plea not Guilty. Issue & gen. verd. for plts, whereupon Deft. prayed an an[7] Appeal.

Marshal, insisted here is no cause of action shewn. The Sheriff was bound to plts. to take proper bail—their remedy was agt. Sheriff.[8]

Baker,[9] Contra. The protection is a further cause of action.

Judgement reversed, Per Cur: unani.[1]

---

verdict of a jury was so imperfect or ambiguous that no judgment could be given upon it, and a new trial was therefore required.

6. Tucker neglected to supply names in this space and one in the following sentence.

7. The second "an" is a slip of the pen.

8. In other words, the sheriff was responsible to a plaintiff in the event he did not secure bail for the defendant and released him from jail. The bondsman who promised to post bail, but did not actually do so, should not be held liable. See Bacon, *Abridgment*, I, 206–208.

9. Jerman Baker.

1. That is, the judgment for the plaintiff against the bondsman was reversed, upon the basis of JM's argument. "Per Cur: unani." indicates that the judgment was per curiam (by the whole court) and that it was unanimous.

Fallen v. Green

Notes on Argument in the General Court

Extract from Casebook, Tucker-Coleman Papers, Swem Library, College of William and Mary

Richmond, April 9, 1787

In Detinue for Slaves. The Question turned upon a Devise in the will of Tho. Thornton, *whether the Slaves were legally entailed* or not. The will is in these words—as for such *worldly Goods & Estate* as I die possessed of, I give devise & bequeath the same to A. B. & C.— & it is my will that my Slaves etc. shall be to my Children to them & the *heirs of their Bodies lawfully begotten* forever. But these Slaves were not *annexed* to any Lands, Although Lands were *devised to some of his Children in Tail*, but with different Limit[ation]s.

The Question is simply this—could Slaves, *not expressly annexed* to Lands be entailed? under the act of 1727, Sect: XII.[2]

Lee, urged that the Limitations both of the Land & Slaves, were the Same, being, *in tail General*, although by the provisions of the will, in Case the *Estate tail should cease* the Slaves were to go in one Course, & the Lands in another quite different.[3]

Marshall, Contra, insisted that the Law must be strictly complied with in order to direct the Limitation of Slaves in a different course from what the policy of the Law requires.[4]

2. Slaves were at first considered chattels personal and therefore could not be entailed. The first taker of an entailed estate in a slave was held to be entitled to an absolute estate, defeasible on death by an executory interest in favor of the issue of his body. Slaughter v. Whitelock (Apr. 1737), Barton, *Va. Colonial Decisions*, II, B251–B252; John C. Gray, *The Rule Against Perpetuities*, 4th ed. (Boston, 1942), 735–739. However, the 1727 act provided that slaves might be annexed to real property, either by deed or by will, and that when so annexed they would descend in the manner that the realty descended. 4 Hening 222. In Oct. 1768 the Virginia General Court heard extensive arguments over the annexation of slaves to real property under the terms of the 1727 act. Attorneys John Randolph (1728–1784) and George Wythe presented outstanding briefs on this point, and at the conclusion of their arguments the General Court held that slaves could never be entailed unless they were annexed to lands. Blackwell v. Wilkinson, Jefferson (Va.) Rep. 73–84.

3. The 1727 statute provided two methods by which an entail in slaves through annexation to land might take place. The first was by express provision in the deed or will, clearly enunciating the intention to annex the slaves to the land. The second was by a similar disposition of land and slaves, from which an intention to annex might be inferred. Charles Lee here argued in support of the second method as being applicable in this case. An estate "in tail General" is one that is entailed to all issue, male or female, of a named individual.

4. JM's argument also dealt with an implied annexation to land, his assertion being

Taylor, for plts. This Cause depends on Construction of the latter part of Sect: XII, of Act 1727. He contended that there was no *remainder* in the Slaves, but merely an *executory devise*, and until defeated by the Contingency should happen the Slaves should remain with the Land in Tail.[5]

April 10, 1787

Tazewell. The Slaves & Lands are subjected to difft. Limitations, act of Assembly not pursued—Ergo—no Intail.[6]

Fleming, accordant. Lyons & Carrington accordant.

Judgt. for the Defendant.

Bailey v. Morris's Estate

Notes on Argument in the General Court

Extract from Casebook, Tucker-Coleman Papers, Swem Library, College of William and Mary

Richmond, April 13, 1787

Appeal from Brunswick Court. Detinue for Slaves, brought agt. *Thomas Lundie*, Admr. of Henry Morris dec[eas]ed.[7] Decl[aratio]n charges the Slaves to have come to the possession of H. Morris in

---

that the statute required that there be the same provisions concerning the slaves as there were concerning the land; otherwise the provisions of the 1727 act would not be complied with. We may surmise that he argued that statutes in derogation of the Virginia common law should be strictly construed and that, for this reason, the party claiming an entail of slaves was required to prove full compliance with the statutory requirements.

5. John Taylor's argument was in support of the validity of the life estate in the testator's children, as well as the entailed estates that would succeed them, since these paralleled the disposition made of the real property. Until the entail ceased, an annexation of the slaves could be inferred from similar disposition of the land and slaves, but thereafter the separate disposition of the lands and the slaves precluded further validity of the annexation. At the happening of the contingency, that is, the termination of the entail, Taylor urged that the rule stated in Slaughter v. Whitelock, n. 2 above, be applied. Taylor's argument is an ingenius one but is inconsistent with a strict construction of the statute as advocated by JM and subsequently upheld by the General Court.

6. Judge Henry Tazewell's decision, roughly synopsized by St. George Tucker, seems to follow JM's argument.

7. The administrator may have been the Thomas Lundie (d. 1798) who filed a claim in the Brunswick County Court in 1782. A Henry Morris voted in Brunswick County in 1748, and an individual of the same name had negotiated with the Nottowacks and Cherokee Indians in 1741 and 1742.

his Lifetime, & *that Deft. detains*, etc. but does not charge possession in the Defendant.

After issue joined the Court annulled the Adm[inistrati]on of Lundie, & granted Adm[inistrati]on de bonis non[8] to Henry Morris Grandson of the first Henry. Then *Morris*, with the *Consent of all parties* & with the *approbation of the* Court, made a party Defendant in the room of *Lundie*.

There was an Exception to the Evidence by which it appeared that plts claimed under a verbal Gift before the year 1748.[9]

Marshall, took Exception to the Decl[arati]on, for that there is no possession charged in the Deft. Lundie.[1] He also objected to the proceedings in making the Deft a party in the room of Lundie.

Lyons, Justice. You can never maintain Detinue agt. a person in whom you do not charge a possession.

Tazewell. An Ex[ecut]or can never be charged in Detinue upon the poss[ess]ion of his Testator.

Carrington & Fleming, accordant on the same point.

Judgt. reversed, unanimously.

Bates v. Fuquay

Notes on Argument in the General Court

Extract from Casebook, Tucker-Coleman Papers, Swem Library, College of William and Mary

Richmond, April 13, 1787

Appeal from Charlotte Court. There was a Case agreed[2] in the County court. Whereby it was agreed, that one John Alford May

---

8. "Administration of the goods not administered." When the original administrator ceases to act, his successor is named administrator de bonis non of all goods left unadministered by the previous administrator. Lundie may have been a creditor who obtained administration but subsequently was ousted by the deceased's grandson as next of kin.

9. The significance of the 1748 date is obscure. A 1734 Virginia statute required that all bills of sale wherein slaves were transferred would be void unless proved, acknowledged, and recorded in the provincial secretary's office. However, such bills of sale, although unrecorded, would be valid between the parties to the transaction. 4 Hening 398–399. In 1748 a statute concerning slaves was refused the royal assent. See Tucker, *Blackstone's Commentaries*, II, app. E, 89–90. The only other statute that could conceivably apply was one requiring a bill of sale to be executed before a magistrate in connection with the sale of cattle. 6 Hening 124–131.

1. To support an action in detinue the defendant must be alleged to have possession of the chattel. Chitty, *On Pleading*, I, 92.

2. A "case agreed," or a "case stated," is one in which the parties stipulate the

1, 1726, made his will, whereby he devised a tract of Land in New Kent County to his eldest Daughter, Eliza Alford in Tail. To his Daurs. Unity & Charity he devised another tract of Land, as Tenants in common in Tail. To his three Daurs. Eliza[be]th, Unity & Charity he devises all his Slaves & their increase, to be equally divided among them when either should arrive at the age of Eighteen years also in Tail.[3] There were cross remainders established between all the Daurs. It is also agreed that John Bates intermarried with Elizabeth,[4] & became possessed of Sue from whom the Slaves in Question descended. *It is admitted* that *Certain papers* to the Case annexed purporting to be writs of Ad quod damnum[5] & Deed of Conveyance for docking[6] the *entail of certain Lands* in the Will mentioned are true & genuine *copies of the record in* the General court. It is agreed that Eliza Bates died in 1757, that John Bates died in 1765, intestate leaving John Bates father of plt HIS eldest Son by the said Elizabeth, & that plt is the eldest son & heir at Law of the last mentioned John. That Defendant purchased the Slaves of John Bates, father of the plt for a valuable consideration.

I[7] was unwell & did not come into court when the Cause was opened. Carrington jr. for Bates the plt below & now the appellant, was concluding his argt. when I came in. He contended that Slaves might be intailed under 1705, being both a Tenement & Hereditament. He cited Blackstone's Com: & Co. Inst.

2: Blacks. Com: 113; 1: Inst: 6.[8]

---

facts of the case for the purpose of narrowing issues to be raised on appeal. For an excellent discussion of the "case stated," see Julius Goebel, Jr., ed., *The Law Practice of Alexander Hamilton* (New York, 1964–), I, 790–793, II, 24.

3. The will of John Alford (d. 1726) is set forth in a jury verdict in the case of Bates v. Watkins, decided in Halifax County in 1771. *VMHB*, XXIII (1915), 420–422.

4. Bates held title to Sue in the right of his wife since he had an estate by the marital right that entitled him to rents, profits, use, and enjoyment of her property. See *The American Law of Property*, I (Boston, 1952), 759–768.

5. A writ *ad quo damnum* orders a sheriff to conduct an inquiry concerning the damage a specified act, if done, will cause.

6. "Docking," or barring an entail, converted the fee tail to a fee simple absolute by means of a common recovery in court or by way of a deed executed by the tenant-in-tail and his heir-at-law.

7. St. George Tucker.

8. Paul Carrington, Jr.'s, argument revolved about a contention that slaves were hereditaments, that is, fixtures annexed to the realty for its enhancement. Blackstone, *Commentaries*, II, 113, discusses the applicability of entail to real property and personal property. The passages on this page limit entails to real property and certain offices or dignities that are related to fixed and certain places or that concern land. However, "mere personal chattels, which favour not at all of the realty, cannot be entailed." The passage from Coke on Littleton is more liberal in its interpretation of what constitutes a hereditament. "Whatsoever may be inherited is an heriditament, be it cor-

Marshall, for Deft. Took an Exception to the Case agreed, because it was not found that plts father was heir at Law to Elizabeth Bates. From ought that appeared to the contrary it might be inferred that she was married to some other person before Bates, & might have had issue by such Marriage: that Slaves are not found to descent ex parte materna.[9]

1: Wilson 55.[1]

Taylor,[2] on the same side insisted, that under 10. sect. of Act of 1705, it was clear, that Slaves of persons dying intestate having Children, should be inventoried & value divided. This is perfectly inconsistent with the nature of an intail. He also insisted, that if there was an original Estate tail, yet the same was destroyed by the writ of ad Quod damnum, although the Slaves are not taken notice therein.

Nelson for the plt. The doctrine in 1. Wilson 55. is not to be to be[3] construed so as to preclude any aid which may be given to a special verdict. He said that that part of the Case agreed which finds the Slaves in Question to be the *descendants* of Sue, ought not to be construed insufficient, because there is no Ceremony of marriage between these people who cohabit promiscuously, therefore, that the finding that they are descended from Sue, must be intended in the *maternal Line* only. Act of 1705, sect. 10, only relates to intestacy. Besides *exceptio probat regulam*,[4] therefore Slaves real Estate in all Cases not expressly excepted, ergo intailable.

poreall or incorporeall, real or personal or mixt." Sir Edward Coke, *The first part of the Institutes of the laws of England; or, A commentary upon Littleton* . . . , 16th ed. (London, 1809), 6a.

9. That is, "on the mother's side." The implication of this argument is not clear. JM may have intended to argue that the husband of Elizabeth Alford could not be her heir-at-law whether or not children by a prior marriage survived her; if so, the statement was inadequate because it did not stipulate that this was the only marriage of Elizabeth Alford. On the other hand, he may have argued that the statement was deficient because it did not specify that the offspring of slave mothers descended with their mother in their mistress's estate. The latter argument seems to be the one advanced since William Nelson's rebuttal, below, addresses itself to this point.

1. Witham v. Lewis ex dem Derby, 1 Wilson 55–57, 95 Eng. Rep. 485–490 (K.B., 1744), involved a special verdict in an ejectment case upon which a new trial was requested. The court there stated that in common law cases "there is nothing more settled than that the Court can intend nothing in a special verdict but what is found by the jury." JM's argument undoubtedly was that a "case agreed" was, for these purposes, identical to a special verdict by a jury and that imperfections in the statement of agreed facts could not be altered by the appellate court.

2. John Taylor.

3. A slip of the pen.

4. "The exception proves the rule." In nearly every other situation except intestate succession, the 1705 statute treated slaves as personal property. See 3 Hening 333–335.

April 27, 1787

Tazewell. Will give an opinion on the merits—under 1705 he did not concieve Slaves could be considered as Tenementum.[5] Slaves were in many cases excepted from the Case of real Estate—could not be entailed, under that Act.

Fleming. They could not be entailed til 1727, nor then but by a particular method, strictly pursued.

Lyons. Slaves were an improper subject to be made real Estate—nothing in the Act of 1705 authorises such a Construction as that they could be entailed.

Carrington. Had given an opinion in the Cause fifteen years ago, to the same effect.[6]

Judgement for the Defendant.

Muir & Wiatt v. Martin Key

Notes on Argument in the General Court

Extract from Casebook, Tucker-Coleman Papers, Swem Library, College of William and Mary

Richmond, April 18, 1787

This was an Action on the case.[7] The Declaration sets forth, that the Defendants & one Wm. Henderson[8] in behalf of the plts entered into an agreement under their respective hands & Seals, for a certain Quantity of Tobo. to be delivered at a future day, for which Henderson promised to pay 25/. There is a N.B. at the foot of the Agreement in these words—"NB. I purchase this Tobacco

5. "Tenementum," freehold realty. See discussion in Blackstone, *Commentaries*, II, 110–113.

6. The 1770 case has not survived. It is possible that Judge Carrington may have referred to the 1768 case of Blackwell v. Wilkinson, Jefferson (Va.) Rep. 73–84, discussed in Fallen v. Green, Apr. 9, 1787, n. 1.

7. An "action on the case" was a form of action to permit recovery for damages in situations where the older forms of action would not lie. The term was also used as an abbreviated form of reference to an action of trespass on the case, which appears to be the usage in this instance of an action in assumpsit. Edmund M. Morgan, *Introduction to the Study of Law*, 2d ed. (Chicago, 1948), 107–111; Frederic W. Maitland, *The Forms of Action at Common Law*, ed. A. H. Chaytor and W. J. Whittaker (Cambridge, 1968), 53–56.

8. Martin Key was probably the individual of the same name from Albemarle County who had been commissioner in charge of disposing of the estate of loyalist William King in 1780 and 1781.

for Mess. Muir & Wiatt, Merchants in Fredericksburg."[9] The agreement is set forth verbatim with a profert in Curia,[1] Whereby plts were entituled to demand the said Tobacco. Breach assigned, the not delivering the Tobacco, but no avermt. that they ⟨performed⟩ paid for Tobo.

Marshal, for Deft. excepted to Decl[arati]on, the rule being that no action on the Case can be supported [on a] Contract under Seal.[2]

Taylor, for plt. Covenant would not lie, for plts were not *parties* to the Agreement.[3] Nothing but a special action on the Case could be maintained by them, & it is evident they are entituled to that Action, the contract being on their Behalf.

Tazewell, Judge. Will it be any injury to your Cause if you wave the Exception for the present & move in arrest of Judgt.[4]

Marshall. It might save time to make it now, but I am willing to go on with the trial at present.

Taylor, now applied to the court, to inform the Jury whether in an action upon mutual promises, where plt doth not aver paymt. on his own part, mutual actions may not be maintained; for Deft. may bring suit for the price of the Tobacco; Consequently Jury may give Damages to the amount of the whole Tobo. not delivered. Law of Evid. 196. vi: 1. Wilson 88.[5]

9. The firm of Muir & Wiatt was founded about 1772. One of the partners, William Wiatt, came from Liverpool; despite strong loyalist sympathies, he remained in Virginia throughout the American Revolution.

1. A "profert in curia" is an offer to produce the original agreement in court for examination by the court and the parties to the case.

2. Chitty, *On Pleading*, I, 89, stated that "assumpsit [i.e. an action on the case] . . . was not in general sustainable where the contract was originally under seal." Whenever a party had security of a nature superior in form and solemnity of execution to that cognizable in an action of assumpsit, he had to use the appropriate action, either debt or, as in this case, covenant. *Ibid.*, 75.

3. John Taylor questioned whether the plaintiffs were parties to the contract under seal, since they did not execute the agreement, but their names were merely inserted in the agreement by Henderson. Ultimately the determination in such a case would depend upon the existence of an agency relationship between Henderson and the defendants, since a signature would not be required if an agency relationship could be proved to exist.

4. This was a trial before the General Court in the exercise of its original common law jurisdiction. Judge Henry Tazewell's question was directed toward avoiding immediate argument on the point of law, reserving to the parties their right to raise it in argument on a motion in arrest of judgment after the jury verdict.

5. Sir Geoffrey Gilbert, *The Law of Evidence* (Dublin, 1754), 196–197, discusses the right of a tenant to prove the expenditure of rent to make repairs that his landlord agreed to make. According to Gilbert the amount spent for repairs could not be proved by the defendant tenant unless he had alleged a counter-agreement by the landlord covering the repairs. Martindale v. Fisher, 1 Wilson 88, 95 Eng. Rep. 507, 508 (K.B., 1745), held that in an action founded upon mutual promises, the promise itself was

Marshall, admitted the Doctrine—but cui bono?[6] What End will it serve.

Lyons, Judge. In Ass[umpsi]t you may give in Evidence whatever fact will defeat the plts action. The Case is otherwise in Covenant. There performance [must] be averred, by plt, &

Tazewell, Judge. The Law is as stated by Taylor,[7] but if Deft. can shew any thing in mitigation of Damages, it ought to go to Jury.

Fleming, Accordant.

Carrington. The Jury may find any Damages, or no Damages as they think proper.

The Jury found a Verdict for £379.10.

Motion for new Trial.

Tazewell. I find myself inclined to support this Verdict. It is true that in An Action upon mutual promises the parties may maintain reciprocal Actions: it is also true that Deft may give any thing in Evidence in mitigation of Damages. The Jury in the present Case had the whole matter before them, & ought to have assessed Damages according to the difference of price, or any other *Special Damage* which plt could have proved but here no special Damage appears; the plt has failed in proving that he paid the whole money. The Damages therefore are excessive & a new Trial must be granted. Hard.[8]

Fleming, accordant.

Lyons. This Verdict cannot be Sustained. He reasoned as Tazewell had already done, & added, that the Deft could not recover on a mutual Action, since he could not give in Evidence that he had delivered the Tobacco. Here is a general Verdict from which nothing of the kind can be inferred. Consequently Defendant in his cross Action must be non-suited.

Carrington. This is a most extraordinary Verdict. I expected a Verdict for Deft, from the Evidence.

New Trial, granted, Per tot. Cur.[9]

---

good consideration and that there was no need to aver delivery of the goods; in other words, after 1745 a promise for a promise was valid consideration.

6. That is, "for what good or purpose?"

7. In other words, assumpsit would lie and damages might be awarded according to the jury charge proposed by Taylor.

8. Judge Tazewell termed this a "hard" case because of his tendency to support the jury verdict and hence deny a new trial. However, he was compelled to hold the verdict excessive, because the plaintiff did not prove payment on his part and the jury assessed no special damages based upon nondelivery.

9. "By the whole court."

October 15, 1787

The new Trial in this Cause came on today. Marshall ex parte Deft, submitted to the Court whether the plt must not prove paymt. on his part, in order to maintain the present Action. The Court dissentiente Tazewell & Absentibus Lyons & Fleming,[1] determined that he must.

The Question whether the writing under Seal should be given in Evidence on this Action was reserved.[2]

Verdict for Deft & Motion for new Trial, granted.

Ex Rel; Nelson.[3]

Hannah v. Davis

Notes on Argument in the General Court

Extract from Casebook, Tucker-Coleman Papers, Swem Library, College of William and Mary

Richmond, April 20, 1787

Special Verdict in these words—We of the Jury find that Bess was an Indian & was brought from some Indian nation into the County of Richmond since the year 1705, viz. 1712, and *held* & claimed as a Slave to the day of her death. We find that find that[4] plaintiffs are *Descendants* of the said Bess; and if upon the whole Matter etc.

Tho. Nelson, all the acts of assembly relative to Indians as Servants or Slaves, are Acts of 1662, of 1670, Both of which inflict a temporary Servitude on Indian captives—1682. inflicts perpetual Servitude. 1705. perhaps repealed the last.[5] But if act of 1682. be

1. Tazewell dissenting, Lyons and Fleming absent.

2. A point of law might be reserved for argument before the judge after the jury had returned with its general verdict; this was also termed a "special case." Blackstone, *Commentaries*, III, 378; Julius Goebel, Jr., ed., *The Law Practice of Alexander Hamilton* (New York, 1964–), II, 18–19.

3. This is an indication that St. George Tucker may have copied this report from William Nelson's notes.

4. A slip of the pen.

5. Thomas Nelson (d. 1803), the future attorney general of Virginia, presented a reasonably accurate summary of the Virginia law relative to Indian slavery. The act of 1662 provided a method for determining the term of service of servants brought into Virginia for an undefined period of servitude. The act of 1670 differentiated between

unrepealed yet it being contrary to the Law of God & the Law of nature to make Slaves of the Subjects of foreign powers, which the Indians certainly were, this Act is null & void.

Taylor, Pro Deft. The Argument against Slavery applies equally to African as to Indian nations. This court will concieve itself bound by Acts of the General Assembly.[6] Act of 1682. repeals a former Act providing that Indians should not be made Slaves, & enacts that they shall be Slaves when Sold by neighbouring Indians. Act of 1705.* does not repeal this Act. Nor does it require that Slave holder should prove the Slave to have been a Servant, or heathen, in his native Country. Were the onus probandi[7] upon the Slave holder, it must be attended with almost universal Emancipation. No distinction made in any Act of Assembly between Indian & negroe Slaves. If Act of 1782.[8] be repealed by the Act of 1705. ch: 49. the same Act must repeal the Act of 1705. making Slaves real Estate. This has never been supposed.

The Verdict finds Bess to have been brought hither as a Slave & to have been held as such unto the time of her death—plaintiffs as her Descendants, if on the part of the mother must therefore be Slaves. On the other hand if not ex parte mâternâ The court cannot presume that they are descended from a free person ex parte maternâ.

Munroe.[9] Pro plts. Act of 1692.† Opens a free trade with Indians; can it be supposed the Legislature passed this Act with a view only to entrap the Indians & make Slaves of them. Indians must be *Servants* under 1682. to make them Slaves. But it is a most unquestionable fact that they have no Servants among them. Slavery is unknown among them. Their *Women* are the only *Servants*

---

non-Christian servants brought into Virginia by sea, who were to be considered slaves, and non-Christian servants brought into Virginia by land, who would serve for 30 years if boys or girls and 12 years if men or women. 2 Hening 169, 283. In 1682 the act of 1670 was repealed, and all servants, except Turks or Moors in amity with Great Britain, not Christians at the time of their purchase, and all Indians thereafter sold by neighboring Indians were to be considered slaves. 2 Hening 490–492. The 1705 act referred to was probably the act opening trade with the Indians; sec. 7 of this statute provided that "the Indians tributary to this Government, shall be well secured and defended in their persons, goods, and properties . . . as if . . . an Englishman." 3 Hening 464–467. Another 1705 act dealing with the status of slaves in Virginia does not make specific provision for Indian slaves. See 3 Hening 447–462.

6. John Taylor's argument was that the court should defer to the legislative policy toward Indian slavery.

7. "The burden of proof."

8. That is, 1682.

9. James Monroe.

they have. Act of 1705. ch: 14. repeals all former acts relative to Indians (this is a mistake—See the purview of the Act).

Marshall, for plts. The Act of 1705. Authorises a free trade with Indians. Will the Court Countenance a flagitious Act done after that Act? Bess though detained in Slavery, if wrongfully detained could still transmit the right of freedom to her posterity. The Act of 1705. ch: 5. only relates to such Indians as were already Slaves.

Taylor. By which of these Acts of 1705. is the Act of 1682. repealed. Examine the purview of both—neither of them does, or can be construed to relate to the Subject of the Act of 1682.

Baker[1] for Defendant. In this special verdict the Jury ought to have found the Law which they concieved comprehended the plt's Case, in order that the Court may Judge if in force. This was the practice in the former General Court.

W. Nelson,[2] for plts. These are public Acts, unnecessary to have been specially found by Jury. Could the people of Virginia make Slaves of a nation with whom they were at peace? Yet the act of 1705. Makes such a peace, & authorizes a free trade with them. The *holding* & *claiming* Bess as a Slave, can not be construed to destroy her freedom. The bare *holding* or *claiming* her, could have no such effect. No marriage Ceremony among Indians, therefore *Descendants* shall be understood to apply to the maternal Line. In pleading the onus probandi lies on him who affirms a fact. The Deft. in his plea, affirms the plt's to be *Slaves*. But it is said plts must shew a title to an Action. All persons primâ facie are entituled to an Action. Their dissability to maintain one must be Specially pleaded.

The court seemed unanimously of opinion that the Act of 1682. was absolutely repealed by the Acts of 1705. "Concerning Servants & Slaves"—and "for opening a trade with the Indians"—therefore, that no Indian brought into this Govt. from the back Country since that period could be made a Slave.[3] They were also of opinion, that the word *Descendants*, in the Case of Slaves, must mean lineal descendents in the maternal Line.[4]

Judgement for plts.

1. Jerman Baker.
2. William Nelson.
3. A citation to the 1792 case of Jenkins v. Tom, in 1 Washington (Va.) Rep. 123–124, was inserted in this manuscript at a later date by St. George Tucker.
4. This point had been considered in Bates v. Fuquay, decided by the General Court on Apr. 13, 1787, and argued by JM on that date.

*Concerning Servants & Slaves. ch: 49. Edo. of 1733.[5]
[†]Title. "For a free trade with Indians." Which may be found in the Edo. of 1733.[6]

Braxton v. Beall

Notes on Argument in the General Court

Extract from Casebook, Tucker-Coleman Papers, Swem Library, College of William and Mary

Richmond, April 1787

Sups. from the Court of Hustings Williamsburg. The Decl[ara-ti]on charges that Deft was indebted to plt in £6000, for Goods he sold & delivered to Deft, at his Spl instance & request by a certain Thomas Webb & co—but does not alledge who Thomas Webb & co, are, or by what means a Debt to them became a Debt to the plt.[7]

The writ was tested[8] March 24th. 1784. March 26. 1784. The

5. *A Collection of all the Acts of Assembly, Now in Force, in the Colony of Virginia* (Williamsburg, Va., 1733), 218–228, particularly 219, sec. 4.

6. *Ibid.*, 94. The 1733 printing of the statutes indicates that 3 Wm. & Mary c. 9 (1692), text not given, was repealed by 4 Anne c. 52 (1705). The repealing statute, printed in 3 Hening 464–469, does not expressly repeal either the 1682 or the 1692 act. In 1772 the Virginia General Court held that the 1705 act repealed the 1682 act and that Indians brought into Virginia after 1705 might not be considered slaves. Robin v. Hardaway, Jefferson (Va.) Rep. 109–123; see also Tucker, *Blackstone's Commentaries*, I, Pt. 2, app. H, 45–47.

7. This transcript of the argument, taken by St. George Tucker, does not provide a clear statement of the parties plaintiff and defendant in the Williamsburg City Hustings Court below or in the General Court on appeal. However, the internal evidence indicates that the plaintiff in the lower court was Beall and the defendant was Braxton. Beall had delivered goods to Braxton at the request of Thomas Webb & Co., the delivery giving rise to the £6,000 indebtedness for which he subsequently instituted this action of debt against Braxton. Braxton authorized confession of judgment; he subsequently appealed by writ of supersedeas and, as plaintiff in error, was represented by John Taylor and John Francis Mercer. The plaintiff in the court below, defendant in error (Beall), was represented in the General Court by JM, William Nelson, and Jerman Baker.

Normally Taylor as counsel for the appellant would argue first and have the right to make a statement in reply to the legal arguments of appellee's counsel. However, the first matter considered, the contents of the record on appeal, was a preliminary motion made by the appellee. The argument against the insertion of the warrant of attorney in the record, made by Nelson and JM, was rejected by the court, and John Taylor then commenced his argument on the substantive issues of the case.

8. That is, attested, or signed by the clerk of the court.

Defendant wrote a Letter to Joseph Prentis esqr.[9] telling him plaintiff *will* institute an Action agt. him, and authorising him to confess Judgement to the *plaintiff* for £2126.17.3. & £2168.12.4. with some stay of Execution to carry interest, from *that* time (qu. whether time of Judgt. or of payment) *being Ballances due from me for Account of Thomas Webb & company*, by virtue of which Letter, or warrant of Attorney, Prentis confessed Judgement, according to the Terms thereof, april court 1784.

vi: Virga. Laws pa: 181. ch: 5. Sect. 7.[1]

It is to be observed that the writ does not appear to have been served on Braxton, & probably never was, as his Letter to Prentis bears date at Eltham, in New Kent County.[2]

This Cause came on to be argued in October Term 1787.

Nelson & Marshall contended, that the warrant of Atty. is no part of the record.

Taylor cited one of the Statutes of Jeofails, where the Lack of warrant of attorney shall not be deemed Error.[3] This Shews a Warrant of Atty. to be properly part of the record.

Tazewell gave no Opinion. The rest of the Court were unanimously of opinion it might be read. What weight it might have as a part or not part of the record they would not now decide.

Taylor. From the Tenor of this Warrant it is evident it was made before action brot. therefore void under the Act.[4]

2. There is no Consideration between plt & deft, whereon to ground a general Ind: Assumpsit. It must be a collatoral promise for which a special Action & not Ind. Assump. will lie.[5]

9. Joseph Prentis (1754–1809), member of a prominent mercantile family, was at this time a practicing attorney but after 1789 was a judge of the General Court.

1. 22 Geo. 2, c. 5, sec. 7 (1748), provided that, "all Powers of Attorney for confessing or suffering Judgment to pass by Default or otherwise . . . , made or to be made by any Person or Persons whatsoever within this Colony, before Action brought, shall be and are hereby declared to be absolutely null and void. . . ." *The Acts of Assembly Now in Force in the Colony of Virginia* (Williamsburg, Va., 1769), 181, printed in 5 Hening 240, 241, but incorrectly dated 1744.

2. A writ issuing from a Virginia hustings court did not run beyond the magisterial limits of the city. Hence Braxton could not have been served properly unless he had goods within the city of Williamsburg or had been physically present there at the time of service.

3. Several English statutes concerning jeofailes mention warrants of attorney, but the one most applicable to John Taylor's argument is 32 Hen. 8, c. 30, sec. 1 (1540), which saved the plaintiff's cause of action but fined the defendant's attorney for not filing his warrant. On statutes of jeofaile in Virginia see Gilbert v. Taylor, Apr. 1786, n. 7.

4. See n. 1 above.

5. Indebitatus assumpsit was available only in those cases where an action of debt

October 12, 1787[6]

Taylor Pro Braxton. Where the doing a thing is a good Consideration, there an Assumpsit founded thereon will be good. 12. Mod: 459.[7] Consideration should always be stated in Decl[arati]on in order to bar the plt of a second demand for the same thing. Strange 592. Skinner 196.[8] Mutual promises must be stated specially because mutual Actions may be necessary. The Ground of such an Assumpsit as is here laid, must be a promise on the part of Beall to discharge Braxton from the Debt to Webb & co. This must, or at least might be a condition precedent. There is a difference between an Assumpsit in Law & an Ass. in Deed. On the latter, Ind. Ass. will not lie, for it is founded on a Special Consideration. Action on the Case for several Promises one was for money lent to Deft's son at the Special Instance of Deft. Obj. That Ind. ass. will not lie in this Case agt. Deft.—& so adjudged. Carth. 446.

1. Salk. 23, 364; Carthew 446; Cro. Jas. 500; 1. Ba: Abr: 163; Strange 648, 592; 1. Burrow 373.[9]

---

might be brought; a collateral promise to pay the debt or satisfy the obligation of another could form the basis of an action in special assumpsit but not in indebitatus assumpsit. Bacon, *Abridgment*, I, 163. There is reason to believe that, in colonial Virginia, either indebitatus assumpsit or special assumpsit might be brought upon the promise to pay the debt of another. See Eppes v. Redford (Apr. 1732) and Meggs v. Bates (Oct. 1733), Barton, *Va. Colonial Decisions*, I, R74–R76, II, B39–B40.

6. Apparently the court adjourned the case to the next term and Taylor resumed his argument on Oct. 12, 1787.

7. The case of Thorp v. Thorp, 12 Modern Rep. 455–466, 88 Eng. Rep. 1448–1454 (K.B., 1701), involved the release of an equity of redemption in real property and the promise of the recipient to pay the sum of £7 in consideration of the release. The issue was whether the execution of the release had to be pleaded in an action to recover the balance due on the £7. The court held that the execution of the release had to be pleaded since it was a condition precedent to the payment of the £7.

8. Crow v. Rogers, 1 Strange 592, 93 Eng. Rep. 719, 720 (K.B., 1737), held that one who gained no benefit from his promise, and whose promise brought no detriment to the plaintiff, might not be sued in assumpsit since he was not a party to the agreement. The anonymous case in Skinner 196, 90 Eng. Rep. 90 (C.P., 1684), involved an agreement by *A* to pay £20 to *B*, when *A* received £100 that *C* owed to *A*. It was held that indebitatus assumpsit would not lie.

9. Hard's Case, 1 Salkeld 23, 91 Eng. Rep. 22 (K.B., 1697), laid down the rule that wherever debt would lie, indebitatus assumpsit also was available; however, assumpsit would lie in many cases where debt would lie, as well as in many others not actionable in debt. Courtney v. Strong, 1 Salkeld 364, 91 Eng. Rep. 316 (Q.B., 1705), held that a promise to forebear doing something that the promissor could not do was inadequate consideration to support an enforceable agreement. Butcher v. Andrews, Carthew 446, 90 Eng. Rep. 858 (K.B., 1698), also reported in 1 Salkeld 23, 91 Eng. Rep. 22–23, involved the promise by a father to reimburse the plaintiff for money lent to his son; the court held that a promise to repay the plaintiff for money paid to his son would support indebitatus assumpsit but that a promise to pay money lent was actionable only in special assumpsit. Batesby v. Brooksbeck, 3 Croke 500, 79 Eng. Rep. 427 (K.B., 1618), held that, in an action brought against a surety, the nonperformance of the principal

Nelson, for Deft. This warrant of Atty. bears date after the Institution of the suit—& being in the future Tense cannot be intended to belong to this Case—it can not be a part of the record. Therefore no respect to be had to it.[1]

2d. The court can not take notice of any Error upon a sups. but what appears on the face of the record.

    3. Bl. Com: 405; vi: Gen. Co. Act 1777.[2]

3. Objected that there is no Consideration, Webb & co. being alledged to be to no way concerned with Beall. Strange 592. determined after the Statute of frauds & probably upon that footing. That is not in force here.[3] Collatoral promise defined 1. Salk. 28.

    1. Salk: 28, 23; 1. Ba: abr: 172.[4]

Decl[arati]on lays that he was *indebted to plt.* This is not collateral. The Case from Carthew does not apply, for there the Money was lent *to the Son.* See the report of it, Salk. 23.[5] After this Judgt. Webb & co. must be intended to be partners of Beall. If A. pay money to B to pay to C. C, may bring Debt or Case agt. B for this money. This being by Confession, if the Assumpsit were irregular, or to a third person, it is cured. Therefore the Judgement well founded.

    Tho. Raym: 67; 1. Rol. Abr: 82, pl. 13; 2. Blacks. rep. 1269; 3: Black: Com: 154: 155.[6]

---

and his default had to be alleged, in addition to a demand by the plaintiff unsatisfied by the principal debtor. The marginal note in Bacon, *Abridgment,* I, 163, cites the foregoing cases. Weaver v. Boroughs, 1 Strange 648, 93 Eng. Rep. 757–758 (K.B., 1725), held that, in a declaration drawn in indebitatus assumpsit and special assumpsit, the plaintiff's action would be dismissed if he failed to prove a special agreement. Crow v. Rogers, 1 Strange 592, is discussed at n. 8, p. 223. Harris v. Huntbach, 1 Burrow 373–376, 97 Eng. Rep. 355–357 (K.B., 1757), held that an action of debt on a note for the benefit of an infant would be sustained, since the infant principal could not be liable. In the course of the opinion William Murray, first Lord Mansfield (1705–1793), commented that there existed a want of sufficiency concerning the definition of what undertakings should be considered collateral and what should be held original.

    1. Nelson's argument is based upon the 1744 statute, discussed at n. 1, p. 222.

    2. Blackstone merely indicated that a writ of error involved only matters appearing on the face of the record. *Commentaries,* III, 405. The Virginia statute is in 9 Hening 412–413 (1777).

    3. The English statute of frauds required that any suretyship promise to answer for the debt or default of another be in writing. 29 Car. 2, c. 3, sec. 4 (1677). The statute was not applicable to the overseas colonial possessions and apparently had not been accepted in Virginia either by usage or by act of the assembly.

    4. Hard's Case, 1 Salkeld 23, and Butcher v. Andrews, 1 Salkeld 23, are discussed at n. 9, 4 notes above. The material in Bacon consists of examples of undertakings that are actionable in indebitatus assumpsit.

    5. Nelson distinguished Butcher v. Andrews, probably on the ground that the special language in Butcher, "money lent to," was the basis for the holding in that case. The court there held that the process of lending money implied delivery to the recipient, even if made at the request of defendant.

    6. Although the text would indicate Nelson shifted his attention to the effect that a

After a trial & verdict Consideration shall be presumed. If a Man promise a Surgeon money for curing a poor Man, ind: ass. lies.

Hobart 216; Tho Raym.[7]

After Confession the court will intend Beall to have been a partner of Tho. Webb & co.

1. Wilson 1; 2. Wilson 5; 1. Salk: 9; 5. Co. 40 a & b.[8]

Marshall for Deft. Did not fear the operation of the Warrant of atty when he objected to its Admission, but with a view to Shorten Argt. In the manner it is certified it does not appear to be any part of the record.

But if any imperfection in the Decl[arati]on it is cured by the Confession—he would consider it in the same light as a Judgt. after verdict. Courts have gone a great way in support of Judgts. after verdict. Comb: 149, 150, 283, 284. (Lyons said this last Case has been denied to be law.)[9] The Cases in the margin all shew that a

---

confession of judgment or a verdict would have upon defects in the declaration, the marginal citations continue his argument concerning collateral and original undertakings. Stonehouse v. Bodvil, T. Raymond 67, 83 Eng. Rep. 37 (K.B., 1663), involved an action in indebitatus assumpsit for medicines provided to the defendant's daughter at his request; it was held that debt, and hence indebitatus assumpsit, would lie for goods delivered *for* the daughter, but not *to* the daughter. However, delivery to the daughter would be held intended by the verdict, and judgment for plaintiff was upheld. Fenner v. Meares, 2 Blackstone Rep. 1269-1272, 96 Eng. Rep 746-748 (C.P., 1779), permitted assumpsit to be brought upon a specialty (an instrument under seal), based upon an endorsed promise to pay the debt to any assignee without set-off. However, the justice, Sir William Blackstone (1728-1780), limited the case to the special circumstances and customary trade usages it presented. His earlier discussion in *Commentaries*, III, 154-155, analyzed the procedural aspects of assumpsit, debt, and indebitatus assumpsit. The other citation is to Sir Henry Rolle, *Un Abridgment des Plusiers Cases et Resolutions del Common Ley* . . . (London, 1668).

7. Bidwell v. Catton, Hobart 216, 80 Eng. Rep. 362-363 (K.B., 1618), involved an action in assumpsit based upon a promise to forebear from prosecuting an action. The plaintiff desisted, but the defendant failed to pay the 50s. promised. After the verdict the defendant moved in arrest of judgment, alleging that the declaration should have asserted that the action had a sound basis. It was held that there could be no presumption that the action foreborne was without basis. The example cited concerning a surgeon curing a poor man is a reference to Stonehouse v. Bodvil, discussed at n. 6, immediately above.

8. Morris v. Barry, 1 Wilson 1, 95 Eng. Rep. 458 (K.B., 1742); Adams v. Freeman, 2 Wilson 5, 95 Eng. Rep. 655 (K.B., 1753); Poulter v. Cornwall, 1 Salkeld 9, 91 Eng. Rep. 9 (Q.B., 1706); and Dorner's Case, 5 Coke Rep. 40a-41a, 77 Eng. Rep. 115-118 (Q.B., 1593). All involved various defects in pleading held cured by verdict.

9. JM's citations covered various situations in which English courts had held that defects in pleading were cured by the jury's verdict. Lewis v. Weeks, Comberbach 149-150, 90 Eng. Rep. 397-398 (K.B., 1689), involved a judgment in a local hundred court that did not recite the declaration but that was upheld by the appellate court. Young v. Sarum, Comberbach 150-151, 90 Eng. Rep. 398 (K.B., 1689), involved a defective declaration in a prosecution under a criminal statute, where the court stated that "after a verdict . . . [the missing allegation] . . . shall be intended to have been given in evidence," although omitted in the pleading. Austin v. Burscoe, Comberbach 283-284,

special Agreement may be given in Evidence on a general Ind. Ass. (Sed Qu.[1] for I think they do not.)

12. Mod. 510, 511; 1. Sid: 218; 10. Mod. 300, 330; 1 Ventris 211, 268; Gilb. Cases 305, 4; 3. Lev. 150; Hard: Cases 366; Buller's ni: pr: 139.[2]

---

90 Eng. Rep. 480–481 (K.B., 1694), involved an action for treble damages in which the damages were incorrectly computed in the declaration; the court held that the defect was corrected by the verdict, although it might have been deemed fatal to the case if raised on demurrer. There is no indication that the English courts had overruled this case, and thus it is probably to an unreported Virginia decision that Judge Peter Lyons referred.

1. That is, "but query." St. George Tucker's statement referred to the cases discussed at n. 3, 2 notes below.

2. Palmer v. Stavely, 12 Modern Rep. 510–511, 88 Eng. Rep. 1483–1484 (K.B., 1701), held that it was not a good verdict in an assumpsit action that there was a debt, for the debt might arise from a judgment, recognizance or a speciality, in which case assumpsit would not lie. In this instance the verdict could not cure the omission in the declaration and the proof. Bikerstaff's Executor v. Purdue, 1 Siderfin 218, 82 Eng. Rep. 1067 (K.B., 1664), held that in an action in debt for rent, where possession was not alleged in the declaration, this omission was cured by the verdict, and it would be intended that possession had been proven. In Muston v. Yateman, 10 Modern Rep. 300–303, 88 Eng. Rep. 737–738 (K.B., 1715), the court was confronted with an action for trespass to land where the plaintiff had failed to allege precisely the nature of the title by which he claimed possession. The court observed that "defects in pleading are cured by verdicts because it is to be supposed, that the verdict could not have been found unless there had been evidence given at the trial of that matter wherein the pleading is defective." Here the nature of plaintiff's title was not directly in issue and hence could not be intended to have been given in evidence. A title defectively set forth could have been cured by verdict, but a title that was actually defective could not be.

Child v. Pierce, 10 Modern Rep. 330–331, 88 Eng. Rep. 751 (K.B., 1716), was a judgment by default on several actions brought in indebitatus assumpsit on several promises made by the defendant, who had borrowed money from one who later became a bankrupt. The court held that it would be intended that the money was that of the bankrupt and that the transactions did create a debt. This intendment would provide the lack in the declaration, and the court would also intend an allegation of delivery in the declaration. Since this case, like the one being argued by JM, involved a judgment by default, it was one of the most persuasive precedents to be cited to the court.

Pollexfen v. Crispin, 1 Ventris 122–123, 86 Eng. Rep. 84–85 (K.B., 1671), involved an action for trespass to fish, presumably trespass *de bonis asportatis,* in which the declaration failed to allege the basis for the plaintiff's title but in which the court, on a motion in arrest of judgment, held that the verdict cured the defect in pleading. Hawes v. Smith, 1 Ventris 268, 86 Eng. Rep. 179 (K.B., 1677), involved a promise between an executor and a creditor of an estate for an accounting, which was made the subject of an assumpsit action. The defendant executor claimed, upon motion in arrest of judgment, that the plaintiff had not alleged a consideration for his promise. However, the court held that the consideration would be intended after the verdict and denied the motion to arrest judgment. Muston v. Yeatman, Gilbert 305–307, 93 Eng. Rep. 337–338 (Q.B., 1714), discussed previously in this note, stated the rule that, if a matter material to the issue were deleted from the declaration, it would be intended to have been proved at trial after the submission of a verdict.

Johnson v. May, 3 Levinz 150, 83 Eng. Rep. 624 (K.B., 1684), involved the surrender of a copyhold term by defendant to plaintiff, the plaintiff agreeing to allow the defendant to continue his enjoyment of the land upon the annual rental of 50s. Upon the defendant's failure to pay, the plaintiff brought assumpsit, and the defendant de-

A note of hand may be given in Evidence on a general ind: assump-sit—Per Ld. Mannsfield 1. Burr: 373; 1. Vent: 40; Buller 130.[3] Suppose Webb & co. to have been Beal's factors—will not such an Intendment support the decl[arati]on? vi. Buller 130; Strange 1182.[4]

Mercer; An Act of Assembly was passed authorising suits in the name of the principal for Goods sold & delivered by Factor. V.L. 324.[5]

Such a Case is ours—every syllable of the Decl[arati]on upon this Confession must be intended to be true. The Court will there-fore intend Webb & co. to have been Beall's factors. 10. Mod. 330, a strong Case.[6] The word *indebitatus* does necessarily imply the Goods sold were the goods of the plt.—it does of itself create a Con-sideration. 3. Burr. 1406; Carthew 276; Hob. 5; 1. Lev. 141; 2. Wilson 141; Carthew 446.[7]

Hard. 72; Doct. & Stu: 24; Ventris 311.[8]

---

murred, asserting that assumpsit was not the correct form of action. However, the court held that assumpsit would lie and gave judgment on the demurrer for the plaintiff.

King v. Holmes, Cases in the Time of Lord Hardwicke, 365–367, 95 Eng. Rep. 236–237 (K.B., 1737), was a criminal case concerning appeals by certiorari. The citation is no doubt incorrect.

The citation to Buller, Nisi Prius, refers to Sir Francis Buller, *An Introduction to the Law relative to Trials at Nisi Prius*, 5th ed. (London, 1768).

3. King v. Milwich, 1 Burrow 373–374, 97 Eng. Rep. 355–357 (K.B., 1757), held that indebitatus assumpsit might be brought for a debt and a note of hand—that is, a promissory note—might be given in evidence and that this would be considered an original undertaking. The citation to Wells v. Wells, 1 Ventris 40, 86 Eng. Rep. 29 (K.B., 1669), supports the points of law concerning formal defects cured by verdict discussed at n. 2, immediately above. The remaining citation is to Buller, *Introduction to Trials at Nisi Prius*, 130.

4. Buller, *Introduction to Trials at Nisi Prius*, 130. Scrimshire v. Alderton, 2 Strange 1182–1183, 93 Eng. Rep. 1114–1115 (K.B., 1743), held that a factor's sale created a contract between the owner of goods and the purchaser.

5. 28 Geo. 2, c. 2, secs. 6, 7 (1755), *Va. Acts in Force* (1769), 324, 325, printed in 6 Hening 480–481.

6. See the discussion of Child v. Pierce, 10 Modern Rep. 330–331, at n. 2, 4 notes above.

7. Mayor of Yarmouth v. Eaton, 3 Burrow 1402–1408, 97 Eng. Rep. 896–899 (K.B., 1763), was an action on the case in assumpsit for port duties unpaid by the defendant, who exported goods from Yarmouth. The defendant demurred that the plaintiffs had not alleged consideration, and it was held that the arrival in port was, in itself, ade-quate consideration. However, the court strictly limited the holding to port duty cases. Hibbert v. Courthouse, Carthew 276, 90 Eng. Rep. 764 (K.B., 1693), was an assumpsit for labor rendered, upon which a judgment by default was entered. On writ of error the defendant claimed that the plaintiff did not allege performance on his part and that his failure to specify the type of work was also a flaw, since illegal work could not form a valid consideration for the defendant's promise to pay. The court held that it was unnecessary to allege performance or the nature of the work and that the only reason to allege the type of indebtedness was to show that it did not arise on a matter of

Taylor as to Intendment cited Douglas 654 to 658.[9]

Baker, replied the next day. I did not hear his Argt.

October 19, 1787

The Court now proceeded to give Judgt.

Tazewell gave no opinion.

Mercer. When Cause first opened to him it appeared a very clear case—well argued on both sides. Not withstanding Appellants Councils abilities he still adhere[s] to his first opinion that it is a clear Case in favor of Deft. Confession of Judgt. on the void warrant of Attorney appeared to him of great weight at first—but upon inspection of the record he finds it a mere private paper—it does not appear Cty Court[1] ever took notice of it. In this Country Law does not require warrant of Atty—otherwise in England—hence the law as laid down in the Books. But co[uld] not Prentis have ap-

---

record or a specialty, for in such cases assumpsit would not lie. In Gardiner v. Bellingham, Hobart 5, 80 Eng. Rep. 155 (Exch. Ch., 1611), the Court of Exchequer Chamber asserted that, while it was necessary to plead the type of obligation in a general indebitatus assumpsit, this was not required in matters arising from the delivery of goods, provision of pasturage, and sale of wares, for those were personal matters in which assumpsit might lie. Wright v. Beal, 1 Levinz 141, 83 Eng. Rep. 338 (K.B., 1664), held that indebitatus assumpsit would be held to intend delivery and sale of goods after a verdict.

Marriott v. Lister, 2 Wilson 141–142, 95 Eng. Rep. 731–732 (K.B., 1762), involved an action in indebitatus assumpsit for money lent to a third person, and the court held the pleading bad after verdict, for this was a special undertaking by the defendant that must be specially pleaded. In passing the court noted that, in an action in indebitatus assumpsit for money lent the defendant, the law presumes a promise, which is not traversable (in other words, the matter could not be put into issue by a denial in the pleadings), and for that reason the promise need not be proved. See the discussion of Butcher v. Andrews, Carthew 446, at n. 9, p. 223.

8. Bern v. Bern, Cases in the Time of Lord Hardwicke, 72, 95 Eng. Rep. 45 (K.B., 1734), held that under the statute of jeofaile, 32 Hen. 8, c. 30 (1540), no judgment might be stayed by any discontinuance after the verdict. Kent v. Derby, 1 Ventris 311, 86 Eng. Rep. 200–201 (K.B., 1677), involved an action in indebitatus assumpsit where the plaintiff's declaration alleged that a stranger requested him to lend money to the defendant. The court held that the action was well brought since the allegation of the indebtedness and use of the word *indebitatus* implied the existence of a debt. The remaining citation is to Christopher Saint German, *Doctor and Student* (London, 1761).

9. The reference is to Whitcomb v. Whiting, 2 Douglas 652–654, 99 Eng. Rep. 413–414 (K.B., 1781), an action in assumpsit on a promissory note drawn by several individuals. After a verdict for the plaintiff against one of the drawers, there was a motion in arrest of judgment, and the court held that the law after the verdict would intend that the admission of indebtedness by one defendant would be an admission by them all. Similarly the court observed that the law would presume a promise to pay when the pleadings before the verdict admitted a debt to be due. The case in 2 Douglas 654–657, Bree v. Holbach, is not in point.

1. That is, the Williamsburg City Hustings Court, which had jurisdiction equivalent to that of a county court. 4 Hening 542 (1736).

peared & confessed the Judgt. without any warrant. He will therefore presume Court never saw the Warrant, filed by prentis for his own Justification—it appears to him more properly a Letter than a Warrant of Atty.

2d. point. Whether Ind: Ass: will lie in the Cases stated in Decl[arati]on (He then stated the Decl[arati]on). The party comes into Court & confesses the Action. Suppose Webb & co. Beal's Agents—it is necessary they should be mentioned—Beal did Business also under the firm of Norton & Beal. Upon such an Assumpsit would the court have admitted proof of a Debt due to Norton & Beal upon a genl. Ind. Ass. But say the Appellants here is a nudum pactum.[2] Braxton assumes payt. to Beall for Goods sold by another person—but the Goods might have been Beal's though delivered by Webb. But it is objected the word *Sold* implies the Debt due to *Webb*—but this is not so—the word sold might well stand with such a transaction made on the part of Webb for Beal. The words *being indebted* in the former part of the Decl[arati]on, ex vi Termini[3] imports a Consideration—and the mentioning of Tho. Webb & co. is only as a relation to shew whence the consideration arose. This Case does agree with the Case of the father & the Son.[4] Here the Decl[arati]on shews the debt & the manner by which it accrued. So far the Decl[arati]on good on it's own merits. But suppose here was a title defectively set out, by not averring that Webb & co. were Beal's Agents. The Law directs him to intend after a Verdict that proof of the Agency was made out at the trial a fortiori upon a Confession—never saw a clearer Case.

Fleming. After mature deliberation he has formed an opinion different from Mercer. In every Decl[arati]on the plt must shew that he has a right of Action—in this case he thinks plt has failed. Should Webb & co bring an Action for the same Goods, the recovery in this Action could not be pleaded in Bar. Upon the reason of Courtney & Strong his Judgt. formed.

Courtney v Strong, Salkeld 364.[5]

Lyons. Great doubts. Did not consider warrant of atty any part of record for reasons assigned by Mercer. As to 2d. point—plt must shew such a Cause of Action as is specified in Decl[arati]on. Con-

---

2. That is, an agreement devoid of consideration and, therefore, unenforceable.

3. That is, "from the meaning of the expression."

4. The reference is probably to Butcher v. Andrews, 1 Salkeld 23, Carthew 446, discussed at n. 9, p. 223. However, a similar factual situation was presented in Harris v. Huntbach, 1 Burrow 373, also discussed in the same note.

5. See discussion at n. 9, p. 223.

fession goes no farther than what is stated in Decl[arati]on—it is of no more weight than a verdict—if Consent takes away all Error why were the Statutes of Jeofails made—but the Deft confesses nothing more than Decl[arati]on alledges—it ought to shew some privity between parties.

Comb. 447.[6]

Ind. Ass: will not lie but for the seller—not for a third person.[7] The seller may certainly maintain Ind. Ass.—but can he at *whose request* they were delivered to a third person bring ind: ass: agt. that third person. Clearly not. Perhaps action for money had—a remedy equal to a Bill in Equity, as he thinks very properly so continued. To support Decl[arati]on, something must be presumed which does not appear on the record. Modern Judges have said you are to presume all you can to Support a verdict. Lord Holt,[8] who was a bold Man was the first Judge that held Gen. Ind. Ass. would lie for Goods sold, without specifying of what nature. This before the last Statutes of Jeofails he considered as going a great way. Where Judges as is frequently the Case in this Country are not attentive to Evidence offered there is less reason for presumption than in England where great attention is paid to these matters. But to examine the Decl[arati]on—how does it appear that there was any privity or Consi[de]ration between plt. He has no right to presume Tho Webb & co. were his factors. The Case from Douglas[9] shews presumption may not be carried too far—it might be that T Webb & co gave Beall an order on Braxton. The Act of Ass.[1] does not mend the matter, it should have been averred they *were his factors* if the Action had been brot. upon that Act.

Carrington. No less clear than Mercer but on the other side. He reasoned as Lyons had done on both points. But he must take the whole record as brot. up—by the Judgt. entered with a reciept annexed in Bealls own hand he confesses the Goods to have been the property of Webb & co. throwing every thing else out of the Case. This part alone shews him there is manifest Error.

Judgement reversed!

6. The reference appears to be to Barrett v. Scrimshaw, Comberbach 477, 90 Eng. Rep. 601 (K.B., 1699), where the plaintiff, by demurring to the defendant's answer, was held to have admitted that title to the animals was in a third party.

7. See discussion at n. 5, p. 222.

8. Chief justice of the Court of King's Bench from 1689 to 1710.

9. Whitcomb v. Whiting, discussed at n. 9, p. 228.

1. 28 Geo. 2, c. 2, secs. 6, 7 (1755), *Va. Acts in Force* (1769), 324, 325, printed in 6 Hening 480–481, which concerned factors.

Muse v. Lee

Declaration

Record Book Copy, District Court Records, Office of the Clerk of the Circuit Court, Fredericksburg, Va.

[*April 1787, Richmond.* A declaration in debt on bond to secure payment of £40, filed in the General Court by JM as attorney for the plaintiff and signed by JM.[2]]

Randolph v. Carter

Declaration

Record Book Copy, District Court Records, Office of the Clerk of the Circuit Court, Fredericksburg, Va.

[*April 1787, Richmond.* A declaration in debt on bond to secure payment of £266 9s., filed in the General Court by JM as attorney for the plaintiff and signed by JM.[3]]

Ware v. Conway

Declaration

ADS, University of Virginia Library

[*April 1787, Richmond.* A declaration in detinue brought in the General Court, for a mare valued at £30, by JM as attorney for the plaintiff. The animal was claimed by James Ware and allegedly had been held by Cornelius Conway since Jan. 10, 1786. Endorsements indicate that the case was continued until Sept. 1791, when the verdict and judgment were given for the plaintiff.[4]]

2. The case was subsequently transferred to the newly established District Court at Fredericksburg, where the defendant withdrew his plea and judgment was entered for the plaintiff on Oct. 3, 1789. District Court Records, 1789–1792, 45, 46, Office of the Clerk of the Circuit Court, Fredericksburg, Va.

3. The case was subsequently transferred to the newly established District Court at Fredericksburg, where the defendant withdrew his plea and judgment for £127 15s. 8d. was entered for the plaintiff on Oct. 7, 1789. District Court Records, 1789–1792, 92, Office of the Clerk of the Circuit Court, Fredericksburg, Va.

4. After the reorganization of the courts in 1788, this case was transferred to the District Court at Winchester. Superior Court Order Book, 1789–1793, 35, 74, Office of the Clerk of the Frederick County Circuit Court, Winchester, Va. See Account Book, Receipts, Apr. 11, 1787.

To John Breckinridge

ALS, Breckinridge Family Papers, Library of Congress[5]

Dear Sir　　　　　　　　　　　　　Richmond, May 1, 1787

I have just received yours of the 23d. of April.[6] I shall with very much pleasure make you any communications on legal or any other subjects whenever you chuse. I cannot promise you that they will be worth receiving but such as they are—take them.

Upon a certificate such as you have now sent down the clerk will issue a writ of habeas corpus. The writ ought to find the person in custody. For this purpose the bail which is usually given after the certificate may surrender the defendant when the writ is about to be put into the hands of the sheriff. The sheriff will then execute the writ & the defendant is immediately in his custody under process from the Genl. Court. He will then act as he woud on any other writ with this only exception that the proceedings must be returnd with the writ to the General court. It has been the usual practise for the sheriff to execute the writ & return it with the proceedings tho the defendant shoud not be in custody at the time the writ is servd. If the sheriff will do this 'tis well enough but shoud he refuse he will be in his duty when he refuses. The better way therefor always is to let the writ find the defendant in custody, this is no difficult matter because the bail may surrender the principal & then put the writ into the sheriffs hands to whom he was surrenderd.

I wish you great success at the bar[7] & am dear Sir with great esteem, your obedt. Servt.

J. MARSHALL

Bill of Sale

DS, Welling Collection, Connecticut Historical Society[8]

[Richmond], July 3, 1787

I do hereby bargain sell & convey in absolute property to John Marshall for seventy pounds which I have this day receivd from

5. Addressed to Breckinridge, spelled Breckenridge, at Albemarle.

6. Not found.

7. Breckinridge had begun practicing law in 1785 and frequently asked JM's advice. On occasion JM enlisted Breckinridge's services in the Albemarle County area. See Lowell H. Harrison, *John Breckinridge: Jeffersonian Republican* (Louisville, Ky., 1969), 22–26.

8. The text of the bill and the attached receipt are in JM's hand.

him one negroe wench namd Dicey with her child & do bind myself my heirs executors & administrators to warrant and defend a
complete title totally unincumberd to the said slave & her issue.

JOHN B. JOHNSON

For the within mentiond sum of seventy pounds which I have
received I bargain & sell the within mentiond slaves to Jaqueline
Ambler Esquire.[9]

J MARSHALL

Commission

DS, Executive Papers: Militia, Virginia State Library[1]

Richmond, July 5, 1787
THE COMMONWEALTH OF VIRGINIA, To John Marshall Esquire
Greeting:

KNOW you that from the special trust and confidence, which is
reposed in your fidelity, courage, activity, and good conduct, our
Lieutenant Governor (the Governor being absent, and having
previously notified his intention of being absent to the Privy Council, and such intention having been entered on their Journals) with
the advice of the Privy Council doth appoint you the said John
Marshall Colonel in the Militia of the County of Henrico to take
rank as such from the date hereof. IN TESTIMONY whereof these our
Letters are made patent. Witness the honorable BEVERLEY RAN-
DOLPH, Esquire, our said Lieutenant Governor, at Richmond, this
5th. day of July 1787.
(REGISTERED.)   BEVERLEY RANDOLPH[2]
T. MERIWETHER[3]

9. See Account Book, Disbursements, July 4, 1787.
1. A printed form with name, rank, county, and date entered by hand.
2. Randolph served as president of the Council of State from Nov. 6, 1783, until
Nov. 12, 1788, when he assumed the governor's office. The president of the Council
was considered lieutenant governor. JVCS, III, 305, and passim.
3. Thomas Meriwether (1763–1802) served as assistant clerk and clerk of the Council intermittently during the 1780s. Ibid., passim, and ibid., IV, passim.

To Beverley Randolph

ALS, Executive Papers: Militia, Virginia State Library

Sir   Richmond, August 6, 1787
    I receivd today the enclosd commission.[4] Permit me to thank you
& through you the Honble. members of the privy council for the
distinction conferd upon me. I have indeed sir a very high sense of
it & coud only be inducd to decline acting under so honorable an
appointment by a conviction that the immense load of professional
business under which I at present labor woud render it impossible
for me to discharge the duties of an office becoming so important
in a manner reconciliable to the public interest or my own feelings.
I have the honor to be sir, with every sentiment of respect, Your
Obedt. Servt.

                                                    J MARSHALL

Acknowledgment

DS, Executive Papers, Virginia State Library

[*August 23, 1787, Richmond.* As a magistrate of the City of Richmond,
JM takes the oath of William Cunningham (d. 1789), pursuant to the
statute concerning naval officers and the collection of duties (11 Hening
182 [1782]), that the schooner *Betsy and Polly* was built in Virginia and is
owned by Cunningham, an inhabitant of Virginia.]

Havely v. Hammersly

Declaration

Printed DS, Marshall Papers, University of Virginia Library

[*August 31, 1787, Richmond.* A declaration in debt brought in the General
Court for £45 in Maryland currency (£36 in Virginia currency), on a
writing obligatory from Garret Hammersly to Frederick Havely, made by

4. Commission as colonel of Henrico County militia dated July 5, 1787, printed
above.

JM as attorney for the plaintiff; endorsements indicate that the case was continued until Apr. 1790, when the verdict and judgment were given for the plaintiff.[5]]

To John Breckinridge

ALS, Breckinridge Family Papers, Library of Congress

My dear Sir   [Richmond], September 28, 1787
I have just receivd your letter[6] accompanying the appeal Hill v Henley. I have lookd it over but do not think there is any error in it. Will you please to mention what mistake the clerk has committed? I see some thing not entirely usual but I think there is nothing material. You will when you see him mention this to Mr. Hill. I wrote you the other day by Mr. Harvie[7] an answer to your queries. I am dear Sir, yours etc.

J MARSHALL

Brickhouse v. Brickhouse

Notes on Argument in the General Court

Extract from Casebook, Tucker-Coleman Papers, Swem Library, College of William and Mary

Richmond, October 2, 1787
Marshal moved for a mandamus to the County Court of
to allow an appeal from a Judgement of that Court on a Replevin Bond.[8] The Court doubted of the regularity of the motion for a mandamus in the first instance, without a previous rule to shew

5. Because the case had originated in Berkeley County, it was transferred to the District Court at Winchester after the court reorganization of 1788. See Superior Court Order Book, 1789-1793, 76, Office of the Clerk of the Frederick County Circuit Court, Winchester, Va.
6. Not found.
7. Probably John Harvie of Augusta County. JM's letter not found.
8. A replevin bond was obtained for the indemnification of the sheriff who executed a writ of replevin, which transferred custody of a chattel from the defendant to the plaintiff, pending determination of the dispute concerning ownership.

cause;[9] but there appeared to be no doubt with them that a mandamus would be proper after such a rule. Marshal said he would endeavour to satisfy the doubts of the court tomorrow.[1]

3. Blacks. 110.[2]

Mandamus granted, Mercer absent.

Duncan & Company v. Dameron & Company

Notes on Argument in the General Court

Extract from Casebook, Tucker-Coleman Papers, Swem Library, College of William and Mary

Richmond, October 6, 1787

The suit brought by Starke,[3] on a bond, which after decl[arati]on filed was burnt in his Lodgings at the fire of Richmond.[4] Office Judgement[5] confirmed.

Starke, moved the court to direct the Clerk to fill up the Judgt. & issue Ex[ecuti]o[n] on Affidavit that Bond was burnt.

Marshall, moved to be permitted to appear & plead.

Rule to shew Cause, 8th. day of next Term.[6]

NB. Lyons said, where oyer[7] is claimed the Bond is to lie in court one Term—[qy].

9. In other words, the motion should have been made upon notice by means of an order to show cause why a writ of mandamus should not issue. Mandamus, in this case, was a writ by a superior court to an inferior court, directing the lower court to perform a particular act required by the court's public, official, or ministerial duties. More generally, mandamus was also used to command the performance of official duties by executive, administrative, or judicial officers and to command that a party be restored certain privileges of which he had been wrongfully deprived.

1. Apparently the necessary order to show cause was obtained the following day.

2. The citation is to the discussion of mandamus in Blackstone, *Commentaries*, III, 110-111.

3. Burwell Starke, an active practitioner in the Virginia courts, had been educated at Donald Robertson's school (1767-1770) and the College of William and Mary (1773-1774).

4. For a brief discussion of this Richmond fire, see Account Book, Disbursements, Feb. 9, 1787.

5. Under Virginia procedure the clerk of a court might enter a default judgment after the term of a court at which a rule to answer or to plead had been entered. Such an "office judgment" was final where the action was in debt and the amount due was certain. 6 Hening 335 (1753).

6. An order to show cause why judgment should not be entered.

7. Oyer in this context is a request by a defendant that the plaintiff bring the bond into court and that it be read into the records of the court.

April 25, 1788

Rule to shew cause why Judgt. for plt should not be entered up according to Decl[arati]on, on affidavit that the Bond whereon suit brot. was burnt—there being an Office Judt.

Rule discontinued. The court concieving he might proceed in Equity.[8]

Jacobs v. Nottingham

Notes on Argument in the General Court

Extract from Casebook, Tucker-Coleman Papers, Swem Library, College of William and Mary

Richmond, October 8, 1787

Debt for Rent. The Question arose upon this point, whether the taxes paid by the Tenant in 1780. & 1781. in paper money shall be admitted as a disc[oun]t agt. the Rent which plt demands. There is one point, however, the parol Acknowledgement of Deft in August 1781. that he owed plt £246. Plt & Defendant lived in the same County, but had no notice until payment of the Taxes.

If for plt Judgt. for a larger—if for Deft, a lesser Sum.

This Question arises under Act of assembly, revd. Code 60. ch: 2. Sect: 6. & 8.[9]

Baker. Where Landlord & Tenant reside in the same County Tenant may if he pleases pay the rent—not so where the Landlord resides in another County. See Sect: 8.[1] Policy of the Act did not require Tenants to advance more than the Rent they were bound to pay by their Leases. Taxes were often (*nominally*, at least) more than the rent.

8. The loss of the declaration and office judgment in the fire was therefore held to preclude the plaintiff from proceeding at law, and the order to show cause was vacated. The plaintiff was left to obtain equitable relief, perhaps by a bill in chancery supported by depositions explaining the circumstances in which the documents were lost.

9. The reference is to *A Collection of all the Public Acts of the General Assembly and Ordinances of the Conventions of Virginia, passed since the year 1768, as are now in force* (Richmond, 1785), 60. The statute printed on this and the subsequent page of the "Chancellor's Revisal" is "An Act for Raising a Supply of Money for Public Exigencies," and it is c. 2 of the acts of the Oct. 1777 session of the General Assembly. See 9 Hening 356–357 for the text of sec. 6; 9 Hening 358–359 for the text of sec. 8.

1. It is difficult to accept Jerman Baker's assertion that sec. 8, providing the mode of collecting taxes when the proprietor resided in another county, limited the provisions of sec. 6, which upon its face permitted the tenant to pay the taxes assessed against his landlord, regardless of the landlord's place of residence.

Lee.[2] Tenant cannot pay more than the annual Rent. If he has paid a sum of money which the Law will not justify him in paying, the Case agreed is defective. It is certain a certain sum of money might have been lawfully paid by the Tenant under the Law, but he concieved it was incumbent on the Tenant to shew every thing necessary to make his payment lawful.

NB. The Case is somewhat perplexed, I concieve the Question to be, whether arrears due by the Teneant before that Law could *by him* be paid in discharge of the Landlords proportion of the tax under the Act.[3]

Marshall cited the Act for regulating the Scale of Dep[*reciation*][4] and insisted Tenant had a right to pay, though the Landlord was not consulted thereon. Sect: 8. does not apply to this Case. Sect. 6. intended to apply to all Cases between Landlord & Tenant; but the 8th. Sect. the Law has *unoccupied* Lands only in contemplation. Nothing in the Law to warrant Lees distinction that Tenant shall not pay more than the *annual rent*.

Lee. Deft was bound to pay £82. Per ann. rent. He has paid a much larger sum so as to sweep off the Arrears of several former years. This the Law did not warrant, therefore he ought not to have credit for the Excess, but according to the value as fixed by the Scale, not according to the nominal amount.

Tazewell gave no opinion.

Mercer. Judgt. for the Lesser Sum.

Lyons. Same opinion—payt. to the Sheriff the same as if to the Landlord himself.

Carrington; Same opinion.

Judgement for Defendant to pay the lesser sum.[5]

2. Charles Lee.

3. St. George Tucker's reservation was not raised in the argument, namely, that the statute would be retroactive in effect if it pertained to rents accrued prior to the date of enactment.

4. Probably "An Act directing the Mode of Adjusting and Settling the Payment of Certain Debts and Contracts and for Other Purposes," 10 Hening 471–474 (1781).

5. In other words, the tenant could pay only the taxes due under the assessment of the year in which he paid the taxes; any additional amount could not be set-off against his accrued rent.

Byrd v. Holcombe

Notes on Argument in the General Court

Extract from Casebook, Tucker-Coleman Papers, Swem Library, College of William and Mary

Richmond, October 15, 1787

Debt on a penal Bill—Decl[arati]on in the common form on a Bond.

Marshal, objected to the penal Bill as improper Evidence on this Declaration.[6] Of which opinion absente Lyons, was the whole Court.

Plt. nonsuited.

NB. The Tenor of the Bill was that Deft should have one month's notice of demand. Marshall objected that this was a material Circumstance omitted, notice not being averred. But the Court inclined, as I thought, to the Opinion that this was cured by the plea of payment which admitted (as they said) the notice. See the Cases in the Margin. See Also. 2. Cro. 183, 640, 523, 382.[7]

vi: Hob: 217, 51, 68; 1. Ld. Ray. 735, 792; Douglas 640 to 644; 1. Ld. Ray. 365; 4. Mod. 230; Brownl. 13; 3. Salk: 246.[8]

6. Apparently the declaration set forth some of the terms of the bond but not the conditions contained in the bond. Chitty, *On Pleading*, I, 260, says that "no covenants or matter unconnected with the cause of action should be stated; on the other hand a variance will frequently be fatal, and any matter which qualifies the contract must be stated, or the plaintiff will be nonsuited on the plea of *non est factum*." Also, "if the . . . contract proved in evidence vary from that stated in the pleadings, the plaintiff will be nonsuited." *Ibid.*, 224.

7. St. George Tucker's discussion deals with another aspect of the case: the requirement that notice be pleaded as a material aspect of the plaintiff's action on the bond. The cases cited hold that if an action be brought on a collateral promise, or on an arbitration bond requiring notice, notice must be specifically alleged and proved. Selman v. King, 3 Croke 183, 79 Eng. Rep. 159-160 (K.B., 1607); Hill v. Wade, 3 Croke 523, 79 Eng. Rep. 447-448 (K.B., 1619); Waters v. Bridge, 3 Croke 639-640, 79 Eng. Rep. 551 (K.B., 1620). However, in an action upon a bond conditioned upon notice of a specific act being done, it was held that the plaintiff might, by replication, correct his failure to plead notice in the declaration. Gold v. Death, 3 Croke 381-382, 79 Eng. Rep. 325-326 (K.B., 1615).

8. The marginal citations support the rule that a plaintiff must allege notice of all information that is within his private knowledge but that will give rise to the defendant's liability on a bond. Holmes v. Twist, Hobart 51, 80 Eng. Rep. 200 (Exch. Ch., 1612); Richard v. Carvamel, Hobart 68, 80 Eng. Rep. 217 (K.B., 1618); and a passage entitled "Notice" in 3 Salkeld 246, 91 Eng. Rep. 804 (K.B.). However, where the defendant is charged with gaining information at his peril, he is not entitled to notice. Pitman v. Biddlecombe, 4 Modern Rep. 230, 87 Eng. Rep. 364-365 (K.B., 1693).

Record of Attendance

House of Delegates Records, Virginia State Library[9]

[*October 15, 1787, Richmond.* JM signs the attendance book as a qualified member of the House of Delegates representing Henrico County.[1]]

Deed

Deed Book, Office of the Clerk of the Fauquier County Circuit Court, Warrenton, Va.

[*October 18, 1787, Markham.* JM buys 268 acres of land in fee simple from Aquila and Lucy Dyson, located in Fauquier County, paying £160 for it. The deed was recorded in Fauquier County Court on Feb. 25, 1788.[2]]

Receipt

ADS, Patton Family Papers, Virginia Historical Society[3]

[Richmond], October 29, 1787

Recd. five pounds in a suit in chancery for Doctor Walker at the suit of Colo. Syme.[4]

J MARSHALL

Sherwood v. Adderly, 1 Lord Raymond 735, 91 Eng. Rep. 1391 (Nisi Prius, 1699), and Pierce v. Paxton, 1 Lord Raymond 692, 91 Eng. Rep. 1361 (K.B., 1701), hold that a bond must be read into evidence and that a deed of acquittance must also be read into evidence to show payment. Gore v. Colthorp, 1 Brownlow & Gouldsborough 13, 123 Eng. Rep. 634–635 (C.P., 1607), held that one collaterally concerned in a debt on a bond must be given notice of the demand upon the principal obligor. Jackson v. Pigott, 1 Lord Raymond 364–365, 91 Eng. Rep. 1140 (K.B., 1698), and Ancher v. Bank of England, 2 Douglas 639–641, 99 Eng. Rep. 404–406 (K.B., 1781), both involve negotiable instruments—the first, the effect of acceptance of a bill of exchange after the due date, and the second, the status of a holder who has ignored the existence of a restrictive endorsement on a bill of exchange.

9. This list is in a book labeled "Resolutions of House of Delegates, 22 May 1776 and 28 May 1781–24 July 1784" and is headed "Richmond, October 15th 1787, List of members of Assembly qualified for the present year." The book is filed with House of Delegates Attendance Books, 1781–1782, Virginia State Library.

1. JM had been elected to the House of Delegates on Apr. 2, 1787, and took his oaths of office on the same day he signed this list. Election Certificate, Apr. 2, 1787, and Qualification Certificate, Oct. 15, 1787, Election Records, Va. State Lib.

2. JM was not in Fauquier County in Oct. 1787, so he must have had someone handle the transfer. He went there on Feb. 22, 1788, and recorded the deed during that visit. See Account Book, Disbursements, Feb. 22, 1788.

3. This is item no. Mss1P2284a1660 in the Virginia Historical Society collections.

4. Thomas Walker (1715–1794), a physician in Albemarle County who had ex-

Pickett v. Claiborne

Argument

Printed, Daniel Call, *Reports of Cases Argued and Decided in the Court of Appeals of Virginia* (Richmond, 1833), IV, 99–106

[*October 30, 1787, Richmond.* JM and John Taylor argue for appellant Pickett in the Court of Appeals. The judgment is for Pickett on Nov. 1, 1787.[5]]

Wilson v. Hart

Declaration

Record Book Copy, District Court Records, Office of the Clerk of the Circuit Court, Fredericksburg, Va.

[*October 1787, Richmond.* A declaration in indebitatus assumpsit, filed in the General Court by JM as attorney for the plaintiff and signed by JM.[6]]

Petition of James Markham

AD, Legislative Petitions: Fauquier County, Virginia State Library[7]

[Richmond], November 3, 1787

To the Honble. the Speaker & Members of the house of Delegates the petition of James Markham[8] humbly sheweth

plored the Kentucky country in 1750, served in the Council of State in the 1770s and headed the Virginia commission to draw the border with North Carolina westward. John Syme (*ca.* 1728–1805), of Hanover County, whose mills had helped supply troops with flour in 1781, was a member of the House of Delegates at several sessions from 1776 to 1782 and served in the Virginia Senate from 1784 to 1788. See Account Book, Receipts, Mar. 3, and June 20, 1787.

JM entered this fee in Account Book, Receipts, Oct. 29, 1787.

5. Court of Appeals Order Book, 1779–1789, 106–108, Virginia State Library.

6. The defendant pleaded non assumpsit, and the case was then transferred to the newly established District Court at Fredericksburg. After jury trial and verdict, judgment was entered for the plaintiff for damages of £611 10s. ½d. and court costs. District Court Records, 1789–1792, 186, Office of the Clerk of the Circuit Court, Fredericksburg, Va. See Account Book, Receipts, Aug. 17, 1787.

7. The entire petition is in JM's hand.

8. Markham (1752–1816), of Fauquier County, had submitted a petition to the

That your petitioner early in the late war with Great Britain engagd in the service of his country as an Officer in the Navy of this State & remained therein performing the duties of his office till the 27th. of April 1781 when your petitioner was taken a prisoner by the Enemy & his vessel captured. In a few days your petitioner was paroled, but not being exchanged he was not discharged from his parol till the end of the war. So that your petitioner was deprived of the power of going on board any vessel during the war & of consequence prevented from supporting his family by the exercise of that profession to which he had been trained from his infancy. That when your petitioner presented his accounts to the Auditors of this State for a settlement, they refused to issue Certificates or warrants to him for a later period of time than the 5th. day of Novr. 1781 alledging that the officers of the navy of this Commonwealth were then discharged from the service of the state. ⟨They likewise charged your petitioner with monies which he had never received.⟩ Your petitioner prays that your honorable house will take his case into consideration & grant him relief in the premises. And your petitioner as in duty bound shall ever pray etc.

JAMES MARKHAM

Petition of John Kelly

AD, Legislative Petitions: Henrico County, Virginia State Library[9]

[Richmond], November 22, 1787

To the Honble. the Speaker & Members of the genl. Assembly the petition of John Kelly humbly sheweth that during the late war sometime in the year 1780 a certain Nathaniel Henderson[1] with a party of Virginia Soldiers took possession of the dwelling house the property of your petitioner. The house was taken into the public

Oct. 1784 Assembly "praying that the auditors may be directed to liquidate his accounts as an officer of the navy of this State, and grant him certificates for the balance due to him." *JVHD*, Oct. 1784, 40. No action was taken until Dec. 12, 1785, when the claims committee advised the House to accept his claim. The House tabled the resolution. *JVHD*, Oct. 1785, 89. At the Oct. 1787 session, however, the claims committee approved Markham's petition, and the House of Delegates accepted it on Nov. 10. The Senate concurred on Nov. 14. *JVHD*, Oct. 1787, 38, 45. JM wrote the petition even though he was representing Henrico County at this session.

9. The petition and the signature are in JM's hand.

1. Henderson (1736–1794).

service in order to lodge in it the aforementioned party of men who were at work on the labaratory at Westham. While they were in possession of the said house they burnt it down. Your petitioner prays that the honble. the genl. assembly may take his case into consideration & grant him relief and your petitioner will ever pray etc.[2]

JOHN KELLY

Birth of Jaquelin Ambler Marshall

Entry, Marshall Family Bible, Collection of Mrs. Kenneth R. Higgins, Richmond

[*December 3, 1787 (Richmond)*. A notation in JM's hand indicates that his son, Jaquelin Ambler Marshall,[3] was born on this day.]

To Commissioners on Illinois Accounts

Certified Copy, RG 360, National Archives[4]

Gentlemen,   Richmond, December 31, 1787

The Committee appointed by the House of Delegates, to call on you for a state of your proceedings in liquidating and adjusting the Expenses incurred by the Commonwealth of Virginia for the North Western Territory ceded to Congress, return their thanks to Col: Heth and Col: Henley for their ready compliance in laying the proceedings of your Board before the Committee; and to Col: Heth for laying before the Committee in compliance with their request a Statement of the whole claim of Virginia for the ceded Territory, together with a Statement and Estimate of his own, of the sum which Virginia ought [*to*] be reimbursed after making every just and reasonable deduction, in conformity to certain determinations already had by your Board.[5]

2. The petition was rejected without referral to a committee. *JVHD*, Oct. 1787, 62.
3. JM's second son became a physician but never practiced medicine. He married Eliza L. S. Clarkson on Jan. 1, 1819. An avid reader of theology and literature, he spent his life quietly at Prospect Hill, 10 miles south of Markham, Va., in Fauquier County, where he died on July 7, 1852.
4. Contemporary copy made by John Beckley (1759–1807), clerk of the House of Delegates. Addressed to Messrs. Pierce, Heth, and Henley, Commissioners for settling the Illinois Accounts.
5. When Virginia had ceded Congress its claim to the northwest territory, it was

The Committee cannot entertain a doubt that the true Intent and meaning of the Contracting Parties, was that Virginia should be fully reimbursed the amount of what she had actually expended and paid in the conquest and protection of the Territory ceded to the United States; nor can they conceive it consistent with the honor and Justice of Congress that any principles operating against this should be established or even proposed by the Commissioners. The sale of the Lands Virginia has ceded to the United States will produce a sum more than sufficient to discharge her proportion of the whole debt of the United States both foreign and domestic; and surely nothing can be more incompatible with the Act of Cession construed upon the principles of common Justice, than now to refuse, allowing the comparatively small Sum which that Country has bona fide cost her: especially when it is notorious that in far the greater part of the Expenditures on this Object, she consulted in the best manner she could, her own individual Interest without any Expectation of being reimbursed by the United States. In this situation and for the purpose of liquidating & settling such Expenditures as it was impossible for want of proper evidence and information to adjust here, public Commissioners were appointed in the back Country, where only, a proper investigation of the subject could be made, as the nature of the Service as well as the price and difficulty of procuring many Articles depended upon vivâ voçê testimony and a variety of local Vouchers. The settlement made under these circumstances by the said Commissioners, We conceive to be in it's nature final, and affording now the best possible evidence, so far as their settlement has extended. It is therefore with equal surprize and concern, that upon examining the papers and

---

agreed and included in the act of cession in 1784 that the "necessary and reasonable expenses" incurred by Virginia in acquiring and defending the territory since July 1776 be reimbursed by Congress. Commissioners were to be appointed—one by Congress, one by Virginia, and the last by the two chosen—to determine the amount Congress should reimburse Virginia. John Pierce (d. 1788), commissioner of Army accounts, was appointed commissioner by Congress; William Heth was appointed by Virginia; and David Henley (1748–1823) was chosen by Heth and Pierce to complete the panel. Virginia had arrived at a determination of how much money was owed the state as early as 1781, when the General Assembly appointed commissioners to make a study. *JVHD*, May 1781, 27–28. When Pierce, Heth, and Henley began deliberations, Pierce was hesitant to accept the early findings and convinced the others to make a new study, which resulted in the elimination of several items, thus reducing the amount Virginia had expected to receive. At that point the General Assembly appointed this special committee to inquire into the work of the commissioners. *Ibid.*, Oct. 1787, 105. Heth and Henley replied that the committee could look at their journal. Pierce dissented, saying he could not approve such a thing without approval from Congress. See *ibid.*, 137–139; *Mason Papers*, III, 1027–1037; and E. James Ferguson, *The Power of the Purse: A History of American Public Finance, 1776–1790* (Chapel Hill, N.C., 1961), 216–217.

statements laid before Us, with the arguments of the Commissioners in support of their respective Opinions, We find the said settlements departed from, and an Enquiry substituted in the nature, amount, and prices of the Supplies, at this distance of time and place impracticable, and depending merely upon opinion, which under such circumstances is only another Name for Caprice. Besides this We also find some principles adopted and others' urged, which appear to us evidently calculated to reduce the consideration to be allowd VIRGINIA to a pittance, not worth her Acceptance contrary to the former Intentions and present Interest of the contracting Parties; as it may bring into doubt the validity of the deed of Cession and thereby greatly affect the sales of the Lands to the injury of the whole Union. Among other objections to the claims of Virginia, We observe that the establishment and support of Forts Jefferson, and Nelson, is denied by the Commissioners on the part of Congress, to be comprehended within the Intent and meaning of the Act of Cession, and upon principles and arguments which appear to us equivocal & unjust: it being matter of public notoriety that the charge of these Ports,[6] would not have been incurred, had not Virginia been engaged in the conquest and protection of the Illinois Country, they being established by Government at the instance of General Clark,[7] the Officer employed for those purposes, and therefore within the knowledge and contemplation of the Contracting Parties. The Committee are unanimously of opinion that the Legislature upon being informed of the present state of this important business, will protest against the further proceedings of your Board, from the fullest conviction that an Official public Officer under Congress was an improper person, to have been employed on a subject, wh. required the utmost impartiality and consequently independence of Situation: and the Committee must consider it as their duty in making their Report, to recommend it to the General Assembly, to remonstrate to the United States, in the most respectful but unequivocal terms, informing them, that unless Congress will direct their Commissioner to admit such principles in the settlement of the Accounts, as will clearly tend to reimburse Virginia the amount of what she has actually and bonâ fidê, expended and paid for the conquest and protection of the ceded North Western Territory, she will withold all monies on the requisitions of Congress, untill such amount shall have been reimbursed, or will take such other measures therein as Justice, Good Faith, and regard for

6. The writer obviously meant "Forts."
7. George Rogers Clark.

her own, as well as the common Interest of the Union shall dictate. The Committee from the papers and statements before them find, that the sum of about two hundred and twenty thousands pounds specie would remain due to Virginia, after deducting to the amount of twenty odd thousand pounds, for such Articles as are doubtful, and some of which may perhaps have been improperly charged; and that from the first mentioned sum, a further deduction of near sixty thousand pounds would be made, if the accounts should be closed on the principles already determined by your Board:

These sums are too great to be sacrificed, although the loss of many thousands would probably be preferred, to the risque of involving either herself or the United States in any disagreeable Dispute or Consequences, especially at so critical a Season, as the present.

Impressed with these ideas, the Committee cannot refrain expressing their most earnest wish that the Board, would reconsider, some of the leading general principles, upon which the settlement of the Accounts depends: so as to meet the propositions from Virginia upon just and equitable grounds: And in this hope the Committee will defer making their Report for a day or two, expecting to be informed in the mean Time of the Sentiments of the Board thereon.[8] We are Gentlemen, Your Mo Obt humle Servants,

(Signed)   GEORGE MASON
GEORGE NICOLAS
FRAN: CORBIN
JOHN MARSHALL
BENJ: HARRSION[9]

Acknowledgment

ADS, Executive Papers: Militia, Virginia State Library

[*December 31, 1787, Richmond.* JM, as a magistrate of Richmond, affirms that Nathaniel Wilkinson[1] appeared before him and swore that he had received no money while commander of the Henrico County militia.]

8. See Commissioners on Illinois Accounts to House of Delegates Committee, Jan. 2, 1788, below.

9. Mason (1725–1792) was a delegate from Fairfax County; Nicholas, a delegate from Albemarle County; Corbin, a delegate from Middlesex County; and Harrison, a delegate from Charles City County.

1. Wilkinson was appointed county lieutenant (commanding officer) of the Henrico County militia on July 5, 1787. *JVCS,* IV, 121.

From Commissioners on Illinois Accounts

Letterbook Copy, RG 93, National Archives

Gentlemen   [Richmond], January 2, 1788

The Commissioners have been h[o]nored by your Letter of the 30th.[2] ulto. and we take the Liberty to assure your Honorable Committe that the principles already established by us were determined on a full view of the subject & from the purest intentions—that we have endeavoured to discharge our duty hitherto without fear, favor, affection, partiality or hopes of Reward from either of the Parties—and that untill they shall think proper mutually to revoke our appointments we shall to the best of our Abilities proceed in the further discharge of it upon the same principles. We have the honor to be, Gentlemen, Yours etc.

JNO. PIERCE
DAVID HENLEY

I am in my own person as free, as ready and can as conscientiously declare that the opinions which I have given have been as uninfluenced [by] fear, favor, affection partiality or hopes of reward from either of the contracting parties as the above Gentlemen and that such opinions proceeded from the purest intentions as well as the fullest view & most perfect knowledge of the subject as Testimony recently examined will clearly evince. Having long since acquieced in the determination already had by this Board I shall as readily consider myself bound to prosecute the objects of our appointments so long as the means are in our power for so doing.[3] I have the honor to be, Gentlemen your mos obt huml. Svt.

WILLIAM HETH

2. The clerk meant 31st. See the preceding document to Commissioners on Illinois Accounts.

3. Other copies of this letter indicate the first part was written by Pierce and the latter by Heth. See *Mason Papers*, III, 1031. After the commissioners refused to change their position, Mason reported to the House of Delegates on Jan. 7, 1788, and the House resolved to demand that Congress reject the findings of the commissioners, especially Pierce, and award Virginia what she had claimed all along was her due. The tenor of the resolutions put Pierce in bad light, and he submitted a lengthy report of his own to Congress in which he stated that Virginia refused to cooperate with the commissioners when she learned things were not going in her favor. John Pierce to Board of Treasury, Jan. 10, 1788, RG 93, National Archives. Pierce became ill and could not continue meeting with Heth and Henley. These two agreed that $500,000 was a reasonable sum. Some in Congress thought this excessive, and nothing was decided until 1791, when the figure had risen to $1,253,877. *JVHD*, Oct. 1787, 137–139; *Mason Papers*, III, 1037; E. James Ferguson, *The Power of the Purse: A History of American Public Finance, 1776–1790* (Chapel Hill, N.C., 1961), 217, 324.

Legislative Bill

AD, House of Delegates Papers, Virginia State Library[4]

Richmond, January 3, 1788
   Be it enacted by the General Assembly that the act entitled an
act for establishing courts of Assise shall be & the same is hereby
repeald.[5] And that so much of every act or acts of Assembly[6] as prohibits an Attorney from practising at the same time in the superior
& inferior courts shall be & the same is hereby repeald except only
that no attorney shall be permitted to prosecute in a superior court
an appeal from a Judgement or decree of any inferior court where
he shall have appeard in the inferior court for the appellant.[7]

Land Grant

Registry Book, Grants, XIV, 393–397, Land Office Papers, Virginia State Library

[*January 8, 1788, Richmond*. JM receives a grant of 40,000 acres in Fayette County, Ky., based upon a survey conducted on Mar. 15, 1785, on
land located one-half mile above the mouth of Salt Lick Creek into the
Ohio River.]

Subscription

Copy, Richmond City Hustings Deeds, Virginia State Library[8]

Richmond, January 9, 1788
WE the underwritten Subscribers taking into consideration the present defenceless situation of the City, and our total inability to provide against Accidents by fire, unless Order and discipline be

4. JM introduced this bill on Jan. 3; this draft is in his hand. It was accepted on
Jan. 4, amended by the Senate on Jan. 5, and adopted. *JVHD*, Oct. 1787, 132, 136.
The bill with the amendment is printed in 12 Hening 497.
   5. The repealed act is 11 Hening 421; it had never gone into effect, having been
consecutively suspended. 12 Hening 45, 267.
   6. 7 Hening 399.
   7. In other words, the same attorney could not appeal a case to the higher court,
but if the adversary party did so, the same attorney could appear in the higher court
for the appellee.
   8. In a clerk's hand, this subscription is on microfilm reel 1 (1782–1792), p. 198.

introduced among the Citizens, do hereby associate ourselves, (under an Act of Assembly intituled an Act to authorize the establishment of fire companies[9]) into a company to be known and called by the name of "The fellowship fire company of Richmond"[1] and hereby agree to abide by and perform all such by Laws, rules and regulations, as shall be enacted, and agreed to by a majority of the said company WITNESS our hands this Ninth day of January One thousand seven Hundred & Eighty eight.

J. MARSHALL[2]

At a Court of Hustings for the City of Richmond, held at the Courthouse on Monday the 28th. of January 1788.

This Instrument of writing composing the "FELLOWSHIP fire Company of Richmond," was exhibited into Court by Thomas P. Johnson one of the subscribers thereto, acknowledged by the said Johnson and proved by his Affirmation as to the rest of the subscribers except John Ker, & John Hicks,[3] which is Ordered to be Recorded.

Examined   Teste ADAM CRAIG C.C.

To John Beckley

[*ca. March 10, 1788, Richmond.* A letter resigning from office of recorder of the city of Richmond, mentioned in Minutes of the Richmond City Common Hall, I, 160, Virginia State Library. Not found. Beckley was mayor from Feb. 21, 1788, to Mar. 9, 1789.]

9. The act provided that towns with populations exceeding 40 people could legally form companies "for the purpose of extinguishing fire." Those desiring to form a fire company were required first to record their names with their county or corporation court, after which they could adopt rules and regulations and obtain "engines and other necessary implements." The act also allowed collection of fines for nonattendance or delinquency if the offender were brought before a magistrate and the fine did not exceed 25s. The act passed the General Assembly on Jan. 7, 1788, just two days before this subscription was prepared. 12 Hening 530–531.

1. The existence of this fire company has escaped notice by historians. The earliest fire company in Richmond, according to all accounts, was established in 1816. See R. A. Brock, *The Richmond, Virginia, Fire Department, Its Organization and Equipment, with an Account of Its Precursors from the Initial Organization of "Effective Friendship" in 1816* (Richmond, 1894); Mary Dudley Cappelmann, *A Brief History of the Fire Department and the Police Department of Richmond, Virginia* (Richmond, 1931); and Donald Lee Morecock, "A History of the Richmond, Virginia, Fire Department" (M.A. thesis, University of Richmond, 1958). Unfortunately no records of this earlier fire company have been found.

2. JM was one of 44 signers, among whom were William Foushee and John Beckley.

3. Johnson, Ker, and Hicks, all Richmond residents, also signed the subscription.

Power of Attorney

ADS, Land Office, Kentucky Secretary of State's Office[4]

[Prince William], March 12, 1788

I Charles Tyler of the County of Prince William & State of Virginia do hereby Constitute Nominate and appoint my trusty friend John Marshall jr[5] of the City of Richmond, my true and Lawful Attorney, for me and in my behalf to subscribe my name to an Assignment of a certain Tract or parcel of Land now lying in the Registers Office at Richmond; containing twenty five thousand Acres on Salt Lick Creek one half to Abraham Foe & his Heirs and Assigns the other moiety to Christopher Greenup and Humphrey Marshall[1] as Tenants in Common and their Heirs or Assigns forever hereby ratifying and confirming whatever my said Attorney may legally do in the premises. In Witness whereof I have hereunto set my hand and Seal this 12th. day of March A D. 1788.

Attest   CHARLES TYLER [LS]
CHARLES MARSHALL[2]

Kirman Holmes & Company v. Duncan

Notes on Argument in the General Court

Extract from Casebook, Tucker-Coleman Papers, Swem Library, College of William and Mary

Richmond, April 26, 1788

The Writ in this Case was served on the Deft Turner, only, & was returnable to the 23d: day of the court. Turner came into Court to confess Judgt. not only in this suit but in three others, for

---

4. The document is endorsed "Tyler to Marshall, Po. Atto." It is located in the bundle for Survey 8118, Virginia Land Grants. The related survey is recorded in Survey Book 10, 101, Land Office, Kentucky Secretary of State's Office. Charles Tyler formerly was an ensign in the Eleventh Virginia Regiment and resigned his commission on Dec. 23, 1777.

5. In Kentucky JM was known as "John Marshall, Jr.," to distinguish him from an older John Marshall (d. *ca.* 1783), who was a resident of Kentucky.

1. Greenup (1750–1818) was first lieutenant in Grayson's Additional Continental Regiment from Feb. 2, 1777, to Apr. 1, 1778. Humphrey Marshall was actively engaged in securing Kentucky land grants, at times in association with JM and Col. Thomas Marshall.

2. Probably JM's brother (1767–1805), one of the twins about whom little is known. He practiced law at Warrenton, Va., and is thought to have been paralyzed. He married Lucy Pickett on Sept. 13, 1787.

very large sums. Turner resides in new york. Duncan in Louisa:[3]

Taylor, for Duncan opposed the Deft. Turner's being permitted to confess a Judgt. which should bind the property of Duncan, who might or might not be a partner. It was admitted that Duncan did not know anything of these suits. Taylor cited a Similar Case in the old General Court, between Edbeck & Ross & Ross & Trigg. Ross appeared & confessed Judgt. in the name of Ross & Trigg—Judgt. & Ex[ecuti]o[n]. thereon—but the court at the next Term set aside the Judgt. & quashed the Ex[ecuti]o[n]; & permitted Trigg to defend the suit—April 14, 1775. See the record.

Marshall for the plt. One partner certainly can bind the property of the company by confessing a Judgt.—this is a power resulting from their mutual confidence in each other.

Tazewell, Judge, to Marshal. Would not this confession bind the Individual private property of Mr. Duncan, as well as the property of the Company.

Marshal. Yes, but it is his own act by becoming a partner.[4]

Tazewell. Where one partner wishes to confess Judgt. & the other desires to defend the suit, he should not choose to suffer the Confession. The Gen. Court did right in Ross's Case.

Mercer & Carrington Concurred.

Hindman & Company v. Ball

Declaration

Record Book Copy, District Court Records, Office of the Clerk of the Circuit Court, Fredericksburg, Va.

[*April 1788, Richmond.* A declaration in debt on a bill of exchange for £100 9s., filed in the General Court by JM as attorney for the plaintiff and signed by JM.[5]]

3. That is, Louisa County, Va.

4. The law concerning the ability of a partner to obligate his copartners had not yet been fully articulated. In legal proceedings on partnership contracts, it was the rule that all partners had to be named in the action, lest some advantage be gained by the omission of the other partners. However, on matters within the law merchant, such as the acceptance of a bill of exchange, the act of one partner might bind the partnership. See William Watson, *A Treatise of the Law of Partnership* (Albany, N.Y., 1795), 123, 232, 246, 252. A century after JM's argument, the rule in Virginia was that as a general principle a confession of judgment by one partner would not be binding on his copartners. Alexander v. Alexander, 85 Va. 353, 365 (Ct. App., 1888).

5. The case was subsequently transferred to the newly established District Court at Fredericksburg, and, after trial, judgment was entered for the plaintiff on Oct. 1, 1790. District Court Records, 1789-1792, 221-222, Office of the Clerk of the Circuit Court, Fredericksburg, Va.

McKean v. Bowyer

Declaration

Copy, District Court Order Book, Office of the Clerk of the Augusta County Circuit Court, Staunton, Va.

[*April 1788, Richmond.* A declaration in debt on three bonds to secure payment of a total of £482 15s. 6½d., filed in the General Court by JM as attorney for the plaintiff and signed by JM.⁶]

The Virginia Ratifying Convention

EDITORIAL NOTE

Few of the conventions called to ratify the Constitution of the United States can compare with the Virginia convention for dramatic impact and sophisticated discussion of the delicate issues of political structure and governmental power. John Marshall served as a member of the convention, having been elected a delegate from Henrico County. Although his support for the proposed form of government was strong and active, his role in the floor debates was relatively minor when compared with the efforts of his colleagues Edmund Pendleton, James Madison, Edmund Randolph, and George Nicholas.⁷

Marshall delivered three speeches to the assembled delegates.⁸ His oration on the judicial powers of the federal government is the best known of the three be-

6. The case was transferred to the newly established District Court at Staunton, where it came on for trial on Apr. 6, 1791, at which time the jury returned a verdict for defendant. District Court Order Book, 1789–1793, 235, Office of the Clerk of the Augusta County Circuit Court, Staunton, Va.

7. JM and Gov. Edmund Randolph were elected to represent Henrico County on Mar. 3, 1788. Election certificate, Election Records, Virginia State Library. Pendleton (1721–1803), president of the Virginia ratifying convention and a delegate from Caroline County, was also president of the Virginia Court of Appeals; Madison, who had been active in the Virginia delegation to the Philadelphia Convention, coauthor of *The Federalist*, and a delegate from Orange County, was most prominent in floor debate during the Virginia ratifying convention. Nicholas, who later moved to Kentucky and became that state's first attorney general, was a delegate from Albemarle County; he was probably the most colorful debater in the federalist camp.

8. JM's appearance is described by Hugh B. Grigsby (1806–1886) from eyewitness reports as "a tall young man, slovenly dressed in loose summer apparel, with piercing black eyes. . . . His habits were convivial almost to excess; and he regarded as matters beneath his notice those appliances of dress and demeanor which are commonly considered not unimportant to advancement in a public profession. Nor should those personal qualities which cement friendships and gain the affections of men, and which he possessed in an eminent degree, be passed over in a likeness of this young man." *The History of the Virginia Federal Convention of 1788* . . . , ed. R. A. Brock (Virginia Historical Society, *Collections*, N.S., IX–X [Richmond, 1890–1891]), I, 176.

cause of his subsequent identification with that branch, but the two other speeches, one on the general distribution of powers under the new form of government and the other on the control and training of the militia, were a valued addition to the federalist argument. At the same time these speeches are significant because they represent the first clear enunciation of Marshall's political and constitutional philosophy.

John Marshall's first speech before the Committee of the Whole was delivered on the morning of June 10, 1788, following a short, scholarly discussion of ancient and contemporary political systems by antifederalist James Monroe. Marshall's address clearly was not prepared in answer to Monroe's remarks, nor does it seem to have been drafted to complement the speeches of Henry Lee and Edmund Randolph, delivered on June 9. Rather, Marshall's maiden speech seems to have been written to state his personal support for the proposed Constitution and his opposition to the general views expounded by Patrick Henry on June 7 and 9.[9]

Although Marshall was not refuting the speech of his boyhood friend Monroe, the plain style of his oration stands in sharp contrast to the classical allusions used by the delegate from Spotsylvania County. Indeed, it may well have been this first speech that drew the attention of Madison, Randolph, and Pendleton, causing them to obtain Marshall's assistance in replying to two major points raised by Patrick Henry: his woeful predictions that the standing army of the proposed federal government, coupled with the removal of the militia from state control, would leave Virginia prostrate at the feet of the national military machine and his claim that the creation of federal courts of law would deprive Virginia courts of their traditional role as protectors of the liberties of Virginians, thus subjecting her citizens to distant trials before courts that were not required to use juries.

Marshall's second speech before the convention, delivered on June 16, came after an extended argument on the militia provisions of the proposed Constitution. The discussion of those measures had brought forth a violent attack from George Mason, followed by Henry. Mason assured the convention that "I abominate and detest the idea of a Government, where there is a standing army," for where such an institution existed the people lost their taste for liberty. Furthermore, under the terms of the proposed Constitution, the Congress alone had the exclusive right to arm and discipline the militia. Should the federal government neglect to arm the militia forces of the states, the people of the various states would be left defenseless against invasion. According to Mason, if the Congress did not properly train and equip the militia, the states should have an unequivocal right to do so by virtue of an express provision of the Constitution.[1]

Patrick Henry took up the same theme, despite James Madison's well-reasoned clarification that the power to arm and equip the militia was, in fact, concurrent,

9. The debates are reported at length in [David Robertson], *Debates and other Proceedings of the Convention of Virginia, Convened at Richmond, on Monday the 2d of June, 1788 . . .* (Petersburg, Va., 1788; 2d ed., Richmond, 1805). Unless otherwise stated, the first edition is the source for materials concerning speeches on the floor of the Virginia ratifying convention. When an obvious typographical or grammatical error or omission occurs in the 1788 edition and a correction appears in the 1805 edition, the editors have silently supplied the correction. Other variations between the editions have been identified by a footnote giving the source of the version printed. The problems of preparing the first edition and an explanation of the errors subsequently discovered are set forth in the 1805 edition, pp. vii, viii.

1. *Ibid.*, II, 164–165.

as any man might see by a careful reading of the Constitution. On Monday, June 16, Henry reverted to this argument, using to good effect the maxim that in a free government the same hand should not control the purse and the sword. Madison's assertion that the militia would be used for the enforcement of state laws, as they had been in the case of the smugglers in Alexandria, brought a retort from William Grayson that the militia, under the Constitution, could be called into such service only upon the humble supplication of the state authorities to the federal government.

The strongest and most original contention in Marshall's speech on the militia clause was the claim that the proposed Constitution did not in fact alter the military powers of the federal and state governments as they existed under the Articles of Confederation. Pointing to the preexisting law concerning the maintenance and discipline of militia forces, Marshall argued that the Constitution at no point divested the states of their traditional authority in this field. The state governments, although denied other powers by the Constitution, were never expressly denied the right to arm and train their militia. In length Marshall's speech on the militia clause was a modest effort, but it illustrates his intimate grasp of the precise terminology in the new frame of government.

The judiciary article in the new federal Constitution had drawn attack from the very opening days of the Virginia ratifying convention. Patrick Henry had pictured destitute men dragged great distances from their homes to stand trial on false charges before courts sitting without juries.[2] As the convention debates moved forward toward consideration of this third article, Edmund Pendleton became ill on June 14 and did not return to the convention floor until June 19, just in time to hear George Mason's extended speech on the defects of the judiciary clause and the dangers to individual liberties that lurked within the broad grant of powers to the federal courts and Congress. Pendleton rose to reply, but his physical weakness, manifested in his delivery, prevented the shorthand reporter from hearing and recording his words.[3] The task of replying point-by-point to Mason fell to John Marshall, and on June 20 he rose to speak for the last time in favor of the proposed Constitution.

Parallel readings of Marshall's speech and that delivered the previous day by Mason leave little doubt that the federalists believed Mason's effort required specific and precise refutation. Undoubtedly Marshall studied Mason's speech closely during the evening of June 19. The speech he delivered the next day does not appear to have been altered to accommodate the debate that preceded it on the convention floor on June 20. We concur with Pendleton's able biographer that John Marshall was selected by the federalists to take the elder statesman's place in supporting the judiciary article in the new Constitution.[4]

The judiciary speech by Marshall, marked by insistent logic and an active practitioner's knowledge of legal procedure, struck at the points where the opposition was weakest. It is possible that Marshall excelled even Edmund Pendleton in his familiarity with the modern development of Virginia's law and its court sys-

2. *Ibid.*, I, 169–170, II, 112, 119.

3. *Ibid.*, II, 152.

4. David J. Mays, *Edmund Pendleton, 1721–1803; A Biography* (Cambridge, Mass., 1952), II, 262–263. The accuracy of JM's refutation leaves little doubt that he either took careful notes on Mason's speech or had access to a transcript of David Robertson's shorthand notes. No documentary record of JM's preparation of this speech has survived.

tems, and he certainly eclipsed James Madison and Patrick Henry in this field. It was this effort rather than his two other speeches that constitutes his greatest contribution toward ratification.

Marshall's duties at the convention also included committee service, but no record of this survives other than the appointment of the committees and their reports. One group, on privileges and elections, was charged with gathering evidence and adjudicating disputed elections, of which there were several. However, only one seated delegate, William White from Louisa County, was superseded by another. The election contest between White and Richard Morris had been initially won by White with a four-vote majority; when fourteen voters' qualifications were examined and found wanting, the committee reported Morris's election to the convention. This occurred on June 21, in time for Morris to cast a vote against ratification in the final balloting but well after the main floor debates of the convention.

The membership of the Committee on Privileges and Elections contained a substantial portion of the leadership of both antifederalist and federalist camps. However, there was a slight majority of federalists on the committee, that faction having at least thirteen and perhaps fourteen of the twenty-four members. Since the federalist margin of victory in the ratifying vote was ten members in favor, it is clear that the work of the committee did not have any significant impact upon the outcome. For Marshall it was probably routine duty, conducted in accordance with the generally accepted rules of the Virginia House of Delegates and devoid of any political significance.

John Marshall's other committee appointment was to the committee that prepared the form of ratification and later the text of the amendments to be submitted to the first Congress to convene under the new government. We have no basis for an opinion concerning Marshall's role in preparing these formal documents, although it seems unlikely that he exercised anything but a restraining influence concerning the drafting of the proposed amendments. When the final vote upon amendments was taken on the floor of the convention, following the committee's report, Marshall cast his vote against the clause in the amendments that would have perpetuated the requisition system for raising federal revenue.[5] From this we must conclude that Marshall left the convention as he entered it, an uncompromising advocate for increased federal power and a strong supporter of an independent federal taxing authority. Although many of his fellow federalists were willing to make concessions to the opposition in regard to these proposed amendments, Marshall did not swerve from his original convictions.

The Virginia ratifying convention decision did much to turn Virginia from her provincial self-satisfaction and to direct her abundant energies toward the construction of a viable federal government based upon the new Constitution. Similarly the convention vote had a substantial impact upon Marshall's own life. Although he continued to devote his skills to the development of a lucrative law practice in Richmond, his associations in the years after 1788 included many men who were active in the new federal administration, and he was to be periodically offered official appointments at the federal level. While he refused most of these offers, Marshall's career was nevertheless substantially changed by the adoption of the Constitution by his native state, and his participation in the debates of the convention may justly be considered the climatic point in his early life.

5. For JM's vote on amendments see [Robertson], *Debates*, III, 224.

Speech

Printed, *Debates and other Proceedings of the Convention of Virginia, Convened at Richmond, on Monday the 2d of June, 1788* . . . (Petersburg, Va., 1788), II, 28–40

Richmond, June 10, 1788

Mr. *John Marshall*.—Mr. Chairman,[6]—I conceive that the object of the discussion now before us, is, whether Democracy, or Despotism, be most eligible. I am sure that those who framed the system submitted to our investigation, and those who now support it, intend the establishment and security of the former. The supporters of the Constitution claim the title of being firm friends of liberty, and the rights of mankind. They say, that they consider it as the best means of protecting liberty. We, Sir, idolize Democracy. Those who oppose it have bestowed eulogiums on Monarchy.[7] We prefer this system to any Monarchy, because we are convinced that it has a greater tendency to secure our liberty and promote our happiness. We admire it, because we think it a well regulated Democracy. It is recommended to the good people of this country[8]—They are, through us, to declare whether it be such a plan of Government, as will establish and secure their freedom. Permit me to attend to what the Honorable Gentlemen (Mr. *Henry*) has said. He has expatiated on the necessity of a due attention to certain maxims—to certain fundamental principles, from which a free people ought never to depart.[9] I concur with him in the propriety of the observance of such maxims. They are necessary in any Government, but more essential to a Democracy than to any other. What are the favourite maxims of Democracy? A strict observance of justice and public faith, and a steady adherence to virtue. These, Sir, are the principles of a good Government. No mischief—no misfortune

6. George Wythe, chairman of the Committee of the Whole. JM's speech is discussed at length in Hugh Blair Grigsby, *The History of the Virginia Federal Convention of 1788* . . . , ed. R. A. Brock (Virginia Historical Society, *Collections*, N.S., IX–X [Richmond, 1890–1891]), I, 176–183.

7. See Patrick Henry's speech of June 9. [David Robertson], *Debates and other Proceedings of the Convention of Virginia, Convened at Richmond, on Monday the 2d of June, 1788* . . . (Petersburg, Va., 1788), I, 166–167. In 1832 JM reportedly told Thomas H. Bayly that the speeches of George Mason and Edmund Randolph were well reported in Robertson, that James Madison was reported badly, and Patrick Henry was reported the worst of all, "and as to what is given to me . . . , if my name had not have been prefixed to the speaches I never should have recognized them as productions of mine." Bayly's memorandum of conversation with JM [1832], Collection of Alexander H. Sands, Richmond.

8. The term "country" refers to Virginia and not to the United States of America.

9. Patrick Henry's speech of June 7. [Robertson], *Debates*, I, 142.

ought to deter us from a strict observance of justice and public faith. Would to Heaven that these principles had been observed under the present Government! Had this been the case, the friends of liberty would not be so willing now to part with it. Can we boast that our Government is founded on these maxims? Can we pretend to the enjoyment of political freedom, or security, when we are told, that a man has been, by an act of Assembly, struck out of existence, without a trial by jury—without examination—without being confronted with his accusers and witnesses—without the benefits of the law of the land?[1] Where is our safety, when we are told, that this act was justifiable, because the person was not a Socrates?[2] What has become of the worthy member's maxims? Is this one of them? Shall it be a maxim, that a man shall be deprived of his life without the benefit of law? Shall such a deprivation of life be justified by answering, that the man's life was not taken *secundum artem*,[3] because he was a bad man? Shall it be a maxim, that Government ought not to be empowered to protect virtue?

The Honorable member, after attempting to vindicate that tyrannical Legislative act to which I have been alluding, proceeded to take a view of the dangers to which this country is exposed. He told us, that the principal danger arose, from a Government, which if adopted, would give away the Mississippi.[4] I intended to proceed regularly, by attending to the clause under debate,[5] but I must reply to some observations which were dwelt upon, to make impressions on our minds, unfavourable to the plan upon the table. Have we no navigation in, or do we derive no benefit from, the Mississippi? How shall we attain it? By retaining that weak Government which has hitherto kept it from us? Is it thus that we shall secure that navigation? Give the Government the power of retaining it, and then we may hope to derive actual advantages from it.

1. An oblique reference to the Josiah Philips case, a topic that occurred frequently in debate with the purpose of embarrassing Patrick Henry. See Grigsby, *History*, ed. Brock, I, 122–124, 178, 185–186, 220.

2. A more pointed reference to the Philips case. The allegation that Philips was condemned without due process of law—by an act of attainder passed during Henry's term as governor of Virginia—was first raised by Edmund Randolph on June 6, and on the following day Henry asserted that Randolph had misstated the facts. Randolph returned to the subject on June 9. [Robertson], *Debates*, I, 77–78, 144–145, 192.

3. "According to the art" of the law.

4. Henry made this assertion in his speeches of June 7 and 9. [Robertson], *Debates*, I, 145–146, 154.

5. A resolution of June 3 required clause-by-clause debate, but Henry ranged broadly in his comments upon the provisions of the proposed Constitution, causing his opponents to resort to frequent comment on this breach of the convention's rules.

Till we do this, we cannot expect that a Government which hitherto has not been able to protect it, will have power to do it hereafter. Have we not attended too long to consider whether this Government would be able to protect us? Shall we wait for further proofs of its inefficacy? If on mature consideration, the Constitution will be found to be perfectly right on the subject of treaties, and containing no danger of losing that navigation, will he still object? Will he object because eight States are unwilling to part with it? This is no good ground of objection. He then stated the necessity and probability of obtaining amendments. This we ought to postpone till we come to that clause, and make up our minds, whether there be any thing unsafe in the system. He conceived it impossible to obtain amendments after adopting it. If he was right, does not his own argument prove, that in his own conception, previous amendments cannot be had; for, Sir, if subsequent amendments cannot be obtained, shall we get amendments before we ratify? The reasons against the latter do not apply against the former. There are in this State, and in every State of the Union, many who are decided enemies of the Union. Reflect on the probable conduct of such men. What will they do? They will bring amendments which are local in their nature, and which they know will not be accepted. What security have we, that other States will not do the same? We are told, that many in the States are violently opposed to it. They are more mindful of local interests. They will never propose such amendments, as they think would be obtained. Disunion will be their object. This will be attained by the proposal of unreasonable amendments. This, Sir, though a strong cause, is not the only one that will militate against previous amendments. Look at the comparative temper of this country now, and when the late Federal Convention met. We had no idea then of any particular system. The formation of the most perfect plan was our object and wish. It was imagined that the States would accede to, and be pleased with the proposition that would be made them. Consider the violence of opinions, the prejudices and animosities which have been since imbibed. Will not these greatly operate against mutual concessions, or a friendly concurrence? This will, however, be taken up more properly at another time. He says, we wish to have a strong, energetic, powerful Government.[6] We contend for a well regulated De-

6. On June 5 Henry stated that the British became a "great, mighty and splendid" nation, not because their government was "strong and energetic," but rather because "liberty is its direct end and foundation." [Robertson], *Debates*, I, 65.

mocracy. He insinuates, that the power of the Government has been enlarged by the Convention, and that we may apprehend it will be enlarged by others.[7] The Convention did not in fact assume any power. They have proposed to our consideration a scheme of Government which they thought advisable. We are not bound to adopt it, if we disapprove of it. Had not every individual in this community a right to tender that scheme which he thought most conducive to the welfare of his country? Have not several Gentlemen already demonstrated, that the Convention did not exceed their powers?[8] But the Congress have the power of making bad laws it seems. The Senate, with the President, he informs us, may make a treaty which shall be disadvantageous to us—and that if they be not good men, it will not be a good Constitution.[9] I shall ask the worthy member only, if the people at large, and they only, ought to make laws and treaties? Has any man this in contemplation? You cannot exercise the powers of Government personally yourselves. You must trust agents. If so, will you dispute giving them the power of acting for you, from an existing possibility that they may abuse it? As long as it is impossible for you to transact your business in person, if you repose no confidence in delegates, because there is a possibility of their abusing it, you can have *no* Government; for the power of doing good, is inseparable from that of doing some evil.

We may derive from Holland, lessons very beneficial to ourselves.[1] Happy that country which can avail itself of the misfortunes of others—which can gain knowledge from that source without fatal experience! What has produced the late disturbances in that country? The want of such a Government as is on your table, and having in some measure such a one as you are about to part with. The want of proper powers in the Government—The consequent deranged and relaxed administration—The violence of contending parties, and inviting foreign powers to interpose in their

7. Henry's speeches of June 4 and 5 demanded to know by what right the Philadelphia Convention had presumed to create a new government. *Ibid.*, 36, 37, 64.

8. Edmund Pendleton on June 5, Henry Lee on June 5, and Francis Corbin on June 7. *Ibid.*, 50, 54–55, 111.

9. See Henry's speech of June 9. *Ibid.*, 167.

1. Patrick Henry on June 9 claimed that the newly constituted government of Holland, organized under the stadholder, had a constitution similar to the one under debate and presently was groaning under its miseries. The republic of Holland had been ruined by the stadholder. Edmund Randolph replied that the Dutch republic would have been ruined long before if it did not have its stadholder. *Ibid.*, 156–157, 163, 189–190, II, 9.

disputes, have subjected them to all the mischiefs which have interrupted their harmony. I cannot express my astonishment at his high-coloured eulogium on such a Government. Can any thing be more dissimilar than the relation between the British Government, and the Colonies, and the relation between Congress and the States. We *were not* represented in Parliament. Here we are represented. Arguments which prove the impropriety of being taxed by Britain, do not hold against the exercise of taxation by Congress. Let me pay attention to the observation of the Gentleman who was last up, that the power of taxation ought not to be given to Congress.[2] This subject requires the undivided attention of this House. This power I think essentially necessary, for without it, there will be no efficiency in the Government. We have had a sufficient demonstration of the vanity of depending on requisitions. How then can the General Government exist without this power? The possibility of its being abused, is urged as an argument against its expediency. To very little purpose did Virginia discover the defects in the old system—To little purpose indeed did she propose improvements[3]— and to no purpose is this plan constructed for the promotion of our happiness, if we refuse it now, because it is possible that it may be abused. The Confederation has nominal powers, but no means to carry them into effect. If a system of Government were devised by more than human intelligence, it would not be effectual if the means were not adequate to the power. All delegated powers are liable to be abused. Arguments drawn from this source go in direct opposition to every Government, and in recommendation of anarchy. The friends of the Constitution are as tenacious of liberty as its enemies. They wish to give no power that will endanger it. They wish to give the Government powers to secure and protect it. Our enquiry here must be, whether the power of taxation be necessary to perform the objects of the Constitution, and whether it be safe and as well guarded as human wisdom can do it. What are the objects of the national Government? To protect the United States,

2. James Monroe. *Ibid.*, II, 22–25.

3. While JM unduly emphasized Virginia's role in attempts to amend the Articles of Confederation, it is true that Virginians had been active in the 1783 attempts to grant an impost to the Confederation Congress and the 1784–1785 efforts to grant commercial regulatory powers to Congress. Andrew C. McLaughlin, *The Confederation and the Constitution, 1783–1789* (New York, 1905), 79, 171–172; Edmund C. Burnett, *The Continental Congress* (New York, 1941), 634–635; for a good general survey see Merrill Jensen, *The New Nation* (New York, 1950), 399–421. These and all other endeavors to amend the Articles to increase congressional power were defeated by the nonconcurrence of one or more states.

and to promote the general welfare. Protection in time of war is one of its principal objects. Until mankind shall cease to have ambition and avarice, wars will arise. The prosperity and happiness of the people depend on the performance of these great and important duties of the General Government. Can these duties be performed by one State? Can one State protect us, and promote our happiness? The Honorable Gentleman who has gone before me (Governor *Randolph*) has shewn that Virginia cannot do these things.[4] How then can they be done? By the national Government only. Shall we refuse to give it power to do them? We are answered, that the powers may be abused. That though the Congress may promote our happiness, yet they may prostitute their powers to destroy our liberties. This goes to the destruction of all confidence in agents. Would you believe that men who had merited your highest confidence would deceive you? Would you trust them again after one deception? Why then hesitate to trust the General Government? The object of our inquiry is,—*Is the power necessary—and is it guarded?* There must be men and money to protect us. How are armies to be raised? Must we not have money for that purpose? But the Honorable Gentleman says, that we need not be afraid of war.[5] Look at history, which has been so often quoted. Look at the great volume of human nature. They will foretell you, that a defenceless country cannot be secure. The nature of man forbids us to conclude, that we are in no danger from war. The passions of men stimulate them to avail themselves of the weakness of others. The powers of Europe are jealous of us. It is our interest to watch their conduct, and guard against them. They must be pleased with our disunion. If we invite them by our weakness to attack us, will they not do it? If we add debility to our present situation, a partition of America may take place. It is then necessary to give the Government that power in time of peace, which the necessities of war will render indispensable, or else we shall be attacked unprepared. The experience of the world, a knowledge of human nature, and our own particular experience, will confirm this truth. When danger will come upon us, may we not do what we were on the point of doing once already, that is, appoint a Dictator? Were those who are now friends of this Constitution, less active in the defence of liberty on that trying

4. See Randolph's speeches of June 6 and 10. [Robertson], *Debates*, I, 82–86, 89, II, 5–6.

5. Discounting the possibility of warfare with foreign nations, Henry accused his opponents of creating "imaginary dangers." *Ibid.*, I, 155–159.

occasion, than those who oppose it? When foreign dangers come, may not the fear of immediate destruction by foreign enemies impel us to take a most dangerous step? Where then will be our safety? We may now regulate and frame a plan that will enable us to repel attacks, and render a recurrence to dangerous expedients unnecessary. If we be prepared to defend ourselves, there will be little inducement to attack us. But if we defer giving the necessary power to the General Government, till the moment of danger arrives, we shall give it then, and with an *unspairing hand*. America, like other nations, may be exposed to war. The propriety of giving this power will be proved by the history of the world, and particularly of modern Republics. I defy you to produce a single instance where requisitions on the several individual States composing a confederacy, have been honestly complied with. Did Gentlemen expect to see such punctually[6] complied with in America? If they did, our own experience shews the contrary. We are told, that the Confederation carried us through the war. Had not the enthusiasm of liberty inspired us with unanimity, that system would never have carried us through it. It would have been much sooner terminated had that Government been possessed of due energy. The inability of Congress, and the failure of the States to comply with the Constitutional requisitions, rendered our resistance less efficient than it might have been. The weakness of that Government caused troops to be against us which ought to be on our side, and prevented all the resources of the community from being called at once into action. The extreme readiness of the people to make their utmost exertions to ward off[7] the pressing danger, supplied the place of requisitions. When they came solely to be depended on, their inutility was fully discovered. A bare[8] sense of duty, or a regard to propriety is too feeble to induce men to comply with obligations. We deceive ourselves if we expect any efficacy from these. If requisitions will not avail, the Government must have the sinews of war some other way. Requisitions cannot be effectual. They will be productive of delay, and will ultimately be inefficient. By direct taxation, the necessities of the Government will be supplied in a peaceable manner without irritating the minds of the people. But requisitions cannot be rendered efficient without a civil war—with-

6. "Punctuallity" in the 1788 edition. We have substituted "punctually," as reflected in the second, corrected edition. [Robertson], *Debates*, 2d ed., 167.

7. "Of" in the 1788 edition. We have substituted "off," as in the 1805 edition. *Ibid.*, 167.

8. "Bad" in the 1788 edition. We have substituted the word "bare" as in the 1805 edition. *Ibid.*

out great expence of money, and the blood of our citizens. Are there any other means? Yes, that Congress shall apportion the respective quotas previously, and if not complied with by the States, that then this dreaded power shall be exercised. The operation of this has been described by the Gentleman who opened the debate.[9] He cannot be answered. This great objection to that system remains unanswered. Is there no other argument which ought to have weight with us on this subject? Delay is a strong and pointed objection to it. We are told by the Gentleman who spoke last, that direct taxation is unnecessary, because we are not involved in war.[1] This admits the propriety of recurring to direct taxation if we were engaged in war. It has not been proved, that we have no dangers to apprehend on this point. What will be the consequence of the system proposed by the worthy Gentleman? Suppose the States should refuse. The worthy Gentleman who is so pointedly opposed to the Constitution, proposes remonstrances.[2] Is it a time for Congress to remonstrate, or compel a compliance with requisitions, when the whole wisdom of the Union, and the power of Congress are opposed to a foreign enemy? Another alternative is, that if the States shall appropriate certain funds for the use of Congress, that Congress shall not lay direct taxes. Suppose the funds appropriated by the State for the use of Congress, should be inadequate; it will not be determined whether they be insufficient till after the time at which the quota ought to have been paid, and then after so long a delay, the means of procuring money which ought to have been employed in the first instance, must be recurred to. May they not be amused by such ineffectual and temporising alternatives, from year to year, till America shall be enslaved? The failure of one State will authorise a failure in another. The calculation in some States that others will fail, will produce general failures. This will also be attended with all the expences which we are anxious to avoid. What are the advantages to induce us to embrace this system? If they mean that requisitions should be complied with, it will be the same as if Congress had the power of direct taxation. The same amount will be paid by the people.

It is objected, that Congress will not know how to lay taxes so as

9. Edmund Randolph's opening speech of the day, June 10. [Robertson], *Debates*, II, 6-7.

1. James Monroe. *Ibid.*, 21.

2. We have been unable to find Henry's use of the term "remonstrances" in place of the word "requisitions"; presumably the statement may have developed from JM's misunderstanding of Henry's words or, in the alternative, may have been designed to express JM's attitude toward the ineffectuality of "requisitions."

to be easy and convenient for the people at large.[3] Let us pay strict attention to this objection. If it appears to be totally without foundation, the necessity of levying direct taxes will obviate what Gentlemen say, nor will there be any colour for refusing to grant the power. The objects of direct taxes are well understood—They are but few—What are they? Lands, slaves, stock of all kinds, and a few other articles of domestic property. Can you believe that ten men selected from all parts of the State, chosen because they know the situation of the people, will be unable to determine so as to make the tax equal on, and convenient for, the people at large? Does any man believe, that they would lay the tax without the aid of other information, besides their own knowledge, when they know that the very object for which they are elected, is to lay the taxes in a judicious and convenient manner? If they wish to retain the affection of the people at large, will they not inform themselves of every circumstance that can throw light on the subject? Have they but one source of information? Besides their own experience—their knowledge of what will suit their constituents, they will have the benefit of the knowledge and experience of the State Legislatures. They will see in what manner the Legislature of Virginia collects its taxes. Will they be unable to follow their example? The Gentlemen who shall be delegated to Congress will have every source of information that the Legislatures of the States can have, and can lay the tax as equally on the people and with as little oppression as they can. If then it be admitted, that they can understand how to lay them equally and conveniently, are we to admit that they will not do it; but that in violation of every principle that ought to govern men, they will lay them so as to oppress us? What benefit will they have by it? Will it be promotive of their re-election? Will it be by wantonly imposing hardships and difficulties on the people at large, that they will promote their own interest, and secure their re-election? To me it appears incontrovertible, that they will settle them in such a manner, as to be easy for the people. Is the system so organized as to make taxation dangerous? I shall not go to the various checks of the Government, but examine whether the immediate representation of the people be well constructed. I conceive its organization to be sufficiently satisfactory to the warmest friend of freedom. No tax can be laid without the consent of the

3. Monroe had claimed that Congress could not lay taxes equally or justly throughout the widespread territories of the United States. Speech of June 10, [Robertson], *Debates*, II, 22.

House of Representatives. If there be no impropriety in the mode of electing the Representatives, can any danger be apprehended? They are elected by those, who can elect Representatives in the State Legislature. How can the votes of the electors be influenced? By nothing but the character and conduct of the man they vote for. What object can influence them when about choosing him? They have nothing to direct them in the choice, but their own good. Have you not as pointed and strong a security as you can possibly have? It is a mode that secures an impossibility of being corrupted. If they are to be chosen for their wisdom, virtue and integrity, what inducement have they to infringe on our freedom? We are told that they may abuse their power. Are there strong motives to prompt them to abuse it? Will not such abuse militate against their own interest? Will not they and their friends feel the effects of iniquitous measures? Does the Representative remain in office for life? Does he transmit his title of Representative to his son? Is he secured from the burthen imposed on the community? To procure their re-election, it will be necessary for them to confer with the people at large, and convince them that the taxes laid are for their good. If I am able to judge on the subject, the power of taxation now before us, is wisely conceded, and the Representatives are wisely elected.

The Honorable Gentleman said, that a Government should ever depend on the affections of the people.[4] It must so. It is the best support it can have. This Government merits the confidence of the people, and I make no doubt will have it. Then he informed us again,[5] of the disposition of Spain with respect to the Mississippi, and the conduct of the Government with regard to it. To the debility of the Confederation alone, may justly be imputed every cause of complaint on this subject. Whenever Gentlemen will bring forward their objections, I trust we can prove, that no danger to the navigation of that river can arise from the adoption of this Constitution. I beg those Gentlemen who may be affected by it, to suspend their judgment till they hear it discussed. Will, says he, the adoption of this Constitution pay our debts?[6] It will compel the States to pay their quotas. Without this, Virginia will be unable to pay.—Unless all the States pay, she cannot. Though the States will not coin money, (as we are told) yet this Government will

4. Opening his speech of June 10, Henry said, "No Government can flourish unless it be founded on the affection of the People." *Ibid.*, I, 154.

5. *Ibid.*, 155.

6. *Ibid.*, 159*ff.*

bring forth and proportion all the strength of the Union. That oeconomy and industry are essential to our happiness will be denied by no man. But the present Government will not add to our industry. It takes away the incitements to industry, by rendering property insecure and unprotected. It is the paper on your table that will promote and encourage industry. New-Hampshire and Rhode-Island have rejected it, he tells us.[7] New-Hampshire, if my information be right, will certainly adopt it. The report spread in this country, of which I have heard, is, that the Representatives of that State having, on meeting, found they were instructed to vote against it, returned to their Constituents without determining the question, to convince them of their being mistaken, and of the propriety of adopting it.[8] The extent of the country is urged as another objection, as being too great for a Republican Government.[9] This objection has been handed from author to author, and has been certainly misunderstood and misapplied. To what does it owe its source? To observations and criticisms on Governments, where representation did not exist. As to the Legislative power, was it ever supposed inadequate to any extent? Extent of country may render it difficult to execute the laws, but not to Legislate. Extent of country does not extend the power. What will be sufficiently energetic and operative in a small territory, will be feeble when extended over a wide extended country. The Gentleman tells us, there are no checks in this plan.[1] What has become of his enthusiastic eulogium on the American spirit? We should find a check and controul when oppressed, from that source. In this country, there is no exclusive personal stock of interest. The interest of the community is blended and inseparably connected with that of the individual. —When he promotes his own, he promotes that of the community. When we consult the common good, we consult our own. When he desires such checks as these, he will find them abundantly here. They are the best checks. What has become of his eulogium on the Virginia Constitution? Do the checks in this plan appear less excellent than those of the Constitution of Virginia? If the checks in the

7. *Ibid.*, 160.

8. JM was correct, for on June 21, 1788, New Hampshire voted to adopt the Constitution, having recessed its convention to enable instructed delegates to consult their constituencies. A good description of the events is contained in Jere R. Daniell, *Experience in Republicanism: New Hampshire Politics and the American Revolution, 1741–1794* (Cambridge, Mass., 1970), 206–216.

9. Patrick Henry's speech of June 9, referring to an earlier statement by George Mason. [Robertson], *Debates*, I, 163*ff.*

1. *Ibid.*, 167*ff.*

Constitution be compared to the checks in the Virginian Constitution, he will find the best security in the former.

The temple of liberty was complete, said he, when the people of England said to their King, that he was their servant.[2] What are we to learn from this? Shall we embrace such a system as that? Is not liberty secure with us, where the people hold all powers in their own hands, and delegate them cautiously, for short periods, to their servants, who are accountable for the smallest mal-administration? Where is the nation that can boast greater security than we do? We want only a system like the paper before you, to strengthen and perpetuate this security.

The Honorable Gentleman has asked, if there be any safety or freedom, when we give away the sword and the purse?[3] Shall the people at large hold the sword and the purse without the interposition of their Representatives? Can the whole aggregate community act personally? I apprehend that every Gentleman will see the impossibility of this. Must they then not trust them to others? To whom are they to trust them but to their Representatives who are accountable for their conduct? He represents secrecy as unnecessary, and produces the British Government as a proof of its inutility.[4] Is there no secrecy there? When deliberating on the propriety of declaring war, or on military arrangements, do they deliberate in the open fields? No, Sir. The British Government affords secrecy when necessary, and so ought every Government. In this plan, secrecy is only used when it would be fatal and pernicious to publish the schemes of Government. We are threatened with the loss of our liberties by the possible abuse of power, notwithstanding the maxim, that those who give may take away. It is the people that give power, and can take it back. What shall restrain them? They are the masters who give it, and of whom their servants hold it.

He then argues against this system, because it does not resemble the British Government in this, that the same power that declares war has not the means of carrying it on.[5] Are the people of England more secure, if the Commons have no voice in declaring war, or are we less secure by having the Senate joined with the President? It is an absurdity, says the worthy member, that the same man should

---

2. Henry said, "When the *Commons* [emphasis added] of England, in the manly language which becomes freemen, said to their King, *you are our servant*, then the temple of liberty was complete." *Ibid.*, 167.

3. *Ibid.*, 171.

4. Henry's remarks are partially reported and partially paraphrased. *Ibid.*, 172.

5. *Ibid.*, 173.

obey two masters—that the same collector should gather taxes for the General Government and the State Legislature.[6] Are they not both the servants of the people? Are not Congress and the State Legislatures the agents of the people, and are they not to consult the good of the people? May not this be effected by giving the same officer the collection of both taxes? He tells you, that it is an absurdity to adopt before you amend.[7] Is the object of your adoption to amend solely? The objects of your adoption are Union, and safety against foreign enemies—Protection against faction—against what has been the destruction of all Republics. These impel you to its adoption. If you adopt it, what shall restrain you from amending it, if in trying it, amendments shall be found necessary? The Government is not supported by force, but depending on our free will. When experience shall shew us any inconveniences, we can then correct it. But until we have experience on the subject, amendments, as well as the Constitution itself, are to try. Let us try it, and keep our hands free to change it when necessary. If it be necessary to change Government, let us change that Government which has been found to be defective. The difficulty we find in amending the Confederation, will not be found in amending this Constitution. Any amendments in the system before you, will not go to a radical change—a plain way is pointed out for the purpose. All will be interested to change it, and therefore all will exert themselves in getting the change. There is such a diversity of sentiments in human minds, that it is impossible we shall ever concur in one system, till we try it. The power given to the General Government over the time, place, and manner of election, is also strongly objected to. When we come to that clause, we can prove that it is highly necessary, and not dangerous.

The worthy member has concluded his observations by many eulogiums on the British Constitution.[8] It matters not to us whether it be a wise one or not. I think, that for America at least, the Government on your table is very much superior to it. I ask you, if your House of Representatives would be better than it is, if a hundredth part of the people were to elect a majority of them? If your Senators were for life, would they be more agreeable to you? If

6. "Absurdity" occurs, *ibid.*, 175, but JM probably refers to a statement in Henry's speech of June 9, concerning sheriffs collecting both federal and state taxes. *Ibid.*, 169.

7. *Ibid.*, 175.

8. Henry's conclusion of his speech on June 9, as reported, does not seem to support this statement, although if JM's comment is applied to the entire text of Henry's speech, it will be found to be accurate.

your President were not accountable to you for his conduct; if it were a constitutional maxim, that he could do no wrong, would you be safer than you are now? If you can answer *yes* to these questions, then adopt the British Constitution. If not, then good as that Government may be, this is better. The worthy Gentleman who was last up, told us, that the Confederacies of ancient and modern times were not similar to ours, and that consequently reasons which applied against them, could not be urged against it.[9] Do they not hold out one lesson very useful to us? However unlike in other respects, they resemble it in its total inefficacy. They warn us to shun their calamities, and place in our General Government, those necessary powers, the want of which destroyed them. I hope we shall avail ourselves of their misfortunes, without experiencing them. There was something peculiar in one observation he made. He said, that those who governed the cantons of Switzerland were purchased by foreign powers, which was the cause of their uneasiness and trouble.[1] How does this apply to us? If we adopt such a Government as theirs, will it not be subject to the same inconvenience? Will not the same cause produce the same effect? What shall protect us from it? What is our security? He then proceeded to say, that the causes of war are removed from us—that we are separated by the sea from the powers of Europe, and need not be alarmed.[2] Sir, the sea makes them neighbours to us. Though an immense ocean divides us, we may speedily see them with us. What dangers may we not apprehend to our commerce? Does not our naval weakness invite an attack on our commerce? May not the Algerines sieze our vessels?[3] Cannot they, and every other predatory or maritime nation, pillage our ships and destroy our commerce, without subjecting themselves to any inconvenience? He would, he said, give the General Government all necessary powers. If any thing be necessary, it must be so, to call forth the strength of the Union, when we may be attacked, or when the general purposes of America require it.[4] The worthy Gentleman then pro-

9. James Monroe on June 10, drew this conclusion after a lengthy marshaling of evidence. [Robertson], *Debates*, II, 16–18.

1. *Ibid.*, 18.

2. *Ibid.*, 19.

3. The "Barbary states," Morocco, Tripoli, Tunis, and Algiers, declared war on the United States in 1784, began seizing American vessels, seamen, and passengers, and demanded ransom. The Moroccan treaty of 1787 concluded that nation's depredations, but the others continued because Congress had insufficient funds and military power either to purchase or compel peace or to ransom the captives.

4. [Robertson], *Debates*, II, 21–22.

ceeded to shew, that our present exigencies are greater than they will ever be again.[5] Who can penetrate into futurity? How can any man pretend to say, that our future exigencies will be less than our present? The exigencies of nations have been generally commensurate to their resources. It would be the utmost impolicy to trust to a mere possibility of not being attacked, or obliged to exert the strength of the community. He then spoke of a selection of particular objects by Congress, which he says must necessarily be oppressive.[6] That Congress for instance, might select lands for direct taxes, and that all but landholders would escape. Cannot Congress regulate the taxes so as to be equal on all parts of the community? Where is the absurdity of having thirteen revenues? Will they clash with, or injure, each other? If not, why cannot Congress make thirteen distinct laws, and impose the taxes on the general objects of taxation in each State, so as that all persons of the society shall pay equally as they ought?

He then told you, that your Continental Government will call forth the virtue and talents of America.[7] This being the case, will they encroach on the powers of the State Governments? Will our most virtuous and able citizens wantonly attempt to destroy the liberty of the people? Will the most virtuous act the most wickedly? I differ in opinion from the worthy Gentleman. I think the virtue and talents of the members of the General Government will tend to the security, instead of the destruction of our liberty. I think that the power of direct taxation is essential to the existence of the General Government, and that it is safe to grant it. If this power be not necessary, and as safe from abuse as any delegated power can possibly be, then I say, that the plan before you is unnecessary; for it imports not what system we have, unless it have the power of protecting us in time of peace and war.

5. Perhaps an oversimplification of Monroe's statement that with certain fiscal adjustments the old Confederation would meet the exigencies of the day. *Ibid.*

6. *Ibid.*

7. Monroe's point was that men of ability would prefer federal to state offices. See *ibid.*, 23.

To Gouverneur Morris

ALS, Marshall Papers, Swem Library, College of William and Mary

[Richmond, June 11, 1788]

J Marshall presents his compliments to Gouverneur Morris Esquire, & requests the favor of his company to dinner tomorrow

Thursday evening[8]

Extempore at the Convention in Virginia[9]
The State's determined Resolution
Was to discuss the Constitution
for this the Members come together
Melting with Zeal and sultry Weather,
And here to their eternal Praise
To find it's Hist'ry spend three Days
The next three Days they nobly roam
Thru ev'ry Region far from Home
Call in the Grecian Swiss Italian
The Roman [*Russian?*] Dutch Rapscullion
Fellows who freedom never knew
To tell us what we ought to do
The next three Days they kindly dip yee
Deep in the River Mississippi
Nine Days thus spent eer they begin

8. The invitation to Morris (1752–1816) is in JM's hand and the extempore verse was written by Morris. It is impossible to learn which was written first. It was not unlike JM to use any available piece of paper to write a note, so conceivably he did this when he received Morris's poem. The argument that Morris wrote the poem on the invitation to dinner, however, is equally plausible. Although the document was acquired by the College of William and Mary from Miss Ellen Harvie Wade, a descendent of JM, her ownership is no indication that she inherited the item. Were it known that she had inherited it, we might conclude JM sent the invitation first, then received the poem in return. Miss Wade's collection, however, contained several recipient's copies of JM letters, and she might have purchased this one.

The absence of a date on the document adds confusion. JM's reference to Thursday evening may have been the time he penned the invitation but it could have been the time he wanted Morris to come to dinner. Morris's counting of the days the convention had been in session signifies he wrote his poem on June 11, the ninth working day of the convention, or on June 12, at the start of the tenth working day. The editors have decided JM's reference to Thursday evening was the time Morris was to come to dinner, and that JM penned his invitation on June 11. The date of Morris's poem remains uncertain, as does the sequence of the writing by the two men.

9. In Morris's hand, this is written on the reverse side of the invitation and address leaf.

Let us suppose them fairly in
And then resolve me gentle friend
How many Months before they End

Speech

Printed, [David Robertson], *Debates and other Proceedings of the Convention of Virginia, Convened at Richmond, on Monday the 2d of June, 1788* . . . (Petersburg, Va., 1788), III, 11–13

Richmond, June 16, 1788

Mr. *John Marshall*, asked if Gentlemen were serious, when they asserted that if the State Governments had power to interfere with the militia, it was by implication?[1] If they were, he asked the Committee, whether the least attention would not shew that they were mistaken? The State Governments did not derive their powers from the General Government. But each Government derived its powers from the people; and each was to act according to the powers given it. Would any Gentleman deny this? He demanded if powers not given, were retained by implication?[2] Could any man say so? Could any man say, that this power was not retained by the States, as they had not given it away? For, says he, does not a power remain till it is given away? The State Legislatures had power to command and govern their militia before, and have it still, undeniably, unless there be something in this Constitution that takes it away. For Continental purposes Congress may call forth the militia; as to suppress insurrections and repel invasions. But the power given to the States by the people is not taken away: For the Constitution does not say so. In the Confederation Congress had this power. But the State Legislatures had it also. The power of Legislation given them within the ten miles square is exclusive of the States, because it is expressed to be exclusive. The truth is, that when power is given to the General Legislature, if it was in the State Legislatures before, both shall exercise it; unless there be an

1. Patrick Henry on June 16 asserted that the Constitution gave Congress the exclusive power to suppress insurrections. If any portion of that power remained with the states, it did so only by implication. [David Robertson], *Debates and other Proceedings of the Convention of Virginia, Convened at Richmond, on Monday the 2d of June, 1788* . . . (Petersburg, Va., 1788), III, 9. William Grayson referred to a "constructive implied power" concerning the militia, which remained with the states. *Ibid.*, 10.
2. See Henry's speech of June 14, 1788. *Ibid.*, II, 171–172.

incompatibility in the exercise by one, to that by the other; or negative words precluding the State Governments from it. But there are no negative words here. It rests therefore with the States. To me it appears then unquestionable, that the State Governments can call forth the militia, in case the Constitution should be adopted, in the same manner as they could have done, before its adoption. Gentlemen have said, that the States cannot defend itself without an application to Congress, because Congress can interpose![3] Does not every man feel a refutation of the argument in his own breast? I will shew, that there could not be a combination between those who formed the Constitution, to take away this power. All the restraints intended to be laid on the State Governments (besides where an exclusive power is expressly given to Congress) are contained in the tenth section, of the first article. This power is not included in the restrictions in that section.—But what excludes every possibility of doubt, is the last part of it.—That "no State shall engage in war, *unless actually invaded, or in such imminent danger as will not admit of delay.*" When invaded, they can engage in war; as also when in imminent danger. This clearly proves, that the States can use the militia when they find it necessary. The worthy Member last up, objects to the Continental Government possessing the power of disciplining the militia, because, though all its branches be derived from the people, he says, they will form an Aristocratic Government, unsafe and unfit to be trusted.[4]

Mr. *Grayson* answered, that he only said it was so constructed as to form a great Aristocratic body.

Mr. *Marshall* replied, that he was not certain whether he understood him. But he thought he had said so. He conceived that as the Government was drawn from the people, the feelings and interests of the people would be attended to, and that we would be safe in granting them power to regulate the militia. When the Government is drawn from the people, continued Mr. *Marshall*, and depending on the people for its continuance, oppressive measures will not be attempted, as they will certainly draw on their authors the resentment of those on whom they depend. On this Government, thus depending on ourselves for its existence, I will rest my safety, notwithstanding the danger depicted by the Honorable Gentleman. I cannot help being surprised that the worthy Member thought this power so dangerous. What Government is able to pro-

3. See Henry's speech of June 5. *Ibid.*, I, 59, 63.
4. See Grayson's speech of June 16. *Ibid.*, III, 10.

tect you in time of war? Will any State depend on its own exertions?—The consequence of such dependance and withholding this
power from Congress will be, that State will fall after State, and be
a sacrifice to the want of power in the General Government. *United
we are strong, divided we fall.* Will you prevent the General Government from drawing the militia of one State to another, when the
consequence would be, that every State must depend on itself? The
enemy possessing the water, can quickly go from one State to another. No State will spare to another its militia, which it conceives
necessary for itself. It requires a superintending power, in order to
call forth the resources of all to protect all. If this be not done, each
State will fall a sacrifice. This system merits the highest applause in
this respect. The Honorable Gentleman said, that a general regulation may be made to inflict punishments.[5] Does he imagine that a
militia law is to be engrafted on the scheme of Government, so as
to render it incapable of being changed? The idea of the worthy
Member supposes, that men will renounce their own interests. This
would produce general inconveniences throughout the Union, and
would be equally opposed by all the States. But the worthy Member fears, that in one part of the Union they will be regulated and
disciplined, and in another neglected. This danger is enhanced by
leaving this power to each State; for some States may attend to
their militia, and others may neglect them. If Congress neglect our
militia, we can arm them ourselves. Cannot Virginia import arms?
Cannot she put them into the hands of her militia men? He then
concluded by observing, that the power of governing the militia
was not vested in the States by implication; because being possessed
of it antecedent to the adoption of the Government, and not being
divested of it, by any grant or restriction in the Constitution, they
must necessarily be as fully possessed of it as ever they had been:
And it could not be said, that the States derived any powers from
that system, but retained them, though not acknowledged in any
part of it.

5. See Grayson's speech, *ibid.*, and that of George Mason on June 14. *Ibid.*, II,
185–186.

Speech

Printed, [David Robertson], *Debates and other Proceedings of the Convention of Virginia, Convened at Richmond, on Monday the 2d of June, 1788* . . . (Petersburg, Va., 1788), III, 124–133

Richmond, June 20, 1788

Mr. *John Marshall*,—Mr. Chairman.—This part of the plan before us, is a great improvement on that system from which we are now departing. Here are tribunals appointed for the decision of controversies, which were before, either not at all, or improperly provided for.—That many benefits will result from this to the members of the collective society, every one confesses. Unless its organization be defective, and so constructed as to injure, instead of accommodating the convenience of the people, it merits our approbation. After such a candid and fair discussion by those Gentlemen who support it—after the very able manner in which they have investigated and examined it, I conceived it would be no longer considered as so very defective, and that those who opposed it, would be convinced of the impropriety of some of their objections. —But I perceive they still continue the same opposition. Gentlemen have gone on an idea, that the Federal Courts will not determine the causes which may come before them, with the same fairness and impartiality, with which other Courts decide. What are the reasons of this supposition?—Do they draw them from the manner in which the Judges are chosen, or the tenure of their office?—What is it that makes us trust our Judges?—Their independence in office, and manner of appointment. Are not the Judges of the Federal Court chosen with as much wisdom, as the Judges of the State Governments?—Are they not equally, if not more independent?—If so, shall we not conclude, that they will decide with equal impartiality and candour?—If there be as much wisdom and knowledge in the United States, as in a particular State, shall we conclude that that wisdom and knowledge will not be equally exercised in the selection of the Judges?

The principle on which they object to the Federal jurisdiction, seems to me to be founded on a belief, that there will not be a fair trial had in those Courts. If this Committee will consider it fully, they will find it has no foundation, and that we are as secure there as any where else. What mischief results from some causes being tried there?—Is there not the utmost reason to conclude, that Judges

wisely appointed, and independent in their office, will never countenance any unfair trial?—What are the subjects of its jurisdiction?
Let us examine them with an expectation that causes will be as
candidly tried there, as elsewhere, and then determine. The objection, which was made by the Honorable Member who was first up
yesterday (Mr. *Mason*) has been so fully refuted,[6] that it is not
worth while to notice it. He objected to Congress having power to
create a number of Inferior Courts according to the necessity of
public circumstances. I had an apprehension that those Gentlemen
who placed no confidence in Congress, would object that there
might be no Inferior Courts. I own that I thought, that those Gentlemen would think there would be no Inferior Courts, as it depended on the will of Congress, but that we should be dragged to
the centre of the Union. But I did not conceive, that the power of
increasing the number of Courts could be objected to by any Gentleman, as it would remove the inconvenience of being dragged to
the centre of the United States.[7] I own that the power of creating a
number of Courts, is, in my estimation, so far from being a defect,
that it seems necessary to the perfection of this system. After having
objected to the number and mode, he objected to the subject matter of their cognizance.—(Here Mr. *Marshall* read the 2d section.)[8]
—These, Sir, are the points of Federal jurisdiction to which he
objects, with a few exceptions. Let us examine each of them with a
supposition, that the same impartiality will be observed there, as in
other Courts, and then see if any mischief will result from them.—
With respect to its cognizance in all cases arising under the Constitution and the laws of the United States, he says, that the laws
of the United States being paramount to the laws of particular
States, there is no case but what this will extend to.[9] Has the Government of the United States power to make laws on every subject?—Does he understand it so?—Can they make laws affecting
the mode of transferring property, or contracts, or claims between

6. Mason concluded his speech late in the afternoon of June 19, leaving James Madison little time for rebuttal. Madison resumed his remarks on the morning of June 20
and was followed by Edmund Pendleton. JM's speech printed here followed a short
reply by Mason. [David Robertson], *Debates and other Proceedings of the Convention of
Virginia, Convened at Richmond, on Monday the 2d of June, 1788* . . . (Petersburg, Va., 1788),
III, 106–125.

7. Compare Mason's statements attacking congressional powers to erect inferior
federal courts with his objections concerning trials and appeals in courts distant from
the residence of the parties. *Ibid.*, 99, 101.

8. Art. III, sec. 2, Constitution of the United States.

9. [Robertson], *Debates*, III, 99.

citizens of the same State? Can they go beyond the delegated powers? If they were to make a law not warranted by any of the powers
enumerated, it would be considered by the Judges as an infringement of the Constitution which they are to guard:—They would
not consider such a law as coming under their jurisdiction.—They
would declare it void. It will annihilate the State Courts, says the
Honorable Gentleman. Does not every Gentleman here know, that
the causes in our Courts are more numerous than they can decide,
according to their present construction? Look at the dockets.—You
will find them crouded with suits, which the life of man will not see
determined.[1] If some of these suits be carried to other Courts, will
it be wrong? They will still have business enough. Then there is no
danger, that particular subjects, small in proportion, being taken
out of the jurisdiction of the State Judiciaries, will render them useless and of no effect. Does the Gentleman think that the State
Courts will have no cognizance of cases not mentioned here? Are
there any words in this Constitution which excludes the Courts of
the States from those cases which they now possess? Does the Gentleman imagine this to be the case? Will any Gentleman believe it?
Are not controversies respecting lands claimed under the grants of
different States, the only controversies between citizens of the same
State, which the Federal Judiciary can take cognizance of? The
case is so clear, that to prove it would be an useless waste of time.
The State Courts will not lose the jurisdiction of the causes they
now decide. They have a concurrence of jurisdiction with the Federal Courts in those cases, in which the latter have cognizance.

How disgraceful is it that the State Courts cannot be trusted,
says the Honorable Gentleman![2] What is the language of the Constitution? Does it take away their jurisdiction? Is it not necessary
that the Federal Courts should have cognizance of cases arising
under the Constitution, and the laws of the United States? What
is the service or purpose of a Judiciary, but to execute the laws in a
peaceable orderly manner, without shedding blood, or creating a
contest, or availing yourselves of force? If this be the case, where can
its jurisdiction be more necessary than here? To what quarter will
you look for protection from an infringement on the Constitution,
if you will not give the power to the Judiciary? There is no other
body that can afford such a protection. But the Honorable Member
objects to it, because, he says, that the officers of the Government

1. On docket congestion see Beveridge, *Marshall*, I, 453, n. 1.
2. George Mason, in [Robertson], *Debates*, III, 103–104.

will be screened from merited punishment by the Federal Judiciary.[3] The Federal Sheriff, says he, will go into a poor man's house, and beat him, or abuse his family, and the Federal Court will protect him. Does any Gentleman believe this? Is it necessary that the officers will commit a trespass on the property or persons of those with whom they are to transact business? Will such great insults on the people of this country be allowable? Were a law made to authorise them, it would be void. The injured man would trust to a tribunal in his neighbourhood. To such a tribunal he would apply for redress, and get it. There is no reason to fear that he would not meet that justice there, which his country will be ever willing to maintain. But on appeal, says the Honorable Gentleman, what chance is there to obtain justice? This is founded on an idea, that they will not be impartial. There is no clause in the Constitution which bars the individual member injured, from applying to the State Courts to give him redress. He says that there is no instance of appeals as to fact in common law cases.[4] The contrary is well known to you, Mr. Chairman, to be the case in this Commonwealth. With respect to mills, roads, and other cases, appeals lye from the Inferior to the Superior Court, as to fact as well as law. Is it a clear case, that there can be no case in common law, in which an appeal as to fact might be proper and necessary? Can you not conceive a case where it would be productive of advantages to the people at large, to submit to that tribunal the final determination, involving facts as well as law? Suppose it should be deemed for the convenience of the citizens, that those things which concerned foreign Ministers, should be tried in the Inferior Courts—If justice would be done, the decision would satisfy all. But if an appeal in matters of fact could not be carried to the Superior Court, then it would result, that such cases could not be tried before the Inferior Courts, for fear of injurious and partial decisions.

But, Sir, where is the necessity of discriminating between the three cases of chancery, admiralty, and common law? Why not leave it to Congress? Will it enlarge their powers? Is it necessary for them wantonly to infringe your rights? Have you any thing to apprehend, when they can in no case abuse their power without rendering themselves hateful to the people at large? When this is the case, something may be left to the Legislature freely chosen by ourselves, from among ourselves, who are to share the burdens imposed

3. This recurrent theme had been most recently voiced by Mason. *Ibid.*, 101.
4. *Ibid.*, 102.

upon the community, and who can be changed at our pleasure. Where power may be trusted, and there is no motive to abuse it, it seems to me to be as well to leave it undetermined, as to fix it in the Constitution.

With respect to disputes between a State, and the citizens of another State, its jurisdiction has been decried with unusual vehemence. I hope no Gentleman will think that a State will be called at the bar of the Federal Court. Is there no such case at present? Are there not many cases in which the Legislature of Virginia is a party, and yet the State is not sued? It is not rational to suppose, that the sovereign power shall be dragged before a Court.[5] The intent is, to enable States to recover claims of individuals residing in other States. I contend this construction is warranted by the words. But, say they, there will be partiality in it if a State cannot be defendant—if an individual cannot proceed to obtain judgment against a State, though he may be sued by a State. It is necessary to be so, and cannot be avoided. I see a difficulty in making a State defendant, which does not prevent its being plaintiff. If this be only what cannot be avoided, why object to the system on that account? If an individual has a just claim against any particular State, is it to be presumed, that on application to its Legislature, he will not obtain satisfaction? But how could a State recover any claim from a citizen of another State, without the establishment of these tribunals?

The Honorable Member objects to suits being instituted in the Federal Courts by the citizens of one State, against the citizens of another State.[6] Were I to contend, that this was necessary in all cases, and that the Government without it would be defective, I should not use my own judgment. But are not the objections to it carried too far? Though it may not in general be absolutely necessary, a case may happen, as has been observed, in which a citizen of one State ought to be able to recur to this tribunal, to recover a claim from the citizen of another State. What is the evil which this can produce?—Will he get more than justice there?—The indepen-

5. See Mason's remarks and those of Patrick Henry concerning states being made parties defendant in federal courts. *Ibid.*, 103, 116–118. JM was not alone in denying the possibility that states would be made defendants in these courts. See the speech of James Madison, June 20, 1788. *Ibid.*, 109.

The difficulties that have arisen from a state appearing before the Supreme Court as a party defendant are discussed in Henry M. Hart, Jr., and Herbert Wechsler, eds., *The Federal Courts and the Federal System* (Brooklyn, 1953), 218–260, with specific reference to enforcement of judgments and decrees at 246–247.

6. Mason. [Robertson], *Debates*, III, 102–103.

dence of the Judges forbids it. What has he to get?—Justice. Shall we object to this, because a citizen of another State can obtain justice without applying to our State Courts? It may be necessary with respect to the laws and regulations of commerce, which Congress may make. It may be necessary in cases of debt, and some other controversies. In claims for land it is not necessary, but it is not dangerous. In the Court of which State will it be instituted, said the Honorable Gentleman? It will be instituted in the Court of the State where the defendant resides,—where the law can come at him, and no where else. By the laws of which State will it be determined, said he? By the laws of the State where the contract was made.[7] According to those laws, and those only, can it be decided. Is this a novelty?—No—it is a principle in the jurisprudence of this Commonwealth. If a man contracted a debt in the East-Indies, and it was sued for here, the decision must be consonant to the laws of that country.—Suppose a contract made in Maryland, where the annual interest is at six per centum; and a suit instituted for it in Virginia— What interest would be given now, without any Federal aid?—The interest of Maryland most certainly; and if the contract had been made in Virginia, and suit brought in Maryland, the interest of Virginia must be given without doubt.—It is now to be governed by the laws of that State where the contract was made. The laws which governed the contract at its formation, govern it in its decision. To preserve the peace of the Union only, its jurisdiction in this case ought to be recurred to.—Let us consider that when citizens of one State carry on trade in another State, much must be due to the one from the other, as is the case between North-Carolina and Virginia. Would not the refusal of justice to our citizens, from the Courts of North-Carolina, produce disputes between the States? Would[8] the Federal Judiciary swerve from their duty in order to give partial and unjust decisions?

The objection respecting the assignment of a bond to a citizen of another State, has been fully answered. But suppose it were to be tried as he says, what could be given more than was actually due in the case he mentioned? It is *possible*, in our Courts as they now stand, to obtain a judgment for more than justice. But the Court of

7. Mason had asserted that disputes should be determined by the law of the forum in which the case was being tried. *Ibid.*, 103. Here JM stated the conflict-of-laws rule that contractual rights are governed by the law of the place at which the contract was made.

8. "Should" in the 1788 edition of [Robertson], *Debates*. We have substituted "would," as in the 1805 edition. *Ibid.*, 2d ed., 395.

Chancery grants relief. Would it not be so in the Federal Court? Would not depositions be taken, to prove the payments, and if proved, would not the decision of the Court be accordingly?

He objects in the next place to its jurisdiction in controversies between a State, and a foreign State.[9] Suppose, says he, in such a suit, a foreign State is cast, will she be bound by the decision? If a foreign State brought a suit against the Commonwealth of Virginia, would she not be barred from the claim if the Federal Judiciary thought it unjust? The previous consent of the parties is necessary. And, as the Federal Judiciary will decide, each party will acquiesce. It will be the means of preventing disputes with foreign nations. On an attentive consideration of these Courts, I trust every part will appear satisfactory to the Committee.

The exclusion of trial by jury in this case, he urged to prostrate our rights.[1] Does the word Court only mean the Judges? Does not the determination of a jury, necessarily lead to the judgment of the Court? Is there any thing here which gives the Judges exclusive jurisdiction of matters of fact? What is the object of a jury trial? To inform the Court of the facts. When a Court has cognizance of facts, does it not follow, that they can make enquiry by a jury? It is impossible to be otherwise. I hope that in this country, where impartiality is so much admired, the laws will direct facts to be ascertained by a jury. But, says the Honorable Gentleman, the juries in the ten miles square will be mere tools of parties, with which he would not trust his person or property; which, he says, he would rather leave to the Court.[2] Because the Government may have a district ten miles square, will no man stay there but the tools and officers of the Government?—Will no body else be found there?— Is it so in any other part of the world, where a Government has Legislative power?—Are there none but officers and tools of the Government of Virginia in Richmond?—Will there not be independent merchants, and respectable Gentlemen of fortune, within the ten miles square?—Will there not be worthy farmers and mechanics?—Will not a good jury be found there as well as any where else?—Will the officers of the Government become improper to be on a jury?—What is it to the Government, whether this man or that man succeeds?—It is all one thing. Does the Constitution say, that juries shall consist of officers, or that the Supreme Court

9. [Robertson], *Debates*, III, 103.
1. *Ibid.*, 104.
2. Mason. *Ibid.*, 21–22, 104.

shall be held in the ten miles square? It was acknowledged by the Honorable Member, that it was secure in England.[3] What makes it secure there?—Is it their Constitution?—What part of their Constitution is there, that the Parliament cannot change?—As the preservation of this right is in the hands of Parliament, and it has ever been held sacred by them, will the Government of America be less honest than that of Great Britain? Here a restriction is to be found. The jury is not to be brought out of the State. There is no such restriction in that Government; for the laws of Parliament decide every thing respecting it. Yet Gentlemen tell us, that there is safety there, and nothing here but danger. It seems to me, that the laws of the United States will generally secure trials by a jury of the vicinage, or in such manner as will be most safe and convenient for the people.

But it seems that the right of challenging the jurors, is not secured in this Constitution. Is this done by our own Constitution, or by any provision of the English Government? Is it done by their Magna Charta, or Bill of Rights? This privilege is founded on their laws. If so, why should it be objected to the American Constitution, that it is not inserted in it? If we are secure in Virginia, without mentioning it in our Constitution, why should not this security be found in the Federal Court?

The Honorable Gentleman said much about the quitrents in the Northern Neck.[4] I will refer it to the Honorable Gentleman himself. Has he not acknowledged, that there was no complete title? Was he not satisfied, that the right of the legal representative of the proprietor did not exist at the time he mentioned? If so, it cannot exist now. I will leave it to those Gentlemen who come from that quarter. I trust they will not be intimidated on this account, in voting on this question. A law passed in 1782, which secures this.[5] He says that many poor men may be harrassed and injured by the representative of Lord Fairfax. If he has no right, this cannot be done. If he has this right and comes to Virginia, what laws will his claims be determined by? By those of this State. By what tribunals

3. Mason demanded a bill of rights in his speech of June 16 but did not mention British guarantees. *Ibid.*, 33. On the other hand, Patrick Henry made numerous references to English historical experience and the need for a written bill of rights in the Constitution. *Ibid.*, 34–36, 93, 111–112. Edmund Pendleton on June 12 scorned the antifederalist demand as a request for a "Paper-Bill of Right" that obscured the fact that the sole security of the American people was in the primary right of power vested in the people. *Ibid.*, II, 96.

4. For Mason's discussion see *ibid.*, 104–107.

5. 11 Hening 112, 128.

will they be determined? By our State Courts. Would not the poor
man, who was oppressed by an unjust prosecution, be abundantly
protected and satisfied by the temper of his neighbours, and would
he not find ample justice? What reason has the Honorable Member
to apprehend partiality or injustice? He supposes, that if the Judges
be Judges of both the Federal and State Courts, they will incline in
favour of one Government. If such contests should arise, who could
more properly decide them, than those who are to swear to do justice? If we can expect a fair decision any where, may we not expect
justice to be done by the Judges of both the Federal and State Governments? But, says the Honorable Member, laws may be executed
tyrannically. Where is the independency of your Judges? If a law
be executed tyrannically in Virginia, to what can you trust? To
your Judiciary. What security have you for justice? Their independence. Will it not be so in the Federal Court?

Gentlemen ask what is meant by law cases, and if they be not
distinct from facts. Is there no law arising on cases in equity and
admiralty? Look at the acts of Assembly.—Have you not many
cases, where law and fact are blended? Does not the jurisdiction in
point of law as well as fact, find itself completely satisfied in law and
fact? The Honorable Gentleman says, that no law of Congress can
make any exception to the Federal appellate jurisdiction of fact as
well as law.[6] He has frequently spoken of technical terms, and the
meaning of them. What is the meaning of the term *exception?* Does
it not mean an alteration and diminution? Congress is empowered
to make exceptions to the appellate jurisdiction, as to law and fact,
of the Supreme Court.—These exceptions certainly go as far as the
Legislature may think proper, for the interest and liberty of the
people.—Who can understand this word, *exception,* to extend to one
case as well as the other? I am persuaded, that a reconsideration of
this case will convince the Gentleman, that he was mistaken. This
may go to the cure of the mischief apprehended. Gentlemen must
be satisfied, that this power will not be so much abused as they
have said.

The Honorable Member says, that he derives no consolation
from the wisdom and integrity of the Legislature, because we call
them to rectify defects which it is our duty to remove.[7] We ought
well to weigh the good and evil before we determine—We ought to
be well convinced, that the evil will be really produced before we

6. [Robertson], *Debates,* III, 102.
7. *Ibid.,* 104.

decide against it. If we be convinced that the good greatly preponderates, though there be small defects in it, shall we give up that which is really good, when we can remove the little mischief it may contain, in the plain easy method pointed out in the system itself?

I was astonished when I heard the Honorable Gentleman say, that he wished the trial by jury to be struck out entirely. Is there no justice to be expected by a jury of our fellow citizens? Will any man prefer to be tried by a Court, when the jury is to be of his countrymen, and probably of his vicinage?[8] We have reason to believe the regulations with respect to juries will be such as shall be satisfactory. Because it does not contain all, does it contain nothing? But I conceive that this Committee will see there is safety in the case, and that there is no mischief to be apprehended.

He states a case, that a man may be carried from a federal to an antifederal corner, (and *vice versa*) where men are ready to destroy him. Is this probable? Is it presumeable that they will make a law to punish men who are of different opinions in politics from themselves? Is it presumeable, that they will do it in one single case, unless it be such a case as must satisfy the people at large? The good opinion of the people at large must be consulted by their Representatives; otherwise mischiefs would be produced, which would shake the Government to its foundation. As it is late, I shall not mention all the Gentleman's argument: But some parts of it are so glaring, that I cannot pass them over in silence. He says that the establishment of these tribunals, and more particularly in their jurisdiction of controversies between citizens of these States, and foreign citizens and subjects, is like a retrospective law. Is there no difference between a tribunal which shall give justice and effect to an existing right, and creating a right that did not exist before? The debt or claim is created by the individual. He has bound himself to comply with it. Does the creation of a new Court amount to a retrospective law?[9]

We are satisfied with the provision made in this country[1] on the subject of trial by jury. Does our Constitution direct trials to be by jury? It is required in our Bill of Rights, which is not a part of the

---

8. JM was referring to Mason's rhetorical flourish expressing his dismay at the idea of trial by a jury impaneled from the proposed federal district. See *ibid.*, 104.

9. Mason referred to the Northern Neck claims and demanded an amendment that would deny the Constitution a retrospective effect, thereby precluding federal courts from adjudicating those claims. *Ibid.*, 106. Earlier he and Patrick Henry had made a similar argument concerning British merchants' claims against Virginia debtors. *Ibid.*, 58–60, 63.

1. Virginia.

Constitution. Does any security arise from hence? Have you a jury when a judgment is obtained on a replevy bond, or by default? Have you a jury when a motion is made for the Commonwealth, against an individual; or when a motion is made by one joint obligor against another, to recover sums paid as security? Our Courts decide in all these cases, without the intervention of a jury; yet they are all civil cases. The Bill of Rights is merely recommendatory. Were it otherwise, the consequence would be, that many laws which are found convenient, would be unconstitutional. What does the Government before you say? Does it exclude the Legislature from giving a trial by jury in civil cases? If it does not forbid its exclusion, it is on the same footing on which your State Government stands now. The Legislature of Virginia does not give a trial by jury where it is not necessary. But gives it wherever it is thought expedient. The Federal Legislature will do so too, as it is formed on the same principles.

The Honorable Gentleman says, that unjust claims will be made, and the defendant had better pay them than go to the Supreme Court.[2] Can you suppose such a disposition in one of your citizens, as that to oppress another man, he will incur great expences? What will he gain by an unjust demand? Does a claim establish a right? He must bring his witnesses to prove his claim. If he does not bring his witnesses, the expences must fall upon him. Will he go on a calculation that the defendant will not defend it; or cannot produce a witness? Will he incur a great deal of expence, from a dependance on such a chance? Those who know human nature, black as it is, must know, that mankind are too well attached to their interest to run such a risk. I conceive, that this power is absolutely necessary, and not dangerous; that should it be attended by little inconveniences, they will be altered, and that they can have no interest in not altering them. Is there any real danger?—When I compare it to the exercise of the same power in the Government of Virginia, I am persuaded there is not. The Federal Government has no other motive, and has every reason of doing right, which the Members of our State Legislature have. Will a man on the Eastern Shore, be sent to be tried in Kentuckey; or a man from Kentuckey be brought to the Eastern Shore to have his trial? A Government by doing this, would destroy itself. I am convinced, the trial by jury will be regulated in the manner most advantageous to the community.

2. [Robertson], *Debates*, III, 105.

Colloquy

Printed, [David Robertson], *Debates and other Proceedings of the Convention of Virginia, Convened at Richmond, on Monday the 2d of June, 1788* . . . (Petersburg, Va., 1788), III, 148–151

[*June 23, 1788, Richmond.* Henry states his belief that the new government will be "an empire of men and not of laws." Since the right to organize the federal judiciary is given to the Congress, that body may decide whether to institute a jury system. He declares that JM is mistaken in his opinion, expressed in his speech on June 20, that the right of trial by jury is better secured under the proposed Constitution than under the British government or the Virginia Bill of Rights. Following the clerk's reading of the eighth Article of the Bill of Rights concerning trial by jury, JM rises to point out that Mr. Henry misunderstood him when he said that "trial by jury was as well secured, and not better secured, in the proposed new Constitution, as in our Bill of Rights." Henry continues to insist that the proposed Constitution does not insure trial by a jury of one's neighbors or peers but enables Congress to decide the matter. Amendments to secure this point must be obtained, or "the liberty and happiness of our citizens (will be) gone."]

ACCOUNT BOOK

September 1783–June 1788

Account Book

EDITORIAL NOTE

Faced with the absence of a diary and the paucity of letters in the first thirty years of John Marshall's life, scholars are fortunate that he began keeping a record of his personal accounts in 1783. The Account Book reveals a great deal of new information about Marshall's professional, domestic, and social activities.

When work began on Marshall's papers, the Account Book had already been laminated and rebound in a leather binding. That bound volume consists of two sections, one containing accounts and the other containing the law notes. When Marshall began to record his accounts, he apparently turned the book of law notes over and made what had been the back cover of the law notes the new front cover of his Account Book. Because sufficient pages remain at the center of the book for Marshall to have continued his accounts, it is not clear whether this is the last account book he maintained or the only remaining one of a series. There must have been an earlier book, since accounts are carried forward to the beginning of this volume; however, Marshall's failure to use the blank pages lends support to the editors' conclusion that he discontinued keeping detailed accounts in 1795.

A group of pages has also been laminated and bound in a separate volume boxed with the Account Book in the Swem Library at the College of William and Mary. Known as "Fragments of an account book, 1776," these consist of military accounts maintained from about January 1776 to about August 1776. They do not appear to be in Marshall's hand, nor do the dates coincide with those of his service in either the Culpeper Minutemen Battalion or the Virginia Line. The records of the library indicate that these were used as endpapers to the Account Book before it was restored, and the editors believe they may have been kept by Colonel Thomas Marshall or some other military officer in the Marshall family. They are not printed in this collection of Marshall papers.

When Marshall began keeping this book, he followed the standard procedure of separating his accounts into receipts and disbursements, consistently entering the former on the left-hand page of the book and the latter on the opposite page. He usually totaled the figures on both pages when they were filled, and he often subtracted the disbursements from the receipts in order to carry the balance over to the next page. When this occurred, the editors have inserted *Receipts*, *Disbursements*, and *Balance* in brackets. Readers should be cautioned that Marshall ran a negative balance for much of 1785, although he did not indicate it with a minus sign. After a few years, Marshall became more casual about his current balance and at times only totaled the receipts, appearing unconcerned whether disbursements exceeded that figure. Most often he totaled both categories for the year, but he reopened his books every January with a zero balance, failing to keep a cumulative record of his net worth in this document. Marshall was frequently careless with his figures. He sometimes added two sums incorrectly, suggesting either he was poor in arithmetic or he simply entered the wrong amount for an item. Sometimes his monthly totals were added incorrectly. A warning not to accept his addition at face value should be sufficient editorial interference with this trait of Marshall's financial bookkeeping.

Although Marshall's Account Book is primarily a record of financial transactions, it is perhaps equally important as a reflection of the man who prepared it for his own use. As a young man, Marshall was typically concerned with his net worth, systematically subtracting his expenditures from his monthly receipts to measure the increment to his worldly goods gained through the month's activities. After a time he tired of the bookkeeping function as such, but throughout his life he seems to have exhibited a strong interest in the acquisition of wealth. During the period covered by this Account Book, and indeed throughout his lifetime, Marshall took an active role in the management of his household, shouldering those tasks that normally would have been undertaken by his wife. His accounts show his close relationship with his father, sisters, and brothers; his mother is mentioned infrequently. When his father moved the family to Kentucky, Marshall gave financial help to those who wanted to remain in Virginia. Elizabeth, Mary, and Lucy lived with their brother for different periods in the 1780s, and his entries show how generously he cared for their needs, furnishing them with clothing, paying for such things as Lucy's dancing lessons, and frequently giving them money. This applies as well to James Markham Marshall, whose name appears more often than any other sibling.

Because of the frequent appearance of members of Marshall's family in the Account Book, each is identified only the first time he or she appears or in entries that are ambiguous about which Marshall relative is intended. All references to Thomas Marshall, "Colo. Marshall," or "Colo. M." are to Marshall's father, and the name is not identified as such after the first mention. Other references to Thomas are identified as Marshall's brother or son, unless his entry is unmistakable, such as "To my Brother Tom." In all cases the volume index may be consulted for clarification.

Entries under disbursements provide a clear picture of Marshall's sociable nature. He obviously enjoyed gambling, even though he often lost. He attended the seasonal balls held in Richmond and was a frequent visitor to the city's taverns, especially Formicola's. He was an active Mason and participated in most of the city's social activities, including dances, horse races, theater productions, and celebrations held on at least two saint's days, one in June and another in December each year. He supported the Richmond Subscription Library and invested in various business enterprises. Marshall's generosity to those outside his family is reflected in numerous contributions, such as the £21 gift he made to sufferers of the January 1787 fire that destroyed much of the center of Richmond. Given the lack of substantial secondary literature on any of these subjects, a close study of Marshall's Account Book fills a gap that has long existed in Richmond's history.

Most of his expenditures were commonplace. Medical bills, postage, books of poetry, sermons, or law, the purchase and maintenance of slaves, trips to conduct legal or personal business in Winchester, Fauquier County, Fredericksburg, or Williamsburg, and of course expenses for the birth of a child appear with predictable regularity. He made many visits to the market, one of the social centers of daily life, and he faithfully noted each expenditure in its proper place. Because of the entry of items costing only a few pence, it seems likely that Marshall entered figures almost daily, even though he often omitted recording the date of the entry. Where the date could be supplied from available evidence, it is printed in brackets in its proper place. When Marshall wrote the name of the month at the top of the page, we have moved it to the left margin.

Entries under receipts are primarily legal fees. As a neophyte lawyer, however, Marshall's professional income was small, and his civil list fees as a member of the Council of State played an important part in his support. These were supplemented by his extensive activities in the acquisition of Kentucky land warrants, in securing and negotiating military pay certificates and military land bounty warrants, and in conducting a few law cases, at first in county courts, but increasingly in the General Court and the Court of Appeals. By the time of the Virginia ratifying convention, Marshall's income appears to have been based entirely on his professional activities, which concerned litigation in the courts and relatively little office practice such as preparing deeds, wills, or legal opinions.

The bare record of the Account Book demonstrates the rapid growth of Marshall's law practice, as well as the number of cases in which he was retained during the course of a year. Since the record does not identify the courts in which these matters were pending, it is difficult to draw definite conclusions about the locality of his practice, nor can we be certain of the nature of these cases, because the records of the higher courts were destroyed in the 1865 Richmond fire. In his calendar of Marshall papers, Irwin Rhodes identified as many of these cases as possible, using the microfilm of extant court records, especially District Court Order Books, all of which are on file in the Virginia State Library. When a case was identified for which Marshall received a fee, this information has been included in a footnote with a citation to the proper court records. When these records contain documents or copies of documents executed by Marshall, they have been printed or calendared with other Marshall papers in proper chronological order.

Unfortunately for the record of Marshall's legal practice, most of the references to cases in the Account Book in the 1780s are not evidence that Marshall actually tried the case. This is especially true of district court cases. Most of them, in fact, were taken over by other attorneys after 1788. When Marshall moved to Richmond and began practicing in the state courts, the judicial system was centralized in the capital. There was a General Court, a High Court of Chancery, a Court of Admiralty, and a Court of Appeals composed of the judges of the other three. Each court held terms in Richmond in April or May and October or November.[1]

By 1788 it had become evident that the system needed to be decentralized, and after a lengthy and sometimes heated struggle marked by resistance from the county courts a new system was approved in 1788. The Court of Appeals was given a separate staff of five judges, three of whom were promoted from the old General Court and two of whom came from the old High Court of Chancery. George Wythe remained as the sole chancellor of the High Court of Chancery. The Court of Admiralty was abolished, since the recently adopted U.S. Constitution placed admiralty jurisdiction in the federal courts. Its three judges were transferred to the newly reorganized General Court, and seven judges were elected to complete that bench. The old General Court was broken down into district courts, each to be constituted by two judges. These district courts had the same jurisdiction as the old General Court,[2] and cases then pending were reassigned to their

1. For statutes creating these courts, see 9 Hening 202, 389, 401; 10 Hening 89. The Court of Admiralty was moved to Richmond when the capital was relocated in 1779, but almost immediately it was allowed to continue holding its sessions in Williamsburg.

2. Certain constitutional jurisdiction, such as impeachment trials, remained with the General Court, as did some classes of cases brought by the state.

proper districts.[3] Consequently most of the cases Marshall had entered on the docket of the General Court were transferred to such places as Winchester, Dumfries, Accomack County, Staunton, and Fredericksburg. This reorganization had a great effect on the Richmond bar. Marshall could have become a circuit rider, traveling throughout the state to any of the eighteen districts. Understandably most Richmond attorneys chose to remain in the Richmond area, limiting their practice to the Court of Appeals, the High Court of Chancery, and the district courts meeting at Richmond or at other nearby locations. Marshall took cases before the District Court at Fredericksburg and those at Petersburg, Richmond, and probably Williamsburg. Most of the cases begun by Marshall prior to 1789, when the new system went into effect, were therefore transferred to distant courts, and he turned them over to others who established practices in the new courts. Where we have determined that Marshall actually tried or argued a case, more annotation is given to that case's entry in the Account Book, and a cross-reference may appear to his argument, or to an extant litigation paper in his hand, printed elsewhere in the text of this volume.

Despite occasional references to trips to Fauquier County and other places "up country," Marshall did not continue to practice before county courts once he began practicing before the General Court when he moved to Richmond. There are entries for fees received in Fauquier County for cases in 1785, for example, but the legal business he conducted on these trips probably concerned matters his clients wanted brought before the courts in Richmond. They might also engage Marshall's help in submitting a petition to the Council of State or the House of Delegates, as James Markham did on November 3, 1787, or they might request him to enter a caveat in the Land Office. Fees recorded for county court cases are representative of business Marshall had already concluded prior to his move to Richmond.

Because of what the Account Book tells us about Marshall, it is the most significant single document in his papers. Despite an occasional entry or group of entries that have defied editorial explanation, the mere fact that Marshall engaged in certain activities when he did is often more than we knew before. His connection with Robert Morris in the 1780s is notable, for example, though the nature of it is hard to clarify. Also Marshall's frequent entries for money spent at "Rose's" suggest the existence of a tavern in the Richmond area that has escaped the historical record, even though we have identified several others he visited. The picture of Marshall's domicile before he built his own house around 1790 remains cloudy, but without this Account Book we would know nothing about his rental from William Cocke in 1784 and his possible rental or purchase of a house from Benjamin Lewis in 1785–1786. The editors are hopeful that some of these mysteries will eventually be solved.

The complete Account Book covers Marshall's financial record continuously through 1795. The editors have divided it into two parts, ending this, the first, at June 1788, to correspond with the closing date of this volume. The remainder of the Account Book will be included in Volume II. The accounts in that segment, from 1788 to 1795, are those of an established attorney in the state and federal courts, and they reflect Marshall's continuing financial growth.

3. For a discussion of the court reorganization of 1788 and its consequences, see Cullen, "St. George Tucker," 100–134. The statute that established the district courts is in 12 Hening 730.

GUIDE TO ABBREVIATIONS

ads.   *ad sectam*, "at the suit of." When listing cases, ads. is used when it is desired that the name of the defendant should come first. Thus, *A* v. *B* would become *B* ads. *A*.

appl.   appeal

att.   attachment

case   An abbreviated form of the title "trespass on the case," the common law action for the recovery of damages for injury resulting from the wrongful act of another, unaccompanied by direct or immediate force.

chy.   chancery

Comth.   Commonwealth of Virginia

covt.   covenant

Do.   ditto

H. C.   habeas corpus

ha. cor.   habeas corpus

injn.   injunction

L wart.   land warrant

Ld. wt.   land warrant

Pd.   paid

rep.   replevin

Sups.   supersedeas

T.A.B.   trespass, assault and battery

ux   *uxor*, "a wife"

AD, Marshall Papers, Swem Library, College of William and Mary

	[*Disbursements*]	
[*September*]	Given Polly[1] 6 Dollars & £4 [ ]	
	2 yds. Lustring[2] 16/, a coffee pot 4/, 1 yd. Gauze 3/6	
	2 Sugar boxes £1–7–6, Candlestick etc. 3/6	
	1 yd. linnen for P.[3] 2/6, 2 pieces of bobbin[4] 1/6	
	Tea pot 3/, Edging 3/6, Sugar pot 1/6	
	milk pot 1/, Thimble 4 1/2, Irons 9/	
	2 yds. Hummins 14/, Tea 20/,	

1. Mary W. Marshall, JM's wife.
2. A glossy silk fabric.
3. Polly.
4. A fine cord or narrow braid.

	£		
Stockins for P.[5] 6 Dollars, mustard pot 9	5	14	
	5	17	9
7 yds. Oznabrugs[6] at 1/3		8	9
Inkstand 8/, pomatum[7] 1/6		9	6
Land warrants for my Father[8]	1	15	
Fee to the Attorney[9] for Do.	1	2	6
Fee to the Register[10] for a Patent for Do.	0	15	10
For Oats 36 Bushels	3	10	6
To one pair of Stockings	1		
To trimmings for Mr. Keith	1	4	9
To advice fee given the Attorney for opinion on surveyors fees[11]	1	2	6
For sundries		5	9
To one hat £1–18–6, to making a coat etc. 1–8–6	3	7	
To [ ] pair spectacles		3	9
[To 1] box Candles for James[12] £3–9, to one Do. for self £3–1–4	6	10	4
To one Firken[13] butter	1	13	3
To b[ooks] sent James	10	8	
To cambrick[14] for self		8	
To fee given Mr. Stewart (for Colo. Powell)[15]	2	10	

5. Polly.

6. A coarse linen cloth.

7. Pomade, a scented ointment for the hair and scalp.

8. On Sept. 17, 1783, JM purchased a land warrant for Thomas Marshall covering 10,000 acres for £16,000; on the same date he purchased a similar warrant for his brother Thomas Marshall, Jr., and two warrants for himself covering 31,121 acres. The £1 15s. was for Land Office fees, as were the following two disbursements. See a discussion of JM's activities in Kentucky land speculation in Marshall's Kentucky Lands: Editorial Note, Sept. 4, 1783.

9. Edmund Randolph was attorney general of Virginia at this time.

10. John Harvie was register of the Land Office established at the 1779 session of the General Assembly. "Return of the Inhabitants," 1782, Richmond City Common Hall Records, 311, Virginia State Library; 10 Hening 50.

11. An opinion of Edmund Randolph, no doubt obtained for Thomas Marshall, JM's father, who was surveyor of Fayette County.

12. James Markham Marshall, JM's brother. After Thomas Marshall's move to Kentucky, JM frequently aided his young brother.

13. A small cask, about the size of a quarter of a barrel.

14. A fine white cloth of linen or hand-spun cotton.

15. See JM to Leven Powell, Dec. 9, 1783.

		£			
[To 4] yds. Durantz for P.[16] a 3/6 pr. yd.				14	
[To] for writing desk			3	19	
		£	[		][17]

[Receipts]

[October]		£			
Brought over[18]		£	63	1	3½
Recd. from Mr. Keith Thomas			1	14	9
Recd. from Mr. Crohan part of fees			3		
By my civil list warrants[19]			15		
By Do.			5		
Recd. from Treasury			20		
Recd. one fee from Mr. Ernest			2	10	
By my civil list warrants			44		
Recd. from Colo. R.C. Anderson for Colo. Marshall[20]			2	18	9
Recd. from Treasury			30		
Won at whist 24/			1	4	
At backgammon 30/			1	10	
By civil list warrant 40/			2		
			191	18	9½
[Disbursements]			169	11	2½
[Balance]			22	7	7 0

[Disbursements]

October 23		£			
Pd. for linnen due Majr. Lewis[21]		£	2	[	]
For advertisement for 1 of F.C.[22] 8/, fir soap 15/			1	3	

16. Durance for Polly; durance is a stout durable cloth.

17. Page torn, obscuring JM's total.

18. The amount carried over indicates perhaps that only a page of earlier accounts is missing from this book. It is possible, however, that an earlier account book was kept from 1780 to Sept. 1783.

19. JM was a member of the Council of State at this time, and "civil list warrants" is probably a reference to receipt of pay for service in that body. Councillors were paid quarterly in specie from an annual sum of £3,200. At each quarter £800 was divided among them according to records of attendance. See 10 Hening 493.

20. Richard C. Anderson and JM's father, Thomas Marshall.

21. William Lewis (*ca.* 1740–1812).

22. JM frequently abbreviated Fauquier County as F.C., but it is unclear what "1 of F.C." means. It could be a reference to a reprinting of an advertisement pertaining

For coarse cloth 20/ &			
blanket 8/, thread 1/3	1	8	3
For Flour			
Fodder	1	5	
Table furniture 25/3,			
calicoe 7/, skean silk 2/	1	14	3
24 yds. sheeting at 4/	4	16	
Stockings for self 14/, for			
Moses[23] 5/, shoes 6/8, Curry			
comb & brush 3/9, thread			
for P.[24] 1/	1	10	5
Shoes for Hannah[25] 6/8		6	8
Stockings for self 12/, Buttons			
for Moses 2/2		14	2
Dutch oven 14/8, bringing			
coal 1–14	2	8	8
150 bushels coal for self £7–10	7	10	
50 Do. for James £2–10,			
freight on Do. 18/	3	8	
For Cloth etc. for Coat 2–14	2	14	
Pd. Mr. Booker for			
Mr. Cocke[26]	4		
Pd. plasterer for Do. £1–2	1	2	
Nails for Do. 5000 at 5/ pr.			
1000	1	5	
remnant calicoe 12/, Do.			
£1–12–7, Teaboard 17/6	4	6	
ten yds. Diaper £5, 2 pr.			
stockins £1–2, needles 10½	6	2	10½

to Fayette County that appeared in the *Virginia Gazette, or, the American Advertiser* (Richmond) on May 10, 1783: "Any persons who may have surveying business to be done in the County of Fayette, are hereby informed that the money paid to my son John Marshall in Richmond, or to my son Thomas in Shanandoah, and either of their receipts sent out to me, expressing the sum, and for what purpose the money was paid, will be accepted by me as so much cash, and if it amounts to more than my fees, the overplus shall be paid, or applied in any manner the owner shall direct, immediately on the receipts being presented to Thomas Marshall, S.F.C."

23. Apparently JM bought Moses (b. *ca.* 1765) at this time; see below where he paid £74 for him.

24. Polly.

25. It is not known when Hannah (b. *ca.* 1758), a slave, was purchased.

26. JM was renting a house in Richmond owned by William Cocke (1758–1835) and located on lot 630, a few blocks west of the present John Marshall House but on the south side of what is now Marshall Street. "Assessment of Lots and Tenements . . . ," 1784, Richmond City Common Hall Records, 361, Va. State Lib.

25 lb. Sugar 18/9, 7 do. Coffee 10/6, 3 blankets £1–10	4	14	3
Oznabrugs 1/6, Hose 5/, Given Polly £1–8	1	14	6
Carpet £2–8, Knives etc. £1–7, Dishes etc. £2–6	6	1	
sent James £5–4, Dinner for self 10/	5	14	
Wine 6/, oranges 3/, Apples 3/, Silk for sister M[27] £3–10	4	2	
Plates [etc. £] 1–13–6, shoes 12/, 4 yds. w. ribband for sister 8/	2	13	6
a pair of buckles for James 7/, one yd. silk 10/		17	
Ironing table 18/, lost at whist £3–14	4	12	
Paid for Moses £74, for grate £3, putting it up 18/	77	18	
For rum £9–15, Pot 11/, skillits 6/, corn £2–12	13	4	
	169	11	2[½]

[Receipts]

[December]	Brought over £	22	7	7
	Won at whist 22/	1	2	
	By my civil list warrants	20		
	Won at Whist 24/	1	4	
	Do. 18/		18	
	By my civil list	6	10	
	Won at Backgammon	3	12	
	Received from Colo. Anderson[28] for Colo. Marshall	46		
	By my warrants for a Watch	18		
	Do. for Tobacco	13	1	3

27. Mary Marshall, JM's sister, lived with him in Richmond until Sept. 1784, when she married Humphrey Marshall of Kentucky. See JM to James Monroe, Dec. 2, 1784. JM called this sister Molly. See entries for Disbursements, Jan. 1784 and Apr. 24, 1787.
28. Richard C. Anderson.

Recd. of Mr. Reid for one fee		2	8	
Recd. from Doctor Lee[29] for Colo. Marshall		45		
Recd. from Hancock Lee[30] for one fee		2	11	
Recd. from James Cochran[31]		3		
		185	13	10
[Disbursements]		183	10	4
[Balance]		2	3	6

[Disbursements]

[December]	For Moses shoes 6/, for saltpetre 3/, Jar 12	£	1	1	
	Bought pork 15–1, 9¾ lbs.	[		15	1]
	Tub & pales 9/, 2 pots 55/, wine 6/, at whist £10		13	12	
	one Mutton a 6d. lb. £1–11, wine 8/, bowl 12/		2	11	
	lock 2/, brushes 2/6, Mats & brooms 5/, 2 Jars £1–1		1	10	6
	whist 30/, given Jack 6/, salt 6/, wood 12/, eggs 5/		2	19	
	Petticoat for Hannah 15/, Stirrup Leathers 2/6, taps[32] 1/6			19	6
	Corn 30/, nails 1/3, whist 12/, cow £3–12–8		5	15	11
	For my Land warrant 13/3, poker 6/, To Parson 30/		2	19	3
Jan. 14 [1784]	For Colo. Marshall's land wt. £1, Spit 13/, sheldrake[33] 3/		1	16	

29. Arthur Lee. Lee was a delegate to the Continental Congress at that time. See JM to Lee, Jan. 2, 1784.

30. Hancock Lee later became clerk of the Essex County Court.

31. Cochran (1756–ca. 1820), ensign in the Virginia Continental Line, was appointed a justice of the peace of Monongalia County by the governor on Aug. 26, 1784. *JVCS*, III, 376.

32. A tap is a piece of leather with which the worn-down heel or sole of a boot is "tapped."

33. A duck.

	£	s	d
Mats 3/4, Subscription to Library[34] £7, Market 3/, Tea 12/	7	18	4
Wood 12/, Chocolate 6/, halfsoling boots 6/, Breeches 19/6	2	3	6
Tea kettle 24/, Paid for Colo. Marshalls L wart. 24/	2	8	
Turkys 12/, blacking[35] 1/6, Wood 24/ Whist etc. £18	19	17	6
Wood 10/, Beef 26/8, Backgammon £6	7	16	8
Wood 10/, Blankets 24/, Shoes 10/ Paid for steps to be repaid by Cocke[36] 12/	2	16	
Watch £18, Beef 22/6, Gauze 14/, Fruit Birds 11/	20	7	6
Tobacco £13–1–3, Balls[37] £3, To my Brother[38] £22–1–4	38	2	7
Moses Breeches 6/3, pepper 4/, powder etc. 4		13	7
Wood 10/, Mustard 2/4, Corn 18/, Given Polly £2–8	3	18	4
Physick 3/, eggs 1/, wood 10/,			

34. At a meeting on Jan. 16, 1784, the Library Society in Richmond, presided over by Edmund Randolph, held a meeting and published a notice regarding subscriptions. Subscribers were required to pay the chairman (until a treasurer could be appointed) a fee of 5 guineas before Feb. 3, 1784. It seems clear that JM was one of these original subscribers and that he paid his 5 guineas before Feb. 3. *Virginia Gazette, and Weekly Advertiser* (Richmond), Jan. 17, 1784.

JM noted £7 rather than the required fee of 5 guineas because he was recording Virginia currency here. In the 18th century a guinea was an English gold coin worth 21 shillings, rather than a fictional unit of currency as it is today, and in 1776 it was valued at £1 6s. 3d. in Virginia currency. It is understandable that by 1784 this amount would have become inflated to £1 8s. Further evidence that 5 guineas equaled £7 is seen in JM's entry under Disbursements, [*ca.* Mar.] 1784. See Thomas Jefferson's "Notes for the Report on the Value of Gold and Silver Coins," [Sept. 2, 1776], in *Jefferson Papers*, I, 511–514.

35. Lampblack, or black polish for boots and shoes.

36. William Cocke, JM's landlord. See entry under Disbursements, [Oct. 23], 1784.

37. JM joined the Richmond Assemblies, annual social activities held every two weeks during the winter months and supported by subscriptions. These were most often dances held at the Eagle Tavern. See JM to William Pierce, Feb. 12, 1783; *Va. Gaz. & Wkly. Adv.*, Dec. 10, 1785; and annual entries in the Account Book for Assemblies.

38. This was either James Markham Marshall, whom JM was helping financially during this period, or Thomas, who lived in Fauquier County. JM traveled to Fauquier at about the time of this entry.

given Polly £2–14	3	8	
Peas 6/, shoes for Moses 7/6, Wood 10/, beef £3	4	3	
Pd. for Mr Turner 29/, Wine 6/	1	15	
Sister Molly's[39] trimmings & Eliza[40] 26/, Coat 22/ & £3–10	4	12	
sent James £4–10, Pd. Mr. Webb for corn £9–12	14	2	
Butter 55/, spent in travelling[41] £4–15	7	10	
Given Eliza £2–8, pd. Dr. Horner 6/8	2	14	8
	181	14	4
	1	16	
	[183	10	4][42]

[Receipts]

[ca. March] Brought over	2	3	6
Recd. from Eliz. Nailer 33/4	1	13	4
By my warrants	60	12	
Rcd. from Mr Durrett 50/	2	10	
Recd. from Nat. Pope[43] for Colo. Marshall	5	02	
Recd. from Mr. Thompson one fee for a suit brought in the name of Lacy	2	10	
Recd. from Dr. Belt 2 fees	5		
Recd. from Mr Broddus for			

39. Mary Marshall. The 1784 "Return of the Inhabitants," Richmond City Common Hall Records, 330, Va. State Lib., lists a Moll, age 30, who lived on JM's property. This probably was Mary, although her correct age in 1784 would have been 27. The ages listed for inhabitants are frequently incorrect by several years. There is no evidence to suggest JM ever owned a slave named Moll.

40. Elizabeth Marshall (1756–1842) apparently stayed in Virginia when her father moved the family to Kentucky. JM helped her, as well as other members of the family, until she married Rawleigh Colston (1747–1823) on Oct. 15, 1785. JM's last gift to her was £43 6s. 8d. on Sept. 26, 1785. She is not to be confused with Elizabeth Ambler Brent (later Carrington), JM's sister-in-law, known also as Eliza.

41. JM had gone to Fauquier County to test the political climate before entering the race for the House of Delegates. See JM to James Monroe, Apr. 17, 1784.

42. Page torn, obscuring JM's total.

43. Nathaniel Pope, of Chilton in Hanover County. Pope later practiced law in Hanover County in 1788 and 1789.

motion	2	5	
From Sheriff of Albemarle[44]			
Do.	2	8	
From Mr. Cochran in full 52/	2	12	
From Mr. Garland for			
Motion[45]	2	10	
From Mr. Fowler one fee[46]	2	16	
From Mr. Smith Do.	2	16	
Recd. from Mr. Hugh Hill Do.	2	10	
Recd. from Mr. Archer[47] Do.	2	8	
By my civil list	19	14	
By my civil list	100		
Recd. from Mr. Latham one			
fee T.A.B.[48]	2	10	
From Mr. Ross 3 fees £7–10	7	10	
	228	19	10
[Disbursements]	172	2	5
[Balance]	56	[17]	5[49]

[Disbursements]

[ca. March]	For wood 32/, For watch			
	chain 18/	2	10	
	To Polly for house 24/, Do. 30/	2	14	
	sugar 16/6, Tea 9/, for a			
	cask 6/, wood 11/	2	2	6
	Punch & Tea 10/, forms 2/6,			
	Calicoe 20/6	1	13	
	Given my brother James 48/	2	8	
	Greens & eggs 7/6, bowl 1/3,			
	vest 24/	1	12	9

44. Clifton Rhodes was appointed sheriff of Albemarle County on Nov. 6, 1783, while JM was a member of the Council of State. He was replaced on July 28, 1785, and removed as a justice of the peace on Sept. 13, 1786. Apparently Albemarle County had a history of sheriffs failing to send tax revenues to the state treasurer. Rhodes was no exception. *JVCS*, III, 305, 464, 578, 591, IV, 53, 275.

45. See fee entered for Garland v. Lee on Apr. 3, 1787.

46. Balance of fee paid in Fowler v. Campbell on Mar. 30, 1785.

47. Additional fee entered in Archer v. Dabney on Oct. 6, 1784.

48. See fee collected after the case of Latham v. Camp was finished under Sept. 5, 1785. Trespass, assault and battery is an action charging physical violence to the person of the plaintiff based on the wrongful act of the defendant.

49. Page torn, obscuring JM's total.

To my Brother James	8		
Paid Doctor Fowshee[50]	4	2	
Jug & wine 40/	2		
Wood 10/, given Eliza £4–4	4	14	
Lost at backgammon £6	6		
To one piece of linnen	6		
Paid the University in the hands of Mr. Tazewell for Colo. Marshall as Surveyor of Fayette County[51]	100		
Tea 12/, market 6/, paper 3/	1	1	
Coat 2–18, Flower 38/6	4	16	6
To Polly for Servts. & house 5 guineas	07		
To Eliza £2–16/, Lemons & gridiron 6/8	3	2	8
To straw 10/, To house 20/	1	10	
Lemons etc. 6/, 2 Mattresses £10–10	10	16	
	172	2	5

[Receipts]

[ca. May]	Brought over	51	17	5
	Recd. from Mr. Muschit one fee in a chancery suit	7		
	Recd. from Mr. Kimbro one fee ads. Cary & others	2	10	
	Recd. from Mr. Bins by Colo. Peyton	2	10	
	Recd. from Colo. Tunstal	12		
	Recd. from Mr. Colston Smith	9	12	
	Recd. from Mr. Love	5	2	
	Recd. from Mr. John			

50. William Foushee.

51. Thomas Marshall had been appointed surveyor of Fayette County on Nov. 1, 1780, and established his office in Kentucky in Nov. 1782. His fees were fixed by statute, and the College of William and Mary was entitled to one-sixth of all the fees collected by him. 10 Hening 57, 126, 231; 11 Hening 352, 353. Henry Tazewell was a resident of Williamsburg and that city's representative to the House of Delegates. Apparently he had been asked by the college to act as a receiver of surveyors' fees in Richmond. See entry under Disbursements, Oct. 16, 1784.

Ambler[52]	9	12
Recd. from Mr. Michael Burke for advice[53]	1	8
Recd. from Mr. Lawson for a suit against Mr. Wm. Neilson	2	10
From Elicia Lightfoot ver C. McCarty	1	10
From Genl. Stevens[54]	2	8
From Wm. Massie ads. N.L. Savage[55]	2	8

	119	[7]	5[56]

[Disbursements]

[ca. May]	Given my Brother[57] 1 [0] dollars	3	[0]
	To the house 9/, Do. 12/	1	01
	Saint Taminy[58] 11 Dollars	3	6
	The house 15/, Sundries for Polly 12/	1	7
	The house 20/, Stockings for self 48/	3	8
	Shoes 9/, handkerchiefs for Polly 9/		18
	Table £3, house 17/	3	17
	To my Brother James	36	18

52. Ambler was a first cousin of JM's wife. See JM to Ambler, May 7, 1784.

53. See Michael Bourke ads. Meade, Receipts, Oct. 10, 1784.

54. Edward Stevens (1745–1820) distinguished himself in the Revolution and afterwards represented Culpeper County in the Virginia Senate until 1790.

55. William Massie (d. ca. 1804), of New Kent County, and Nathaniel Littleton Savage, a former member of the House of Delegates and a justice of the peace in New Kent County. See entry for Receipts, Oct. 12, 1784.

56. Page torn, obscuring JM's total.

57. James Markham Marshall.

58. Saint Taminy was the patron saint of America, facetiously canonized around 1770. He was sometimes called St. Tamina, and his day was celebrated on May 1. The name originated from Indian Chief Tamenende, or Tammany, a respected leader of a Delaware tribe. The Sons of St. Tammany was an offshoot of several patriotic societies loosely organized during the Revolution. They performed charitable works, such as poor relief. These are forerunners of the political organization in New York known as Tammany Hall. See Mitford M. Mathews, ed., Dictionary of Americanisms (Chicago, 1951). This year the society produced "a sumptuous entertainment at the public buildings," at which were present the governor and most other public officials. Va. Gaz. & Wkly. Adv., May 8, 1784.

	£	s	d
Sugar 19, Sope 1/8'			
Breeches 22/	1	3	8
Stockings 18/, Gloves 3/4,			
house 5/	1	6	4
Wood 12/, house 6/8, milk 6/	1	4	8
Mrs. Younghusbands[59] 14/,			
Tea 21/6	1	5	6
To my Sister[60] £4–16	4	16	
To the house 5/3, Do. 6/,			
Boots 42/	2	13	3
house 6/, punch 3/		9	
pasturage & ferriage 12/,			
Given Servt. at D.G. 6/		18	
House 12/, Do. 6/, Do. 8/3,			
Do. 5/3	1	11	3
Handkerchiefs 6/8, wine 14/,			
Lemons 6/	1	6	8
House 6/3, Do. 7,			
Cambrick 18/	1	11	3
House 13/, wood 10/	1	3	
	73	19	7
[Receipts]	119	7	5
[Balance]	35	7	8

[Receipts]

		£	s	d
	Brought over	35	7	8
June 9th.	Recd. from Mr. Smith[61]	4	10	
17th.	Recd. from Mr. Cochran[62]			
	the balance of his fees	2	8	
21st.	Recd. from Mr. West in			
	part of a fee	4	10	
26th.	Recd. from Mr. Dabny[63] in			
	part for two chy. suits	7	10	

59. Mrs. Pleasant Younghusband (d. 1808) operated a boarding house in Richmond. JM might have dined there.

60. Mary or Elizabeth Marshall.

61. Presumably the case of Rawley Smith, administrator of Joseph Smith, v. William Smith, Minute Book, 1784–1786, 51, Fauquier County, Va. State Lib. See the next n. 75 for an explanation of cites to Virginia court records in the Account Book. See also fee entered at May 5, 1787, below.

62. James Cochran.

63. See entry under Receipts, Oct. 6, 1784, Archer v. Dabney.

July 1st.	By my warrants		72		
	To my service in the Assembly[64]		34	4	
[3]d.	By cash recd. on warrants some Colo. Monroes[65]		65	6	
	Recd. from Colo. Henry Lee[66] for Colo. Marshall, by Mr. Byrne in Petersburg		22	10	
12th.	By my warrants		2	15	11
	Colo. Marshalls warrants		20	4	
			271	5	7
	[Disbursements]		242		½
	[Balance]		29	5	6½

[Disbursements]

June 9th.	Spoons £7–16, vest 1–12–6	£	9	8	6
11th.	Oznabrugs 50/, house 6/7½		2	16	7½
12th.	Water Glasses & Tumblers 12/			12	
15th.	Polly 6/, House 3/, Do. 3/, Polly 14/		1	6	
	Tea etc. 4/, Eliza £2–8		2	12	
19th.	Sugar 12/9, House 24/		1	16	9
22d.	Lost at whist £19, Hous 12/8		19	12	8
25th.	House 10/, Polly £1–8		1	18	
26th.	Colo. Monroe & self at the play[67]		1	10	
July 1st.	Paid for Ben[68]		90	4	

64. In 1779 the General Assembly set the pay of delegates at 50 pounds of tobacco per day, plus 2 pounds per mile travel as well as all ferry charges. A system for converting the value of tobacco into treasury warrants was adopted at each session to May 1780, and in May 1783 the delegates voted to cut their pay by 25% during the economic crisis. 10 Hening 30, 104, 137–138, 229; 11 Hening 280. See the Pay Voucher, June 30, 1784.

65. James Monroe. See JM to Monroe, Apr. 17, 1784.

66. Henry "Light Horse Harry" Lee.

67. A company of actors under the direction of Dennis Ryan (d. 1786) opened the first post-Revolution season in Virginia in Richmond on June 3, 1784. Several plays were performed before the summer season ended in July, among them *Douglass*, *The Padlock*, and *The Cheats of Scapin*. Suzanne Ketchum Sherman, "Post-Revolutionary Theatre in Virginia, 1784–1810" (M.A. thesis, College of William and Mary, 1950), 17–19. Standard seats sold for 6s.; apparently James Monroe and JM bought box seats, or the £1 10s. represents more than theater tickets.

68. The price JM paid for Ben would suggest he was at prime work age, but apparently he caused JM some trouble. On May 4, 1786, JM paid fees to get him out of jail, and the last Account Book entry for Ben is Feb. 4, 1789.

2d.	Given Polly £1–8, Play 12/	2		
2d.	To my subscription[69]	50		
	To one Quarter cask wine	14		
3d.	To the play 13/, pd. for Colo. Monroe[70] £16–16	17	4	
Do.	To 2 pair stockings 14/, Limes 3/		17	
	House 6/; 5th. House 14/, to Eliza 1–12–6	2	2	6
12th.	To Polly £2–8, To St. John's[71] £1–8	3	16	
13th.	house 6/3; [14]th. Do. 6/, play[72] 15/	1	07	3
15th.	Serge[73] £3–13–9, Paper £2–2 £	5	15	9
15th.	Sent my Brother James	11	8	
15th.	sugar 32/; 18th. house 11/	1	13	
		242		½

[Receipts]

	Brought over	£	29	5	6½
	won at whist	£	10		
July 20th.	Recd. from Robert Price in two certiorari's[74] ads. of				

69. It is not certain to what JM had subscribed. The May 1784 session of the General Assembly had recently enacted a subscription program to raise money for the construction of government buildings. JM might be expected to invest in such an undertaking, although his name is not on a list of subscribers submitted to the governor on Nov. 5, 1785. *CVSP*, IV, 63–65. Another enterprise had been discussed on June 23, 1784, when those who had been supporting the movement to extend the navigation of the James River met "to determine whether they still intend to contribute to carry on so useful and beneficial an undertaking." The amount JM paid for a subscription strongly suggests an investment in one of these projects. It is possible, however, that JM was subscribing to the construction of a library or the Masons' hall, both of which were being planned at this time. 11 Hening 400; *Va. Gaz. & Wkly. Adv.*, June 12, 1784; JM to George Muter, Jan. 7, 1785.

70. James Monroe.

71. June 24 is the festival day of St. John the Baptist, and it was usually observed by the Masons, who attended a church service and concluded with a banquet. It is unclear why JM entered this expense so late, unless the observance had been postponed. It is possible, although unlikely, that JM was making a contribution to St. John's Episcopal Church in Richmond.

72. According to Sherman, "Post-Revolutionary Theatre," 256, the summer theater season ended on July 12. JM's purchase of tickets on the 14th suggests a more accurate date.

73. Serge is a durable woolen worsted fabric.

74. See partial return of fees to Price deducted from receipts at the end of Oct. 1784. Certiorari is a writ issued by an appellate court, usually in criminal matters, to stay

	Harvie & Ross	5		
22d.	Recd. from Fitzhugh ver			
	Saunders[75]	8	8	
23d.	Recd. from Mr. Bourke[76]	5		
27th.	Recd. from Mr. Dormont[77]			
	in part of fees in chy.	3	2	6
	ver Quintana &	1	17	6
31st.	won at whist	4	6	
	Recd. from Mr. Humston			
	one fee ver Love[78]	3	12	
	Mr. Chinn ver West	4	16	
	Hume 20/, Colo Brooke 51/	3	11	
	John Green ads. Thornberry	1	8	
	Recd. in Fauquier for County			
	business[79] £2–14	2	14	
	Advice fee from Mr. Beale	1	2	6
	Do. from Mr. Stewart	1	8	
	From Mr. Smith in chy. ver			
	Arthur Campbell	2	8	
	Recd. Warrants for Colo.			
	Marshall	7	9	8
	Do. for self	48		
		143	8	8½

[Disbursements]

July 20th.	Chickens 40/, beef 3/2	£	2	3	2
22d.	To one coat 15/;				

---

proceedings before the matter proceeds to trial in the lower court and to order the transmission of the record to the higher tribunal for trial there. See Bacon, *Abridgment*, I, 349–359. This common law procedure is quite distinct from the statutory certiorari jurisdiction of the Supreme Court of the United States.

75. This case, filed in the General Court in Oct. 1785, JM for the plaintiffs, ended in the District Court at Dumfries in 1792. See Sarah Fitzhugh *et al.* v. Lewis Saunders, in Land Causes, 1789–1793, 361–421, Office of the Clerk of the Prince William County Circuit Court, Manassas, Va., hereafter cited as Land Causes, 1789–1793, Prince William County, Va. State Lib. The records for the Virginia courts have been collected on microfilm at the Va. State Lib.; hereafter in the Account Book all references to Virginia court records will be to those collections and will specify the location, city or county, under which the records are filed.

76. Michael Bourke. See entry for Bourke ads. Meade, Oct. 10, and Nov. 11, 1784.

77. See also entry for Receipts, Nov. 16, 1784.

78. See also entry for Disbursements, Sept. 27, 1784, and Receipts, Aug. 1786, where the case is identified as in chancery.

79. JM received this fee for performing some legal function for someone in the county, not for handling a case before the county court. Once lawyers began practicing before the General Court in Richmond, it would have been considered irregular for

		£	s	d
	23d. House 6/	1	1	
26th.	Given Mrs. Granger[80]	11	18	
Do.	Expense sending Mrs. Granger home		6	
Do.	Child 4/3		10	3[81]
28th.	Given My Brother James	4	4	
29th.	Tea £1–1–6, pasturage etc. 1–2–6	1	4	
[August] 2d.	mending Phaeton[82] 12/, Given my Brother[83] £7–4	7	16	
4th.	2 pr. saddlebags £3, left with Polly £5–15	8	15	
	Given James £2–16, rum £4–10	7	6	
	Expences travelling[84] £8–8–6	8	8	6
	paid for two negroes[85] £30	30		
	In part for two servants £20	20		
	For a horse £22–10	22	10	
	Linnen for servts. 15/		15	
	Paid taxes for Colo. Marshall[86]	8	13	7½
		135	0	6½
	[Receipts]	143	8	8½
	[Balance]	8	8	2

them to take new cases before the county courts.

80. Mrs. Granger, obviously a midwife, had attended the birth of JM's first child, Thomas, on July 21, 1783.

81. JM included the amount spent in sending Mrs. Granger home with the 4s. 3d. spent on his son Thomas when he entered the total expenditure.

82. A light, four-wheeled open carriage usually drawn by a pair of horses. JM was no doubt preparing for his trip to Fauquier County.

83. James Markham Marshall.

84. JM went to Fauquier County. See JM to Charles Simms, June 16, 1784, and Receipts for Aug. 1784.

85. These were probably Edey and Harry, two slaves that JM owned when he filed his Henrico personal property list in 1784 and that he had not owned when his Richmond list was filed earlier that year. They were listed as nontithable, that is, either under 16 years old or too old to work. The price JM paid for them supports this also. Henrico County Personal Property, 1784, 20, Va. State Lib.

86. Because Thomas Marshall's land tax in 1784 amounted to only £5 6s. 1d., this figure must include also his personal property tax on his slaves, horses, and cattle. JM had listed on the Fauquier County personal property list one nontithable Negro and two horses. The total tax he recorded here probably included his tax as well. Fauquier County Land Books, 1783–1795, and Fauquier County Personal Property, 1784, both in Va. State Lib.

		£	s	d
	To my Brother James for Saddle bags & expenses 37/6	1	17	6
	[Balance]	6	10	8

[Receipts]

		£	s	d
	Brought over £	6	10	8
Septr. 1st	Recd. from Mr. J:W. Semple in part for a caveat enterd agst. Jo. Griffith[87]	1	4	
2d.	Recd. from Mr. Gilbert for supersedeas[88]	4	16	
3d.	Recd. from Johnston for injunctn. vs. Walker	5		
	Recd. from Mr. Perfect to bring a suit against Page's Exrs. on a bond to convey etc.[89]	3		
	From Mr. Myers in part	3		
	From Mr. Okely retaining fee	4	16	
	From Jo. Leacy ads. Garner detinue[90]	3		
	From Wm. B. Seers ads. Turberville	3		
	From T. Williams ads. Carter[91]	1	16	
	County Court 15.		15	
	From Mr. Love	2	10	

87. John Walker Semple (d. 1822) and Joseph Griffith. The issuance of land patents in this period inevitably produced conflicting claims to all or part of the same parcel of land. In this instance Semple and Griffith claimed the same land. Semple paid JM to enter a caveat in the Land Office. A caveat was an order preventing the issuance of a grant to Griffith until the conflict could be settled. Land Office Caveats, Sept. 2, 1784, 112, Va. State Lib.

88. A supersedeas was a writ issued by an appellate court designed to supersede enforcement of a trial court's judgment, pending determination of an appeal.

89. Christopher Perfect v. John Page, executor of Mann Page. JM filed suit in the General Court to force Page to honor a bond of indebtedness that had existed between Perfect and Page. The case ended in the District Court meeting in Fredericksburg on Oct. 2, 1789. See District Court Law Orders, A, 1789–1793, 33, Fredericksburg, Va. State Lib. See n. 75 above for an explanation of citations to Virginia court records.

90. Detinue is an action for the recovery, in specie, of personal chattels from one who acquired possession of them lawfully but is retaining them without right, together with damages for the detention.

91. This case, Charles Carter v. Jesse Williams, was dismissed from Fauquier County Court in May 1783. Minute Book, 1781–1784, 128, Fauquier County, Va. State Lib. That JM received fees in Sept. 1784, Feb. 1785, and Apr. 1785 suggests the case was revived in the higher courts.

	From H Funk ads. Nixon		2	10	
Septr. 25th.	From Mr. White—Ann ver				
	John White		2	10	
	From Mr. G Pickett fees pd.				
	in his store[92]		8	8	
	Deliverd me by Colo. Marshall		139	18	
Septr. 30th.	From Capt. W. Bentley [ver]				
	Mazaret debt[93]		2	10	
	From Mr. Teagle ads				
	Minthurston		3	10	
			198	13	8

[*Disbursements*]

Augt. 31st.	Stockings 28/, paper 3/6	£	1	11	6
	To home for christening[94] 12/,				
	Do. 2/6			14	6
	sugar 16/, Shoes 12/,				
	Waiters 6/		1	14	
	Limes 6/, house 6/, Linnen				
	for Polly 4–14–9		5	6	9
Septr. 1st.	Paid Gilbert for Colo.				
	Marshall		2	14	
	Enterd two caveats agt.				
	Craig for Do.[95]			10	
2d.	Tea 21/6, Shoes for Polly 10/		1	11	6
3d.	Given Polly for house £4–16–8		4	16	8
	Cap etc. for Ben[96] 6/3,				
	paper 2/6			9	[ ]
	Spent in my absence from				
	Richmond[97]		8	12	3
	Hats for Servts. 8/, Given my				

92. George Pickett (*ca.* 1755–1821) was a Richmond merchant and apparently accepted fees due JM in his store. He originally lived in Fauquier County, and his niece, Lucy, married JM's brother Charles in 1787. Valentine Museum, *Richmond Portraits in an Exhibition of Makers of Richmond, 1737–1860* (Richmond, 1949), 152–154.

93. William Bentley (*ca.* 1755–*ca.* 1818) served as captain in the Third Virginia Regiment during the Revolution. Debt is an action to recover a certain specific sum of money or a sum that can readily be reduced to a certainty.

94. This is either what it cost JM to return home from Fauquier County for his son Thomas's christening or a sum spent for the occasion.

95. Even though these caveats were entered for JM's father, the Land Office recorded them as John Marshall, Jr., v. John Craig, and only one caveat appears in the book. Land Office Caveats, Sept. 3, 1784, 113, Va. State Lib.

96. A slave purchased on July 1, 1784.

97. This could represent an additional amount JM spent while on his trip to Fau-

	Brother[98] 12/	1	0	
	Paid for servants £25, for a horse £20	45		
	Pd. my Father for a Silk purchasd by my sister Eliza for Sukey[99] & returnd	6	18	
25th.	For one hat 30/, Pen knife 3/	1	13	
	To Eliza 16/, To Polly for silk 56/, To my Mother[1] for silk 56/	8	8	
27th.	Paid for Mr. Humston to Mr Atty.[2]	2	8	
	For shoeing my horses		8	
		93	15	2
	[Receipts]	198	13	8
	[Balance]	104	18	6

[Receipts]

October 1st	Brought over	104	18	6
	Recd. from McMahon with Colo. Marshall	2	10	
2d.	From Mr. Eppes on a will	10		
	From Thomas Humphries in part of a fee for defending him—robbery[3]	3		

quier County in August, although that might suggest that he returned to Fauquier after his son's christening. He dated no entries in his Account Book between Sept. 3 and Sept. 25, and his disbursements during this time certainly could have been made in Fauquier County.

98. James Markham Marshall.

99. The name Sukey does not appear anywhere else in the Account Book or JM's papers. There are no slaves known to be owned by the Marshall family with this name, nor does it seem likely that Elizabeth Marshall would be buying silk for a slave, unless Sukey was a seamstress who was to make something for her. It seems more probable, however, that Sukey was Susan Tarleton Marshall (1774–1858), JM's 10-year-old sister. The entry suggests that Thomas Marshall had sent money for Eliza to buy silk for Sukey; Eliza bought it and sent it to Sukey in Kentucky, but for some reason it was returned. JM then returned his father's money.

1. Mary Randolph Keith Marshall (1737–1809), who had married Thomas Marshall in 1754.

2. "Mr. Attorney" was Edmund Randolph, the attorney general of Virginia.

3. Thomas Humphreys was convicted at the Oct. 1784 session of the General Court. Robbery was a felony punishable by death. He, with other criminals, appealed to the Council of State for mercy on Jan. 27, 1785. The Council reprieved his sentence until Feb. 4, 1785, and on Feb. 3 extended the reprieve to Mar. 1. After another reprieve,

3d.	Recd. from Mr. Lattime[r] ads. Archer	2	16	
4th.	From Capt. Williams ads Doctor Fulwell	2	10	
5th.	From M Everet ads. Penner Slander	5		
	Clarkes Admrs. ads. Watkins debt	2	10	
6	Robt. Harlowe part for motion in chy.		12	
	From Mr Tabb in Archer ver Dabney debt.	2	16	
7th.	From Mr. Kennan in part ver Webb.	1		
	From Mr. Dickie in Crawford ver Sans.	2	10	
8th.	From Mr. Woodlief ads. Norton debt	2	10	
	From Mr. Sudbury ads. Totty	2	16	6
9th	From Capt. Marshall[4]	6	4	
	From Dixon Nailor ads. Anderson Exr.	1	16	
	From Daniel Brown ver Uriah Jones	2	10	
10th	From Michael Bourke[5] ads. Meade	2	16	
	From Lane ads. Mitchel	2	12	
12th	From Mr Love in full	2	8	
	From Mr. Massie ads. Savage additional[6]	2	8	
	From Mr. Saunders ver Jude	2	10	

the Council ordered on Mar. 10 that Humphreys be pardoned, on the condition that he work on constructing the public buildings for three years. One member of the Council of State, Joseph Jones, dissented from this decision, objecting that the executive lacked constitutional authority to issue conditional pardons. *JVCS*, III, 414, 416, 419, 422.

4. This was most probably JM's brother Thomas Marshall, who had served as captain of a Virginia State Regiment from May 1778 to Apr. 1780. He remained in Fauquier County when his father moved the family to Kentucky. After a visit to Kentucky in 1788 and 1789, he moved to Mason County, Ky., in 1790. He became clerk of the county and attended the convention that wrote Kentucky's first constitution. He later settled in Washington, Ky., where his father moved to live with the family in 1800.

5. See entry from Michael Burke in Receipts, *ca.* May 1784.

6. See entry under Receipts, *ca.* May 1784.

		£	s	d
	From Major West ads. Ashton[7]		7	
		175	12	
	[Disbursements]			
October 1st.	black silk stockings 20/	1		
	Paid Colo. Marshall in the hands of McMahon	2	10	
	waist coat & breeches £3–13–9	3	13	9
4th	To the house 26/, Shoes 10/6, ribband 1/6, club[8] 1/6	1	19	6
7th.	one yd. Dimmety[9] 4/4, Wood 12/, House 12/8	1	8	8
8th.	Sugar 13/, Given Polly for Cloak 56/	3	9	
10th.	Chickens 1/3, peaches 7½		2	
11th.	Given Polly for hat	3		
	Dimety for Tom[10] 3/, oranges 3/		6	
12th.	House 9/		9	
	My subscription to Mr. Buchanan[11]	3		
		20	17	11
	[Receipts]	175	12	
	[Balance]	154	14	1
	[Receipts]			
	Brought over	154	14	1
[October] 13th.	Recd. from Major Magill[12]	8		

7. See above, JM's oral argument for the widow of Hugh West in an ejectment action brought by Ashton, Oct. 13, 1786.

8. JM belonged to a social club that met at a tavern owned by Serafino Formicola (*ca.* 1743–1790). See entry under Disbursements, May 9, 1785.

9. A stout cotton cloth, woven with raised stripes and fancy figures, used for bed linen and garments.

10. Thomas Marshall, JM's son.

11. It is uncertain what subscription JM was buying. Mr. Buchanan was probably the Rev. John Buchanan (1743–1822), rector of St. John's Episcopal Church in Richmond; JM might have been helping to pay his salary in a manner customary in Virginia.

12. Charles Magill had served as a lieutenant in the Eleventh Virginia Regiment

	From Mr. Myers in full	2		
	From Majr. Kirkpatrick ver Thomas	2	10	
14th.	From Mr. Miller ads. Mayo (caveat)	2	10	
	From Charles Shoemaker for Collinson Reid (out of state) ver Armstead[13]	2	2	
	Baytop ads. Wyat	2	10	
	Easterly ver Foland & al (caveat)[14]	2	10	
15th.	From Mr. Moore ads. Mr. Mason debt	2	8	
16th.	From Mr. Strother ver Brown	2	10	
	From Gaar etc. ver Broyles	2	10	
	From Gaar ver same	2	10	
	From Mr. Wyatt on motion	2	8	
	From Mr. Mccoul for Tobacco belonging to Colo. Marshall	54	16	8
	Mr. Harrison in the appeal of North ver Hair for appellee	3		
17th	Mr. Hume in part ver Payne etc.	3		
	Rogers ads. Rogers	2	10	
25th.	From Mr. Harlow [in] part		18	
26th.	From Mr. Allen ads. Page[15] in part		18	
	From Mr. Webb for fees	14		
		268	4	9
	Returnd Mr. Price[16] to be deducted from fees	2	14	
		265	10	9

and subsequently as a major of a Virginia State Regiment. See JM to William Branch Giles, Sept. 22, 1786.

13. Charles Shoemaker (b. *ca.* 1756) was a Richmond merchant in 1784. "Return of the Inhabitants," 1784, Richmond City Common Hall Records, 357, Va. State Lib. "Out of state" probably signifies Reid was not a resident of Virginia.

14. George Easterly v. John Benson, Frederick Kaylor, assignee, and Frederick Foland, assignee. Land Office Caveats, Oct. 19, 1784, 124–125, and Oct. 23, 1784, 124–125, Va. State Lib.

15. Robert Page v. William Allen. JM was defending Allen in a contract case that began in the General Court in Oct. 1784. Litigation did not end until Apr. 2, 1790, when a verdict was reached by the District Court meeting in Staunton, where the case had been transferred in 1788. District Court Order Book, 1789–1793, 34–36, Augusta County, Va. State Lib.

16. See entry under Receipts, July 20, 1784.

[*Disbursements*]

[October]				
13th.	Paid Major Magill[17] for a Mare	24		
15th.	Paid the Register for entering five caveats for Owens ver Craig chargeable to Colo. Marshall[18]	1	10	
16	To house 10/, Do. 10/	1		
	Paid Mr. Tazwell as receiver for the College on account of Colo. Marshall as surveyor of Fayette County[19]	112	2	
	Putting up the grate		9	
17	House 5/6, Do. 10/		15	6
18	For repairing Cox's grate 6/		6	
	Tea 18/, wood 12/	1		
21st.	House 8/, For Counter pin 35/	2	3	
	Decanters & Glasses 26/, Crane 2/6	1	8	6
22d.	To my Brother James	9	12	
	Knives & forks 14/, butter 56/	3	10	
23d.	House 24/, my subscription for race[20] £4–4	5	8	
	Decanters & glass 12/, bridle crupper[21] 8		14	

17. Charles Magill. See Receipts, Oct. 13, 1784.

18. The Land Office register was John Harvie. JM actually entered only one caveat for John C. Owings v. John Craig. The others were entered for Owings and chargeable to Thomas Marshall, but they were caveats against other individuals. Land Office Caveats, Aug. 31, 1784, 111, Va. State Lib.

19. Henry Tazewell was receiver of surveyors' fees, in this case those of Thomas Marshall, for the College of William and Mary. See Disbursements, *ca.* Mar. 1784, for information on the collection of surveyors' fees by the college.

20. Twice each year, in May and October, horse races were held in Richmond and other Virginia towns, and the occasion was the central feature of the season's social activity. Jockey Clubs, one of which JM joined, set the rules of the races and helped raise purses for each event. Formal balls were held (see entry for Disbursements, Nov. 1), and theater productions were set to coincide with the races (see entry under Disbursements, Oct. 26). JM's subscription for the race was no doubt the amount levied by his Jockey Club. The following advertisement appeared in a Richmond newspaper in Oct. 1784: "The Richmond Races, which were intended to have begun on the third Thursday in the month, are put off on account of interfering with other purses which are to be run for about that time. They will commense the last Tuesday in this month, on Richmond Hill." JM paid his subscription on Saturday, Oct. 23, before the races began on Oct. 26. [Samuel Mordecai], *Richmond in By-Gone Days* (Richmond, 1856), 178–179; *Va. Gaz. & Wkly. Adv.*, Oct. 2, and May 15, 1784.

21. JM must have meant a bridle and a crupper. A crupper is a leather strap buckled

Date	Description	£	s	d
26	Paid Mr. Webb for two tables	14		
	Blankets 28/, paper 16, race[22] 14/	2	18	
	Sent my Brother James 20/, play[23] 10/	1	10	
		182	6	
	[Receipts]	265	10	9
	[Balance]	83	4	9

[Receipts]

Date	Description	£	s	d
	Brought over	83	4	9
Novr. 1st.	From Mr. Jones ads. Lewis appeal	2	8	
	From Mrs. Pieden ads. St. Clair Ejectmt.	2		
6th.	Recd. from Mr. Webb for Colo. Marshall money advancd for Mr. Fleming	20		
7th.	From Mr. Blount ads. Sheffield	2	10	
	From Mr. Gaddis Winston[24] for Colo. Marshall	5		
11th.	Recd. from Mr. Bourke[25] the balance	5		
	Recd. from Mr. Martin ads. Brown motion	2	10	
13th.	From Mr. Burnley	9	8	
	From Mr. Harlow in full	3	5	
16	From Mr. Dormont in full £5	5		
	Recd. from my Father	9	06	
23	From Mr. Palmer ads. Palmers chy.	2	16	
	From Mr. Nelson for warrants	14	18	
		167	5	9

to the back of a horse's saddle and passed under the tail to keep the saddle from slipping forward. There is no known piece of equipment called a bridle crupper.

22. The Richmond races began on Oct. 26, 1784, and this is either the amount JM paid to attend or the amount he lost betting on a horse. See *Va. Gaz. & Wkly. Adv.*, Oct. 2, 1784.

23. The theater season opened with the horse races, rather than in November as stated in Sherman, "Post-Revolutionary Theatre," 256. Among the productions that season were *The Roman Father*, *Tony Lumpkin in Town*, *Miser*, and *A Trip to Scotland*. *Ibid.*, 21–22.

24. Geddes Winston (1720–ca. 1792), of Hanover County, Va.

25. See Bourke ads. Meade, Receipts, Oct. 10, 1784.

	[Disbursements]	139	19	
	[Balance]	27	6	9
	[Disbursements]	1	4	6
	[Balance]	26	2	3

[Disbursements]

Novr. 1st.	Paid my subscription to the ball[26] 20/	1		
	To my Brother James 38/	1	18	
	House 6/, For shoeing boots 24/	1	10	
Novr. 3	Corn 54/, house 33/	4	7	
Novr. 6	To my Brother James 45/	2	5	
8th.	Wood 10/	0	10	
	Given James in Mr. Digges note on which he has recovered judgement £7	7		
10th.	House 28/, Flour 47/, Bed tick[27] 49/	6	4	
13	House 19/8, pd. for Capt. Markham 48/	3	7	8
15.	Razor 3/, club[28] 3/, Given my Brother[29] 28/	1	14	
17.	Sheeting £7–1, Oznabrugs 11/8	7	12	8
	House 12/, pd. for Coal £12–10	13	2	
19.	Tea 18/, wood 12/, blankets for negroes 42/	3	12	
23d.	House 8/, play[30] 15/, Kate & Esau[31] £63	64	3	

26. This was the ball held in conjunction with the Richmond races. Although usually held at the Eagle Tavern, the event this year was held at the capitol, probably because of the larger crowd expected to attend to welcome George Washington and the marquis de LaFayette (1757–1834). The governor and the members of the General Assembly also attended. [Mordecai], *Richmond in By-Gone Days*, 179; *Va. Gaz. & Wkly. Adv.*, Nov. 20, 1784.

27. A cover to contain feathers or straw to form a mattress.

28. See entry under Disbursements, May 9, 1785.

29. James Markham Marshall.

30. See entry under Disbursements, Oct. 26, 1784.

31. JM entered no other expenditures for these two slaves throughout his Account Book, but his Henrico County personal property lists in 1785 and 1786 indicate he probably still owned them. Unfortunately the names of slaves were not recorded on Henrico County property lists after 1784. See Henrico County Personal Property, 1785, 1786, Va. State Lib.

	Carpet 10/, Sundries 13/6, House 7/		1	10	6
24	House 10/, Fodder 36/, Oysters 10/		2	16	
29th.	Flour 36/, sundries 16/6, Do. 9/		3	01	6
Decr. 1st.	House 9/, pd. Mr. Anderson for plaistering the house[32] £10–2		10	11	
	For Dockets[33] £3–14–8		3	14	8
			140	[7]	0
	sugar 12/6, House 4/			16	6
			141	03	6
			01	4	6

[Receipts]

	Brought over	£	26	
Decr. 1st	Advice fee from Mr. A. Jones		1	8
4th	Recd. from Mr. Barksdale one fee		2	16
	From Mr. Wm. Brown 3 Guineas		4	4
11th.	From McGehee Asse. of Lynch ver Carter[34]		2	10
13.	Recd. from my Father		26	4
	Recd. from Mr. Tyler one fee		12	
18th	From Mr. Rogers in part for three suits in Genl. Ct.		5	10
19.	From Mr Lewis in part for Moses[35]		9	6
	From Colo. Simms[36] to be repaid		33	

32. Henry Anderson (b. ca. 1758) was a mason living in Richmond in 1784. "Return of the Inhabitants," 1784, Richmond City Common Hall Records, 332, Va. State Lib.

33. This disbursement would be for the purchase of books used to maintain an office docket of cases pending or for the payment of term fees to one or more court clerks.

34. John McGeehee, assignee of Charles Lynch, v. Charles Carter had begun in Stafford County Court. JM filed a petition for McGeehee in the General Court in Apr. 1785, and the case was continued to Oct. 1789, when, after having been sent to the new District Court meeting in Fredericksburg, judgment for the plaintiff was confessed. District Court Records, 1789–1792, 33, Fredericksburg, Va. State Lib.

35. Moses, one of JM's slaves, was hired out to Mr. Lewis. See entry under Receipts, Jan. 29, 1785.

36. Charles Simms, of Alexandria. See JM to Charles Simms, Mar. 20, 1785, for additional financial dealings between them.

	From Mr. Stead one fee	24		
		146	18	

[Disbursements]

Decr. 2d.	play[37] 6/, House 18/	1	4	
5th.	House 6/, wood 12/, House 10/	1	8	
	Given Harry[38] for expenses to Wms.burg		12	
8	Chickens 7/3, house 3/, Do. 7/9		18	
12th.	Oysters 10/, Grate 39/, flour 36/	4	5	
	House 18/, Do. 8/, Corn 27/	2	13	
	Candles 50/, House 12/, wood 12/	3	14	
15th.	House 15/, Do. 47/4, House 14/	3	16	4
20th.	Butter £4, house 12/	4	12	
	Pd. Mr. Mason in part for furniture	10		
31st.	Pd. balance of my rent[39]	43	13	
	Great Coat for Ben	2	5	
	Expenses at St Johns[40]	2	3	
	Chease 24/	1	4	
		82	7	4

[Receipts]

Jany. 1st.	By my warrants[41] £122 £	122		
	One fee from Mr. Adams ads Allen	2	10	
10th.	One fee from Mr. Stewart injunction ver John Baird & Co	5		
15th.	From Mr. Rootes one fee ads. Radford	3		
18	From Hite v Conn one fee	2	10	

37. See entry under Disbursements, Oct. 26, 1784.

38. Harry was one of JM's slaves, probably purchased in 1784. He does not appear on the 1784 Richmond list of inhabitants with JM's other slaves, but his name is on the Henrico County personal property list taken that year. Henrico County Personal Property, 1784, 20, Va. State Lib.

39. JM was renting a house on Shockoe Hill in Richmond, owned by William Cocke. See entry under Disbursements, Jan. 1784.

40. The festival of St. John the Evangelist was celebrated on Dec. 27 by the Masons in Richmond, usually with a church service followed by a banquet or dance. See subsequent entries around this date each year.

41. It is uncertain what these warrants represent. They are not payment for service in the General Assembly; they may represent the sale of land warrants.

		£	s	d
	From Mr. Nelson for money lent him	15		
	From Mr. Duval for Do.	12	17	9
	From Major Magill in part for a mare[42]	16	17	
24th	Advice fee from Mr. Wilson	1	2	6
25th.	From Mayo v Hundley injunction bill	5		
27th.	From Mr. Peachy v. Skelton	2	10	
29th.	From Mr. Lewes one fee	3		
	Balance of hire for Moses[43]	3	16	
30th.	From Genl. Morgan Throckmorton v Beall	2	14	
		167	17	3
	[Disbursements]	130	1	
	[Balance]	37	16	3

[Disbursements]

		£	s	d
Jany. 1st. & 8 11th.	House 36/, Wood 24/, bedstead 30/	4	10	
	Corn 9/, Corn crib £4, Corn & fodder 10/	4	19	
15	House 4/, Sundries for Polly £8-6-8-½	8	10	[8½]
	sundries for house £1-9-9, for Tom[44] £1-0-3	2	10	
	For myself £5-2-6, Negroes 10/	5	12	[6]
	For Lucy[45] £1-8-3	1	8	3
18.	Corn £3-1-3, Given Polly 6/	3	7	3
	My subscription to Assemblies[46]	4	4	
	To my Brother Tom	2	10	
22d.	Given Eliza for Lucy	4	16	
	For Fodder 32/, Wood 12/, Wine 10/	2	14	

42. Perhaps JM was returning the mare he had purchased from Charles Magill on Oct. 13, 1784.

43. See entry under Receipts, Dec. 19, 1784.

44. JM's son.

45. JM's sister Lucy came to live with him in Richmond at about this time. She stayed until she married John Ambler in 1792.

46. Each winter the men of Richmond organized the Richmond Assemblies, a series of social activities held every other week during the winter months and supported by subscriptions. These were most often dances held at the Eagle Tavern. See JM to William Pierce, Feb. 12, 1783, and Va. Gaz. & Wkly. Adv., Dec. 10, 1785.

		£	s	d
	making a great coat		19	
24th.	Provisions 12/6, wood 12/	1	4	6
25th.	Laid out in purchasing certificates	35	4	10
	Cow £5, Casimir[47] for Polly 11/7½	5	11	7½
26th.	Paid Mr. Mason in the hand of Mr. Hay	12		7½
27th.	Books £4–12, Club 10/6, Gloves 3/6	5	6	
29th.	For Pork	16	12	9
	Annual subscription for Library[48]	1	8	
	Given Polly for a hat 36/	1	16	
31st.	repairing watch 18/, wood 24/	2	2	
	Tea 6/, beef £1–14–8, wine 14/	2	14	8

[Receipts]

		£	s	d
Feby. 1st.	Brought over	37	16	3
	From T. Williams in part	4	18	
	From Mr. Rector[49] v.	2	10	
	From Mr. Taylor v Parker	2	10	
	From Mr. Kennan v Webb balance	1	10	
	Miller ads. Fugate appeal	4	5	
	Glasscock ads. Currie	2	10	
Recd. in	Peyton ads. Fallen	2	14	
Fauquier	From J. Markham[50] v Harrison etc.	1	8	
	Grigsby Wm. ads. Minor Trespass	2	13	4
	Powell v Burwells Exrs.[51]	4	4	
	Harrison v Peyton	2	10	
	Nelson v. Maddox	2	18	
	Morehead ads. Thornberry	2	10	
	McGuire advice fee	1	8	
March 22d.	Anderson Exr. etc. to			

47. Casimire, a plain or twilled woolen cloth, is a variation of cashmere.

48. JM was a regular subscriber to the support of a library in Richmond. See entry under Disbursements, Jan. 14, 1784. The new library opened in the summer of 1785, probably in July. See *Va. Gaz. & Wkly. Adv.*, July 30, 1785.

49. Benjamin or Frederick Rector, both of Fauquier County. See Minute Book, 1781–1784, 300, 339, Fauquier County, Va. State Lib.

50. James Markham. See the petition JM wrote and submitted to the House of Delegates for Markham, Nov. 3, 1787.

51. See JM to Leven Powell, Dec. 9, 1783, and entry under Receipts, Apr. 8, 1786.

	Hundley	2	10
	& Jones ads. Ross	2	11
	From Mr. Wyatt	2	16
	From McMahon v. Grayham	2	10
	From Mr. Dupriest caveat Appleberry v Anthony[52] for Deft.	2	10
24.	From Hartshorne & Co. v	2	10
	Grozart	2	10
25	From T. Smith for William-son v Kings Exrs.	2	10
	From Eggleston v. Chiles etc.[53]	1	8

95	9	7

[*Disbursements*]

Feby. 10th.	Laid out in Books £9-10-6	9	10	6
	Backgammon table	2	8
12th.	repairing the Phaeton	2	8
	wood 12/, spent at Trowers[54] 23/	1	15
	Given Eliza £2-8 for Lucy	2	8
	Paid for caveats for Colo. Marshall	3	
	Ld. Wt. for G.W.[55]		5
	Corn 17/		17
March	Expended in going to &		

52. John Dupriest (b. *ca.* 1759) was a carpenter in Richmond in 1784. "Return of the Inhabitants," 1784, Richmond City Common Hall Records, 337, Va. State Lib. The caveat was related to a contest over the estate of James Anthony. The case, an appeal from a county court to the High Court of Chancery, was entitled Elizabeth and Jane Applebury *et al.* v. James Anthony's executors. The High Court of Chancery decreed in favor of the defendants, JM's clients, on May 24, 1793, and the Court of Appeals affirmed that decree on Oct. 20, 1794. 1 Washington 287–290; Court of Appeals Order Book, III, 5, 7, Va. State Lib.

53. Elizabeth Eggleston v. Thomas and John Chiles and John Sutton, Jr., was a debt action on a 1782 penal bill that JM filed for the plaintiff in the General Court at its Apr. 1785 term. The case was transferred after the reorganization of 1788 to the District Court at Fredericksburg, which had jurisdiction over Caroline County, where the case originated. On Oct. 1, 1789, judgment was entered for the plaintiff. District Court Records, 1789–1792, 29–30, Fredericksburg, Va. State Lib.; see also JM's petition calendared at Apr. 1785.

54. Samuel Trower's (b. *ca.* 1758) tavern in Richmond. W. Asbury Christian, *Richmond: Her Past and Present* (Richmond, 1912), 30; "Return of the Inhabitants," 1784, Richmond City Common Hall Records, 357, Va. State Lib.

55. The amount paid indicates JM was paying the register of the Land Office a fee for issuing the land warrant. No documentary evidence exists that would indicate "G.W." was George Washington.

		£	s	d
	returning from Oak hill[56]	8	14	
	Do. at Winchester	1	10	
	On Servants at Oak hill	1	7	
	Given Polly 7/, laid out 24/	1	11	
	Boot for a horse	15		
22d.	Spoons £6–14, wood 12/	7	6	
	To Colo. Marshall in hands			
	McMahon	2	10	
	Corn 6/, fodder 30/, market 6/	2	2	
23d.	Corn 33/, house 7/, Polly 5/	2	5	
25	Tax on property in			
	Richmond[57]	4	9	
		69	5	6
	[Receipts]	95	9	7
	[Balance]	26	4	1

[Receipts]

		£	s	d
	Brought Over £	26	4	1
March 25	From Mucklehany v Early &			
	Wade	2	4	
	From Arthur ads. Holt 2 suits	5		
27th.	By Moses[58] 40/	2		
29th.	From Mr. Hebburn in West v.			
	Mason etc. eject.	7		
30th.	From Mr. Smith the balance			
	of my fee in Fowler agt.			
	Campbell	2	2	
	From Mr. Noland ads.			
	Edmonds	4	16	
		49	6	1
	[Disbursements]	25	11	11
	[Balance]	23	14	2

56. Oak Hill was the Marshall family home in Fauquier County, which his father transferred to JM on Mar. 16, 1785, just before his final departure for Kentucky. See above, Deed, Mar. 16, 1785.

57. JM purchased lot 480 from Jaquelin Ambler. Title was transferred by a deed dated Mar. 15, 1785, and recorded in Richmond on Mar. 21, 1785. No land tax records for Richmond or Henrico County exist for 1785, and the amount JM entered here suggests tax paid on land. The Henrico County Personal Property records and the Henrico County Tithable Book, both in Va. State Lib., show JM owning different amounts of property during the year. The former registers ownership of 5 tithable and 4 nontithable Negroes and no livestock, while the latter indicates ownership of 2 tithable Negroes, 2 horses, and 12 cattle.

58. JM had hired Moses out. See entry under Receipts, Jan. 29, 1785.

[*Disbursements*]

			£			
March 25	Cloths etc.		£	5	13	3
	Shoes & Stockings			1	15	
	For Lucy 10/6				10	6
	For Polly				17	6
30th.	For butter			1	13	
	Making my cloths etc.			2	10	8
	Paid Tazewell[59] cash lost			12	12	
				25	11	11

[*Receipts*]

	Brought over	23	14	2
Apl. 1st.	From Mr. Bronaugh ads. Whaley	2	16	
2d.	From Mr. Muse ads. Smith	2	14	8
	From Capt. Slaughter in Suttle ads. Dade[60]	2	10	
	From Moffett v Williams	2	10	
3d.	From Colo. Heth[61] 2 suits	5		
	From Mr. Cary 2 suits	5		
	From Mr. Lamb ads. Eppes etc. appeal	4	4	
4th.	From Brent v Masterson	2	8	
	From Gibbs v Richardson 2 suits	5		
6th.	From Lundy ads. Hynes Assignee Peebles	2	10	
	From Rogers in part		6	
	From Galligo ads. Robert	4	4	
7th.	From Ingram v. Ball in part	1	8	
8	From Mrs. Burns a finishd suit	2	10	
9th.	From Oliver v Lewis 2 suits	5		
	From Oliver ads. Lewis chargd on next side			
	From Love Exr. etc. v Page			

59. Henry Tazewell.
60. Philip Slaughter (1758–1849) had served with JM during the Revolution. JM appeared in the Apr. 1785 General Court for the defendant in Langhorne Dade v. Frances Suttle. The case was continued and judgment was finally given against Suttle in the Fredericksburg District Court on Oct. 5, 1789. District Court Records, 1789–1792, 69–70, Fredericksburg, Va. State Lib.
61. William Heth.

	Exr. etc.	2	10	
10th.	From Burks v. Halcomb acct. render	2	16	
11th.	From Mr. J. Peyton ads. Fallen	2	8	
	From Mrs. Peyton Do.	2	8	
	From Colo. Carrington for probate of will[62]	5		
	From Gooch ads. Bib	2	10	
		86	16	10

[*Disbursements*]

Apl. 1st.	Market 40/, Watch 3/, club 3/	2	6	
	Stockings 20/	1		
	wood 12/, to Polly for necessaries 6/8		18	8
7th.	Corn 6/, wood 12/, market 14/	1	12	
8th.	sugar 13/4, coal £2–16–3	3	9	7
10th.	given Ben 6/, taxes for town[63] 2–7	2	13	
		11	9	3
	Paid Stewart for Colo. Simm[64] cash lost last winter	31		
		42	9	3
	[*Receipts*]	86	16	10
	[*Balance*]	44	7	7

[*Receipts*]

	Brought over	44	7	7
Apl. 12th.	From Mr. Piper	2	10	
13	From Triplet ads. Miller	2	16	
14th.	From Maddox v Neale, in full	3	16	
	From Hudson an abated suit	2	8	
	From Throckmorton ads. Moores Exrs.	2	10	

62. Edward Carrington had no doubt asked JM to probate the will of his parents, who died in Feb. 1785 in Cumberland County. See Garland Evans Hopkins, *Colonel Carrington of Cumberland* (Winchester, Va., 1942), 35, 76.

63. Tax records for Richmond and Henrico County in 1785 are incomplete. This amount paid could be either a tax on land or an amount paid for personal property taxes. See note to entry under Disbursements, Mar. 25, 1785.

64. Charles Simms.

	From Wright & Co. v Roche etc. irish debt in chancery by Deane	2	16	
	From Oliver in full	2	8	
15.	From Majr. Marbury in chy. 2 suits	7	4	
	From Kerchival in full	1	8	
16th.	From Burks ads. Johnston[65]	4	4	
	From McDaniel	4	16	
	From Coon ads. Norton	2	12	
17th.	From Conn ads. McCrae & al. appeal	4	16	
	From Harrison ads. McMichen	2	8	
18th.	From T. Williams ads. Carter[66]	4	16	
	From B. Rust ads. Carter	7	4	
19th.	From Bowman (by Hite) v Maderas	2	10	
	From Dennison v Earnest	2	10	
	From Collett v. Banks	2	10	
		110	9	7

[Disbursements]

Apl. 14	At market 12/			12	
15	Corn 12/, wood 12/		1	4	
	market 12/, Do. 4/6			16	6
	To John Jones[67] for currying horse			6	
	mustard 1/3, wine 3/4			4	7
			3	3	1

[Receipts]	110	9	7
[Balance]	107	6	6

65. Richard Burks v. Martha, Peter, Andrew, and Charles Johnston, executors, etc., of Peter Johnston. This case, probably in the General Court in 1785, was moved to the District Court for Prince Edward County after the 1788 reorganization of the courts, was dismissed on Sept. 4, 1792, and was revived before the same court on Apr. 3, 1793. District Court Order Book, 1789–1792, 285, 1793–1799, 17, 57, Prince Edward County, Va. State Lib.

66. See entry under Receipts, Sept. 3, 1784.

67. John Jones (b. *ca.* 1744) was a barber in Richmond. "Return of the Inhabitants," 1784, Richmond City Common Hall Records, 358, Va. State Lib.

	[Receipts]			
Apl. 20th.	Brought over	107	6	6
	From Stewert Hopkins v Littlepage	2	8	
	From Young v Rorock[68] supersedeas	2	10	
	From Mr. Kinnol ads. Roland Estidge slander case	2	16	
22	From Mr. Harwood Judgemt. agt. him	2	1	
	From Capt. Ashby v. Young in full	7	10	
	From Buck v. Mercher	2	10	
	From Johnston v. Monroe[69]	2	10	
24	From Cleveland 2 suits	5		
25	From Payne v. Cabell T A B	2	10	
26	From Kello (for Meacom) v. Kirby supersedeas	2	10	
27	From Hylton & Hunter for conveyance	2	10	
29th.	From Mr. Bland in part for rule for Mandamus[70]	7	4	
		149	5	6
	[Disbursements]	64	18	5
	[Balance]	84	7	1

	[Disbursements]			
Apl. 20th.	Given Eliza 36/	1	16	
	Market 4/6, Given Polly 56/	3		6

68. JM represented the defendant in Michael Rorrock v. Edwin Young. See fee received on May 9, 1787. The case went to the District Court meeting in Winchester after the reorganization of the General Court, and on Apr. 17, 1792, was dismissed for lack of prosecution. Superior Court Order Book, 1789–1793, 286, Frederick County, Va. State Lib.

69. James Monroe v. Benjamin Johnston. The case was probably in a county court at this time, because after being filed in the General Court in Apr. 1788 (JM for the defendant), it was sent to the District Court in Fredericksburg for argument. There judgment was given for Monroe on May 7, 1790. District Court Records, 1789–1792, 210–211, Fredericksburg, Va. State Lib.

70. Mandamus is the name of a writ issued from a court of superior jurisdiction commanding performance of a specific act that the law enjoins as a duty resulting from an office, trust, or station.

24th.	For Corn	20	10	
	For Wine	26	10	
	Market 11/8, kitchn table 4		15	8
	Biscuit 24, Tea 8/, bier 4d.	1	12	4
25	Wood 12/, Market 26/8	1	18	8
	Given Lucy		6	
	China & Glass £4–1–6,			
	Glass 7/	4	8	6
	market 27/7	1	7	7
	Gin 30/	1	10	
	Pamphlets 8/, Dinner 7/,			
	nails 3/, lock 5	1	3	
		64	18	5

[Receipts]

May 1st.	Brought over	84	7	1
	From Cartwright v Morgen			
	finishd	5		
	From Blackwell ads. Blackwell	6	6	
	From Thilmans Exr. in			
	Coleman v Littlepage			
	finished	2	10	
4	From Violett ads. Willis[71]	2	10	
	From Reid ads. Campbell[72]	2	10	
	For one horse sold Colo.			
	Marshall[73]	22	10	
12	From Mr. Deane 3½ Jo[c]s	7	4	
13	From Colo Lynch v Madison	7		
	From Oldham v Wall	2	10	
	From Ward ads. Ward chy.	5		
19th.	From Mr. J Smith v Loury &			
	McPhetters[74]	2	10	

71. Francis Willis, Jr., v. Thomas Violett was continued several times until the District Court at Winchester "discontinued" it on Sept. 3, 1792. Superior Court Order Book, 1789–1793, 212, 354, Frederick County, Va. State Lib.

72. Duncan Campbell v. Thomas Reed was also moved to the District Court in Winchester sometime after 1788, and judgment was given for the plaintiff on Apr. 20, 1790. *Ibid.*, 60–61.

73. See entry under Disbursements, May 1, 1785.

74. John Smith v. John Lowry and John McPheeters was a debt action filed in the General Court in Feb. 1783. JM appeared for Smith, arguing the defendants owed Smith £500 for failure to deliver two male Negroes to Smith in exchange for a wagon and four horses that he had delivered to Lowry and McPheeters. In May 1786 the General Court decided against McPheeters and in Jan. 1787 against Lowry, but the

	£	s	d
From Colo. Peachy[75] admr. of Flood v. Cockes Exrs. & v. John Lawson		4	6
	154	3	1

[Disbursements]

		£	s	d
May 1st.	For Masons poems[76]			9
	Pd. for T. Mason[77]		2	8
	Given Polly		2	16
	Pd. Colo. Marshall in a horse[78]		22	10
	Pd. Register[79] for Colo. Marshall	12	16	3
	Pd. Register for Capt. H. Marshall		3	10
9th.	Expended in going up the Country[80]		4	10
	Repairing the corn crib		1	10
	St. Taminy's[81]		2	
	My club at Formicolas[82]		6	6
14	Market 8/, barber 1/			9
	Shoes 10/, books 17/8	1	7	8
	Market 5/, Do. 7/6, Do. 15/	1	7	6
16	Ball 30/, music 9/, market 5/, tea 3/		2	7
19	Oznabrugs 50/, Linnen for self 5-15-6	8	5	6

case was continued. After the reorganization of the courts, it was sent to the District Court in Staunton, where on Sept. 3, 1789, the defendants failed to appear. A judgment of £500, payable by £159, was finally awarded in May 1792. District Court Order Book, 1789-1793, 36-39, and 1789-1797, 26, Augusta County, Va. State Lib.

75. William Peachy (1729-1802).

76. John Mason, *Spiritual Songs: or Songs of Praise. With Penitential Cries to Almighty God, upon Several Occasions [By Thomas Shepard]: Together with the Song of Songs, which is Solomons*, 18th ed. (Norwich, 1783), printed by John Trumbull.

77. Thomson Mason, who was practicing law in Richmond. See Notice of Richmond Lawyers, Oct. 25, 1784.

78. The spring horse races were to begin in May, although this expenditure could have been unrelated. See also Receipts, May 4, 1785.

79. John Harvie was register of the Land Office.

80. JM had gone to Fauquier County to see his father and his family before their final departure for Kentucky, Thomas Marshall having returned for them. See JM to George Muter, Jan. 7, 1785, Deed, Mar. 16, 1785, and JM to Charles Simms, Mar. 20, 1785, the last written from Falmouth.

81. See Disbursements, ca. May 1784.

82. A tavern owned by Serafino Formicola.

Date	Description	£	s	d
	Gloves for self 3/6, book 5/6		9	
	Blackstones Commintaries[83] 36/	1	16	
20	Market 10/, Books 6; 24th. Market 6/8	1	2	8
24th.	Afternoon Tea 3/, club 4/[84]		7	
25th.	bringing books in stage 25/, market 27/	2	12	
	wood 12, Jockie club[85] 4–4	4	16	
28th.	Market 15/, sugar [&] Tea 24/	1	19	
30th.	Advertizements 28/, market 3/	1	11	
		72	5	1
	[Receipts]	154	3	1
	[Balance]	81	18	0
	By my civil List Warrants[86] £	177	16	
	By my interest £	120		
		297	16	
April 29th.	Recd. for Justinian Cartwright one certificate with an interest warrant amounting to 22–13–10[87] £	22	13	10
	Lent Capt. Markham[88]	27	13	10
	Also £2–8 formerly lent him	2	8	
	Pd. for Pork[89] £	19		

83. Sir William Blackstone, *Commentaries on the Laws of England* (Philadelphia, 1772), printed by Robert Bell. Volume IV of this edition with JM's signature on the title page is in the Swem Library, College of William and Mary. For more information on JM and this book, see Law Notes: Editorial Note, *ca.* June 1780.

84. JM probably attended the meeting of the Virginia Constitutional Society at Anderson's Tavern scheduled for this day. See copy of the Society's Subscription Paper, Apr. 13, 1785.

85. The Jockey Club met before the horse races in May and October to draw ground rules and to raise money for the event. See Disbursements under Oct. 1784 for additional information.

86. This entry and the one after, dated Apr. 29, are on the first page following the May accounts. The bottom half of the page is filled with "Colo. Thomas Marshall" written in a hand other than JM's.

87. Cartwright (1752–1832) was a Revolutionary soldier who moved his family to Kentucky in 1790 but who had lived in Amherst County, Va. He was described as "quite a poor man and not so much a bad as a good-for-nothing kind of man." Susannah Johnson, *Recollections of the Rev. John Johnson* (Nashville, Tenn., 1869), 32.

88. James Markham, of Fauquier County.

89. This entry, ending with "Recd. for myself £50," is on the second page following the May accounts.

				£		
for linnen to H. Hampton				£	9	10
By cash from Treasury					60	12
By Do. from Warrants					19	14
By Do. from Do.					100	
By Do. from Do.					72	
					280	14
By Do.					17	2
					297	16
Recd. for my Father & others on their warrants				£	48	4
Recd. for myself				£	50	

Lent Mr. Randolph[90] the
  property of Colo Marshall

James Alexander	1	11	9
Wm Warwick	5	17	11
repaid me	7	9	8

Land Warrants

Thomas Marshall[91]	1860
Do.	1300
H. M.[92]	800
Do.	560
Do.	100

[Receipts]

			£		
	Brought over		£	81	18
June 1st.	Recd. from Mr. Ryan for convce.[93]			1	8
	From Colo. Grayson[94] in part			60	
6th.	From Mr. Thompson in an appeal Winston & Radford v. Gaines			2	16

90. Edmund Randolph. This entry and the remainder to the beginning of the June accounts are on the third page following the May accounts. The fourth page is filled with Col. Marshall's name, not in JM's hand.

91. JM's brother.

92. Humphrey Marshall, JM's cousin in Kentucky.

93. Conveyance.

94. William Grayson. See JM to Charles Simms, Mar. 20, 1785.

9th.	Hughes v Hughes & al. Chy.[95]	5		
14	From Kebble in part criminal	2	2	
	From Jones[96] criminal	8		
	From McDonal v Musgrave	2	10	
	From Teele Assignee etc. v Whalys Exrs.	2	10	
16	From Shacklet v. Glasscock bond	2	10	
	From Majr. Cock	6	9	7
	From Robinson (advice fee)	1	2	
28th	From Mr. Annesly (advice fee)	2	8	
		176	13	7
	[Disbursements]	182	12	6
	[Balance]	5	18	11

[Disbursements]

June 1st.	To Mr. Lewis[97] in part	150		
3d.	Market		12	
5th.	market 6/, in store 3/		8	
	Strawberries & cherries 3/9,			

95. The outcome of this case, John Hughes, Sr., v. Henry Clayton and wife, Theodosia, administratrix of Anderson Hughes, her late husband, in the High Court of Chancery is unknown, but it was later taken to the District Court at Petersburg, which issued a judgment on Sept. 22, 1789. From there it was appealed to the Court of Appeals, where the decision was confirmed on July 10, 1790. 3 Call 478; Court of Appeals Order Book, II, 24, 25, Va. State Lib.

96. This was no doubt Reubin Jones, who was convicted by the General Court of a felony and sentenced to hang. On July 21, 1785, the Council of State gave him one week's respite from his July 22 execution date. Three days later Jones and 18 others escaped from jail by forcing the door when food was passed in. Jones and 7 others were apprehended within hours and chained to the floor of the jail. Jones was executed on July 29, on schedule. *JVCS*, III, 462; *Va. Gaz. & Wkly. Adv.*, July 30, 1785.

97. It is very likely that JM bought a house from Benjamin Lewis (b. *ca.* 1745) in 1785. Between June 1 and Oct. 11 he paid Lewis £250, and in 1786 he paid an additional sum of slightly more than £195, between Oct. 7 and Dec. 28. When the Dec. 28 payment was made, JM entered "Paid Mr. Lewis in full." JM also made entries for the maintenance of his house, for which he expected no reimbursement such as that he had received from William Cocke in 1783 and 1784. On Dec. 1, 1784, he paid Mr. Anderson for plastering his house, and at the end of Nov. 1785, he paid Anderson a partial payment of £38, possibly for masonry work on the house he had bought. On Apr. 3, 1787, he paid 16s. to have the house whitewashed. The strongest evidence favoring this theory is that JM paid no rent after 1784, except for a charge of £12 10s. paid to William Cocke on Jan. 4, 1787, for rent covering 1786. This was probably the rental for JM's law office. We know his law office was not in the same place it had been when he rented a house from Cocke in 1784, because he paid £12 to have his office moved on Feb. 15, 1786.

	Cowpers reports[98] 10/	13	9
8th	Chicken coal 8/, Ben 3/,		
	raffling 24	1	15
	Market 6/8, Do. 3/, Do. 3/,		
	punch 2/6		17	3
	Docket 28/, fish 24/	2	12
14	Market 10/, fruit 6/, Map 8/	1	4
15	punch 3/, Do. 4/, market 6/		13
16th.	punch 6/, making Breeches		
	etc. 28/	1	14
18th.	House 28/	1	8
	Pd. for Mr. James Key on a		
	patent	1	
	For H. Marshall[99] 5 patents	7	10
	To Colo. Marshall (pd. for		
	Genl. Wilkinson[1])	1	10

It is possible, of course, that JM continued to rent a house from William Cocke or Benjamin Lewis and kept a record of his rental expenses elsewhere. In 1787 and 1788 he was clearly paying some expenses from a different account than that kept here. He never recorded any expense connected with the purchase of land in Fauquier County on Oct. 18, 1787. On May 24, 1788, he paid for the construction of a porch and then deducted the amount at the end of the month rather than including it with his regular expenses. He did the same thing in July, when he bought a lot, and again in Jan. 1790, when he paid Philip Turpin for the lot he had purchased in 1789.

The lack of a deed for Lewis's house is little indication JM did not buy it. The act requiring the recording of deeds for conveyances did not become effective until Jan. 1, 1787 (12 Hening 154), well after JM might have purchased Lewis's house. When he finally recorded the deed to the property he resided on for most of his life, construction had been under way for 10 months; construction began in Oct. 1788, but JM did not record the deed for the property until July 7, 1789. Land tax records for Richmond show no improved land owned by JM through 1788, but land tax records for Henrico County for the 1780s are missing from the Va. State Lib., and many Richmond residents actually resided within the county. (The house JM rented from William Cocke in 1784 was outside the city boundary in Henrico County.) Deed books for Henrico County show JM bought a lot from Jaquelin Ambler in 1785, located in Richmond City, and another lot from Philip Turpin in 1789, also located in the city. No deed exists for the lot JM bought from "Mr. Clay" in July 1788, just as there is no record of a deed between JM and Benjamin Lewis. Deeds could be recorded with the General Court as well as with the county, and if JM did in fact buy property from Lewis and Clay, the deeds were probably recorded with the General Court. Unfortunately all the pre-Civil War records of that tribunal have been destroyed. Because of the loss of these records and of the Henrico County land tax books, as well as the incomplete collection of Richmond City land records, JM's definite property holdings in the 1780s must remain a mystery.

See entries under Disbursements, Oct. 11, 1785, Oct. 7, Nov. 19, Dec. 20, and Dec. 28, 1786.

98. H[enry] Cowper, *Reports of Cases Adjudged in the Court of King's Bench 1774–78* (London, 1783).

99. Humphrey Marshall.

1. James Wilkinson. See JM to Wilkinson, Jan. 5, 1787.

Date	Description	£	s	d
	To Do. (pd for M. Marshall² 2 patents)	1	5	
	To Do. (pd for Wm. Marshall³ one patent)		10	
23d.	Spent going to & returning			10
	from Belleveue⁴	4	4	
	For Blairs lectures⁵	1	10	
24th.	Market 3/, fruit 3/, quills 6/6		12	6
27th	Market 12/, Gilberts evidence⁶ 10/, Foster⁷ 10/	1	12	
28th.	Market 12/, wood 10/	1	2	
		182	12	6

[Receipts]

Date	Description	£	s	d
July 4th.	Recd. from Mr. Masterson	3	16	
5th.	From Parsons fees taxd ads. Johnstons Exrs.	5		
7th.	From Mattart ads Clark case	2	5	
11th.	From Mr. Briggs v Capt Gray 50/	2	10	
12th.	From Mr. Booker £1–8 advice	1	8	
16	From Mr. Harrison v Byrd 50/	2	10	
20th.	From Capt. Chilton ads. Thornberry	2	10	
21st.	From Dyer v Haden (a finishd suit)	2	10	
		22	9	
[Disbursements]		82	8	1¾
[Balance]		59	19	1¾

2. Markham Marshall (b. *ca.* 1736), JM's uncle, who moved to Kentucky in 1779 and began surveying lands.

3. This could be either JM's brother William (1767–1815) or his uncle, the Rev. William Marshall (1735–1809), who moved to Kentucky in 1780 and died with a sizable landed estate. It is most likely his brother, the twin who later had a successful practice at the Richmond bar.

4. Bellevue, the former home of Thomas Ludwell Lee (1730–1778), was in Stafford County near Fredericksburg. JM had gone there to bring his sister-in-law, Eliza Ambler Brent, home to Richmond following the death of her husband, William Brent. Eliza Ambler Brent to Mildred Smith, July 18, 1785, Ambler-Carrington Letters, Collection of Mrs. John L. Lewis, Colonial Williamsburg Foundation, Williamsburg, Va.

5. Hugh Blair, *Lectures on Rhetoric and Belles Lettres* (Philadelphia, 1784), printed by Robert Aitken.

6. Sir Geoffrey Gilbert, *The Law of Evidence* (Dublin, 1754). JM's signed copy is in the Swem Library, College of William and Mary.

7. Sir Michael Foster, *A Report of some Proceedings on the Commission of Oyer and terminer and goal delivery for the Trial of the Rebels in the year 1746 in the County of Surry and other Crown Cases* (Oxford, 1762; 2d ed., 1776; Dublin, 1763, 1767).

Sold my horse for £35

[*Disbursements*]

		£	s	d
July 4th.	balance agt. me	5	18	11
	Market 6/		6	
	Military certificates pd. for self £13–10–2 at 4 for one £3–7–7, Interest for 3 years £2–8–9½	5	16	4½
Pd. com-missioners	Pd. for Colo. Marshall £57 at 4 for one £14–5, Interest for three years £10–5–2¼	24	10	2¼
	Pd. for H. Marshall £41–19 @ 4 for one £10–9–9, Interest for 3 years 7–11	18	0	9
5.	Club 6/, Making coat etc. 20/	1	6	
6	Market 9/, do. 5/, do. 10/	1	4	
12th.	21/8, given Eliza £2–8	3	9	8
	wood 10/, fruit 3/, chickens 2/		15	
17th	market 6/, Do. 2/3, Map 4/6, ink 3/, boots 60/	3	18	9
19th	Market 3/3, Do. 14/, fruit 4/	1	1	3
22d.	Wood 10/, pd. for buttons 2/6, market 9/6	1	2	
24	Market 18/, do. 4/6, Do. 6/9	1	9	3
25	For my Brother Wm. to T. & R. Young	12	10	
	To Colo Marshall assignmets		7	6
26	To fruit 1/6; July 31st. Market 10/		10	6
	P. Mr. Lewis[8] £35	82	8	1¾

[*Receipts*]

		£	s	d
Augt. 1st	From Mann v Caperton[9] caveat —in part (to receive £10 on recovering)	1	8	
5th.	From Mr. Cuth. Harrison[10] v Wheelock Same v. Beaty—no tax recd.	5		

8. See entry under Disbursements, June 1, 1785.

9. Adam Mann v. Hugh Caperton and Paul Lang, Land Office Caveats, Aug. 1, 1785, 212–213, Va. State Lib.

10. Cuthbert Harrison (1749–1824) was a merchant in Fauquier County.

9th.	Sir Jonn. Becquith[11] ads. Settle Slander		4	16	
16.	From Mr. Richardson Ejectmt.		5		
	From Mr. D'orr by Bernard Markham[12] for Colo Marshall		11		3¼
	From Mr. Bernard Markham for Colo. Marshall		6	12	
	From Bernard Markham for Colo. Marshall		8	8	1½
18	From Robins in part agt. Martin & Hale		1	8	
22d.	From Mr. Harrison v Byrd T A B & F.J.[13]		2	10	
	From Majr. Young for Colo. Marshall		35	16	2
			81	18	6¾

[Disbursements]

Augt. 1st.	balance agt. me	£	59	19	1¾
	Market 3/, Do. 1/, Do. 4/, Soap 4/			12	
	Pd. for Lucy entering into dancing school		2	2	
	Pd. for Linnen for Eliza		4	6	2
2d.	Wood 10/, pail 1/6, Market 1/6			13	
	Book case £6–12, Window shutter 10/		7	2	
4th.	St. Johns[14] £1–16, Market 5/		2	1	
6th.	Pd. for a barbacue in town 20/9		1		9
	Market 3/, Oil 20/, buttons 3/		1	6	
13.	Pd. for barbacue at Prossers[15]		1	12	8

11. Sir Jonnathan Becquith (1720–1796), of Richmond County, Va.

12. Markham (1737–1802) lived in Chesterfield County, Va., and was appointed sheriff in 1786. *JVCS*, III, 549.

13. Trespass, assault and battery, and "false judgment"(?).

14. JM was late entering (and perhaps paying) his expenses for celebrating the anniversary of St. John the Baptist on June 24. The Masons had a morning parade that ended with a church service and an evening dinner at Formicola's tavern. *Va. Gaz. & Wkly. Adv.*, June 25, 1785.

15. Thomas Prosser (d. 1798), a former sheriff of Henrico County, had been appointed in 1784 one of a committee to solicit subscriptions for constructing public

	market 7/6, Do. 1/3, Do 1/6		10	3
14	Peaches 1/6, to Moses for shirts 6/		7	6
	market 9/, wood 10/, Tea 14/, books 1/3	1	14	3
17	market 6/, Do. 9/, Do. 11/	1	6	
23d.	market 21/, Do. 7/6	1	8	6
24th.	Pd. Colo. Anderson[16] for surveying etc. Military lands £7–17–3, Pd. Register[17] for £1–16–3	9	13	6
29th.	Wood 12/, Toys for Tom[18] 3/		15	
30th	pd. into Registers office for tax on patents for Colo. Marshall	94	15	
	Market 12/		12	
		191	15	5¾
	[Receipts]	81	18	6¾
	[Balance]	109	16	11

[Receipts]

Septr. 1st.	From Mr. Ruxel v Colo. Syme 2 guineas	2	16	
3d.	From the Assignees of Torris & Wante Chy.	7		
5th.	From Latham ads. Camp[19] (finishd)	2	10	
	a Warrant from Treasury	1	17	6
6	From Price ads Smith[20] (finishd)	2	10	

buildings in Richmond. Christian, *Richmond*, 23.

16. Richard C. Anderson.

17. John Harvie.

18. JM's son.

19. JM took this case, Thomas Latham v. Richard Gaines, John McBargon, and John Camp, from Edmund Randolph, who had filed it in the General Court in Apr. 1783. Latham had charged the defendants with assault in the Culpeper County Court. JM represented Latham while the case was continued on the docket, at least until this fee was paid. Judgment was not given until Oct. 8, 1789, when the District Court in Fredericksburg awarded £100 damages, far short of the £5,000 originally asked. District Court Records, 1789–1792, 112–116, Fredericksburg, Va. State Lib.

20. After this case, Guy Smith v. Bourne Price, was transferred from the General Court to the District Court at New London, it was discontinued by Smith on Sept. 24, 1790. District Court Order Book, I, 1789–1793, 129, Franklin County, Va. State Lib.

		£	s	d
7th.	From Colo. Meade in chy.	7		
	From Mr. Blackwood (advice)	1	8	
	From Wilson ads. Shore & McConico[21] appeal	2	10	
	From Booker for Robertson v Ogleby Ejectmt.	5		
12	From Mr. Taylor v Edmondson	2	10	
	From Mr. Kenner ads. Roane	2	10	
	Recd. for on[e] Hoxhead Tobacco	11	18	3
26	From Ege v Allen 50/	2	10	
	From Lewes v Banks 50/ H. corpus	2	10	
29.	From Sir Peyton Skipwith[22]	6	4	
	From Capt. Douglass[23]	4	4	
30th	From Mr. Harrison for three suits in chy for Randolphs Exrs.	15		
	From Mr. Payne v Hylton	2	10	
		82	7	9

[Disbursements]

		£	s	d
Septr. 1st.	Balance agt. me	109	16	11
6th.	Pd. Mr. Nelson[24] for a saddle	5	10	
	settled with Mr. Deane[25] to this date	10		5
	Fruit 2/, Physic 1/3, fruit 3/		6	3
7th	Market 14/9, Quire of declns.[26] 5/		19	9
8	Shoes for Tom[27] 3/9, blank book 5/, morter 19/	1	7	9

21. Shore & McConnico was a mercantile firm in Petersburg, Va.

22. Skipwith (ca. 1737–1805) lived at Prestwould, his home in Mecklenburg County, Va.

23. Hugh Douglass (ca. 1760–1815), of Loudoun County. See Declaration calendared at Mar. 30, 1786.

24. Alexander Nelson (b. ca. 1752) was a merchant in Richmond. "Return of the Inhabitants," 1784, Richmond City Common Hall Records, 358, Va. State Lib.

25. James and Thomas Deane were merchants in Richmond. "List of Merchants," Richmond City Hustings Court Order Book, II, 50, Va. State Lib.

26. A quire of declarations was a small pamphlet or bundle of several pages containing printed declarations for law office use.

27. JM's son.

9	Market 7/4; 13th Do. 4/, bason 1/6		17	10
13	pd. Masons hall subscription[28] for	10		
15	Sugar 8/, Wood 9/, chickens 8/9	1	05	9
1[7]	Sundries 3/9, Market 17/, bacon £3–6–8	4	7	5
20	Market 3/, Bacon 18/6	1	1	6
26th.	Spoons £6–16	6	16	
	Given Eliza £43–6–8	43	6	8
28th.	Hay £12, books £1–6	13	6	
	Paid the Physicians for Tom[29]	4	16	
29	Sundries for self £4–10	4	10	
	Wood 10/, Market 8/		18	
30th.	Shoes for self 9/6, money scales 6/		15	6
	Hat for Ben 6/		6	
		216		9
	[Receipts]	82	7	9
	[Balance]	133	13	

[Receipts]

October 1st.	Recd. from Capt. Craine ads. Ball	2	8	
	From Mr. Coats chd. with passing forged note	12		
	From Peachums—Murder	8	8	
	From Doctor Turpin[30]	5	12	
	From Miller & al. ads. Miller & al. Chy.	5		

28. The Free Masons of Richmond were about to construct a meeting hall, the money being raised by subscriptions such as this one, as well as by a lottery authorized by the General Assembly. The cornerstone was laid Oct. 29, 1785, and the building was completed by June 1786. Christian, *Richmond*, 28; 12 Hening 229; *Va. Gaz. or Am. Adv.*, June 28, 1786.

29. JM's son.

30. Philip Turpin (*ca.* 1743–1828) later sold JM the property in Richmond on which the John Marshall House still stands. Turpin's loyalty during the Revolution was in question after the war. His status was prisoner of war on parole until Dec. 1783, when the General Assembly removed the stigma and permitted him full citizenship. *Madison Papers*, VII, 233; Henrico County Deed Book, July 7, 1789, III, 74–75, Va. State Lib.

Date		£	s	d
	From Miller ads. Anderson	2	10	
3	From Hansons ads. Sutton in part of 3 suits	4	16	
	From Jones ads. Ward Tres.	2	10	
4	From Mr. Dormont v. Quintana	5		
	From Adams ads. Common-wealth	2	10	
	From Edmundson ads. Mitchel	2		
	From Simonds ads. Pertil	2	11	
	From Leitch v. Thomas[31]	2	10	
5	From Burton[32] in part (for horse stealing)	5	12	
	From Coats the balance for passing f. T.)	2		
	From Mr. Atkinson ads. Shore & Co.[33]	2	16	
	From Mr. Dickinson in part advice fee		13	4
7	From Irby v Redford 2 Suits)	5		
8.	From Mr. Bland for Mandamus[34]	11	8	
	From Mr. Pierce 50/ in Do.	2	10	
9th.	From Ball ads. Tabb in part	1	10	
		89	4	4

[*Disbursements*]

Date		£	s	d
	Balance against me	133	13	
October 1st.	Spent at Rose's, 3/, Market 6/, Do. 7½		9	7½
3	Taylor for making Breeches		10	

31. JM filed a petition in the General Court in Oct. 1785 for the plaintiff in Benjamin Leitch, assignee of Charles Holloway, v. James Thomas. The case was continued through 1788, then transferred to the District Court in Fredericksburg, where one penny damages were awarded on Oct. 5, 1789. District Court Records, 1789–1792, 47–49, Fredericksburg, Va. State Lib.

32. John Burton had a long history of incarceration and escape from jail. While being brought to the public jail in Richmond in Sept. 1784, he escaped from the custody of the sheriff of Chesterfield County. A reward of £40 was offered by the state at that time. He was not captured until June 1785. On July 24, he escaped from the public jail with 18 others (see entry under Receipts, June 14, 1785) but was almost immediately apprehended and chained to the floor of the jail. It seems he escaped again, sometime in Nov. 1785. *JVCS*, III, 377, 453, 487n; *Va. Gaz. & Wkly. Adv.*, July 30, 1785.

33. Shore & McConnico was a mercantile firm in Petersburg, Va.

34. See entry under Receipts, Apr. 29, 1785.

	Market 28/, butter 45/, Flower 47/	6		
	Barber 3/6, Given Polly for house 18/	1	1	6
5th.	Market 10/3, Do. 10/, Laws[35] 36/	2	16	3
7.	Wood 9/, Market 6/8, Tea 12/	1	7	8
8th.	Market 24/, Chese 19/6	2	3	6
	Kaims principles of equity[36]	1	4	
	Fruit 6/, Potatoes 2/		8	
		149	13	6½
	[Receipts]	89	4	4
	[Balance]	60	9	2½

[Receipts]

October				
10th.	From Coffer ads. Baugns	3		
	From Young v. Allen[37]	2	8	
	From Hudson	1	10	
12	From Mr. Pierce appl. Cheek v Pierce	2	10	
	From Holliday v Jones	2	10	
	From Reid & al v Machir Sups.	2	10	
13	From Mr. Darnal in an Ejectmt.	3	2	
	From Mr. Jones v Mattox[38]	2	10	

35. Two sets of Virginia laws were published in 1785, and the amount JM paid suggests he bought the longer set, *A Collection of all such public acts of the general assembly, and ordinances of the conventions of Virginia, passed since the year 1768, as are now in force; with a table of the principal matters. Published under inspection of the judges of the high court of chancery, by a resolution of general assembly, the 16th day of June, 1783* (Richmond, 1785), printed by Thomas Nicolson and William Prentis. This is generally known as the Chancellors' Revisal. The other published set of laws was *Acts passed at a general assembly of the commonwealth of Virginia, Begun and held at the public buildings in the city of Richmond, on Monday the seventeenth day of October, in the year of our Lord, one thousand seven hundred and eighty-five* (Richmond, 1785), printed by John Dunlap and James Hayes. Earl G. Swem, "A Bibliography of Virginia, Part II, Containing the Titles of the Printed Official Documents of the Commonwealth, 1776–1916," Virginia State Library, *Bulletin*, X (1917), 40–41.

36. Henry Home, Lord Kames, *Principles of Equity* (London and Edinburgh, 1760; 2d ed., 1767; 2 vols., 1778).

37. Edwin Young v. John Allen was dismissed on Apr. 20, 1790, after being transferred to the District Court in Winchester. Superior Court Order Book, 1789–1793, 61, Frederick County, Va. State Lib.

38. William Jones v. Thomas Maddox was an old case from Fauquier County Court.

	From Whitly in part for defence in Ejectmt.	2	10	
14	From Winn & al ads. Tisdale T.A.B.	2		
	From Mr. Jones balance finished appeal	1	10	
15	From Mr. Miller in part of finishd suits	7		
	From Harrison Habeas corpus	2	10	
	From Thorogood in part v Scarboro	5		
	From Harle	1	8	
17	From Nelson v Butler	2	10	
	From Martin (one of Fallens suits)	2	10	
18	From Edmondson T.A B. finishd	[ ]	16	
20	From Bryan v Noble four suits	[ ]		
22	From Funk 2 advice fees	2	16	
26	From Mr. Dixon motion	7		
27	From Mr. Rust	2	8	
		71	16	

[*Disbursements*]

	balance against me	60	9	2
[October]				
10th.	barber 1/, Spent 1/3, bread 1/3		3	6
11th.	Pd. Mr. Lewis³⁹	65		
	Market 25/6, Do. 30/	2	15	6
15.	Market 8/6, for Episcopal meeting⁴⁰ 8/4		16	10
1[7]	Market 10/, Coal £5-15	6	5	

JM won a judgment for Jones on Apr. 26, 1785. Minute Book, 1784–1786, 125, Fauquier County, Va. State Lib.

39. Probably Benjamin Lewis. See entry under Disbursements, June 1, 1785.

40. The Episcopal church in Virginia held its annual diocesan convention in May 1785 in the midst of a controversy that lasted several years. Delegates to that meeting were the same men who had been involved in the political life of Virginia, and they were determined to make the church as democratic as the state. The General Convention of the church, meeting in Philadelphia in Sept. 1785, took a dim view of Virginia's activities, and it is possible the Oct. meeting JM attended was held to consider the action of the General Convention. The best account of the church in Virginia during this period is George MacLaren Brydon, *Virginia's Mother Church and the Political Conditions Under Which It Grew*, II (Philadelphia, 1952), 456–461.

18	Butter 58–6, Market 6/	3	4	6
22	Wood 9/, Market 7/		16	
26	Market 18/, at Rose's 6/	1	4	
	Books £6–12	6	12	
	Market for past £3–5	3	5	
		150	10	10
	[*Receipts*]	71	16	
	[*Balance*]	78	6	10

28	To Mr. Miller for one hindquarter of beef 13/6, Do. 21/3	1	14	9
	2 chafing dishes		16	
	Spirit of laws [41]		12	
	[ ]athers	5	3	
	[*Balance*]	86	12	7

[*Receipts*]

Novr. 1st.	From Majr. Gill in T.A.B. ads. McNab	4	16	
2	From Mr. French v. Jenkins	2	10	
5	From Mr. Brown v Beale injunctn.	6	4	
10th.	For a finishd supersedeas	3	8	
15th.	Penny v Burton injn.	5		
17th.	Edmunds ads. Maddox [42]	2	16	
	Adam Banks & Scott Exrs. v. Overton	2	2	
29th.	Recd. from Colo. Monroe [43] for Humphry Marshall	27	16	
	Recd. from Do. for Colo. Marshall	4	16	
	Two interest warrants for Colo. Marshall	5	10	

41. Charles Louis de Secondat, Baron de Montesquieu, *The Spirit of the Laws* (Dublin, 1751).

42. Maddox v. Edmonds was an old case from Fauquier County, finally discontinued on Apr. 26, 1785. Minute Book, 1784–1786, 120, Fauquier County, Va. State Lib.

43. James Monroe.

	From Colo. Henry Lee for Colo. Marshall balance of former order[44]	5	18	6
		70	16	6

[*Disbursements*]

Novr. 1st.	Balance agt. me	86	12	7
	Stays for Polly	3		
2	Subscription to a ball[45] 18/.		18	
	Spent 3/, [ ]ps 12/		15	
6	Market 9/, Do. 6, Do. 6/, Do. 3/	1	4	
9	Market 6/, Barber 2/, Hack 1/6		9	6
10	Market 18/3, do. 6/, do. 9/.	1	13	3
15	Market 9/, Wood 10/		19	
20th.	Market 9/, Do., 18/	1	7	
23	Market 50/, chrystal in watch 3/	2	13	
29th.	Market 6/8, Apples 20/	1	6	8
	Trunk lock 1/3		1	3
	Paid my subscription to Powtomac river company[46]	30		
		130	19	3
	Pd. Mr. Anderson in part[47]	38		
		168	19	3
	[*Receipts*]	70	16	6
	[*Balance*]	98	2	7

[*Receipts*]

Decr. 1st.	From Mr. Saunders ads.	2	10	
4th.	From Mr. Barret ads. Floyd injunction[48]	5	4	

44. See entry under Receipts, July [3], 1784.
45. This was the ball held in conjunction with the fall horse races.
46. The Potomac River Company was chartered by the General Assembly at its Oct. 1784 session. The act sought to improve the navigation of the river by clearing the falls. *JVHD*, Oct. 1784, 110; 11 Hening 510–525; *JVCS*, III, 400; JM to George Muter, Jan. 7, 1785.
47. Henry Anderson was a Richmond brick mason.
48. David Barrett v. Berry Floyd, Archibald Garrison, John Floyd, and John

13th.	From Beale ads. Jones Exrs.	2	11	
	From Mr. Pendleton	2	8	
	From Robertson ads. Robertson[49] appeal from Halifax on will	2	8	
20th.	From Wren v Mallory debt	2	10	
	From George ads. Payne[50]	2		
	From Dabney v Hawkins[51] covt.	2	14	
	From Stannard v Buckner in Chy.	5	12	
	From Angus for exr. Groves	7		

[*Disbursements*]

Decr. 3d.	Balance against me	98	2	7
	For making suit of cloaths 40/	2		
	market 1/3, brush 2/, paper 18/	1	1	3
	To entering two caveats agt. Tibbs etc. & one agst. Henry Lee[52]		15	
5th.	Ducks 29/4–1/2, oranges 1/	1	10	4½
	To a papent for Genl Wilkinson[53] to be chargd to Colo. Marshall	1	10	
	To a patent for H. Marshall		5	
10th.	Wood 12/, ribband 1/3, Market 6/		19	3
18	Market 12/, Pork £21–8	22		
	Flour £4–4/, Market 16	5		
22	Tea £3–11, Sugar 12/8,			

Widgeon was an appeal from the High Court of Chancery. JM appeared for the appellant. See 3 Call 531–537 (1790).

49. JM's argument on Robertson's will before the General Court is printed at Oct. 1786.

50. Aminidab Seekright, lessee of Merryman Payne, v. Francis George was transferred to the District Court at Northumberland. It was an ejectment action, with JM appearing in the General Court for George. Judgment was given for the plaintiff on Apr. 10, 1790, with one penny damages awarded. District Court Order Book, 1789–1792, 72, Northumberland County, Va. State Lib.

51. JM's receipt for this fee is printed at Dec. 21, 1785.

52. The two caveats entered against John Tibbs were John Marshall v. Henry Autcher and John Tibbs (where JM is listed as John Marshall, Jr.). Land Office Caveats, Nov. 25, 1785, 247, Va. State Lib. The caveat entered against Henry Lee was in the name of Thomas Marshall. *Ibid.*, 248.

53. James Wilkinson.

	purse 6/, cask 16/8	5	6	4
23d.	Wood 12/, Market 12/	1	4	
	Pd. for Lucy dancing	5	2	
	Subscription to Richmond			
	assem.[54]	3		

[Receipts]

[ca. December][55]	Receivd for Broadhead on interest warrants	85	3	4
	Recd. for Do. on Military fund Do.	727	17	10
	Recd. for Do. on Military Do.	80	16	
	Recd. for Do. on Do.	45		
	Recd. for Do. on interest Do.	14	11	
	Recd. for Do. on Military fund Do.	100		
	Recd. for Do. on interest Do.	27	10	10
	Recd. on Military Do.	130		
		1210	19	
[Disbursements]		1037	15	8
	Cash to be pd.	173	3	4
	Warrants to be pd.	192	10	4
		19	7	

[Disbursements]

[ca. December]	Remitted for Broadhead to Philadelphia £	500		
	By a bill in favor of Messieurs Williams & Rochester & Co.	82	7	6
	By a bill in favor of John Belli & Co.	39	12	0
	By a bill in favor of Wm. Vanleer	8	10	
	R.C. Anderson[56]	27		

---

54. See entry under Disbursements, Jan. 18, 1785. This year the men of Richmond organized the Richmond Assembly on Dec. 12 at Gilbert's Coffee House. *Va. Gaz. & Wkly. Adv.*, Dec. 10, 1785.

55. This page follows two blank pages, the bottom half of which is filled with figures with no apparent significance.

56. Richard C. Anderson.

	Willis Green[57]	88		
	Phillip Barbour[58]	18	11	9
	Harry Innis[59]	65		
	Gilbert Imlay[60]	30		
	Wm. Leas	29	12	10
	Capt. Morrison	19	1	7
	John Moylan	80		
	John Moylan	50		
		1037	15	8
		127	5	2
		910	10	6
	warrants sold	1011	11	7
		101	3	1¾
		910	8	6¼
	James Alder	89	8	
	Aylet Lee	50		
		1049	18	6

Jany. 1st. 1786	Recd. for Colo. Marshall Interest warrants	£	107	4	11
	For self		130	11	6
	From Capt. McClanahan for Colo. Marshall		50		
	I have recd. from Colo. Monroe[61] for H Marshall		32	14	
	I have paid for H. Marshall		29	3	3
			3	10	9
	I have recd. from Monroe		8	13	1
	I have paid to H. Marshall for him.		5	14	
			2	19	1 [62]

[Receipts]

Feby. 1st.	Recd. from Mr. Cavans in part of fees for four suits	5	10	4

57. Green (1752–1813) was clerk of the Lincoln County Court and a surveyor for locating land warrants. He attended the convention that wrote the Kentucky constitution in 1792.

58. Barbour (*ca.* 1750–1790) lived in Orange County, Va.

59. Harry Innis was attorney general of Kentucky. See JM to George Muter, Jan. 7, 1785.

60. See JM to Arthur Lee, Mar. 5, 1787.

61. James Monroe.

62. This page is followed by a page of figures that seem to be related to the figures

4th.	From Singleton v Singletons Exrs. Chy.	3	16	
	From Hubbard & al v same	2	8	
	From Nester & North v Kearns in part for two suits	2	8	
	From H. Banks[63] for fees	14		
	From Wilson v Claiborne[64]	2	10	
15	From Trozvint v. Southall (finishd)	3		
16	From Mr. Bisset[65]	2	10	
	From Gratz in a caveat Gibson v Benlys admr.	2	16	
	From Do. for drawing a deed	1	8	
18th.	From Scot ads. Brickhouse[66] appeal	2	10	
24th.	From Mr. Ronald for advice	1		
		43	16	4
	[Disbursements]	37	17	5
	[Balance]	5	18	11

[Disbursements]

Feby. 1st.
 to 6th. | Market 30/, plays[67] 36/,

on the third preceding page. They appear to have been entered after the accounts were listed.

63. Henry Banks (1761–1836) was a Richmond merchant. Joseph I. Sherlin, "Henry Banks: A Contemporary Napoleonic Apologist in the Old Dominion," *VMHB*, LVIII (1950), 335–345.

64. JM probably meant Willis v. Claiborne. He was defending Claiborne in Francis Willis, Jr., v. William Dandridge Claiborne, assignee of Fendall Southerland, before the General Court. The case was transferred to the District Court at Williamsburg sometime after 1788. JM's client won there, but Willis appealed to the Court of Appeals. The case was dropped on Apr. 14, 1792. Court of Appeals Order Book, II, 156, Va. State Lib.

65. James Bisset (b. *ca.* 1759) was a ropemaker and later a merchant in Richmond. "Return of the Inhabitants," 1784, Richmond City Common Hall Records, 333; "List of Merchants," Richmond City Hustings Court Order Book, II, 50, both in Va. State Lib.

66. Michael Dunton and Sarah, his wife, administrator and administratrix of Mary Scott, v. Major and John Brickhouse and John Kendall, Sr. This was a debt action in which JM appeared for the plaintiffs. After 1788 the case was transferred to the District Court in Accomack and Northampton, where an office judgment was set aside on Oct. 18, 1793. The case was not ended, however, until May 19, 1794, when judgment was confessed. District Court Order Book, 1789–1797, 285, 336, Accomack County, Va. State Lib.

67. There is no evidence of a theater company performing in Richmond at this time. This entry suggests the existence of a company hitherto unknown.

		£	s	d
	Wood 12/	3	18	
	barber 2/, Market 25/, flour 41/3	3	8	3
14th.	Market 6/, plates 5/, spit 2/		13	
15	For moving my office £12	12		
17th.	Market 3/, Buckles 24/5, for Polly 32/	2	19	5
	Wood 12/, Market 13/6	1	5	6
	To cloths for myself	1	10	
20	Market 6/, Do. 6/, Straw 10/	1	2	
24th.	Market 48/, Wood 12/	3		
	Paid for Mr. Colsten to Colo. Anderson for survey in name of J.F. Mercer[68]	2	14	3
24th.	Coal £5, Salt & salt petre 6/	5	6	
		37	17	5

[Receipts]

		£	s	d
March 2d.	Brought over	5	18	11
	From George ads. Payne Eject. balance of my fee (deft. lives in lancaster[69])	3		
3d.	Advice fee from Mr. Booker on a Will	1	7	
4th.	From Brodhead in three suits	14	13	
6	From Laurance v Johnston injn.	5	18	
8th.	From Young v Nevill (finishd)	2	10	
12	From Macon v Dandridge	2	16	
14th.	From Pollard v Gaines[70]	2	10	
16th.	From Mr. Brent	11	4	
17	From Short v. Jones	2	10	
18	From [ ] Samson ads. Waid	2	14	
20	From Clem. Biddle & Co. in chy.	20		

68. Rawleigh Colston to Richard C. Anderson in name of John Francis Mercer.

69. See entry under Receipts, Dec. 20, 1785. Lancaster County, Va., lies at the tip of the peninsula north of the Rappahannock River, on the Chesapeake Bay.

70. Robert Pollard v. Richard Gaines. JM filed a petition for Pollard to appeal this debt case from Culpeper County to the General Court in Oct. 1785. The case was continued through 1788 and was then transferred to the District Court in Fredericksburg. On Oct. 5, 1789, judgment was given for Pollard. District Court Records, 1789–1792, 54–55, Fredericksburg, Va. State Lib.

		£	s	d
	From Sampson ads. Payne Eject.[71]	5		
24th.	From Marshall ads. Shore & Co.	2	10	
	From Marshall ads. Chew Exrs. etc.	2	10	
30th.	From Holmes ads. Willis— det.[72]	2	10	
31st.	From Williamson ads. Rutherford Eject.	2	8	
	From Henderson ads. Johnston[73]	2	8	
	From Brown ads. Johnston	2	8	
	From Massie ads. Chiles	2	11	
		97	5	11
	[Disbursements]	51	17	7¾
	[Balance]	[45	8	3¼][74]

[Disbursements]

		£	s	d
March 1	Market 6/, Polly 4/, wheel-barrow 12/	1	2	
3	For assignment from Young & Arnold chargeable to H. Marshall		2	6
5th.	Market 6/6, Wood 12		18	6
7th.	To Mr. Deane[75] for my Brother Wm. to be charged Colo. Marshall	6	18	11½
	To Mr. Deane for sundries	10	19	10¾
12th.	Market 20/, Do. 3/	1	3	

71. Agatha Payne v. Stephen Sampson was an ejectment action that was won by the plaintiff on Apr. 16, 1786. 2 Washington 155–156; District Court Order Book, I, 1789–1793, 253, 308, II, 1794–1796, 192, Franklin County, Va. State Lib.; Court of Appeals Order Book, III, 78, 88–89, Va. State Lib.

72. Francis Willis, Jr., v. Joseph Holmes, detinue. This case in detinue was continued until, after being transferred to the District Court at Winchester, it was discontinued on Sept. 3, 1792. Superior Court Order Book, 1789–1793, 354, Frederick County, Va. State Lib.

73. Henderson, Ferguson, and Gibson, merchants, v. Benjamin Johnston. Litigation in this debt action did not commence until Sept. and Oct. 1790 in the District Court at Fredericksburg. Judgment was given for the plaintiffs on May 7, 1792. District Court Records, 1789–1792, 705–707, Fredericksburg, Va. State Lib.

74. JM's total is partially obscured at the bottom of the page.

75. James and Thomas Deane were merchants in Richmond. "List of Merchants," Richmond City Hustings Court Order Book, II, 50, Va. State Lib.

		£	s	d
14th.	Wood 12/, sundries £1–18	2	10	
16	Coal 35/4	1	15	4
18	making suit of cloaths	1	10	
	Market 5/4, rope 1/3		6	7
20	Market 6/, Do. 3/, Wood 12/	1	1	
23d.	Shoes 9/, market 3/, club 3/		15	
25th.	Market 6/, Do. 6/, Hat £3	3	12	
	one piece of linnen for Polly	5	7	5
27th.	market 2/6, do. 9/, postage 9/	1	00	6
	a piece of linnen for self	6	7	
29th.	market 1/, Garden pails 44/	2	5	
	Oil & brush 34/6, [tarp] 1/,			
	paint 24/, books 24/	4	3	6
		51	17	7¾

[Receipts]

		£	s	d
	Brought over	45	9	5¼
April 1st	From Conway v Bullett	2	16	
	From Rattle ads. Anderson etc.	4	4	
	From Beale Exr. of Hite ads. Walker Exr.[76]	2	10	
	From West ads. Ashton[77]	2	16	
	From Johnston v Dade	2	10	
	From Scott ads. Wilson	2	16	
3d.	From Pope ads. Pope appl. in chy.	4	10	
	From Overstreet v Randolph[78] in part injn.	2	16	
	From Mason v Tabb	2	10	
	From Hooe v Becquith[79] Chy.	8	8	

76. Lewis Walker, executor of Jolliffe, v. Tavenor Beale, executor of John Hite, was a debt action in which JM appeared for the defendant. On Apr. 20, 1790, the District Court in Winchester awarded judgment to the plaintiff. Superior Court Order Book, 1789–1793, 63, Frederick County, Va. State Lib.

77. See JM's argument in Ashton v. West, printed at Oct. 13, 1786.

78. An opinion in John Holcomb Overstreet v. Richard Randolph and David Meade Randolph, executors of Richard Randolph, and William Griffin, was given by Chancellor George Wythe in Aug. 1789. Wythe 47.

79. Sarah Hooe, who survived her husband, Gerrard Hooe, and John Alexander and Elizabeth, his wife, v. Mary Kelsick, who survived her husband, Younger Kelsick, and Jonathan Beckwith, who survived his wife, Rebecca, was heard in the High Court of Chancery on Mar. 8, 1793. At the same time, Beckwith and Mary Kelsick sued Sarah Hooe, and Beckwith sued John Alexander and his wife. The question was the distribution of the estate of the father of the women in these suits, all of whom were sisters. Wythe, 190. Wythe's decision in the case was appealed by JM and reversed in

	From Trammel jr v. Scott	1	8	
	From McCarty ads. Boggus 2 suits	2	5	
	From White ads. Smith in part	1	12	
6th.	From Murray ads. Randolph assee. of Randolph	2	12	
	From Lewellen a criminal in part	5	12	
8th.	From Cleveland v Posey	2	16	
	From Powell v Burwells Exrs.[80] (finishd)	10		
	From Lane ads. Odaniel	2	10	
	From Scott Ogleby v Baker & Blow	1	2	
		101	2	5¼

[Disbursements]

April 1st	rake & wheelbarrow		6	
3d.	Sternes works[81] 33/	1	13	
	Blairs sermons[82]	1	4	
	Paint for the office	2	17	
6th.	Scrapers 12/, bowl 24/	1	16	
	Market 18/		18	
	Sugar 11/, Jug 2/, Wood 12/	1	5	
		9	19	

[Receipts]	101	2	5¼
[Balance]	91	3	5¼

[Receipts]

April 11th	From Fauntleroy in Tomlin ads. Jones to send alias v

the Court of Appeals. See Court of Appeals Order Book, II, 271, III, 28–35, 42, 307–309, 315, Va. State Lib.

80. See JM to Leven Powell, Dec. 9, 1783.

81. This may have been the American edition of Laurence Sterne, *The Works of Laurence Sterne In Five Volumes* (Philadelphia, 1774).

82. It is most likely this was Samuel Blair, *The Works of the Reverend Samuel Blair, Late Minister of the Gospel at Foggs-Manor, in Chester County, Pennsylvania. Containing a Collection of Sermons on Various Subjects: Together with Several Treatises, viz., A Vindication of the Brethren, etc.; The Doctrine of Predestination, etc.; A Sermon on his Death, by Rev. Mr. Finley* (Philadelphia, 1754), printed by William Bradford. Blair (1712–1751) was a popular Presbyterian clergyman who trained other ministers, many of whom preached in Virginia after the Revolution.

	principal in Pittsylvania[83]	2	10
	From Hume v King & al (finished)	3	2
	From Legross v Jetts Exrs.	2	10
	Same v Mitchel	2	10
	From Butler ads. Ryding	2	10
13	From Ashby v Bruin	2	10
	From Clarke v Ferree[84]	2	10
14	From Sowther v Thomson[85]	2	10
	From Moffett v Bronaugh	2	8
	From v	2	10
	From Orr in Fairfax Justices v Carlysles Exrs.	4	16
	From White ads. Willis[86]	2	16
	From Lynaugh advice etc.	1	8
18	From McRoberts[87] for difft. persons	9	12
	From Palmer ads. Palmer (finished)	2	8
24	From Sampson Royster ads Commonwealth.	2	10
	⟨From Ladd ads. Faris ads. Ladd detinue.⟩[88]	2	10
	From Smith v Cowden (finishd)	2	8
	From Lee v Conway	5	12
		59	10

83. Pittsylvania County is in southwest Virginia.

84. Jonathan Clark v. Cornelius Free. See receipt for a bond and legal fee, calendared at Apr. 8, 1786.

85. Jacob Souther v. William Thompson was a debt action appealed to the General Court from Spotsylvania County. JM filed a declaration for Souther on May 13, 1785. After being continued through several terms, the case was transferred to the District Court in Fredericksburg, where judgment was awarded Souther on Oct. 5, 1789. District Court Records, 1789–1792, 52–53, Fredericksburg, Va. State Lib.

86. Francis Willis, Jr., v. Robert White was an action in detinue in which JM appeared for White. The case was finally discontinued in the District Court in Winchester on Sept. 3, 1792. Superior Court Order Book, 1789–1793, 50, 212, 282, 354, Frederick County, Va. State Lib.

87. Alexander McRoberts, or McRobert, was a merchant in Richmond who must have received fees for JM much as George Pickett had on Sept. 25, 1784. He was also an alderman and a Mason with JM. "Return of the Inhabitants," 1784, Richmond City Common Hall Records, 353; "List of Merchants," Richmond City Hustings Court Order Book, II, 50, both in Va. State Lib.

88. JM crossed out this fee and entered it under Receipts, Apr. 26, 1786.

	[*Disbursements*]			
April 12th.	repairing dressing table	1	13	4
	plank to Ramsbottom	1	13	4
	spent 9/, Market 12/	1	1	
20th.	Flour 45/, market 20/	3	5	
27th.	Wood 12/, Market 20/	1	12	
		9	4	8

	[*Receipts*]			
April 26th.	From Faris ads. Ladd[89]	2	10	
	From Booker advice	1	8	
28th.	From Anderson ads. North	2	8	
	From Devier ads. Carr	2	10	
	From Mullen Devier v Thomas			
	supersedeas	2	8	
	From Hare ads. North			
	(finishd)	14		
		25	4	

	[*Disbursements*]			
April 28th	sugar 28/	1	8	
	Market thro the month	4	4	
		5	12	

	[*Receipts*]			
May 2d.	From Randolph ads. Nelson			
	& Co.	2	16	
12th.	From Allen v. McCrae Chy.	4	16	
22d.	Two advice fees	2	5	
26th.	Advice fee on Hardaways			
	will[90]	1	8	
	Do. from Mr. Dukes on			
	contract to lease a tavern to			

89. William Faris v. William Ladd. Since this case was decided in Apr. 1791 at the District Court at Richmond, it must have begun in the General Court at about the time this fee was paid. When the reorganization of the courts took place in 1788, the case then would have been transferred to the district court. JM appeared for Faris but lost the case in the district court. The decision was appealed to the Court of Appeals, which reversed the judgment of the lower court on Nov. 26, 1791. Court of Appeals Order Book, II, 144, Va. State Lib.

90. See Receipts, June 26, 1786.

	Mr. Hawkins	1	2	6
29th.	From McElhany v Hughes	2	2	
	From Mr. Robertson in Sinclair & al ads. of Montgomery & Allan	2	16	
	From Matthews v Zane injunction	2	8	
31st.	From Slaughter v. Harrisons injunction	5		
	From Colo. Peachy[91] advice on the will of Mr. Samuel Peachy	1	8	
		26	1	6

[*Disbursements*]

May 3d.	Boots, Shoes 15/	3	15	
4th.	Market 10/		10	
	City taxes[92] £5–9	5	9	
	Goal fees for Ben	1	1	4
	expended at Mr. Roses		9	
	Hankerchief 4/, fruit 3/		7	
5th.	Wood 12/		12	
17th.	Wood 12/, Sturgeon 20/	1	12	
22	Sturgeon 20/, barbacue 9/, Market 11/	2	6	
	at Mr. Rawlins's[93] 6/		6	
29th.	Market 3/9, Do. 15/		18	9
		17		1

[*Receipts*]

June 2d.	From Gregory ads. Dudley[94] (issue)	2	8
26th.	From Mr. Wiseman in Partler v Kennedy, debt	2	10

91. William Peachy.
92. Richmond tax records for 1786 are not extant.
93. A tavern owned by Robert Rawlings (d. 1789).
94. William Dudley, executor of Edwin Fleet, executor of William Fleet, v. James Gregory, executor of David Ker. This case no doubt began in the General Court but was continued until 1788, when it was transferred to the District Court at King and Queen County. Gregory won a judgment on Sept. 25, 1792. Dudley took the case to the Court of Appeals, but on Nov. 20, 1795, it was dismissed when Dudley failed to appear. Court of Appeals Order Book, III, 101, Va. State Lib.

			£	s	d
	Recd. from Hardaway ads. Hardaway in part in chy. 45/		2	5	
			7	3	
	From Booker v Davies		2	10	
			9	13	

[*Disbursements*]

			£	s	d
June	1st.	market 6/, corn 22/6	1	8	6
		Counterpane £2–8	2	8	
	7th.	Wood 10/, market 5/		15	
	11th.	market 7/, punch 6/, barbacue 7/	1		
	12th.	Corn 24/, taxes[95] £4–13	5	17	
	15th.	sending for & sending back Mrs. Granger[96]	1	6	
		Given Mrs. Granger	6	4	
		paid for wine	7	7	6
		To Mr. Barrett[97] for suit of cloaths	6	15	
	16	To paper 18/, market 3/	1	1	
	23d.	To James river Compy.[98]	12		
	26th.	corporation dinner[99]	2	2	6
		Fruit 3/, sugar 8/9, barbacue 6/		17	9
	28th.	Bark for Polly		14	
		Flour 30/, wood 10/	2		
			51	16	3

95. Presumably this entry refers to Henrico County property taxes. Land tax records for this period are not extant, but JM was listed in 1786 as owning five tithable and five nontithable Negroes and two cattle. Henrico County Personal Property, 1786, Va. State Lib.

96. Mrs. Granger assisted in the birth of Rebecca, JM's second child, who lived only five days. See the family Bible notation at June 15, 1786, above. Mrs. Granger had assisted in the birth of Thomas Marshall also. See entry under Disbursements, July 26, 1784.

97. John Barret (1748–1830) was a merchant in Richmond. He became mayor of Richmond in 1791 and held that office again in 1793 and 1798. "Return of the Inhabitants," 1784, Richmond City Common Hall Records, 355, Va. State Lib.; Valentine Museum, *Richmond Portraits*, 12.

98. The James River Company was incorporated by act of the General Assembly at its Oct. 1784 session. The company was created to raise funds to use in clearing and improving the navigation of the river. Turner Southall and James Buchanan were appointed managers of subscriptions in Richmond, and subscription meetings were scheduled for the first Monday of Oct. every year. 11 Hening 450–462; JM to George Muter, Jan. 7, 1785; Wayland Fuller Dunaway, *History of the James River and Kanawha Company* (New York, 1922), 9–28.

99. This undoubtedly refers to a dinner held by the Richmond City Common Hall.

[*Receipts*]

July	1st.	From Levy v Phillips injn.	5	
	13th.	From Booker (advice fee etc.)	1	8
	26th.	From Cottrel v Jordan det.		
		(Buckingham)[1]	2	10
		From Mr. Carrol ads. Edins		
		T.A.B. removed by H.C.	3	
		From Same v Charlton & al	3	
		Same v Veal	2	14
	26th.	From Pringle & Co.		
		admiralty[2]	70	
			87	[12][3]

[*Disbursements*]

July	1st.	Corn 26/, for Moses 9/	1	15	
	4th.	Dinner at Andersons[4]	1	8	
	12th.	Market 28/	1	8	
	15	Barbacue 12/, postage 6/		18	
	20th.	Corn 7/6		7	6
	26th.	Paid Colo. Heth[5] for China	10	2	
		Corn 15/, soap 1/		16	
		Paid for subscription in			
		Potowmac river Compy.[6]	30		
	27th.	Paid for St. Taminy's[7] feast	2		
		for Hack to go up the country	3		
		For Market 15/, Oats 6/,			
		Harness 6/	1	7	
		expences going to Wms.burg	7		

1. Charles Cotteral v. Benjamin Jordan. This action in detinue from Buckingham County was continued through the reorganization of the General Court and was transferred to the District Court at Prince Edward County. It was continued from Sept. 7, 1789, until Apr. 2, 1791, when it was dismissed. District Court Order Book, 1789–1792, 40, 78, 131, 163, Prince Edward County, Va. State Lib. See also fees paid under Receipts, Oct. 2, 1786.

2. Until admiralty jurisdiction was transferred to the federal courts established under the U.S. Constitution in 1789, Virginia exercised admiralty jurisdiction through a state Court of Admiralty.

3. An ink blot obscures this figure.

4. Anderson's Tavern in Richmond.

5. William Heth.

6. See entry under Disbursements, Nov. 29, 1785.

7. See entry under Disbursements, *ca.* May 1784. There is no indication why the celebration, usually held in May, was postponed until July. Possibly JM meant St. John's, referring to the annual celebration of St. John the Baptist Day, but that day was June 24, which would mean its celebration was also delayed several weeks.

Sundries for self 50/	2	10	
Pd. the Taylor	4		
	64	7	6

[Receipts]

August	From Genl. Stevens ads.			
	Syme in chy.	7		
	From Rozzel ads. Gregg	2	10	
	same v Lee Ejectmt.	4		
	From Pierce ads. Cheek			
	(appeal)	2	10	
	From Noble ads. Fitzgeral[8]			
	2 suits habeas corpus	4	8	
	same ads. Shamblin TAB to			
	plead N.G.[9] & justification	2	10	
	From Humston v Love[10] Chy.	5		
	From Mr. Warren for advice	1	2	6
	From Williams v Thomas	2	10	
	From James Exx. etc. v Faris	2	10	
	From Ravenhill ads. Treasurer	3		
	From Hite v Conn	2	10	
	From Bruebaker v Miller in			
	chy in part		13	4
	From Colo. Kennedy advice			
	fee	1	8	
	From Dowdale ads. Glasscock[11]	4	16	
		46	7	10

[Disbursements]

August	Expenses going to & returning			
	from Winchester	15		
	Expenses at Berkley Ct. house	2	5	
	Do. at Winchester	2	18	10

8. John Fitzgerald v. George Noble was a debt action that ended on Sept. 7, 1789, in the District Court at Winchester. JM's entry suggests he became involved when the case was removed from a county court to the General Court by the issuance of a writ of habeas corpus. Superior Court Order Book, 1789–1793, 34, Frederick County, Va. State Lib.

9. "Not guilty."

10. See fee entered under Receipts, July 31, 1784.

11. William Glascock v. James G. Dowdall was transferred to the District Court in Winchester after the reorganization of the General Court, and on Sept. 5, 1789, judgment was awarded for JM's client, Dowdall. Superior Court Order Book, 1789–1793, 24, Frederick County, Va. State Lib.

at Fauquier		12	
Sundries for self, spurs & saddle cloth	2		3
Sundries for Polly	2	12	6
Pd. Mr. Wright[12] for rum	14	10	
Do. for a gross of bottles	2	2	
Pd. Potowmac Company[13]			
Left with Polly	10	4	

[*Receipts*]

September				
18th.	Recd. From Overton v Price	4	16	
22d.	Bell ads. Muir advice fee[14]	1	6	
	Turner ads. Hooker	2	10	
25th.	From Mr. Bernard for Oxley & Hancock in their chy. suits	21		
	From Mr. Thomson in his appeal & judgement on rep. bond[15] & for advice	5	12	
27th.	From Mr. Yancy for advice on appl.	1	8	
	From Mr. Carrol v Alexander	2	8	
30th.	From Simpson ads. Hunter	2	13	8
	From Withers v Harris & ux	2	10	
	From Blackwell v Sydnor & Armstead	2	10	
		46	13	8

[*Disbursements*]

September				
16.	Postage on letters		4	4
20th	Paid for two grates	5	2	6
	Paid for letter case	1	10	
	Paid postage 6/		6	

12. Matthew Wright was a merchant in Richmond. "Return of the Inhabitants," 1784, Richmond City Common Hall Records, 358, Va. State Lib.

13. See Disbursements, Nov. 29, 1785.

14. See JM to William Branch Giles, Sept. 22, 1786, for the advice JM gave Bell.

15. Replevin means redelivery to the owner of the thing taken. A replevin bond was executed to indemnify the officer who executed a writ of replevin and to indemnify the person from whose custody the property was taken for such damages as he might sustain.

22d.	Paid Doctor Fowshee[16]	5	13	9
	also	5	6	9
	Paid Doctor McClurg[17]	30	7	6
	Pd. Doctor Mackie	1	8	
	Flour	1	16	
	Market		14	
	wood 10/, moving corn house 24/	1	14	
	Books 6/6, punch 5/		11	6
23d.	Two grates £5–5–10	5	5	10
	Sugar 8/2, a cow £4–4	4	12	2
27th.	Flour 45/, corn 15/, market 6/	3	6	
28th.	Pd. Mr. Robinson for dockets	2	8	

[*Receipts*]

October

1st.	From Porter v Burnley	2	16
2d.	Morris ads. Hollingsworth & Johnston & Co.[18]	2	10
	Same ads. same	1	18
	From Mr. Cotrel v Jordan detinue in Full[19]	1	8
	From Smith in part (robbery)	3	
	From Sheet ads. Laurance in part	1	8
	From Smith ads. Lithgo	2	10
3d.	From Colvert for indictment	2	16
	From Rattle ads. Andersons	2	16
	From Ashby v Grant[20] Appeal	1	8
	From Smith Blaky (for New) v May appeal	3	
	From Cuninghame & Smith ads. Loyd Eject.[21]	13	

16. William Foushee.

17. James McClurg.

18. Hollingsworth & Johnston & Co. was a Richmond mercantile firm. "List of Merchants," Richmond City Hustings Court Order Book, II, 50, Va. State Lib.

19. See entry under Receipts, July 26, 1786.

20. This was an appeal to the General Court from a Fauquier County Court decision of Aug. 27, 1784, against Ashby (JM's client) in John Ashby v. William Grant. Minute Book, 1784–1786, 47, Fauquier County, Va. State Lib.

21. JM had entered a plea of not guilty for the defendant in Ephraim Lloyd v. Zara Osborne, Barnet Lambert, and John Smith before the General Court in Apr. 1786. See calendars of declarations printed at Jan. 10 and 11, 1786.

4th.	From Valentine v Wisharts			
	Exrs. Supersedeas	2	14	
	From Smith v Gilmore injn.			
	(in part	2	10	
	West ads. Ashton[22]	4	4	
5th.	From Brooke ads. Henderson[23]	2	8	
	From Roman ads. Campbell			
	caveat[24]	2	10	
	From Montgomery ads.			
	Campbell	2	10	
6th.	Calvert ads. Loyal	2	10	
	Valentine v Wishart			
	supersedeas	2	6	
	Winston ads. Whitlock	2	8	
		62	10	

[*Disbursements*]

October 1.	Market 15/, do. 3/		18	
2d.	Market 6/, limes 3/		9	
	For a mare	13		
3d.	Market 6/, putting up			
	grates 15	1	1	
4th.	Tea 12/, Market 9/, Hackney			
	coach	1	2	6

[*Receipts*]

October				
7th.	Parish ads. Harfield appeal	2	10	
	Hockerdy ads. Williams do.	2	10	
	Vaughan ads. Couts do.	2	10	
	Martin v Walkers exrs. & al			
	att[25] in chy.	6	14	
			6	
	Mohen exr. etc. v Logan			
	Gilmore & Co.	2	10	
	also	2	10	

22. See JM's argument in Ashton v. West printed at Oct. 13, 1786.

23. Richard Henderson, etc., v. William Brooke was transferred to the District Court in Winchester after the 1788 court reorganization and was dismissed by consent on Apr. 17, 1790. Superior Court Order Book, 1789–1793, 52, 57, Frederick County, Va. State Lib.

24. JM entered a caveat for Isaac Roman against Arthur Campbell on Apr. 14, 1786. Land Office Caveats, Apr. 14, 1786, 286, Va. State Lib.

25. "Attachment."

9th.	Ford v Kinnon (Mason plf.[26]) Chy.	5		
10th.	Ramsay ads. Daltons exrs.	3	12	
	Sampson ads. Comth.	2	14	
14th.	Quarles ads. Miller	3	2	
	From Majr. Little (retaining fee)	3	12	
	From Mr. Young for advice	1	2	6
15th.	From Mr. Roberts for will establishd	2	16	
16	Clark ads. Griffin	2	10	
	Parfect v Page	2	8	
17	Ravenhill ads Treasurer	2	10	
	Cuninghame ads. Easom	2	10	
	Machir v Windle	2	10	
	Pitman ads. Harris & al chy.	2	8	
20th.	Glanvil ads. Evans	5		
		60	4	6

[Disbursements]

October

7th.	Paid Mr. B. Lewis in part for his house £70 cash[27] & 5£ in an order in favor of James Taylor	75		
	Corn 12/, Wood 10/	1	2	
8th.	Market 3/9, do. 24/, punch 3/	1	10	9
10th.	Sugar 13/4, cheese 10/6, limes 5/, porter 15/	2	3	10
14th.	Market 7/6, Tea kettle 14/, punch 3/	1	4	6
15th.	Market 7/4, barber 15/	1	2	4
16	Play[28] 6/, Jocky club[29] 28/	1	14	

26. Stephens Thomson Mason (1760–1803) for the plaintiff. Mason served in the House of Delegates in 1783 and 1794 and ultimately was a senator from Virginia from 1794 until his death.

27. See entry under Disbursements, June 1, 1785, and monthly entries below through December.

28. Alexander Marie Quesnay (1755–1820) opened a new theater in Richmond known as Quesnay's Academy Theatre. The new season opened under the direction of Lewis Hallam (ca. 1740–1808) and John Henry (1746–1794) on Oct. 10, 1786, when their Old American Company presented *School for Scandal*. Other productions included *Alexander the Great*, *The Poor Soldier*, and *Love-a-la-Mode*. The company gave a repeat performance of *School for Scandal* on Nov. 16. Sherman, "Post-Revolutionary Theatre,' 37–45.

29. The Jockey Club met before the horse races each season to draw rules and to

17th.	Market 7/, wood 10/, play 12/	1	9
19th.	Corn 3/, thread 3/		6

[*Receipts*]

October
22d.	From Page ads. Montgomery	1	7
23d.	Tyler v Hardin injn.	1	10
⎰24th.	Campbell etc. v Baine	2	10
Deane ⎱
	Same v Bairden	2	10
25	Jones Mrs. ads. Shelton re.		
	bond	2	16
	Adams in a caveat	2	16
27th.	From Clark ads. Jones	2	10
	From Tutt for motion agt.		
	Sheriff	2	10
	From Reid for motion abt.		
	admn.	1	8
28th.	From Branch ads. Donald		
	Eject.	2	10
	From McCaul v Woodson chy.	5	
29th	From Ellis ads. Willing chy.	5	12
31st.	From Mr. Elean v	2	10
		35	9

[*Disbursements*]

October
22d.	Market 11/6, sugar 12/6	1	4
23d.	Corn 20/, Butter 56/	3	16
24th.	Market 6/, do. 12/		18
	Pd. Mr. Deane in 2 suits	5	
28th.	Shoes 12/, wood 10/,		
	Market 3/	1	5
	For Negroes 50/	2	10

[*Receipts*]

November
1st.	From Jesse Chapels	2	8

---

take subscriptions from members to provide a purse. See entries under Disbursements, Oct. 23, 1784, for more information on the horse races in Richmond.

	From Kirkly ads. Head Chy.	5	
	From Arnot ads. Grider	2	10
2d.	From Hughes ads. Clayton[30]	2	8
	From Ewing ads. Pratt chy.	4	10
3d.	From Mr Allen in supersedeas		
	Wilson v Powel[31]	2	10
7th.	Smith ads. Hainsford chy.	2	16
10th.	From Cheadle in part two		
	Chancery suits	4	12
11th.	Brickhouse ads. Brickhouse[32]		
	appeal	2	8
	Granvil v Kendal appeal	2	8
14th.	From Keith ads. Vass &		
	ux.[33] det.	2	16
	Graham ads. Henderson & al	5	
	Henderson ads. Cosby admr.	2	10
19th.	Ranken v Donahoe	2	
	Legrand v Tabb	2	10
	Clopton v Earnest appeal	2	8
	Chapman v	10	
24th.	From Norfolk borough[34]	14	
		72	14

[Disbursements]

November			
1st.	plays[35] 18/, market 18/	1	16

30. John Hughes, Sr., v. Henry Clayton and wife, Theodosia, administratrix of Anderson Hughes, her late husband. In 1788 this case in detinue was transferred to the District Court at Petersburg, where judgment was given against Hughes on Sept. 22, 1789. JM appealed for Hughes to the Court of Appeals, which affirmed the judgment on July 10, 1790. 3 Call 554; Court of Appeals Order Book, II, 24–25, Va. State Lib.

31. William Wilson v. Robert Powell was not settled until Oct. 14, 1793, when the District Court in Dumfries found for JM's client, Wilson. District Court Records at Large, 1793, 37, Prince William County, Va. State Lib.

32. William and Smith Brickhouse, executors of Hezekiah Brickhouse, v. Major John, Sr., and George Brickhouse, Jr., originated in Northampton County Court in 1786. JM filed the appeal to the General Court on Mar. 15, 1787. After the reorganization of the courts in 1788, the case was transferred to the District Court at Accomack and Northampton counties, where the county court's judgment was confirmed in 1799. District Court Order Book, 1789–1791, 36, 1794–1797, 243, 1789–1797, 247, 339, 356, 394, 402, 423, 428, Accomack County, Va. State Lib.

33. Vincent Voss v. Rosey Keith was filed in the General Court at its Apr. 1786 session, JM appealing the decision of Spotsylvania County Court for Keith. After the reorganization of the courts in 1788, the case was transferred to the District Court at Fredericksburg, where the lower court's judgment was overturned on Oct. 6, 1789. District Court Records, 1789–1792, 82, Fredericksburg, Va. State Lib.

34. Norfolk was incorporated as a borough by George II on Sept. 15, 1736. 4 Hening 541–542.

35. See information on the 1786 theater season under Disbursements, Oct. 16, 1786.

2d.	Pd. for Mr. Colston[36] in a tax on deed from Peachy to him	7	10
3d.	play 6/; 5th. Market 18/	1	4
7th.	Corn 12/, Wood 10/, Market 2/	1	4
10th.	Corn £5–17	5	17
11th.	Sugar 25/, Market 12/	1	17
17th.	Flour 33/, wood 10/, Market 15/	2	18
	To expences up to Lowry[37] for Money	1	4
	To do. to Fredericksburg for Polly	2	8
	To Potowmac river company[38]	80	
19th.	Paid Mr. B. Lewis[39] in part for the house	50	
	Market at difft. times	4	10
	For quarter cask of wine	12	10
	To Barber		18

[Receipts]

December	Gee v Eason & al. TAB & Trespass[40]		12
	Hawlet ads. Osborne	2	8
	Advice fee from Mr. Hallam	1	8
	From Mr. Young ads. Young	2	10
	From Mr. Higbee on a protested bill	4	4
	From Parker v Cowper	5	12
2d.	Woods ads. Jerdon debt	2	16
4th.	From Carters Exrs. ads. Goodlow[41]	3	

36. Rawleigh Colston.

37. Lowry was located on the south bank of the Rappahannock River on the boundary separating Essex and Middlesex counties, a few miles south of Hobb's Hole, or Tappahannock, as it is called today.

38. See entry under Disbursements, Nov. 29, 1785.

39. See entry under Disbursements, June 1, 1785.

40. Trespass, assault and battery, would be an actual violence to someone. The reference to simple trespass may be intended to cover an implied violence, such as peaceable but wrongful entry upon a person's land.

41. Robert Goodloe v. Joseph Brock, William and John Carter, executors of John Carter, was an action in detinue in which JM appeared for Brock and the Carters. After the court reorganization of 1788, the case was transferred to the District Court at Fredericksburg, where on May 3, 1791, it finally abated by the death of Goodloe. District Court Law Orders, A, 1789–1793, 58, 156, 232, Fredericksburg, Va. State Lib.

	From Edjer v Greenhil[42]		
	appeal	1	4
8th.	From Jones ads. Verrel & ux	5	2
	From Henry Leipner for advice	1	2	6
12th.	From Nichols v Nichols	4	10
	Recd. in part of two fees		
	from Ham	4	4
14th.	For writing a conveyance etc.		
	for Beale from Clayton	2	8
15th.	From Mr. Brag v Fowke		
	(old suit)	2	10
21st.	From Mr. Hunter on Wm.		
	Hunters will	2	8
22d.	From Beard v Dickie in chy.	4	2
25th.	From Mordecai[43] for advice	3	10
26th.	From Faris for do. on will	1	
	Cooper ads. Montgomery &		
	Allen[44]	2	10
		53		6

[Disbursements]

December	Market 8/, plays[45] 30/	1	18
	Given Polly £1–8, chocolate 6/	1	14
	Shovels, pokers, & Tongs	1	4
	Books 14/, for tax for D.		
	Brent[46] 30/	2	4
	Wood 9/, market 3/, do. 7/6		19	6
	Pd. Mr. Lewis in part for		

42. William Edgar v. Daniel Grinnan was an appeal from a county court to the General Court in which JM appeared for Edgar. The case was transferred to the District Court at Fredericksburg after the court reorganization of 1788, and on Apr. 9, 1790, the parties agreed to a dismissal. *Ibid.*, 75.

43. This would no doubt be either Jacob Mordecai (1762–1838), Joseph Mordecai (b. *ca.* 1766), or Isaac Mordecai, all merchants in Richmond. "Return of the Inhabitants," 1784, Richmond City Common Hall Records, 345; "List of Merchants," Richmond City Hustings Court Order Book, II, 50, Va. State Lib.

44. Alexander Montgomery (b. *ca.* 1757) and Timothea Allen (b. *ca.* 1758) were both merchants in Richmond. "Return of the Inhabitants," 1784, Richmond City Common Hall Records, 350, Va. State Lib.

45. See entry under Disbursements, Oct. 16, 1786.

46. Daniel C. Brent (1759–1814), of Stafford County, had married a daughter of Thomas Ludwell Lee in 1782. JM perhaps was helping Brent pay his taxes following the death of his brother, William Brent, in 1785. JM's sister-in-law Eliza Ambler had been married to William Brent at the time of his death. See entry under Disbursements, June 23, 1785.

	house[47]	27	4	
4th.	Market 12/, do. 12/8	I	5	8
7th.	Sugar 10/6, market 4/		14	6
	postage on letters 7/6, Gloves for Polly 7/6		15	
	Market 4/, Tea 15/		19	
8th.	Market 2/, wood 10/, do. 7/		19	
10th.	spent at Rose's 6/		6	
14th.	Market 9/, Given for docket 28/	I	17	
15th.	Market 12, do. 3/, spent 6/	I	I	
16	Sugar & Coffee 12/, Market 34/	2	6	
20th.	Paid Mr. Lewis[48] 16£	16		
21	Pork 6£, flour 37/6	7	17	6
22	For butter £4–2, wood 12/	4	14	
24	Wood 3/, Tar 1/6, Saddle-bags 28/	I	12	6
25	Raffling for Braxton 28/, given 1/3	I	9	3
26	Shoes for boy 7/6, market 12/		19	6

[Receipts]

December 28th.	From Mr. Mayo for advice	I	8	
	From Mr. Bibb for do.	I	2	6
	Receivd in the year 1786 according to the forgoing account	508	4	10
	[1786 Disbursements]	432		
	[1786 Balance]	76	4	10

I recd. on the 2d. of March ⎫
from Colo. Grayson,[49]   ⎪
which discharged his   ⎬
bond to Marye assignd   ⎪
to me the sum of £70   ⎭ £70

---

47. See entry under Disbursements, June 1, 1785.
48. Benjamin Lewis, on a house. See Disbursements, June 1, 1785.
49. William Grayson.

I have in my hands on ⎫
   the exn. v[50] Goode ⎬ both
   42–5 & the amount ⎬ paid
   of the exn. v Wood ⎭ off

[Disbursements]

Decr. 28th. Wood 10/, St. Johns[51] 38/	2	8	
market 6/, shoes 9/		15	
Given Polly 28/	1	8	
assignments for Mr. Colston[52] in Land office 7/6, do. for Colo. Marshall		15	
Paid Mr. Lewis in full[53]	26	17	1¼
For sundries at Mr. Boyds[54] paid	24	14	
To my expenses	432		
	1	8	
[Balance]	433	8	

[December]   Paid my father through my
    brother Tom in interest
    warrants   £30–6

[Receipts]

January 4th. Recd. from Brown ads. Brown[55]	2	10
From Hugert ads. Burnsides supersedeas	2	10

50. Perhaps JM meant "execution against."
51. Spent observing the festival of St. John the Evangelist.
52. Rawleigh Colston.
53. See entry under Disbursements, Oct. 7, 1786.
54. Robert Boyd was a Richmond merchant and alderman. "Return of the Inhabitants," 1784, Richmond City Common Hall Records, 343, Va. State Lib.
55. John Brown v. Elizabeth Brown, administratrix of Thomas Brown, was appealed to the General Court in Oct. 1786. The case was continued until after the reorganization of the courts in 1788, when it was transferred to the District Court at Staunton. On Sept. 5, 1789, judgment was given against the estate of the intestate. District Court Order Book, 1789–1793, 28–30, Augusta County, Va. State Lib. See also Brown and others v. the administratrix of Thomas Brown, deceased, which was an appeal from a decree of the High Court of Chancery in 1793. That case was appealed to the Court of Appeals and is reported in 2 Washington 151–154 (1795).

	From Estil v Fitzpatrick (Chy.)	3	12	
	From Parson Couts £4–10			
	advice etc.	4	10	
6th	From Bowles v Richardson	1	17	
7th.	From Fauntleroy v Turner	1	19	
	From Colo. Cropper[56] for			
	advice	1	2	6
8th.	From Bibb in part,			
	usury		13	
10th.	From Stuart exr. of Alex-			
	ander v Rutherford	2	10	
	From Jones v Anderson &			
	Ross[57] (Chy.)	5		
13	From Mr. Gregory for			
	conveyance	2	8	
20th.	From Winfrey v May injn.	5	9	
22d	From Hitt ads. Williams	2	10	
	From Cohen v Woodson	1	3	
23d.	From Colo. A.W. White[58]	4	4	
	From Whitehurst for advice	1	8	
29th.	From Woodson v Montague			
	appeal	2	10	
30th.	From Machir in Carnegys			
	exrs. v Montgomery	2	10	
		48	5	6

[Disbursements]

January				
1st.	corn 2/6, market 6/		8	6
4th.	market 2–6, do. 14/, spent 6/	1	2	6
	Paid Cock for last years rent[59]	12	10	

56. Probably John Cropper from Accomack County. After serving with various regiments and rising to the rank of colonel during the Revolution (during which time he was JM's lieutenant colonel), Cropper represented Accomack County in the House of Delegates from 1784 to 1790. He later represented the same district in the Senate from 1813 to 1817.

57. Joseph Jones v. Henry Anderson, Smith Tandy, and David Ross & Co. was heard by the High Court of Chancery sometime before Sept. 1, 1792, because at that time the decision was appealed by JM to the Court of Appeals. That tribunal affirmed the chancery decree on Oct. 22, 1793. Court of Appeals Order Book, II, 240, 243, Va. State Lib.

58. Anthony Walton White (1750–1803), of New Jersey and New York, had been an aide to George Washington, then colonel of the Third Battalion of New Jersey troops, during the Revolution. During the Whiskey Rebellion, Pres. Washington appointed him a general of cavalry under Gen. Henry Lee.

59. William Cocke. See entries under Disbursements, Jan. 1784, and June 1, 1785.

6th.	market 3/, do. 19/	1	2	
9th.	Pork 16£, salt 3/, wood 10/	16	13	
10th.	Pork 9£, Salt 6/	9	6	
12th.	Chocolate 6/8, apples 36/	2	2	8
13th.	Market 3/6, do. 5/, wood 9/		18	6
16th.	Making a suit of cloths	2	5	8
17	beer 40/, wood 9/, salt 6/,			
	market 6/	3	1	
20th.	Market 1/, wood 10/,			
	Market 3/		14	
23d	market 2/, house 6/, market 9/		17	
25th.	paper 24/, salt barrel 7/	1	11	
	corn to Colo. T. Randolph[60]	7		
26th.	Market 5/, Declarations 15/	1		
27th.	Market 6/, postage 7/6		13	6
29th.	Wood 8/, market 6/		14	
	To Duval for Coal	4	10	
		66	9	4

[Receipts]

February
1st.	From Delacour v New Kent			
	Justices[61] supersedeas	2	3	
	From Mr. Mayo for advice			
	on will	1	8	
2d	From Mr. Braxton drawing a			
	deed	1	2	6
	From Mr. Hartshorne &			
	Lingley for Corp assee.			
	of Wilkes v Sharkie	2	16	
	Chy.	3		
	Recd. from Mr. Alexander in			
	Morris ads. Braxton[62]	8	10	

60. Thomas Mann Randolph of Tuckahoe owned farm property near Richmond. JM bought corn and flour from him on several occasions this year. The corn he would buy in Jan. and on Apr. 23 would be for horse feed, although slaves might make hominy from part of it.

61. Claudy Delacour had petitioned the Council of State to remit a fine the New Kent County justices of the peace had imposed on him at a meeting of the county court. He had been fined for failing to submit a list of his taxable property. On Jan. 18, 1787, the Council refused remission, claiming lack of power to remit fines that went toward paying the county levy. Obviously Delacour retained JM to ask for a supersedeas from the General Court that would block execution of the county court's ruling. *JVCS*, IV, 32.

62. Carter Braxton v. Willing, Morris, & Co. Braxton (1736–1809), a member of

4th.	From Colo. Taylors estate	11	4	
19th.	From Buford v Deane injn.	5		
21st.	From Southampton Justices[63] for advice	1	8	
22d.	From Kimbro's exrs. ads. Smith	2	10	
	From Wilson & Wilkins v Kearnes & al. Chy.	4	3	
25th.	Waring ads. Weeks	5		
28th.	Advice on Cavenaughs will	1	2	6
	From Mr. E. Smith v Lyde & Co. chy.	5		
		54	7	0

[Disbursements]

February				
2d.	Market 14/, expences 5/3, Market 3/	1	2	3
	Candles 43/6, flour £6	8	3	6
	Paid Bets[y] Munkes[64] 15/, Given Polly 14/	1	9	
3d.	Paid Quarrier for swingle trees[65] 36/	1	16	
5th.	For Bedsteads £10–10, Glazing windows 1/6	10	11	6
6th.	Shoeing a horse 4/, Market 6/, house 12/	1	2	

the Council of State during this time, was trying to obtain settlement of some commercial accounts with Willing, Morris, & Co. Thomas Willing (1731–1821) and Robert Morris (1734–1806) were partners of the Philadelphia company. Willing was president of the Bank of North America and later the Bank of the United States, and Morris was a U.S. senator during most of this litigation. The case began in Henrico County Court on Mar. 10, 1787. On Nov. 11, 1791, judgment was entered against the defendants, but an appeal to the High Court of Chancery was allowed. That court found for Willing, Morris, & Co. Braxton then appealed to the Court of Appeals, which heard the case between Apr. 13 and Nov. 23, 1794. Henrico County Order Book, II, 660, III, 70, 101, IV, 69, 115, 175, 200, 481, V, 41, Va. State Lib.; 1 Washington 380–381; 4 Call 288; Court of Appeals Order Book, II, 275, III, 40, 73, 74–78, 80, 81, 83, 86–89, 90–96, 102–107, Va. State Lib.

63. Southampton County is south of Petersburg and borders North Carolina.

64. Betsy Munkus appears almost every month until June 1788, receiving 16s. each time except Jan. 1788. Although no biographical information survives, it is most probable she worked as a maid or a nurse during this period of Polly's illness. Her last entry in the Account Book is Apr. 2, 1790.

65. A swingletree is a crossbar, pivoted at the middle, to which the traces of the harness are fastened in a cart or a carriage. Also, singletree, or whiffletree.

		£	s	d
7th.	sope 3/, peas 5/, mending my boots 5/		13	
	To my subscription to sufferers by fire[66]		21	
9th	To my subscription to the assemblies[67]		3	
	Market 6/, postage 1/, Market 4/		11	
	Paid Bell for my Brother William	1	4	
15th.	Market 15/, do. 7/6, wood 20/	1	12	6
17th.	Market 12/3, do. 15/	1	7	3
21st.	Market 15/, expences 12/	1	7	
	To Majr. McRoberts[68] for sugar & coffee	9	7	7
	To do. for Hay	4	13	
	To Mr. Donald for sugar	7	7	9
27th.	expences 6/, Market 9/, do. 2/6		17	6
	Manure 24/, postage 4/6	1	8	6
28th.	Piece of linnen for myself	5		
	book 5/		5	
		83	18	4

[Receipts]

		£	s	d
March 3d.	Walker v Syme[69] debt	2	10	
	Bratton ads. Joseph[70] supersedeas	2	16	

66. Early in the morning of Jan. 8, 1787, a fire that started in a house occupied by Mrs. Julia Hartshorne spread to Anderson's Tavern, and in a short time high winds had caused "a general conflagration" in the center of Richmond. By dawn the four-hour fire had destroyed 40 or 50 buildings. The Speaker of the House of Delegates, Joseph Prentis, and six other delegates had moved the money and papers from the treasury office to the chamber of the Council of State, and when that was threatened they took the papers to the governor's house. The fire was stopped only when the wind shifted and two houses were pulled down. Gov. Randolph called a town meeting at Trower's Tavern the same afternoon and appointed a committee to solicit contributions to help the sufferers. JM's gift came in response to this fund raising drive. Va. Gaz. & Wkly. Adv., Jan. 11, 1787; Christian, Richmond, 30.

67. See entry under Disbursements, Jan. 18, 1785. This year's Assemblies, scheduled to begin Mar. 23, had to be postponed one week because several people failed to pay their subscriptions. Va. Gaz. & Wkly. Adv., Mar. 22, 1787.

68. Alexander McRobert.

69. Dr. Thomas Walker v. Col. John Syme. See entries under Receipts, Oct. 29, 1787, Oct. 19, 1789, and Aug. 1792. A receipt is printed under Oct. 29, 1787. JM also wrote a letter to Walker about the case on July 9, 1789.

70. Daniel Joseph v. Robert Bratton. JM represented Bratton and asked the Gen-

4	From Mr. May for advice	I	8
	From Mr. C.B. Harrison v Skipwith[71]	2	8
5th.	From Colo. R. Randolphs exrs. retainer	I 4	
	From Calvert v Loyal £4–17	4	17
	From Allens ads. Allason debt	2	10
7th.	From Atkinson ads. White[72] chy.	5	
11th.	advice on John Smiths will	I	4
	drawing a deed Braxton to Randolph	I	8
15th.	Hobson ads. Richardson (new suit) 23/ & 5/	I	3
19th.	From Binns v French	3	10
20th.	From Mason v Lee	4	4
	From G. Mason jr.[73]	9	16
22d.	From Thomson v Byrne (finishd)	2	10
23d.	From Mrs. Fox in part for two writs of supersedeas two guineas (taxes to be deducted) advice	2	16
	receivd from Petersburg	50	
26th.	From Barret in Floyd & al. v Williams & al. for deft in chy.	5	
	From Judges exrs. v Harris (finishd)	4	2
27th.	one advice fee	I	4
		122	6

eral Court for a writ of supersedeas to stay the May 18, 1785, judgment of the Augusta County Court. The case was transferred to the District Court at Staunton after 1788, and on Apr. 6, 1790, the cause was abated by the death of Bratton. District Court Order Book, 1789–1797, 39, Augusta County, Va. State Lib.

71. Carter Basset Harrison (1761–1808), the son of Gov. Benjamin Harrison, represented Surry County in the House of Delegates from 1784 to 1786 and later was a member of the U.S. House of Representatives from 1793 to 1799.

72. Rawleigh White v. Roger Atkinson and Stephen Coleman was a suit White brought before the High Court of Chancery for specific performance of a contract to purchase land. White appealed the decree to the Court of Appeals, and the Chancery Court's decree was affirmed on Nov. 10, 1795. 2 Washington 94–106; 2 Call 376–378; Court of Appeals Order Book, III, 72, 91, Va. State Lib.

73. George Mason, Jr. (1753–1796), was the son of George Mason, father of the Virginia Declaration of Rights.

[Disbursements]

Date	Item	£	s	d
March 1st.	Wood 10/, shoes for Tom 4/, house 12/	1	6	
2	Market 3/9, do. 5/, cloaths horse 4/		12	9
4th.	expences 14/, do. 20/	1	14	
6th.	market 13/4, pair of breeches for self 33/	2	6	4
7th.	fish 11/3, for Betsy Munkus 16/	1	7	3
9th	expenses 6/, market 6/, wood 9/	1	1	
10th.	drawing manure for garden	1		
	given for lime for the office 28/	1	8	
	postage for letters 7/9, laws[74] 12/, grains 2/	1	1	9
13th.	Market 30/, wood 10/, books 24/, hat £3	6	4	
15th.	Market 8/9, meal 11/3, Tea 12/, nails 2/	1	14	
21st.	papering & painting the office £3–7	3	7	
22d.	butter 34/, bed cover 31/	3	5	
24th.	expenses £3	3		
26th.	house 30/, market 46/	3	16	
	Pd. John Hopkins[75] for Coy	75		
	subscription to barbacue		3	
		33	12	1

[Receipts]

Date	Item	£	s	d
March 27th.	From Catesby Jones[76] for Fauntleroy at the suit of Crawford (Chy.	2	10	
	From Jesse Brown in part	5	12	
28th.	From Alexander for advice	1	8	

74. JM no doubt purchased *Acts passed at a general assembly of the commonwealth of Virginia. Begun and held at the public buildings in the city of Richmond, on Monday the sixteenth day of October in the year of our Lord, one thousand seven hundred and eighty-six* (Richmond, 1787), printed by Dixon, Holt, Nicolson and Davies. The acts were advertised for sale on Mar. 22, 1787, in *Va. Gaz. & Wkly. Adv.*

75. John Hopkins (*ca.* 1757–1827) was a merchant in Richmond and from 1780 until sometime after 1794 was commissioner of the continental loan office for Virginia. In 1781 he was accused of fraud by the House of Delegates but was legally charged only with wrongdoing. "Return of the Inhabitants," 1784, Richmond City Common Hall Records, 357, Va. State Lib.; *Madison Papers*, III, 325–326.

76. Jones (*ca.* 1755–1800).

30th.	From Powell v Carr[77] (chy.)	4	16	
	From North v Appeal	2	10	
		16	16	

	[*Disbursements*]			
March 27th.	black casimir & trimmings for myself	2	13	6½
	To Mr. Deane[78] for sundries	7	18	6¾
	load of wood 10/		10	
	expences 10/, lodge 6/, market 3/		19	
	Given Polly 28/	1	8	
28th.	wood 9/, eggs 2/6, given Polly 28/	1	19	6
30th.	expences 3/		3	
		15	11	7¼

	[*Receipts*]		
April 1st.	From Mr. Muse[79] 7–10	7	10
3d.	From John Churchill[80]	6	
	Carters & Suttons	2	8
	From Tatum for Clayborne ads. Dunnivant 2 suits	5	
	From Hewit (To write to him)	2	10
	Garland v Lee	2	10
	From Shiffen Yancy	2	10
	Brewer ads. Turberville	2	10
5th.	From Mr. Johnston for advice	2	6
	Hughes v Trent supersedeas (old suit)	2	16
	From Hudson ads. Armstrong	2	16
6th.	From Parker ads. Fowler[81]	2	16

77. Thomas Powell v. Thomas Carr was an appeal from the Spotsylvania County Court filed by JM at the Apr. 1787 General Court. The case was continued until it was transferred to the District Court at Fredericksburg, which reversed the lower court's decision on Oct. 6, 1789. District Court Records, 1789–1792, 299–302, Fredericksburg, Va. State Lib.

78. This would be Thomas or James Deane, both merchants in Richmond. "List of Merchants," Richmond City Hustings Court Order Book, II, 50, Va. State Lib.

79. Battaile Muse lived in Berkeley County. See JM to Muse, *ca.* Apr. 1, 1787.

80. Churchill (b. 1767) was born in Fauquier County but moved to Kentucky with his wife and father in 1787.

81. John Fowler, surviving obligee of John and George Fowler, v. Richard Parker,

		From Muse v Roane appeal	2	16	
	7th.	From Gatewood v Beverley	2	10	
		From Mark & Co. 2 suits	5		
		Calvert v Shropshire appeal	1	8	
		Claiborne ads. Spotswood	5		
		Brown ads. Anderson appeal	2	10	
		Baker ads. Sutton	8	18	
		Dick ads. Lyle[82] 3 suits	5	12	
	8	From Wickliffe in Graham v			
		Atwell	1	10	
			76	16	

[*Disbursements*]

April 1		Oats	4		
	2d.	paid Taylor for making			
		breeches etc.	1	4	8
	3d.	hankerchiefs 10/, expences 9/,			
		wood 9/	1	8	
		Whitewashing the house		16	
	4th.	Market 40/, do. 14/	2	14	
	5th.	market 6/, postage 1/,			
		expenses 1/		8	
	7th.	paid Mr. Hayes	3	11	6
		market 20/	1		
			15	2	2

[*Receipts*]

April 9th.	From Gee v Eason	2	5
	From May v Johnns 2		
	supersedeas's	10	
	From Robertson v Hobson &		
	al & Ransom v same[83]	6	

and Henry S. Redman, security for his appearance. This debt action ended in Apr. 1790, after it had been transferred to the District Court at Northumberland County. District Court Order Book, 1789–1793, 64, Northumberland County, Va. State Lib.

82. One of these suits was William Hunter, Andrew Wailes, Robert Lyle, and Thomas Hewet, executors of Robert Lyle, v. Elisha C. Dick. This was a debt action brought to the General Court from Fairfax County. After 1788 it was transferred to the District Court at Dumfries, where judgment was entered on Oct. 17, 1793. District Court Records at Large, 1793, 285, Prince William County, Va. State Lib.

83. Edward Robertson v. William Thomas, Jr., and John Hobson, Jr., John Clarke, Edward Dillon, Crud Haskin, and Denny Hatcher was a trespass, assault and battery, action from Cumberland County. After 1788 the case was transferred to the District

	Davies ads. Donahoe	2	10	
	Sutton ads. Segar [84]	1	8	
10th.	Archer v Davies appeal	1	17	
	Durret v Marshall on rep. bond	2	10	
	From Pettit in same suit as Fauntleroy [85]	2	10	
11th.	Ware v Conway [86]	2	10	
	Weir (George) v Upshaw	2	10	
12th	Advice on Welbournes deed	1	2	6
	From Kennedy ads. Beards exrs. [87] appeal	2	5	
	Brown ads. Reynolds	2	10	
	same ads. Putnam	2	10	
	From Mr. Lewes (Gloster) [88]	2	16	
	From Boggess v Hugh Conn TAB	2	7	
	From Thompson (Judgement confessd by Allerson on protested bill)	2	10	
13	From Mr. Orr two suits	4	4	
	From Thornly ads. Picket appeal	2	10	
		56	14	6

[Disbursements]

April	Paid for Israel [89]	55		
12th.	Market 14/, do. 2/, wood 10/	1	6	

Court at Prince Edward County, where in Sept. 1790 judgment was entered against Thomas, Hobson, and Clarke. The others were acquitted. William Ransom v. same was a joint action. District Court Records at Large, 1789–1792, 282–284, Prince Edward County, Va. State Lib.

84. Elizabeth Segar, by Richard Segar, guardian, v. Joseph Sutton was an action in which an appearance for Sutton was filed by JM in the General Court. The case was later transferred to the District Court at Fredericksburg and dismissed on Oct. 6, 1789. District Court Law Orders, A, 1789–1793, 52, Fredericksburg, Va. State Lib.

85. See under Receipts, Mar. 27, 1787.

86. James Ware v. Cornelius Conway. See JM's declaration in the case printed at Apr. 1787.

87. David Kennedy, Samuel Reid, and George Riley v. Beard's executor was an appeal from Berkeley County Court to the General Court. After 1788 the case was transferred to the District Court at Winchester, which reversed the county court's decision on Apr. 23, 1790. Superior Court Order Book, 1789–1793, 91, Frederick County, Va. State Lib.

88. Gloucester County.

89. JM kept this slave until Feb. 1792. At that time he wrote in his Account Book, "taking up Israel 21/," probably spent taking him to Fauquier County.

Coal 44/, expences £6, do. 24/	9	4		
Corn £17	17			
	82	10		

[Receipts]

April 13	Advice to Mr. Jones	1	2	
	Long ads. Bruce (dismissed)	2	10	
	Southerland ads. Braxton (motion)	2	10	
	Thornley ads. Pickett (2 old suits of the Govr.)[90]		16	
	Coleman v Voss & al motion on rep. bond	2	10	
	Grymes v Maury (old suit	2	8	
	Smith v Cary (finished)	2	10	
14	Welbourne v Corbin two ejectments £3	3		
	Murry v Sale & al	2	8	
	Mr. Copeland	3		
16th.	From Mr. Gracie for Hazzle-green & Co. Merchts. of Amsterdam	4	16	
	Ransom ads. by Mr.	4	2	
	Dalby v Richardson for deft.	2	10	
	Booker admr. of Wager ads. Chapman Guardian for Baines	2	10	
17	Degraffenreidt ads. Moore	3	2	6
	From Bland (finishd)	7		
	From Hennings & al. ads. Mills[91]	2	10	
18th.	From Clapham for advice	2	16	
	Johnston ads. Bibb motion	2	10	
	Adam Hunter[92]	14		
	Poindexter v Grubb (appeal	2	15	
		71	5	6

90. Upon being elected governor of Virginia in 1786, Edmund Randolph turned over his law practice to JM. *Virginia Independent Chronicle* (Richmond), Nov. 15, 1786. A portion of the notice is reprinted in Christian, *Richmond*, 30.

91. Overton Cosby and James Gregory, surviving partner James Mills & Co., v. David Hening, executor of Samuel Hening, was a debt action filed in the General Court in Apr. 1786. It was continued until after the court reorganization of 1788 and was then transferred to the District Court at Fredericksburg, where on Oct. 6, 1789, judgment was awarded to the plaintiffs. District Court Records, 1789–1792, 86–87, Fredericksburg, Va. State Lib.

92. Hunter was a merchant in Falmouth, Va. See Daniel Lawrence Hylton v. Adam

[*Disbursements*]

April 13	Paid Miss B Munkus 16/		16
	Given Polly		12
	Postage 4/, Market 30/	1	14
16th.	Market 8/, do. 3/		11
17th.	Market 6/, flour 33/	1	19
	Tea 12/		12
19th.	expenses 6/, Market 12/		18
		7	2

[*Receipts*]

April 19th.	Advice 28/	1	8	
	From Key ads. Muir	5	5	
	From Hernden ads. Crutchfield[93]	2	8	
	From Morris ads. Posey	3		
20th.	From Branch ads. Donald		12	
	From Hecks ads. Crawford & Co.	7	10	
	From Jones v Skelton 49/4	2	9	4
	advice fee	1	2	6
	do. to Higbee	3		
	From Stevens v Preston (by Higbee)	5		
21st.	From Williams Cary & Co. ads Lyles	2	11	
	For motion on repln. bond for Ritchies exrs.	2	3	
	Waring v Weeks (for trial)	2	10	
22d.	From Currel ads. Lawson	4	14	
23d.	From Kuhn v Hoomes T.A.B.[94]	3		
	From Capt. Douglass[95] £3 int. warrants	2	10	

Hunter and Abner Vernon, Wythe 195–211, for the case JM became involved in for Hunter.

93. John Crutchfield v. Edward Herndon was an action in detinue that ended in the District Court at Fredericksburg on Oct. 4, 1790, when the parties agreed to a dismissal. District Court Law Orders, A, 1789–1793, 71, 73, 153, Fredericksburg, Va. State Lib.

94. Jacob Kuhn v. John Hoomes was an action for trespass, assault and battery, brought in the General Court in Oct. 1786. See JM's declaration printed at Oct. 1786.

95. Hugh Douglass. See JM's pleading calendared under Douglass's executor v. Bruin, Mar. 30, 1786, and entry under Receipts, Sept. 29, 1785.

Mosby v Johnston & Garrat (old suit		1	14	
Westbrooke & al. ads. Byrd		4	16	
Tomlin v Kelly[96]		2	8	
Jackson ads. Farrar[97] appl. chy.		4	16	8
		63	17	6

[Disbursements]

April 19th.	furnishd by brother Wm.	18	9	
	Sent my Father by my brother Tom	34	16	
20	sent to market 12/		12	
23d.	To Colo. T. Randolph[98] for 3 barrels of corn	2	10	
		38	16	9
		3	2	

[Receipts]

April 25th.	From Colo. T. Randolph in 3 barrels of corn[99]	2	10	
	Kellys exrs. ads. Alexander chy.	2	3	8
	From Neilson v Willis	2	8	
26th.	From McChesny ads. Cosby etc. surviving part. of Mills & Co.	2	10	
	From Tisdale v Winn (balance)		10	
	From Davies v Ross & Hook chy.	5		

96. Tomlin, Mitchell, and How v. Kelly was first brought in the General Court by JM for plaintiffs. After 1788 it was transferred to the District Court at Northumberland Courthouse and was taken over by another attorney. District Court Order Book, 1789–1792, 106, 142, 1793–1802, 1, Northumberland County; Court of Appeals Order Book, II, 193, 211, both in Va. State Lib.; 1 Washington 190–192 (1793).

97. William Farrar v. Francis Jackson was an appeal to the High Court of Chancery from Amelia County Court. JM's client, Jackson, won a reversal by a division of the court, George Wythe dissenting. Wythe 1.

98. Thomas Mann Randolph. See entry under Disbursements, Jan. 25, 1787.

99. The entry under Disbursements, Apr. 23, to Thomas Mann Randolph and the return of the money registered here suggests that the corn was bad and JM got a refund for the purchase. He bought no more corn from Randolph, although he did buy flour from him in Sept. 1787.

		£	s	d
	From Lucas v Crawford	2	10	
	same v Colemans exrs.		10	
	From Morris (habeas corpus)	2	10	
	Kinnon v Webb on repn. bond[1]	2	10	
	Glasscock v Shacklett	2	3	
29th.	From Fuqua ads. Bates	7		
	From Lewis v Christian admr.	2	10	
	From Lewis ads. Smith & ux.	2	10	
		36	19	8

[Disbursements]

		£	s	d
April 24th.	tea tongs 22/6	1	2	6
	to Polly 15/, wood 10/, expenses 11/	1	16	
	In presents to My Mother & sister Molly	4	16	
26th.	Market 12/, expenses 7/, for stocks 20/	1	19	
	paid for cloth for my father	6	16	2
	Flour £4, wood 6/8	4	6	8
27th.	expenses 4/, barber 24/	1	8	
29th.	postage for letters 2/		2	
	Market 9/		9	
	Browns chancery reports[2]	3	5	
		26		4
		6	16	2
		19	4	2

[Receipts]

		£	s	d
May 1st.	Woody ads. Wilson Appl. chy. £	5		
2d.	Mr. Watkins for advice	1	2	
	Whiting v Washington[3]			
	Trespass	2	4	
	Neale v Stubbs TAB		18	

1. See definition under Receipts, Sept. 25, 1786.
2. William Brown's *Reports of Cases argued and determined in the High Court of Chancery
. . . Trinity Term . . . 1778 (to Hilary Term, 34 Geo. III)* (London, 1785–1794). The publication date indicates that JM bought only a portion of the four-volume set. See entry under Disbursements, Jan. 12, 1788.
3. This case may be Robert Coan, surviving executor of Thomas Whiting, v. Warner Washington's executor, although that was a debt action that ended in the District Court at Winchester on Sept. 12, 1794. Superior Court Order Book, 1794–1797, 109, Frederick County, Va. State Lib.

5th.	Smith ads Smith apl. in Case	5	
	Same ads Same[4] Same	5	
9	Young ads of Roirick[5] (Hab Corps)	2	10
12th.	From Samson ads. Dixon (motion)	2	8
	Sampson was involvd with Foxe.		
16th.	From Doctor Stuart[6]	16	16
	From Gratz v Lee (in name of Simons)	2	3
22d.	From Hill v Tinsley (finishd)	2	16
	From Doctor Fowshee in Neilson v Middlesex justices[7] supersedeas	1	8
	From Bell v Carrs Exrs. appeal	2	11
26.	From Butler v Butler in chy.	1	8
29th.	Burtons exrs. ads. Stringer[8] repln.	2	11
30th.	From Mr. Eyre ads. Savage[9] Appeal	2	11
		56	6

4. JM had appeared in this case, Rawley Smith, administrator of Joseph Smith, v. William Smith, in Fauquier County Court on Aug. 27, 1784. He was obviously filing an appeal in the General Court or the High Court of Chancery in 1787. Minute Book, 1784–1786, 51, Fauquier County, Va. State Lib.

5. See same case under Receipts, Apr. 20, 1785.

6. David Stuart (1753–1811) studied medicine at Edinburgh after attending the College of William and Mary. He settled in Alexandria, Va., and represented Fairfax County in the House of Delegates from 1785 to 1788. He also attended the ratifying convention in 1788 and became an ardent Federalist and strong friend of George Washington, who appointed him one of the first commissioners of the District of Columbia. In 1791–1792 he helped fix the boundary lines of the proposed U.S. capital.

7. Apparently William Foushee was delivering a fee in this case against the Middlesex County justices of the peace.

8. John Stringer v. Thomas Dolby and John Guy, executors of John Burton, originated in Northampton County Court, where that court ordered Burton to return some slaves to the possession of Stringer. JM appealed the decision to the General Court for Dolby and Guy. The case was transferred to the District Court at Accomack and Northampton, but that court adjourned the case to the General Court in Oct. 1790. In May 1792 the General Court found for Stringer and ordered a jury impaneled to assess the values of the slaves. This was done in Accomack County on Oct. 15, 1792. District Court Order Book, 1791–1794, 259–264, Accomack County, Va. State Lib.

9. John Eyre, executor of Littleton Eyre, v. John Savage was a debt action on appeal to the General Court. After 1788 the case was transferred to the District Court at Accomack and Northampton, where it was finally dismissed on May 15, 1792. Ibid., 1789–1797, 177, 199.

[*Disbursements*]

May 1st.	To Betsy Munkus		16	
	Saddle & bridle for Polly	5		
2d.	for water cask 9/, Market 4/		13	
	punch ladle 22/6, knee			
	buckles 5/, postage 2/	1	9	6
9th.	To Polly expended about			
	house	2	10	0
12th.	My expenses going to Gloster[10]			
	etc.	5		
	Expences in county £4–4	4	4	
15	razors etc.		6	6
16th.	Tea 10/6, wood 8/, for			
	Polly 10/, market 5/4	1	13	10
18th.	Paid for a Woman bought in			
	Gloster[11]	55		
	Market 13/9, do. 13/,			
	Cowhide 2/	1	8	9
	Subscription Jocky club[12]	2	2	
	Shrub 6/, capers 2/6, nuts 1/3		9	9
	plants 3/3, market 2/6, do. 2/		7	9
22d.	Market 20/, do. 10/4,			
	expenses 8/	1	18	4
	Shoeing my horse 3/		3	
23d.	Lost at race[13] 34/, wood 9/	2	3	
25th.	Market 3/, taxes in			
	Henrico[14] £7	7	3	
30th.	Market 11/6		11	6
		37	19	2
	the Negroe[15]	55		
		92	19	2

10. Gloucester County is on the north shore of the York River and borders on the Chesapeake Bay.

11. Apparently this was not the only slave JM bought in Gloucester County, but it was the only one he paid cash for. See entry under Disbursements, Aug. 20, 1787. This purchase was the first of several JM made in 1787. See *passim* below.

12. This subscription was in preparation of the spring horse races in Richmond. See note for entry under Disbursements, Oct. 23, 1784.

13. This is the first gambling entry JM recorded from horse races.

14. All Henrico County land tax records after 1786 are missing.

15. Purchased in Gloucester County.

[*Receipts*]

June	1st.	advice 28/	1	8	
	2d.	advice 22/6	1	2	6
		drawing a conveyance	1	8	
		Grey v McKewan case	2	17	
		From Rees v Taite T.A.B. dam. 500[16]		15	
	9th.	From Clayborne ads. Dunnivant	3		
		From the sheriff of Louisa[17]	2	8	
	13th.	From Shepherd v Stribling & Ball two suits	4	6	
		From Fleming ads. Hollingsworth	2	10	
		same ads.	2	4	
	19th.	From Haynes ads. Parker two suits	5		
		From same ads. Tabb	2	10	
	20th.	Armstrong ads. Ladd debt	1	8	
		Custer ads. Hall & ux. ch.	2	8	
	27th.	Recd. from Majr. Lee for Colo. Marshall	13	10	
		From Allen v Wallace & al & from same & ux v same		18	
		From Mr. Bryan for a suit with Withers concerning land in Fauqr.[18]	2	12	
			49	14	6

[*Disbursements*]

June	1st.	a pair of shoes for self 12/		12
		Gown for Polly 24/, knife 5/	1	9
	3d.	To Betsy Munkus 16/, market 3/		19
		expenses 6/		6

16. Damages of £500 were being asked in this case of trespass, assault and battery.

17. The sheriff of Louisa County, Waddy Thompson, had been ordered to pay damages as part of a judgment for the 1785 taxes. Upon appeal to the Council of State, probably handled by JM, part of the damages were remitted on Nov. 12, 1787. *JVCS*, IV, 166.

18. Fauquier County.

		£	s	d
	Paid Mr. Lewis in part for two negroes[19]	10	13	8
	Fruit & blacking 4/		4	
6th.	Market 6/, flour £3–16	4	2	
12th.	Taxes for Fauquier[20]	8	5	2
	Market 7/6, expences 4/		11	6
	market 6/, Tea 12/		18	
	Chickens 7/6,[21] raffling 28/	1	15	6
18th.	market 2/3, expenses 4/, postage 4/		10	3
	chamber utensils 9/, paper 13/4	1	2	4
19th.	In a present to Nancy[22]	1	10	
	cherries 1/, chickens 9/6		10	6
20th.	Flour from Colo. Syme[23] 40/, expenses 6/	2	6	
	linnen for Sam 9/		9	
	coffin for Sam[24] 12/		12	

19. This may be Benjamin Lewis, from whom JM probably bought a house in 1785. The amount could be for hiring rather than purchasing slaves, but see at the end of this month where JM deducted this amount from his expenses.

20. Fauquier County tax records indicate JM was taxed £5 6s. 1d. for Oak Hill and £2 6s. 9d. for personal property of 1 tithable and 2 nontithable Negroes, 7 horses, and 11 carriage wheels. This of course totals only £7 12s. 10d. Possibly JM paid his brother Tom's land tax of £1 6s. 3d., but this would raise the total to £8 19s. 1d. It is conceivable that in Virginia currency, this last figure equaled £8 5s. 2d. in 1787. Fauquier County Land Book, 1787, and Personal Property, 1787 (oversize), Va. State Lib.

As explained in the editorial note, JM's Account Book also contains the law notes at the other end of the volume. At the end of those notes and separated by a few pages, JM entered the following expenses for Oak Hill:

> Fauquier Plantation
>
> 1787 Taxes
>
> | | |
> |---|---|
> | expenses on negroes | £20 |
> | bought a horse | 20 |
> | Corn | 17 |
> | do. | 30 |

21. Not in JM's hand.

22. Nancy Marshall (b. 1781), JM's youngest sister.

23. John Syme, of Hanover County, owned flour mills that had helped supply the troops in 1781.

24. Nothing is known about when JM acquired this slave. Jaquelin Ambler owned a slave named Sam who was 34 years old in 1784. JM might have bought him from Ambler sometime between 1784 and his death in 1787. In any event, it is likely JM bought him on credit. See entry under Disbursements, Apr. 16, 1788, where JM paid someone £60 for this same slave, although Sam had been dead almost one year. For Ambler's slaves in 1784, see "Return of the Inhabitants," 1784, Richmond City Common Hall Records, 330, Va. State Lib.

29th.	paid Doctor Leiper[25] for				
	do. £3-11		3	11	
	Market 6/			6	
			39	12	11
			10	13	8
			28	19	3

[Receipts]

July		Johnston ads. Commonwealth	2	10
		Johnston ads. Heaths exrs.	2	10
		same ads. Webb Claiborne		
		& Co.	2	10
	7	Southerland v. Quarles &		
		al. chy.	5	2
		From Reigley ads. Harris		
		appeal	2	16
	17th.	From Bryan 50/ v Withers	2	10
		From Capt. Darnal 28/	1	8
		From Page v Randolph sups.	2	10
		advice on Aldens will	1	1
	31st.	From Hoomes v Dixon	2	10
			25	7

[Disbursements]

July	1st.	barrel of shads	4	10	
	2d.	making a crane	4	12	3
		putting up Do.		7	6
		expences 12/		12	
		To Miss Betsy Munkus 16/		16	
		wood 8/, chickens 8/9		16	9
	4th.	Market 4/3, postage 2/6		6	9
		market 2/, do. 9/, taking up			
		Moses[26] 10/	1	1	
		Pd. Johnston for Dise & child			
		on acct. of Mr. Ambler[27]	70		
		Paid Mr. Ambler for Negroes[28]	14	8	

25. Andrew Leiper, or Leeper (b. *ca.* 1752), was a Richmond physician. *Ibid.*, 350.
26. JM was taking Moses, a 22-year-old slave, to Fauquier County.
27. Dicey and her child were purchased from John B. Johnson for Jaquelin Ambler on July 3, probably in Fauquier County. See Bill of Sale, July 3, 1787. See end of the month where JM deducted this expense from his regular disbursements.
28. JM made an additional payment in Aug. for the slaves he bought in Gloucester

18th.	expenses up & down to & from Fauquir	4	12	
	For a book 6/, quills & pencil 3/, postage 3/8		12	8
	Market 6/, kitchen furniture 30/	1	16	
23d.	Market 21/7½	1	1	7½
25th.	Wood 8/, Market 9/, do. 2/		19	
30th.	Cart £6–6, expences 15/, wood 6/	7	7	
31st.	market 8/3, do. 37/6, do. 2/	2	7	9
		116	6	3½
	70²⁹			
	14	84	8	
	84 8	31	18	3½

[Receipts]

August 1st.	From Green v Miller supersedeas		17	
	From Gayle & ux v Billups exrs. old chy. suit	1	8	
	From Compton v Hickman	2	10	
4th.	From Southerland on a bill exchange v Braxton Hill & al[30]	2	10	
6th	Advice fee	1	1	
	Advice fee	1	1	
	Matthews v McClenahan superses.	2	10	
7th.	Howle v Christian appeal	1	15	
9th.	Dohrman v Anderson[31] 2 suits	4	4	

in May. See Disbursements, Aug. 20, 1787. See end of the month where JM deducted this expense from his regular disbursements.

29. This is the total JM paid for slaves on July 4.

30. James Hill and Carter Braxton v. Roger Gregory, executor of Fendall Souther-land. Hill was the endorser of a protested bill of exchange drawn by Braxton in favor of Southerland in 1776. Various judgments were obtained until in 1787 Southerland filed a new suit against Hill. After he won a new judgment, Hill sought an injunction in the High Court of Chancery. The case finally ended in the Court of Appeals in Oct. 1792. Wythe 73; 1 Washington 128–134; Court of Appeals Order Book, II, 186, 197–198, Va. State Lib.

31. Henry H. Dohrman v. George Anderson was transferred to the District Court at Prince Edward County after the reorganization of the courts in 1788 and was con-tinued from Sept. 7, 1790, until it was finally dismissed on Sept. 7, 1795. District Court

14th.	Markham ads. Page exr. of Cary	2	5
17th.	Wilson (Leiper) v Hart admr. of Marshall[32]	5	
21st.	Stoval & al (Jeter) v Stovals exrs.[33]	2	10
	Kellum v West[34] case	2	10
	Hambleton ads. Wells[35] eject.	4	16
	From Mr. Deane in chy. v Smythe Wilson & al.	5	
	For drawing a deed 20/	1	
29th.	From Jones & ux. v Ransones chy.	2	4
30th.	On the attachments v. Conrad etc.	8	
		51	1

Order Book, 1789–1792, 131, 276, 1793–1799, 52, 140, 168, 213, Prince Edward County, Va. State Lib.

32. Robert Wilson v. Robert Hart, administrator of John Marshall, deceased, of Louisa County was an action in assumpsit brought before the General Court by JM in Oct. 1787. The case was subsequently transferred to the District Court at Fredericksburg, where judgment was entered for the plaintiff on May 6, 1790. District Court Records, 1789–1792, 185–188, Fredericksburg, Va. State Lib. See JM's declaration calendared at Oct. 1787.

33. Augustine Leftwich and wife v. Bartholomew Stovall et al. The Bedford County Court had awarded judgment to Leftwich on Aug. 28, 1786. JM filed an appeal in the General Court for Stovall. The case was transferred to the District Court at New London but did not end until it reached the Court of Appeals in 1794. 1 Washington 303–306 (1794); and Court of Appeals Order Book, III, 9, 11; District Court Order Book, I, 1789–1793, 128, 359–360, II, 1794–1796, 42, 107, 136, Franklin County, both in Va. State Lib.

34. Severn Kellum v. Jeremiah West was a slander case in which West claimed damages from Kellum for perjuring himself as a witness. JM obtained a writ of inquiry to determine damages from the General Court after West defaulted on Feb. 29, 1788. The case was continued until it was transferred to the District Court at Accomack and Northampton after the reorganization of the courts. JM turned the case over to George Parker at that time. District Court Order Book, 1789–1791, 4–7, 1789–1797, 21, Accomack County, Va. State Lib.

35. James Hambleton, David Bradford, and John Decker v. Solomon Saveatt, lessee of Alexander Wells. The plaintiffs' action in ejectment was unsuccessful in the court below, and JM filed an appeal in the General Court. The case was transferred to the District Court at Monongalia County after 1788, and a judgment was entered on Sept. 20, 1790. In Dec. 1790 an appeal was filed with the Court of Appeals, which reversed the district court's judgment on June 29, 1791. Court of Appeals Order Book, II, 60, 102, 105, Va. State Lib.

	[*Disbursements*]			
August 1	market 4/3, blackball[36] 1/3		5	6
2d.	Paid Register[37] for two Military Surveys for Colo. Marshall	1	16	3
	for coal to Duval	3	4	
3d.	To Betsy Munkus 16/, market 8/	1	4	
	Expences 20/, Herrings 20/	2		
9th.	Given Polly 6/, market 4/, house 2/		12	
	water melons 2/6, postage 4/		6	6
13th.	expenses 2/, market 2/, postage 2/		6	
	shoes for Israel 6/		6	
17th.	market 4/		4	
20th.	paid Mr. Ambler balance for negroes bought on his credit in Gloster[38]	30		
21st.	given Polly 12/, market 2/		14	
22	Market 3/, postage 1/3, Hinges etc. 6/, shoeing bay horse 2/6		12	9
23d	paid for oats 9£	9		
	For coal £7–10	7	10	
25th.	Tongs etc. for upstairs		12	
	counterpane 30/	1	10	
	For a negroe man from F. Webb[39]	47	2	
28th.	market 2/, do. 4/, furniture for cart 31/6	1	17	6
29	For case £5–2, postage 2/3, market 2/, do. 4/	5	10	3
		114	12	9
		78	16	5
		35	16	4

36. A composition of wax and lampblack used in polishing shoes, sometimes called heelball.

37. John Harvie was register of the Land Office.

38. See entries under Disbursements, May 18, July 4, 1787.

39. Foster Webb, Jr.

[Receipts]

September				
5th.	from Colo. Gaskins ads. Heath	I	10	
	For defending Mr. Forsythe	7		
	Mr. Cox v Calloway (to be brought down)	I	4	8
	Mr. Lee exr. of Keene v Aldingtons exx. super.	2	3	
	Bates v Boyd slander	2	10	
10th.	From Mr. Smith in Maxwell v McClenahan supersedeas (to be tried in October)	2	10	
13th.	From Wharton v Spraggens	2	10	
	From Ruffin exr. in sevl. suits[40]	4	12	10
18th	from Alexander	II	0	0
23d.	from Muse vs. Stark appl.	2	10	6
	From Mr. Brown for Mr. Donald	2	16	
	Advice	2	16	
24	From James v Cobbs[41] appeal	2	10	
	Garrison ads. Garrison (old eject)	I	4	
25	Scott ads. writ o[f] error	2	10	
25	Cole & Alloway v Nelson appeal	I	4	
	Priddy v Richardson		18	
	Jacob ads. Robins appeal about a road	5		
	Morton ads. Johnston (enquire of C. Pendleton & search			

40. William Jones, surviving partner Farrell & Jones, v. Francis Ruffin, executor of John Ruffin, was one of the suits. It was based on goods sold and delivered in 1769 and finally came before the U.S. Circuit Court for Virginia, which dismissed the case on Nov. 28, 1798. U.S. Circuit Court, Va., Order Book, I, 44; U.S. Circuit Court Restored Case Papers, both in Va. State Lib.

41. Richard James and William Spears v. John Cobbs was an appeal from Cumberland County Court filed by JM on Mar. 28, 1787. The case was transferred to the District Court at Prince Edward County after 1788, was dismissed on Sept. 2, 1790, reinstated the next day, and dismissed again on Apr. 4, 1791. District Court Order Book, 1789–1792, 112, 115, 134, 165, Prince Edward County, Va. State Lib.

records) [42]		1	8	
Jacobs ads. Nottingham		1	8	
Holliday ads. Coleman & ux				
(old suit in chy)		3		
		62	4	4

[Disbursements]

September

1st.	Veal 11/9, Market 2/		13	9
4th.	Market 3/6, do. 1/, wood 7/		11	6
5th.	Paid Betsy Munkus 16/,			
	given Polly 2/		18	
6	paid for newspaper 7/6		7	6
	Market 9/, given Polly 4/		13	
8th.	Fruit 1/, book for Tom [43] 1/6		2	6
9th.	Market 7/6, do. 6/		13	6
15th.	postage 4/6, expenses 6/		10	6
	Flour paid for to Colo. T.			
	Randolph [44]	3	12	
	Market 4/6, expences 1/6		6	
	Tea 12/6, wool 6/, fruit 1/6	1		
25th.	postage 3/4, do. 7½, market 3/		7	
28th.	Market 18/, fruit 1/		19	
		10	14	3

[Receipts]

September	Cotrel v Eales 30/ an old petn.	1	10	
	Young v Nale	2	10	
	Moore v Moore [45] appeal	2	10	
	Power ads. Brown appeal	2	10	

42. Gabriel Johnston, administrator of John Drake, v. Elijah Morton, executor of William Morton, was a debt action that finally abated on Oct. 5, 1789, by the death of Morton. The case had been transferred to the District Court at Fredericksburg. C. Pendleton probably refers to Chancellor Edmund Pendleton, one of the chancery judges at this time. District Court Law Orders, A, 1789–1793, 41, Fredericksburg, Va. State Lib.

43. JM's son.

44. Thomas Mann Randolph.

45. John Moore v. Reubin Moore, Jr., was an appeal from a judgment of the Shenandoah County Court of June 2, 1787. It was transferred after 1788 to the District Court at Winchester, which affirmed the lower court's decision on Apr. 25, 1791. Superior Court Order Book, 1789–1793, 193, Frederick County, Va. State Lib.

	[Disbursements]			
September 30th.	Shoemaker 25/, corks 1/3	1	6	3
	[Receipts]			
October 1	Kirtley v Head	2	10	
	Armstrong ads. Lad	1	2	
	Henman v Wooster (rep. bond)	2	10	
	Meux ads. Syme Appeal	2	10	
	Richardson v high shrf. of hanover[46]	5	12	
	Rennolds ads. Vawter (Caroline)[47]	2	10	
	Rennolds ads. Johnston[48] (in part)	1	8	
	From Capt. Rust	2	16	
2	Hite v Hites Orphans & al (chy.)	3	6	
	do. 48/	2	8	
	do. 6/		6	
	From John Perkins on rep. bond	1	4	
	From Mr. Wormington (2 suits)	6		
	Cox v Rootes H.C. (to inspect)	2	10	
	Richardson ads. Lewis[49]	2	10	
	Gooch ads. Eppes & al H.C.	1		
3	Howle v Christian appeal		15	
	Harfield (appeals in part)	2	8	
	Whitehurst 2 suits to be dismissd	5		

46. The sheriff of Hanover County was William Overton Winston (1747–1815). See Clayton Torrence, *Winston of Virginia and Allied Families* (Richmond, 1927), 43.

47. Elliott Vawter v. James Reynolds was an appeal from Caroline County to the General Court. It was transferred after 1788 to the District Court at Fredericksburg, where it abated by the death of Reynolds on Oct. 7, 1789. District Court Law Orders, A, 1789–1793, 58, Fredericksburg, Va. State Lib.

48. James Johnston v. William Reynolds was an appeal from Caroline County to the General Court, filed in Oct. 1786. The case was continued until it was transferred to the District Court at Fredericksburg, where judgment was entered for Reynolds on May 5, 1791. District Court Records, 1789–1792, 487–488; District Court Law Orders, A, 1789–1793, 53, 108, 241, Fredericksburg, both in Va. State Lib.

49. George Lewis v. William Richardson ended in the District Court at Winchester, where judgment was entered for Richardson on Sept. 7, 1790. Superior Court Order Book, 1789–1793, 127, Frederick County, Va. State Lib.

White	Campbell ads. Wellch Appeal	2	10	
	same ads. [S]wilbys do.	2	10	
	Hites orphans v Martin	7		
4th.	Taylor ads. Payne etc. exrs. etc.[50]	2	10	
	Jones ads. Smith T.A.B. (henrico)	2	10	
		64	5	

[*Disbursements*]

October				
2d.	Market 12/		12	
	Market 29/, Betsy Munkus 16/	2	5	
4th.	market 6, expenses 4/, eggs 3/		13	
		3	10	

[*Receipts*]

October				
5th.	Mackee ads. Yancy appeal	2	7	
6	Smith ads. Taylors exrs.[51]	2	3	
	Wilkinson caveats[52] 5£	5		
7th.	From Lewis ads. Jones eject.[53]	2	6	8
	From Norrel ads. Boyd	2	10	
8th.	Markham ads. Cock (appeal)	1	8	

50. William and Joseph Payne, executors of John Elliott Payne, v. William Tailor, Elijah Kirtley, and Zachariah Tailor was a debt action filed in the General Court in Apr. 1787. Various court orders were issued against various defendants, represented by JM, in May and Oct. 1787, and Apr., June, and July 1788. The case was then transferred to the District Court at Fredericksburg, where judgment was confessed against the remaining defendants on Oct. 7, 1789. District Court Records, 1789–1792, 96–98, Fredericksburg, Va. State Lib.

51. John Smith v. Ralph Wormeley, Jr., Mann Page, Francis Lightfoot Lee, George Plater, John Taylor Corbin, Warner Lewis, Jr., Edward Loyd, Thomas Lawson, surviving executors of John Taylor, came before the General Court sometime before 1788. It was then transferred to the District Court at Northumberland County, which entered a judgment against Smith on Sept. 10, 1791. Smith appealed to the Court of Appeals, which affirmed the decision on Oct. 15, 1792. Court of Appeals Order Book, II, 184, Va. State Lib.

52. William Kennedy v. Thomas Turk, Sr. Kennedy was "claiming the same by virtue of two entries made prior to 1780, one by John Wilkinson, and the other by James Kennedy Senr. & by them assigned to him." Land Office Caveats, II, Oct. 31, 1787, 34, Va. State Lib.

53. John Dreadnought, lessee of Robert Jones, v. John Lewis was transferred to the District Court at Prince Edward after 1788, where the case was dismissed on Sept. 5, 1789. District Court Order Book, 1789–1792, 37, Prince Edward County, Va. State Lib.

		£	s	d
	Jordan ads. Armstead[54]	2	10	
9th.	From R Scott	3	10	
	From Shelton v Sheltons exrs. chy.[55]	5		
10	Garlington v Clutton appeal[56]	2	10	
	From Mr. McCarty (chy)	5	8	
12	Dade ads. Roe & Hammond (old suit)	2	8	
13th.	Tabb ads. McNeal Chy.	5		
	advice Barton ads. Livesay	1	4	
15th.	advice 22/6	1	2	6
	Jones v Skelton (chy. old suit)	2	10	
16	Mr. Harminson	2	8	
	Mr. Brockenboro	2	6	
	McClain v Baine	2	2	
	From Philips in old suits		16	
		52	11	2

[Disbursements]

		£	s	d
October 6	market 16		16	
8th.	Market 20/, wood 3/7½	1	3	7½
	market 3/, wood 3/		6	
12th.	corn £3, sundries in store 5£	8		
	Tea 12/, grains 1/6		13	6
16	Butter	2	8	
	Butter	6	15	9
		20	2	10½

54. William Armistead v. Mathew Jordon began in the Charlotte County Court, which found against Armistead on Aug. 6, 1787. The case was then appealed to the General Court, where JM represented Jordon. After 1788 the case was transferred to the District Court at Prince Edward, which affirmed the judgment on Sept. 4, 1790. The Court of Appeals also affirmed the decision on June 22, 1791. Court of Appeals Order Book, II, 88, Va. State Lib.

55. David, William, and Samuel Shelton, executors of Joseph Shelton, v. John Shelton was brought before the High Court of Chancery sometime prior to Aug. 5, 1790, when it issued a decree for John Shelton, JM's client. This decree was appealed to the Court of Appeals, which heard argument in June and Nov. 1791 and reversed the decree on Nov. 10, 1791. Ibid., 50, 66–67, 110, 113, 117.

56. William Garlington v. Jesse Clutton was brought before the General Court on appeal from Northumberland County Court sometime before 1788. After that date it was transferred to the District Court at Northumberland County. There were two trials during the 1790s and a final appeal to the Court of Appeals in 1799. Ibid., III, 299.

[*Receipts*]

October 16	From Noland ads Edmonds old suit	1	8
	From Elzey	3	
17	Jones v Latane	2	10
	Booth v Bradley's exrs. motion to be made to the next court & I am to send notice	2	10
	From Webb on rep. bond	2	5
18	Thilman assee. of Guerant	1	3
	From Van Bibber	5	12
	From Biggars v Bibb	1	4
	From Wyat ads. Johnston[57]	2	
19th	From Barksdale ads. Posey	2	10
	Bevers v Waterson in part		13
	From Reid in Hook v Meade & al)	5	
21st.	From Mr. Latham	5	2
24th.	advice fee	1	2
	drawing an answer	1	8
	From Slaughter ads.[58]	2	10
28th	From Devier v Callender etc. two appeals	5	
	From Shermers exrs.[59]	28	
		72	17

[*Disbursements*]

October 16th.	wood	8

57. Christopher and Robert Johnston v. William Wiatt was filed in the General Court in 1783. The parties agreed to arbitration in 1784, and the case was continued until a trial was held in Apr. 1788. After 1788 the case was transferred to the District Court at Fredericksburg, which gave judgment for Wiatt on Oct. 1, 1789. District Court Records, 1789–1792, 4–8, Fredericksburg, Va. State Lib.

58. Culpeper justices at instance of John Thompson and Jane, his wife, v. John Slaughter *et al.*, administrators of Thomas Howison, filed in the General Court in Oct. 1787 by James Monroe, charged Slaughter *et al.* with improper administration of Howison's estate. The case was transferred to the District Court at Fredericksburg after 1788, and on Oct. 4, 1790, that court found for the Culpeper justices. *Ibid.*, 261–271.

59. William Shermer v. Dudley Richardson, John Shermer's executor, was decided by the High Court of Chancery on Sept. 27, 1792, for JM's client, Dudley Richardson. William Shermer appealed to the Court of Appeals, which affirmed the decree on Oct. 18, 1794. 1 Washington 266–268; Court of Appeals Order Book, II, 262, III, 2, 6, Va. State Lib.

		£	s
20th.	market at various times		18
	do. 9/, Jockey club[60] 42/	2	11
		3	17

[Receipts]

		£	s
October			
27th.	From Rees v. Taite (old suit)	1	10
	Reamy & King ads. Feagans		18
	same ads. Combs (debt		
	From Mr. Harrison in a suit		
	in chy. from Philadelphia		
	(Ritsons heirs I beleive)	10	
	From do. chy. in Randolphs		
	exrs. ads Maury	5	
	Craddock v Jones supersedeas	2	5
29th.	Walker ads. Syme[61] (chy.)	5	
	McGan v Powell (T.A.B. old		
	suit)		12

[Disbursements]

		£	s
October	Market 18/, wood 8/,		
	postage 4/	1	10
	Potatoes 7/6, market 4/6		12
		2	2

[Receipts]

			£	s
November				
2d.	Towns admr. of Clough ads.			
	Williams	£	5	
	Mayo ads. H.C.		2	10
	McGan v Powell (old suit)			12
3d.	Booker v Taylor		5	6
	Geddy v Roane rep. bond		2	10
4	From Mrs. McKewan		5	
5th.	Pleasants ads. Smith (chy.)		2	10
6	Holliday v Coleman		2	4
	Fitzhugh ads. Hansbro chy.			
	att.		5	
7	Keller ads. Alexander injn.		3	

60. See entry under Disbursements, May 25, 1785.
61. See Receipt from Thomas Walker, printed at Oct. 29, 1787.

	Ellington v Traylor injn.	2		
	Dickie v Hind (injn.)	3	16	
	McCall ads. Rountree injn.	5		
	Mosely v Mosely chy.	5		
	Baird v Muir injn.	2	16	
	From Mr. Anderson finishd	2	10	
8th.	From Wilkinson ads. Trents	7	4	
	McKee & al ads. Wilson ha. cor.	2	10	
	Genl. Stephens[62]	3	12	
9	Roach v Hudson injn.	5		
	about naval office Fees[63]	1	8	
		74	8	

[Disbursements]

November 3d.	Market 11/6, do. 20/	1	11	6
	cart 12/6, Market 4/		16	6
	Betsy Munkus		16	
5th.	Turkies & Chickens 36/, Market 5/, do. 4	2	4	
9th.	Market 6/, postage 18/	1	4	
	beef 20/8, market 3/	1	3	8
		7	15	8

[Receipts]

November 12th	Slaughter ads. Slaughter chy.	7		
	Mordecai v Myers	4	16	
	Griffin to dismiss appeal	2	8	
13	Advice fee	1	8	
15th.	From Pollard for Biddle & Co	7		
	From Arch Stuart[64]	4	16	
25th.	From Tibbs	4	12	

[Disbursements]

November 10th	Wood 8/, market 3/7½, Teal 12/8	1	4	3½

62. Edward Stevens.

63. Several questions relating to the naval office in Virginia came before the Council of State in late 1787, one of which was referred to the attorney general, James Innes. It is likely that JM was consulted on one or more of these issues and paid a fee for his services. *JVCS*, IV, 151–152, 164, 172.

64. Archibald Stuart. See Notice of Richmond Lawyers, Oct. 25, 1784.

12th.	Market 6/8, do. 6/8		13	4
	Market 5/		5	
15th.	Market 36/	1	16	
	expenses 30/	1	10	
20th.	Wood 24/, house 1/3	1	5	3
	Coffee	1	16	
25	Market 12/8		12	8
27th.	Market 37/6, do. 6/8	2	4	4
	Oysters 6/		6	
	Market 8/6		8	6
		12	1	6

[*Receipts*]

December 1	From Mr. Eppes v Tucker[65]	7		
3	From Murry (old suit)	2		
4	Morris v Posey injn.	5		
	Advice fee from Moody	1	8	
5th.	Lampkin ads. Straughan[66]			
	writ of error	2	10	
7th.	advice fee from Stith on will	1	8	
15	West v King (Pitsylvania)[67]	2	10	
	advice 28/	1	8	
19th.	Purdie v Ball (suit to be brot.)	2	10	
	Cock v Webb	2	10	
	same v same	2	10	
21st.	advice fee	1	8	
22d.	do.	1	8	
	from Mr. Morris one fee	2	10	
	from Mr. Colston in paymt.	10	4	3
24	advice fee 22/6	1	2	6
			6	9

65. Francis Eppes v. St. George Tucker began in the High Court of Chancery but was appealed to the Court of Appeals in 1784. It was continued until May 3, 1785, when it was argued, but was continued for a rehearing until June 22, 1790. An opinion was issued on June 24, 1790, by which time Tucker was a judge of the General Court. 4 Call 346–353 (1790); Court of Appeals Order Book, I, 36, 46, 54, 93, 102, 106, 119, II, 2, 4, Va. State Lib.

66. Samuel L. Staughan v. Lewis Lamkin came to the General Court on a writ of error to the Northumberland County Court. The case was transferred to the District Court at Northumberland after 1788, and on Apr. 5, 1792, that court reversed the county court. District Court Order Book, 1789–1793, 193, Northumberland County, Va. State Lib.

67. Joseph West v. Edmund King involved a controversy over the sale of land in Pittsylvania County. The case did not end until after it was transferred to the District

[*Disbursements*]

December				
	Betsy Munkus		16	
	Mrs. Granger[68]	4	4	
	expences sending her & bringing		18	
	Barber	1	1	3
	Meal 12–		12	
9th.	market 6/, candles 6/		12	
10th.	market 4/3, Bacon 24/4	1	8	3
	Tea 12/, Corn £4–10	5	2	
12th.	Corn £7–10, market 6	7	16	
	Tax on deed from Colo. Peachy[69] to Colo Marshall	3		
15	Oysters		4	
	Candles £3–3, Market 14	3	17	
21st.	Market 12/, barly sugar 4/		16	
	wine & sundries at Mr. Harrisons[70]	25		
	pork 24/, market 12/	1	16	
	Given gown to Judy Brook[71]	1	10	
	Paid Mr. Colston for sundries	14	0	3
	Paid Mr. Morris[72] for hay	3	5	
24th.	oysters 4/, rent for stable 10/, wood 6/, eggs 4	1	4	
	market 8/6, Masons ball[73] 12/	1	0	6
		75	2	3

[*Disbursements*][74]

Decr. 28th.	market 40/	2		
	Paid Mr. Pickett[75] for sundries	24£		

Court at Prince Edward County, which entered a judgment for King on Sept. 8, 1791. District Court Records, 1789–1792, 426, Prince Edward County, Va. State Lib.

68. Mrs. Granger, the midwife who had earlier assisted Polly in the delivery of her children, aided in the delivery of Jaquelin Ambler Marshall on Dec. 3.

69. William Peachy.

70. Benjamin Harrison (b. *ca.* 1751) was a merchant in Richmond. "Return of the Inhabitants," 1784, Richmond City Common Hall Records, 356, Va. State Lib.

71. Judith Marshall Brooke (b. 1766), JM's sister, had married George Brooke about 1783.

72. Joshua or Turner Morris were both merchants in Richmond in 1787. "List of Merchants," Richmond City Hustings Court Order Book, II, 50, Va. State Lib.

73. The Masons in Richmond celebrated the festival of St. John the Evangelist on Dec. 27 with a parade from their hall to a church where they heard a sermon. The day was concluded with a grand ball. *Va. Gaz. & Wkly. Adv.*, Jan. 3, 1788.

74. This page is preceded by a blank page on which JM apparently had intended to enter receipts.

75. George Pickett was a Richmond merchant.

[Receipts][76]

Septr. 88	Recd. from Mr. Voss for Majr. Young	2		
No. 88	Recd. from Treasury for do.	20		
		22		
	[Disbursements]	12	14	11
	[Balance]	9	5	1

[Disbursements]

Paid horse here for J.T. at reqt. of H.Y.	1	16	
let Jack Tucker have at request of Majr. Young	3	12	8
Pd. Barrett for powder etc. for do.		6	3
Pd. Doctor Leiper for curing do.	7		
	12	14	11

[Receipts]

Jany. 1st.	From Dabny ads. Powell	2	10	
	advice fee	1	1	
	From Squire Lee[77]	1	1	
11th.	From Colo. Mason v Hooe on account of [debt] v Fowke in chy.	5		
16th.	From Thomson in Smith & al ads. Dandridge sci. fa.[78]	2	10	
20th.	advice 26/8	1	6	8

76. These receipts and the disbursements that follow are obviously figures JM entered out of their proper order. They are on a page with the Dec. 28, 1787, disbursements, printed directly above. "J.T." is no doubt Jack Tucker, and "H.Y." and "Majr. Young" must be Henry Young. "Barrett" is John Barret, the merchant, and "Doctor Leiper" is of course Andrew Leiper. It is unclear whether the expenses to Barret and Leiper were for Tucker, Young, or the horse.

77. Richard Lee (1726–1797) lived at Lee Hall in Hague, Va.

78. An abbreviation for "scire facias," which is a writ founded upon some matter of record, such as a judgment or recognizance, that requires the person against whom it is brought to show cause why the party bringing the writ should not have advantage of such record, or why the record should not be annulled and vacated.

21st.	From J. Peyton ads. Fallen (finishd)	7		
	From do. advice	1	4	
30th.	Polston v Fitcher injn. in part	2	1	
		22	13	8

[Disbursements]

Jany.	Betsy Munkus		18	
	Tea		12	
	My Father		6	
7th.	Market sundry times	3		
9th.	cart 6/, wood 6/8, mutton 21/6	1	14	4
	Pork	21	4	
10th.	wood 9/, potatoes 6/, market 1/3		16	3
12th.	Vinegar 4/, paper, [cork] wafers 9/		13	
	Continuation of Browns reports[79]		12	
15th.	paid for coal £3-1-8½, Hominy 2/4	3	4	½
19th.	wood 18/, expenses 4/, mending cellar door 11/4	1	13	4
22d.	market 9/, wood 8/, ink stand 10/	1	7	
23d.	market 6/, soap 3/, wood 36/	2	5	
24th.	Market 12/, kitchen 6/		18	
26th.	Market 4/, do. 6/, wine 15/	1	5	
	market 6/8, do. 6/, stockings negroe 5/		17	8
		41	5	7½
30th.	wood 9/, market 1/		10	
		41	15	7½

[Receipts]

February				
22d.	Advice fee from Mr. Briscoe	1	2	6
	Riddick v Carrs exrs.	3	16	
		4	18	6

79. JM no doubt bought an additional volume of Brown's *Reports of Cases . . . in the High Court of Chancery*. See entry under Disbursements, Apr. 29, 1787.

[*Disbursements*]

February				
1st.	Wood 8/		8	
	Pork £10–12–8	10	12	8
4th.	Tea 12/, Betsy Munkus 16/	1	8	
	Paid Olly on account of Colo. Marshall		6	
	Given Olly on account of do.	1	8	
11th.	wood 16/, sundries 2/		18	
	Subscription to birth night[80]	1	8	
	Stable 7/4, ribband 1/4		8	8
22d.	expences to Fauquier[81]	2	10	
24th.	Market 8/, Corn 12/	1		
28th	Market 6/8, do. 4/		10	8
29th.[82]	Shoes for Ben & Moses		13	4
	Wood 24/, for Tom 15/, sundries 6/	2	5	
	Taxes[83] & clerks notes	10	16	
	Newspaper & postage 28	1	8	
		36	0	4

[*Receipts*]

March 1st.	From Mr. Jennings two suits	5		
8th.	Keisel v Donally[84] appeal	2	10	
9th.	From Paynes exrs. v Riddle	4	18	4
13th.	From Mr. Archibald McColl[85]	10	8	

80. George Washington's birthday was still being observed on Feb. 11, using the old-style calendar. The day of celebration began with cannon salutes and a parade, after which the participants "proceeded to Mr. Mann's tavern, (joined by a number of citizens) where they spent the remaining part of the day in the greatest harmony and conviviality." There was a formal dinner and a grand ball at Anderson's rebuilt tavern, called the Union Tavern. JM's entry was no doubt for a subscription to the ball. *Va. Gaz. & Wkly. Adv.*, Feb. 14, 1788.

81. While in Fauquier County, JM recorded a deed to a farm he had purchased. See Deed calendared at Oct. 18, 1787.

82. 1788 was a leap year.

83. JM paid in 1788 the same taxes in Fauquier County as he had paid in 1787 (entered under Disbursements, June 12, 1787). Henrico County and Richmond City taxes were not paid until later in the year.

84. George Keisel v. Andrew Donnally was an appeal from the Aug. 22, 1787, judgment of the Augusta County Court to the General Court. It was continued until after the court reorganization of 1788, at which time it was transferred to the District Court at Staunton. On Sept. 3, 1790, the county court's decision was reversed. District Court Order Book, 1789–1793, 107–108, 1789–1797, 42, 56, Augusta County, Va. State Lib.

85. McCall (1734–1814) was a merchant in Tappahannock, Va. When the Revolution began he went to England to retrieve his children who were visiting there, and he

		£	s	d
	Trent v Wilson injn. in chy.	3	16	
14th.	From Edmund Harrison Esquire[86] advice	5		
	From Mr. Bell for advice	1	2	6
15th.	From Mr. Eppes exr. of Wayles	2	8	
	From Bell ads. Carys exrs.	5		
16	Mason v Holt advice	1	2	
20	Smith v Thornton[87] appeal	2	10	
	Hill v appeal	2	10	
21	Mr. Redford for advice	1	2	6
22	From Mr. Norton for three judgts. on replevin bonds	7	10	
	Mr. Jerdon advice fee	1	2	6
	do. suit in chy. ads. Middleton & ux	5		
24th.	From Mr. Coats v Haynes	7	10	
25th.	From Wilson & al. v Wilson chy.[88]	4	16	
26th.	Miller v Atkinson old ejectmt.	2	8	
	Mitchel ads. [ ] appeal	2	9	
		78	2	10

[Disbursements]

		£	s	d
March 11th.	corn 19/6, expences 7/6	1	7	
12th.	pair of shoes for self 13/		13	
	postage 1/8, mending boots 6/		7	8

was forced to stay until the war ended. He had left part of his lucrative business in the hands of his cousin, George McCall, who sued for remuneration in 1787. Perhaps McCall consulted JM on this legal matter. Joseph S. Ewing, ed., "The Correspondence of Archibald McCall and George McCall, 1777-1783," *VMHB*, LXXIII (1965), 312-353, 425-454.

86. Harrison (1764-1826), of Prince George County, later lived at The Oaks in Amelia County. After serving in the House of Delegates from 1788 until 1793, he was elected to the Council of State. From 1800 to 1807 he represented Amelia County in the House of Delegates.

87. Jesse Thornton v. William Smith was a slander case appealed to the General Court from the Richmond City Hustings Court judgment of Sept. 25, 1787. Although JM sat on the Hustings Court that decided against Smith, he obviously was now representing Smith in his appeal to the General Court. The case was transferred to the District Court at Richmond after 1788, which reversed the Hustings Court decision on Sept. 5, 1791. This decision was appealed to the Court of Appeals and affirmed on Apr. 28, 1792. 1 Washington 81; and Court of Appeals Order Book, II, 146, 159, 169; Richmond City Hustings Court Order Book, II, 220-221, both in Va. State Lib.

88. James and Bruce Wilson, London merchants, v. James Wilson began in the High Court of Chancery but ended in the U.S. Circuit Court when it was dismissed on May 25, 1792. U.S. Circuit Court, Va., Order Book, I, 99; U.S. Circuit Court Restored Case Papers, both in Va. State Lib.

14th.	waistcoats		19	6
	Coal 30/	1	10	
20th.	piece of linnen £6–14	6	14	
	card table £5–10, cards 8/, paper 2/	6		
	expences & lost at billiards at dift. times	3		
	Pd. Potowmac river co.[89]	24		
	barrel of flour	1	13	
	cloth etc. for self	6	7	
	Given Waggoner for carrying negroes		12	
	hat 48/	2	8	
	corn 6/, market 9/		15	
24th.	Net for fishing 5/, market 1/		6	
26	Market 15/, castor oil 8	1	3	
	Sugar 13/4, Tea 12/, expenses 30/	2	15	4
28th	Wood 8/, Sugar 31/6	1	19	6
		62		
	Paid potowmac co. to be deducted	24		
		38		

[Receipts]

March 29th.	Carter ads. Dade[90] appeal	2	10
	Eggleson v Chiles[91] (old suit)	1	2
	From Mr. Beale[92]	20	
31st.	From Genl. Stephens[93]	2	8
	McKean ads. McKewan[94]	2	10

89. For information on the company, see entry under Disbursements, Nov. 29, 1785. Also see below, Mar. 28, where JM deducted this entry.

90. Francis Dade and Lawrence Taliaferro v. Charles Carter was appealed from the Orange County Court. It was transferred to the District Court at Fredericksburg after the reorganization of 1788, and the parties agreed to a dismissal on Apr. 30, 1791. District Court Law Orders, A, 1789–1793, 163, Fredericksburg, Va. State Lib.

91. See entry under Receipts, Mar. 25, 1785.

92. Samuel Beale v. Martin Cockburn was brought before the High Court of Chancery, which issued a decree on Mar. 11, 1789. Afterwards JM appealed to the Court of Appeals for Beale, and in July 1790 that court affirmed the decree. 4 Call 162–195; Court of Appeals Order Book, I, 150, II, 19, 27, Va. State Lib.

93. Edward Stevens.

94. Michael McKewn v. William and John McKeen was a debt action filed in the General Court but transferred to the District Court at Winchester, where judgment

Scott v Field TAB[95]	2	12	
Webb ads. Grier appeal	2	10	
	33	12	

$$\begin{array}{rrr} 78 & 2 & 10^{96} \\ 33 & 12 & \\ \hline 111 & 14 & 10 \end{array}$$

[Disbursements]

March 29th.	paid the Taylor for suit of cloths	1	17	6
	market 2/6, expences for self 16/, paper 1/3		19	9
	paper 10/, quills 2/		12	
	barbacue 29/	1	9	
		3	16	3

[Receipts]

April 1st	Cox admr. etc. (Colo. Parker pd. fee ads. Sorrel appeal	2	16
	Rightmire ads. Doherty	2	10
	Roach & al. ads. Davies ha. cor.	2	8
2d.	Braithwhaite ads. Mandeville chy.	2	16
	Matthews ads. Byrd	4	16
	Markham ads. Cock (balance appeal)	1	4
	drawing an instrument of writing	1	8
3d.	Hudnal v Lewis	2	10
	Myrick v Vaughan appeal chy.	5	10
	Wingfields exrs. ads. Claybrook Chy.	2	10

was entered for McKewn on Apr. 20, 1790. Superior Court Order Book, 1789–1793, 66, Frederick County, Va. State Lib.

95. Mary Sloman Scott, executrix of Thomas Scott, v. William Call, surviving partner of Field and Call, was a debt action that JM appealed to the Court of Appeals in 1791 after the District Court at Petersburg found against Scott on Sept. 3, 1790. Possibly this is the same case and JM was filing it before the General Court in 1788, but it certainly was not a case of trespass, assault and battery as he noted. 1 Washington 115–116 (1792); Court of Appeals Order Book, II, 109, 169, 180, 184, 202, Va. State Lib.

96. JM totaled his March receipts here.

4th.	Cheadle ads. Cheadle chy.	3	
5th.	Dawson ads Lingan[97]		
	ejectment	3	16
	Booker with Tabb & Fields		
	exrs. chy. & common law	7	12
6th.	Thorntons exrs. in writ of		
	error v Robinsons admrs.	5	12
7th.	Thurman ads Leipner appeal	2	8
	Colliers ads. Dedlake three		
	ejects.	2	10
8th.	Dameron ads. Duncan & Co.	2	10
	Wilson ads. Wells supersedeas	2	10
	same ads. same supersedeas	2	10
		60	16

[Disbursements]

April 1st.	Silk stockings 24/	1	4
2d.	bottles 36/, corks 6/,		
	market 7/	2	9
	Paid P. Lee[98] for Colo.		
	Marshall	1	16
3d	Paid B. Munkus 16/, wood 8/	1	4
	Needles for my Mother		9
5th.	Stockings for myself 28/	1	8
	Nankin for breeches for self	1	16
		11	6
	deduct pd. P. Lee for Colo.		
	Marshall	1	16
		9	10

[Receipts]

April 10th.	Adams ads. Taylor	2	16	
11th.	From Stribling v Hite	5	15	8

97. Lessee of James M. Lingan v. John Dawson was an ejectment action in Hampshire County. When a declaration was filed in the General Court for Lingan by Charles Lee on Sept. 7, 1787, JM entered a not guilty plea. The case was transferred to the District Court at Winchester after the court reorganization of 1788, and judgment was entered for the plaintiff on Apr. 21, 1790. Dawson v. Lingan Declaration, Fairfax and Lee Papers, Alderman Library, University of Virginia; Superior Court Order Book, 1789-1793, 26, Frederick County, Va. State Lib.

98. This is probably Philip Richard Francis Lee, who had been a captain in the Continental Line. See end of column where JM deducted this amount.

12th.	Thompson v Hamilton & others	4	10
	Hamilton ads. Allison in part	1	8
14th.	Gatewood ads. Poindexter[99] in part	2	8
	Bledjer ads. Brickhouse appeal	2	10
15th.	Lees exrs. ads. Carr[1]	2	10
	Conway admr. v Rootes (Pinkard)	2	15
	Lee ads. Muschet & Co	2	15
	Lees exrs. ads. Kent & al. chy.		12
	Haskins ads. Ellyson[2] appeal	2	10
	Nicholsons exr. v Baker	2	16
16th.	Britton v Riddick (old suit)	2	8
	Thorp v Richardson for deft. appeal	5	
	From Ruffin ads. Brown (old suit)	2	8
	Mathews ads. Byrd do.	1	8
	Brooks v Anderson do.	2	8
	Hazlegreen v Cock do.	4	4
	Thornton (old suit finishd)	2	8
	From Randolphs v Randolphs exrs.	28	

80	9	8

[*Disbursements*]

April 9th.	Market 12/	12
10th.	Market 12/, expences 6/	18
	Oats 50/, market 6/, tumblers 4/3	

99. Joseph Poindexter v. James Gatewood was transferred to the District Court at New London after the reorganization of the courts in 1788, and judgment was entered for Gatewood on Sept. 23, 1790. District Court Order Book, I, 1789–1793, 53, Franklin County, Va. State Lib.

1. Simon Luttrell and Thomas Chapman, executors of William Carr, v. Charles Lee, executor of Henry Lee, was entered in the District Court at Dumfries as a reinstatement by the plaintiffs on Oct. 15, 1794; it is uncertain that JM was representing Lee at this time. District Court Order Book, 1794–1798, 10, 187, 236, 294, 350, 422, Prince William County, Va. State Lib.

2. Creed Haskins v. Garrard Ellyson was an appeal from the Cumberland County Court to the General Court. The case was transferred to the District Court at Prince Edward after 1788, and that court affirmed the county court's decision on Sept. 4, 1790. District Court Records, 1789–1792, 203–204, Prince Edward County, Va. State Lib.

14	market 36/	1	16	
16	wood 8/3, purse 5/		13	3
	Paid for Sam a dead negroe[3]	60		
		66	19	3
	deduct paid for Sam	60		
		6	19	3

[Receipts]

April 17th.	From Mr. Woodson[4] (2 suits in chy.)	10	
18th.	Davies & al. ads. Hill & al. 2 suits	5	
	From Cown in part	1	1
19th.	From Jones v Latane		18
	From Goodwin v Pegram	2	10
	Sampson ads. Yager[5]	2	10
21st.	King ads. Combs.	1	8
	Roe exr. of Gardner ads. Dejarnet	2	10
	Mr. Fox	2	16
22d.	Powel v Ringo in part chy.	2	10
	Richard Lee[6] Esquire	1	8
	From Mr. Warder	12	
	From Mr. Heron[7] law business	14	
28th.	Mr. Hare (old suit)	4	16
	Mr. Wilson judgt.	2	10
	Mr. Gordon supersedeas v. Smith	2	16
	Mr. Payne old suits	5	
		73	19
	Spicer v Mathews (old suit)	2	10
		76	9

3. See entry under Disbursements, June 20, 1787.

4. Joseph Woodson v. John Woodson was an appeal from the Goochland County Court to the High Court of Chancery, which issued a decree on Oct. 31, 1791. Wythe 129–132.

5. Samuel Yager v. Thomas Sampson was an action of trespass, assault and battery, in which JM defended Sampson. After 1788 the case was transferred from the General Court to the District Court at Fredericksburg, where it was dismissed on May 3, 1791. District Court Law Orders, A, 1789–1793, 232, Fredericksburg, Va. State Lib.

6. See entry under Receipts, Jan. 1, 1788.

7. James Heron (1754–1829) was a merchant in Richmond. "List of Merchants," Richmond City Hustings Court Order Book, II, 50, Va. State Lib.

	[Disbursements]			
April 17–18	expences 6/, do. 2/, market 1/		9	
	Given Polly 48/	2	8	
	Paid for Mr. Jeffersons book[8]			
	& Publius for myself[9]		12	
	do. for Colo. Marshall		12	
	Given Polly for knives etc. &			
	trimmings for self	1	8	
	Given Olly, for my father	2	16	
	advancd my brother James			
	for do.	4	4	
26th.	For Coy 28/, expences 15/	2	3	
	To Mr. Heron for sundries	19	17	6
	market 2/, do. 6/		8	
	For negroes	7	4	2
	Wood		7	
	Paid Mr. Payne[10] for sundries	6	16	
		49	4	8

deduct pd. for Colo.

Marshall   £2   16

                        12   3   8

                              45   16   8

76	9[11]				
80	9	8	16	9	3[12]
60	16		45	16	8
217	14	8	62	5	11

8. JM probably bought a copy of the English edition of Thomas Jefferson, *Notes on the State of Virginia* (London, 1787), 200 copies of which were sent to Richmond to be sold. Coolie Verner, *A Further Checklist of the Separate Editions of Jefferson's Notes on the State of Virginia* (Charlottesville, Va., 1950); Thomas Jefferson, *Notes on the State of Virginia*, ed. William Peden (Chapel Hill, N.C., 1954), v, xvi, xix, xxiii; Dumas Malone, *Jefferson and the Rights of Man* (Boston, 1951), 505–506.

9. The first edition of *The Federalist; A Collection of Essays, Written in Favour of the New Constitution, As Agreed Upon by the Federal Convention, September 17, 1787. In Two Volumes* (Philadelphia, 1788) was printed by John and Archibald McLean. JM bought only the first volume at this time. It was published on Mar. 22, 1788, and contained the first 36 essays. Volume II did not appear until May 28, 1788. *Hamilton Papers*, IV, 289–290.

10. Samuel Payne, or Paine, was a merchant in Richmond. "List of Merchants," Richmond City Hustings Court Order Book, II, 50, Va. State Lib.

11. Receipts totals for April.

12. Disbursements totals for April, but note that JM incorrectly added the figures for Apr. 9–16. The total should be £5 19s. 3d.

[*Receipts*]

May 1	Fulgeson v Parker injn. (in part	2	8
	Wallup v Holdens exrs. (appeal)	2	8
2d.	Goadsby, in part of chy. attachmts.	2	16
	advice fee	1	2	3
	Morris (Robt. retainer)	4	4
4th.	Webb ads. Woodson	5	
6th.	Edmunds ads. Cooper & al v Dunlop & Co.	5	
8th.	Ramsay ads. Sutton case	4	4
9th.	Copeland (in King & al. ads. Baker	1	8
	Tunstal a supersedeas	2	10
	Booker v Tab & al. chy. in part	2	8
	From Maynard & ux v Camps exrs. (old suit)	1	8
	From Mr. Donald injunction	5	
12th.	From Price ads. Lawson chy. injn.	5	
13th.	advice fee	2	16
	Clopton v Earnest (chy. old appeal)	2	8
14th.	Slaughter v Slaughter (old suit)	2	10
	From Colo. Lynch in Byrds exr. & al. ads. of Robinsons admrs.	7	
	Spratt ads. Latham[13] appeal	2	10
		62		3

[*Disbursements*]

May 1	Market 3/, expences 3/		6
	paid my barber	1	

13. John Conner and Thomas Latham v. Robert Spratt was an appeal from the Culpeper County Court to the General Court, filed in Apr. 1788. The case was continued until after the reorganization of 1788, when it was transferred to the District Court at Fredericksburg. On Oct. 1, 1790, that court affirmed the county court's decision. District Court Records, 1789–1792, 223–226, Fredericksburg, Va. State Lib.

	Paid Betsy Munkus		16	
	Market 3/, do. 12/8		15	8
	expenses 2/, Tea 12/		14	
8th.	market 24/	1	4	
	Shoes for self 12/, corn 3/		15	
	Market 20/	1		
	Fruit nuts etc. 12		12	
	Paid Mr. Donald for wine	20		
	bottles 9/, bandbox 6/		15	
	sugar 6/8, greens 6/		12	8
	Paid Mr. Moody my sub-			
	scription[14]	1	8	
		29	18	4

[Receipts]

May 16th	From Mr. Blow	4	16
17th.	From do. injn. in chy. v Lyon	2	16
22d.	From Clarke ads. Stockdale		
	(injn.)	5	
	From Mr. Hare[15] advice fee	1	8
	From Mr. Ross	9	12
23d.	From Todds exrs. ads.		
	Pollard & al Chy.	2	8
26	Priddie v Richardson suit at		
	issue	1	12
28	From Mr. Gaven Lawson	7	
	From Mr. Copeland (balance		
	of fee chy.)	3	12
	Williamson v Shermens exrs.		
	injn.	1	4
		39	8

[Disbursements]

May 18th.	Paid Mr. Buckhanan	2	8
	sugar & Coffee	2	8
	Market 9/		9

14. This expenditure was probably for the Jockey Club races to be held that month. Mathew Moody, Richmond City sergeant, was sometimes appointed to receive these subscriptions.

15. JM was receiving a fee for advice in Hare v. Gay, which was heard before the Court of Appeals on May 3, 1788, after being adjourned from the General Court. 4 Call 151–152; Court of Appeals Order Book, I, 122, 125, Va. State Lib.

22d.	Given Polly	1	8	
24th.	Paid Mr. Hart for building porch	26		
	Wood 8/		8	
25th.	Market 4/6		4	6
27	Corn	13		
28	Market 10/, do. 22/	1	12	
	Given Olly	5	12	
	Market 9/, fruit 2/		11	
		54		6
	deduct for building porch	26		
		28		6

[Receipts]

June 1st.	Prilliam v Allen T.A.B.	1	5	
	Hughes exrs. ads. Williams & ux.	5		
	Walker v Roebuck & al appeal chy.	2	12	
12th.	Hobday ads. Newton & Archer Appl.	2	16	
	Portlock ads. Comth.	2	16	
	Calvert ads. Do.	2	16	
	Jerdone ads. Younghusband appeal	3		
	advice fee 28/	1	8	
	do. 22/	1	2	
14	From Robinson v Taylor supersedeas	2	15	
	Advice fee	1	2	
16	drawing a deed for Mr. Madison	1	4	
	advice fee	1	2	6
returnd	⟨Hicks v. Storrs exrs. (new suit)	2	10⟩	
	Carter ads. Armstead (eject.) for trial	5	18	
17th.	Binns ads. Alexander appeal	2	10	
	same ads. same do.	5		
18	advice fee Harris v Watkins	1	2	6

		£	s	d
	Colo. W. Miles Cary	6	4	
	Cobbs etc. ads. Street	5		
26th.	advice for Mr. Pride	1	2	6
	advice fee	1		
		59	15	6
		2	10[16]	
		57	5	6

[Disbursements]

		£	s	d
June 1	Paid Betsy Munkus		16	
2	Paid for coat for self	1		
	sugar 28/	1	8	
3, 4, 5, 6	market 15		15	
8th.	Market 12/		12	
	Tea 12/, market 6/, Wood 7/	1	5	
	painting the porch 12/		12	
14th.	market 14		14	
	apples 1/3, fruit 3/9, market 19/	1	4	
18	fruit 2/6, market 14/6		18	
20	Given to Polly	2	8	
	Market 6/, books 12/		18	
	stockings for self		18	
23d.	linnen for Moses 6/		6	
28	market 20/, expenses 7/	1	7	
		15	1	

16. JM's fee in Hicks v. Storrs exrs., returned. The bottom of the page is torn, partially obscuring JM's total.

LIST OF CASES
IN THE ACCOUNT BOOK

Each case title in John Marshall's Account Book is listed here twice, once under the plaintiff and again under the defendant. Italics indicate cases commented on in the editors' notes. Generally names in the case titles are spelled as Marshall entered them in the Account Book.

The page references in this list are to the Account Book only. Any other mentions of these cases in the volume are given in the Legal Index (see p. 431), which contains case titles that appear in Marshall's correspondence and papers.

INDEXES

LEGAL INDEX

GENERAL INDEX

LEGAL INDEX

The Legal Index contains both legal digest entries and case titles that appear in John Marshall's correspondence and papers. When a case title additionally appears in Marshall's Account Book, those page references are given here also. However, for case titles appearing only in the Account Book, see the list of cases following that document. For names of individuals and general subject entries, see the General Index, which begins on p. 437.

GENERAL INDEX

The General Index contains names of individuals that appear in this volume, as well as general subject entries. Dates of individuals, if known, may be found at their first page reference. For legal digest entries, see the Legal Index, which begins on p. 431; for case titles, also see the Legal Index and the List of Cases in the Account Book (p. 415).